DISCOVERING THE AMERICAS

DISCOVERING THE AMERICAS

THE ARCHIVE OF THE INDIES

by

Pedro González García
Manuel Romero Tallafigo
Alfredo J. Morales
M.ª Antonia Colomar Albajar
M.ª del Carmen Galbis Díez
Purificación Medina Encina
Antonio López Gutiérrez

General Editor
Pedro González García

Published in cooperation with
the Archivo General de Indias
of Seville

THE VENDOME PRESS
NEW YORK • PARIS

Published in the USA in 1997 by
THE VENDOME PRESS
1370 Avenue of the Americas
New York, NY 10019

Distributed in the USA and Canada by
Rizzoli International Publications
through St. Martin's Press
175 Fifth Avenue
New York, NY 10010

Translated from the Spanish by Dominic Currin
Edited by Alexis Gregory

Library of Congress Cataloging-in-Publication Data

Discovering the Americas / by Pedro González García... [et al.].
p. cm.
ISBN: 0-86565-991-5
1. America—Discovery and exploration—Spanish—Sources
2. Archivo General de Indias. I. González García, Pedro.
E123.D57 1997
970.01—dc21 97-14276
CIP

Printed and bound in Spain

The translation of this book was made possible by the assistance of the Directorate General of Books, Archives & Libraries of the Spanish Ministry of Education & Culture

The General Archive of the Indies is one of the finest examples of Spain's rich documentary heritage. Ever since it was founded, its close links to the Americas and the Philippines have aroused the curiosity of researchers, scholars and the general public in a number of countries. This is why the documentary fonds of this Archive are among the most important in the world.

At one of the most lucid moments of the Spanish Enlightenment, the Spanish King Charles III ordered this Archive to be created and housed in Seville's *Lonja* or Commodity Exchange, a magnificent building associated with Spain's New World trade ever since the 16th century. Listed by UNESCO as 'world heritage', it is located next to the Cathedral and the Alcázar of Seville, gateway to the Americas via its port on the Guadalquivir river.

The 18th-century origins of the Archive are particularly significant, in that it was established for the purpose of housing all existing documents relating to the New World and the Philippines, enabling a history of Spain and all those lands to be written. Today, it is equally significant as a model for archives all over the world, in that it has pioneered the incorporation of new technologies in order to keep abreast of today's information-oriented society, while simultaneously ensuring the conservation of all the archival material it houses.

The Archive's willingness to take in additional documentation relating to the Americas, and to further develop its computerized facilities, will undoubtedly contribute to more effective and more dynamic archival services. This is bound to bring changes to its splendid halls, where tradition and modernity have been harmoniously blended with a view to the next millennium, so that future generations may benefit by learning about a past which has brought together the history and culture of so many nations.

The Spanish Ministry of Education and Culture has given priority to the preservation of the wealth of historical, documentary and art heritage that Spain has generated over the centuries. This Archive of the Indies, with its huge documentary fonds and its dynamic, day-to-day operations, is a magnificent testimony to the Ministry's proactive stance in the crucial defense of Spain's heritage.

Esperanza Aguirre Gil de Biedma
Spanish Minister of Education and Culture

16th-Century Spanish Colonial Expansion in the New World

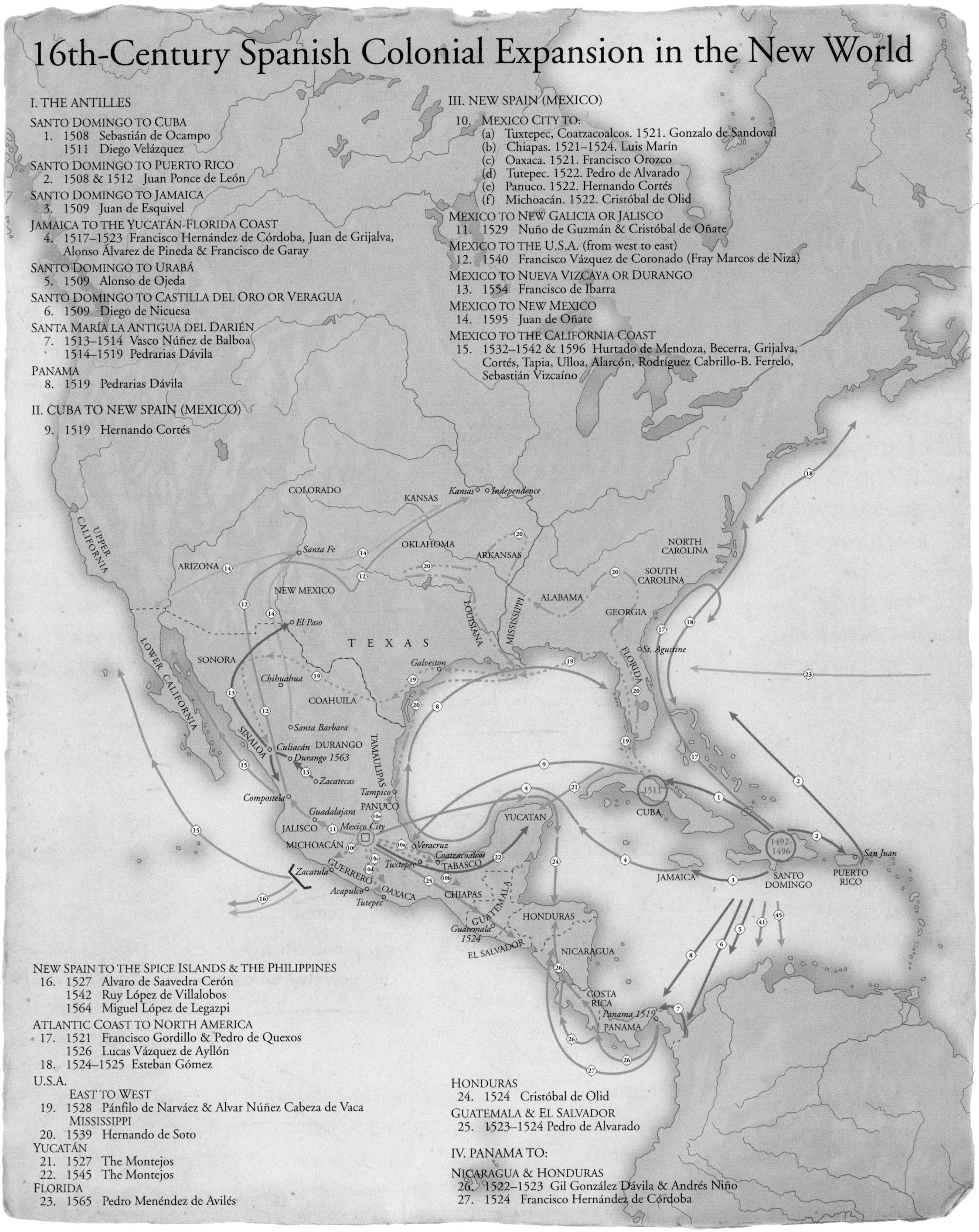
16th-Century Spanish Colonial Expansion in the New World
I. THE ANTILLES
SANTO DOMINGO TO CUBA
1. 1508 Sebastián de Ocampo
1511 Diego Velázquez
SANTO DOMINGO TO PUERTO RICO
2. 1508 & 1512 Juan Ponce de León
SANTO DOMINGO TO JAMAICA
3. 1509 Juan de Esquivel
JAMAICA TO THE YUCATÁN-FLORIDA COAST
4. 1517–1523 Francisco Hernández de Córdoba, Juan de Grijalva, Alonso Álvarez de Pineda & Francisco de Garay
SANTO DOMINGO TO URABÁ
5. 1509 Alonso de Ojeda
SANTO DOMINGO TO CASTILLA DEL ORO OR VERAGUA
6. 1509 Diego de Nicuesa
SANTA MARÍA LA ANTIGUA DEL DARIÉN
7. 1513–1514 Vasco Núñez de Balboa
1514–1519 Pedrarias Dávila
PANAMA
8. 1519 Pedrarias Dávila
II. CUBA TO NEW SPAIN (MEXICO)
9. 1519 Hernando Cortés
III. NEW SPAIN (MEXICO)
10. MEXICO CITY TO:
(a) Tuxtepec, Coatzacoalcos. 1521. Gonzalo de Sandoval
(b) Chiapas. 1521–1524. Luis Marín
(c) Oaxaca. 1521. Francisco Orozco
(d) Tutepec. 1522. Pedro de Alvarado
(e) Panuco. 1522. Hernando Cortés
(f) Michoacán. 1522. Cristóbal de Olid
MEXICO TO NEW GALICIA OR JALISCO
11. 1529 Nuño de Guzmán & Cristóbal de Oñate
MEXICO TO THE U.S.A. (from west to east)
12. 1540 Francisco Vázquez de Coronado (Fray Marcos de Niza)
MEXICO TO NUEVA VIZCAYA OR DURANGO
13. 1554 Francisco de Ibarra
MEXICO TO NEW MEXICO
14. 1595 Juan de Oñate
MEXICO TO THE CALIFORNIA COAST
15. 1532–1542 & 1596 Hurtado de Mendoza, Becerra, Grijalva, Cortés, Tapia, Ulloa, Alarcón, Rodríguez Cabrillo-B. Ferrelo, Sebastián Vizcaíno
NEW SPAIN TO THE SPICE ISLANDS & THE PHILIPPINES
16. 1527 Alvaro de Saavedra Cerón
1542 Ruy López de Villalobos
1564 Miguel López de Legazpi
ATLANTIC COAST TO NORTH AMERICA
17. 1521 Francisco Gordillo & Pedro de Quexos
1526 Lucas Vázquez de Ayllón
18. 1524–1525 Esteban Gómez
U.S.A.
EAST TO WEST
19. 1528 Pánfilo de Narváez & Alvar Núñez Cabeza de Vaca
MISSISSIPPI
20. 1539 Hernando de Soto
YUCATÁN
21. 1527 The Montejos
22. 1545 The Montejos
FLORIDA
23. 1565 Pedro Menéndez de Avilés
HONDURAS
24. 1524 Cristóbal de Olid
GUATEMALA & EL SALVADOR
25. 1523–1524 Pedro de Alvarado
IV. PANAMA TO:
NICARAGUA & HONDURAS
26. 1522–1523 Gil González Dávila & Andrés Niño
27. 1524 Francisco Hernández de Córdoba
COLORADO
KANSAS
Kansas
Independence
UPPER CALIFORNIA
Santa Fe
OKLAHOMA
ARKANSAS
NORTH CAROLINA
SOUTH CAROLINA
ARIZONA
NEW MEXICO
ALABAMA
GEORGIA
LOUISIANA
MISSISSIPPI
El Paso
TEXAS
LOWER CALIFORNIA
SONORA
St. Agustine
FLORIDA
Galveston
Chihuahua
COAHUILA
Santa Barbara
SINALOA
Culiacán
DURANGO
Durango 1563
TAMAULIPAS
Zacatecas
Tampico
Compostela
Guadalajara
PANUCO
JALISCO
Mexico City
YUCATAN
CUBA
1511
MICHOACÁN
Veracruz
Coatzacoalcos
TABASCO
1492
1496
San Juan
Zacatula
GUERRERO
Tuxtepec
JAMAICA
SANTO DOMINGO
PUERTO RICO
Acapulco
OAXACA
CHIAPAS
Tutepec
GUATEMALA
HONDURAS
Guatemala 1524
EL SALVADOR
NICARAGUA
COSTA RICA
Panama 1519
PANAMA

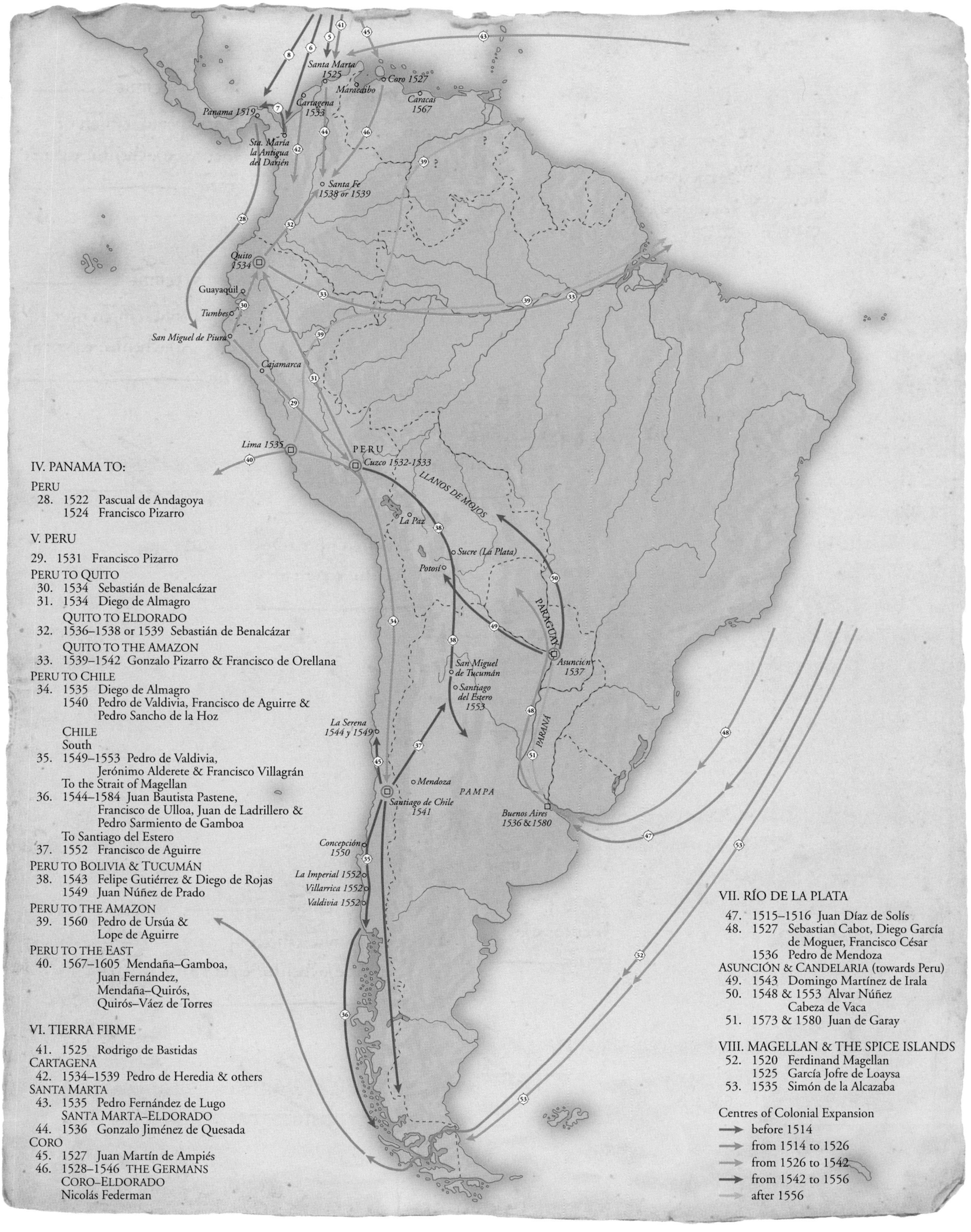
IV. PANAMA TO:
PERU
28. 1522 Pascual de Andagoya
1524 Francisco Pizarro
V. PERU
29. 1531 Francisco Pizarro
PERU TO QUITO
30. 1534 Sebastián de Benalcázar
31. 1534 Diego de Almagro
QUITO TO ELDORADO
32. 1536–1538 or 1539 Sebastián de Benalcázar
QUITO TO THE AMAZON
33. 1539–1542 Gonzalo Pizarro & Francisco de Orellana
PERU TO CHILE
34. 1535 Diego de Almagro
1540 Pedro de Valdivia, Francisco de Aguirre & Pedro Sancho de la Hoz
CHILE
South
35. 1549–1553 Pedro de Valdivia, Jerónimo Alderete & Francisco Villagrán
To the Strait of Magellan
36. 1544–1584 Juan Bautista Pastene, Francisco de Ulloa, Juan de Ladrillero & Pedro Sarmiento de Gamboa
To Santiago del Estero
37. 1552 Francisco de Aguirre
PERU TO BOLIVIA & TUCUMÁN
38. 1543 Felipe Gutiérrez & Diego de Rojas
1549 Juan Núñez de Prado
PERU TO THE AMAZON
39. 1560 Pedro de Ursúa & Lope de Aguirre
PERU TO THE EAST
40. 1567–1605 Mendaña–Gamboa, Juan Fernández, Mendaña–Quirós, Quirós–Váez de Torres
VI. TIERRA FIRME
41. 1525 Rodrigo de Bastidas
CARTAGENA
42. 1534–1539 Pedro de Heredia & others
SANTA MARTA
43. 1535 Pedro Fernández de Lugo
SANTA MARTA–ELDORADO
44. 1536 Gonzalo Jiménez de Quesada
CORO
45. 1527 Juan Martín de Ampiés
46. 1528–1546 THE GERMANS
CORO–ELDORADO
Nicolás Federman
VII. RÍO DE LA PLATA
47. 1515–1516 Juan Díaz de Solís
48. 1527 Sebastian Cabot, Diego García de Moguer, Francisco César
1536 Pedro de Mendoza
ASUNCIÓN & CANDELARIA (towards Peru)
49. 1543 Domingo Martínez de Irala
50. 1548 & 1553 Alvar Núñez Cabeza de Vaca
51. 1573 & 1580 Juan de Garay
VIII. MAGELLAN & THE SPICE ISLANDS
52. 1520 Ferdinand Magellan
1525 García Jofre de Loaysa
53. 1535 Simón de la Alcazaba
Centres of Colonial Expansion
before 1514
from 1514 to 1526
from 1526 to 1542
from 1542 to 1556
after 1556
Santa Marta 1525
Coro 1527
Maracaibo
Caracas 1567
Cartagena 1533
Panama 1519
Sta. María la Antigua del Darién
Santa Fe 1538 or 1539
Quito 1534
Guayaquil
Tumbes
San Miguel de Piura
Cajamarca
Lima 1535
PERU
Cuzco 1532-1533
LLANOS DE MOJOS
La Paz
Sucre (La Plata)
Potosí
PARAGUAY
Asunción 1537
San Miguel de Tucumán
Santiago del Estero 1553
La Serena 1544 y 1549
Mendoza
PAMPA
PARANÁ
Santiago de Chile 1541
Buenos Aires 1536 & 1580
Concepción 1550
La Imperial 1552
Villarrica 1552
Valdivia 1552

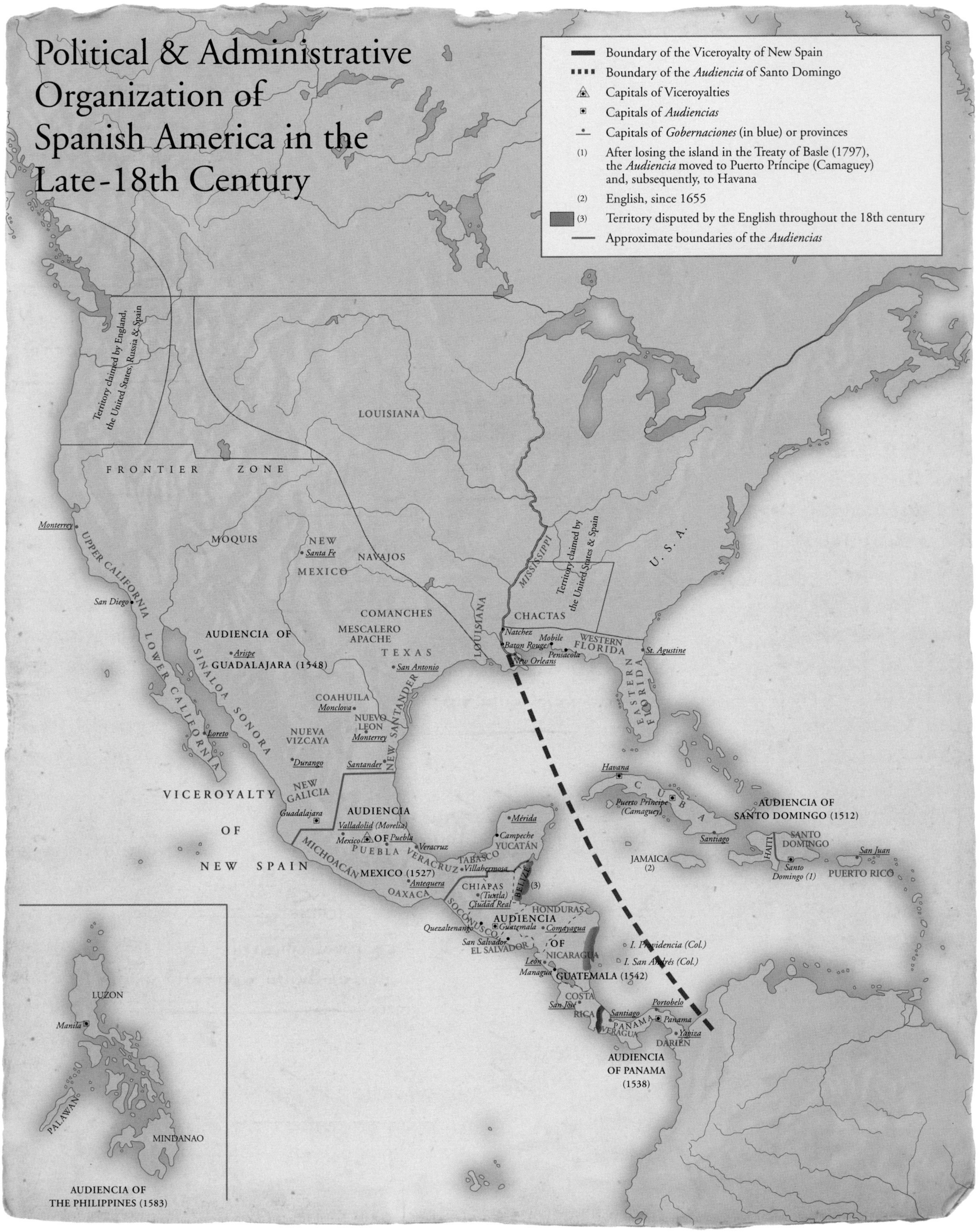
Political & Administrative Organization of Spanish America in the Late-18th Century
Boundary of the Viceroyalty of New Spain
Boundary of the Audiencia of Santo Domingo
Capitals of Viceroyalties
Capitals of Audiencias
Capitals of Gobernaciones (in blue) or provinces
(1) After losing the island in the Treaty of Basle (1797), the Audiencia moved to Puerto Príncipe (Camaguey) and, subsequently, to Havana
(2) English, since 1655
(3) Territory disputed by the English throughout the 18th century
Approximate boundaries of the Audiencias
Territory claimed by England, the United States, Russia & Spain
LOUISIANA
FRONTIER ZONE
Monterrey
UPPER CALIFORNIA
MOQUIS
NEW MEXICO
Santa Fe
NAVAJOS
San Diego
COMANCHES
MESCALERO APACHE
TEXAS
San Antonio
LOUISIANA
MISSISSIPPI
Territory claimed by the United States & Spain
U. S. A.
CHACTAS
Natchez
Baton Rouge
New Orleans
Mobile
Pensacola
WESTERN FLORIDA
St. Agustine
EASTERN FLORIDA
AUDIENCIA OF
Arispe
GUADALAJARA (1548)
LOWER CALIFORNIA
SINALOA
SONORA
Loreto
COAHUILA
Monclova
NUEVO LEON
Monterrey
NEW SANTANDER
NUEVA VIZCAYA
Durango
Santander
NEW GALICIA
Guadalajara
VICEROYALTY OF NEW SPAIN
AUDIENCIA
Valladolid (Morelia)
Mexico
OF
Puebla
PUEBLA
Veracruz
MICHOACAN
MEXICO (1527)
VERACRUZ
Antequera
OAXACA
Mérida
Campeche
YUCATÁN
TABASCO
Villahermosa
BELIZE
(3)
CHIAPAS
(Tuxtla)
Ciudad Real
SOCONUSCO
Quezaltenango
AUDIENCIA
Guatemala
HONDURAS
Comayagua
San Salvador
EL SALVADOR
OF
NICARAGUA
León
Managua
GUATEMALA (1542)
I. Providencia (Col.)
I. San Andrés (Col.)
COSTA RICA
San José
Santiago
VERAGUA
PANAMA
Portobelo
Panama
Yaviza
DARIEN
AUDIENCIA OF PANAMA (1538)
Havana
CUBA
Puerto Príncipe (Camaguey)
Santiago
AUDIENCIA OF SANTO DOMINGO (1512)
HAITI
SANTO DOMINGO
Santo Domingo (1)
San Juan
PUERTO RICO
JAMAICA (2)
LUZON
Manila
PALAWAN
MINDANAO
AUDIENCIA OF THE PHILIPPINES (1583)

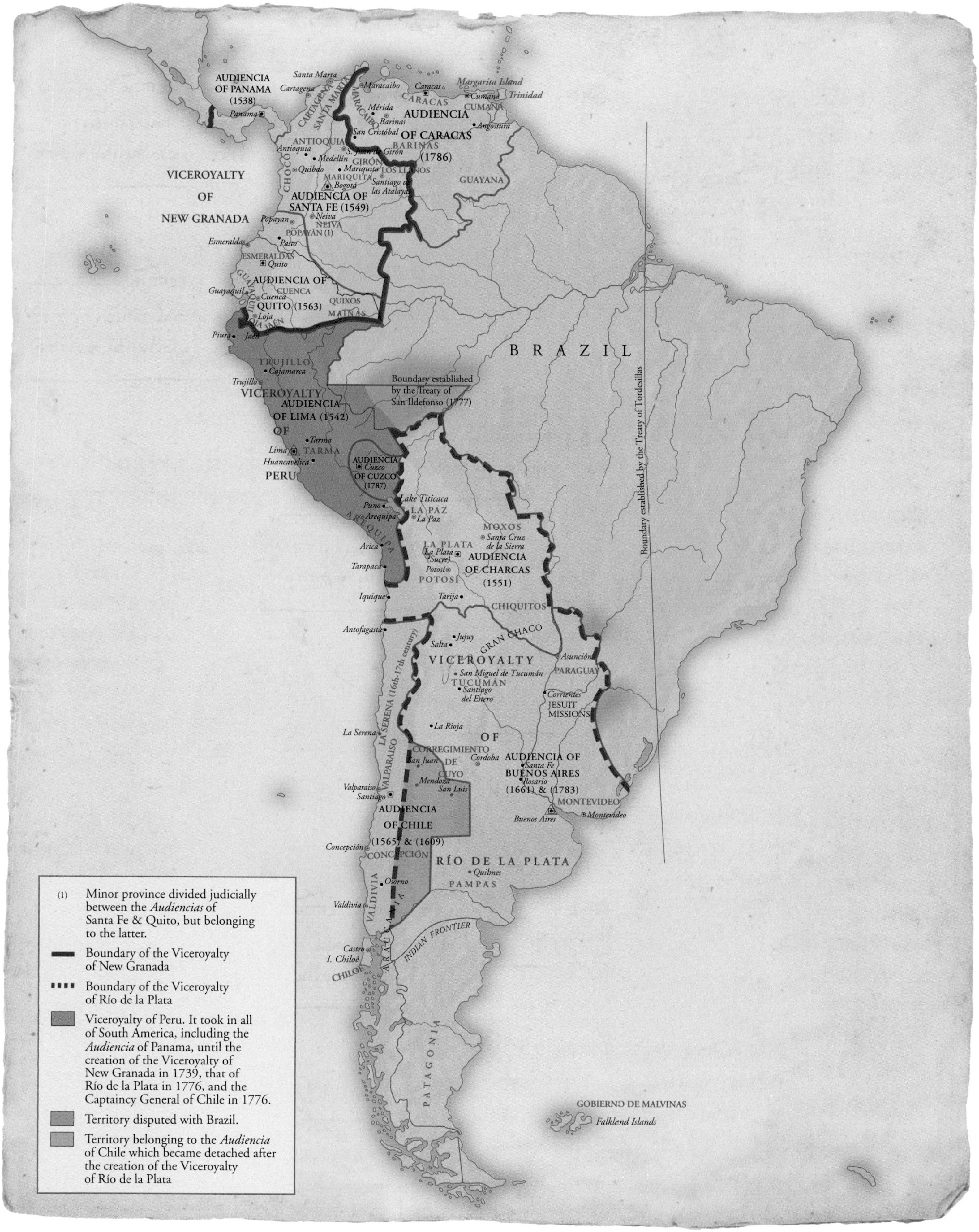

AUDIENCIA OF PANAMA (1538)
Panama
Santa Marta
Cartagena
Maracaibo
Caracas
Margarita Island
Cumaná
Trinidad
CARACAS
CUMANÁ
Mérida
Barinas
San Cristóbal
AUDIENCIA OF CARACAS (1786)
Angostura
BARINAS
ANTIOQUIA
Antioquia
Medellín
GIRÓN
LOS LLANOS
Quibdo
Mariquita
MARIQUITA
Bogotá
Santiago de las Atalayas
GUAYANA
VICEROYALTY OF NEW GRANADA
CHOCÓ
AUDIENCIA OF SANTA FE (1549)
Popayan
Neiva
NEIVA
POPAYÁN (1)
Esmeraldas
Pasto
ESMERALDAS
Quito
AUDIENCIA OF QUITO (1563)
Guayaquil
Cuenca
CUENCA
QUIXOS
MAINAS
Loja
JAÉN
Piura
Jaén
TRUJILLO
Cajamarca
Trujillo
B R A Z I L
Boundary established by the Treaty of San Ildefonso (1777)
VICEROYALTY OF PERU
AUDIENCIA OF LIMA (1542)
Tarma
Lima
TARMA
Huancavelica
AUDIENCIA OF CUZCO (1787)
Cuzco
Lake Titicaca
Puno
LA PAZ
La Paz
Arequipa
AREQUIPA
MOXOS
Santa Cruz de la Sierra
Arica
LA PLATA
La Plata (Sucre)
AUDIENCIA OF CHARCAS (1551)
Tarapacá
Potosí
POTOSÍ
Iquique
Tarija
CHIQUITOS
Boundary established by the Treaty of Tordesillas
Antofagasta
Jujuy
Salta
GRAN CHACO
Asunción
VICEROYALTY OF RÍO DE LA PLATA
PARAGUAY
San Miguel de Tucumán
TUCUMÁN
Santiago del Estero
Corrientes
JESUIT MISSIONS
LA SERENA (16th-17th century)
La Serena
La Rioja
CORREGIMIENTO DE CUYO
San Juan
Cordoba
AUDIENCIA OF BUENOS AIRES (1661) & (1783)
Santa Fe
Rosario
VALPARAISO
Valparaiso
Santiago
Mendoza
San Luis
MONTEVIDEO
Montevideo
Buenos Aires
AUDIENCIA OF CHILE (1565) & (1609)
Concepción
CONCEPCIÓN
Quilmes
PAMPAS
Osorno
VALDIVIA
Valdivia
ARAUCANIA
INDIAN FRONTIER
Castro
I. Chiloé
CHILOÉ
PATAGONIA
GOBIERNO DE MALVINAS
Falklend Islands
(1) Minor province divided judicially between the Audiencias of Santa Fe & Quito, but belonging to the latter.
Boundary of the Viceroyalty of New Granada
Boundary of the Viceroyalty of Río de la Plata
Viceroyalty of Peru. It took in all of South America, including the Audiencia of Panama, until the creation of the Viceroyalty of New Granada in 1739, that of Río de la Plata in 1776, and the Captaincy General of Chile in 1776.
Territory disputed with Brazil.
Territory belonging to the Audiencia of Chile which became detached after the creation of the Viceroyalty of Río de la Plata

The Archive's coat-of-arms.

[11 November 1786]
Design for the coat-of-arms of the General Archive of the Indies, submitted by José de Aguilera, who sought employment in the Archive.
295 x 202 mm.
MP. Europa y África, 50.

The heraldic symbols reflect the overseas calling of the Archive and its identification with a New World dominated by the Crown of Castile. Also featured is a homage to José de Gálvez, the Indies Secretary and key figure in the founding of the Archive.

INTRODUCTION

In the heart of Seville's historical center, on what the classical Spanish writer, Luis Zapata, described as 'the best patch of land' in Spain, stands the General Archive of the Indies. Hard by the Cathedral and the Alcázar, on the former sites of the Mint and the Royal Ironworks, and clothed in some of the finest Spanish Renaissance architecture, it is for most of those who come to pore over its documents the epitome of an archive.

The building housing the Archive is a veritable jewel, both for its artistic value and because it is part and parcel of the history contained in its documents. From the 16th to the 18th century, under the arcades of its courts and in its halls and galleries, the 'Indies merchants' conducted their business or settled disputes before the Consulate Tribunal. Indeed, someone once called it 'the most beautiful archive building in the world'.

The Archive contains a sizeable part of the historical records of the New World, that vast area stretching from the southern United States to Tierra del Fuego. Documentary material on the Philippines and the Spanish Far East is housed here, too. Almost four hundred years of Spain's presence abroad is distributed between the 80 million pages of the Archive: its political, social and economic history, the thinking of the time, the history of the Church and the history of art.

The Catholic Kings and Christopher Columbus, the conquistadors and the discoverers, missionaries and *encomenderos,* masters and slaves, viceroys and natives, seamen and merchants, elite officialdom and emigrants, judges and protectors of Indians in the New World, treasures and shipwrecked galleons, city-building and silver and gold mining, printing works and universities leap from the time-worn pages. Over three hundred years of half the world's history is here condensed into 43,000 bundles.

Day after day, hundreds of researchers from the world over move about the Archive's spacious halls in their quest to delve further into the past. Half of them come from abroad and over 40% from the other side of the Atlantic. Many spend long periods beside the river Guadalquivir, showing 'how to combine duty and pleasure', as Hugh Thomas put it. Others come from time to time, during their holidays or their sabbatical years. There are also those that have been coming here on a daily basis for over fifty years to unearth fresh material for their research.

The Origins of the Archive

> 'History is the intellectual form through which a culture gives an account of its past'. It was this thought that, at the end of the 18th century, inspired Charles III of Spain and his cartographer, Juan Bautista Muñoz, to establish the world's first colonial archive in Seville, in tune with the historiographic ideas of the Enlightenment.
>
> *Prince Bernhard of the Netherlands, when awarding the Erasmus prize to the General Archive of the Indies on 3 December 1992.*

In the last three decades of the 18th century, several factors prompted King Charles III to found the General Archive of the Indies, which is undoubtedly one of the most felicitous creations of Spain's despotic Enlightenment.

For years it was claimed that the decision to set up the institution was largely due to a visit by a high-ranking official and politician of the time to the Simancas Archive in 1773. He was seeking papers that might provide support for the move to canonise the venerable Juan de Palafox y Mendoza, bishop of Puebla de los Ángeles in New Spain from 1639 to 1650 and an out-and-out anti-Jesuit. The politician in question was José de Gálvez, who was likewise seeking documentary evidence to justify the abolition of the Society of Jesus. When the expulsion order, applicable to all Jesuits in the New World, arrived in Mexico, Gálvez, *Visitador* or Inspector General of New Spain in the period 1765–1772, carried it out implacably.

Despite this, the General Archive of Simancas, which had acted as the Spanish Crown's central archive and housed State administration papers since the 16th century, did not provide Gálvez with the evidence he was seeking, either because such evidence did not exist or because the available material was too voluminous to be accurately reviewed for specific information.

This incident might have made itself felt when, a few years later, Gálvez was promoted to the office of Indies Secretary and assumed control of the colonial administration. Whatever the case, there were good reasons for setting up the new archive. After processing incoming papers for over two centuries and with scant resources, the General Archive of Simancas was in dire straits. It was no longer able to take in any more documents and to adequately arrange the ones it already had. Moreover, a proposed extension to the Archive, for which the architect Juan de Villanueva was commissioned in 1774, was never brought to completion. A new idea was gaining momentum at the time in Spain, then at war with England.

Nationalistic fervor was mounting over what in official circles was considered to be a resurgence of the anti-Spanish 'Black Legend' doing the rounds in 16th-century Europe. The term, popularized by the Spanish historian, Julián Juderías, was used by many Protestant historians to imply cruelty and intolerance on the part of the Spanish. Important writings of the time, particularly *Histoire philosophique et politique des etablisements et du commerce des Europées dans les deux Indes,* by Guillaume Tomé Raynal (Amsterdam, 1770) and *History of America,* by William Robertson (London, 1777), helped to fuel the trend. In 1777, Spain's Royal Academy of History officially asked José de Gálvez to furnish certain documents

Aerial view of Seville.

'The best patch of land [in Spain]: Seville Cathedral, the Alcázar, the Casa de la Contratación, *the oil depot, the customshouse, the shipyards, the chapter house, the Commodity Exchange and the royal Audiencia'.*

LUIS ZAPATA: De cosas singulares de España.

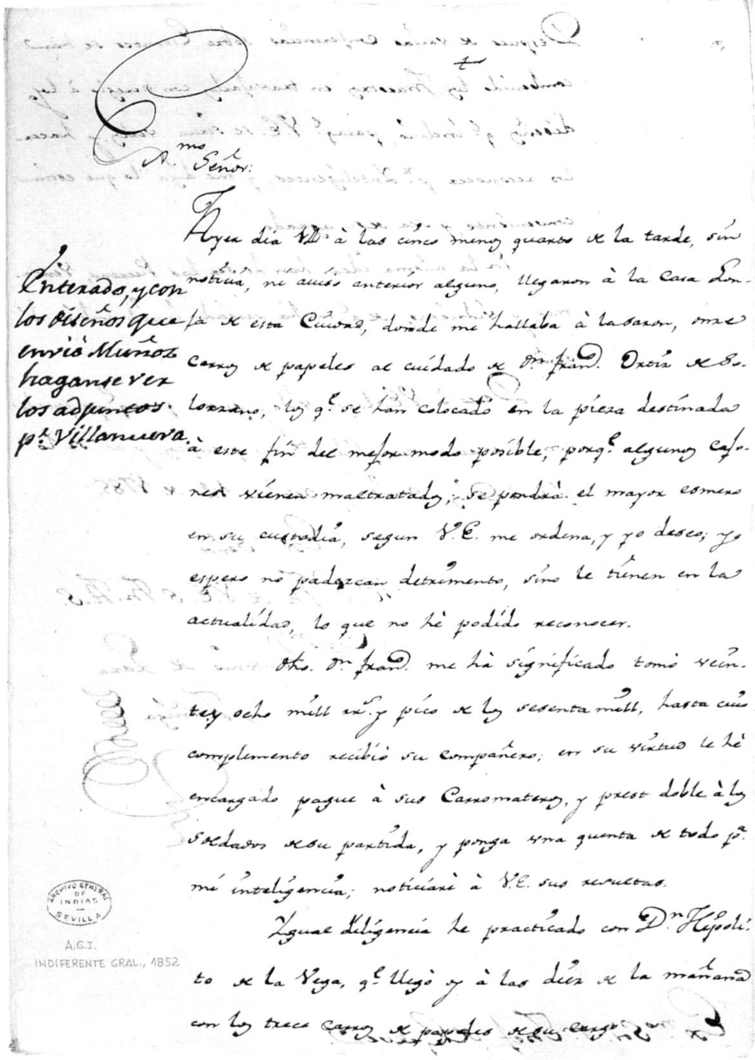

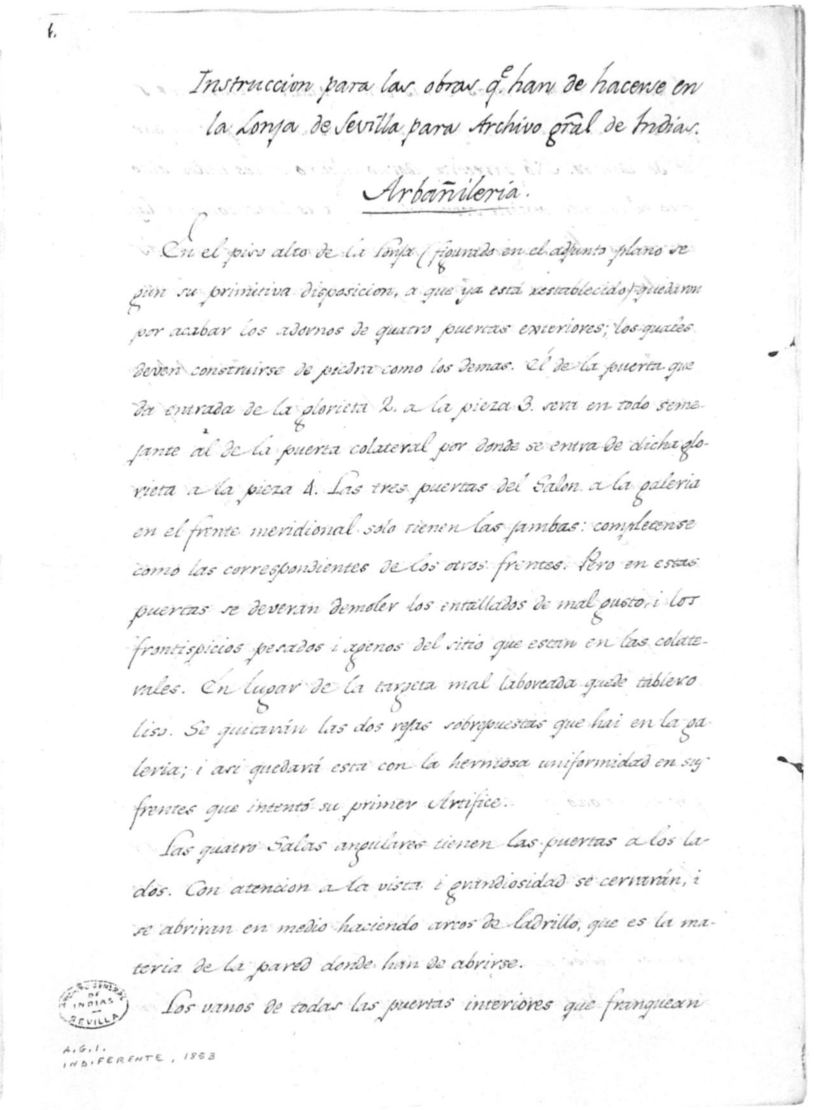

Instruccion para las obras q.e han de hacerse en la Lonja de Sevilla para Archivo gral de Indias.

Arbañileria.

En el piso alto de la Lonja (figurado en el adjunto plano se ...) su primitiva disposicion, a que ya está restablecido, quedaron por acabar los adornos de quatro puertas exteriores; los quales deben construirse de piedra como los demas. El de la puerta que da entrada de la glorieta 2. a la pieza 3. será en todo semejante al de la puerta colateral por donde se entra de dicha glorieta a la pieza 4. Las tres puertas del Salon a la galeria en el frente meridional solo tienen las jambas: completense como las correspondientes de los otros frentes. Pero en estas puertas se deberan demoler los entallados de mal gusto, i los frontispicios pesados i agenos del sitio que estan en las colaterales. En lugar de la tarjeta mal labrada quede tablero liso. Se quitarán las dos rejas sobrepuestas que hai en la galeria; i asi quedará esta con la hermosa uniformidad en sus frentes que intentó su primer Artifice.

Las quatro Salas angulares tienen las puertas a los lados. Con atencion a la vista i grandiosidad se cerrarán, i se abrirán en medio haciendo arcos de ladrillo, que es la materia de la pared donde han de abrirse.

Los vanos de todas las puertas interiores que franqueen

on the Indies in order to analyze controversial aspects of Robertson's work which, for all that, the Academy intended to publish.

The response, with nationalistic, patriotic overtones instigated by the central government, was not long in coming. A better informed, more realistic history had to be written and—bearing in mind the progress made in historical critique during the Enlightenment—that would involve researching the original documents as source material. Thus, in 1779, the Secretary of the Indies, José de Gálvez, Marquis of Sonora, well aware of the problems that had beset the Simancas archive, commissioned Juan Bautista Muñoz to write the new history:

'In 1779, I submitted to the King the need to write an authorized General History of the Indies based on secure, irrefutable documents. As a result, His Majesty honored me with the commission and I set about reviewing various Court archives that belonged to the Indies Department. I soon noticed the absence of some early documents and began to search for them in Simancas, Seville and Cádiz. I looked into the matter with the Marquis of Sonora and, in so doing, touched on the issue of how little we knew of the whereabouts of available documents, how carelessly they had been inventoried and stored over the last two centuries and of what immense benefit it would be to establish a general archive where so many scattered papers might be brought together and properly arranged, without having to make use of a large number of offices.'

The arrival of the first documents.

14 October 1785, Seville.
Letter from Antonio de Lara y Zúñiga, Intendant of the General Archive of the Indies, to the State Secretary of the Indies, José de Gálvez, reporting the arrival of the first documents from Simancas.
1 fol. + 1 blank.
Indiferente General, 1853.

The arrival of the first documents in mid-October 1785 is generally taken to mark the date the General Archive of the Indies came into being.

Remodelling the Commodity Exchange to house the Archive.

27 April 1785, Seville.
Orders given by Juan Bautista Muñoz for remodelling the Commodity Exchange, to convert it into the Archive of the Indies.
6 fols.
Indiferente general, 1853.

The orders which Juan Bautista Muñoz gave the architect, Lucas Cintora, before leaving for Lisbon.

General view of the Archive.

A magnificent building in a splendid setting: the Commodity Exchange of Seville, located next to the Cathedral and the Alcázar, was listed as 'World Heritage' by UNESCO some years ago. Built in the 16th and 17th century on the orders of Philip II and based on an initial design by Juan de Herrera, it houses one of the most important archives in the world—the General Archive of the Indies.

Thus, the General Archive of the Indies was the first archive of its kind to be established in terms of the historical value of its documents for research, rather than the need to serve and uphold the rights of their bearers. The overriding concern for the informative content of the documents housed in the Archive was a wholly new approach to archiving. As Juan Bautista Muñoz wrote:

'In order to achieve such lofty goals, to silence once and for all so much inflamed bickering and backbiting and to render such ignorance inexcusable, it was imperative to go to the heart of the matter and examine irrefutable documents and, as if nothing had ever been written or published on the subject, to create history afresh, so to speak.'

In short, the Archive of the Indies was founded to overcome the inadequacies of the Simancas Archive, the Crown's central archive from the 16th century onwards, and to compile an authoritative history based on original records that could be used to refute the latest foreign writings which, in the view of enlightened currents of opinion in Spain, were rekindling the old issue of the Black Legend.

'It was the Archive of the Indies that gradually rid my mind of childhood adventures, pranks, dreams and memories. The American Indians, pirates, conquistadors clothed in steel, viceroys in their regalia, black slaves and a whole parade of adventure, sound and color that had leaped out from the books I read as a boy, gradually slipped out of their fictitious time and space and turned into files, documents and yellowed papers written in very old ink.'

BAUDOT, Georges: *El Archivo de Indias en mi recuerdo*. Seville, 1985.

The Archive's Grand Premises—the Commodity Exchange

Suitable premises were sought to house such an important archive. Although it was argued that the documents ought to be easily accessible to the Court, the spot finally decided on was the splendid, solid building which still houses the Archive today—the Seville Commodity Exchange or *Lonja*. An important factor in that decision was the part played by Juan Bautista Muñoz, who argued in favor of the Commodity Exchange and supported his arguments in writing. In a report submitted on 24 May 1784, the architects, Carazas and Cintora, commissioned by Muñoz, stated:

'For the purpose in mind, no finer premises could be found in these kingdoms. Indeed, in all Spain, there is no building with such elegance and magnificence, or so well-lit, solid and well-proportioned for storing, arranging and safeguarding the documents.'

However, those views were regarded by Gálvez, a native of Málaga, as merely technical reinforcement of the objective he had set his mind to—that of transferring documents pertaining to the New World to the stately Commodity Exchange in Seville. Designed by Juan de Herrera and commissioned by Philip II, the Exchange was built in the last two decades of the 16th century in response to continuous demands by the Archbishopric and Cathedral Chapter of Seville and the Indies

The exhibition halls.

The area that had housed the archives from the very beginning was subsequently remodelled, but not without some controversy. The thick walls dividing rooms were removed and replaced by powerful arches, setting up a single, U-shaped area made up of three spacious bays. ABOVE: *partial view of the north, east and south wings with their mahogany shelving resting on Málaga marble, where the archival material has always been kept.*

Merchant Guild. In the second half of the 16th century, it is strange that the 'Indies merchants' of cosmopolitan Seville, 'port and gateway to the Americas', should not have had any other place for their commercial transactions than the steps around the Cathedral. Even when the weather was bad, they used to meet in the building's *Patio de los Naranjos* (Court of Orange Trees) or in the very naves of the Cathedral, despite the nearby relief of Christ driving the merchants from the temple which had been set above the Cathedral door as a warning in 1520.

They obviously needed a place to call their own, where they could hammer out their trade deals, and Philip II ended up giving in to Church demands and the merchants' petitions. He gave them permission to conduct their business on the site of the former Mint and the Royal Ironworks. However, in order to finance the venture, he levied a 'commodity tax' on all goods entering or leaving Seville.

Juan de Herrera, who was supervising building work at El Escorial at the time, produced the original design for the project, which was variously interpreted by Juan de Minjares, Alonso de Vandelvira and Miguel Zumárraga. Construction work on the magnificent building lasted from 1583 to 1646.

Main staircase.

The solemn, main staircase was completely refurbished when the Commodity Exchange was remodelled to house the Archive. The other major operation was the removal of the walls dividing the thirteen rooms on the north, east and south wings on the first floor. Lucas Cintora's influence is particularly noticeable in this staircase, where he removed some flaws, replaced the steps and balustrades and added black and red marble facings.

'I have always been awed by the austere architecture, the hushed reading rooms with their monastic atmosphere and the long galleries with their shelves of archives and their air of a cold, imperial mausoleum—at least they are cool in summer. Regulars like us always referred to the building as 'the Archive'. More than affection, familiarity or confidence, it was a question of respect—we were talking about the archive *par excellence,* the archetype of all archives, the scientific Jerusalem of research workers.'

CÉSPEDES DEL CASTILLO, Guillermo: *El Archivo General de Indias en mi recuerdo.* Seville, 1985.

The two-story Exchange is based on a square ground plan, with 56 meter-long sides. The central court, surrounded by columns with ashlar buttresses, leads into two naves—an outer nave and a porticoed inner nave. The entire building is made of stone and the two vaulted stories are linked by a monumental staircase. Despite its rather hermetic appearance, the fact that the building has ten entrances bears out its original function as a public meeting place.

In the 17th century, when Seville went into decline after being superseded by Cádiz as the hub of overseas trade, the Commodity Exchange gradually fell into disuse. By the second half of the 18th century, after the *Casa de la Contratación* or 'House of the Indies' and the Consulate had moved to Cádiz, the building had a markedly dilapidated appearance, even though a consular office was still kept on its premises. Bartolomé Esteban Murillo set up his Public Academy of Painting there and part of the building was even used as a tenement house at one stage.

Thus, when José de Gálvez chose the ailing Commodity Exchange as the site for his General Archive of the Indies, the building took on a new lease of life. Once the occupants had been evicted, the architect Lucas Cintora, under the direction of Juan Bautista Muñoz and, subsequently, Antonio de Lara y Zúñiga, set about the task of remodelling the building. One of the most striking changes was the renovation of the entrance staircase. Its old steps and balustrades were replaced, and the skirting re-tiled in black and red marble. Similarly, the partition walls separating the thirteen rooms on the first floor were removed to form one large hall with U-shaped galleries. Their walls were lined with beautiful mahogany and cedar shelving designed by Juan de Villanueva and built by Blas de Molner.

The Archival Material

The first documents arrived from Simancas on 14 October 1785. Thereafter, a steady flow of documents was sent in consignments from the major Indies institutions: the Council of the Indies, the House of the Indies, the Consulates, and the Secretariats of State and the Indies. The General Archive of the Indies had come into being. All documents dated before 1760 were sent to the new Archive, while later material remained the property of the administrative bodies that had issued it. The Archive continued to take in large consignments in the 19th and even the 20th century.

Arranging the Material

In accordance with the 'Statutes of the General Archive of the Indies', issued in 1790, all documents are arranged by what has come to be known as 'principles of provenance'. However, that procedure has not always been observed in the historical process of absorbing material from the Simancas archive or from administrative sources, or when part of the material was rearranged in the 19th century.

The Archive is currently divided into 15 Sections. Of these, 11 are classified by provenance, and the remaining 4 according to historical criteria or merely to ensure their preservation. The largest section, that of 'Government', is divided into 15 Sub-sections, corresponding to the 14 *Audiencias* or tribunal jurisdictions into which the New World was divided, and the *Indiferente General,* containing all documents of a general nature not related to any particular territorial jurisdiction.

Chest for keeping archival documents.

The Archive of Simancas had a large collection of such chests, used for safeguarding documents, which were designed by the archivist, Diego de Ayala. One of them must have found its way to Seville with one of the original consigments sent from Simancas. The contents of the chest were listed on a parchment scroll bearing the coat-of-arms of Philip II and dated 1567, which was subsequently lost.

The Council of the Indies Documents and the 'Classified Channel'

Here, then, are some of the most salient features of the Archive and the way it is arranged. It should be pointed out that the most important items are considered to be the documents issued by the Council of the Indies:

– The documents generated by the Council of the Indies in its capacity as the Supreme Court of Justice for Indies affairs are arranged into two Sections: IV, Justicia (Justice) and VI, Escribanía de Cámara (Chamber of Justice Records). The archival division parallels the name change—from *Justicia* to *Escribanía de Cámara*—implemented in the Council's justice division in 1571. Documents dated before that change were transferred to the Archive from Simancas, while subsequent material came from Madrid.

– The Council of the Indies also acted as a supreme auditing body via its division known as the *Contaduría General* (Audit Office). Relevant documents are catalogued in Section II, Contaduría (Auditing) and, particularly those issued after 1760, in Section V, Gobierno (Government).

– The 'Government' Section, the largest in the Archive, with over 18,000 files, consists mainly of administrative records issued by the Council of the Indies. However, the system of joint administration based on the Councils underwent a marked change in the 18th century, when the Bourbon monarchs introduced a personalized style of government and dispatch based on Secretariats and the use of the *vía reservada* (classified channel). This triggered radical changes in overseas administration. The duties performed by the Council of the Indies were gradually transferred to the Secretariats, while the role of the Council was restricted to that of an advisory and judicial body. This process affected the Archive in that it prompted the creation of a single Section—that of 'Government'—to house all

The court in the Commodity Exchange.

PARCERISA, F.J.
[Central court in the Consulate]
Plate from Recuerdos y bellezas de España, *T., X, pp. 535.*

This engraving by Parcerisa shows the court in the Commodity Exchange in the days when the Archive was housed on the first floor. The upper arcade was closed off, while the court and the galleries were open to the public, who entered via the impressive bays on the north and south facades now used as document repositories. Those areas were later glassed in and closed to the public.

documents from Simancas, the Council of the Indies and the Secretariats. It was further augmented by records from the Council's Audit Office.

– Some documents from the Council and the 'classified channel' are filed in other Sections of the Archive. For instance, those associated with Royal Patronage (Crown rights in Church affairs), and others from the 15th to the 17th century regarded as historically important or relevant, are filed under PATRONATO (Patronage). The material in question was acquired from the Council of the Indies and is consulted more frequently than any other part of the Archive, as it includes the documents dealing with the early period of discovery, conquest and colonization.

Documents from the House of the Indies

This, the second largest and second most important fond in the Archive, comprises documents from the *Casa de la Contratación* or 'House of the Indies', founded in Seville in 1503. In 1717, it was transferred to Cádiz, where it remained until its dissolution in 1790. The fond consists of almost 6,000 files of considerable importance as they cover all the institution's activities: all matters relating to trade and shipping between Spain and the New World, organization and control of fleets

Shelving.

When the Commodity Exchange was remodelled to house the Archive, Juan Bautista Muñoz chose mahogany and cedar wood for the shelving. He argued that, like all the other materials in the Archive, the woods had to be beautiful and durable, 'particularly in these climes, with the prevailing heat and humidity'. Juan de Villanueva, who designed the fittings, claimed that, as Herrera had done in Simancas, they ought to be made of 'plaster'. However, the mahogany and cedar, which had been ordered from Cuba, had already arrived in Spain. The shelves were built by Blas de Molner, who did justice to Muñoz's original idea: 'the idea will yield so durable, simple, beautiful and noble a work that even the envious will refrain from reprobation'.

Ground floor gallery.

In 1913, at the time of the fourth centenary of the discovery of the Pacific, these galleries, which give onto the court, were glassed in to be used as a repository, and beautiful metal shelves were fitted. The cannon seen in the background was on board the galleon, Santa María de Atocha, when it sank off the coast of Florida in 1622. The ship was built in Seville. Documents in the Archive provided clues which enabled the sunken galleon to be located. The cannon was salvaged by Mel Fisher, who presented it to H.M. Queen Sofía of Spain.

and sailings, the 'Indies passengers', civil litigation between trading companies, freight, administering the estates of the deceased, contracts and so forth.

The Consulates

Without going into detail about all the sections, it is sufficient to draw attention to Section XII, CONSULADOS (Consulates), which contains documents from the old *Universidad de Cargadores de Indias* or 'University of Indies Merchants'. This guild, whose members were merchants engaged in trade with the Indies, was housed in the same Commodity Exchange building, now the seat of the Archive. By royal privilege, it was awarded Consulate status in 1543. It was active in Seville for many years and in Cádiz as from the 18th century.

The General Archive of the Indies and Research

The Archive was founded for the historiographic purpose of promoting research. However, after its inception in the late-18th century, although the premises were sumptuously fitted out, only the most essential facilities and services were available to the public.

To begin with, it was not open to research by the general public and it lacked anything resembling a reading room. To be sure, no one would have been allowed to write a history based on the Archive's records—any such history had necessarily to be in line with the interests of the monarchy. As enshrined in the institution's Statutes, drawn up in 1790, immediately after its inception, access was not permitted to just anyone wishing to consult its documents:

'Nobody may be furnished a copy of any document, or the information it may contain. Indeed, the mere intimation of its existence would be inadmissible. No person is authorized to handle the inventories or indices, or to be present when they are examined and on no account may anyone seek or retrieve documents of any kind.'

All that the Statutes permitted was for institutions or 'bona fide' interested parties to seek confirmation of the existence of a document through the Archive's personnel, after which they could request royal permission to secured authorized copies of the same.

Nevertheless, it is worth recalling that the 'official history', intended to be based on a study of the Indies documents, was never actually written. Juan Bautista

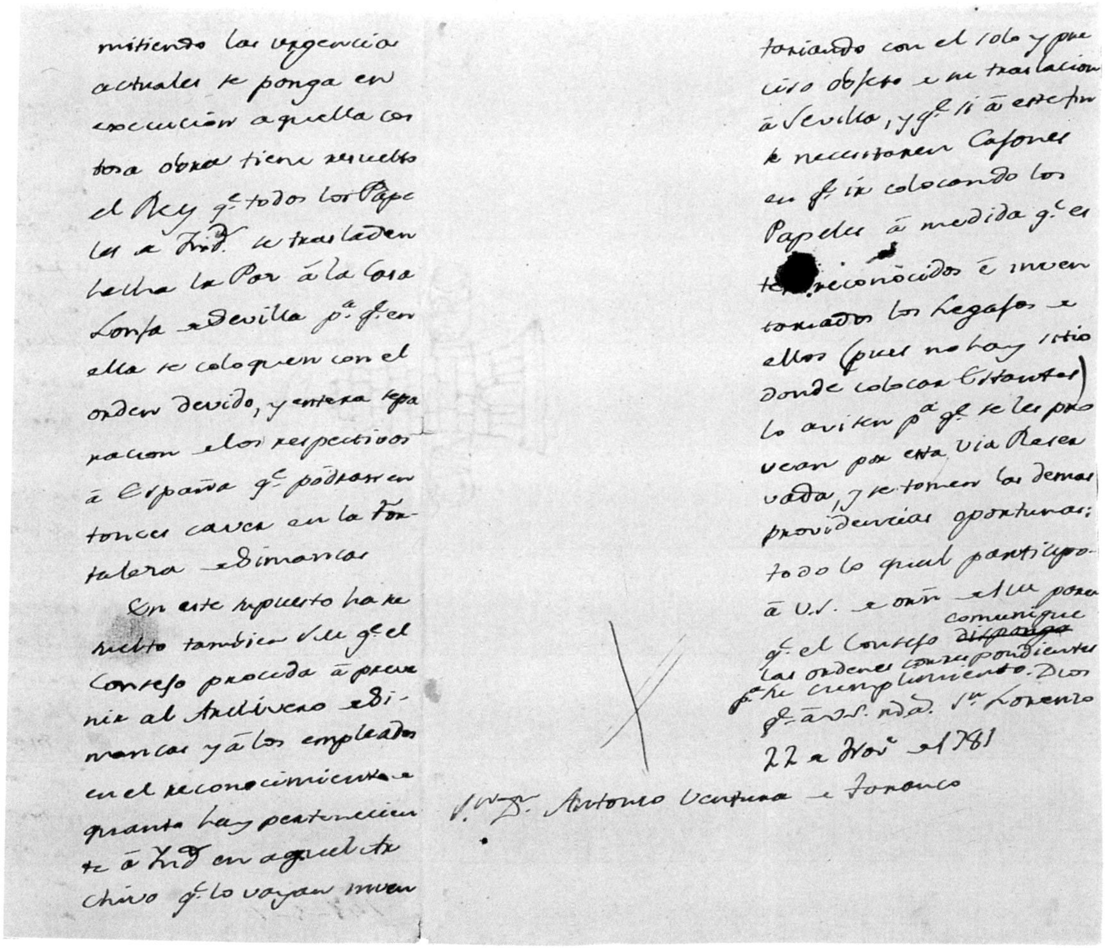

mitiendo las urgencias
actuales se ponga en
execucion aquella con
tra obra tiene resuelto
el Rey q.e todos los Pape
les a Ind.s se trasladen
desde la Por a la Casa
Lonja de Sevilla p.a q.e en
ella se coloquen con el
orden devido, y entera sepa
racion de los respectivos
a España q.e podran en
tonces caver en la For
taleza de Simancas
En este supuesto ha re
suelto tambien S.M. q.e el
Consejo proceda a preve
nir al Archivero de Si-
mancas y a los empleados
en el reconocimiento de
quanto hay perteneciente a Ind.s en aquel Ar
chivo q.e lo vayan inven
tariando con el solo y pre
ciso objeto de su traslacion
a Sevilla, y q.e si a este fin
se necesitaren Cajones
en q.e ir colocando los
Papeles a medida q.e es
tén reconocidos e inven
tariados los Legajos e
ellos (pues no hay sitio
donde colocar Estantes)
lo avisen p.a q.e se les pro
vean por esta Via Reser
vada, y se tomen las demas
providencias oportunas;
todo lo qual participo
a V.S. de orn de S.M. para
q.e el Consejo comunique
las ordenes correspondientes
p.a su cumplimiento. Dios
g.e a V.S. m.s a.s S.n Lorenzo
22 de Nov.e de 1781
S.r D.n Antonio Ventura de Taranco

The founding of the Archive.

22 November 1781, San Lorenzo. Draft of the royal order, conveyed to Antonio Ventura Taranco, Secretary of the Council of the Indies for New Spain, by José de Gálvez, informing of the monarch's decision to have 'all the papers of the Indies' transferred to the Seville Commodity Exchange. It also requests the Council to have the Archive's employees draw up an inventory of the documents to be consigned.
2 sheets, 4to.
Indiferente General, 1852.

This brief document is the first draft of the king's decision to found a new archive for safeguarding all records of Indies affairs in Seville, instead of enlarging the Archive of Simancas for the purpose, as originally intended.

Muñoz, who was formally commissioned by the king to do so, was only able to produce a first volume, which got as far as the year 1500. He did, however, bequeath another, unfinished and unpublished volume that covered the period up to the death of Ferdinand the Catholic.

In the end, it was the passage of time, the liberal currents of opinion of the 19th century and progress in the field of historical critique that enabled the aforementioned history to be laboriously compiled and reworked by the hundreds of researchers who eventually had free access to the Archive's reading rooms.

Archives of a New Era

Today, exactly two centuries after its inception, the General Archive of the Indies has regained its prominence as an innovative institution among the world's archives. The quincentenary celebrations provided a unique opportunity to incorporate the latest information technology for processing the historical archives and settling the complex dilemma facing all archives—that of conservation as opposed to dissemination.

In the Archive's two centuries of existence, its approach to archiving has undergone profound changes, as have the archives themselves. Those changes are commensurate with the worldwide revolution in technology. First, albeit a commonplace, the archives have indeed become veritable 'arsenals of history'. Second,

Juan Bautista Muñoz.

Juan Bautista Muñoz, a historian, was born in Museros (Valencia). The 'Chief Cosmographer of the Indies', he was one of the Archive's founding fathers. Commissioned by King Charles III to compile a 'History of the New World', he journeyed through Spain in search of the requisite documentation. His endeavors influenced the decision to bring all Indies documents together under one roof. The above portrait, housed in the Archive, is a copy painted by Rafael Estalella of an original which has traditionally been ascribed to Goya, although the attribution has never been proved.

Charles III.

Charles III, the great 'King of the Enlightenment', commissioned the founding of the Archive on the urgings of his Indies Secretary, José de Gálvez, the Marquis of Sonora. The above is a copy, housed in the Archive, of an original by Mengs in the Prado Museum.

currents of free thinking have prompted the archives to be fully declassified. Consequently, the reading rooms are now thronged with visitors. However, this poses a serious threat in that continuous and indiscriminate use of the documents is leading to their deterioration.

Apart from the increasing number of researchers in the reading rooms, it is interesting to note the recent changes in their approach, aspirations and academic background. Now that they have rightful access to records, research workers are becoming more demanding when it comes to services offered by the Archive. In short, they have become 'customers' exercising their right to more widely available archival material and improved working conditions, particularly in terms of the new information technologies, global communications and the widespread use of computer technology in research.

In today's world, with information networks providing instant access to huge amounts of data all over the world, is it reasonable to expect researchers to continue working in the Archive's reading rooms with the same old resources?

If the Archive's main purpose is to preserve and disseminate documentary data, how can it possibly serve both interests equally? How can total accessibility be provided when that involves documents being damaged? How can documents be rescued for posterity in the light of intensive, indiscriminate use of them? And,

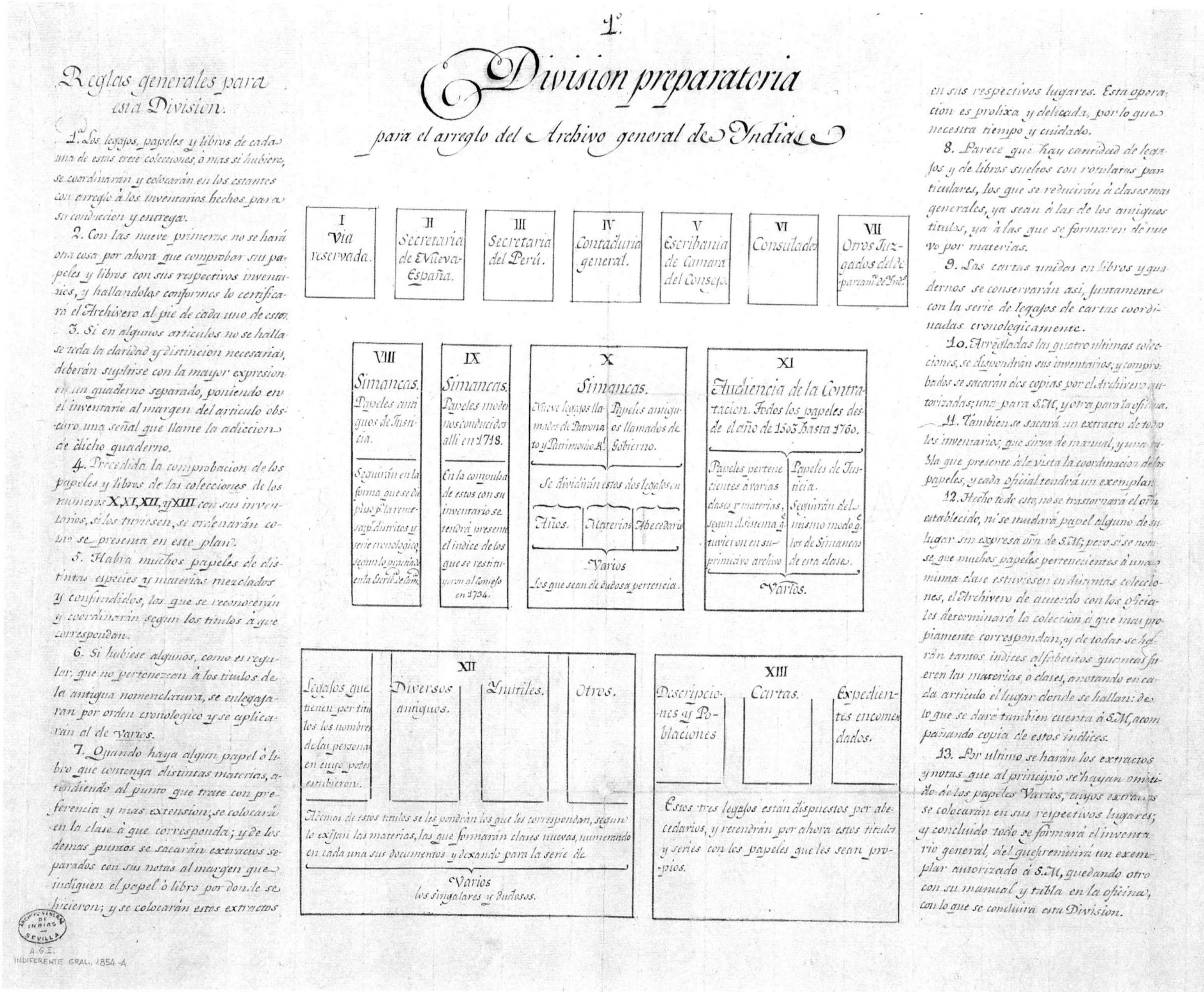

1.º

División preparatoria para el arreglo del Archivo general de Indias

Reglas generales para esta División.

1.º Los legajos, papeles y libros de cada una de estas trece colecciones, o mas si hubiere, se coordinarán y colocarán en los estantes con arreglo á los inventarios hechos para su conduccion y entrega.

2. Con las nueve primeras no se hará otra cosa por ahora que comprobar sus papeles y libros con sus respectivos inventarios, y hallandolas conformes lo certificará el Archivero al pie de cada uno de estos.

3. Si en algunos articulos no se hallase toda la claridad y distincion necesarias, deberán suplirse con la mayor expresion en un quaderno separado, poniendo en el inventario al margen del articulo obscuro una señal que llame la adicion de dicho quaderno.

4. Precedida la comprobacion de los papeles y libros de las colecciones de los numeros X, XI, XII, y XIII con sus inventarios, si los tuviesen, se ordenarán como se presenta en este plan.

5. Habrá muchos papeles de distintas especies y materias mezclados y confundidos, los que se reconocerán y coordinarán segun los titulos á que correspondan.

6. Si hubiese algunos, como es regular, que no pertenezcan á los titulos de la antigua nomenclatura, se enlegajarán por orden cronologico y se aplicarán al de Varios.

7. Quando haya algun papel ó libro que contenga distintas materias, atendiendo al punto que trate con preferencia y mas extension, se colocará en la clase á que corresponda; y de los demas puntos se sacarán extractos separados con sus notas al margen que indiquen el papel ó libro por donde se hicieron; y se colocarán estos extractos en sus respectivos lugares. Esta operacion es prolixa y delicada, por lo que necesita tiempo y cuidado.

8. Parece que hay cantidad de legajos y de libros sueltos con rotulatas particulares, los que se reducirán á clases mas generales, ya sean á las de los antiguos titulos, ya á las que se formaren de nuevo por materias.

9. Las cartas unidas en libros y quadernos se conservarán asi, juntamente con la serie de legajos de cartas coordinadas cronologicamente.

10. Arregladas las quatro ultimas colecciones, se dispondrán sus inventarios; y comprobados se sacarán dos copias por el Archivero autorizadas; una para S.M. y otra para la oficina.

11. Tambien se sacará un extracto de todos los inventarios, que sirva de manual, y una tabla que presente á le vista la coordinacion de los papeles, y cada oficial tendrá un exemplar.

12. Hecho todo esto, no se trastornará el orden establecido, ni se mudará papel alguno de su lugar sin expresa orn. de S.M.; pero si se notase que muchos papeles pertenecientes á una misma clase estuviesen en distintas colecciones, el Archivero de acuerdo con los oficiales determinará la colección á que mas propiamente correspondan, y de todas se harán tantos indices alfabeticos quantas fueren las materias o clases, anotando en cada articulo el lugar donde se hallan: de lo que se dará tambien cuenta á S.M. acompañando copia de estos indices.

13. Por ultimo se harán los extractos y notas que al principio se hayan omitido de los papeles Varios, cuyos extractos se colocarán en sus respectivos lugares; y concluido todo se formará el inventario general, del qual se remitirá un exemplar autorizado á S.M. quedando otro con su manual y tabla en la oficina, con lo que se concluirá esta División.

I	II	III	IV	V	VI	VII
Via reservada.	Secretaria de N. España.	Secretaria del Perú.	Contaduria general.	Escribania de Camara del Consejo.	Consulado.	Otros Juzgados del Departam.to de Ind.

VIII — Simancas. Papeles antiguos de Justicia. Seguirán en la forma que se dió plano p.ª la remesa, distritos y serie cronologica, segun lo ordenado en la Escrib. de Cam.

IX — Simancas. Papeles modernos conducidos allí en 1718. En la comunicacion de estos con su inventario se tendrá presente el indice de los que se restituyeron al Consejo en 1784.

X — Simancas. Nueve legajos llamados del Patronato y Patrimonio R.l — Papeles antiguos llamados de Gobierno. Se dividirán estos dos legajos, en: Años. Materias. Abecedario. Varios. Los que sean de dudosa pertenencia.

XI — Audiencia de la Contratacion. Todos los papeles desde el año de 1503 hasta 1760. Papeles pertenecientes á varias clases y materias, segun el sistema que tuvieron en su primitivo archivo. — Papeles de Justicia. Seguirán del mismo modo que los de Simancas de esta clase. Varios.

XII — Legajos que tienen por titulos los nombres de las personas en cuyo poder estuvieron. — Diversos antiguos. — Inutiles. — Otros. Ademas de estos titulos se les pondrán los que les correspondan, segun lo exijan las materias, las que formarán clases nuevas, numerando en cada una sus documentos y dexando para la serie de Varios los singulares y dudosos.

XIII — Descripciones y Poblaciones. — Cartas. — Expedientes encomendados. Estos tres legajos están dispuestos por abecedarios, y retendrán por ahora estos titulos y series con los papeles que les sean propios.

Preparatory work in the Archive.

[1790]
Tentative arrangement of the archival material in the General Archive of the Indies.
Sent by Juan Agustín Ceán Bermúdez to Antonio Porlier in a letter dated 12 October 1790.
1 sheet (384 x 473 mm).
Indiferente General, 1854.

The archivist, Juan Agustín Ceán Bermúdez, sent this plan showing the initial arrangement of the archives.

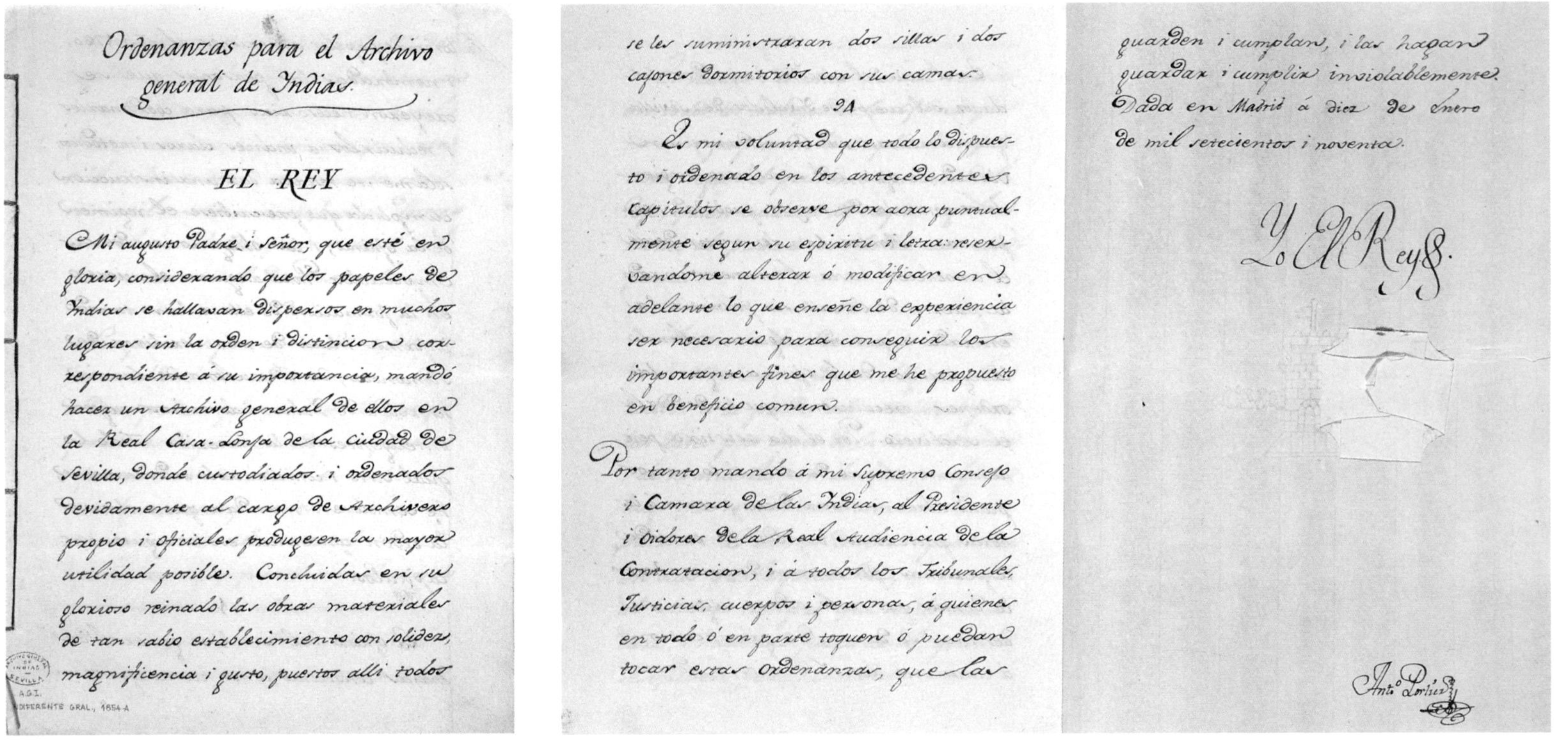

Ordenanzas para el Archivo general de Indias.

EL REY

Mi augusto Padre i señor, que esté en gloria, considerando que los papeles de Indias se hallavan dispersos en muchos lugares sin la orden i distincion correspondiente á su importancia, mandó hacer un Archivo general de ellos en la Real Casa-Lonja de la ciudad de Sevilla, donde custodiados i ordenados devidamente al cargo de Archivero propio i oficiales produxesen la mayor utilidad posible. Concluidas en su glorioso reinado las obras materiales de tan sabio establecimiento con solidez, magnificencia i gusto, puestos allí todos

A.G.I. INDIFERENTE GRAL. 1854-A

se les suministraran dos sillas i dos cajones dormitorios con sus camas.

91

Es mi voluntad que todo lo dispuesto i ordenado en los antecedentes capitulos se observe por aora puntualmente segun su espiritu i letra: reservandome alterar ó modificar en adelante lo que enseñe la experiencia ser necesario para conseguir los importantes fines que me he propuesto en beneficio comun.

Por tanto mando á mi Supremo Consejo i Camara de las Indias, al Presidente i Oidores de la Real Audiencia de la Contratacion, i á todos los Tribunales, Justicias, cuerpos i personas, á quienes en todo ó en parte toquen ó puedan tocar estas Ordenanzas, que las

guarden i cumplan, i las hagan guardar i cumplir inviolablemente. Dada en Madrid á diez de Enero de mil setecientos i noventa.

Yo El Rey

Antº Porlier

The Statutes of the General Archive of the Indies.

10 January 1790, Madrid.
Autograph signatures of Charles IV and Antonio Porlier. Seal of Charles IV.
Indiferente General, 1854.

Those statutes, printed that same year by the 'Viuda de Ibarra' company, were a landmark in the history of Spain's archival administration.

OPPOSITE: *Ground plan of the Archive.*

23 April 1788, Seville.
'Ground floor of the former Commodity Exchange of Seville, showing the layout as used by the Consulate. No essential change has been wrought in the magnificent building, the only minor changes, marked in crimson in one of the corners, being to set apart the treasury department.'
By Felix Caraza.
723 x 506 mm.
MP. Europa y África, 58.

The Archive originally occupied only the first floor, the ground floor still housing the mercantile Consulate. The pressing need for more archival space led to the eviction of the ground floor occupants, which aroused heated protest. The plan shown here was part of a dossier concerning the controversy between the Consulate and the curator of the Archive, Antonio de Lara y Zúñiga.

last, how can methods of data retrieval be speeded up to the satisfaction of computer-literate users when the workings of the Archive are still purely manual?

The Archive's Computer System

In the context of increasingly greater public access to archives and the latter's clamor for speedier services and faster retrieval, a unique initiative is afoot in the world of archiving—that of computerizing the General Archive of the Indies.

A computerized system was developed jointly over the last few years by the Ministry of Culture, IBM España and the Ramón Areces Foundation, who pledged their support on the occasion of the Expo 92 festivities. That move has set the Archive firmly on the threshold of the 21st century.

No historical archive today can claim to have an integrated computer system covering all their services. Neither are they in a position to offer a standardized system of descriptive information, including a data base featuring 'all' the traditional tools for describing information. Similarly, no historical archive in the world is currently able to provide its users with eleven million pages of digitally managed data stored on optical disk for direct, on-screen retrieval or hard-copy print-out.

The two main functions of historical archives—storage and dissemination—are at the heart of the project of computerization. The new technologies will eventually yield the new tools required for instant access to information from any point in the 'global village'.

At present, after years of hard work, those millions of digitized pages stored on optical disk can now be retrieved by a complex system of contextualized data bases. In all, a third of all retrievals and paper reproductions of the Archive's docu-

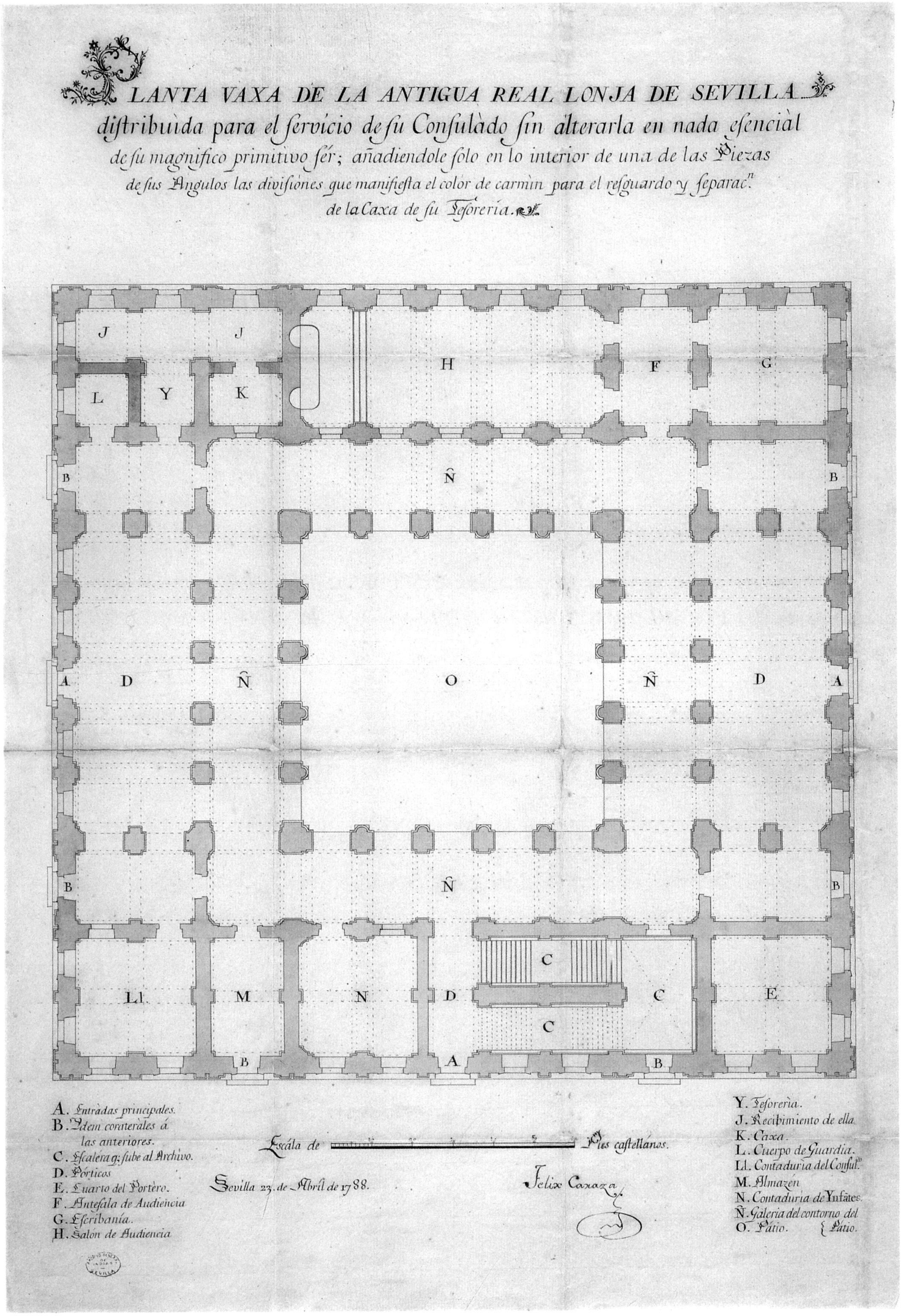
PLANTA VAXA DE LA ANTIGUA REAL LONJA DE SEVILLA
distribuida para el servicio de su Consulado sin alterarla en nada esencial
de su magnifico primitivo ser; añadiendole solo en lo interior de una de las Piezas
de sus Angulos las divisiones que manifiesta el color de carmin para el resguardo y separacn.
de la Caxa de su Tesoreria.
A. Entradas principales.
B. Idem conterales á las anteriores.
C. Escalera q. sube al Archivo.
D. Porticos.
E. Cuarto del Portero.
F. Antesala de Audiencia.
G. Escribania.
H. Salon de Audiencia.
Escala de Pies castellanos.
Sevilla 23. de Abril de 1788.
Felix Caraza
Y. Tesoreria.
J. Recibimiento de ella.
K. Caxa.
L. Cuerpo de Guardia.
Ll. Contaduria del Consdo.
M. Almazen.
N. Contaduria de Yufates.
Ñ. Galeria del contorno del Patio.
O. Patio.

Archive court.

The Commodity Exchange was built around a central court which the merchants used for their 'deals and contracts'. The court is surrounded by two floors of galleries, with pilasters and engaged columns (Tuscan, on the ground floor and Ionic on the first floor). In the early 19th century, the first floor was sealed off with brickwork for archival storage. The ground floor remained open until the second decade of the 20th century, when the first-floor brick frontage was removed and both floors glassed in, as shown above.

ments are processed digitally. In 1996, for instance, 30% of all research queries in the General Archive of the Indies were performed on the Archive's computers.

This is, of course, a merely statistical exposition, but it does give some idea of what has been achieved thus far. Over a quarter of the queries processed in the Archive's reading rooms are done on computer, while the documents themselves are stored intact on their shelves. Their preservation is therefore ensured. Moreover, once communication lines are upgraded to a suitable capacity, the Archive will be able to offer 'remote–access' retrieval of its documentary material.

Other Prospects

As we have seen, the General Archive of the Indies has made enormous progress in recent years in designing, developing and implementing its computerized retrieval system, as attested by many professionals around the world who send us

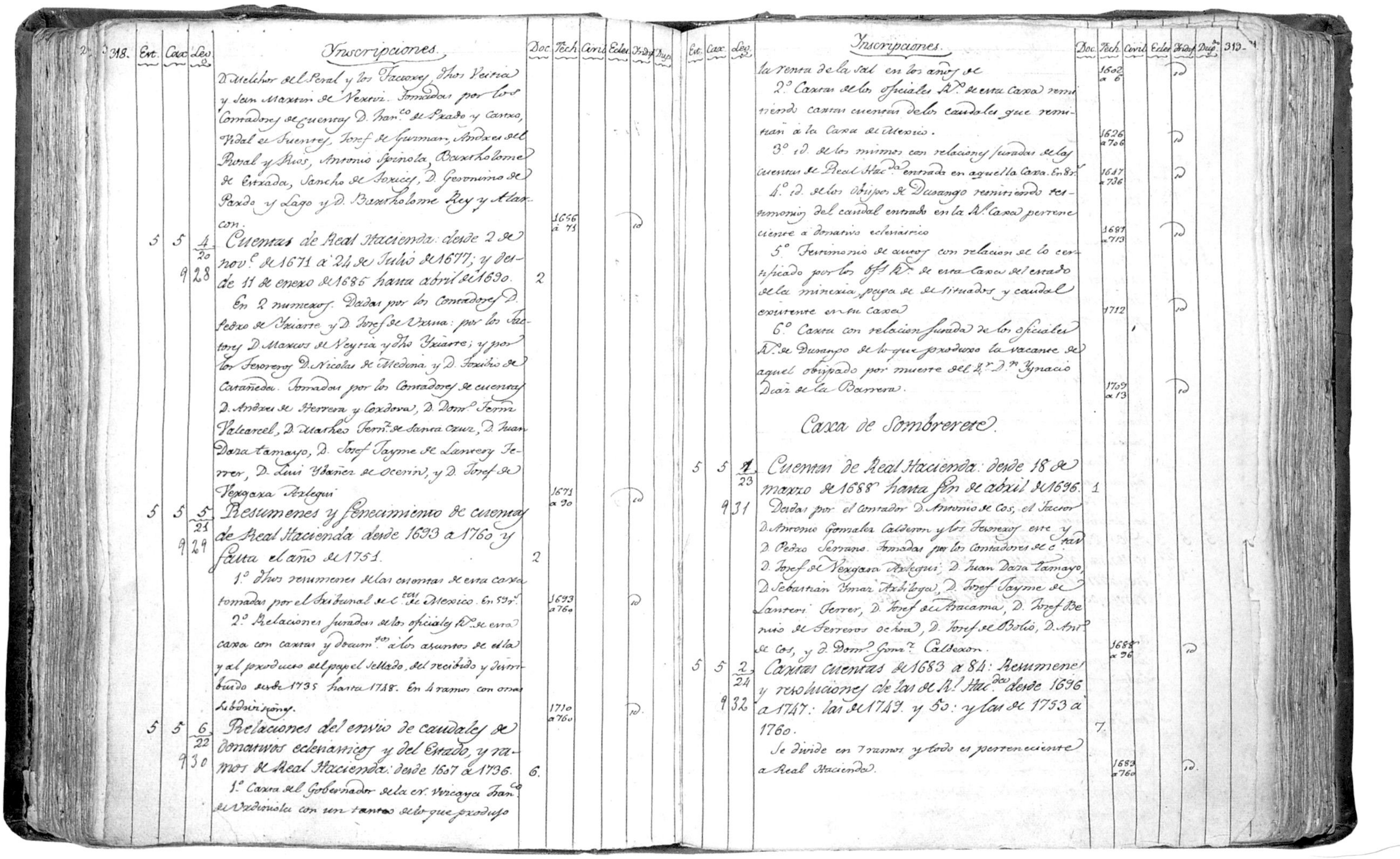

An old Archive inventory.

'Analytical inventory of all the papers sent by the Audit Office of the Council of the Indies...'

From March 1791 to January 1792, the well-known scholar, Juan Agustín Ceán Bermúdez, directed the compilation of documents from the Audit Office of the Council of the Indies, shortly after their arrival at the General Archive of the Indies. Extra signatures have been added to the inventory, which is still in use today.

their queries or come personally to see the system in operation. And, the success of the venture is also confirmed by the improved service this innovation provides.

While new technologies facilitate our endeavor to shape a new approach to historical archiving, other ideas have been put into practice at the Archive. Foremost among them is an ambitious scheme for the building's restoration, renovation and enlargement in order to perform the wide variety of functions expected of a modern archive. The two major facets of the scheme are:

– Restoration of this building, of incalculable art-historical value, to recover its original splendor and to address the conservation issues it poses.

– In keeping with King Charles III's original purpose in the 18th century and the needs of today's world, the search for a more rationalized use of the building's facilities with a view to upgrading services and better preserving its content.

Currently under way is a project for completely restoring the building's frontage and roofing and an ambitious scheme for remodelling and enlarging the building, taking into account each and every one of the Archive's major requirements: functional distribution, additional areas for storage and public use, the security system, air-conditioning and so on.

The 'Cross of Oaths'.

Near the steps of the Commodity Exchange building, this jasper cross, thought to have been designed by Miguel de Zumárraga, presided over the trade dealings of the Indies merchants.

The 'Treasures' of the Archive

At this time of change and renewal, our endeavors to provide improved services include another initiative—the publication of this volume featuring the 'treasures' of the General Archive of the Indies.

Cultural promotion is now perceived as increasingly more important for archives. Indeed, the idea of presenting the general public with the historical legacy contained in the archives, if only in global terms, is gradually gaining momentum. This is, in short, the idea behind this volume—to make the General Archive of the Indies known to those who may not even have heard of it or who might have strolled past it thinking how deeply buried its treasures must be.

The book essentially sets out to describe the metropolitan institutions that controlled the administration of the New World, that is, the Council of the Indies, the *Casa de la Contratación,* the Secretariats of State and the Consulates. Attention is drawn to the documents in which their institutional functions are chronicled, particularly those documents considered to be historically important or visually attractive as illustrations. The selection of full-color reproductions of such documents is designed to give readers an idea of the wealth housed in the General Archive of the Indies and of the history of the Spanish New World.

The essential work was undertaken by a group of Archive officials. They wrote the institutional texts and the commentaries on the documents, which they likewise selected and catalogued. Purificación Medina wrote the chapters on the Council of the Indies and the Secretariats of State. The chapter on the *Casa de la Contratación* was written by Carmen Galbis, and the one on the Consulates by Antonio López. To provide an overview of the project and place it within its historical setting, María Antonia Colomar wrote the chapter dealing with the early period of the Indies: the discovery, exploration and conquest, and the vicissitudes, expectations and disappointments involved in the encounter between two worlds initially alien to each other.

Pedro González
Former Director of the General Archive of the Indies

THE NEW WORLD: THE START OF A GREAT ENTERPRISE

In the Hispano–Portuguese rivalry over Maluku, Portugal took the initiative as of 1434 after securing its monopoly of the route south of the Canary Islands by papal bulls (1455–1480) and the Treaty of Alcáçovas (1479–1480). The arrival of Columbus in the New World marked an initial success for the Castilian cause, which was consolidated in four bulls issued by Alexander VI: an *Inter Caetera* bull of donation (3. V. 1493), which granted the Catholic Kings possession of and authority over everything found west of Europe; an *Inter Caetera* bull of demarcation (4. V. 1493), which established an irregular line a hundred leagues west of the Azores and Cape Verde; an *Eximie Devotionis* bull (3. V. 1493) that granted certain privileges, and a *Dudum Siquidem* bull (26. IX. 1493) authorizing Castile to discover in the west whatever Portugal had failed to discover or occupy in the east. The Treaty of Tordesillas (7. VI. 1494) moved the line of demarcation to 370 leagues west of the Cape Verde islands, thus favoring Portugal.
In 1512, the Portuguese navigator, António de Abreu, reached the Spice Islands via Africa. In 1513, Vasco Núñez de Balboa discovered the Pacific, thereby demonstrating the feasibility of the western route to Maluku once a passage through the new continent had been found. That route was discovered in 1519 by another Portuguese navigator, Magellan, then in the service of Castile. Finally, in the Treaty of Zaragoza (1529), Charles V ceded his claims to Maluku to Portugal in return for 350,000 ducats. Thus, in the end, the competition was won by the Portuguese.

The Search for the Spice Islands

From the Mediterranean to the Atlantic: Precedents for the Discovery

What is traditionally known as the 'Discovery of America' was part and parcel of Europe's long process of medieval expansion and its exploration of the Atlantic, which prepared Europeans for an encounter with the New World by coming to grips with frontier life on land and dangers at sea.

During the 14th century, Europe was involved with the eastern Mediterranean where trading posts in Genoa, Florence and Venice acted as brokers for the luxury trade with the Far East, particularly in silk and spices. By the 15th century, however, only the Venetian settlements had survived pressure from the Turks and Venice still controlled the Asian trade.

At the same time, the Iberian countries—Spain and Portugal—had overspilled their borders and, as out-and-out rivals, had embarked on the conquest of new frontiers, this time in Africa. Their purpose was two-fold: on the one hand, to seek out an alternative to the traditional Mediterranean route, which had become hampered by the Ottoman advance and, on the other, the search for gold, an increasingly more coveted commodity which had become scarcer and more expensive following the depletion of precious metals in Europe by Italian cities.

The shift from the Mediterranean to the Atlantic was facilitated by technological advances in both shipbuilding and navigation, as well as improvements in marine surveys.

The Portuguese took the lead in the competition. From 1434 to 1487, they sailed around the entire Atlantic coast of Africa—in 1487, Bartolomeu Dias rounded the Cape of Good Hope; Vasco da Gama reached India in 1497–1498 and, in 1512, António de Abreu landed in the Moluccas, known as the Spice Islands.

Portugal consolidated its acquisitions through the issue of several papal bulls of concession, donation and privilege wherein the hegemony of those discoveries was established *usque ad Indos,* thereby laying the foundations for future demarcations.

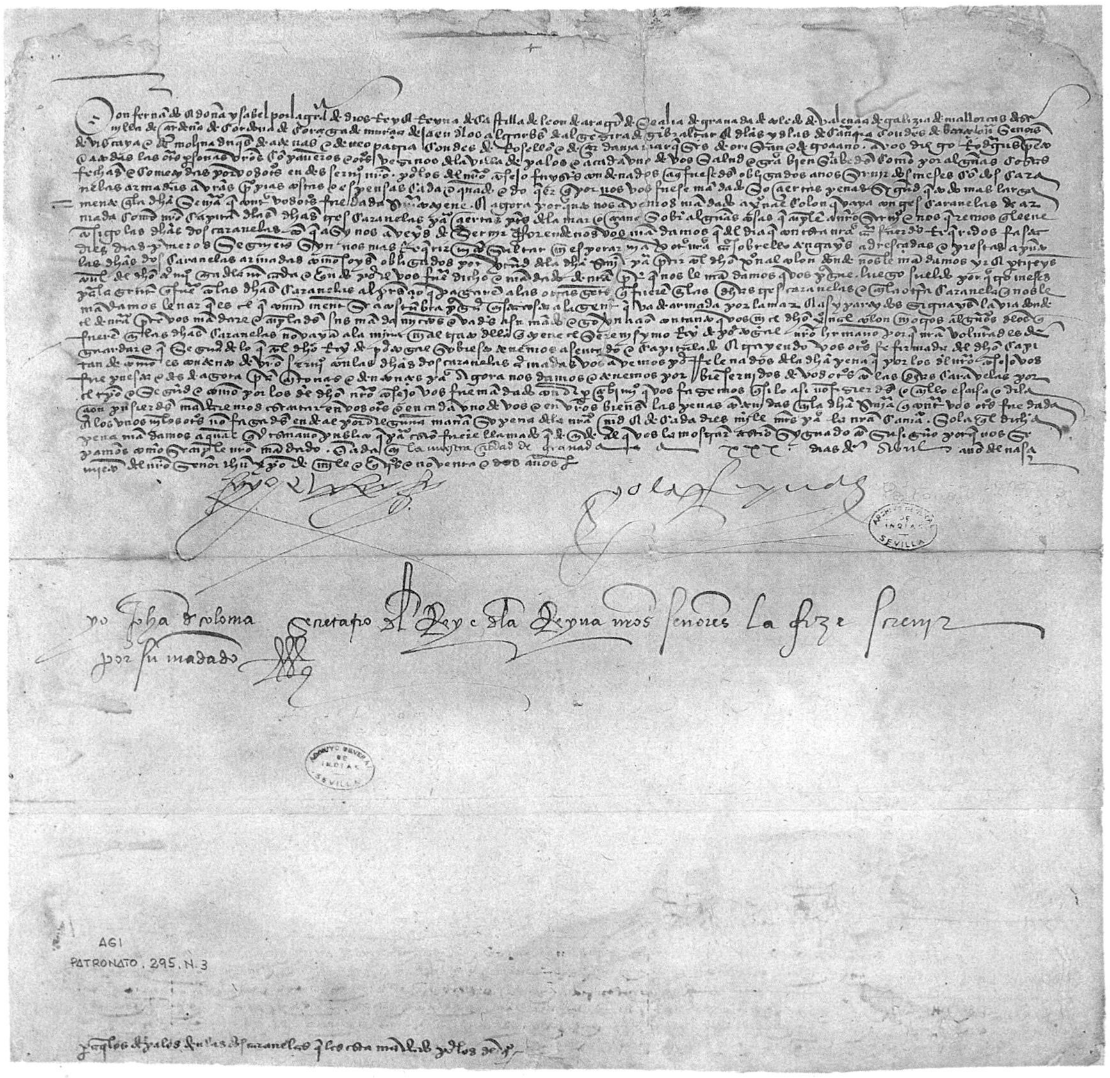

Columbus' first voyage.

30 April 1492, Granada.
The original royal warrant from the Catholic Kings in which Diego Rodríguez Prieto and other inhabitants of the town of Palos are ordered, as a sentence for crimes committed, to ready two caravels to sail with Columbus on his first voyage.
1 fol. (300 x 307 mm).
Patronato, 295, N. 3.

Preparations for Columbus' first voyage were set in motion by royal orders on 30 April and 15 May 1492, both as regards the vessels and crew and provisions. This command is noteworthy in that it impresses on the inhabitants of Palos the compulsory nature of serving the Crown on two caravels for a period of a year as punishment for certain crimes; these caravels had been assigned to the first of Columbus' expeditions. A Crown undertaking, the expedition had to set sail from a royal port but, since Cádiz was being used for the expulsion of the Jews, the Spanish monarchs purchased half the town of Palos from the Silva brothers, forty days prior to setting sail.

Having been relegated to the Canary Islands, the Castilians set about circumventing the Portuguese monopoly by securing licenses from the Catholic Kings to fish, trade, search for slaves and even build settlements in Guinea and Mina. Friction arose with the Portuguese and both sides even seized the other's vessels until, in the end, the Treaty of Alcáçovas (1479–1480) was signed between the two powers assigning zones of influence to each: the Canary Islands to Castile and the rest of Africa to Portugal.

From the Atlantic to the Caribbean and from Alcáçovas to Tordesillas

Parallel to and simultaneously with the Portuguese voyages of discovery, the Spaniards sought the same objective by sailing in a westerly direction, where the Treaty of Alcáçovas was not applicable.

Columbus' right to bear arms.

[1498]
Christopher Columbus' shield, after being embellished with a castle and a lion, authorized by the Catholic Kings in 1493, as a reward for services rendered as Admiral in the discovery of the New World.
Book of Privileges of Veragua.
290 x 210 mm.
Patronato, 295, N. 98.

After returning in March 1493 from his first voyage of discovery, Columbus met the Spanish monarchs in Barcelona between 15 and 20 April. Having publicized the expedition in a letter to the Catholic Kings, Columbus was received effusively by the monarchs, who confirmed his privileges and embellished his coat-of-arms in royal warrants of 20 and 28 May: 'We hereby grant you license to bear, on your banners, coats-of-arms and other heraldic devices, in addition to your arms and above them, a castle and a lion. We grant these to you, it should be stated, as follows: vert a castle or, *in the first quarter of the shield; in the second quarter,* argent a lion purpure; *in the third quarter, golden isles on a wavy sea and, in the fourth quarter, your customary bearings' (Patronato, 9, r. 1, fol. 30. v.). The design shows departures from the original command, as it was probably made according to the description by Gonzalo Fernández de Oviedo.*

This project was devised by Christopher Columbus. Resident in Portugal from 1476 to 1485, he built up a substantial corpus of geographical information based on scientific theories and on public accounts and news. In science, he sided with the current of opinion associated with Paolo del Pozo Toscanelli and Marco Polo who held the western route to the Spicery to be the shortest. When it came to contemporary accounts, Columbus was strategically placed to hear all manner of rumors regarding the Portuguese expeditions and the existence of land west of the Canary Islands, apparently sighted by survivors of shipwrecks. This may have been how he came to hear the confession of a seaman, Álvaro Sánchez de Huelva, who had purportedly reached the Antilles on his return voyage from Mina and subsequently confided his secret to Columbus, giving rise to a theory of 'pre-discovery'.

When John II of Portugal rejected his project, Columbus moved to Spain and, in 1486, submitted it to the Catholic Kings. Then began a protracted, seven-year petitionary procedure at Court during which Columbus' proposals were discussed at the Councils of Salamanca, Cordova and Santa Fe. However, there were two reasons why official sanction was late in coming: his project was regarded as too far-fetched and the privileges he sought in return for his enterprise an important obstacle.

On 17 April 1492, the agreement known as the *Capitulaciones de Santa Fe* was signed on the following terms: Columbus was appointed Admiral, Viceroy and Governor, on a hereditary basis, of all 'discovered' lands and those still to be discovered. As a partner in the enterprise, he was awarded a tenth of all the profit it generated and control over the competition. He was also entitled to invest an eighth of the initial outlay for any further expedition and to receive the same share of the profits. The agreement included two striking points: the allusion to 'discovered lands'—which some authors have associated with the idea of a 'pre-discovery'—and the lack of any reference to the route he was to follow, clearly a precaution to keep Portuguese rivals from getting wind of it.

On his first voyage, Columbus sailed from the port of Palos on 3 August 1492 and sighted land in the Bahamas on 12 October. He made his first landfall in the Americas on Guanahaní (Watling Island), which he renamed San Salvador, followed by Santa María de la Concepción, Fernandina and Isabela, also in the Bahamas. He subsequently made land in Cuba, which he called Juana, and Haiti, dubbed Hispaniola. After exploring the latter, Columbus concluded that he had reached the land of the Great Khan, Ophir, Cipango and other places associated with the East.

Apart from profit and prestige, Columbus' feat brought the Crown into political conflict with Portugal whose king chose to see in the voyage an infringement

Hispano–Portuguese rivalry: the Treaty of Tordesillas.

7 June 1494, Tordesillas. The Treaty of Tordesillas, between the Catholic Kings and King John II of Portugal, was a set of agreements regarding demarcation and ocean limits. It was signed on the aforementioned date and ratified by the Portuguese king at Setubal on 5 September the same year. Autograph signature of John II of Portugal (Portuguese version of the treaty). 1 fol. (330 x 240 mm). Documentos Escogidos, 1, no. 1.

The issue by Pope Alexander VI of papal bulls in favor of Spain met with the disapproval of John II of Portugal who, in August 1493, sent a counterproposal based on a westward shift of the Alcáçoças–Toledo line. When the Spanish rejected this, John II was bound by the demarcation laid down by Alexander VI. However, the Catholic Kings realized that little latitude had been left the Portuguese in the so-called Volta da Mina, *the return voyage with the Gold Coast town of Mina as port-of-call. For this reason they agreed to sign the Treaty of Tordesillas which established a new line of demarcation, from pole to pole, running 370 leagues west of Cape Verde. This treaty marked a diplomatic success for Portugal, as the westward shift ensured their presence in an area that had come under Castilian domination.*

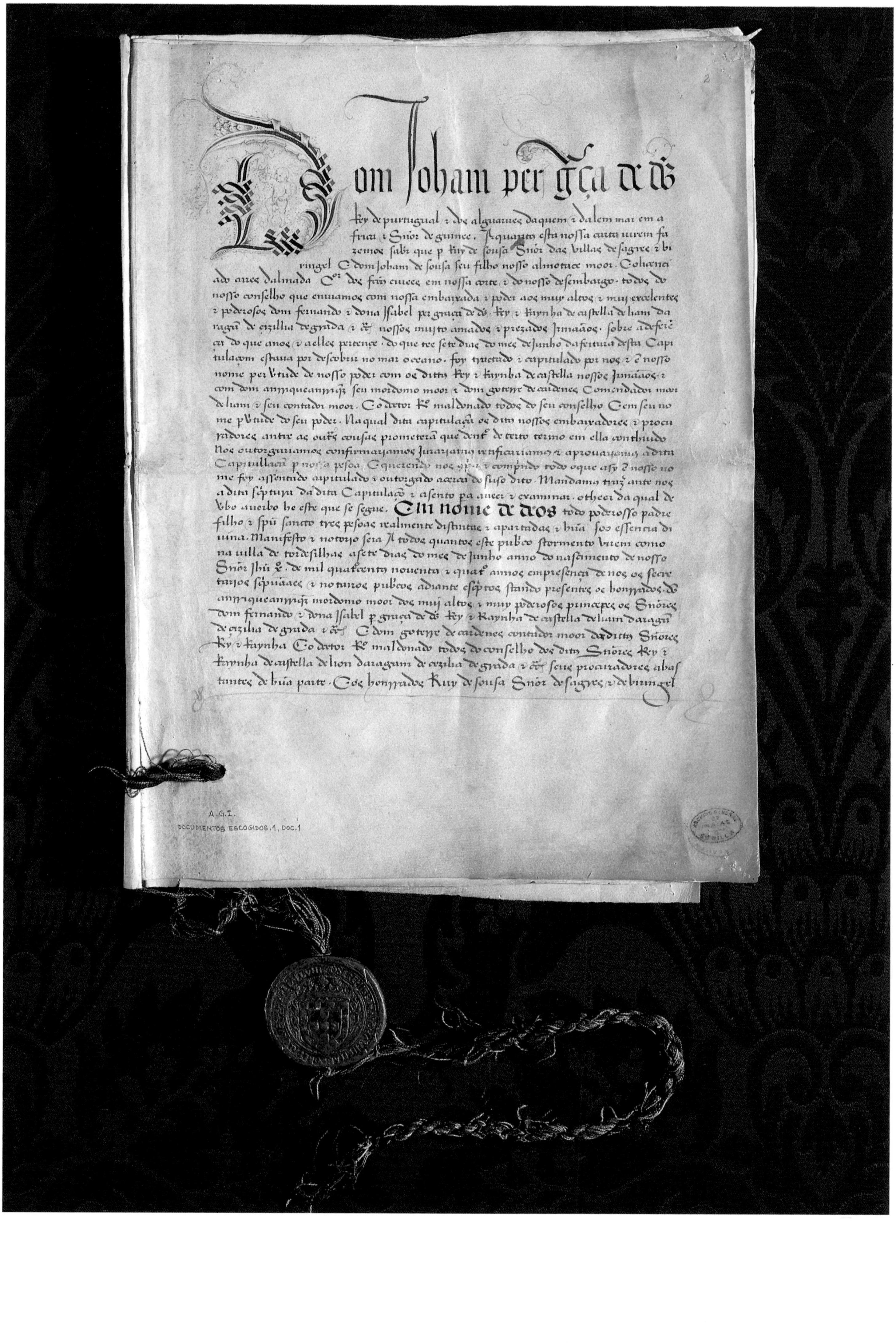
Dom Joham per gça de
A.G.I.
DOCUMENTOS ESCOGIDOS, 1, DOC. 1

of the Treaty of Alcáçovas. The Catholic Kings diligently preempted any action on his part by seeking four bulls of donation, demarcation and privileges from Pope Alexander VI, paralleling those secured by the Portuguese some time before in regard to Africa. This time, the dispute was settled in Castile's favor but, realizing that the Portuguese claim focused on provisions in the papal bulls affecting the 'return' trip via Mina, the Catholic Kings agreed to extend the line established in the same. This led to the signing of the Treaty of Tordesillas, on 7 June 1494.

The treaty provided for a line of demarcation running from pole to pole and passing three hundred and seventy leagues west of the Cape Verde Islands which divided the world between the two powers. This alteration of the line established by Alexander VI prompted the start of Brazil's history, as the eastern tip of the country fell within the Portuguese sector. The issue, however, flared up again owing to the difficulties in determining longitude that arose when Magellan's expedition reached the Moluccas.

Despite these achievements, Columbus had not fulfilled his basic objective of reaching the Spice Islands on his first voyage. This prompted a second voyage, which set sail from Cádiz on 25 September 1493 and returned to the same port on 11 June 1496. Its purpose was to engage in further exploration and to set up The Isabella, a commercial establishment on Hispaniola similar to the Italian ones in the Middle East and the Portuguese ones in Africa. This expedition coasted around the Lesser Antilles or Windward Isles, Cape Virgins, Puerto Rico, Hispaniola, Cuba and Jamaica. Thereafter, Hispaniola became the strategic springboard for further expeditions of exploration.

The third voyage had a favorable start but ended in disaster. In 1497, before leaving, Columbus had his privileges ratified, and he instituted primogeniture in favor of his son, Diego, in 1498. The expedition set out from Sanlúcar on 30 May 1498 and ended in Cádiz on 20 November 1500. This voyage took the explorers to the island of Trinidad and they made their first continental landfall on the Paria peninsula. They then coasted further west, reaching Margarita Island. On arrival in Hispaniola, Columbus became embroiled in uprisings by both the natives and Spaniards that led to royal intervention by Francisco de Bobadilla, who sent Columbus and his brothers back to Spain as prisoners.

News of Columbus' feats triggered a spate of maritime expeditions of discovery, exploration and ransom, which reached a peak from 1495 to 1519, thanks to which the shape of the American continents was gradually revealed. Subsequently, between 1519 and 1555, it also led to expeditions across 'discovered' territories for the purpose of colonization and settlement.

Following in Columbus' footsteps, a number of expeditions were mounted along the Atlantic seaboard of the Americas in search of the Spicery: John Cabot and the Corté Real brothers reconnoitered Newfoundland and Labrador (1497–1502); Pedro Alvares Cabral and Amerigo Vespucci coasted Brazil and South America (1500–1502), and Columbus and members of the so-called 'Andalusian voyages', among others, explored the northern seaboard of South America (1495–1502). By 1502, these expeditions attested to the existence of a new continent separate from Asia: the *Quarta Pars,* New World or West Indies. Amerigo Vespucci, who around this time made two documented voyages around most of the Atlantic seaboard of South America, in the service of both Castile and Portugal, was the first to successfully spread the idea of a new continent in select European circles, while Columbus, on his fourth voyage, still believed he had found the 'Golden Peninsula'.

In 1507, in his new work, *Cosmographiae Introductio,* Martin Waldseemüller put forward the name 'America' for the new continent. The proposal caught on and was adopted by Spain in the 18th century.

Christopher Columbus' letter book.

[16th century, 2nd third?]
Copy of Christopher Columbus' letter book, containing seven accounts of his four voyages and two letters of a private nature, written to the Catholic Kings between 4 March 1493 and 7 July 1503.
A copy, probably dating from the last three decades of the 16th century.
38 fols.
Acquired by the State for the Archive on 14 March 1988.
Patronato, 296.

The outstanding feature of this letter book is that it contains, in a single document, accounts of paramount importance to the study of Columbus' voyages, as well as two private letters in which he reveals his mystic dreams, divine apparitions and plans for conquest. The joy of discovery comes through in the first letter. The incidents on the second voyage (colonizing Hispaniola, the tragedy at Fort Navidad, the founding of Isabela and exploration in Cibao, Cuba, Jamaica and Hispaniola) are described in the second to the fifth letter. Lastly, although published previously, accounts of the third and fourth voyages to the north coast of South and Central America round off this source material of incalculable value.

PLANO D LA VIVORA
DESCRIPCION

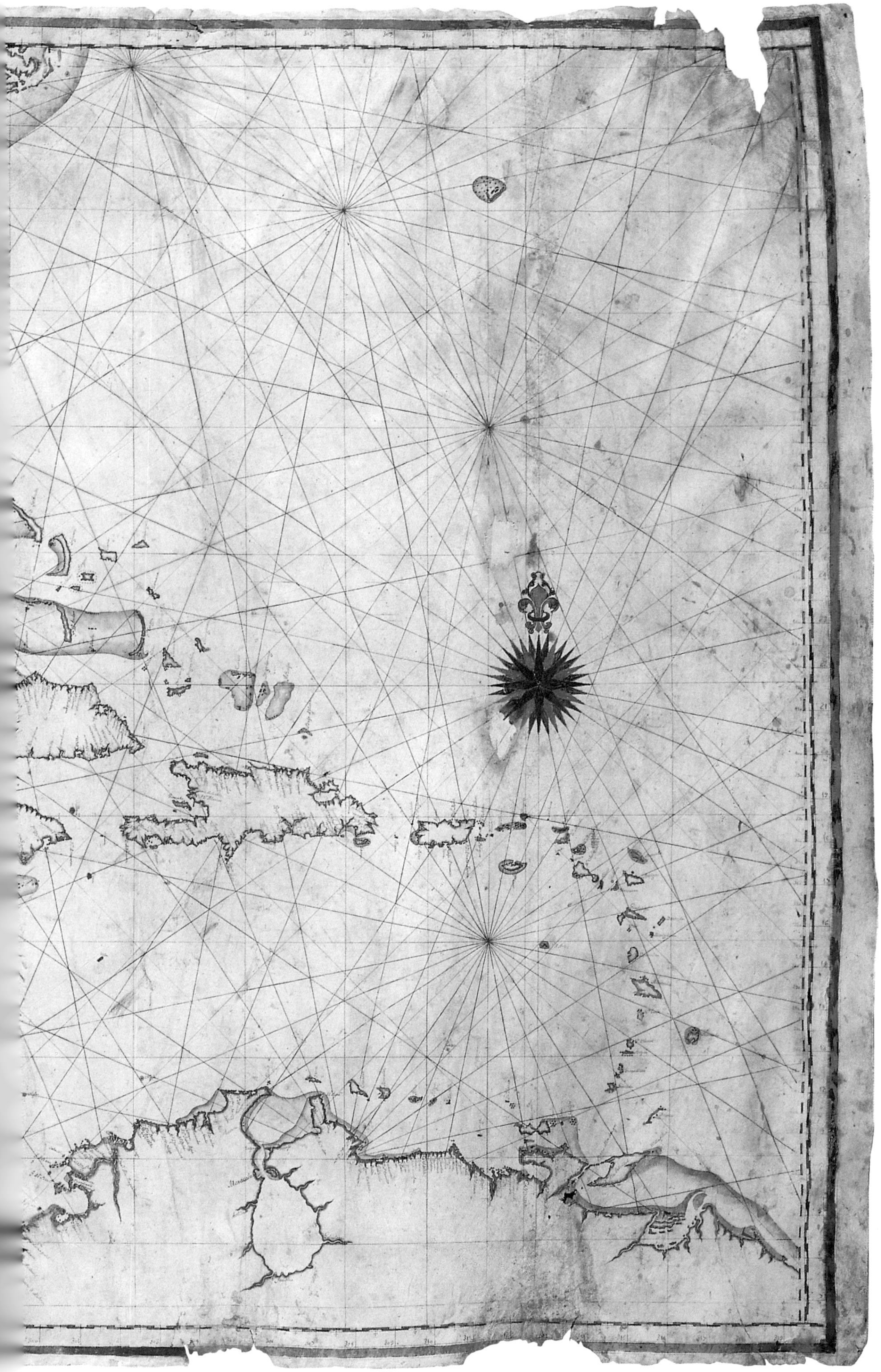

The search for a passage: the Caribbean and Gulf of Mexico.

1734
'Hydrographic survey or coastal chart of Tierra Firme, *North America, the Windward Isles, the Gulf of Mexico, shoals, seabed, bays and fairways, with amendments and some rectifications, from the experience of different pilots and navigators, having been calculated in relation to the meridian of the island of Tenerife.*
'Produced in Nueva Veracruz by the pilot, Antónío de Abreu y Mattos, in the year 1734.'
831 x 1,260 mm.
MP. Santo Domingo, 177.

This nautical map, which attests to the use of portolan charts *until well into the 18th century, displays the area covered by exploratory expeditions on the American seaboard, conducted for the purpose of finding a passage leading from the Atlantic to the Spice Islands. It shows northern South America, coasted during Columbus' third voyage and the so-called 'Andalusian voyages' (1499–1502), and the twin arc from Urabá to Honduras and to Yucatán, reconnoitered during Columbus' fourth voyage. The map also charts the colonizing expeditions led by Ojeda and Nicuesa, the exploratory expedition of Yáñez Pinzón–Díaz de Solís (1502 and 1508), and the arc between Yucatán and Florida, coasted by Juan Ponce de León, Hernández de Córdoba, Grijalva and Álvarez de Pineda. (1512–1519).*

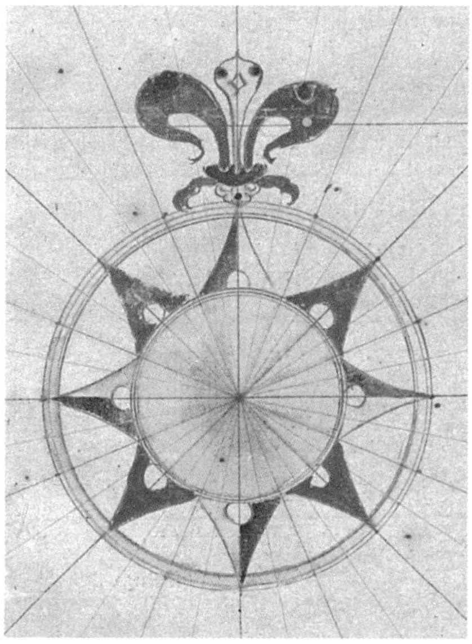

Maritime Expeditions—the Search for the Passage

The phenomenon of Columbus' discoveries sparked a number of Spanish and foreign expeditions around the shores of the Americas that bore out the existence of a continental mass separate from Asia and the need to seek out a passage to the western coast where the coveted Spice Islands supposedly lay.

The earliest of these, commissioned by France, England and Portugal, led to exploration of the eastern coastline of North and South America. The Spanish expeditions were initially mounted in accordance with royal decrees of 1495 and 1499 which overturned the monopoly that had been granted to Columbus at Santa Fe. They were geared to exploration and ransom, authorized by 'contracts of discovery', and yielded a great deal of nautical and geographical information. However, the dealings involving ransom or barter with the natives did not yield much financial profit. These expeditions reached their height between 1499 and 1503 but came to an end in 1513. They fell into two main periods:

– Those between 1495 and 1502. Noteworthy were four which followed the route of Columbus' third voyage around the north coast of South America and part of the eastern seaboard of Brazil. These were the so-called 'Andalusian voyages' led by Alonso de Ojeda, Amerigo Vespucci and Juan de la Cosa (1499–1500), Pedro Alonso Niño and Cristóbal Guerra (1499–1500), Vicente Yáñez Pinzón (1499–1500) and Diego de Lepe (1499–1500).

– Those between 1503 and 1513, directed at the underbelly of the new American continent around the Caribbean and Gulf of Mexico. Part of the area, from Honduras to Panama and Veragua (western Panama), had already been explored by Columbus on his fourth voyage in 1502–1504. The *Casa de la Contratación* or House of the Indies, founded in 1503, took up the task of organizing new expeditions of discovery and colonization. Prominent among these was the expedition led by Diego de Nicuesa and Alonso de Ojeda to found settlements in Veragua and Urabá in 1508–1509 and that of Vicente Yáñez Pinzón and Juan Díaz de Solís, who were assigned the task of finding a passage or fairway to the Spice Islands.

These expeditions, which resulted from decisions taken at the Councils of Toro (1505) and Burgos (1508), as well as a subsequent voyage led by Juan Ponce de León (1512–1513), failed in their endeavor to find the passage to the Pacific.

In this respect, Vasco Núñez de Balboa's discovery of the Pacific in 1513 was a milestone in the history of navigation.

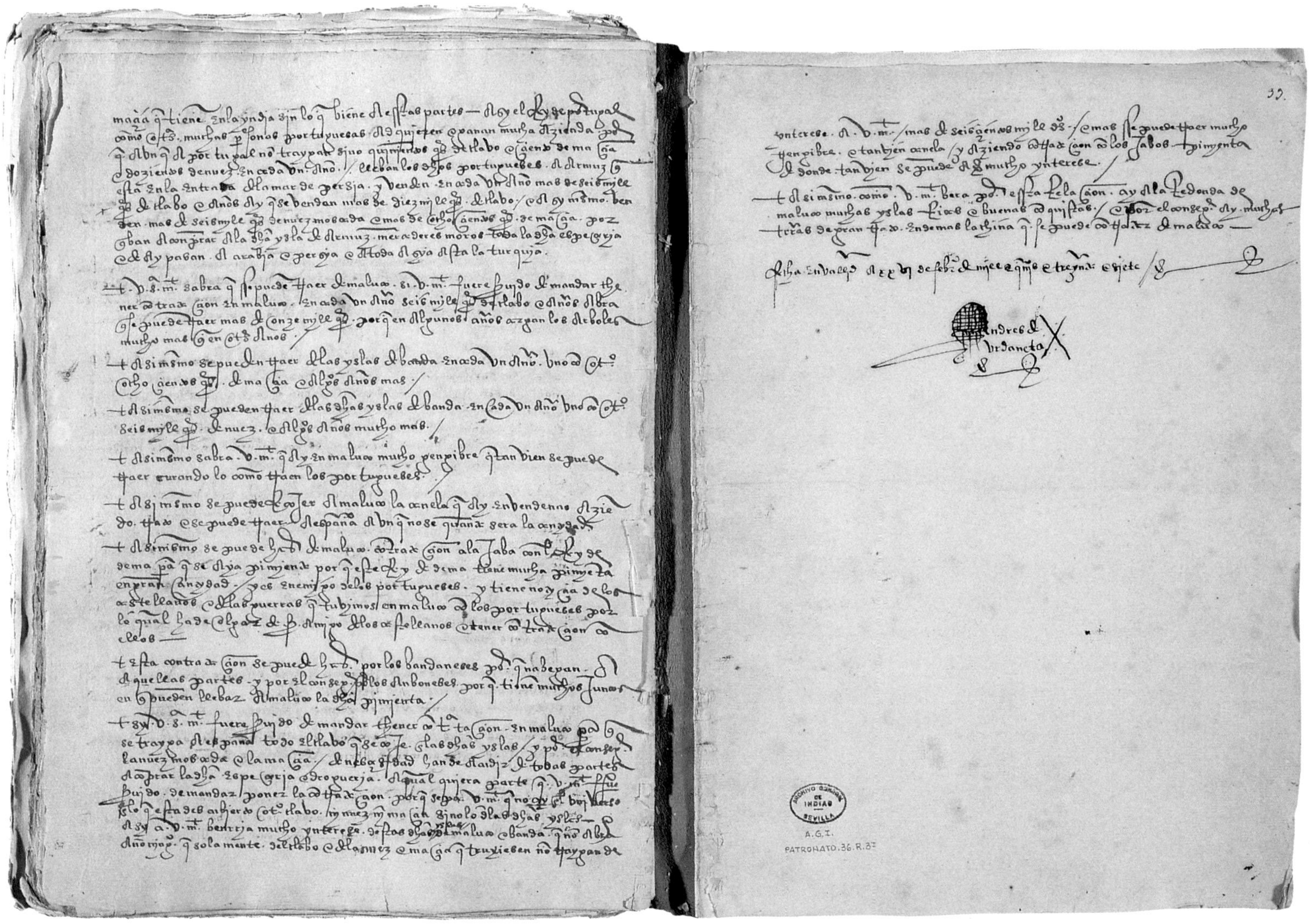

Loaysa–Urdaneta: the ill-fated landfall in Maluku.

26 February 1537, Valladolid.
Detailed account by Andrés de Urdaneta, purser in the squadron of García Jofre de Loaysa, of the disastrous events surrounding the expedition that sailed from Corunna on 24 July 1525, bound for the Spicery. Lasting until 1535, the expedition became embroiled in fighting with the Portuguese over control of the Moluccas.
16 fols. (nos. 18 to 33, copybook 33).
Patronato, 37, R. 36.

The arrival of Magellan's expedition in the Moluccas led Spain and Portugal to convene a Council at Badajoz in 1534 for the purpose of determining the ownership of those islands. The initiative was unsuccessful, prompting Charles V to ready another expedition in Corunna with the aim of securing the Spice Islands, thus driving a wedge into Portuguese-held territory, and finding a sea route from there to New Spain. The squadron, commanded by García Jofre de Loaysa, was decimated by the time it reached the Moluccas and unable to achieve any of its objectives. Finally, after a distressing sojourn in the islands lasting several years, recounted in detail by Urdaneta, the Spaniards received news that Charles V had ceded Maluku to Portugal in return for financial compensation.

The part of the Atlantic coastline that remained to be reconnoitered was the Yucatán–Florida stretch, eventually opened up by Francisco Hernández de Córdoba (1517), Juan de Grijalva (1518) and Alonso Álvarez de Pineda (1519).

From the Atlantic to the Atlantic via the Pacific

Balboa's discovery of the South Sea, now known as the Pacific, caused the Spanish and Portuguese considerable disquiet, as they were both intent on finding a sea route around the southern tip of the continent. They did not, however, relinquish hope of reaching the Spicery on the basis of Balboa's discovery. Espionage intensified, leading to the preparation of a number of secret expeditions, including one mounted by the Portuguese under Nuño Manuel, Cristóbal de Haro and Juan de Lisboa (1513–1514) which reached Patagonia. Another, headed by Juan Díaz de Solís, sailed bound for Maluku, but it reached no further than Río de la Plata.

All that remained was to drive for the southernmost tip of the continent. With that in mind, on 10 August 1519, an expedition of five vessels, with a crew of 265 men organized and funded by the Crown and commanded by Ferdinand Magellan, sailed from Seville to Maluku. Thirty-seven months later, a single ship manned by 18 seamen and skippered by Juan Sebastián Elcano returned to the port of Seville. The appalling voyage, which had decimated the expeditionaries, had led to the discovery of the Strait of Magellan, crossed the Pacific, made a landfall in the Moluccas and circumnavigated the earth, confirming that it was round.

The Magellan–Elcano voyage rekindled the rivalry between Spain and Portugal and in 1524 it became imperative to convene another Council, this time at Badajoz, to determine the ownership and boundaries of Maluku. After considerable wrangling, the Treaty of Zaragoza was eventually signed in 1529. Essentially a repurchase agreement, Spain forfeited to Portugal all its rights over Maluku in return for 350,000 ducats.

Settlement and Colonization

A First, Tentative Settlement—the Antilles

While voyages of exploration and discovery were revealing the shape of the new continent, the Antilles were becoming the springboard for a final thrust towards the mainland.

Christopher Columbus' Book of Privileges.

1498–1501

Known as the 'Book of Privileges of Veragua', it contains three transcriptions, written in Seville and Santo Domingo in 1498, of documents relating to the Admiralty of Castile, as well as privileges granted to Christopher Columbus by the Catholic Kings in 1492 and 1493 and ratified in 1497. Although seemingly incongruous in this book, it also features a transcription of an act dating from 1501 entitling him to primogeniture.
36 fols. on paper; 4 fols. on parchment.
305 x 215 mm.
Patronato, 295, N. 98.

The editing of Columbus' Books of Privileges and of his wills reflects changes in the relationship with his monarchs and endeavors by the latter to keep in check the rights and titles granted to him. They were edited at a time when, having lost royal favor, he attempted to ensure his future and that of his successors. The Book of Privileges of Veragua was compiled in Seville on 15 March 1498, shortly before sailing on his third voyage, and in Santo Domingo, on 4 December. It is an upshot of the unease he felt after falling into disfavor with the Catholic Kings following his second voyage. Two other Books of Privileges, dating from 1502, sent to his friend, Nicolás Oderigo and housed in Florence and Paris, were written shortly before his fourth voyage and reflect the bitterness he felt at his rebuffal in 1500.

According to the terms of the Santa Fe agreement, the islands were initially colonized as a private enterprise by Columbus. However, from 1495 to 1499, the Catholic Kings issued various royal decrees authorizing other expeditions in an attempt to curb Columbus' privileges.

In 1502, Columbus was relieved of his charge and replaced by Nicolás de Ovando. Moreover, even though his son Diego had been appointed Governor of Hispaniola, responsibility for the enterprise was soon transferred to the royal bureaucracy (the first *Audiencia* or Tribunal of the Indies was founded in Hispaniola in 1511). And, at the request of other settlers, it was subsequently declared a public, national enterprise of Castile by a royal decree of 14 September 1519 issued in Barcelona.

Dismantling the remains of the rather ingenuous agreement that had been reached with Columbus did not prove quite as easy. Claims were soon put in by his successors who became embroiled with the Crown in long, interesting and complicated lawsuits which came to an end with a judicial ruling in 1536 whereby the family waived its claim to all authority in return for the title of admiral, a life annuity of 10,000 ducats per annum, the marquisate of Jamaica and the duchy of Veragua.

From 1499 to 1517, Spanish settlements in the Caribbean operated as colonies specializing in gold mining and production, an enterprise that practically wiped out the entire indigenous population of the Greater Antilles and the Bahamas in just forty years. There were serious ethical and legal problems since the natives were the king's subjects and could not therefore be treated as slaves or used in forced labor. It was the Dominican friars who, in 1511, voiced their disapproval of the settlers' methods. The Crown responded by promulgating laws to protect the natives.

The island of Santo Domingo initially became the first nucleus of the Spanish conquest and acted as a platform for 'spreading the gold business' to other islands. This was taken up in Puerto Rico by Juan Ponce de León in 1508, in Jamaica by Juan de Esquivel in 1509, and in Cuba by Diego Velázquez in 1511. Once that had been achieved, the Greater Antilles acted as a bridgehead for the drive towards the mainland by providing ports of departure, supplies and, above all, men such as Cortés seasoned in commerce.

Cuba soon edged out Santo Domingo in the westward advance and Havana was established as Spain's naval base in the Caribbean.

Letter from Christopher Columbus requesting privileges.

5 February 1505, Seville. A letter from Christopher Columbus to his son Diego, who resided at Court, informing him of the imminent departure from the New World of his friend, Diego Méndez, and that of Amerigo Vespucci, who had been summoned by the monarchs to discuss navigational matters, and explaining his having appointed the latter to press his claims for privileges. Autograph letter signed 'Christo ferens', a Latinized version of his name, Christopher, which comes from the Greek, Christophoros, *meaning 'Christ-bearer'. 1 fol. Patronato, 295, N. 59.*

In 1500, after falling out of royal favor, Columbus was relieved of his duties and led back to Spain by Bobadilla. Then ensued a long period of claims that came to a head on his return from the last voyage in 1504, giving rise to correspondence between the infirm Columbus in Seville and his son Diego, who had established himself at Court to safeguard his father's interests. In this respect, it is clear that his purpose in entrusting this letter to Amerigo Vespucci, who had obviously been convened for the Council of Toro, was for Vespucci to pursue claims on Columbus' behalf. Two years later, the New World that Columbus was unable to see and did not wish to recognize was named after his rival, whom he mentions in his letter as having been the victim 'of adverse fortune'.

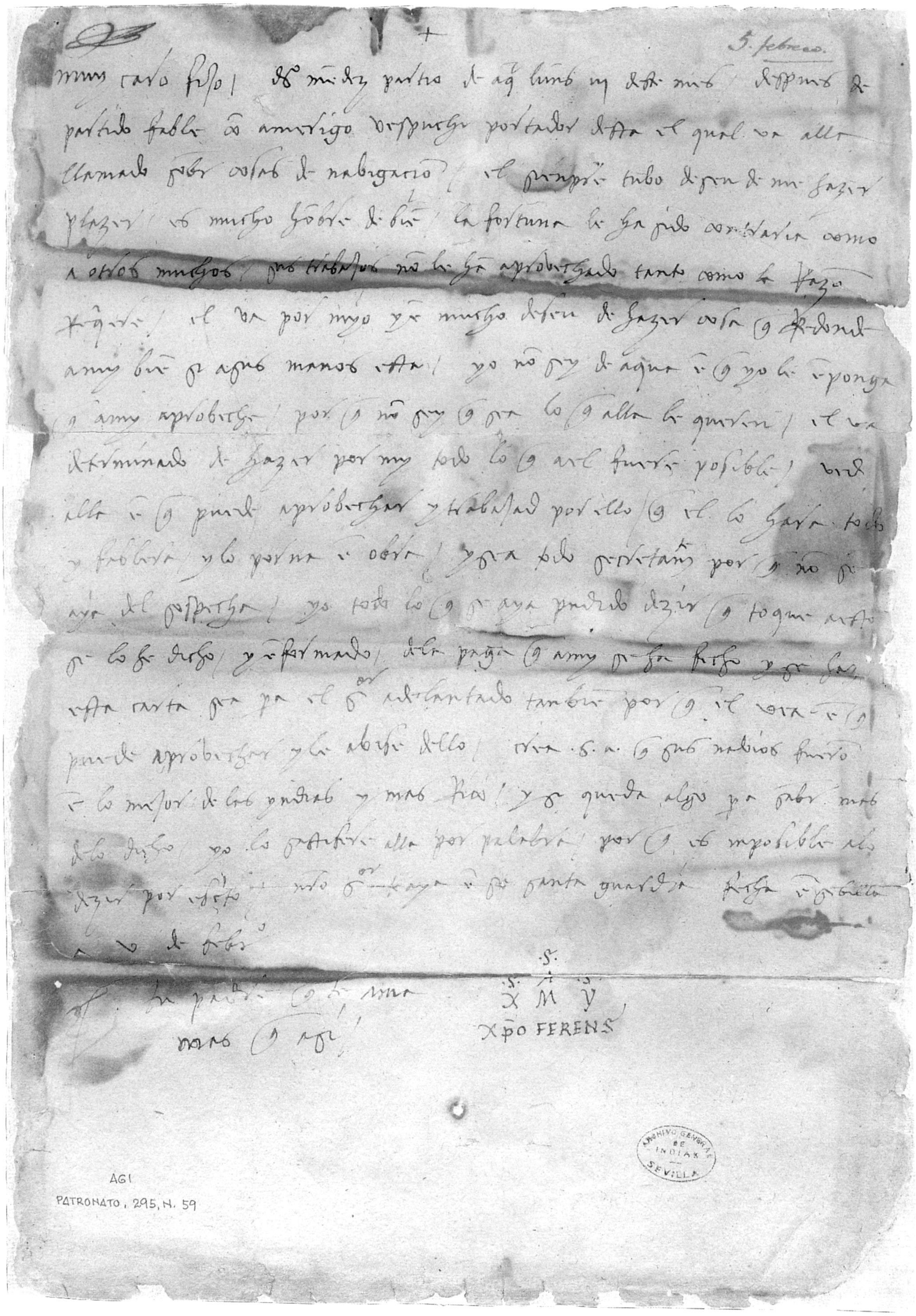
5. febrero.

muy caro fijo / diego mendez partio de aq lunes iij deste mes / despues de
partido fable co amerigo vespuchy portador desta el qual va alla
llamado sobre cosas de nabigacion / el siempre tubo deseo de me hazer
plazer / es mucho hombre de bien / la fortuna le ha sido contraria como
a otros muchos / sus trabajos no le han aprobechado tanto como la razo
requiere / el va por myo y en mucho deseo de hazer cosa q redonde
a my bien si a sus manos esta / yo no se de aqui en q yo le emponga
q a my aprobeche / porq no se q sea lo q alla le quieren / el va
determinado de hazer por my todo lo q a el fuere posible / ved
alla en q puede aprobechar y trabajad por ello q el lo hara todo
y fablara y lo pondra en obra / y sea todo secretamente porq no se
aya del sospecha / yo todo lo q se aya podido dezir q toque en esto
se lo he dicho y enformado de la paga q a my se ha hecho y se haz
esta carta sea pa el sor adelantado tambien porq el vea en q
puede aprobechar y le aviso dello / crea s.a. q sus nabios fueron
en lo mejor de las yndias y mas rico / y si queda algo pa saber mas
de lo dicho yo lo satisfare alla por palabra / porq es ymposible el
dezir por escrito / nro sor te aya en su santa guarda / fecha en sevilla
a v de febro

.S.
.S.A.S.
X M Y
XPO FERENS

tu padre q te ama
mas q a si /

Group of settlements at Bayajá, Hispaniola.
[2nd half of the 16th century]
Perspective view of Bayajá harbor and surrounding areas, on the north coast of Hispaniola.
374 x 620 mm.
MP. Santo Domingo, 3.

One striking upshot of the early conquest was the decimation of the native population of the islands, largely due to the disasters imposed on the Indian inhabitants by the conquistadors, who exploited them in gold mining. The native population was also ravaged by diseases imported by the European settlers. The depopulation of Hispaniola began in 1514. In 1521, Antonio Enríquez Pimentel suggested concentrating the inhabitants of Montechristi and Puerto Real in Bayajá, further north, and using only that harbor. Devastated in 1605, Bayajá was occupied by the French and converted into a magnificent port in the 18th century.

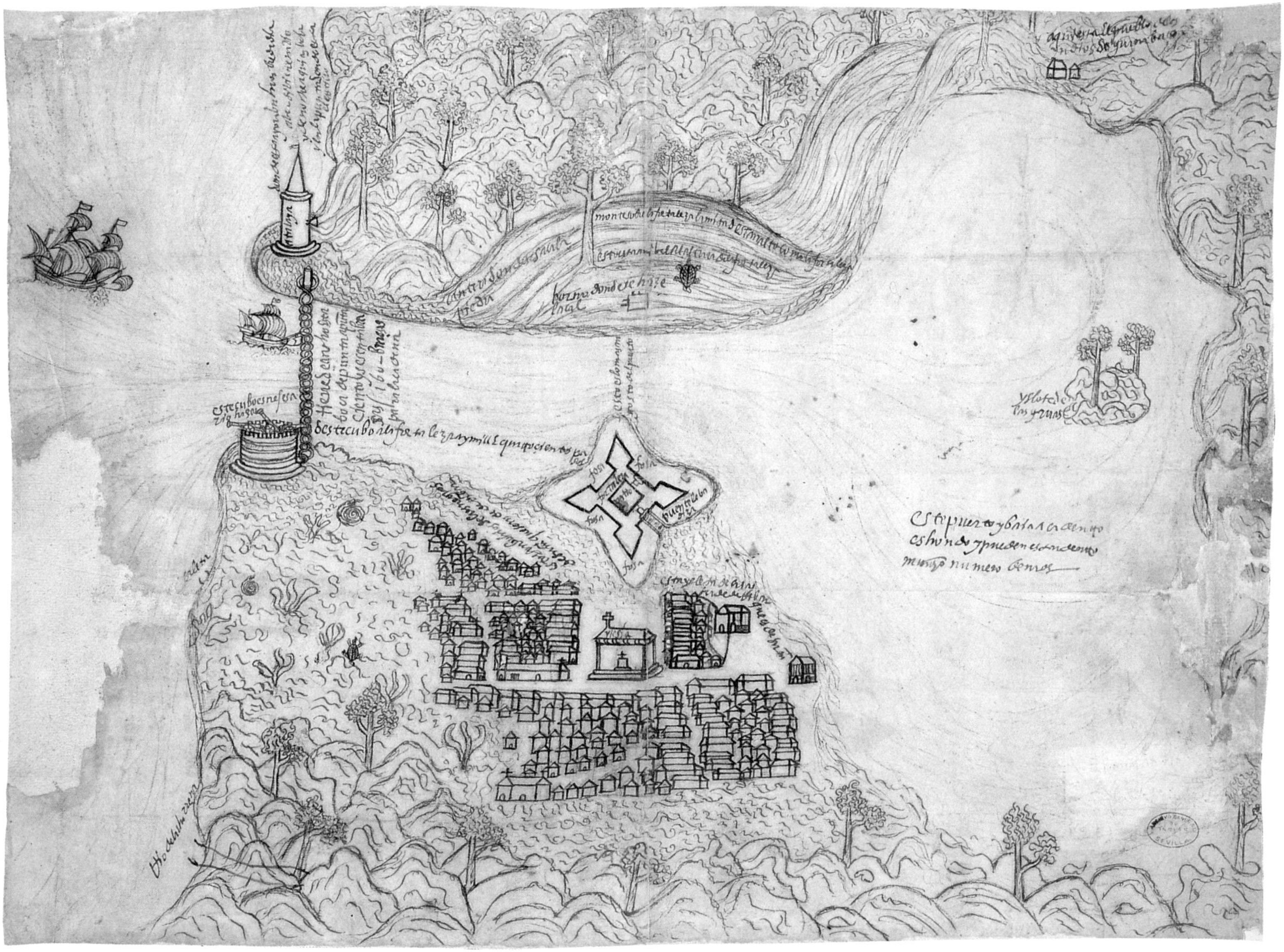

The Drive to the Mainland—Castilla del Oro and Urabá

The first colonizing drive towards the American continent started out from Santo Domingo in 1509. Alonso de Ojeda and Diego de Nicuesa were assigned the task of founding settlements in Urabá and Castilla del Oro or Veragua, respectively, and were appointed governors. Both expeditions failed miserably and they only managed to set up two settlements that were subsequently abandoned—San Sebastián, governed by Ojeda, and Nombre de Dios, by Nicuesa.

The survivors of those expeditions were assembled by Vasco Núñez de Balboa at Santa María de la Antigua del Darién, which he had founded in 1511. Faced with the incompetence of their leaders, the expeditionaries elected to continue under his command, making him the first great leader of the new frontier.

An Extremaduran nobleman seasoned in the Antilles, he was careful to avoid the excesses he had witnessed there. He exacted no tribute, showed respect for native customs and social structures and arbitrated in the frequent disputes between tribal chiefs. As for exploration, Balboa reconnoitered the Atrato basin to the south, although he was unable to locate the source of the gold traded in coins on the coast. Driving west, he came upon the isthmus of Panama and discovered

Havana—Caribbean naval base.

[1567]
Perspective plan of the city of Havana.
342 x 460 mm.
MP. Santo Domingo, 4.

Based on the experience gained in the Canary Islands, the Antilles were used as a base for expansion towards the American continent. The bridgehead was initially located on Hispaniola, from where Diego Velázquez sailed to Cuba in 1511. In a second phase, Cuba came to the forefront and Havana was consolidated as the Caribbean naval base, which necessitated its fortification: 'As you well know, the town of Havana is the main stopover for the Indies, where all vessels from Nombre de Dios and other lands call on their way to these royal domains, and it is necessary and of vital importance that the aforesaid port be well guarded and endowed with adequate defense works...' (Patronato, 177, N. 2, R. 1).

Nombre de Dios, founded by Nicuesa.

[1541]
'Sketch plan of where it would seem fitting to site the fortress of Nombre de Dios.'
320 x 430 mm.
MP. Panamá, 1.

One of the results of the Council of Burgos (1508) was the decision to ready expeditions under Alonso de Ojeda and Diego de Nicuesa to colonize and govern Urabá and Veragua or Castilla del Oro, respectively. Both came to a tragic end: the seven hundred men that sailed with Nicuesa from Hispaniola to Veragua on 22 November 1509 were soon whittled down to seventy, who sought refuge in the fort at Nombre de Dios, founded by Nicuesa (1510). The rest were subsequently rescued, together with the survivors from Ojeda's expedition, at Santa María de la Antigua del Darién. After being fortified on the orders of Philip II, Nombre de Dios became one of the busiest Caribbean ports, until it was superseded by Portobelo.

the South Sea, as mentioned earlier. In terms of organization, he laid the foundations for the first Spanish settlement on the continent, whose capital was Santa María de la Antigua del Darién.

Balboa's uncommonly rapid rise to leadership and the jealousy it aroused proved an obstacle in the way of his appointment as governor. The post was eventually given, in 1514, to the uncouth and inexperienced Pedrarias Dávila who clumsily wrecked Balboa's achievements and persecuted him until his death in 1519.

In 1519, the Castilla del Oro settlement, which marked Balboa's period, was superseded by Panama. Its capital was founded by Pedrarias and it became the new center of expansion towards Central America and the Empire of the Incas.

New Spain

The second great frontier leader to emerge was Hernando Cortés. With obvious parallels to Vasco Núñez de Balboa, his was more of a success story.

Like the latter, he was an Extremaduran nobleman, but with a sounder intellectual background, particularly in the field of law, administration and bureacracy. An accomplished politician and statesman, capable organizer and perspicacious diplomat, his New World experience was also first gained on the islands, particularly in Cuba, alongside Diego Velázquez, the governor of the island. With great acumen and better good fortune he emulated Balboa by taking over the enterprise he had promoted on Velázquez's orders—the rescue expedition the latter commissioned in 1518 turned out to be one of conquest.

To legitimately secure command of the campaign he first relinquished the post conferred on him by Diego Velázquez. His troops, being left without a leader, then exercised their right to vote him captain general during the local elections at the newly founded Villa Rica de Veracruz.

Cortés, who set greater store on diplomacy than war, managed to secure the cooperation of towns he came across on his way to Mexico. One such case was Tlaxcala, which he supported in its struggle against the Aztec Confederation, consisting of Tenochtitlán, Texcoco and Tlacopan. His strategy of taking advantage of dissent among local inhabitants was used later by other conquistadors.

The conquest of Mexico, which lasted from 8 November 1519 until 13 August 1521, was carried out in several stages: the first hinged on a battle of wits between Cortés and Montezuma in an attempt by the former to undermine the latter's will

The Antilles were used as a launching pad to the mainland, where three places in turn acted as nuclei for subsequent expansion: Santa María de la Antigua del Darién—which later shifted to Panama—Mexico and Tierra Firme.
The first was used to drive north to Central America, where it joined the Mexican nucleus, and south to Peru. The Mexican center of expansion spread to places in present-day Mexico and the United States, as well as towards Central America and the Philippines.
At Tierra Firme, Santa Marta and Coro, among others, the settlers became involved in the quest for Eldorado.
The Panama base was used for the thrust into Peru; the latter was first extended north to Quito—which in turn acted as a staging post for Colombia and the Amazon—southeast, to Upper Peru and Bolivia, where it joined the drive originating in Río de la Plata; south, towards Chile, and from there to Argentina (Salta, Jujuy, Tucumán) and the Strait of Magellan and, last, towards Oceania. The province of Río de la Plata was conquered from Spain, as was that of Yucatán.
Each stage in the expansionist drive was accomplished in response to the passing of regulatory 'laws of conquest'—the 'Burgos laws', the *Requerimiento* or 'Injunction' (1512, 1514), the *Ordenanza* (Statute) of 1526, the so-called 'New Laws' (1542) and others (1556).

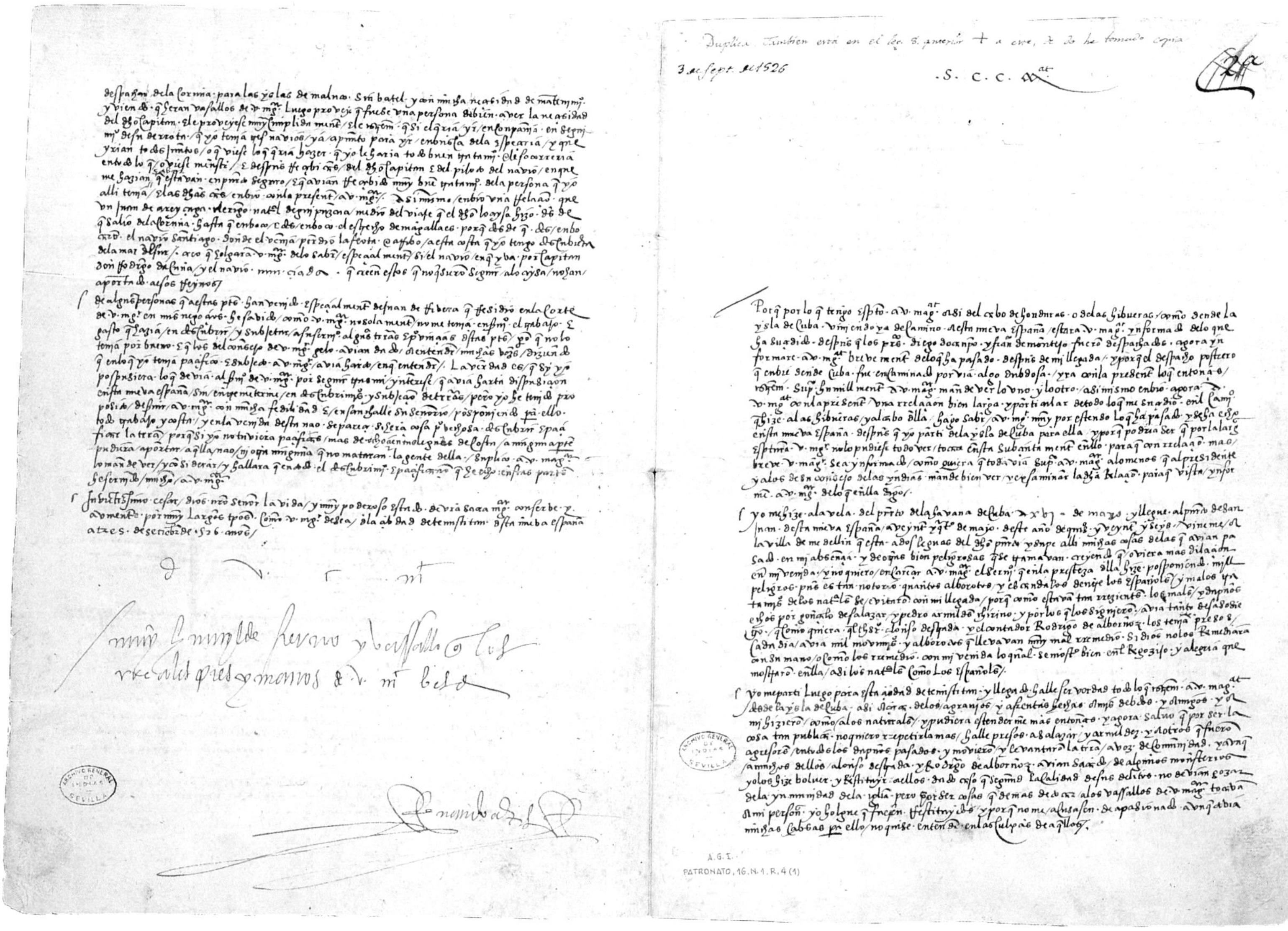

Collaboration with the Indians: Tlaxcala.

25 January 1538, Istapalapa.
Drawing depicting the 'emblem and strength of Tlascala, which are the arms of the generals', which Hernando Cortés presented to Mateo García Xicontecalpopoca Chichimecal, captain general of the Republic of Tlaxcala, along with a staff and title, as a reward for his services in the conquest of Mexico.
412 x 290 mm (491 x 348 mm).
MP. Escudos y Árboles Genealógicos, 6.

Internal strife between the indigenous inhabitants and collaboration with them were decisive factors in the speed of the conquest of the New World. Hernando Cortés backed Tlaxcala and other towns against the Aztec Confederation, earning staunch allies for the conquest of Cholula and Mexico. Prominent among the collaborators was the general of the Tlaxcalteca Indians, Mateo García Xicontecalpopoca Chichimecal, who in 1535 received his surname from his godfather. Tlaxcala was awarded political and religious privileges and exemptions and became the seat of the first episcopal see in New Spain.

Hernando Cortés: rivalry with royal officials.

3 September 1526. Tenochtitlán, Mexico.
Letter from Hernando Cortés to the Emperor, reporting on events in New Spain as of 1524, when he sailed for the Hibueras, until 1526, when he returned to Mexico.
Autograph signature.
2 fols.
Patronato, 16, N. 1, R. 4 (1).

In 1522, Hernando Cortés was appointed governor and captain general of New Spain. However, with a view to curbing the conquistadors' powers, the Crown appointed three royal officials to take over some of his duties. When Cortés left for the Hibueras to put down a rebellion staged by Cristóbal de Olid, the royal officials seized the chance to accuse him of mismanagement and other more serious charges. The period of unrest, which lasted from 1524 to 1526, is described in the above letter, which also reports on the arrival of Luis Ponce de León, a juez de residencia *(a judge who presided over judicial reviews of viceroys' term of office). The letter includes news of a vessel from the Loaysa expedition which had gone adrift, and eventually turned up in Tehuantepec.*

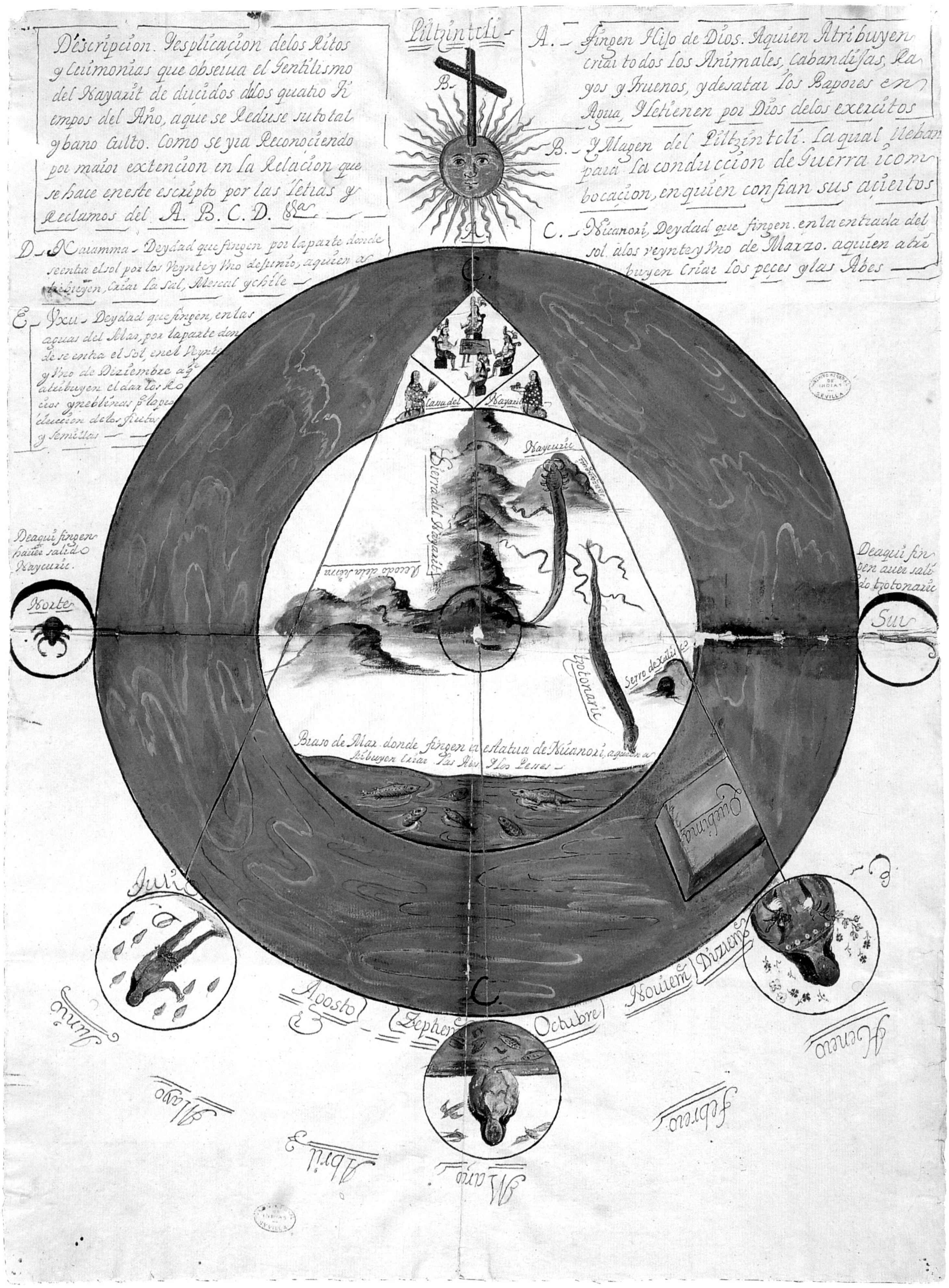
Discripcion. yesplicacion delos Ritos y Ceremonias que obserua el Gentilismo del Nayarit de ducidos dilos quatro Tiempos del Año, aque se Reduse su total y bano Culto. Como se yra Reconociendo por maior extencion en la Relacion que se hace eneste escripto por las letras y Reclamos del A. B. C. D. &a
Piltzintli
A. _ Fingen Hijo de Dios. Aquien Atribuyen criar todos los Animales, Cabandijas, Rayos y Truenos, y desatar los Bapores en Agua, Ytienen por Dios delos exercitos
B. _ Y Ymagen del Piltzintli. La qual llebam para la conduccion de Guerra icombocacion, enquien confian sus aciertos
C. _ Nicanori, Deydad que fingen en la entrada del sol, alos veynte y Vno de Marzo. aquien atribuyen Criar los peces y las Abes
D. _ Naiumma _ Deydad que fingen por laparte donde se entra el sol por los Veynte y Vno de Junio, aquien atribuyen Criar la Sal, Mescal y chile
E. _ Yxu _ Deydad que fingen en las aguas del Mar, por laparte donde se entra el Sol, enel Veynte y Vno de Diziembre
Norte
Sur
Nayarit
Sierra del Nayarit
Tzotonarie
Serro de Xuliste
Braso de Mar donde fingen la estatua de Nicanori, aquien atribuyen Criar las Abes ylos Peces
Junio
Julio
Agosto
Zephem
Octubre
Nouiem
Diziem
Henero
Febrero
Marzo
Abril
Mayo

The Nayarit rites: evangelization and syncretism.

[1672]
Drawing depicting the rites, ceremonies and cult worship performed by the Cora–Nayarit Indians at the 'House of Nayarit', an oracle in Tzacaimuta.
586 x 426 mm.

The drawing illustrates an account by Fray Antonio Arias de Saavedra, a Franciscan who preached in the parish of Nuestra Señora de la Asunción in Acaponeta, New Galicia, describing the recent conversion of the province of Nayarit, evangelized during the period of conquest (1672).
MP. Estampas, 25.

The region of Nayarit, located between the states of Sinaloa, Durango and Jalisco and the Pacific Ocean, and inhabited by Cora, Tepehuan, Huichole and Teco Indians, was conquered in 1531 by Nuño de Guzmán. The indigenous population was indoctrinated by the Franciscans and local chiefs were baptized with names such as Francisco Nayarit and Pedro Guainori. They subsequently took refuge in the northern and northeastern mountains where, isolated amidst impassable terrain, they reverted to their former cults and rites, as depicted in the drawing and described in the account. However, in a display of religious syncretism, they kept a missal and other objects from their initial contact with the friars and worshipped them in their House of Nayarit.

to resist. Montezuma, for his part, was obsessed with a prophecy whereby 'bearded men would come from where the sun rises and become lord over all'. Part of this non-violent strategy involved the Aztecs swearing allegiance to the Crown of Spain and paying a large amount of treasure as tribute. The conquest of the city was postponed, however, when Cortés went out to meet the punitive expedition sent by Velázquez under the command of Pánfilo de Narváez. At Cempoala, Cortés successfully persuaded Narváez's party to side with him and was thus able to head back towards Tenochtitlán with a stronger force.

In the second stage, after being plagued by the misconduct of Pedro de Alvarado, the Aztecs abandoned the peaceful approach embodied by Montezuma and took the offensive under the command of his successor, Cuitláhuac. Montezuma died in an ensuing siege of the Spaniards by the Aztecs inside the city. Cortés had no choice but to beat a hazardous retreat via a lake near the Tacuba road. In the course of the so-called *noche triste* or 'night of sorrow', Cortés lost nearly half his men, as well as the treasure received from the Aztecs. Shortly afterwards, however, by means of a strategic ploy, he managed to defeat the much larger Aztec force on the Otumba plain.

Having opened the road to Tenochtitlán, the siege of the city was able to commence. It began on 21 May 1521 and lasted until 13 August. Led by Cuauhtémoc, Cuitláhuac's successor, the city held out until it was completely devastated. Once the city fell to him, Cortés secured control over the entire territory of the Confederation. He then set about building a new empire over the ruins of the Aztec civilization and called it New Spain.

The conquest then spread in the following directions:

– Ancillary areas: to the east, Veracruz; to the south, Michoacán, Colima, Oaxaca, Tehuantepec and Tuxtepec; to the northwest, New Galicia, (under Nuño de Guzmán and Juan de Oñate), Nueva Vizcaya (under Francisco de Ibarra) and New Mexico (under Juan de Oñate) and, in the direction of 'Cibola', the southwestern United States (under Fray Marcos de Niza and Francisco Vázquez de Coronado).
– Central America.
– California (under Diego Hurtado de Mendoza, Becerra, Grijalva, Cortés, Tapia, Ulloa & others).
– The Spice Islands.
– The Atlantic seaboard, explored from the Antilles: coastal voyages (under Pineda, Quexos & Esteban Gómez) and land excursions, including Florida (under Pánfilo de Narváez, Álvar Núñez Cabeza de Vaca & Hernando de Soto).
– Yucatán (under the Montejos).

The conquest of New Galicia (Jalisco).

[1550]
Map of New Galicia.
318 x 439 mm.
MP. México, 560.

The conquest and government of New Galicia was assigned to Nuño de Guzmán, president of the Audiencia *of Mexico, who wished to emulate the feats of his rival, Hernando Cortés, and consequently gain renown. Noteworthy during the first phase was the founding of Guadalajara, the future state capital, by Cristóbal de Oñate (1529) and that of Compostela by Nuño de Guzmán himself (1535). The second phase of the conquest was mounted sporadically by Oñate and led to the subjugation of the Chichimec Indians and the uprising of the Indians around Guadalajara in 1540, where Pedro de Alvarado died accidentally after coming to the defense of the city.*

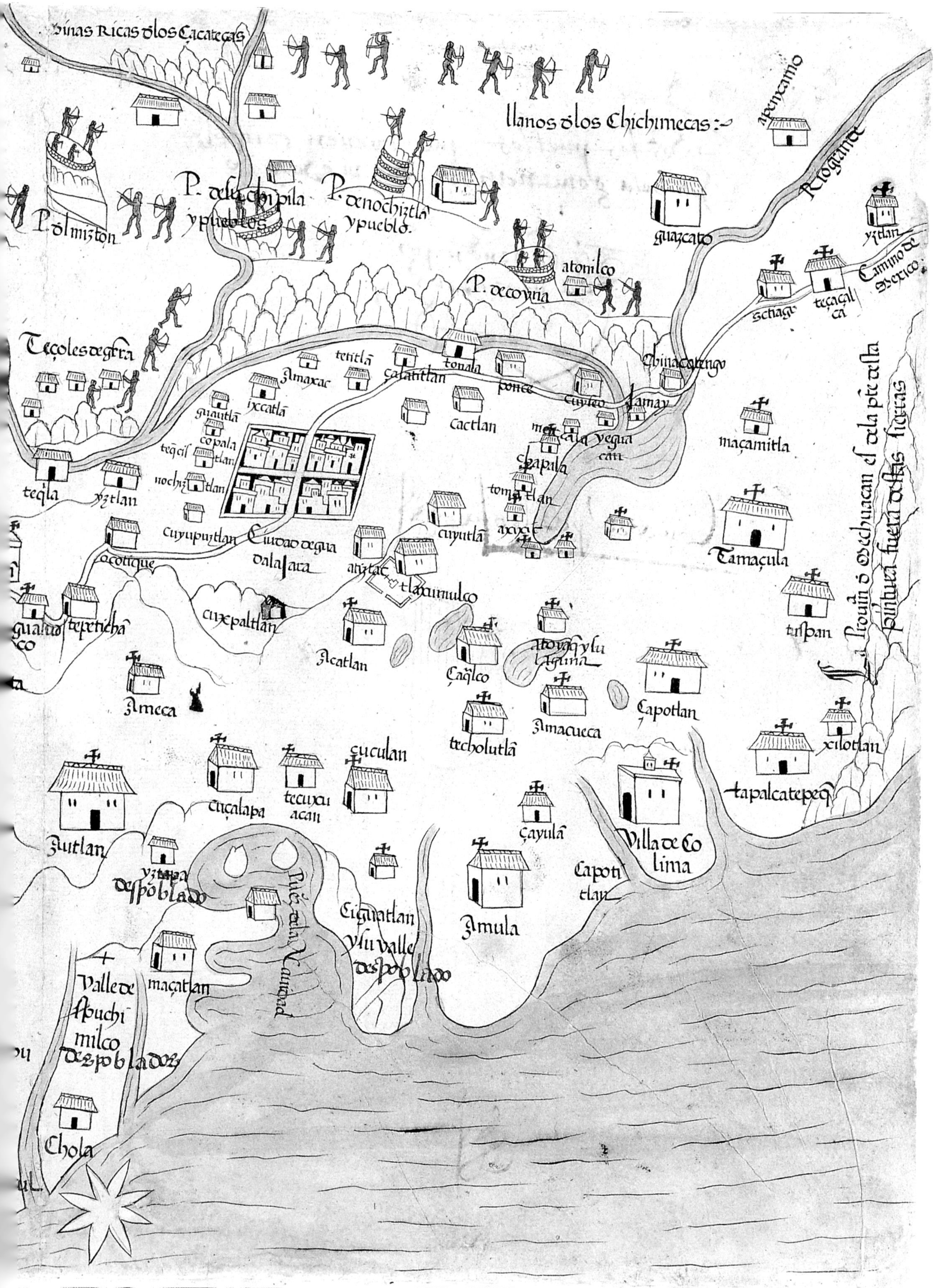

llanos dlos Chichimecas
Rio grande
guazcato
yztlan
atomilco
P. de coyna
tonala
Chinacatengo
cactlan
macamitla
Ciudad de gua dalajara
Tamaçula
Ameca
Acatlan
Capotlan
Amacueca
techolutlã
xilotlan
tapalcatepeq
Autlan
cuculan
çayulã
Villa de Colima
Amula
maçatlan
Chola

The Spice Islands and the Philippines

As mentioned earlier, Magellan and Elcano found the passage to the Spice Islands, but their discovery then raised the issue of the return voyage. A route to the West Indies had to be found and it had to be an alternative to the one used by the Portuguese. However, the expeditions under García de Loaysa, which sailed from Corunna in 1525, and those under Álvaro de Saavedra Cerón in 1527 and Ruy López de Villalobos in 1542, both from Mexico, were unable to accomplish the task.

It was not until 1565 that an expedition from New Spain led by Miguel López de Legázpi finally fulfilled the objective. The feat was actually accomplished by Andrés de Urdaneta, a pilot and Augustinian missionary and a navigator seasoned in those seas, having served under Loaysa. Having secured the return route, Urdaneta opened up the way for the Acapulco–Manila galleon.

Central America

Central America takes in the area covered by the Panamanian expansion, headed by Pedrarias (Nicaragua, Costa Rica and western Panama or Veragua) and the Mexican conquest led by Hernando Cortés (Guatemala, El Salvador and Honduras), who continued to reconnoiter the area in search of the coveted passage. However, the jurisdictional problems created by the overlapping currents of expansion became an ongoing source of conflict.

– Nicaragua and Honduras

In 1522, after an attempt to negotiate a contract with the Crown had failed, Andrés Niño explored the entire western shore of Central America, as far as Tehuantepec, while Gil González Dávila forged inland, reaching Lake Nicaragua and Managua. However, he was forced to retreat to Honduras to avoid a confrontation with Francisco Hernández de Córdoba who had been sent by Pedrarias Dávila to found various settlements. In Honduras, González Dávila met up with Cristóbal de Olid who, in keeping with the tradition of the conquistadors, had emancipated himself from Cortés. Also in the area was Francisco de las Casas, whom Cortés had sent in his pursuit. Thus began a series of fratricidal fights which ended in Olid's execution. By the time Cortés reached the area (1525), the problem had been solved. After the war, Gil González Dávila remained in Honduras and Francisco Hernández de Córdoba in Nicaragua, which was soon occupied by the deposed Pedrarias after being appointed governor of the region.

Pre-Columbian culture: the Mayan ruins of Palenque.

[1794]
Drawing reproducing one of the reliefs found in the Mayan city of Palenque (Chiapas State, Mexico).
300 x 210 mm.

Together with five other drawings, this illustrates the 'Critical American theater or new attempt to solve the great historical problem of the settlement of America', by Pablo Félix Cabrera [undated, circa 1794]
MP. Estampas, 105.

The Mayan civilization spanned a large region that took in southeastern Mexico, Yucatán and Guatemala from the early Christian era until the 16th century. Tical, Copán, Piedras Negras, Yaxchilán and Palenque are some of the cities most representative of the classical period. Prominent in the Maya–Toltec period were Chichén Itzá, Uxmal and Mayapán. Although Chiapas came under the Audiencia *of Mexico from 1528 to 1543 and, subsequently, that of Guatemala, Palenque remained hidden until the 18th century, when its ruins were studied by Antonio Bernasconi and Antonio del Río (1785). Its artistic highlights include stone and stucco reliefwork showing priests set around some central motif.*

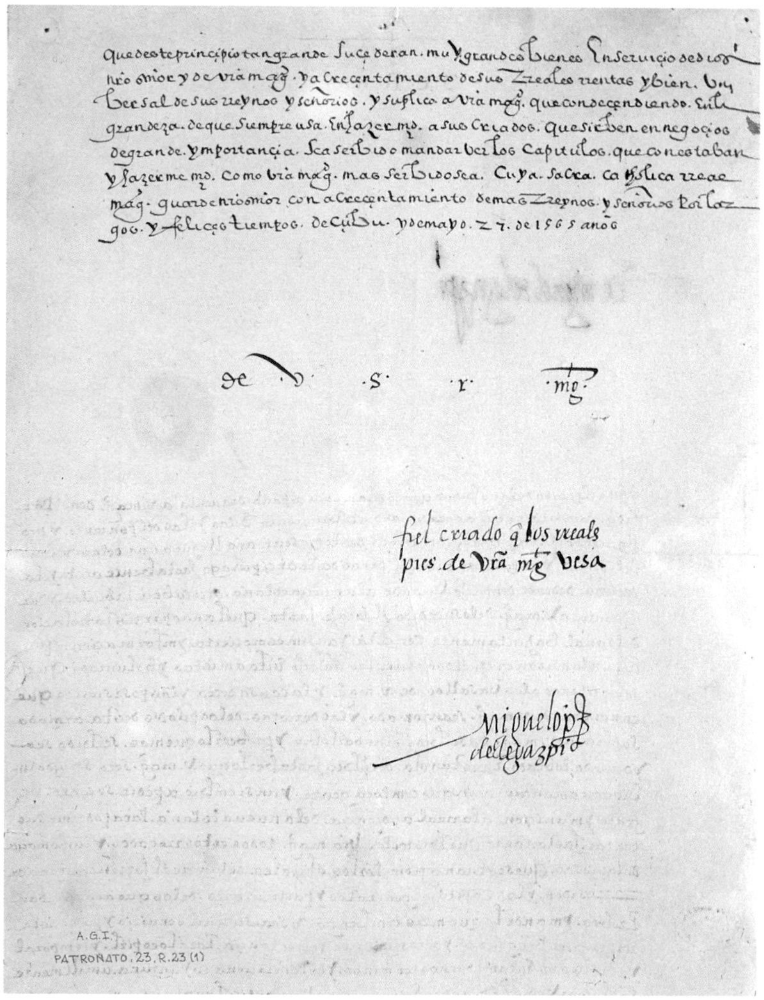

que de este principio tan grande suçederan. muy grandes bienes en seruiçio de dios
nro señor y de vra mag. y acreçentamiento de sus rreales rentas y bien. vni
versal de sus rreynos y señorios. y suplica a vra mag. que condeçendiendo. con la
grandeza. de que siempre usa. en hazer md. a sus criados. que sirben en negoçios
de grande. ymportançia. sea serbido mandar ver los capitulos. que con esta ban
y hazerme md. como vra mag. mas serbido sea. Cuya. sacra. catholica rreal
mag. guarde nro señor con acreçentamiento de mas rreynos. y señorios por lar
gos. y feliçes tiempos. de çubu. y de mayo. 27. de 1565 años

de v. s. r. mg.

fiel criado q los reales
pies de vra mg besa

miguel lopz
de legazpi

A.G.I.
PATRONATO, 23, R.23 (1)

Miguel López de Legázpi: the return route to New Spain.

27 May 1565, Cebú
Letter from Miguel López de Legázpi to Philip II reporting on his arrival in the Western Isles or Philippines and on progress achieved on the Cebú island settlements, from where he sent a vessel to explore the return voyage to New Spain. As a reward for his services, he made a written request for certain favors, adhering to the tradition of other conquistadors.
Autograph signature.
2 fols.
Patronato, 23, R. 23.

After the failure of the Moluccas settlement and an arrangement whereby the islands were sold to Portugal, as reflected in the Treaty of Zaragoza (1529), an attempt was made to build up a Spanish presence in the east on the Philippine islands. However, that settlement project was contingent on the discovery of a return route across the Pacific to New Spain, in order to avoid the Portuguese route around the African coastline. The important route was eventually opened up by Andrés de Urdaneta during an expedition under Miguel López de Legázpi in 1565. He took advantage of the countertrade winds and the Kuro-Sivo current to reach the California coast and Acapulco, thus paving the way for the route plied subsequently by the Acapulco–Manila galleon.

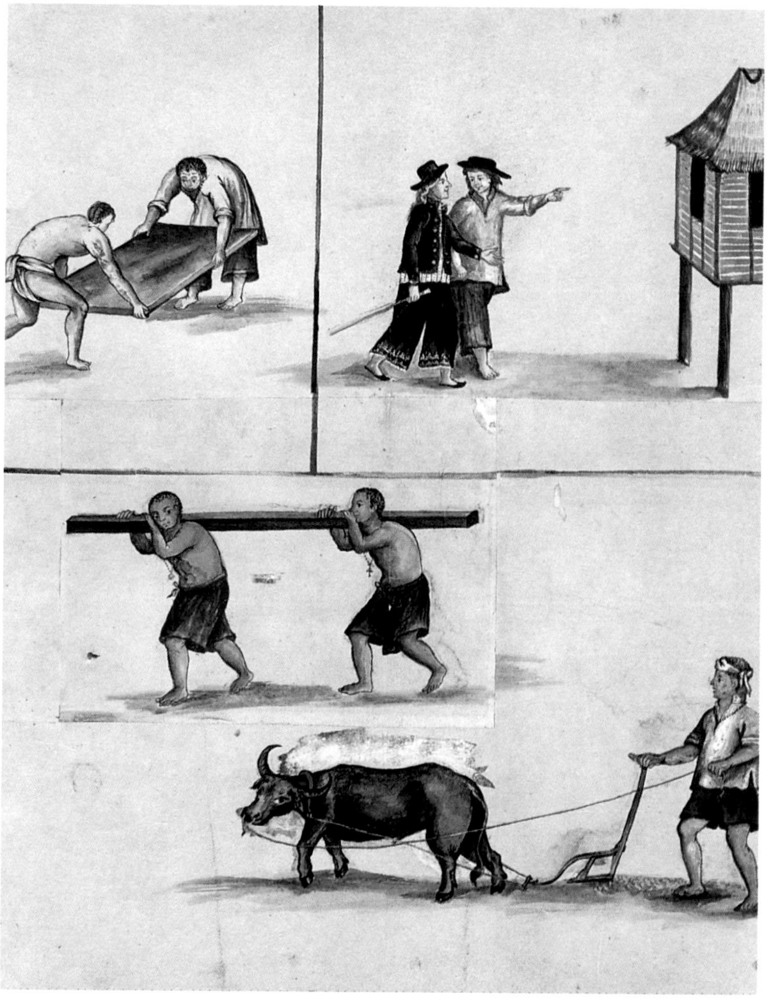

Natives of Cebú island in their traditional dress.

[1815]
Drawings showing the garments worn by natives of the Cebú bishopric (islands of Cebú, Mindanao, Negra, Leyte, Panay, Iloilo, Antiqui, Cagayancito and Cuyo).
380 x 289 mm.
MP. Estampas, 202.

The Philippine archipelago, Spain's trade base in the east, did not attract Spanish immigrants, as the sector was already controlled by the local Chinese community (Sangleys). Among other things, the lack of Spanish influence on the local population accounts for the survival of customs from the settlement period. The clothing shown here, illustrating a report from the Bishop of Cebú dated 1815, is recognizable from an account of 1572: 'The men… have their heads shaven in the manner of the Spanish and wear a kerchief around the head and a small cloth to cover their private parts. From the waist up, some wear an open, loose-fitting jerkin with half-sleeves…' (Patronato, 24, R. 25.)

– Guatemala and El Salvador

Once the peace mission Cortés had sent to southern Mexico had come to an end, Pedro de Alvarado embarked on the conquest of Guatemala. Following Cortés' example, he turned discord among the Indians to his advantage by seeking alliances and collaboration that enabled him to subjugate the territory in a short space of time. From 1523 to 1526 he successfully reduced the Quichés, Tzotzils and Cakchiqueles, the people of Xuchitepec and the Pocoman Indians. He also twice entered El Salvador. Cities such as Zapotitlan and Quetzaltenango fell to him. On 25 July 1524 he founded the city of Santiago de los Caballeros de Guatemala on the site of Tecpan–Iximche, although he was later forced to move it to Xepau, in Atitlán.

Alvarado's adventures did not end there—in 1534 he departed for Peru, lured by news of its wealth. Subsequently, in 1539, he readied a fleet to sail to Maluku. It never reached its destination, however, as he made a detour to assist Juan de Oñate and died in the uprising of Guadalajara in 1541.

City of Guatemala and Iztapa harbor.

[1598]
'Plan of Yztapa harbor, in Guatemala city'.
Drawn by the engineer, Pedro Ochoa de Leguizamo.
575 x 430 mm.
MP. Guatemala, 2.

In 1523, once the conquest of Mexico was over, Pedro de Alvarado, who had proved a loyal colleague to Hernando Cortés, was commissioned by the latter to seek out a passage between the Gulf of Mexico and the Pacific. The venture was unsuccessful, but it did lead Alvarado into the conquest of Guatemala and El Salvador on his own initiative, albeit in the name of Cortés. In 1524 he founded the city of Santiago de los Caballeros de Guatemala in Iximché, but was forced to move the 'old city' to Almalonga, at the foot of the El Agua volcano, three years later. Destroyed in an eruption in 1541, it was moved to present-day Antigua, where it remained until 1776. It was then reconstructed on a lasting basis in the Valley of La Ermita. The plan shows the 'old city' and Antigua.

Peru—in Search of the Incas

It was the tenacity of another leader, likewise a frontier veteran, that made the vague legends reaching Panama about the rich southern lands come true. That man was Francisco Pizarro.

The conquest of the Inca civilization, preceded by the expedition under Pascual de Andagoya, was carried out by Pizarro from the base at Panama on the orders of Pedrarias. The conquest was organized like a business enterprise with Pizarro directing military operations, Diego de Almagro in charge of provisions and Hernando Luque the funds.

Before driving into Inca territory in 1532, Pizarro made two arduous expeditions, in 1524 and 1526, in which he reached Gallo island and San Mateo bay. The harsh conditions on that island led to a momentous decision, whereby Pizarro chose to continue but only thirteen expeditionaries agreed to follow him—they were thereafter known as the 'famous thirteen' and together they reached Guayaquil and the bay of Tumbes, the threshold to the Incan Empire.

As Pedrarias would not authorize another expedition, Pizarro left for Spain where he secured an agreement on 26 July 1529 whereby the enterprise that until then had been private would become a State venture. He was also authorized to conquer Peru, from Temumpalla (Santiago) to Chincha. Almagro was excluded

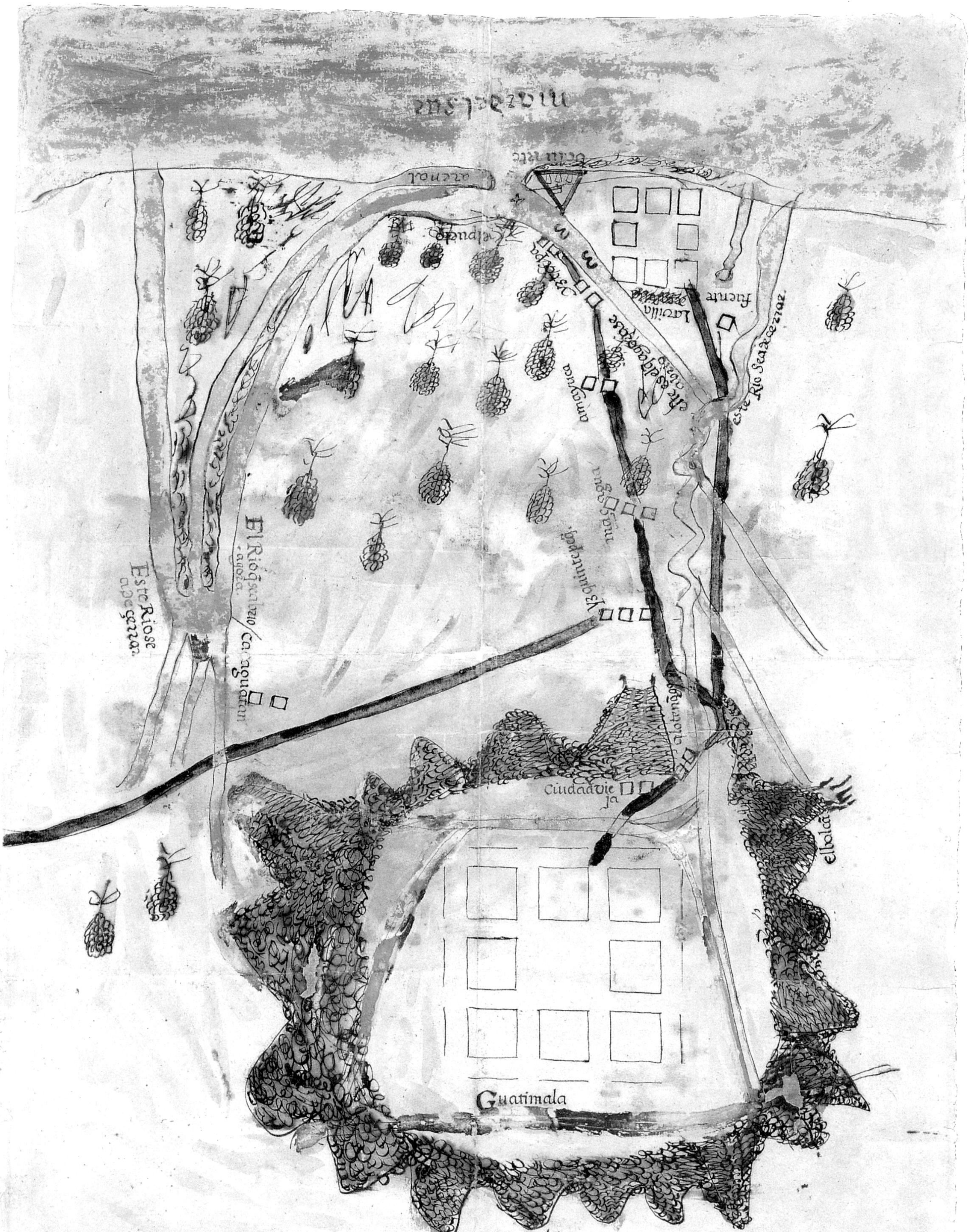
Ciudad vie
ja
Guatimala
norte

from the agreement, a fact that produced friction between himself and Pizarro and would later trigger civil wars.

Early in 1532, in a joint sea and land operation, the expeditionaries reached Tumbes, and shortly afterwards founded San Miguel de Piura as a way station linking them to Panama. On reaching Tahuantisuyo, they witnessed the fratricidal struggle between Huascar and Atahualpa, the sons of Huaina Capac, who had inherited the kingdoms of Cuzco and Quito respectively. As in Mexico and Guatemala, Pizarro took advantage of the dissent to secure his conquest.

Pizarro traversed the land of the Incas as far as Cajamarca, where he met Atahualpa, the victorious Inca. The latter took along an escort but did not attack, as he was confident of his numerical superiority and, like the Aztecs, may have also been influenced by the legends of the arrival of foreigners. He was too trusting, however, as Pizarro took him captive and, in the ensuing fighting, cut down 3,000 Inca warriors.

Accustomed to blind obedience, the Incas offered no resistance when Atahualpa ordered them to pay homage to the conquistadors. Shortly afterwards, following a summary trial on charges of treason, Atahualpa was executed.

After Atahualpa's death, anarchy broke out across the empire. It was again divided into two factions: that of Tupa Inca, Atahualpa's brother, backed by Pizarro and the Quito Indians, and Manco Inca, Huascar's brother, who reigned at Cuzco. Manco Inca was murdered in mysterious circumstances on 15 November 1533 and Pizarro's forces marched unhindered into Cuzco, the capital of the Inca Empire, where they seized magnificent spoils.

The abuses and acts of cruelty perpetrated by the expeditionaries at the time led to an uprising among the Incas, particularly in Quito, which was finally put down by Sebastián de Benalcázar. In 1536–1537, a second uprising, caused by disputes over land concessions, and over grants of Indian labor or tribute, known as *encomiendas,* prompted a second siege of Cuzco. The Incas retreated into the mountains and set up their base at Vilcabamba. Although the town did not pose a serious threat to the Spanish domination, it was eventually destroyed in 1572.

In 1534, Pedro de Alvarado turned up in Peru to take part in the conquest, but was dissuaded from doing so by being offered monetary compensation.

A year later, on 18 January, Pizarro founded Lima on the banks of the river Rimac and called it Ciudad de los Reyes.

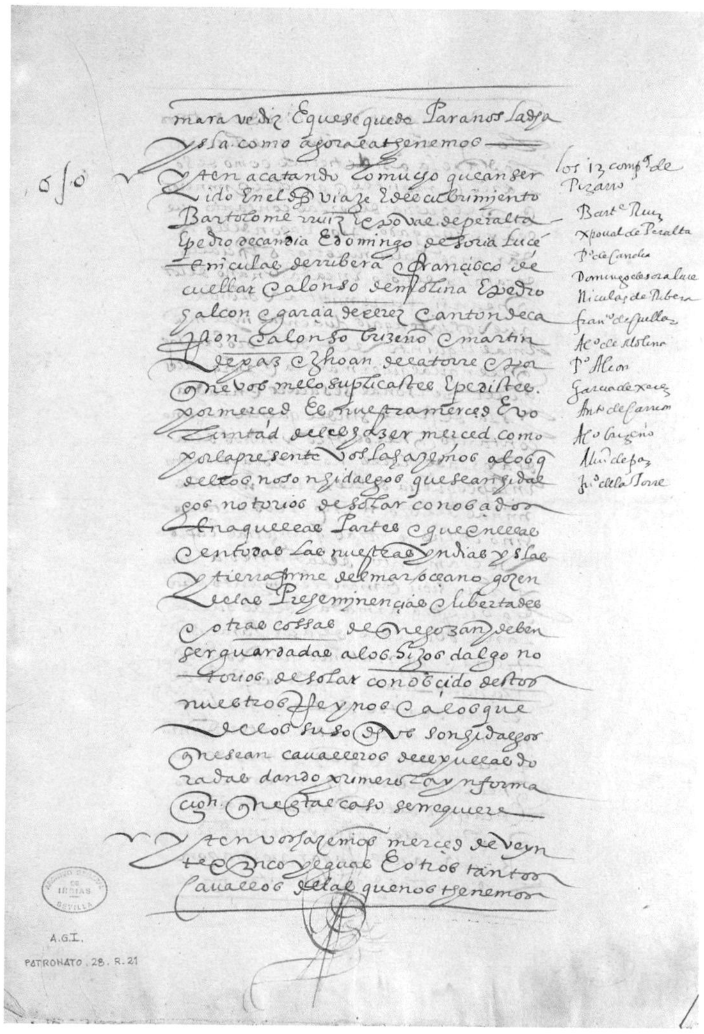

maravedis e que se quede para nos la otra
ysla como agora la tenemos —
Yten acatando lo mucho que an ser
vido en el dicho viaje e descubrimiento
Bartolome Ruiz e xpoval de peralta
e pedro de candia e domingo de soria luce
e nicolas de ribera e francisco de
cuellar e alonso de molina e pedro
alcon e garcia de xerez e anton de ca
rrion e alonso briceño e martin
de paz e joan de la torre e por
que vos me lo suplicastes e pedistes
por merced es nuestra merced e vo
luntad de les hazer merced como
por la presente vos la hazemos a los q
dellos no son hidalgos que sean hidal
gos notorios de solar conoscido
en aquellas partes e que en ellas
e en todas las nuestras yndias yslas
y tierra firme del mar oceano gozen
de las preheminencias e libertades
e otras cosas de que gozan e deben
ser guardadas a los hijos dalgo no
torios de solar conoscido destos
nuestros reynos e a los que
de los suso dichos son hidalgos
que sean cavalleros de espuelas do
radas dando primero la ynformacion
que en este caso se requiere
Yten vos haremos merced de veyn
te e cinco yeguas e otros tantos
cavallos de las que nos tenemos

los 13 compºs de Pizarro
Bartº Ruiz
Xpoual de Peralta
Pº de Candia
Domingo de Soraluce
Nicolas de Ribera
Franco de Cuellar
Aº de Molina
Pº Alcon
Garcia de Xerez
Antº de Carrion
Aº Briceño
Martin de Paz
Jº de la Torre

A.G.I.
PATRONATO. 28. R. 21

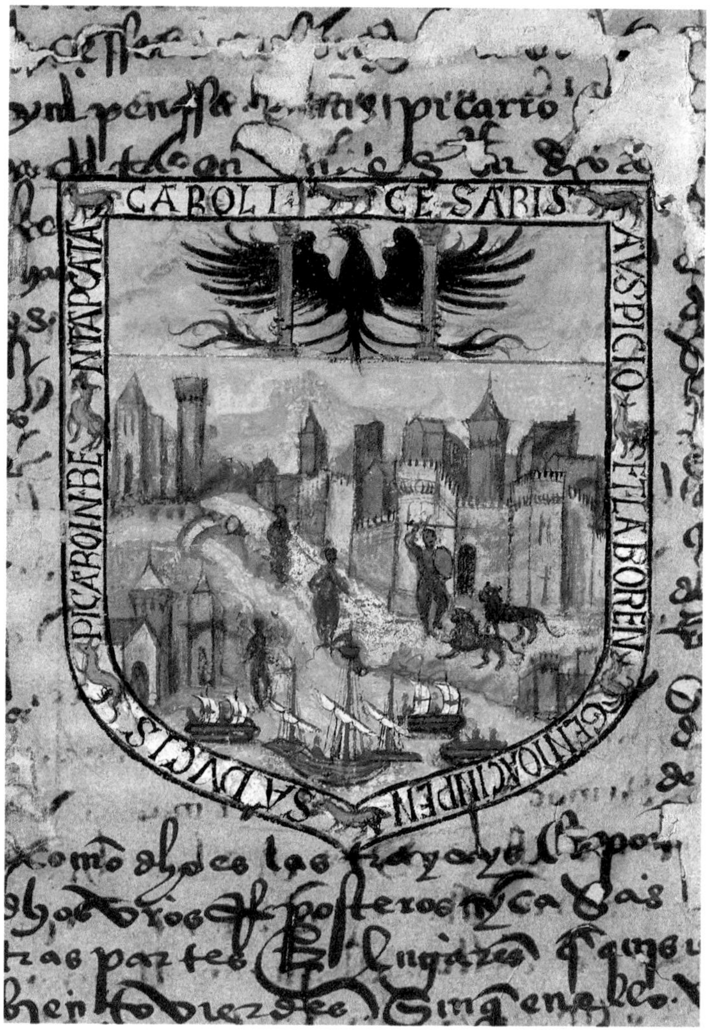

Francisco Pizarro: the conquest of Peru.

26 July 1529, Toledo.
Contract between the Emperor Charles V and Francisco Pizarro authorizing the discovery, conquest, settlement and pacification of the South Sea coast to the east, with the title of hidalgo being awarded to the 'famous thirteen'.
Copy produced in Lima, on 28 January 1573.
12 fols.
Patronato, 28, R. 21.

Francisco Pizarro's coat-of-arms.

13 November 1529, Madrid.
Coat-of-arms of Francisco Pizarro, discoverer and conquistador of Tierra Firme, the South Sea and Peru.
Motto: 'Caroli cesaris auspicio et laboren genio ac inpensa ducis Pizarro inbenta et pacata'.
88 x 75 mm. on fol.
Included in a copy of the 'Privileges' awarded him for his services at arms on the date shown.
MP. Escudos y Árboles Genealógicos, 7.

After the tortuous expeditions that led Francisco Pizarro to the gateway to the Incan empire, in 1529 he signed a contract with the Emperor Charles V whereby he was appointed governor, captain general, adelantado *and* alguacil mayor *(high constable) of the territories that were to be called New Castile, and empowered to pursue the conquest from Temumpalla (in the Gulf of Guayaquil) to the town of Chincha. (*Adelantados *were royal officials who headed military expeditions and held judicial and administrative powers over specific districts. They were usually stationed in frontier zones.) The same document awards the 'famous thirteen' the title of hidalgo for having followed Pizarro on the island of Gallo, in 1527. Shortly afterwards, in November that year, Francisco Pizarro was granted a coat-of-arms.*

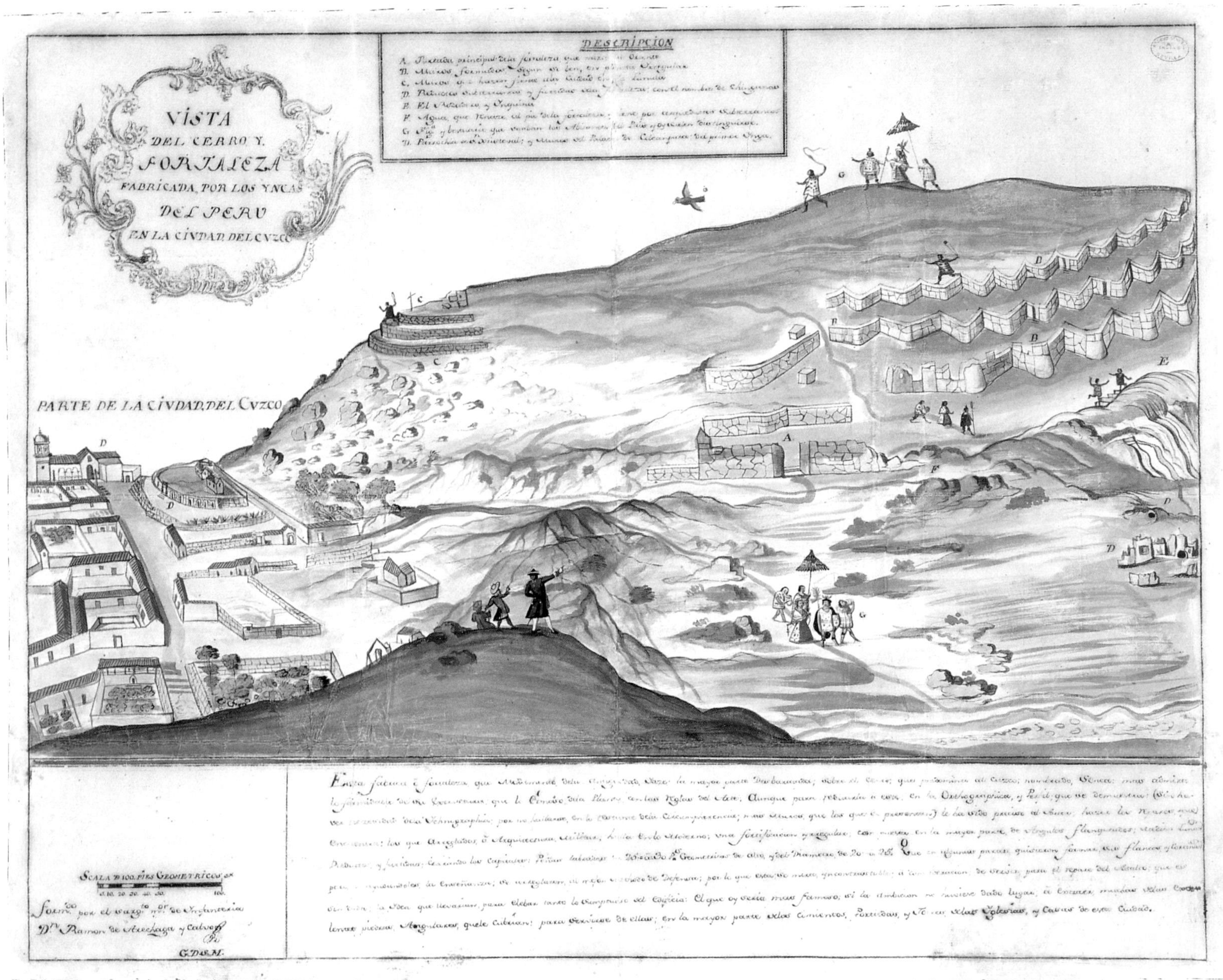

Cuzco, capital of Incan Peru.

[1778]
'View of the hill and fort erected by the Incas of Peru in the city of Cuzco.'
By Ramón de Arechaga y Calvo, sergeant major of the Infantry.
490 x 606 mm.
MP. Perú y Chile, 220.

Founded by the legendary Manco Capac, Cuzco was the grandest of the pre-Columbian cities, and the capital of Peru under Inca rule and during the early conquest. Strategically sited at the crossroads of the immense Andean empire of Tahuantisuyo, the city's layout was based on astronomical dictates and the political and religious organization of the Inca civilization. On 15 November 1533, the Spanish forces entered the virtually deserted city. They roamed the palaces, the 'House of the Sun Virgins', the Coricancha, *the cyclopean walls of the Sacsahuamán fortress, shown in the plan, and seized considerable wealth.*

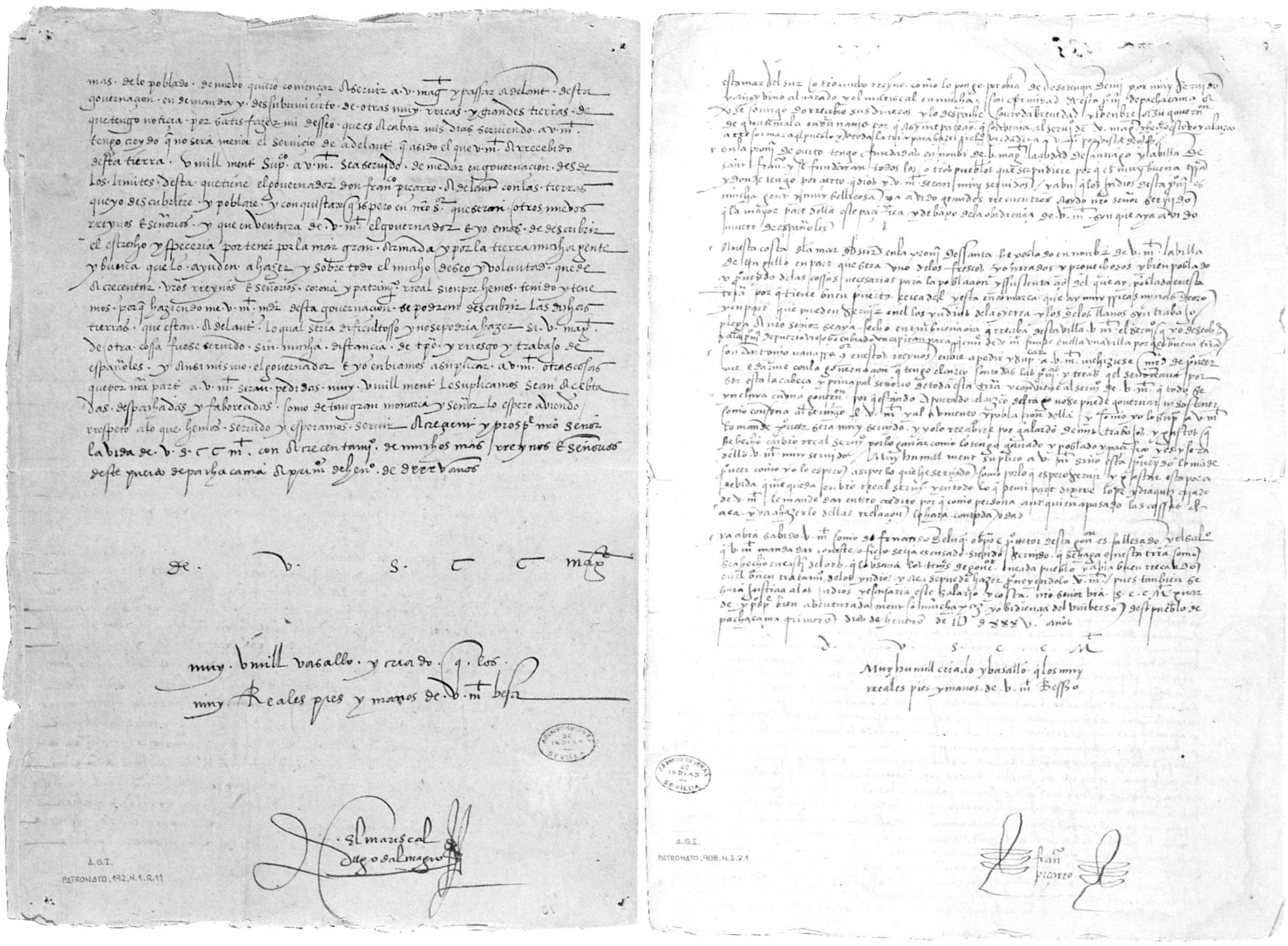

Pizarro and Almagro: rivalry with Alvarado.

1 January 1535, Pachacama.
Letters from Marshal Diego de Almagro and Francisco Pizarro to the emperor, regarding the disturbance caused by Pedro de Alvarado's intrusion in the latter's territorial government and the negotiations held with him. They also give account of the settlements they are founding, both in Quito province and Peru. Lastly, both request territorial privileges, which Pizarro specifies as referring to Cuzco, while Almagro refers to being relieved of his duty as second-in-command.
Autograph signatures.
2 fols. & 2 fols.
Patronato, 192, no. 1, R. 11 & Patronato, 90 B, no. 2, R. 1.

'...Alvarado bore disquieting intentions and a restless greed for rule...' This brief remark by Francisco Pizarro graphically describes the motives that, in his view, led Pedro de Alvarado to trespass on his jurisdiction. In 1534, the governor of Guatemala landed at Puerto Viejo and headed for Quito. Alerted to this development, Sebastián de Benalcázar and Diego de Almagro managed to reach an agreement with him at Riobamba whereby he pledged to return to his government in Guatemala and to make over his vessels and war material in return for 100,000 gold pieces.

The occupation of Peru had been consummated, but Pizarro was unable to impose his authority as Cortés had done in Mexico—internecine war between the Spaniards as well as Inca uprisings soon unleashed a blood bath that would tinge the country for some years to come.

In 1535, the creation of State governments at New Castile in the north and New Toledo in the south, awarded to Pizarro and Almagro, respectively, rekindled the flames of hate. Almagro's departure for Chile to open up new territory there only served to postpone the issue until 1537 when a civil war broke out between supporters of Pizarro and Almagro. It lasted until 1542, after an initial stage in which the confrontation ended with a victorious Pizarro in Salinas valley in 1538 and the execution of Almagro. Following the murder of Pizarro in 1541, the second stage of the conflict, fuelled by supporters of both sides, ended with the defeat of Almagro's forces at Chupas in 1542.

Despite the end to the civil war, peace was not forthcoming as, in the aftermath, the conquistadors led by Gonzalo Pizarro staged a rebellion against the Crown on account of the 'New Laws' governing the welfare of the Indians.

The Peruvian Drive towards Quito

The conqueror of Quito, Sebastián de Benalcázar, had gone to Peru from Nicaragua to rescue Pizarro's forces. The uprising in Quito of Rumiñahui, the pretender to the Inca throne, served as a pretext for him to earn fame and fortune. Despite the chief's resistance, in December 1533, he entered the burning, wealthless city. He seized control of the whole country and founded Guayaquil in 1534.

After the aforementioned Alvarado episode, in 1536 Benalcázar departed in search of Eldorado. There were rumors at the time of a king that covered his body daily in gold dust. Such rumors led the conquistadors to propagate one of the legends that most fuelled the exploratory fever on the continent. Benalcázar followed in its wake and reached the Cundinamarca plain in 1538. There he met up with Jiménez de Quesada and Nicolás Federman who, having journeyed from Santa Marta and Venezuela, respectively, had arrived for the same purpose. On his way, he founded Calli, Popayán, Pasto and Timaná.

The Amazon Expedition

Lured by another myth—that of the 'cinnamon country'—Gonzalo Pizarro left Quito in 1539 with his second-in-command, Francisco de Orellana. The expedition

Lima, capital of Peru.

[1687]
'Lima: Court and emporium of the Empire of Peru, ringed and fortified with walls and bulwarks built according to the tenets of modern architecture.'
'Fray Petrus Nolascus (...) delineavit et sculpsit.'
378 x 535 mm (454 x 640 mm).
MP. Perú y Chile, 13.

Having brought the Inca empire to its knees, the task of settling the land came to the fore, as evinced in the founding of Riobamba and Trujillo. To this end, Pizarro had a new capital city designed, sited on the coast and endowed with a good harbor as, from the outset, he planned it to be both an administrative capital and trade center for the whole of Peru. Thus, on 18 January 1535 he founded the Ciudad de los Reyes *(City of the Kings), in honor of the Spanish monarchs, Charles V and his mother, Queen Joan, on the banks of the river Rimac. Its strategic location soon prompted fortifications to be erected, the structure of which is shown in this magnificent plan.*

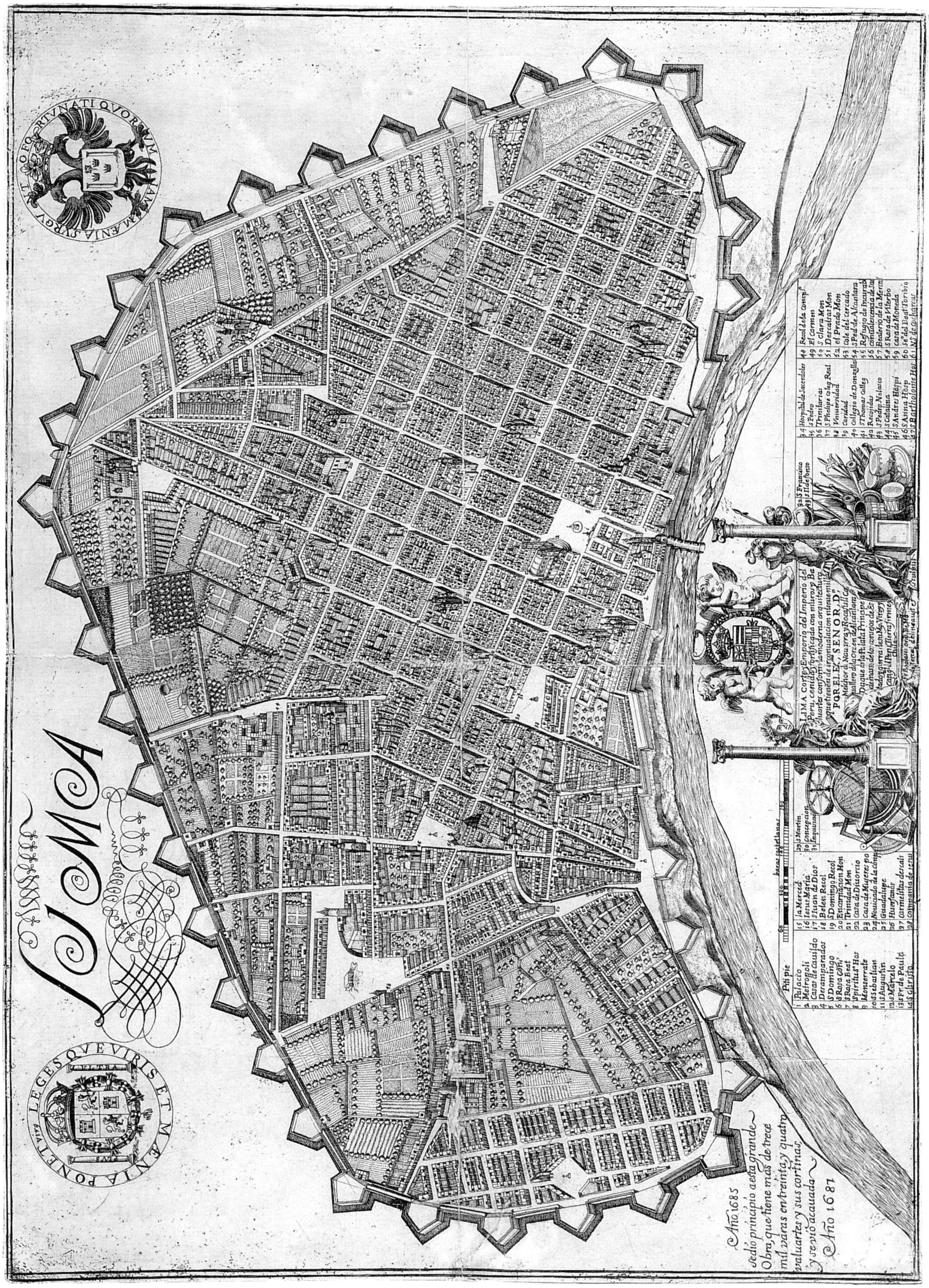
LIMA
Año 1685
se dió principio a esta grande
Obra, que tiene más de treçe
mil varas en treinta y quatro
baluartes y sus cortinas,
y se vió acauada
Año 1687

Inca coat-of-arms.

[9 May 1545, Valladolid]
Coat-of-arms awarded by the Emperor Charles V to Gonzalo Uchu Hualpa and Felipe Tupa Inga Yupanqui, 'the legitimate sons of Guaina Capac and main grandsons of the great Tupa Inga Yupangui, the natural Kings and Lords of those broad Kingdoms and Provinces of Peru, so that they may be regarded as Royal Personages, in representation of our own'.
Caption (below): 'The Great Tupa Ynga Yupangui'.
The caption probably refers to the brothers of Atahualpa and Huascar, Tupa Inca and Manco Inca, protagonists of the fall of Tahuantisuyo.
343 x 432 mm.
MP. Escudos y Árboles Genealógicos, 78.

Prominent among the thirteen emperors of the Inca dynasty were Pachacuti (1438–1471) and Tupac Inca Yupanqui (1471–1493), builders of the great Tahuantisuyo empire, and Huayna Capac, who organized the administrative machine. Under those emperors, the Inca empire extended from Ecuador to central Chile, central Bolivia and El Chaco. During the lifetime of Huayna Capac's sons, Atahualpa and Huascar, internal strife set in, a development the conquistadors turned to their advantage in order to seize the empire. Despite their defeat, the descendants of the Incas were granted privileges associated with the conquering powers, as attested in the above heraldic shield, awarded to relatives of the last four chiefs.

Apart from its spiritual mission, the conquest of Peru had a material objective in the conquistadors' endeavors to improve their financial standing and their social status.
Although not always fuelled by greed, the tireless search for gold, silver, pearls and other valuables endowed those involved in the search with a specific profile, in which some prominent character traits, including cruelty and violence, obstinacy and recklessness, greed and rapacity, and a destructive urge, were highlighted by their detractors. Such traits were, however, offset by a freedom of spirit, piety, firmness and a legalistic spirit, qualities admired by even their rivals. For these reasons, in but a few years the conquistadors, who had been regarded as gods, the reincarnation of Quetzalcoatl or Viracocha, became *cupais*, or 'devils' in the eyes of the Indians.
Moreover, their craving for sex, due in part to the dearth of women among their forces and facilitated by the acquiescence of the native population, earned the conquistadors a somewhat dubious reputation. Cohabitation between the two peoples occurred from the very outset: couples such as Cortés and Malinntzi or Marina, Alvarado and Luisa Xicontecatl, and Pizarro and Inés Huaylas, *La Pizpita* ("Wagtail') were merely the most conspicuous examples of what was actually a widespread phenomenon and gave rise to mestization.
However, the major driving force behind the conquistadors was the thirst for honor and fame, the accession to nobility and lordship in the medieval sense, claims which the Crown sought to restrain from the very beginning, even though coats-of-arms were indeed granted to the most prominent conquistadors.

was decimated by calamities that occurred in the Amazon jungle. Orellana was commissioned to reconnoiter the river Coca in search of provisions. Ignoring that, he sailed with the current to the river Napo and, via either the Marañón or Amazon, reached the Atlantic in 1542. The arduous journey, spanning seven months and 1,880 leagues, took him across the continent at its broadest point.

The second Amazon expedition, apparently mounted by the Viceroy of Peru, the Marquis of Cañete, to get rid of some adventurers, came to a tragic end. It was led by Pedro de Ursúa, accompanied by the mestiza, Isabel de Atienza, who became a veritable bone of contention during the voyage, as did Lope de Aguirre, who gradually earned himself the nickname 'Aguirre the Mad'.

Readied in 1559, the expedition set out along the river Huallaga or Los Motilones up to its confluence with the Amazon, Marañón or Bracamoros. As they advanced, the crew members grew more and more restive. Tension was running high when they reached Machifaro and, in a skirmish that involved Lope de Aguirre on 1 January 1561, Pedro de Ursúa died. From then on, Aguirre's violence knew no bounds. Obsessed with treason, he murdered both friend and foe, ordered Doña Inés to be killed and even assassinated the puppet king he had appointed, succeeding him and appointing himself 'Mighty leader of the Marañones'. After reaching the Atlantic via the mouth of the Amazon (some sources claim it was the Orinoco), he pursued his reign of terror on Margarita Island and then raided Venezuela, escorted by his followers, who were known as 'the Marañón gang'. Lope de Aguirre, 'the Wanderer', who had sworn to be 'a rebel to my dying day' against Philip II, died violently, as he had lived, slain by his own men.

Chile

Further south, central Chile was explored in 1535 by Almagro, but it was not colonized until the Valdivia period. The warlike Araucanians embroiled the Spanish in an ongoing war which marked the territory out as a frontier zone. The unusual shape of the territory, with the Atacama desert to the north and the Andes range to the east, left it hemmed in by land and dependent on the Lima sea route.

Pedro de Valdivia, who hailed from La Serena (Badajoz), was commissioned by Pizarro to further Almagro's mission, for which purpose he struck up an alliance with Francisco de Aguirre and Pedro Sancho de La Hoz.

The expedition departed in 1540 and, in 1541, he founded the city of Santiago de Chile, subsequently destroyed by the Indians and then rebuilt.

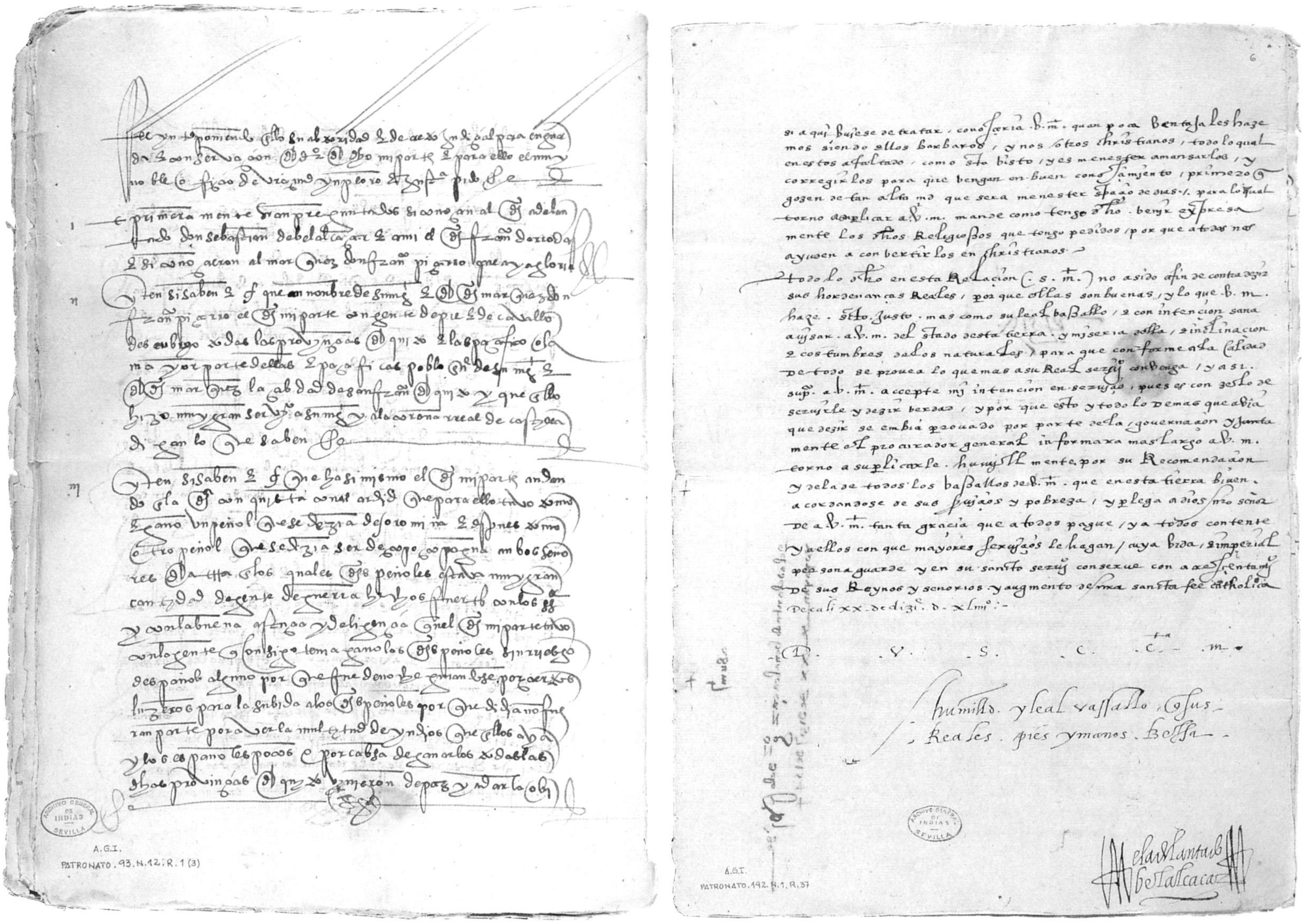

Sebastián de Benalcázar: Quito and Popayán.

2 March 1545 and 20 December 1544, Cali.
'Ad perpetuam rei memoriam' proof of the merits and services rendered by the adelantado *and governor, Sebastián de Benalcázar, in the conquest of the provinces of Quito. Next to it is a letter from him to the Emperor Charles in which he informs the latter in detail about the pacification of some provinces in his jurisdiction, such as Timbas, Páez, Alcón (Popayán) and Arma, near Cartago, and about the widespread disappointment among the conquistadors at the promulgation of the so-called 'New Laws' in 1542.*
10 fols. and 6 fols.
Patronato, 93, N. 12, R. 1 (3) & Patronato, 192, N. 1, R. 37.

These are highly characteristic documents of the period of discovery and conquest of the New World. The declaration of merit and letter–report reproduced above reveal two moments in the life of the conqueror of Ecuador and Popayán, Sebastián de Benalcázar. The first refers to the conquest of Quito, after defeating the local chief, Rumiñahui. Pizarro's companion-at-arms during the conquest of the Inca civilization, the Quito expedition, and from 1535 onwards, Benalcázar comes through as an imposing figure in his own right. The second moment reveals Benalcázar conducting the pacification of the territory under his jurisdiction, after being appointed adelantado *and governor of Popayán in 1541.*

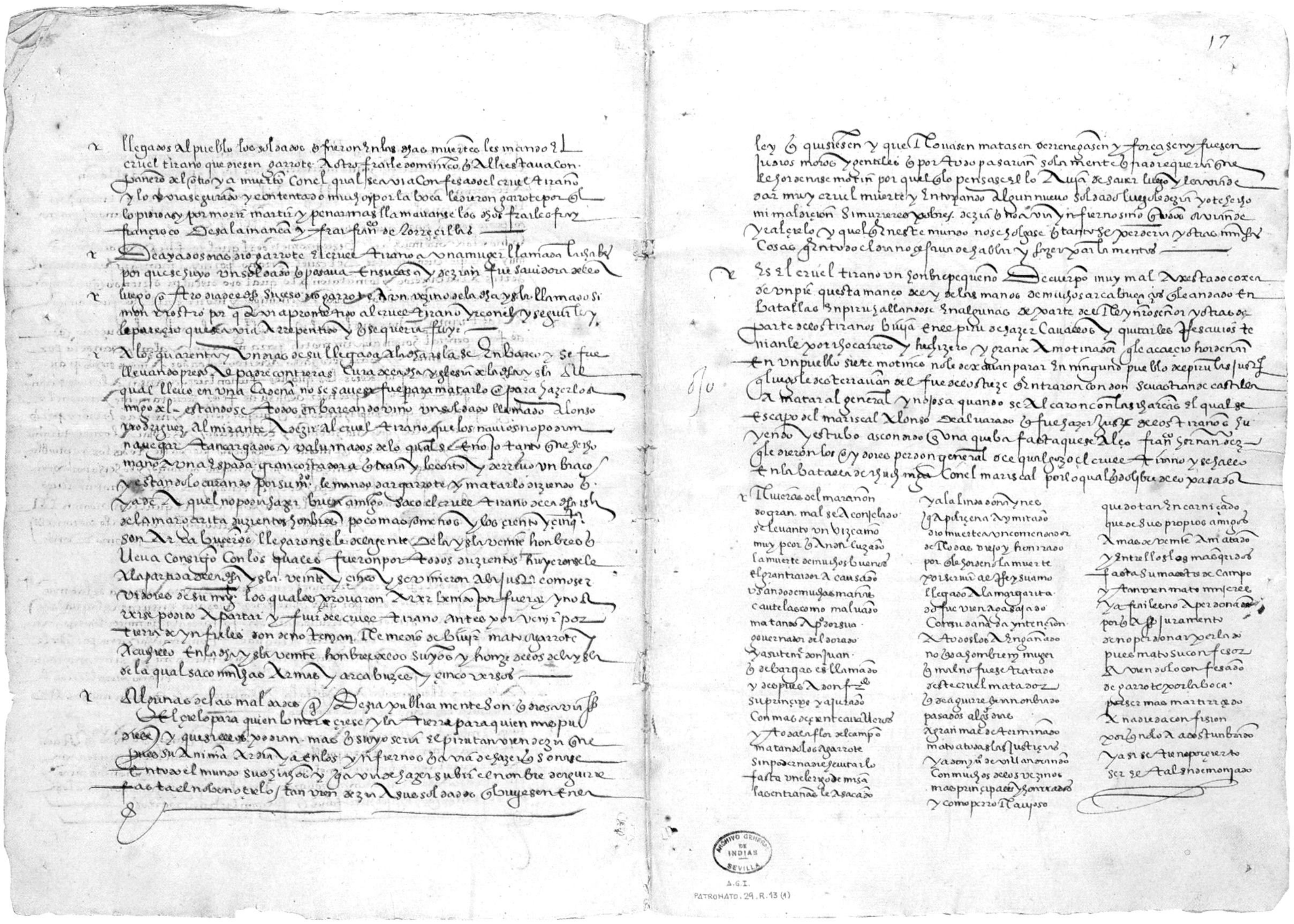

The Amazon expedition: Lope de Aguirre.

[1561]

'Truthful account of what occurred on the river Marañón, in El Dorado province, from the time Pedro Dorsua was sent from the city of Lima by the Marquis of Cañete, Viceroy of the Kingdom of Peru, documenting the death of the aforesaid Pedro Dorsua and the rise of the tyrants, Don Fernando de Guzman and Lope de Aguirre, his successor, and recounting their deeds until the time they reached Margarita Island and departed from there.'

[By Gonzalo de Zúñiga?]

Copy [undated]. In a notebook also containing a copy of a letter from Lope de Aguirre.

23 fols.

Patronato, 29, R. 13.

Within the context of the 'chronicles of conquest', the relación *or 'account' is akin to the present-day documentary for its immediacy and the detail in which events are described. The account shown here recalls the tragic vicissitudes of the second Amazon expedition under Pedro de Ursúa. The author, clearly a detractor of Lope de Aguirre, describes him as being a cruel, paranoid individual, as evinced in the lines of the closing ballad:*

«... Y como perro ravioso quedo tan encarnizado
que de sus propios amigos a mas de veinte a matado,
y entrellos los mas queridos, fasta su Maestre de Campo;
y tanvien mato mujeres y a frayles no a perdonado,
porque a fecho juramento de no perdonar perlado...
Y asi se tiene por çierto ser el tal endemoniado».

('...And like some rabid hound he raged
And of his friends hath he more than twenty slain,
Among them the most beloved, even his field commander
He cut down women, too and spared not even friars
As he has sworn to forgive no prelate
And is thus rightly taken to be the accursed.')

From 1547 to 1549, Valdivia was in Peru helping the judge–president of the *Audiencia* of Lima, Pedro de La Gasca, put down the rebellion staged by Gonzalo Pizarro. He was awarded the governorship of Chile for his services. On his return, he set about conquering Araucanian territory to the south. The Araucanian Indians were highly accomplished warriors and fearful opponents. Valdivia divided his time between founding settlements such as Concepción (1550 & 1552–1553), La Imperial, Valdivia, Angol and Villa Rica, and fighting the Araucanian confederation commanded by Caupolicán, who was subsequently joined by Lautaro after the latter had first sided with the Spaniards. Caupolicán gained the upper hand and, at the battle of Tucapel (1554), took Valdivia prisoner and put him to death after subjecting him to dreadful torture.

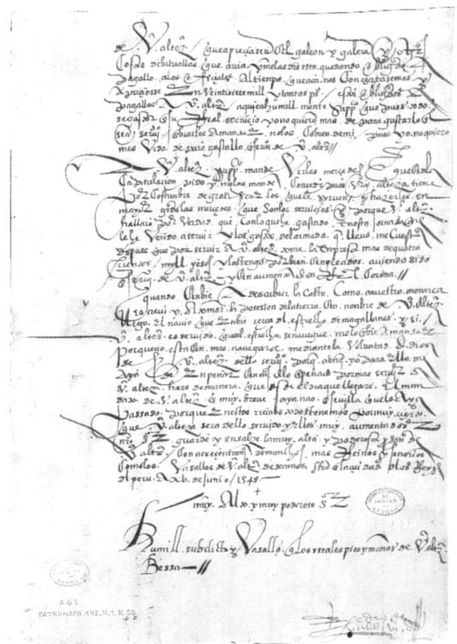

Pedro de Valdivia: Chile and the Strait of Magellan.

15 June 1548, Los Reyes (Lima). Letter from Pedro de Valdivia to Prince Philip seeking confirmation of the privileges granted him by the Audiencia *of Lima as a reward for his services rendered in Peru during the Gonzalo Pizarro revolt and for his government of Nuevo Extremo (Chile). In the letter, he also requests permission to send an exploratory vessel to the Strait of Magellan.*
2 fols.
Patronato, 192, N. 1, R. 50.

Requests for rewards in consideration of services rendered was a constant among the conquistadors throughout the 16th century. In this instance, Valdivia refers to his part in the conquest of Chile and his support of the president of the Audiencia *of Lima in putting down Gonzalo Pizarro's revolt against the 'New Laws' in 1542. The letter also mentions Valdivia's interest in the Strait of Magellan, a region that was still a no-man's land and which he wished to annex. To this end, he sent two exploratory expeditions, one under Jerónimo de Alderete (1544) and the other under Francisco de Ulloa (1555).*

The new governor, García Hurtado de Mendoza, eventually managed to defeat Caupolicán—whose saga is narrated by Alonso de Ercilla in *La Araucana*—after which he pressed further south and founded cities such as Cañete and Osorno in 1558, and Mendoza in 1561.

Tierra Firme

Despite having been the first part of the mainland to be discovered, the coastal strip from the Gulf of Urabá to the mouth of the Orinoco took a long time to settle on account of its climate, rugged, scattered terrain and the belligerence of its native inhabitants. It was visited frequently, however, for the purpose of trading pearls, gold, slaves and other goods. Outposts were also built there and used as bases for venturing into the hinterland.

After the failure of the earliest settlements, it was the mythical sites such as Eldorado and El Sinú, with their *huacas* (Indian tombs), that proved tempting to the expeditionaries and led to the founding of various settlements on their march inland. These include the following:

– El Darién.

This jurisdiction was awarded to Pedro de Heredia who, in 1533, founded Cartagena de Indias. He roamed the territory searching for treasure, thereby attracting hordes of adventurers obsessed with El Sinú. They set about ransacking cemeteries, tombs and everything containing gold or jewels. This led to Heredia being indicted by the jurist, Vadillo. The positive side of these expeditions was that, in geographical terms, they opened up the whole district and enabled settlements to be established, including those of Santa Cruz de Mompox, Cartago, Tamalameque and Pamplona.

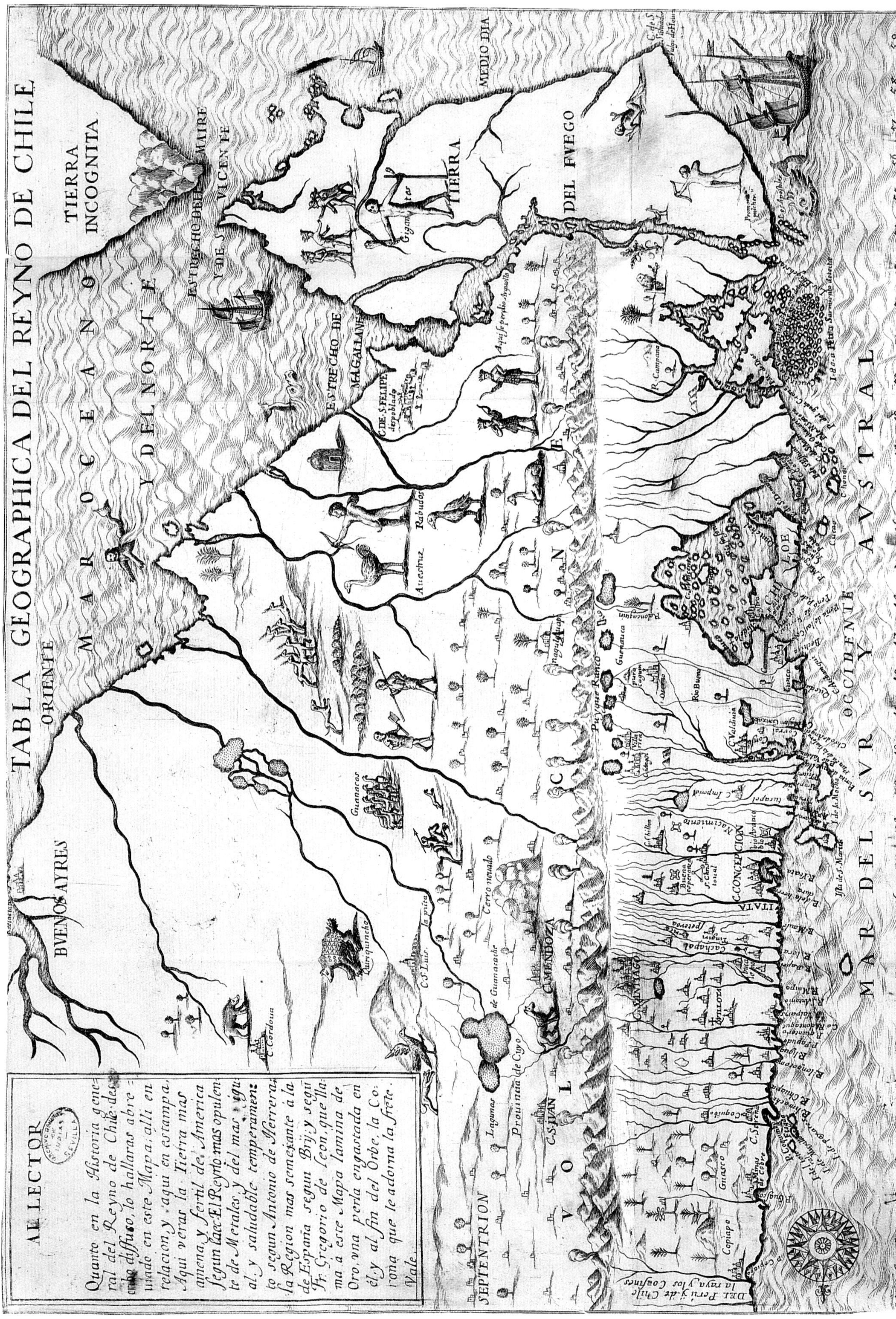

TABLA GEOGRAPHICA DEL REYNO DE CHILE
AL LECTOR
ORIENTE
MAR OCEANO Y DEL NORTE
TIERRA INCOGNITA
ESTRECHO DE MAGALLANES
ESTRECHO DEL MAIRE
TIERRA DEL FUEGO
MEDIO DIA
BUENOS AYRES
SEPTENTRION
MAR DEL SUR Y OCCIDENTE AUSTRAL
C. MENDOZA
C. S. JUAN
C. S. LUIS
C. CONCEPCION
Guanacos
Auestruz
Rabudos

– Santa Marta.

An upshot of coastal trade was the growth of stable settlements such as Cumaná and Santa Marta, founded by Rodrigo de Bastidas. In a season of frenzied forays in search of booty, the bane of those early times were outrages committed against the local population.

The territory was still uncharted when the governor Pedro Fernández de Lugo arrived there in 1535, on one of the largest and best equipped expeditions in the American conquest, accompanied by Gonzalo Jiménez de Quesada. The governor then commissioned the lawyer and jurist, Jiménez de Quesada, to explore the land.

In search of Eldorado, he ventured upstream along the river Magdalena in 1536. Nearly two years later, with his expeditionaries decimated by hunger and disease, he reached the plateaux of the Colombian Andes. The indigenous Indians there were the Muiscas, from the Chibcha family, one of the great American cultures comparable to the Mayas and even the Aztecs or Incas. Practically the whole region fell to him once he had defeated the Zipa tribe of Bogotá Indians, the Zaque of the Tunjas and the Iracas chiefdom, thereby providing him with the treasure the region concealed and details of the whereabouts of emerald mines. On 6 August 1538, Jiménez de Quesada founded the city of Santa Fe de Bogotá, the future capital of the kingdom which he named New Granada, in memory of his birthplace.

– Coro–Venezuela.

A pearl region, Santa Ana de Coro was founded in 1527 by Juan Martín de Ampiés, having been commissioned by the *Audiencia* of Santo Domingo to staunch the traffic of local slaves.

Most likely in return for their financial support in his election, Charles V signed a contract with the Welsers, a family of German bankers, ceding to them the province of Venezuela in return for building two colonies and three fortresses. The emperor's concession lasted from 1528, when the agreement was signed, until 1546, when it was revoked as a result of the Germans' failure to perform.

Maracaibo was founded in 1529 by the explorer Ambrosius Ehinger (or Alfinger), who travelled as far as the river Magdalena. Georg von Hohermuth discovered the source of the river Meta, while his second-in-command, Nikolaus Federmann, departed without his permission in search of Eldorado and arrived at the Bogotá plateau. But, Jiménez de Quesada had preempted him and, while the dispute raged over possession of the land, Sebastián de Benalcázar arrived from

PREVIOUS PAGE
Colonizing the Strait of Magellan.

[1646]
'Geographic map of the Kingdom of Chile'. The map takes in the aforementioned kingdom, Tierra del Fuego and Patagonia and shows the San Felipe settlement in the Strait.
314 x 450 mm (329 x 465 mm).
Featured at the end of:
OVALLE, Alonso de: Historica Relacion del Reyno de Chile, y de las missiones y ministerios que exercita en él la Compañía de Jesús.
Published in Rome by Francisco Cavallo, 1646
Biblioteca, L.A., S. XVII-39.

The earliest conquest and colonizing expeditions of the Strait of Magellan and Tierra del Fuego, including the one led by Simón de la Alcazaba, sailed from Spain between 1534 and 1539 and failed miserably. Subsequent expeditions, commanded by Alderete, Ulloa and Juan Ladrillero between 1544 and 1557, set out from Chile. After inspecting the area in 1578, Pedro Sarmiento de Gamboa persuaded Philip II to let him ready an expedition to settle and fortify the 'Strait of the Mother of God', and was appointed governor of the corresponding province. However, the settlements founded in 1583—Nombre de Jesús and Real Felipe—came to a tragic end, recounted by the sole survivor, Tomé Hernández and by the English pirate, Thomas Cavendish.

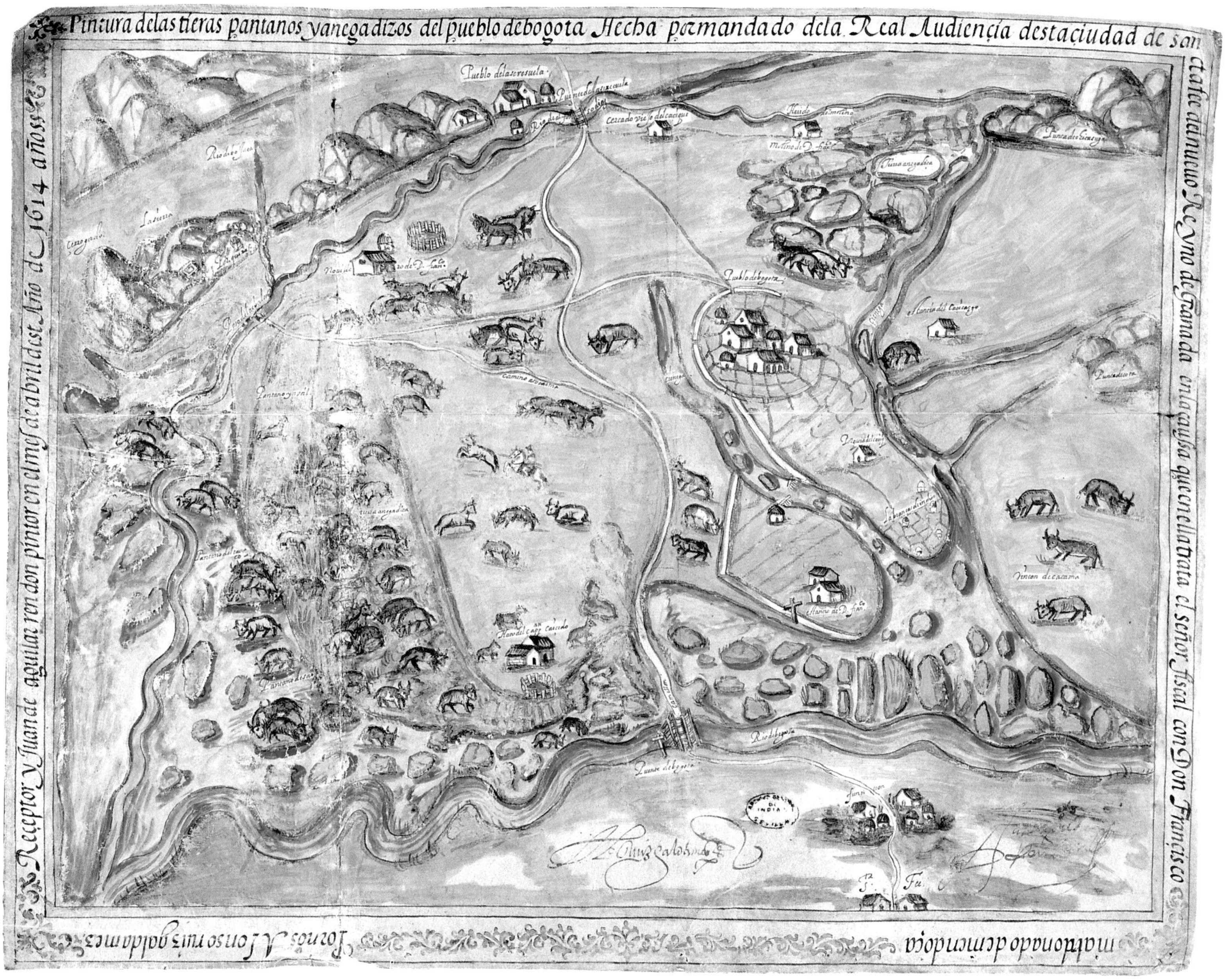

The Bogotá plain and Eldorado.

April, 1614.
'Painting of the lands, marshes and floodland around the town of Bogotá, commissioned by the Royal Audiencia *of Santa Fe in the New Kingdom of Granada.'*
'By ourselves, Alonso Ruiz Galdamez, receiver and Juan de Aguilar Rendon, painter. In the month of April, 1614.'
350 x 430 mm.
MP. Panamá, 336.

The myth of Eldorado, in the Spanish imagination a fabulous land endowed with immense gold riches, was almost certainly based on the legend of a powerful Chibcha chieftain who lived near Lake Guatavitá and was said to smear himself daily with an ointment on top of which he dusted gold. In search of imagined wealth, three expeditionary forces set out from Santa Marta, Coro and Quito, led by Gonzalo Jiménez de Quesada, Nikolaus Federmann and Sebastián de Benalcázar, respectively. In 1538, they met on the Cundinamarca plateau, on the Bogotá plain, inhabited by the Chibchas. On 6 August 1538, Jiménez de Quesada founded Santa Fe in that fertile terrain.

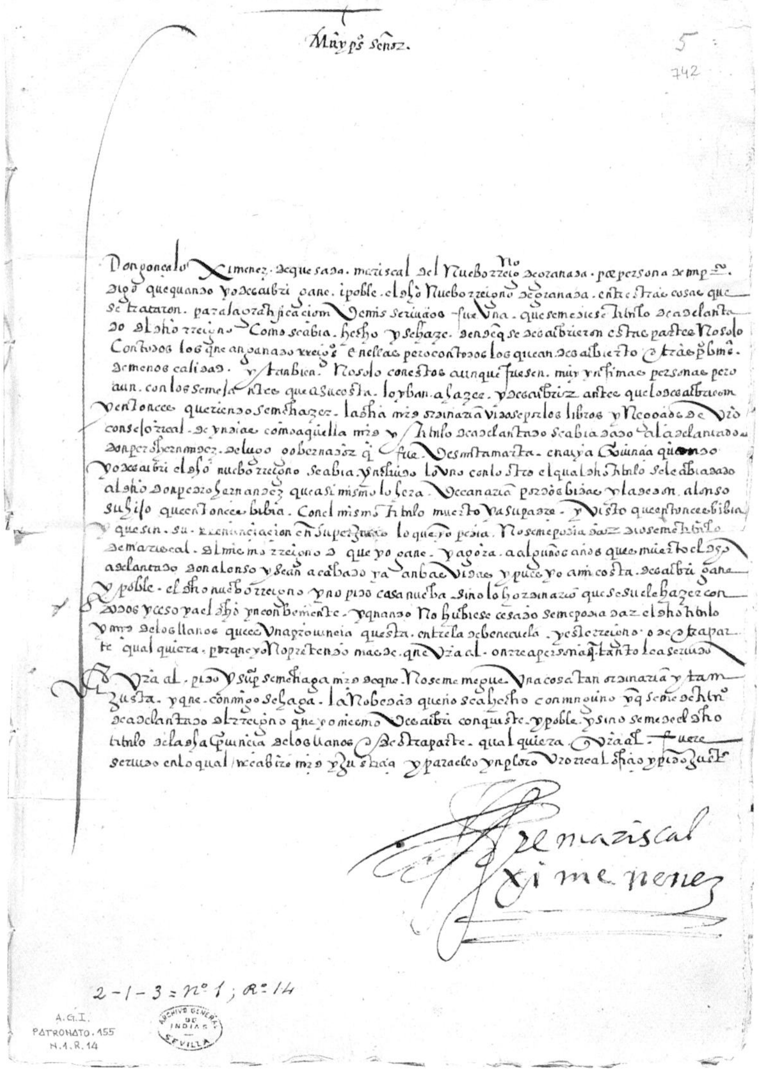

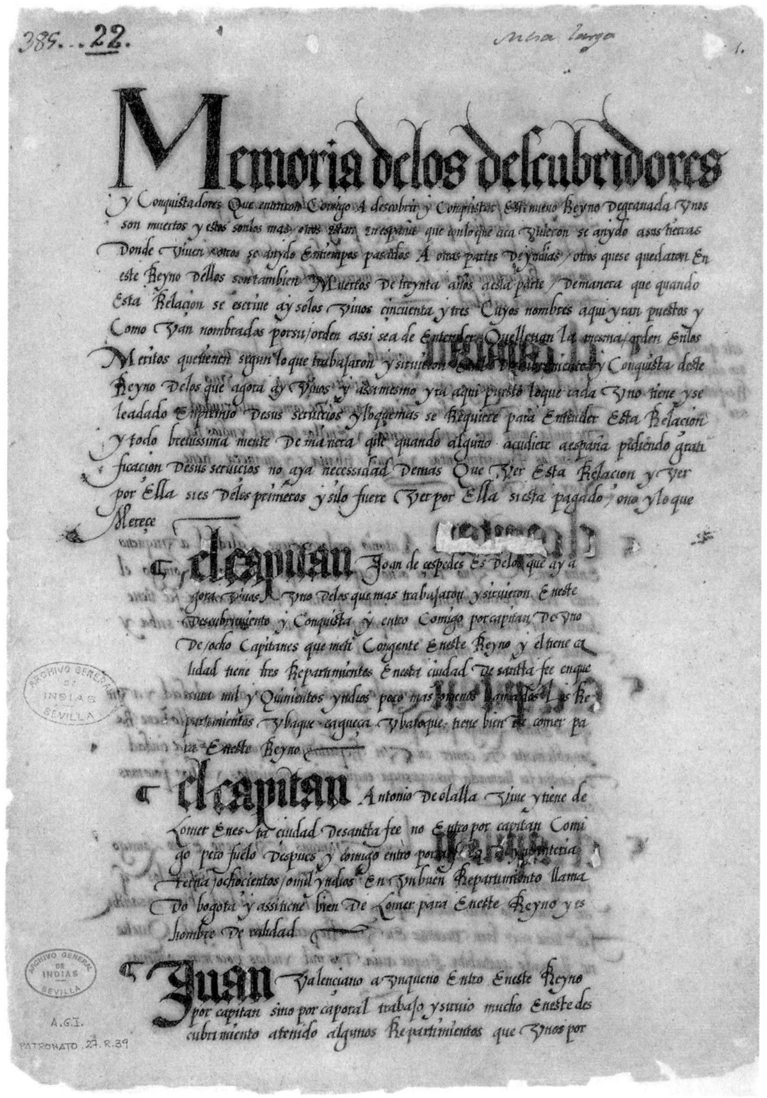

Gonzalo Jiménez de Quesada: the search for Eldorado.

[1563]
Letter from Marshal Gonzalo Jiménez de Quesada, discoverer and conqueror of the New Kingdom of Granada, requesting, in consideration of his services, the title of adelantado *of the territory he had discovered and conquered.*
Autograph signature.
1 fol.
Patronato, 155, N. 1, R. 14.

Roster of the conquistadors of the New Kingdom of Granada.

[undated]
'List of the discoverers and conquerors that ventured with me to discover the New Kingdom of Granada: those who died were in the majority, while those that survived returned to Spain with their riches. Others have long since gone to other parts of the Indies; others stayed behind in this Kingdom and some of them, too, are dead, having perished in the past thirty years, so that, at the time of writing, only fifty-three are still alive and their names are here listed...'
Signed by Gonzalo Jiménez de Quesada.
4 fols.
Patronato, 27, R. 29.

Regarded as the conqueror of New Granada, Gonzalo Jiménez de Quesada headed the expedition sent by Pedro Fernández de Lugo, governor of Santa Marta, to find Eldorado. The expeditionaries, listed in order of merit in the roster shown here, sailed upstream with him along the river Magdalena as far as the plain of Bogotá, in Cundinamarca, where they subdued the Chibcha nation. Jiménez de Quesada was never appointed governor of the territory, which accounts for his repeatedly petitioning for the title of adelantado *to be bestowed in return for his services.*

OPPOSITE
Lake and city of Maracaibo.

21 February 1699
'Layout of Lake Maracaibo, measured in Castilian leagues, with its villages, towns, valleys, harbors, sandbars, forts and castles, encircled by points A, B, C.'
642 x 464 mm.
MP. Venezuela, 286.

After signing a contract with the Germans in 1528, the exploratory mission got under way. Taking a route based on fantastical accounts, believing there to be a passage linking the 'North Sea' or Caribbean to the Pacific near Maracaibo, in 1529 Ambrosius Alfinger reached the shores of Lake Coquibacoa, which he decided to explore. He crossed the lake and founded an expeditionary base, Maracaibo, on its left shore. The town was later resettled by Alonso Pacheco, in 1571, under the name Ciudad Rodrigo and, in 1574, by Pedro Maldonado, who called it Nueva Zamora.

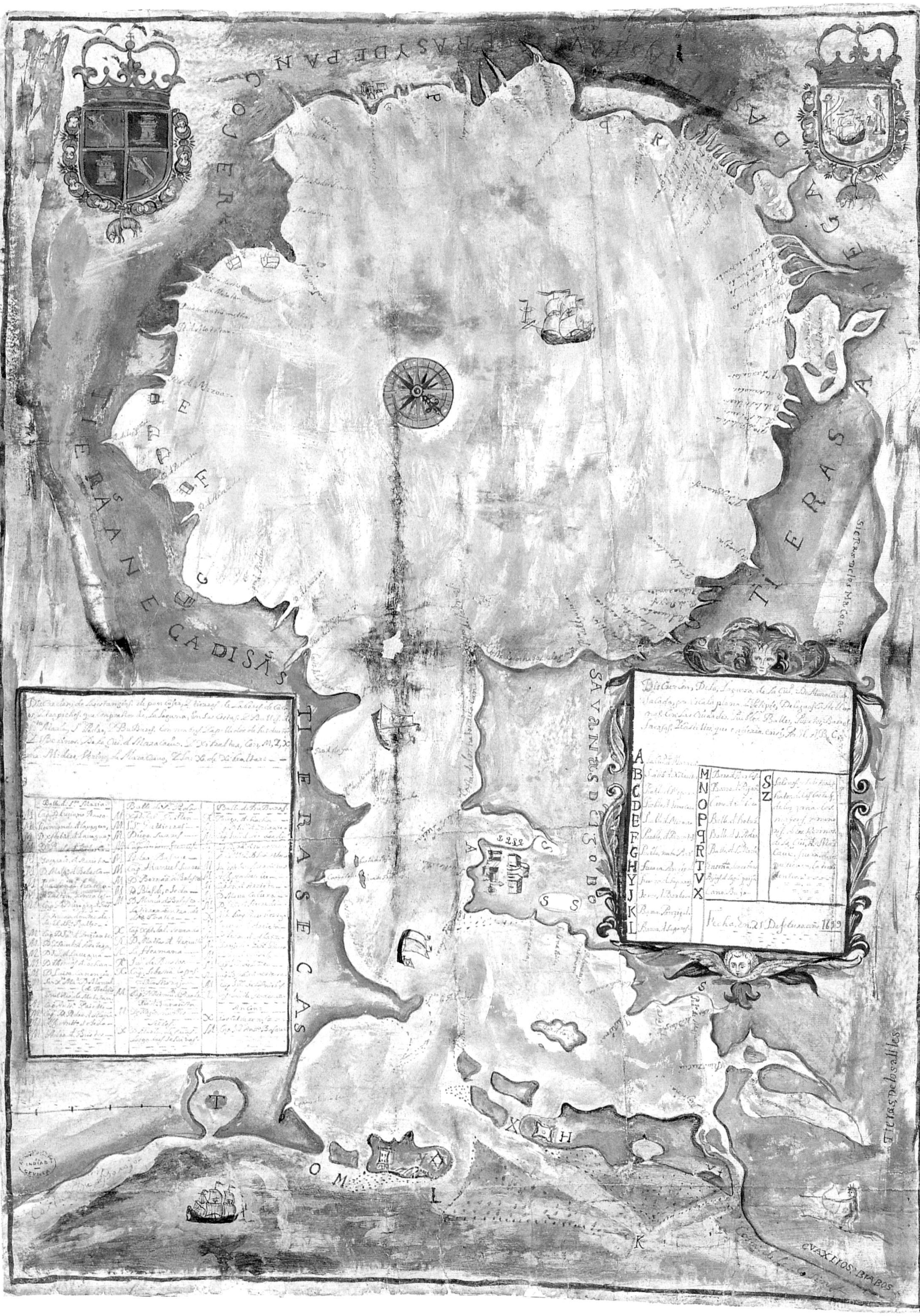

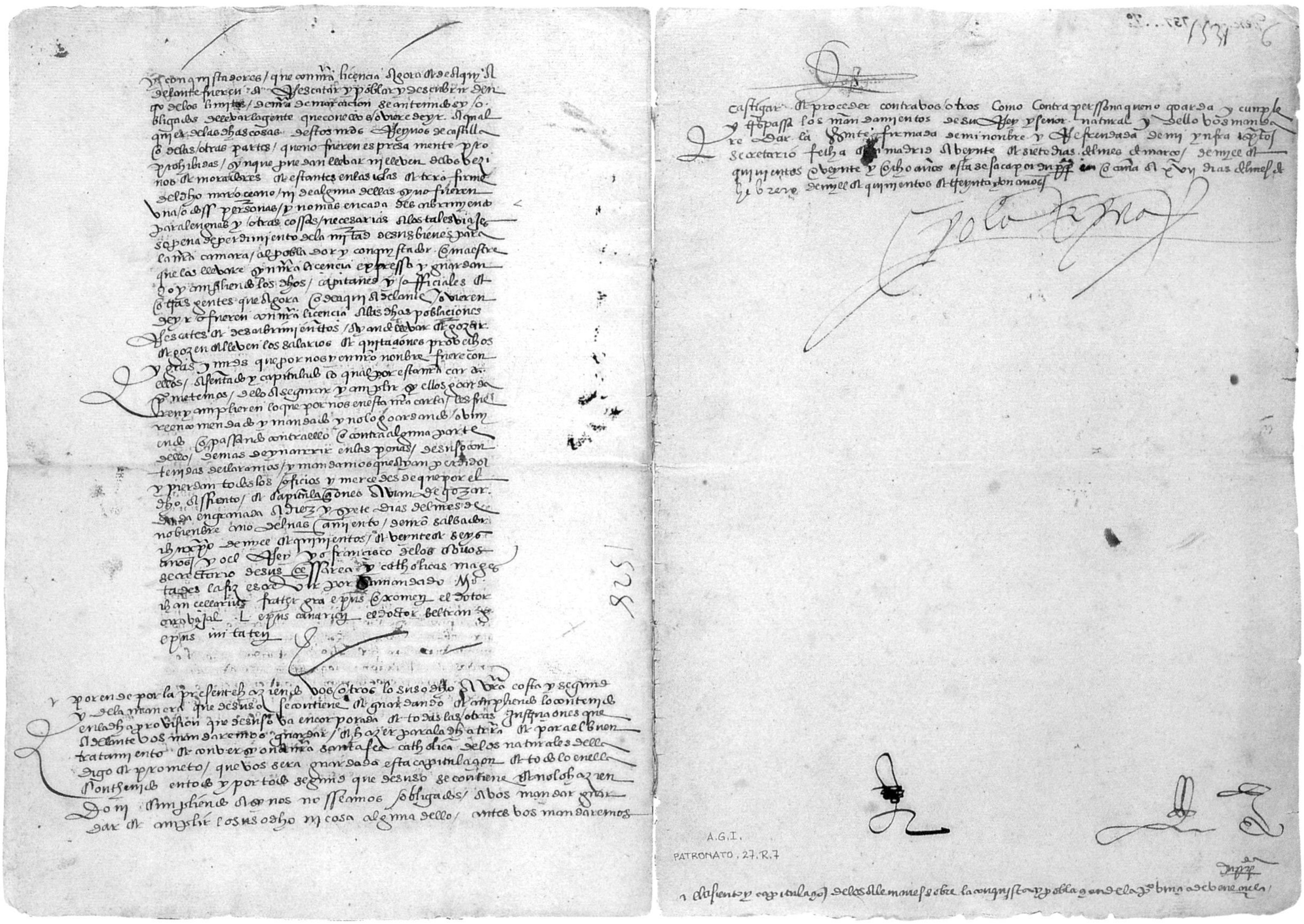

The Welser contract: Venezuela.

27 March 1528, Madrid
Original contract signed by Queen Joan and the Germans, Heinrich Ynguer and Hieronymus Sayler, brokers in Seville for the bankers, Bartholomeus and Anton Welser, assigning to them the land between Cape Maracapana and La Vela in the east, and Santa Marta province in the west, and from the Atlantic to the Pacific, which they were thereby entitled to colonize. A duplicate of the agreement was made in Ocaña on 17 February 1531, the year in which the document was made over to the Welsers.
6 fols.
Patronato, 27, R. 7.

Prior to 1520, the Venezuelan coastline was only used for trading, particularly in pearls and slaves. Settlement there was hampered by hostile natives, stirred up by the conquistadors making forays into their territory to hunt Indians. In 1520, Fray Bartolomé de las Casas made an unsuccessful attempt to settle New Toledo, near Cumaná. In 1527, Juan Martín de Ampiés founded Santa Ana de Coro, the first capital of Venezuela and future center of inland expansion. The following year, Charles V granted the Welsers a concession to rule and exploit the territory on highly favorable terms, in return for founding two cities and building three fortresses. However, their colonizing endeavors foundered and the concession was revoked in 1546.

Quito and claimed his right in Pizarro's name, as the area fell within the latter's jurisdiction. The decision was remitted to the Crown, which in 1542 appointed Alonso Luis de Lugo governor of Santa Marta. Four years later, an *Audiencia* within the jurisdiction of the Peruvian viceroyalty was set up there.

Once the German concession had been withdrawn, the administration set about founding settlements: Burburata in 1548, Barquisimeto in 1557 and Nueva Valencia del Rey (Nueva Trujillo) in 1560. In 1557, San Francisco was rebuilt and renamed Santiago de León de Caracas, and in 1572 it replaced Coro as the capital.

Río de la Plata

The Atlantic seaboard of South America was colonized directly from Europe, although late, slowly and with little success. The drive inland was fuelled by pipe-dreams of a 'White King', the 'Land of the Caesars' and the 'Silver Range'.

Río de la Plata, known as *Mar Dulce,* had first been sighted by Juan Díaz de Solís in 1515, while a member of the ill-fated expedition under his command, Alejo García, was instrumental in disseminating the aforementioned legends.

Commissioned by Charles V to reconnoiter the Magellan route in 1525 and lured by those mythical accounts, Sebastian Cabot headed for the Solís river, which he intended to explore. He sailed up the La Plata, Paraná, Paraguay and Bermejo rivers. His expedition met up with a group led by Diego García de Moguer and together they repeated the fruitless search. One of the expeditionaries, the so-called 'Captain Caesar', started spreading news of the empire of the 'White King'.

In January 1536, after running aground in Río de la Plata, Pedro de Mendoza founded the settlement of Nuestra Señora de Buenos Aires or Santa María del Buen Aire on its banks. He then sent Juan de Ayolas and Domingo Martínez to explore the territory and to find a route overland to Peru. In 1537, Ayolas sailed up the Paraná and Paraguay rivers as far as Candelaria and ventured into Peru, where he died. Juan de Salazar founded Asunción, the capital of Paraguay, in 1537.

With the death of the *adelantado* and deputy, Domingo Martínez de Irala took over as commander and promptly evacuated Buenos Aires and moved the colonial seat of government to Asunción.

Another *adelantado,* Álvar Núñez Cabeza de Vaca, was appointed to replace Mendoza and arrived in Asunción in 1541. In 1543–1544, he and Irala separately sought out a land route to Peru.

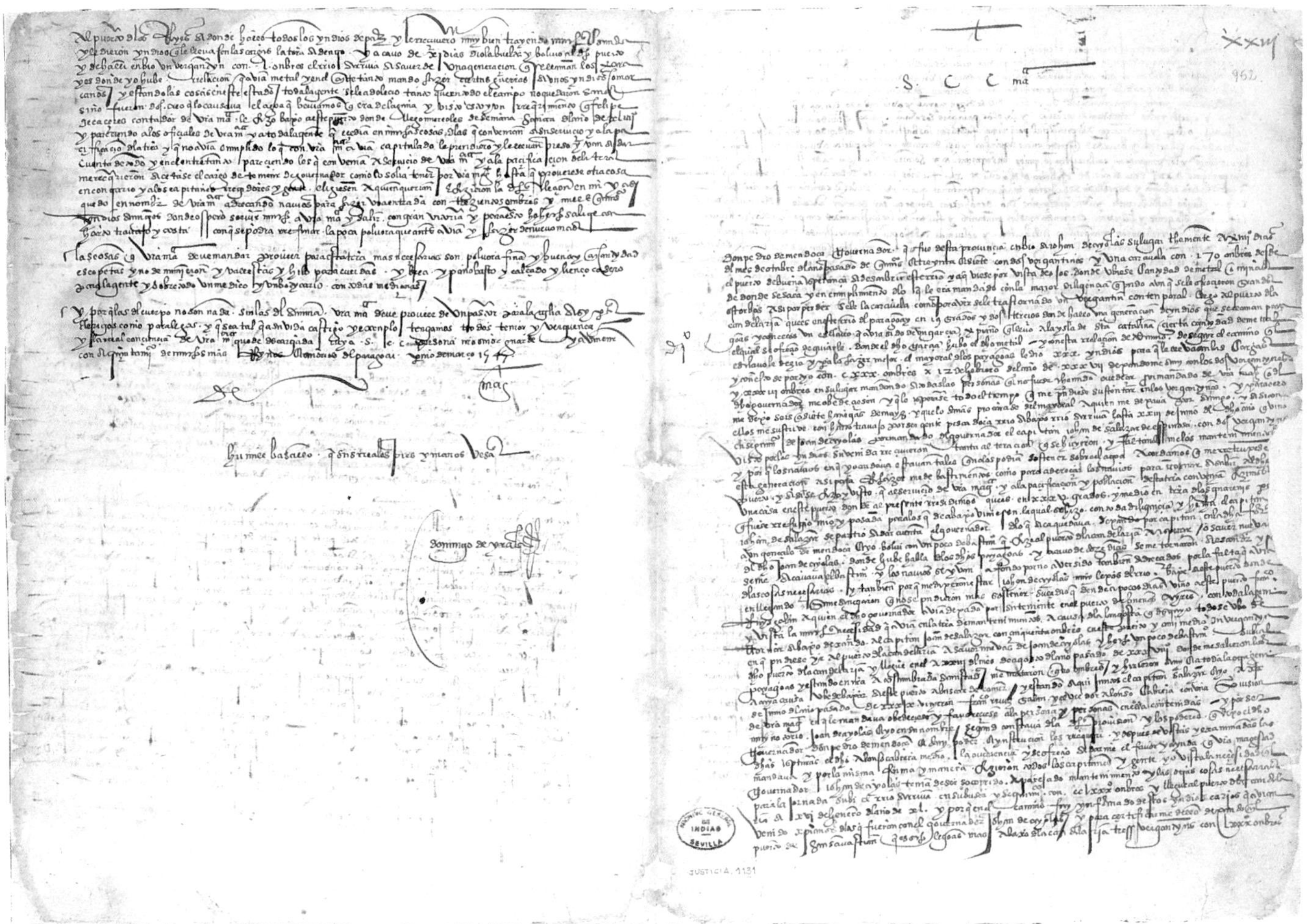

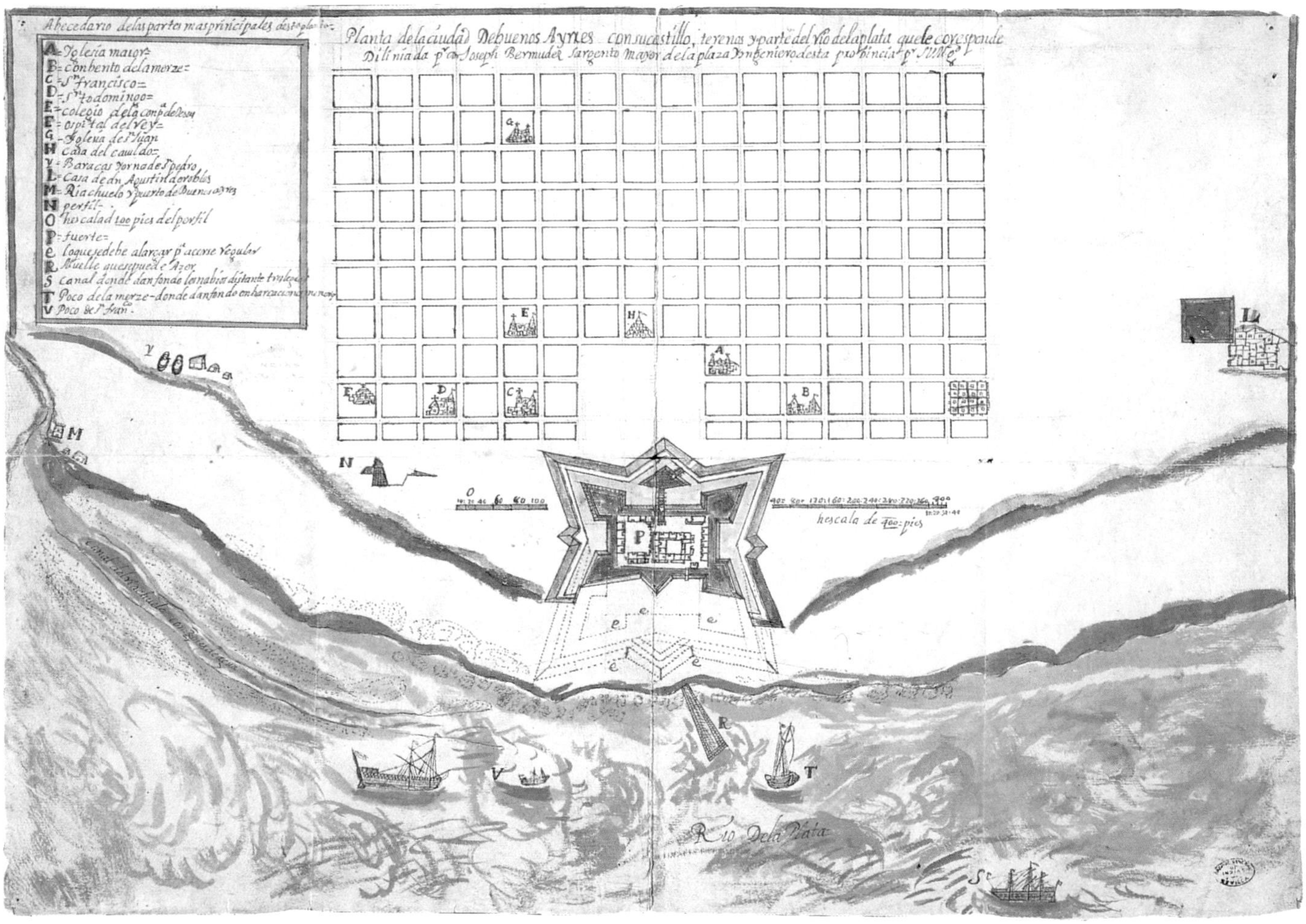
Abecedario dela partes mas principales deste plano
A Yglesia maior
B conbento dela merze
C Sn francisco
D Sto domingo
E colegio dela comp de Jesus
F ospital del rey
G Yglesia de Sn Juan
H casa del cauildo
Y Baracas y orno de Sn pedro
L casa de dn Agustin de robles
M Riachuelo y puerto de Buenos ayres
N perfil
O hescala de 100 pies del porfil
P fuerte
Q loque se debe alargar pa acerse regular
S Canal donde dan fondo los nabios distante tres leguas
T Poço dela merze donde dan fondo embarcaciones menores
V Poço de Sn fran
Planta dela ciudad de buenos Ayres con su castillo, terenos y parte del rio dela plata que le corresponde
Dilineada por Joseph Bermudez Sargento mayor dela plaza Yngeniero desta provincia
hescala de 400 pies
Rio De la Plata

Domingo Martínez de Irala: Río de la Plata.

1 March 1545, Paraguay.
Letter from Domingo Martínez de Irala to the emperor, providing a long, exhaustive account of events in the territory of Río de la Plata, from 1537 to 1544, of his part in its exploration and conquest, together with that of the governors, Pedro de Mendoza and Álvar Núñez Cabeza de Vaca, and of his election as governor by the rebel settlers in the city of Asunción.
Autograph signature.
2 fols.
Justicia, 1131.

The territory of Río de la Plata was explored by some prominent figures who feature in Irala's letter: governor Pedro de Mendoza, his deputy, Juan de Ayolas, the supervisor, Juan de Salazar, who founded Asunción on 15 August 1537, the ill-fated governor, Álvar Núñez Cabeza de Vaca, and, in particular, Domingo Martínez de Irala, the tireless explorer who subsequently reach Upper Peru only to discover that the Spaniards based in Lima had already found the White King (in the Potosí area).

Buenos Aires, opposite Asunción.

1708
Linear plan of Buenos Aires and its castle, and part of Río de la Plata.
By the engineer, José Bermúdez.
580 x 430 mm.
MP. Buenos Aires, 38.

The first settlement of what is now Buenos Aires was founded by the adelantado, *Pedro de Mendoza, in February 1536, on the right bank of Río de la Plata. It lasted five years and in 1541 was moved by Domingo Martínez de Irala to Asunción, where all the Río de la Plata settlers were concentrated. However, the inland expansion of the Paraguayan and Peruvian centers created the need for a settlement near the mouth of the river Paraná to channel local trade. This prompted the second foundation of Buenos Aires, by Juan de Garay, on 11 June 1580, to serve as an outbound port for Peruvian silver to the Atlantic.*

In 1545, the settlers of Asunción revolted and removed the *adelantado* from office, electing Domingo Martínez de Irala as governor. The period 1545–1547 was spent exploring Pilcomayo; in 1547, Irala went to San Fernando, traversing El Chaco and reaching the mountains, where he came across Indians who answered him in Spanish about his inquiries. The myth that had been pursued since 1516 regarding a 'White King', the 'Land of the Caesars' and the 'Silver Range' turned out to be true, but the area in question had already been conquered by Pizarro and Almagro.

The dejected expeditionaries returned to their bases and became farmers and settlers. In 1554, Domingo Martínez de Irala's appointment as governor was finally ratified. A brave soldier, he was also a cautious colonizer. He founded schools, assembled councils, regulated Indian services and kept peace.

Colonization of Río de la Plata, which had begun at the time of Charles V, was given renewed impetus by Philip II, leading to the second foundation of Buenos Aires, by Juan de Garay, on 11 June 1580.

Factors in the Expansion

Expansion on the mainland had been virtually completed by the mid-16th century. The pace of events was quicker in the more civilized areas where the Spaniards inherited the power concentrated in the local military, religious and political elite. The main reasons for their meteoric advance were:

– Technological superiority: the invaders possessed horses, hunting dogs, steel-bladed and fire-powered weapons, and ships.

– War strategy: while the natives had limited objectives, the Spaniards waged swift, decisive warfare that had to end in either triumph or death.

– Religion and mindset: belief in destiny, predestination and prophecies led the American Indians to accept as inevitable the arrival of the Viracochas and the 'bearded men who would become lord over all'.

– The collaboration of the indigenous population, a noteworthy example being the Tlaxcala tribe of New Spain, or the Quiché, Cakchiquel and Tzotzil Indians of Guatemala. The conquistadors' scouts, interpreters and informers were natives—worth recalling here is the role played by Marina or Malinche, Cortés' lover. Starting out with small armies, the invading forces were considerably augmented by large numbers of American Indian auxiliaries, who became allies.

– Internal strife within the indigenous communities, a state of affairs that conquistadors such as Cortés, Pizarro and Alvarado astutely managed to turn to their advantage.

Indigenous collaboration: Tzintzuntzan

[1595]
'Coat-of-arms of the city of "Çintzuntzan Vitzitzilan", in the province of Michoacán.' Legend: 'Harame a nexo a texo vacusti catame'. 'City of Cintzuntzan'. 287 x 207 mm. (315 x 210 mm.) Featured in 'Proceedings for handing over the city of Zintzontza', 1595, which includes details of the city and of its release from the Pázcuaro jurisdiction, fol. 8. MP. Escudos y Arboles Genealógicos, 168.

After conquering Tenochtitlán and, consequently, the land ruled by the Aztec Confederation, Hernando Cortés set about exploring adjacent territories. He sent several expeditions south to the provinces of Michoacán, Colima, Oaxaca, Tehuantepec and Tuxtepec to find a passage linking the Gulf of Mexico to the Pacific. The ruler of Tzintzuntzan, in Michoacán province, offered to join the Spanish forces. Cortés responded by sending two captains to reconnoiter the coastline of the province. By the end of the century, Zintzuntzan had status as a city, its own coat-of-arms and had applied for autonomy from the Pázcuaro jurisdiction.

Justification and Laws of Conquest

The issue of justifying the Spanish conquest is inseparable from the defense of human rights in the Americas and the institution of measures to protect the native populations.

In 1511, Fray Antonio de Montesinos, one of the first Dominican friars to arrive in Hispaniola (1510), publicly denounced maltreatment of the island's indigenous population employed in the gold diggings and as part of the *encomienda* system of concessions. This led to drafting the Laws of Burgos (1512–1513) in which settlers are urged to treat the natives kindly, and to see to their instruction and spiritual needs. The same doctrine was at the heart of the 'Instructions', drawn up for the Hieronymite brothers, who had been sent to Hispaniola in 1516 on a mission of conversion. The Crown's concern for treatment of the natives was set forth in the successive provisions issued, prominent among which was the Statute of 1526 on the correct procedures for conquest, which were included in all susbequent contracts of conquest and colonization.

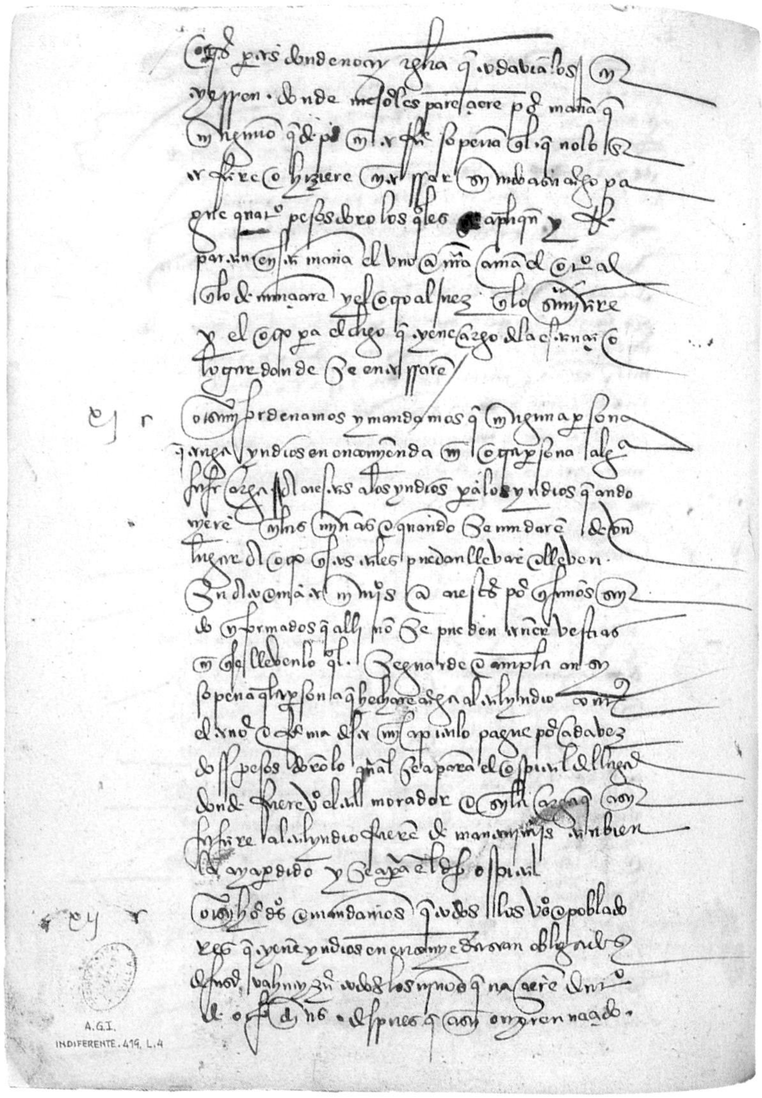

The Laws of Burgos: protecting the natives.

23 January 1513, Valladolid.
Royal statutes for suitably regulating and treating American Indians, issued in Burgos on 12 December 1512 and dispatched to the authorities in the Indies on the dated shown above.
Entry in official royal register.
Indiferente General, 419, L. 4, fol. 83 r.–96 v.

The Dominican Fray Antonio de Montesinos's sermons decrying harsh treatment of the indigenous population of Hispaniola by the conquistadors made such an impact in Spain that King Ferdinand summoned experts in American Indian affairs to a meeting in Burgos, and their deliberations led to the promulgation of the so-called 'Laws of Burgos'; these were amended in a Declaration *regarding their application on the island of Puerto Rico (Valladolid, 28 July 1513. Patronato, 174, R. 1). Those royal provisions formed the basis of doctrines concerning protection of the indigenous population, in particular, their conversion, material well-being, the way they were treated, work conditions, transport and terms of employment under the* encomienda *system.*

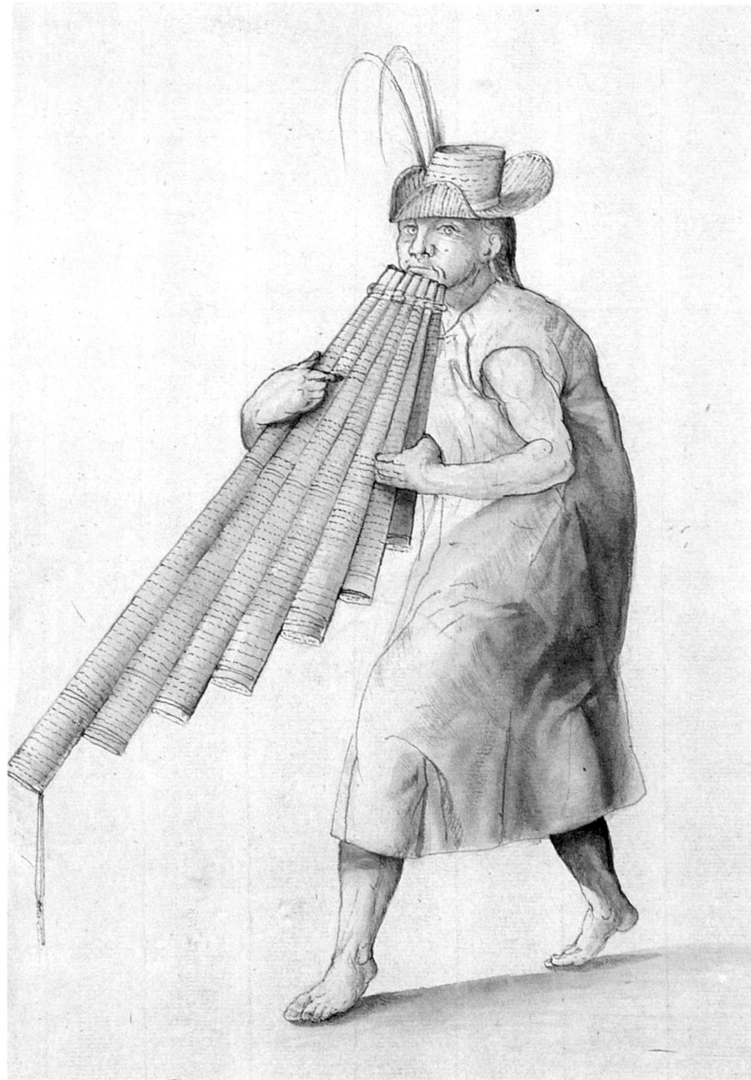

Myth of the 'Great Moxo'.

[1790]
Drawing of a Moxo Indian playing a variety of pan-pipe known as the flautón de palma.
302 x 208 mm.
MP. Estampas, 201.

The Moxos region on the Mamoré river plain in eastern Bolivia was a southern version of the mythical Eldorado. It was the focus of all sorts of fabulous myths which in Paraguay were associated with the Candire, and, in Peru, with the Paititi and the Great Moxo, a chief gleaming with gold and silver who lived on an island in a great lake that could be reached via the land of the Chiquitos. In their search for the Paititi, the Spanish thrust north-west to Cuzco, La Paz and Cochabamba, and south-west to Paraguay and Santa Cruz. The first explorer to enter the Moxos plains was Pedro de Candía, in 1539. However, his and subsequent expeditions were a failure and effective contact with the natives was only established in the second half of the 17th century by the Jesuits.

Modo de entrar à la Provincia de Antioquia desde su Puerto, que nombran las Juntas, en que comienza el camino de montañas altas
y asperas hasta salir de ellas al parage nombrado la Seja, y desde alli à esta Capital, se puede handar en bestias, y en todo él se cuentan setenta
leguas, antes mas que menos; y se hechan de camino desde dho. Puerto hta esta Capital dies, hasta dose dias, y mas en los tiempos de Yvierno.

Indian protection laws: local transport.

[1802]
'Entry into the Province of Antioquia via the pass they call Las Juntas, where the road winds through lofty, rugged mountains until it reaches the place known as La Seja; from there to the capital, one may ride on a beast of burden...'
214 x 310 mm.
MP. Estampas, 257 bis.

An issue outlined in the protection laws was proper treatment of the indigenous population, It was, for instance, explicitly forbidden to use them as porters, although they might be ordered to carry a moderate load, such as in exceptional circumstances when there were no roads: 'We thereby order that in the matter of burdening the Indians... they should not be made to carry loads or, in the event of this... being unavoidable, it should be done in such a way as to avoid any danger to the life, health or preservation of said Indians...' (Leyes Nuevas. Patronato, 170, R. 47). The drawing shows just how often such humanitarian provisions must have fallen on deaf ears.

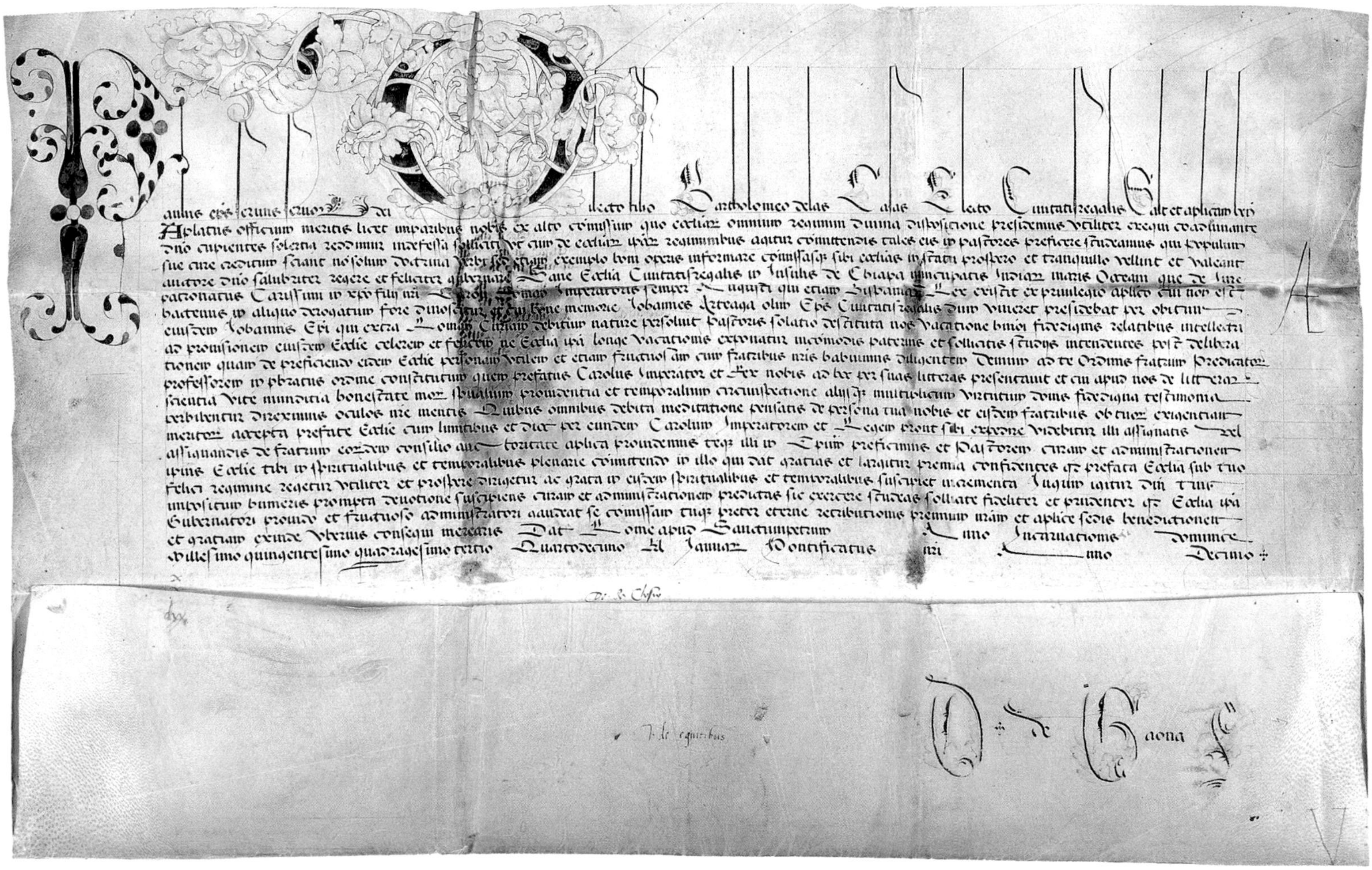

Fray Bartolomé de las Casas: protecting the indigenous population.

19 December 1543, Rome.
Bull issued by Pope Paul III with provisions for succession in the bishopric of Chiapas, which became vacant after the death of Juan de Arteaga y Avendaño, the office being bestowed on Fray Bartolomé de las Casas (O.P.).
580 (441 + 139) x 695 mm.
MP. Bulas y Breves, 26

The encomenderos *were settlers whom the Crown authorized to exact tribute from a number of Indians in gold, labor or in kind, in return for protecting them and instructing them in the Christian faith. Although Fray Bartolomé de las Casas himself started out as an* encomendero *in Hispaniola, he soon reacted to the harsh treatment of natives at the hands of the conquistadors and struck out against the way* encomiendas *and allotments were operated. A controversial figure, he drew hostility from the conquistadors, instrumental, as he was in contributing to the promulgation of the 'New Laws' (1542), the breach of which he likewise denounced. In 1543 he was appointed Archbishop of Chiapas, the diocese having been founded in 1539. He put order into the diocese in the short space of time he resided there, leaving it in 1546 and resigning his office in 1550.*

However, opinion on the matter was divided and there was considerable unease about the possible financial implications of the laws.

Another parallel and related issue discussed at the time was that of the monarchs' rights of ownership in the New World *(justos títulos),* whether they were entitled to wage war against the natives *(guerra justa),* the origin of such rights and the powers invested in the monarchs. Prevalent was the opinion of Francisco de Vitoria and Fray Bartolomé de las Casas who did not recognize either papal theocracy, the emperor's universal authority or the rights to discovery and occupation. This was the spirit that prompted the New Laws of 1542 whereby services rendered in the *encomiendas* were replaced by taxation. Furthermore, *requerimiento* ceased to be a legal cause for 'just war'. This procedure, which was applied from 1513 to 1542 before setting out on expeditions, involved publicly exhorting the indigenous population to pay homage to the Spanish monarch and convert to Christianity. Instead, evangelization became the main purpose of conquest.

The passing of the New Laws caused unease in the Americas and even led to such uprisings as that of Gonzalo Pizarro in Peru and the Contreras in Central America. The dates on which the laws were passed became historic milestones that served to distinguish different phases in the conquest of the Americas.

Objectives and Economics of the Conquest

The conquest of the New World had two major objectives:

– A spiritual aim, medieval in origin, resulting from the Crusades, which was derived from the first papal bull *Inter Caetera* and took the form of spreading the Christian gospel and evangelization.

– A material goal, as seen in the conquistadors' determination to improve their financial situation and the Renaissance desire for honor and fame. Property and renown were the essentials for attaining social status.

With few exceptions, the conquest was an enterprise based on private initiative. The terms of each undertaking were stipulated in 'contracts of conquest' similar to those of discovery and pacification. In such agreements, the expeditionary commander had to meet all expenses, in return for which he was awarded the title of 'royal official' (governor, *adelantado* or captain, depending on the magnitude of the expedition). The Crown, for its part, bestowed rather vague privileges and was careful not to commit itself, instead issuing guidelines for conquest in the form of

With the conversion of Indians to Christianity as its main objective and its most justifiable reason for claiming possession of those lands, in accordance with the first bull *Inter Caetera,* the Spanish Crown underwrote the spiritual conquest of the New World from the outset. To that end it counted on the close collaboration of the Church, in whose affairs it intervened through Royal Patronage, authorized by Pope Julius II in 1508.
The monarchs promoted the Church's influence in the Indies, as the clergy were their best aides in pacifying and civilizing the indigenous population and, on many an occasion, in controlling the Spaniards themselves. Activities such as education and charity were organized almost exclusively by the Church, most often via the religious orders. The expansion of the Church's influence took place at a heady pace and, by the end of the century, its institutions covered practically all the conquered territories.
Mission work was assigned to the mainline clergy: Hieronymites, Capuchins, Franciscans, Dominicans, Augustinians, Mercedarians, Hospitallers and, in the second half of the century, Jesuits, gradually swelled the ranks of the conquest. Evangelization was achieved through education, for which reason great importance was attached to the missions and parishes, *doctrinas* and schools and other educational institutions in which prominent figures included Fray Pedro de Gante, Fray Juan de Zumárraga and Fray Vasco de Quiroga in New Spain.
The collaboration between Church and State extended to the protection of the indigenous population, a fact that influenced Crown policies and legislation.

Marian devotion.

[1795]
'New settlement of San Fernando de Guadalupe at the waterfall on the Tulija river, which flows into Lakes Chichicaste and Terminos...' (Chiapas province).
212 x 305 mm.
MP. Guatemala, 271.

Converting American Indians to the Catholic faith was a dominant issue in the laws of the Indies. The duty to evangelize, implicit in the first bull Inter Caetera, *was embodied in several chapters of the Laws of Burgos (1512) and the New Laws (1542). The former insisted on the obligation to build churches on the estates of all* encomenderos, *with a bell to call the faithful to prayer. There they were to worship before the image of the Virgin. Marian devotion was gradually distilled into the figure of the Virgin of Guadalupe, a spiritual trend that survived over the centuries and comes through clearly in this plan of the foundation of San Fernando de Guadalupe in Tulijá.*

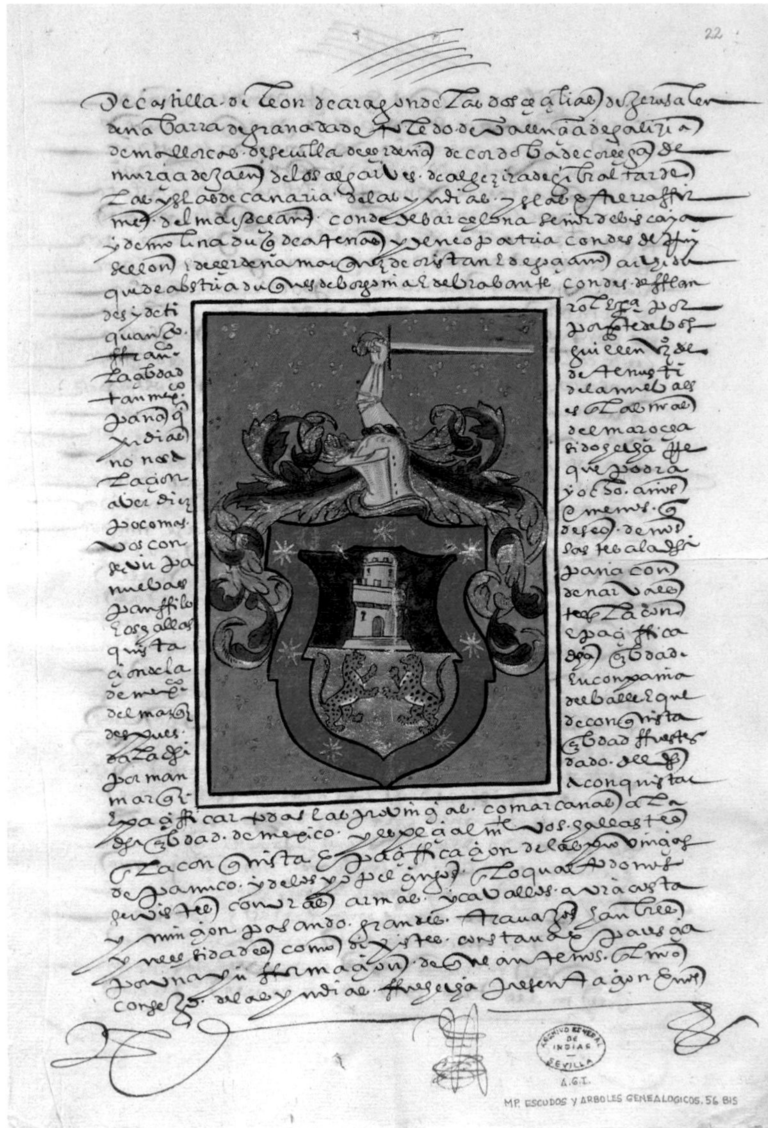

Social status: coat-of-arms of Jerónimo López.

26 June 1530, Madrid.
Coat-of-arms of Jerónimo López, an inhabitant of Mexico, awarded in consideration of the services rendered in the conquest of Pánuco and other parts of New Spain.
120 x 143 mm. in 1 fol.
The above text and illustration are part of the heraldic privilege described in a book on meritorious deeds written by the conquistador's son in 1594.
MP. Escudos y Árboles Genealógicos, 8 bis.

Social status: coat-of-arms of Francisco Guillén.

8 November 1539, Madrid.
Coat-of-arms of Francisco Guillén, a citizen of Tenochtitlán, awarded in consideration of his services under Pánfilo de Narváez and Hernando Cortés.
125 x 94 mm. in 1 fol.
The heraldic privilege was featured in a book on meritorious deeds dating from 1582.
MP. Escudos y Árboles Genealógicos, 56 bis.

The heraldic privilege was granted in these terms: '...And we were entreated that in consideration of your services and in memory of yourselves and them, we should grant you the use of heraldic devices...' Those privileges, which the Crown gradually curtailed, make up a unique collection of heraldic bearings.

The early period of Spanish enterprise in the Americas is open to a variety of interpretations. From a European stance, a noteworthy assessment of Spain's venture by a contemporary rival was that of Sir Walter Raleigh, who had first-hand knowledge of the setting and the events: 'Here I cannot forbear to commend the patient virtue of the Spaniards: we seldom or never find that any nation hath endured so many misadventures and miseries as the Spaniards have done in their Indian discoveries; yet persisting in their enterprises with an invincible constancy, they have annexed to their Kingdom so many goodly provinces as bury the remembrance of all dangers past.' (RALEIGH, Walter: *The History of the World*. London, 1786, Vol. II, pp. 575. *Apud* MORALES PADRÓN, Francisco: *Los conquistadores de América*. Madrid, Espasa, 1974, pps. 93–94).

'Instructions'. It likewise reserved the right to dominate all conquered territories and to receive a 'royal fifth' of all profits derived from the same.

The profit to be had from conquest consisted of booty, which did not always cover the costs involved in acquiring it. Still, the most coveted reward was a title or coat-of-arms and a feudal estate. Set in their medieval ways, the conquistadors dreamed of an almost feudal society, of an aristocracy based on land concessions that would be handed down by inheritance. The Crown was opposed to the pretensions of this would-be aristocracy and, although it respected their financial privileges, it kept their political ambitions in check. That accounts for royal opposition to the perpetuity of *encomiendas* in the form of labor and their replacement by taxation.

The orientation of the conquest was often dictated by myths and legends. In fact, the conquest moved in a geography of wonderland in which a legend was attached to each region: in Florida, the *Fons juventutis,* the fountain of youth that lured Ponce de León; in New Spain, the myth of the *Cíbola* or the 'Seven Cities', which led Fray Marcos de Niza and Francisco Vázquez de Coronado to present-day Arizona and Kansas. In South America, a wealth of such myths abounded, the most famous being the oft-cited Eldorado. Others included the Amazons, the Houses of the Sun, the White Caesar (Cuzco and the Incas), the Silver Range (Potosí), the Land of the Moxos, and the Great Paititi, a mirage of the Incas and Tahuantisuyo.

Driven by a lust for gold, the conquistadors did not always find it, but the search did take them across the geographical expanse of the Americas and led to those vast territories being charted.

THE CASA DE LA CONTRATACIÓN

At the end of the 15th century, Seville was the great capital of southern Spain. Its importance was based more on land than sea, and its wealth on agriculture and industry rather than commerce.

The discovery of the New World was to change the situation, however, and turn Seville into a great maritime and trading center, as all navigational and trade matters relating to the Americas gradually converged on its port.

After Columbus' second voyage, Seville became the great point of departure for the Americas and the hub of trade with the New World.

Seville was well endowed for its new mission. First, its geographical location facilitated communication with the fertile farming hinterland, which yielded the provisions—particularly wheat, wine and oil—used on board ships bound for the Indies and as the basis for trade with the Americas.

– Second, being an inland port, stringent control could be exercised over commercial traffic, the prompt collection of all duties and taxes and the movement of commodities, people, arms and books to and from the New World.

– Third, Seville was a Crown possession and the monarch its rightful lord, so that his authority could not be challenged by local aristocrats from their landed estates.

– Fourth, the city had good natural defenses against enemy attack.

All these considerations led the Crown to choose Seville as the hub of all the activities it planned to conduct in the newly discovered territories and as the site of its *Casa de la Contratación* or 'House of the Indies'.

Foundation

The *Casa de la Contratación* was the first administrative body to be set up for dealings with the New World.

In the foreword to his *Norte de la Contratación de las Indias,* Veitia y Linaje says of the *Casa de la Contratación*: 'I shall not waste time comparing the tribunal I am referring to with others in these kingdoms or abroad, bearing in mind that, regardless of any irregularity in form or substance, the universality and grandeur of the commodities and trade which it handles render it incomparable to any other'.

Ernest Schäffer considers the first rough proposal for what would subsequently become the *Casa de la Contratación* (House of Trade or House of the Indies) to be contained in a report received by the king and written, Schäffer surmises, by Francisco Pinelo.

In that report, he sets forward the idea of operating a building in Seville with a number of suitable rooms for storing all commodities prior to their shipment to the Indies and all incoming consignments from there.

He suggests the trading house should be headed by a factor, a treasurer and two bookkeepers with a sound knowledge of commodities, trade and shipping matters and ship chandlery.

He also describes the procedure for handling gold from the Indies, as well as for mining, treatment of the indigenous population and so on. Similarly, the report raises the issue of whether or not the trading house should also oversee commerce with the Canary Islands and North Africa and the possibility of opening up such commercial activities to private initiative. In the period shortly after the Discovery, trade with the Indies was a Crown monopoly.

By royal order issued in Alcalá de Henares on 20 January 1503, the Catholic Kings decreed the founding in Seville of the *'Casa de la Contratación de las Indias'* and drew up the first statutes.

The statutes closely followed Pinelo's proposals in all matters, except those pertaining to gold and the treatment of the Indians which fell outside the scope of the House.

In effect, in the initial stages the House dealt with all affairs relating to the Indies trade, to chandlery and the scheduling of shipping. It acted as a trading post, a privileged commodity exchange and a storage facility for goods moving to and from the Americas. Its functions likewise included monitoring market fluctuations, buying and selling to the Crown's best advantage and keeping a detailed register of all its operations.

The Catholic Kings issued a royal decree in Alcalá de Henares on 20 January 1503 instituting the foundation of the *Casa de la Contratación* in Seville.
'Firstly, we order and command that in the city of Seville a trading house be established wherein are stored and readied whenever necessary all the commodities and maintenance and all the other provisions that might be required for trading in the Indies and other isles and places we should designate, and to send there whatever may be required, and to receive all commodities and other things that may be taken on board ship there and sent to our kingdoms, so that whatever is deemed suitable for selling and trading in other places might be sent from here in such a manner as to have at their disposal all the abovementioned.'
Thus, the House of the Indies came into being as an exclusive depot for goods sent to or received from the Americas and as a staging post for supplying and scheduling vessels: '...and to designate the time they might be sent and the ships required to transport them, and for all the goods and provisions to be readied for such shipment in fulfillment of the trade on that voyage, and the vessels in which they are to be conveyed, so that no fault or negligence might prevent or postpone the said voyage and that everything might be conducted as befits the adequate completion of said trading.'

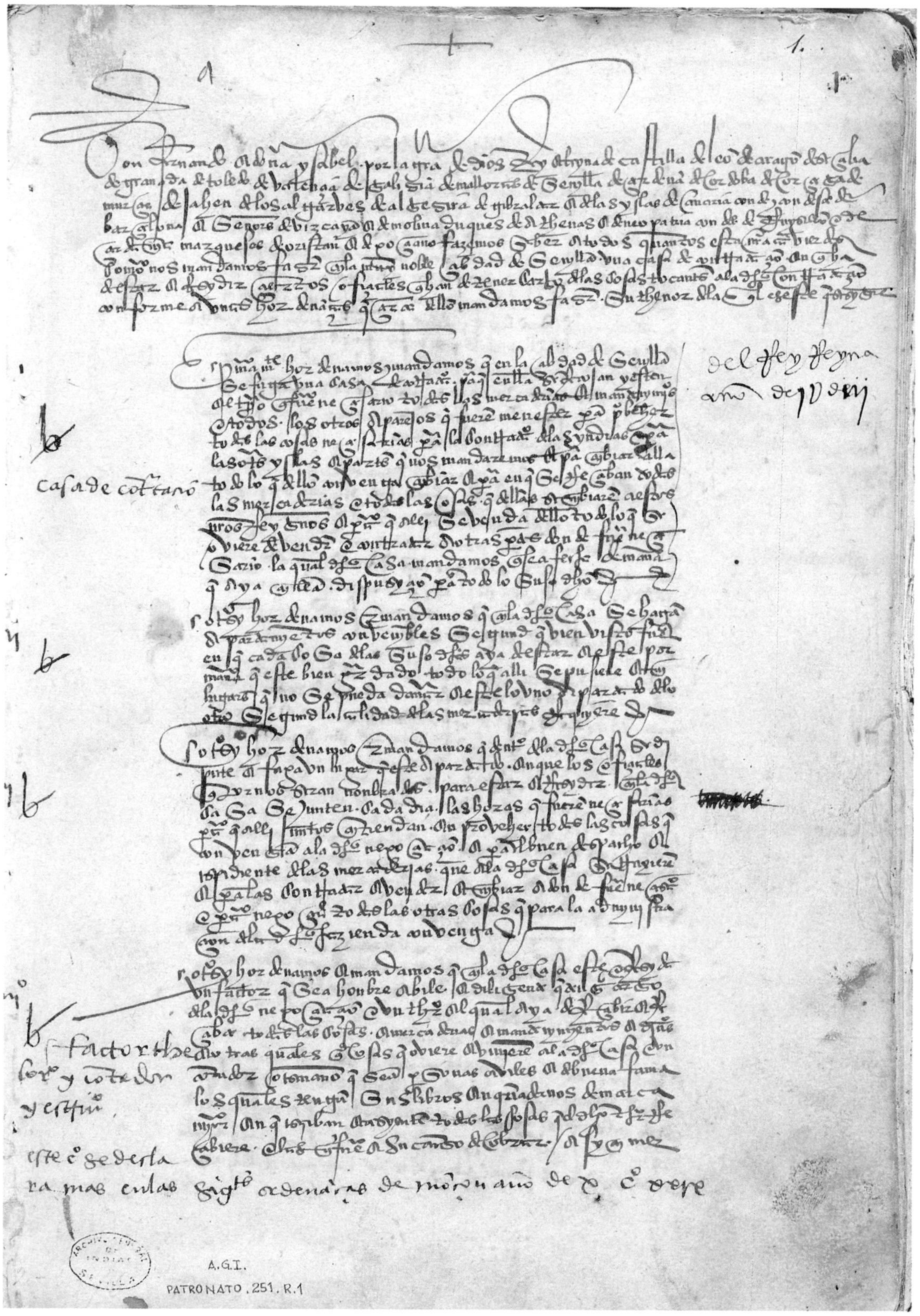

Establishment of the Casa de la Contratación.
20 January 1503, Alcalá de Henares.

Royal warrant issued by the Catholic Kings ordering the establishment of the Casa de la Contratación *and promulgating the statutes governing the affairs of the trading house.*
Patronato, 251, R.1, fol. 1-4 v.

Following Columbus' first voyage, it was in Seville that all preparations were made for subsequent voyages of discovery, a task that was supervised by the archdeacon, Juan Rodríguez de Fonseca. It follows, therefore, that the monarchs should have chosen the city for siting the Casa de la Contratación *in 1503.*

The initial idea was to locate the house in the shipyards but, owing to the humidity there resulting from its proximity to the river, this was not considered suitable for storing commodities. It was thus located in the fortress of the *Reales Alcázares,* in a section known as the *Cuarto de Almirantes.* Subsequently, as activity increased, an adjoining estate that also belonged to the *Reales Alcázares* had to be added. It opened onto a small square, which has been known ever since as the *Plaza de la Contratación.*

The *Casa de la Contratación* remained on that site until 1717, when it was moved to Cádiz.

Statutes

Activities in the *Casa de la Contratación* were regulated by its statutes. The first statutes date from 1503. According to these, officials of the House had legal authority only over trade matters relating to the Indies. They were entitled to impose fines, demand deposits, remand in custody on behalf of the royal authority and file claims against the city's customs authorities. However, their responsibilities were not clearly delimited and they often clashed with Seville's judicial authorities, a fact which seriously hindered the free flow of traffic to the Indies. Indeed, the situation came to a head after countless protests by merchants, officials of the trading house and lawyers on the island of Hispaniola and it was proposed to move the house to Cádiz. The threat was not carried out, however, as the city realized just what benefits it stood to lose and petitioned the King not to move the trading house.

In 1508, the syndic of Seville and all the city's judicial authorities were urged not to interfere in the administration of the House and to recognize its powers, which were reconfirmed.

In 1509, Ferdinand the Catholic asked the officials of the House to send him a detailed report on all the statutes, special instructions, customs duties and so forth in order to facilitate the drafting of a new set of by-laws.

Those new statutes, arranged in thirty–six chapters, were issued at Monzón on 15 June 1510 and completed the following year with the addition of seventeen clauses.

In the main, they amounted to no more than a reiteration of previous regulations and a number of diverse decrees. What was augmented were the sections

Coffer with three locks.

[1537]
Coffer with three locks used to safeguard valuables in the Casa de la Contratación.
Made in iron by Lazarus Norenberguer.

The Casa de la Contratación *acted as the mandatory depot for all gold and silver from the New World earmarked for the monarchs. It was also a repository for the assests of those deceased in the Indies and for goods requisitioned from individuals. The House thus held goods valued at enormous amounts of money at certain stages, which warranted the implementation of stringent security measures. To this end, between 1530 and 1537, chests, coffers and caskets were commissioned, built and imported (one of them is still housed in the General Archive of the Indies). The books kept in the treasury show that, on 9 August 1537, the treasurer, Francisco Tello, paid the German, Lazarus Norenberguer, fifty-two gold ducats for 'an iron box... with three locks and their respective keys...'*

dealing with the inspection of ships and cargoes and everything relating to the functions and duties of its officials.

Detailed regulations were laid down for keeping books and registers: it was compulsory to make copies of all missives sent to the Indies via the House, while all officials in America that corresponded with the Crown via the House over matters of trade and finance had to send copies of their correspondence and a list of all deposits and withdrawals of funds from the royal coffers to be filed in its archives.

The arrangements for emigration, registration of cargoes and instructions for sea captains were reviewed, as were the assets of subjects who had died in the Indies and whose heirs resided on the Iberian Peninsula. In a royal warrant of 1550, Charles V instituted the procedures and reviewed the legal status pertaining to estates of those deceased abroad.

Two different but closely coordinated institutions were instrumental in distributing such assets on either side of the Atlantic—the *Juzgado de Indias* or 'Tribunal of the Indies' and the *Casa de la Contratación.*

The key figure in the Tribunal of the Indies was the *oidor* or civil judge of 'Estates of the Deceased' who was usually the most senior *oidor* of the *Audiencia* or Tribunal. He acted as a custodian of the estates of all those deceased in the Indies, both testate and intestate, while their executors conducted the transactions required for sending relevant assets to the House.

The functions of the *Casa de la Contratación* were likewise clearly laid down: it took delivery of the funds discharged by arriving galleons, made the relevant entry in the register and, three days later, posted the information on the door of the House and on the *Puerta del Perdón* (Door of Pardon) in the cathedral. A month later, a messenger bearing an official document listing the deceased's assets was sent out to the person's hometown in search of heirs.

Public announcements were made in these places and, when various people came forward claiming to be the rightful heirs to an estate, the House instituted legal proceedings. Once witnesses had testified and evidence had been examined, judgement was passed as to who were the lawful heirs and the corresponding assets handed over.

When no heirs were forthcoming, the estate was deposited in a fund to be disposed of by the Crown.

Since the statutes of 1510 did not embrace all mercantile and political arrangements in force between Spain and the New World, previous practices and proceedings had to be referred to on occasion. However, the functions and general administrative procedures of the trading house had been clearly set out and remained in place until the 18th century. Rather than operating as a business enterprise for the Crown's benefit, the House was more of a government department, trade ministry, school of navigation and customs post for colonial trade.

In 1552, all existing laws and procedures of the *Casa de la Contratación* were again assembled and Andrés de Carvajal was commissioned to publish them. They were reprinted in 1585 and formed the basis of the Ninth Book of the Laws of the Indies.

Posts

The foundation–charter of 1503 provided for three positions in the trading house: factor, treasurer and secretary–bookkeeper.

During the 16th century, such positions were filled by people of proven skill and experience but, under Philip IV, it became the custom to appoint favorites, who in turn chose people they trusted to actually fill the posts, which led to a substantial decline in efficiency and productivity.

The factor was in charge of purchasing and embarking all merchandise bound for the Americas, as well as all equipment, provisions, arms, artillery, munitions and naval rigging used on board ship.

In 1588, a 'general purveyor of navies and fleets' was appointed. He took on all the duties implicit in his title, in addition to those of the factor, and had a storekeeper or victualler under his command.

One of the factor's main tasks was to take delivery of and forward cargoes of quicksilver for the silver mines in the New World. The Crown had an export monopoly over quicksilver, which brought in huge profits.

The treasurer was in charge of gold, silver, pearls and precious stones sent to the Royal Treasury from the Americas. After its discovery in 1555, production from the Guadalcanal silver mine was also placed in his charge, as was the collection of customs duty or *almojarifazgo,* as of 1560, the sales tax known as *alcabala,* from the Indies, and administration of those taxes in Andalusia as of 1579.

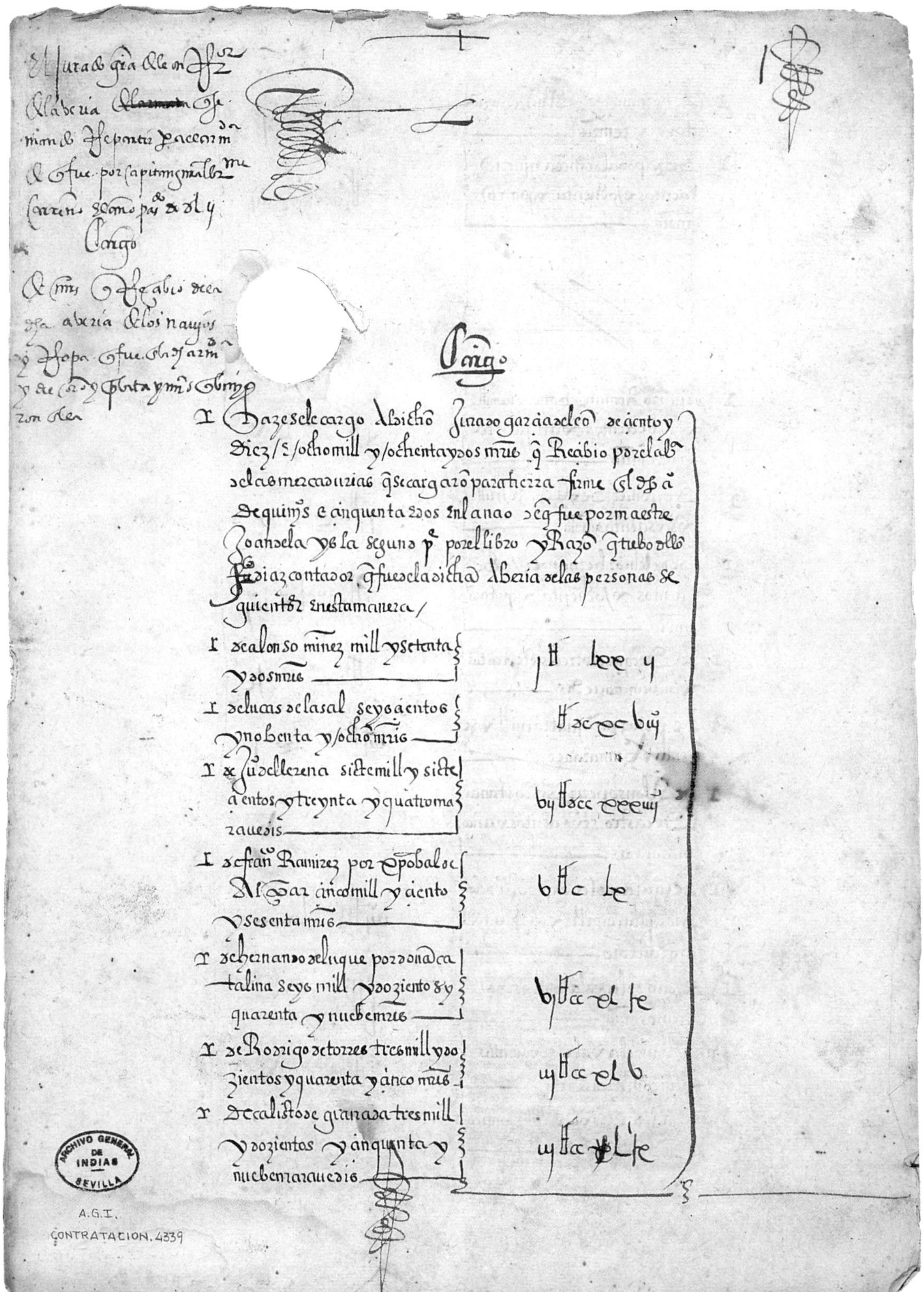

Avería *(Average).*

1552–1553
Book entry by the receiver, García de León, showing the sums assigned to outfitting General Bartolomé Carreño's naval fleet.
(Shown is the first page of the debit account)
1 fol.
Contratación, 4339, no.1.

In the Indies trade, avería *or 'average' was the duty levied as a percentage of all cargoes shipped to and from the New World and used to defray the expense incurred in sending naval escorts to protect shipping from attack by French, English and Dutch pirates and privateers.*

The treasurer also saw to the safekeeping of the Estates of the Deceased and the funds known as *ausentes y depósitos,* amounts temporarily seized by the House from creditors and claimants, as well as sums sent from the Indies whose beneficiaries had not come forth.

The bookkeeper had to keep the accounts of the trading house and make all relevant entries in books and registers.

The expenditure involved in maintaining naval escorts for the Indies' fleets was met by levying an import and export duty known as *avería* (average). For a long period of time, that duty was managed by the three officials of the House, assisted by a collector of funds.

In 1573, the post of *diputado contador de avería* (deputy accountant of average) was created to oversee both the collection of duty and payment of expenses, and was directly answerable to the officials of the House.

In 1580, an *avería* accountant was appointed to keep the relevant books, and four such accountants were active by 1596. Together they made up the so-called *Tribunal de la Contaduría de Averías,* an auditing body which, by a Council decision of 1597, was placed in charge of all accounting areas in the House, except for those of the Royal Treasury and the Estates of the Deceased, which remained under the trading house accountant's authority until 1616.

In October 1557, in a move designed to enhance the dignity and independence of the *Casa de la Contratación,* Philip II created the post of 'president', the first position to be equal or higher than the three original official posts created in 1503. The new position was a logical appointment as it enabled the work of the treasurer, factor and bookkeeper to be better coordinated, and provided for greater consistency in planning and closer liaison with the Council of the Indies, as the appointment always fell on a councillor—either a bona fide lawyer or a swashbuckler.

The president's main functions were administrative but, when the *Sala de Justicia* was subsequently added to the House, that, too, came under the president's authority.

Although he supervised all departments and operations in the *Casa de la Contratación,* his primary task throughout the 17th century was to expedite regular departures of the 'treasury fleets' bound for the Indies.

In May 1541, the office of *correo mayor* (senior postmaster) was created. His duty was to supervise the flow of correspondence between Spain and the Indies, between the colonies and, finally, between Seville and the Court.

In addition to the above, there were junior positions such as *alguacil* (constable) warden, scribe and chaplain.

Duties of the Casa de la Contratación

The functions assigned to the trading house can be divided into three major groups: commercial, nautical and judicial.

Commercial Functions

Since its foundation in 1503, the House of the Indies' main function was to direct and control all trade and shipping to and from the Indies. Such was the specific mandate of the three officials appointed—to control, direct and supervise everything relating to ships, crew, passengers and cargoes.

The original task assigned to officials of the House and the one that remained in force the longest was to register all cargoes and passengers that crossed the Atlantic. It was used to give instructions to Columbus in 1493, was repeated in the statutes of 1503 and its observance determined in subsequent decrees.

At the beginning, when the Crown exercised a monopoly over trade with the Indies, all that was required was for the ship's recorder to draw up a manifest of all cargo taken on board and have it endorsed by the skipper but, when the House started collecting duties on private merchandise, all articles bound for the New World had to be declared before the House officials and included in the royal shipping register of the vessel due to carry them. Once the register had been closed, no further goods could be loaded on board without special permission. The accountant of the House was in charge of keeping and maintaining the registers and was responsible for suing for damages anyone instrumental in their loss or destruction.

In 1535, a special official in Cádiz was appointed to register the cargo carried by all vessels which, on account of their draught, had to anchor in the port of Cádiz. The task had previously fallen to the House officials, who took it in turns. For some time the position became vacant but, in 1556, it was again filled, this time

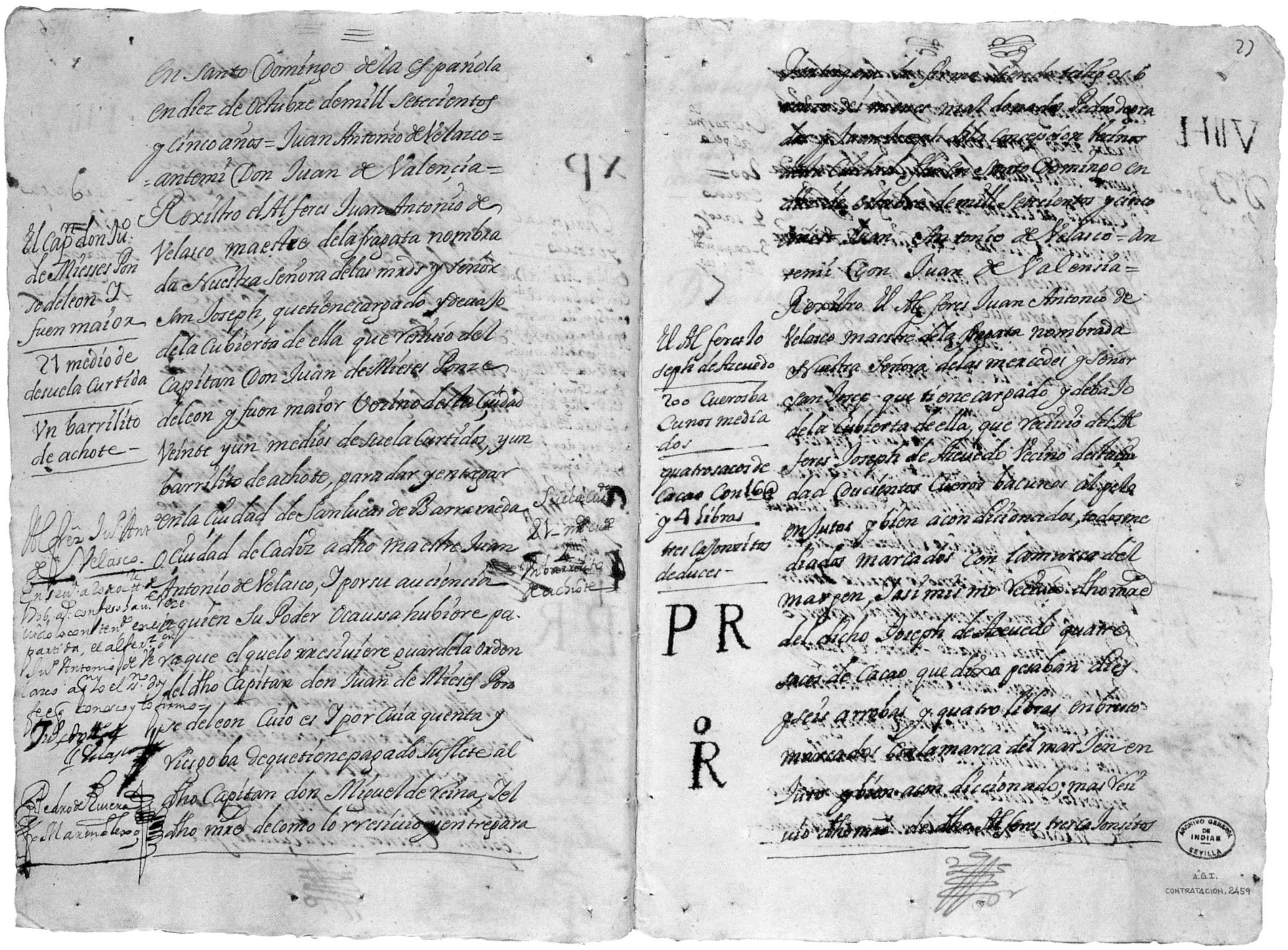

Shipping registration.

1706
'Registry of the ship named Nuestra Señora de las Mercedes y San José: *skipper, Lieutenant Juan Antonio de Velasco, and owner, Captain Miguel de Reyna, recently arrived in this kingdom after sailing from Santo Domingo and making land at Sanlúcar on 15 December 1715.'*
75 fols. + 4 fols. on 4to. + 14 fols. of 80 x 215 mm.
Contratación, 2459.

From the start of the Indies trade, officials of the Casa de la Contratación *were bound by the statutes to keep lists of goods shipped to and from the Indies, thus anticipating the fully-fledged registers to come. Registers were used both to monitor cargoes and vessels, as the list of goods was supplemented by details of the ship, including the names of its owner and officers, equipment, materiel and so on.*

by an official judge from Cádiz. The fleets thereafter assembled in Cádiz and took on their final consigments of cargo before sailing to the Indies. On the return voyage, they had to sail directly up to Seville.

Vessels were registered for the purpose of preventing smuggling and facilitating the collection of the above-mentioned royal levies.

Emigration to America was, from the very, outset, stringently controlled by the Crown. Until the death of Isabella the Catholic, it was limited to inhabitants of Castile and León. However, after her death, Ferdinand allowed the Aragonese to cross the ocean in a private or public capacity, while Charles V extended the privilege to his foreign subjects as well.

A special license was required for sailing to the Indies and it, too, was issued by the *Casa de la Contratación.* A prerequisite was proving one's 'purity of blood' as the voyage to the Indies was forbidden to descendants of Moors, Jews or anyone punished by the Tribunal of the Inquisition. Married men who embarked without their wives could only do so for a limited period of time and only with their wives' express consent.

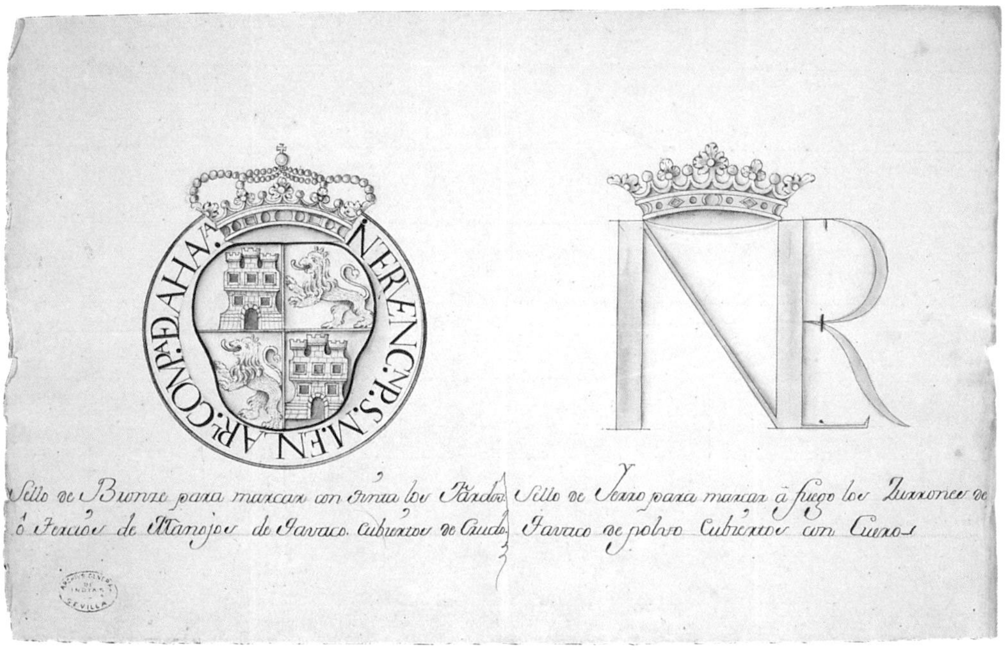

Merchandise.

1744
Two stamp designs: 'Bronze seal for stamping bales of tobacco wrapped in raw tobacco', and 'seal for branding leather tobacco pouches'.
198 x 311 mm.
MP. Varios, 39.

Merchandise.

1748
Drawing of a man branding a case. (Detail of the bottom right-hand corner of a share certificate issued by the Real Compañía de San Fernando, Seville.)
283 x 405 mm (share certificate).
MP. Monedas, 33.

Although the Crown allowed private enterprise to operate in the trade with the Americas from the outset, it did reserve the exclusive right to certain products that proved highly profitable: quicksilver, playing cards, salt, gunpowder, tobacco and official stamped paper. To prevent smuggling and expedite trade, all cargo packages, both privately owned and belonging to the Crown, had to bear relevant seals and identification.

Merchandise.

[18th century]
'Sampler of European fabric coveted in Quito and its province, known by names other than those with which they are marked in the factory and at the customary price.'
35 boards.
MP. Tejidos, 14.

The most widely sought after products in America were wheat, wine, oil, fabric and cloth, which fetched very high prices in places where they could not normally be found. Spain's late move towards industrialization led other countries to export manufactured products to the Americas—combs, hats, paper, haberdashery and a large number of fabrics from centers such as Rouen and Holland.

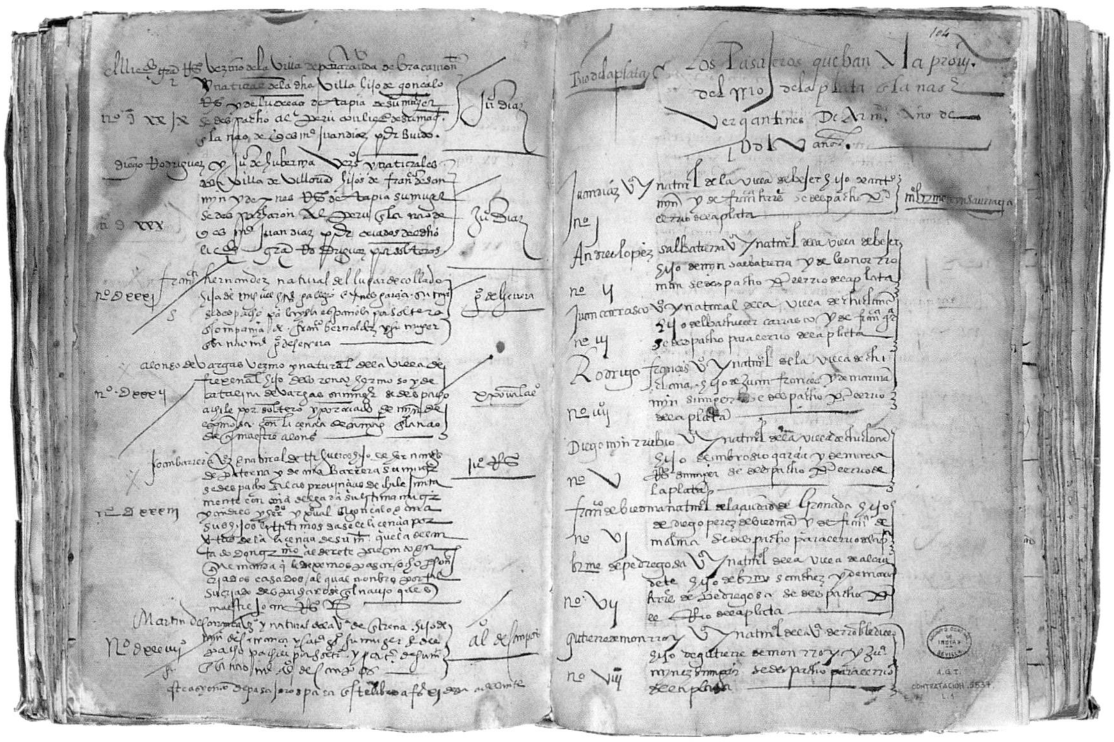

Indies-bound passengers.

1553–1556
Register of passengers bound for the Indies.
Contratación, 5537, L. 1, fol. 104 r.

From the very start, emigration to America was controlled by the Crown. No Jew, convert or anyone sentenced by the Tribunal of the Inquisition was authorized to travel to the Indies. Screening was carried out by the Casa de la Contratación *where all outbound passengers' names were entered in the register.*

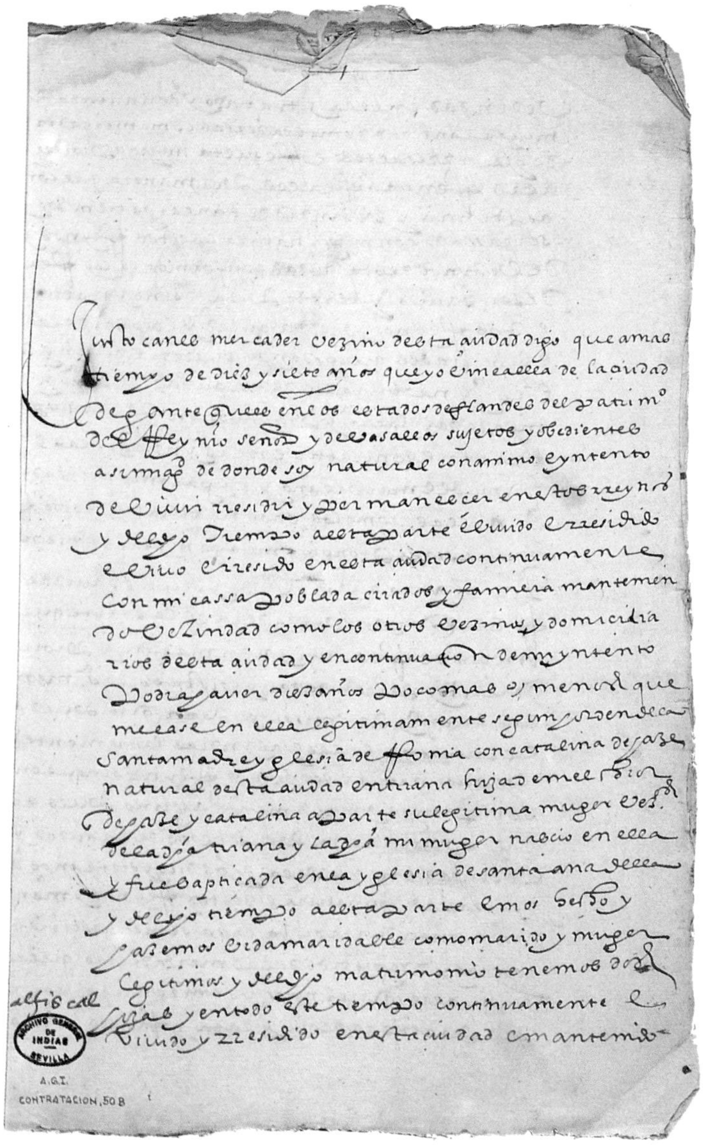

Foreign traders.

23 September 1594, Seville.
Request filed by the merchant, Justo Canes, born in Ghent and resident in Seville, who applied for naturalization in order to trade with the Indies.
5 fols.
Contratación, 50 B.

Under Emperor Charles V, restrictions on foreigners trading with the New World were lifted. To obtain permission, such foreigners had to file a request for naturalization papers, which were processed by the Casa de la Contratación. *These were granted after having verified that the subject in question was Catholic and had resided on the Iberian Peninsula for at least ten years.*

OPPOSITE, ABOVE
The slave trade.

1740
'Map of Cartagena, its harbor and peninsula, from Tierra Bomba to Tierra Chica, showing positions of assault and defense, as provided by His Excellency, Don Blas de Lezo, commander general of the galleons of His Catholic Majesty.'
920 x 580 mm.
MP. Panamá, 140.

The port of Cartagena de Indias, together with that of Veracruz, was the main destination for shipments of slaves from Africa during the early period of trade. From there, they were sent to the various parts of the Americas.

OPPOSITE, BELOW
The slave trade.

1634.
'Description of the island of Curaçao where the Dutch landed on 28 July 1634.'
277 x 420 mm.
MP. Venezuela, 17.

In its second phase, the slave trade was controlled by the Portuguese, Dutch and English. Two main landing posts were set up in the Caribbean, in Curaçao and Jamaica, and from there slaves were distributed to various other Spanish ports.

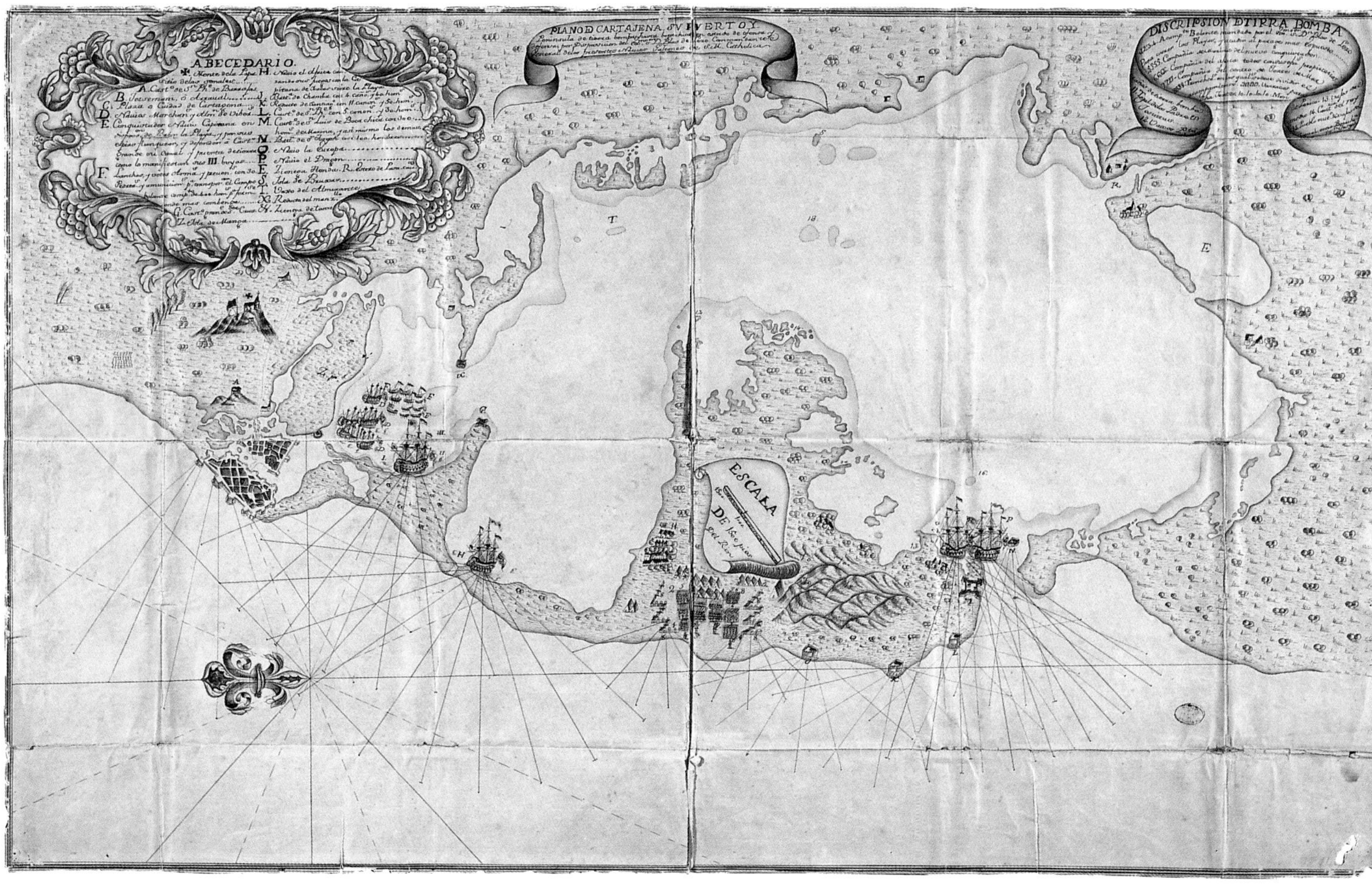

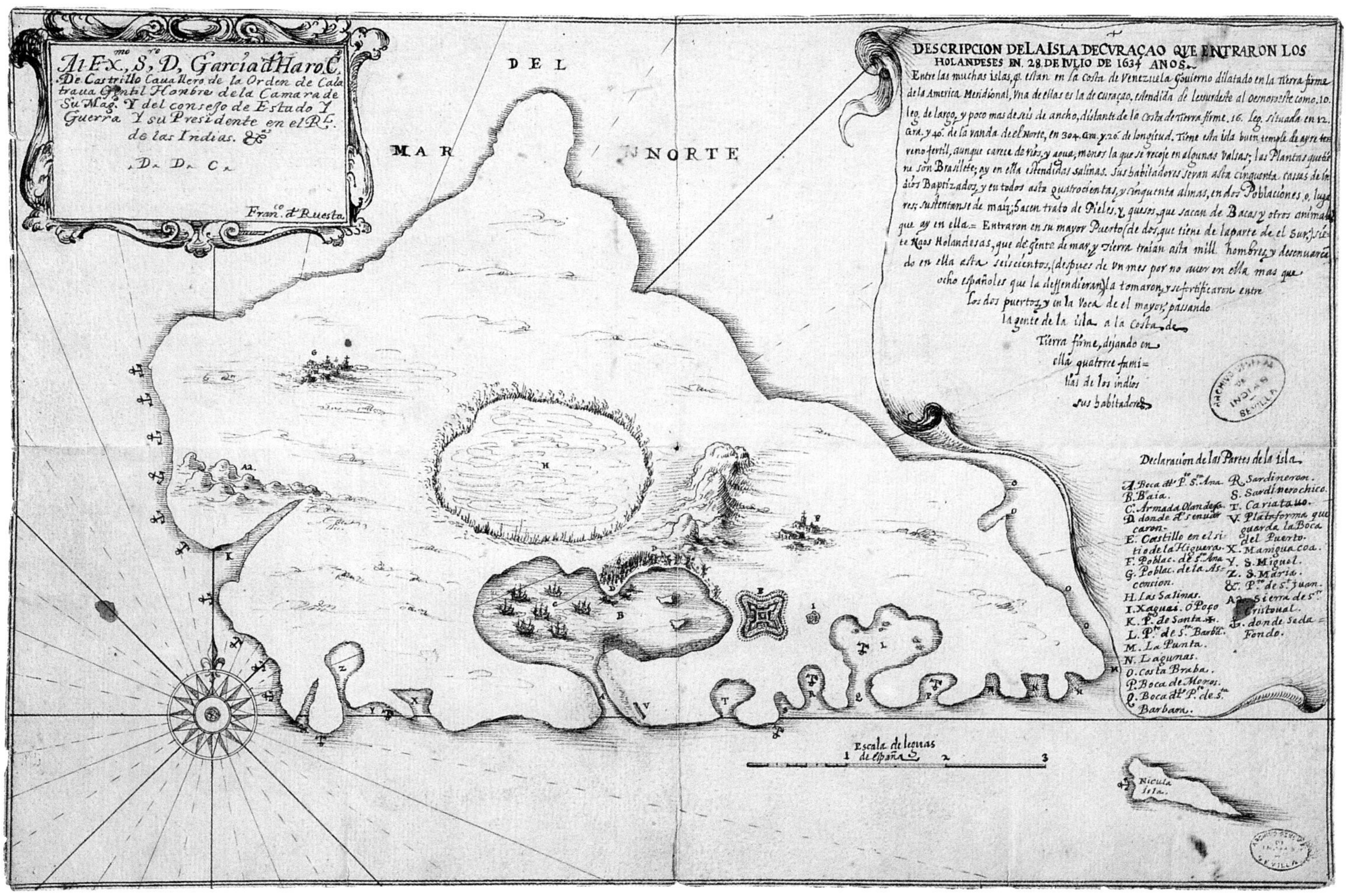

Al Ex.mo S.r D. Garcia d'Haro C.de De Castrillo Caua llero de la Orden de Calatraua Gentil Hombre de la Camara de Su Mag. Y del consejo de Estado Y Guerra Y su Presidente en el R.l de las Indias. &c.
Fran.co d' Ruesta
DESCRIPCION DE LA ISLA DE CVRAÇAO QUE ENTRARON LOS HOLANDESES EN 28 DE JVLIO DE 1634 AÑOS
DEL
MAR
NORTE
Declaracion de las Partes de la isla
Escale de leguas de España
1
2
3
Nicula isla

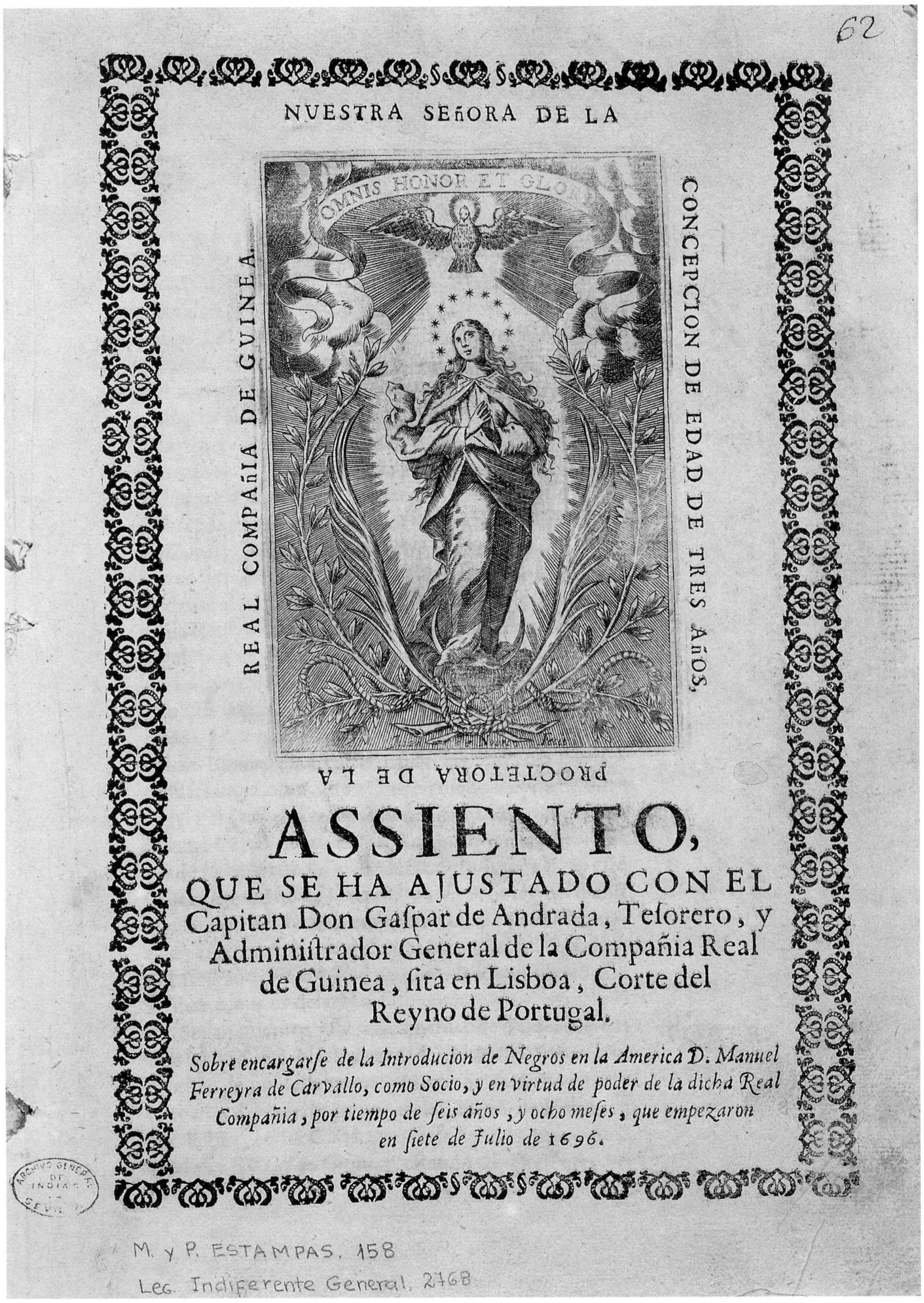

62

NUESTRA SEñORA DE LA CONCEPCION DE EDAD DE TRES AñOS, PROCTETORA DE LA REAL COMPAñIA DE GUINEA.

OMNIS HONOR ET GLO

ASSIENTO,

QUE SE HA AJUSTADO CON EL Capitan Don Gaſpar de Andrada, Teſorero, y Adminiſtrador General de la Compañia Real de Guinea, ſita en Lisboa, Corte del Reyno de Portugal.

Sobre encargarſe de la Introducion de Negros en la America D. Manuel Ferreyra de Carvallo, como Socio, y en virtud de poder de la dicha Real Compañia, por tiempo de ſeis años, y ocho meſes, que empezaron en ſiete de Julio de 1696.

M. y P. ESTAMPAS. 158

Leg. Indiferente General, 2768

1696. Cover of the asiento *or agreement endorsed by Gaspar de Andrada, treasurer and administrator of the Compañía Real de Guinea, to introduce slaves into America.*
M. y P. Estampas, 158.

The discovery of the New World soon opened up such broad horizons for the slave trade that the latter quickly assumed extraordinary proportions.

The trade spanned two clearly distinct periods: in the first period, it was controlled by the Portuguese. Africans were taken straight to foreign ports, mostly Cartagena de Indias and Veracruz. During that early stage, the *Casa de la Contratación* was easily able to control the slave trade.

In the second period, during which the slave trade was run mainly by the Portuguese, Dutch and English, the *Casa de la Contratación* was hard put to control trade developments.

In the 16th century, the slave traffic was regulated by permits; in the 17th century, monopolistic contracts were made with private dealers and, in the 18th, international agreements came into force. Ships engaged in conveying slaves to the Indies required a license issued solely by the *Casa de la Contratación,* regardless of whether the ships were due to sail from the port of Seville or from Lisbon or the Canary Islands, as was most often the case.

The vessels in question were usually small—prior to 1615, none exceeded 100 tons. From then until the middle of the century their size increased to around 100 tons and, as of 1650, there were vessels of 235, 250 or even 375 tons.

A 40-ton vessel could transport up to 100 black slaves, while 100-ton ships had a capacity of over 200.

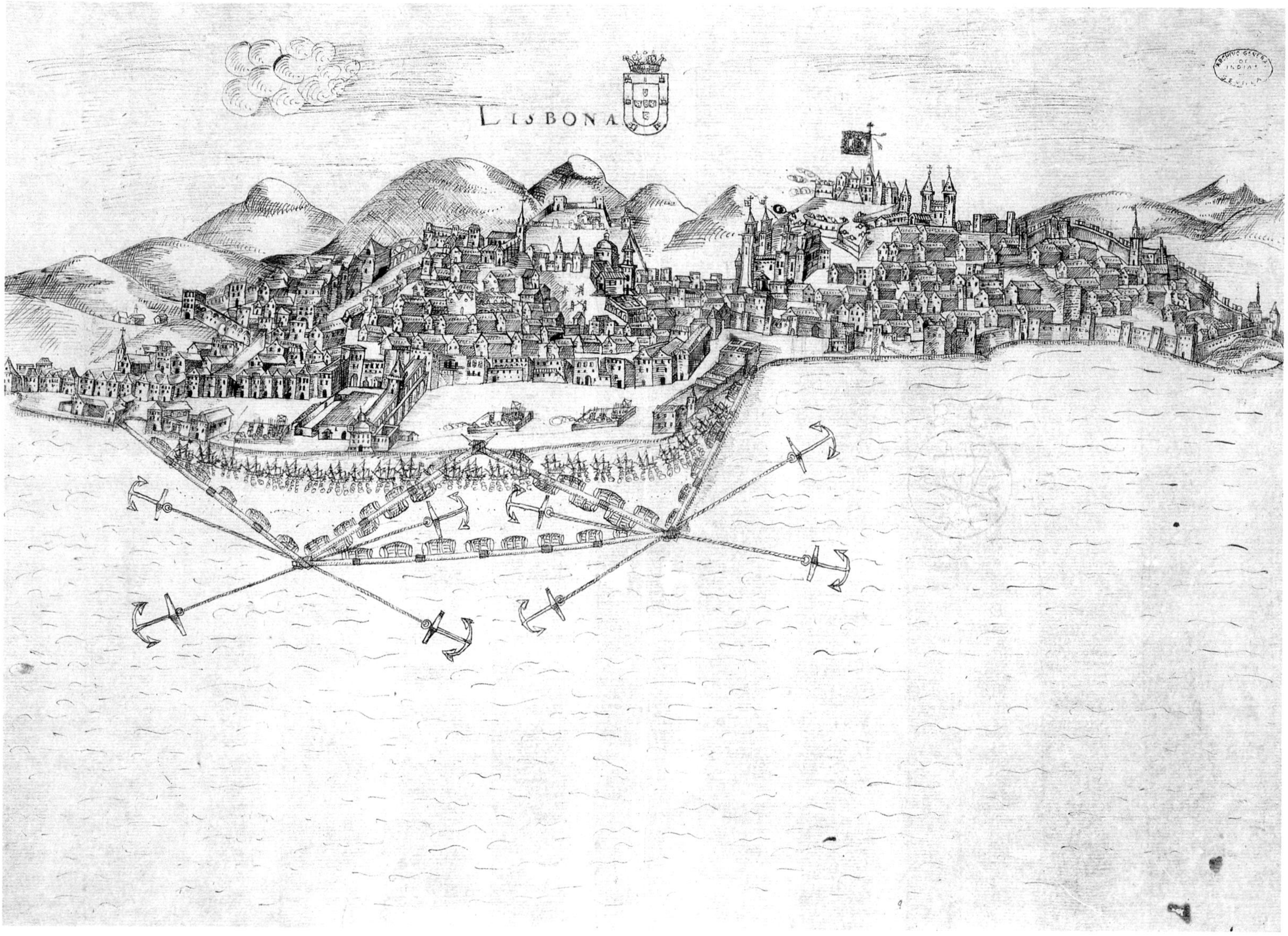

The slave trade.

1596
View of Lisbon.
305 x 424 mm.
MP. Europa y África, 4.

All licenses granted to slave ships were issued by the Casa de la Contratación, *regardless of whether they were due to sail from the Canary Islands, Lisbon or Seville.*

Under Philip II, anyone wishing to trade in the Indies had to be Spanish; this included foreign Catholics who had been residing in Spain for at least ten years, provided they had obtained their 'naturalization papers'.

The discovery of the New World opened up extraordinary prospects for the slave trade. Initially transported in the company of discoverers and conquistadors, the black slaves gradually replaced indigenous Indian labor and were put to work in farming, transportation, mining and pearl fishing.

In the early-16th century, administrative procedures were introduced to regulate and control the legal introduction of slaves under the auspices of the House of the Indies and the Council of the Indies.

Slave dealers were rarely Spaniards, the trade being mainly in the hands of Portuguese, skilled in the enterprise, who had trading posts in Africa and were contracted to provide slaves. They were later joined in the commerce by Dutch, Genoese and English traders.

In the 16th century, the slave traffic to the Americas was regulated by licenses. In the 17th century, it was operated through monopolistic contracts between private individuals and, in the first half of the 18th century, by international agreements.

The *Casa de la Contratación* was likewise responsible for overseeing the contracts of the crews, chandlering, sailing conditions and tonnage. When, for security reasons, a system of naval escorts for convoys bound for the Indies was implemented, all the transactions involved fell under the jurisdiction of the president of the House, assisted by his three officials.

Navigation

In ancient times and for much of the Middle Ages, navigation basically involved coasting along the shore, as seamen rarely dared sail out of sight of the coast.

In the 15th century, the technical progress achieved during the late Middle Ages thanks to the compass, tidal charts and astronomical observation encouraged mariners to tentatively venture out of sight of the coastline.

One of the paramount events of Modern Times was undoubtedly the discovery of America, but this could not have been achieved without first having mastered sailing on the Atlantic. Crossing the great ocean entailed the acquisition of scientific and technical knowledge on the part of contemporary navigators.

From its very inception, the *Casa de la Contratación* was in touch with navigators and cosmographers such as Juan de la Cosa, Amerigo Vespucci and Vicente Yáñez Pinzón. In 1508, the post of chief navigator was created and Amerigo Vespucci was appointed to fill it. That was when a hydrographic office—albeit a rudimentary one—was first set up, as was a school of navigation, the first and finest in modern Europe.

The position of chief navigator was the first scientific post to be created in the colonial administration. Its functions consisted of both examining pilots on the Indies run, drafting and correcting tidal charts, and writing sailing manuals, for which the advice of expert seamen had to be sought.

Several prominent figures held the post of chief navigator during the 16th century, including Juan Díaz Solís, Sebastian Cabot, Alonso de Chaves and Rodrigo Zamorano. They were employed by the House, which also had in its pay a num-

Dispossicion en que lo puso un Ventaxxon
Vracanado por el Oeste en Contraste del Sueste
Frescachon, con que Navegaba al Sudoeste, el
Paquebot Correo de S. M. Nombrado el Pos-
tillon de Mexico, en 29. de Enero de 1771. a las
5 1/2. de la Mañana

Above
Shipwreck.

1771
'Predicament in which His Majesty's mailship, the Postillón de México, found itself after being battered by a westerly hurricane, blowing against a moderate gale from the southwest, on 29 January 1771 at 5 a.m.'
212 x 153 mm.
MP. Ingenios y Muestras, 259.

Spain's vessels and crews were often ravaged by pirates and privateers, and by the weather—the storms, hurricanes and cyclones so frequent in the Atlantic crossing.

Opposite
Slave vessels.

1789
'Plan and sections of a Slave Ship.' Engraving published by James Phillips in London in 1789.
530 x 700 mm.
MP. Ingenios y Muestras, 66.

Until the mid-17th century, slavers bound for the Indies were usually small, with a displacement of under 100 tons. A 40-ton vessel could carry up to 100 slaves, while a 100-ton slave ship had a capacity of over 200.

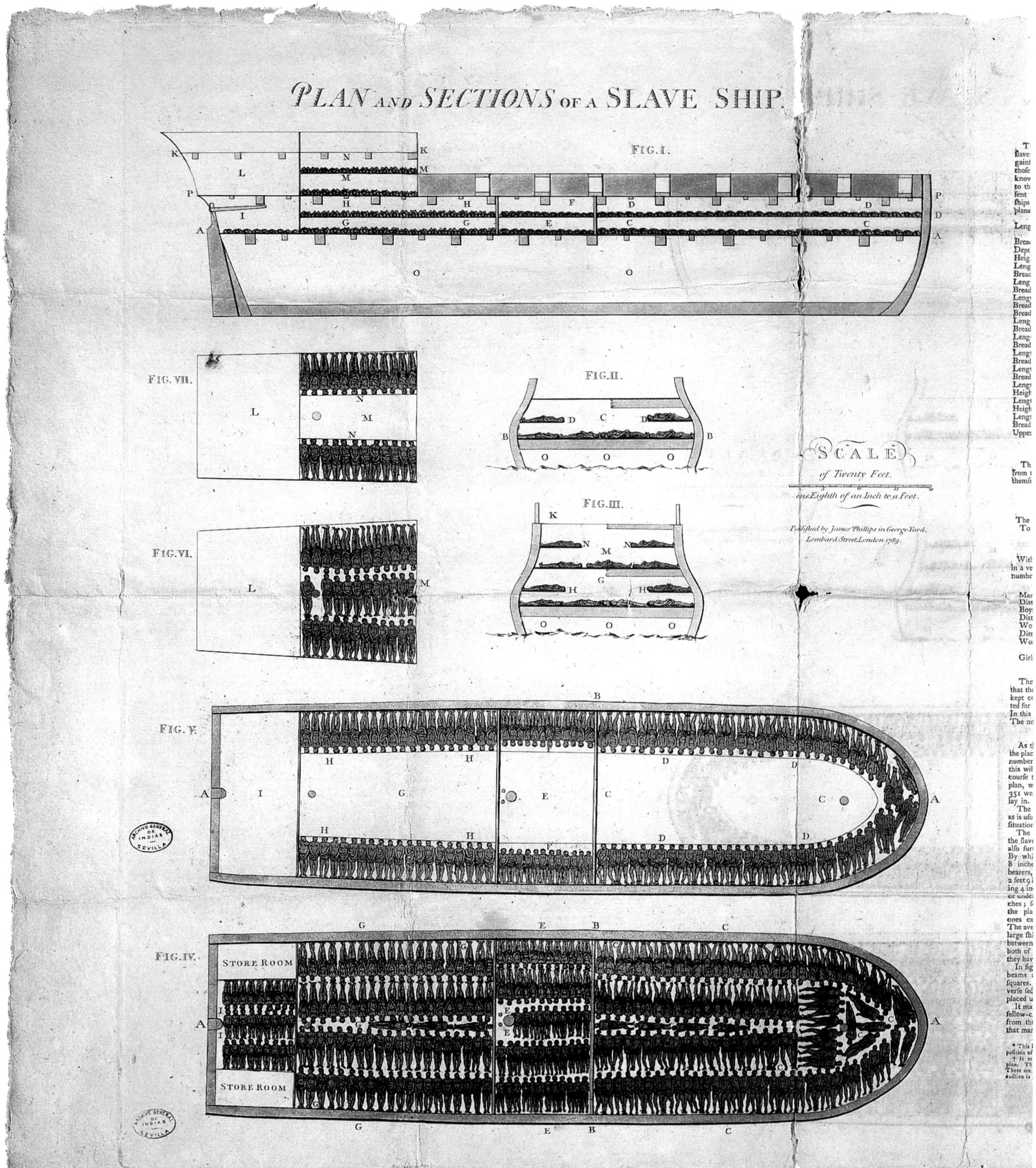
PLAN AND SECTIONS OF A SLAVE SHIP.
FIG. I.
FIG. VII.
FIG. II.
FIG. VI.
FIG. III.
SCALE
of Twenty Feet.
one Eighth of an Inch to a Foot.
Published by James Phillips in George-Yard, Lombard Street, London 1789.
FIG. V.
FIG. IV.
STORE ROOM
STORE ROOM
ARCHIVO GENERAL DE INDIAS SEVILLA

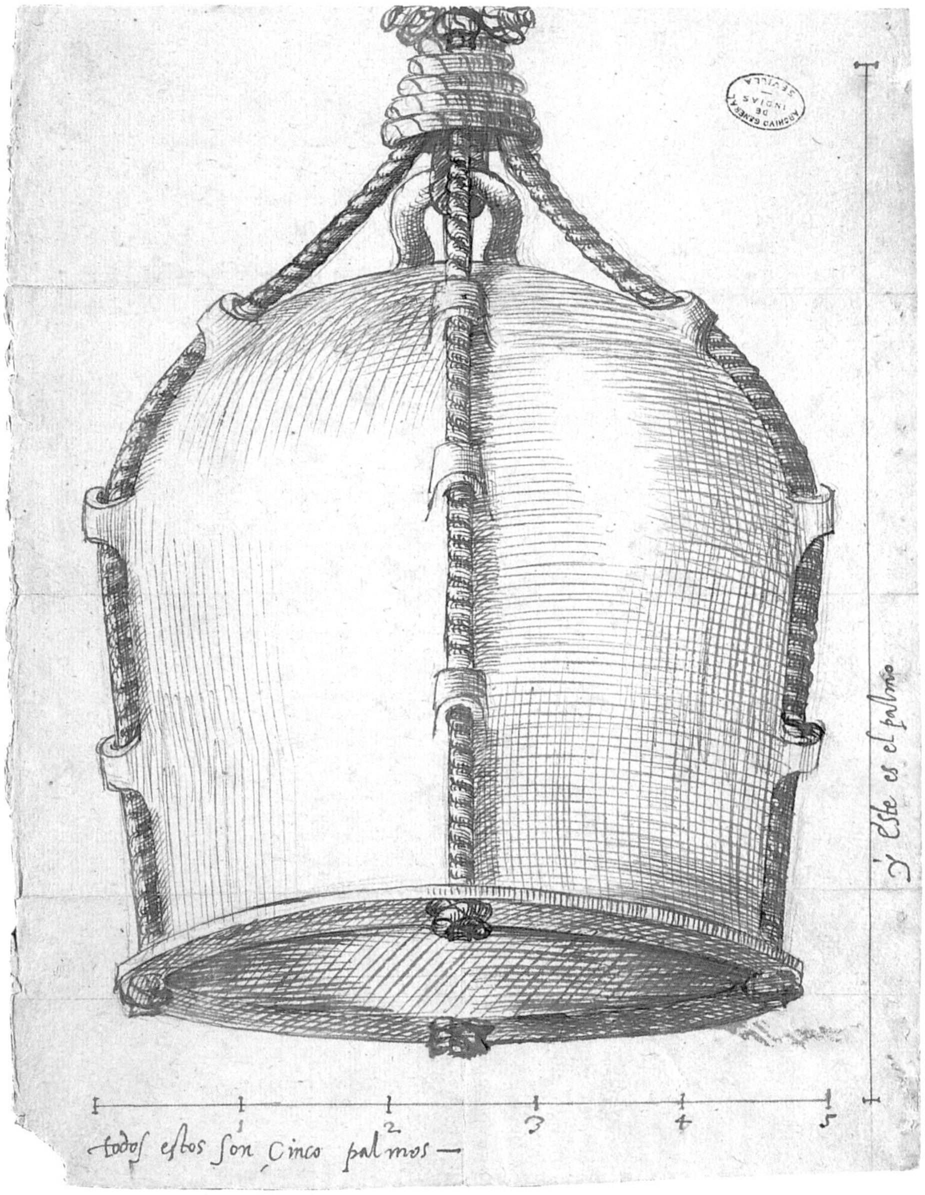

Shipwrecks.

1583
Drawing of a diving bell for rescuing objects from the seabed, invented by Giuseppe Bono of Palermo.
MP. Ingenios y Muestras, 5.

The Sicilian, Giuseppe Bono, presented Philip II with an invention of his which he claimed could be used to remain under the water for more than a quarter of an hour. It consisted of a bronze bell, five spans in diameter, and did not require any ballast, on account of its weight. It was attached by four vertical ropes placed at equal distances around the bell which allowed it to be hauled up or let down.

ber of cosmographers who directed the work of master chart and instrument makers. The office of those cosmographers was legally sanctioned in 1523 when a second scientific post was created under the auspices of the House: that of 'cosmographer, maker of charts and instruments'. The position was held by many a renowned cartographer, including Alonso de Santa Cruz, Alonso de Chaves and Rodrigo Zamorano.

From 1552 onwards, the staff at the *Casa de la Contratación* was augmented by a third scientific post, that of 'professor of the art of navigation and cosmography', which was intended to complement the chair of cosmography that had also been instituted shortly before. The first person to fill the post was Jerónimo de Chaves. Also in 1552, lectures in navigation were assigned to the chair of cosmography and facilities were transferred to the House. Lessons had previously been taught by the chief navigator in his own house.

OPPOSITE
Shipwrecks.

1720
'A hydroandroidal device or garment to be worn by a man under the water. This is the outside covering, which is fitted over an iron hood, jerkin and trousers.'
415 x 282 mm.
MP. Ingenios y Muestras, 248.

The large number of vessels that were lost on the Indies run prompted engineers to try and solve one of the toughest problems in salvaging shipwrecks—how to stay under the water for long periods of time.

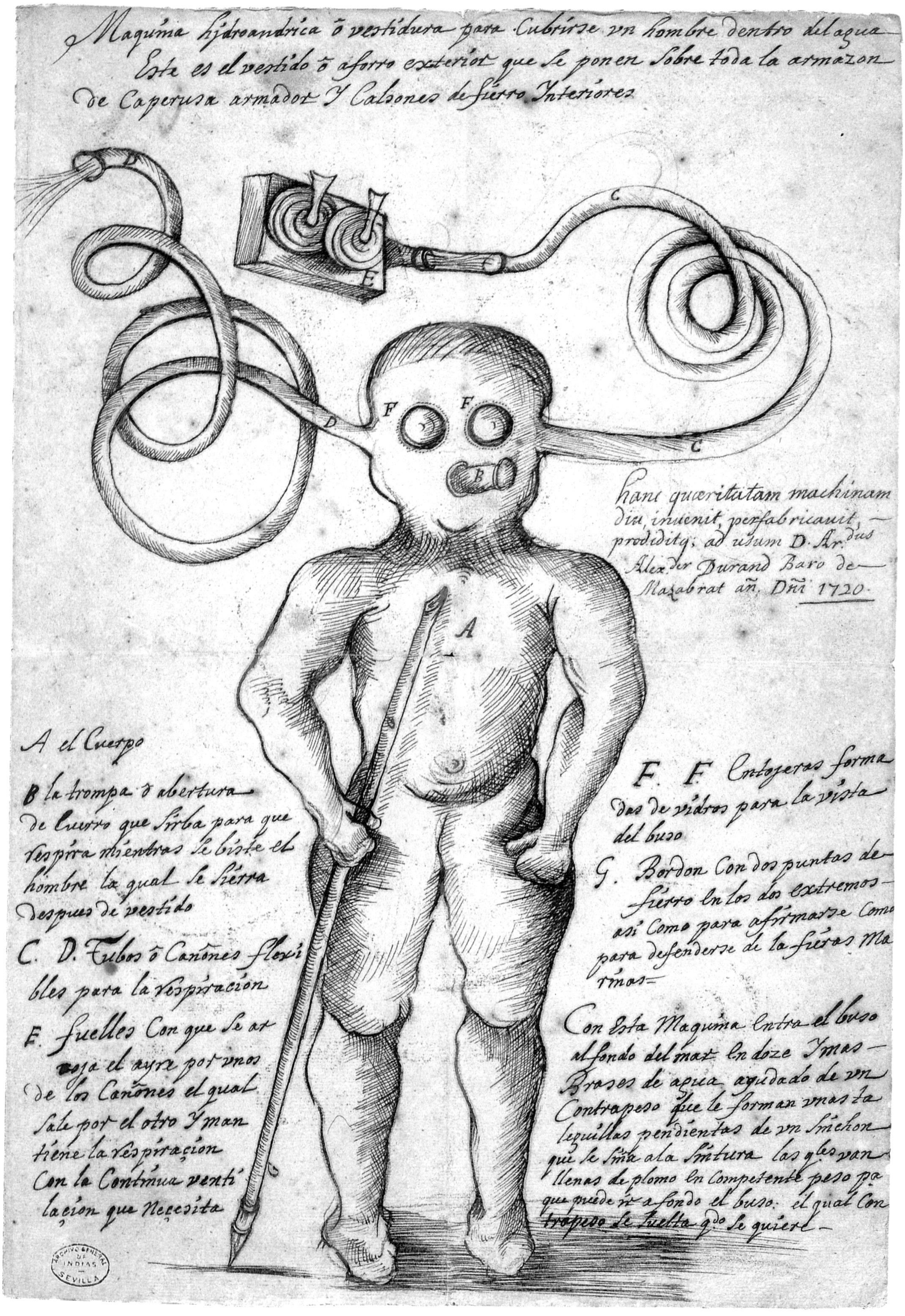

Maquina hydroandrica ō vestidura para Cubrirse vn hombre dentro del agua
Este es el vestido ō aforro exterior que se ponen sobre toda la armazon
de Caperusa armador y Calsones de fierro Interiores
D
E
C
F
F
D
C
B
hanc quæritatam machinam
diu, inuenit, perfabricauit,
proditq; ad usum D. Ar.dus
Alex.der Durand Baro de
Mazabrat añ. Dñi 1720.
A
A el Cuerpo
B la trompa ō abertura
de cuero que sirba para que
respira mientras se biste el
hombre la qual se sierra
despues de vestido
C. D. Tubos ō Cañones flexi
bles para la respiracion
E. fuelles con que se ar
roja el ayre por vnos
de los Cañones el qual
sale por el otro y man
tiene la respiracion
con la continua venti
lacion que necesita
F. F. Antojeras forma
das de vidros para la vista
del buso
G. Bordon con dos puntas de
fierro en los dos extremos
asi como para afirmarse como
para defenderse de la fieras ma
rinos
Con esta Maquina entra el buso
al fondo del mar en doze y mas
brasos de agua ayudado de vn
contrapeso que le forman vnas ta
lequillas pendientas de vn Sinchon
que se siñe ala sintura las q.les van
llenas de plomo en competente peso pa
que puede ir a fondo el buso. el qual con
tropeso se suelta q.do se quiere
ARCHIVO GENERAL DE INDIAS SEVILLA

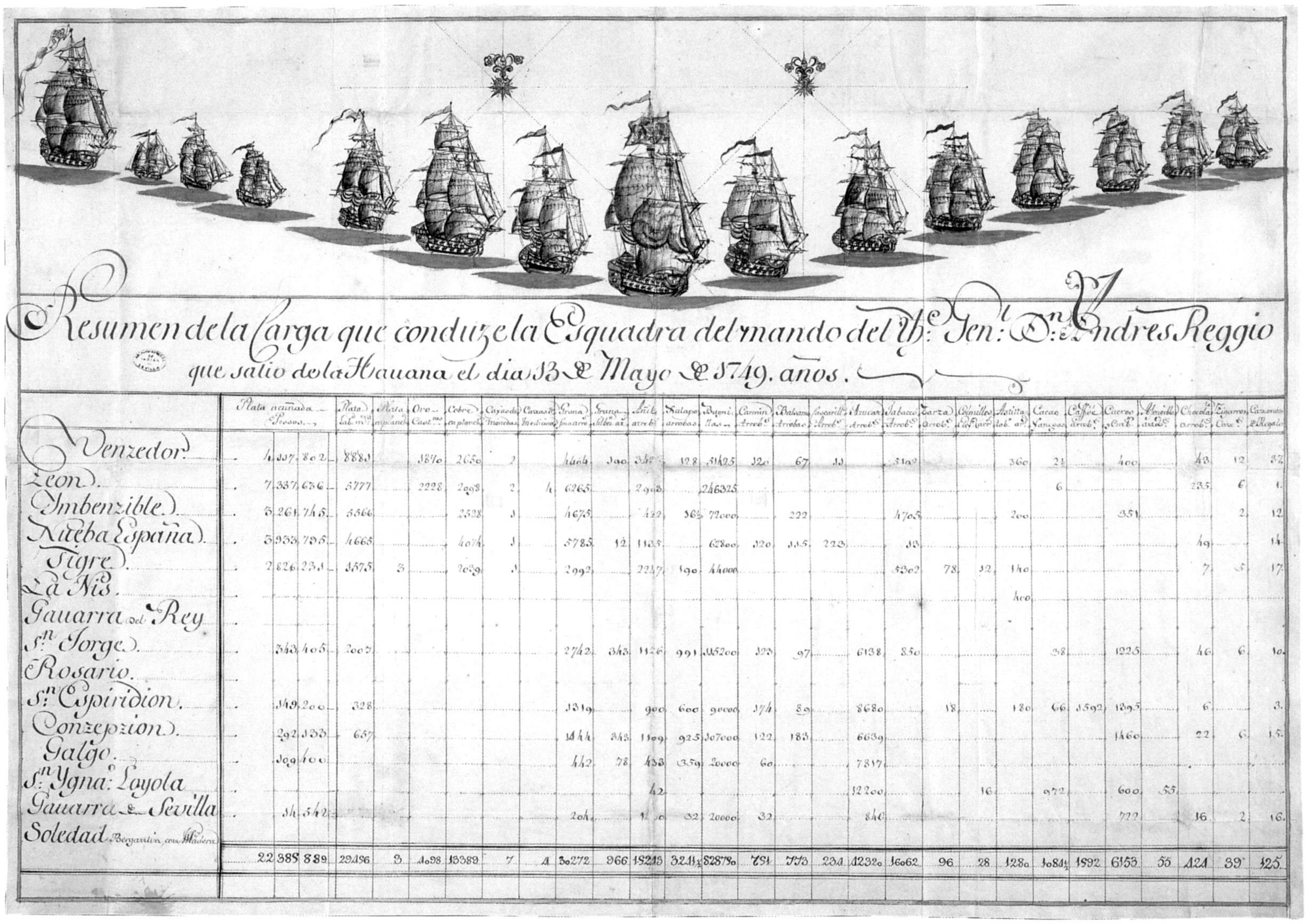

Shipping.

1749
'Summary of the cargoes convoyed by the squadron under the command of Lieutenant General Don Andrés Reggio, which sailed from Havana on 13 May 1749.'
520 x 740 mm.
MP. varios, 23.

During the initial stages of exploration, in the first half of the 16th century, the Indies run was negotiated by isolated ships lacking any protection.

When Castile clashed with the other European monarchies and the promise of riches in the Americas started luring pirates, Spanish vessels became increasingly more exposed to attack.

Merchant ships plying to and from the Indies were thereafter escorted by small naval squadrons in the most dangerous areas, particularly in the area bounded by the Canary Islands, Azores and Cape St. Vincent. A system of fully-fledged naval fleet protection was instituted in 1561.

Two such fleets sailed annually from the port of Seville. One of them, escorted by two large war galleons—the *Capitana & Almiranta*—plied the route to New Spain. The other, with a larger capacity, sailed to Panama, escorted by four or twelve galleons, depending on the season.

The return voyage from the Americas left from the port of Havana, where the vessels assembled before crossing the Atlantic.

Such joint sailings with a security escort substantially slowed down the turnaround time for voyages between Spain and the Americas.

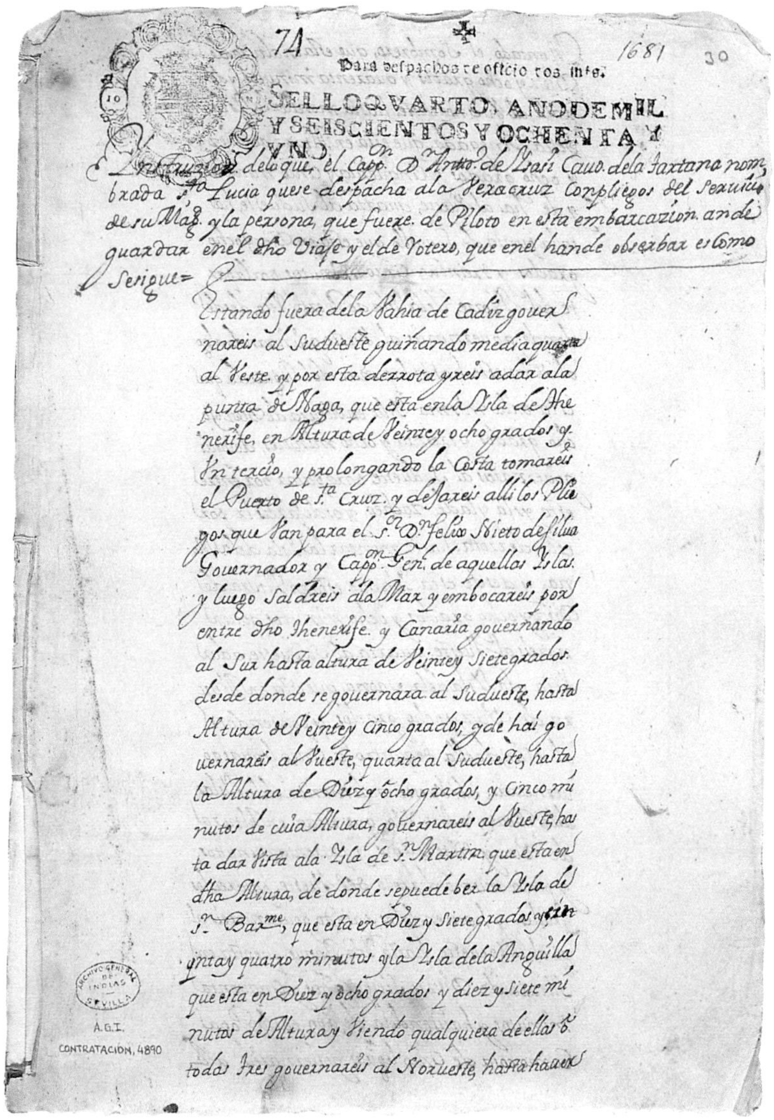

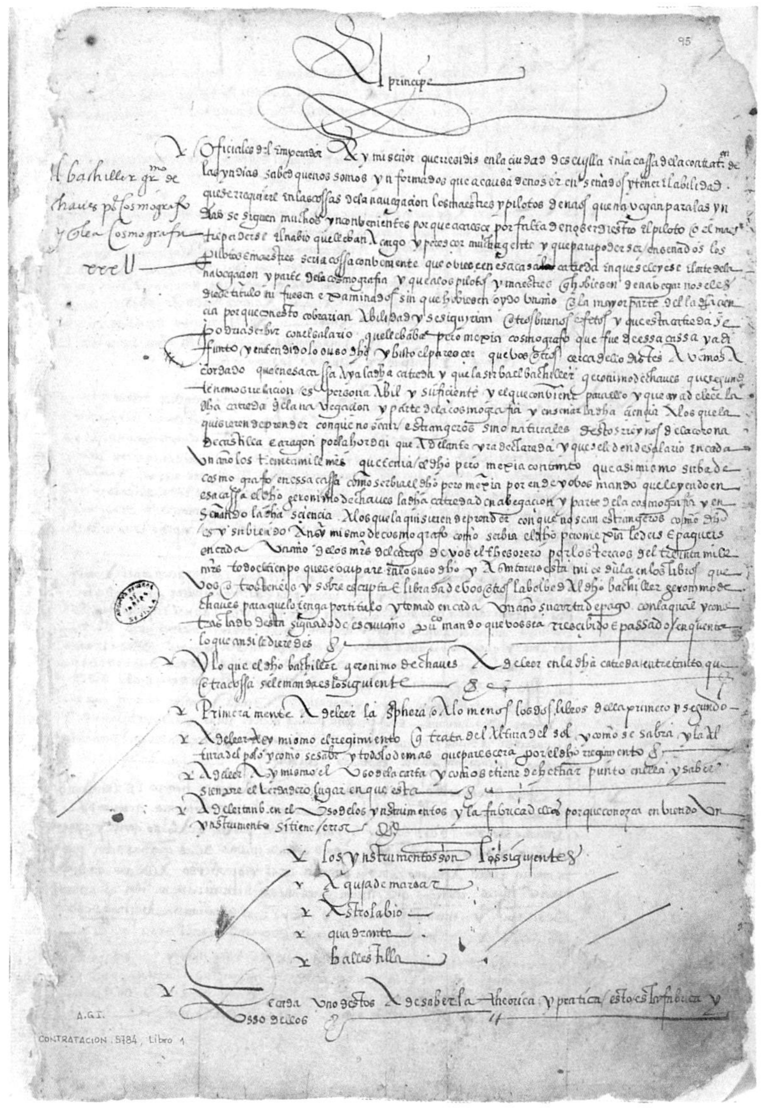

Sailing manuals.

25 April 1681, Seville.
Instructions and sea charts for Antonio de Isasi, quartermaster on the Tartana Santa Lucía, which sailed for Veracruz in the Royal Service carrying documents.
7 fols.
Contratación, 4890.

In the early days of the Indies run, all vessels had to keep a sailing manual written by the chief pilot of the House. However, as routes were opened up and vessels started sailing in formation, the obligation ceased and such manuals were thereafter only used on dispatch boats.

The chair of cosmography.

4 December 1552, Monzón.
Royal warrant issued by Prince Philip, whereby the Casa de la Contratación *would house a department of cosmography headed by Jerónimo de Chaves.*
Contratación 5784, L. 1, fol. 95-95 v.

For a long time, the chief navigator at the Casa de la Contratación *was in charge of all pilots that sailed to the Indies. Apart from the practical piloting experience acquired on numerous expeditions, right from the outset pilots were expected to study the scientific basis of navigation. To this end, the chair of cosmography was created in 1552 and engaged thereafter in training pilots.*

According to Professor Pérez Mallaina, Spain's great contribution in the discovery of America resided not in having reached the New World first but in managing to establish periodical, ongoing communications with the continent. To achieve this, the Atlantic first had to be mastered, for which purpose two disciplines were essential—navigation and cartography.

Ever since its foundation, the *Casa de la Contratación* was associated with pilots and cosmographers. The position of chief pilot was held by the most prominent navigators of each period, such as Amerigo Vespucci, Juan Díaz de Solís and Sebastian Cabot. The leading cosmographers worked for the *Casa de la Contratación* and Seville was where the most distinguished nautical treatises of the 16th century were published.

An extraordinary amount of cartographic work was carried out in the House. American cartography came into being from the time of the discovery of the New World. According to Pedro Mártir de Anglería, in 1498 Columbus sent the monarchs a map of the Paria coastline which he himself had made. In 1500, Juan de la Cosa drew a world map which, for the first time, featured the New World, even though, in terms of technical accuracy, it looked more like a medieval harbor chart. True nautical charts showing latitude and longitude, marine depths, currents and variations in the magnetic needle only appeared after the founding of the *Casa de la Contratación*.

Virtually no exemplary document of 16th-century cartographic activity in the House has survived to the present because, being made of paper, they tended to perish easily, and also because they soon became out-of-date. On their return from the Indies, all pilots reported to the House all the new information and fresh discoveries made on each particular voyage, which was then incorporated into new nautical charts.

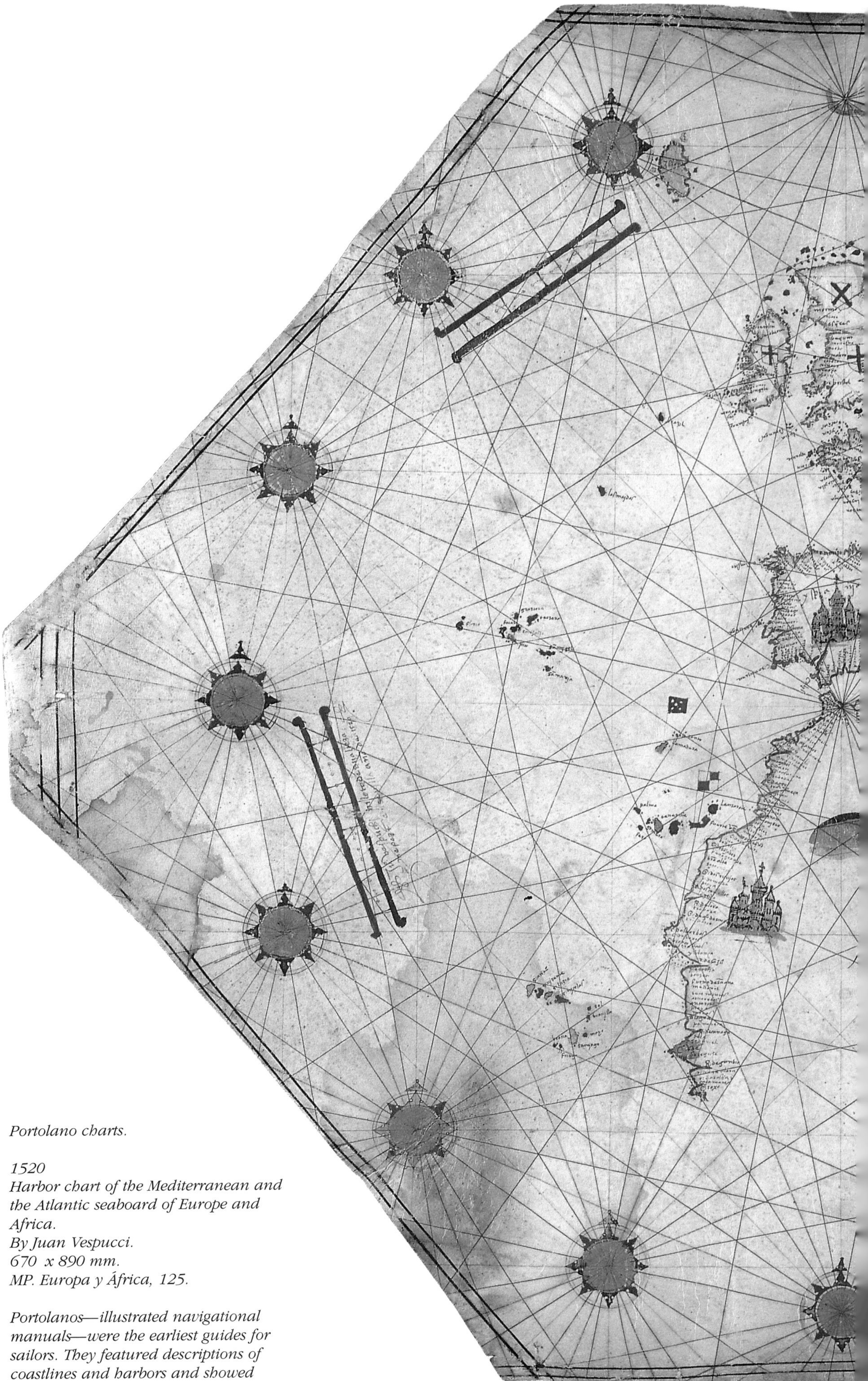

Portolano charts.

1520
Harbor chart of the Mediterranean and the Atlantic seaboard of Europe and Africa.
By Juan Vespucci.
670 x 890 mm.
MP. Europa y África, 125.

Portolanos—illustrated navigational manuals—were the earliest guides for sailors. They featured descriptions of coastlines and harbors and showed distances and courses to follow.

E VR O P A
R I C A

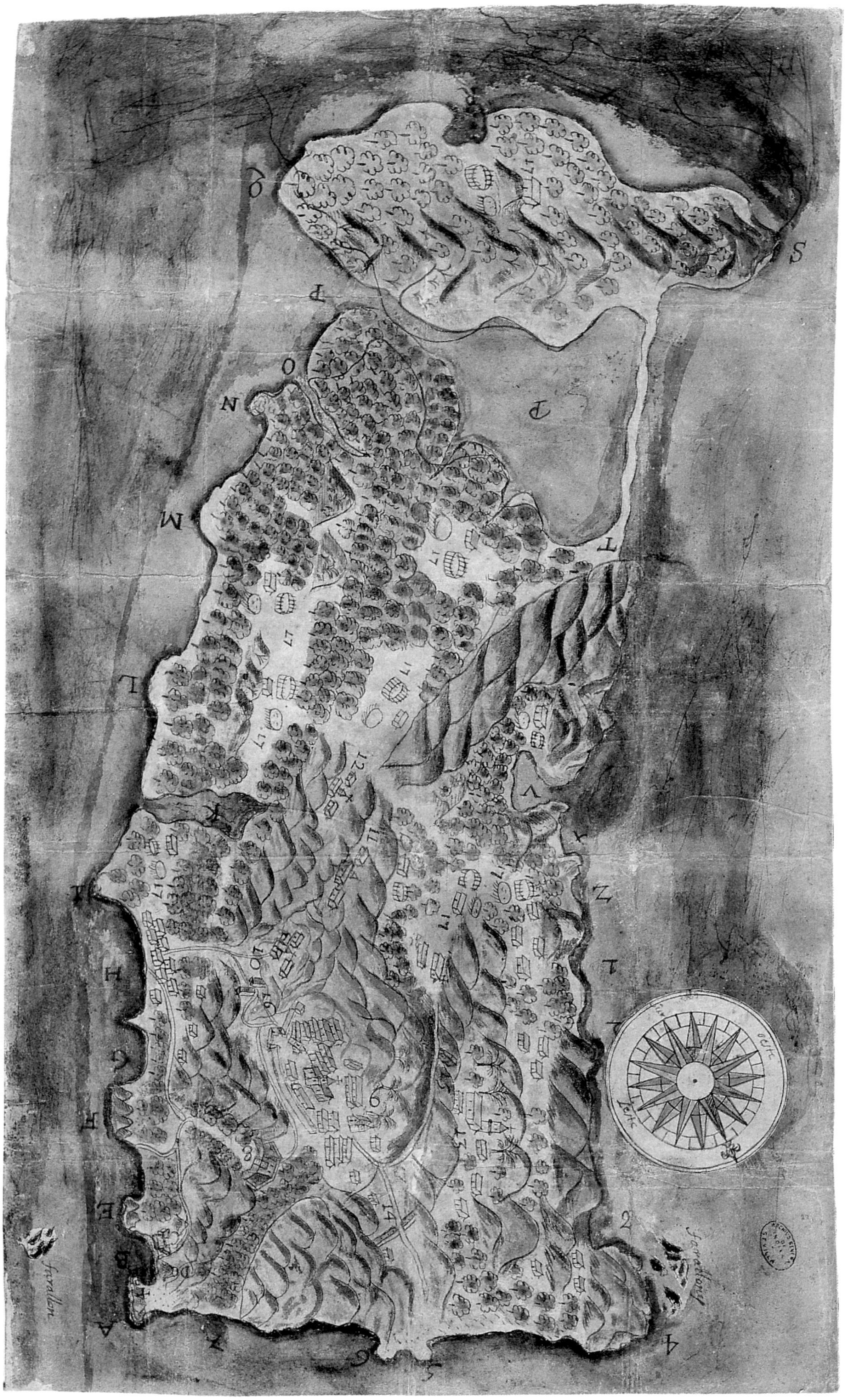

LEFT
'Expeditions of discovery': the voyage of Juan de la Cosa.

1661
'Description of Margarita Island showing its harbors, bays, valleys, hills, roads, saltwater lagoons and trenches dug on the roadside to defend the town.'
315 x 533 mm.
MP. Venezuela, 36.

In 1504, Juan de la Cosa sailed to Tierra Firme. He coasted along the entire Central American seaboard, which Columbus had first discovered, subsequently landed at Margarita Island and reached the mouth of the Orinoco river.

OPPOSITE
'Expeditions of discovery': the voyage of Ferdinand Magellan.

[29 August 1671]
Map of the Strait of Magellan (featured in 'Map of the course sailed by an English frigate and a tender in the Strait of Magellan'. 1671).
420 x 540 mm.
MP. Buenos Aires, 226.

On 27 November 1520, Magellan discovered the strait that bears his name, thus completing reconnaissance of the entire Atlantic coastline of Spanish America and opening up the passage to the Pacific. Subsequently, Juan Sebastián Elcano was to confirm that the world was round.

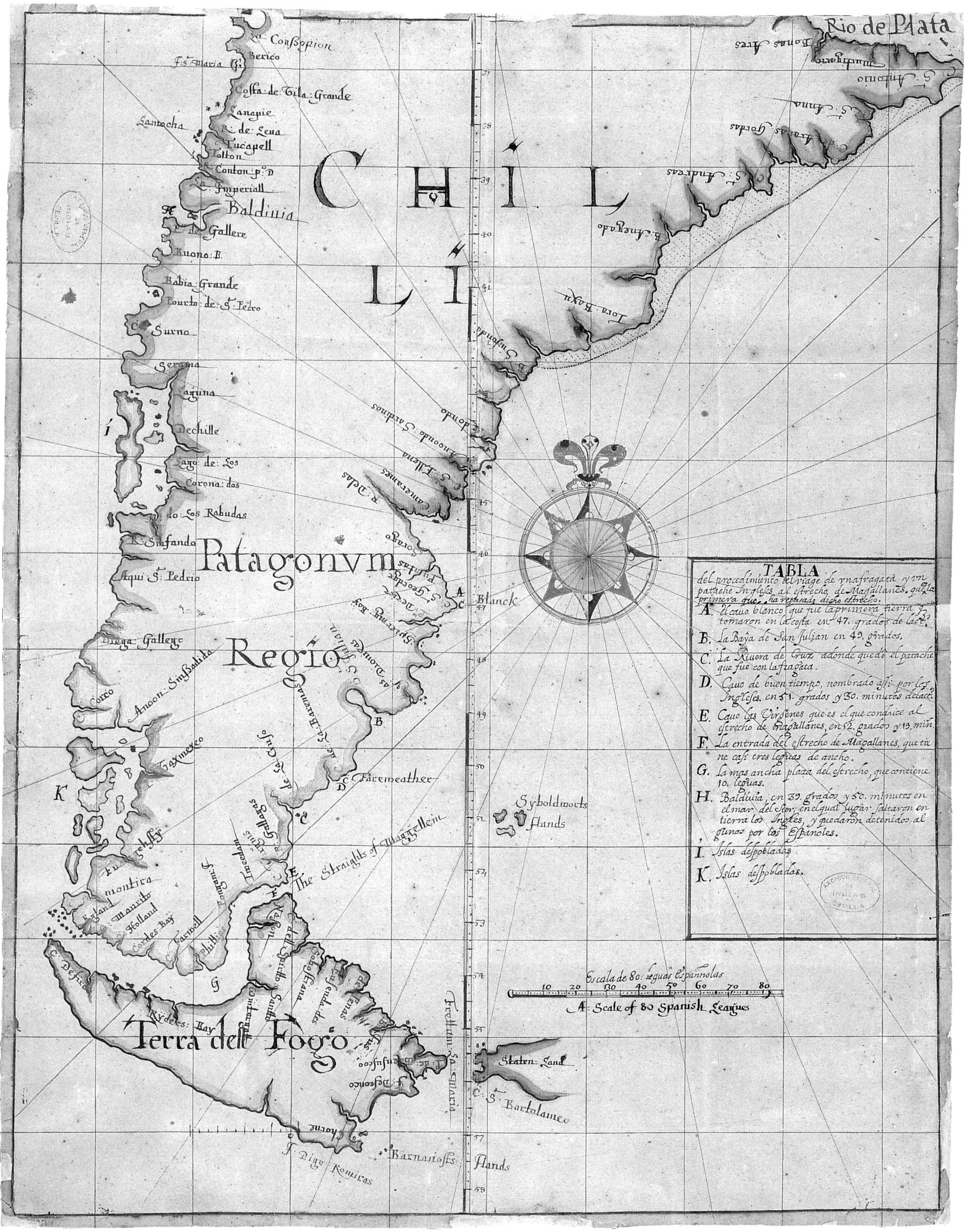
Rio de Plata
CHILI
Patagonvm
Regio
Terra dell Fogo
The Straights of Magellein
Staten Land
C. S. Bartolameo
Sy boldworts Ilands
Barnaiosss Ilands
Blanck
Farewether
Baldiuia
C. Imperiall
Costa de Tila Grande
Bahia Grande
Escala de 80 leguas Españolas
10 20 30 40 50 60 70 80
A Scale of 80 Spanish Leagues
TABLA
del procedimiento del viage de vnafragata y vn patache Ingleses al estrecho de Magallanes. que es la primera que ha repasado dicho estrecho.
A. El cauo blanco que fue la primera tierra q. tomaron en la costa en 47. grados de lat.
B. La Baya de San Julian en 49. grados.
C. La Riuera de Cruz adonde quedó el patache que fue con la fragata.
D. Cauo de buen tiempo, nombrado assi por los Ingleses. en 51. grados y 30. minutos de lat.
E. Cauo las Virgenes que es el que conduce al estrecho de Magallanes, en 52. grados y 19. min.
F. La entrada del estrecho de Magallanes, que tiene casi tres leguas de ancho.
G. La mas ancha plaza del estrecho, que contiene 10. leguas.
H. Baldiuia, en 39. grados y 50. minutos en el mar del Sur; en el qual lugar saltaron en tierra los Ingles, y quedaron detenidos algunos por los Españoles.
I. Islas despobladas
K. Islas despobladas.
ARCHIVO GENERAL DE INDIAS SEVILLA

Punta de santiago.
Ambil
Lubang.
Surgidero
Caponas.
Furton.
SIENDO CORREGIDOR DE LA JURISDIZION de Mariveles el Año de 1698 el sargento mayor D. JOSEPH CORTES MONRROY des Cubrio L A ensenada desubig Adonde porsus Montes Halla Sepueden Fabricar muchos Galeones Con astillero y botadero Como demuestra esta mapa yalpresente seesta Fabri cando Vn Galeon dequenta de Su Magestad Catolica es écho este Mapa En 15 de Marzo de 1715 a.
Bajos.
Limbones.
Fraile.
Lamongja.
Laspuercas.
Ysladecaballo.
Laisla.
Maribeles
Adloloma.
Bagac.
Marigondon.
Riodecana.
Cabcabin.
Lamao.
Pandam.
Odion.
MANILA.
CABITE.
Cabite bieJo.
PARAÑAQUE.
Binacaian.
Bacood.
Laspiñas
Polborista
Tondo.
Bañgcusai.
Bitas.

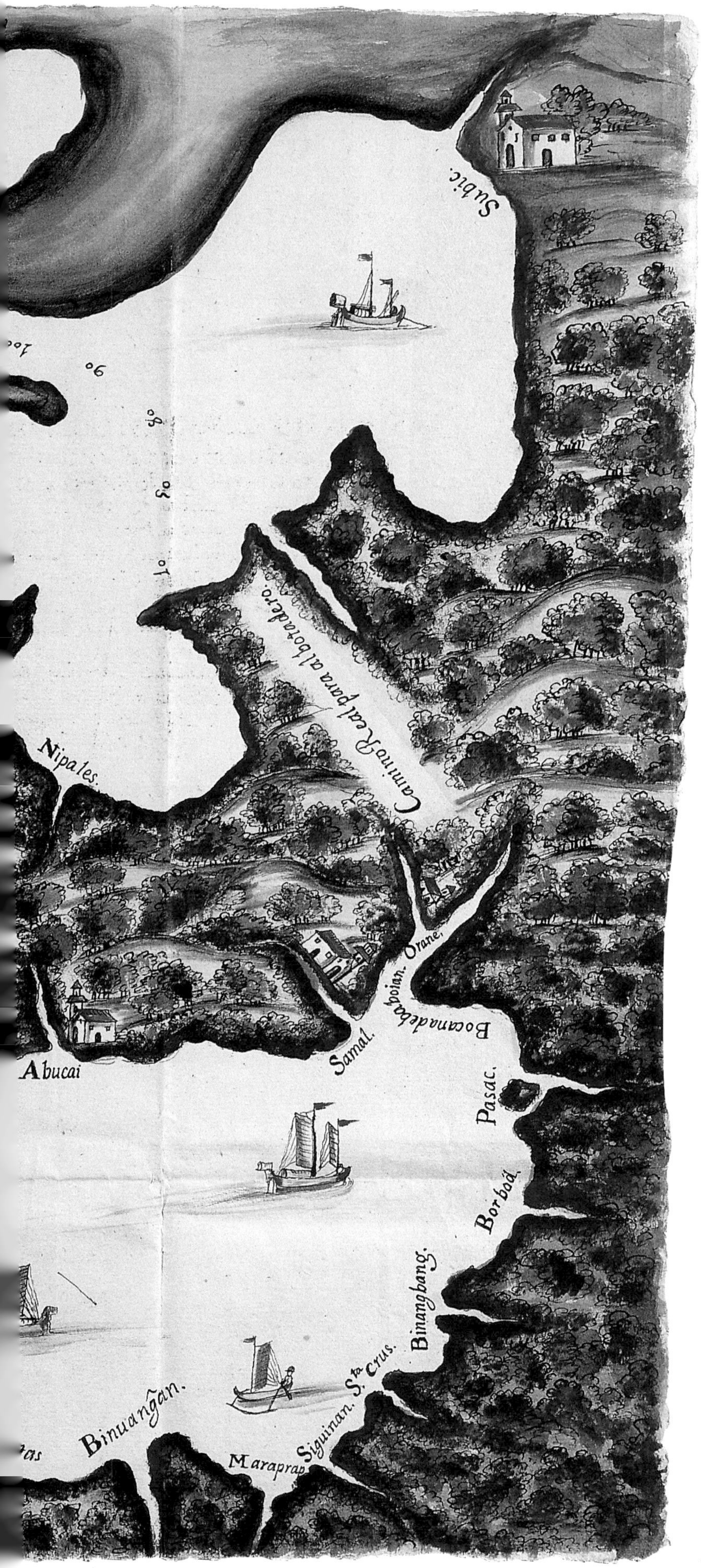

Ever since its foundation, the *Casa de la Contratación* directed and prepared naval expeditions that sailed from the Iberian Peninsula to the Indies to further the task of exploration and discovery pioneered by Columbus.
The voyage of Juan de la Cosa, and expeditions under Alonso de Ojeda, Vicente Yáñez Pinzón and Rodrigo de Bastidas; the discovery of the South Sea by Vasco Núñez de Balboa, and the expeditions of Juan Díaz de Solís and Magellan, among others, were all organized and readied by the House and piloted mainly by navigators in its employ.
Records of the amounts spent on outfitting and victualling the vessels that made these voyages of discovery are kept in the archival fonds transferred to the General Archive of the Indies from the *Casa de la Contratación*.

1715. Plan of Subic Bay and the coast of Cavite and Manila.
430 x 584 mm.
M. y P. Filipinas 146.

The course in navigation originally lasted one year, but circumstances subsequently led it to be reduced to three months. Both the theoretical and practical aspects of the discipline were taught. There were lectures in general cosmography, latitude reckoning, the use of nautical charts, charting a course and the use and manufacture of instruments, including the astrolabe, Jacob's staff, quadrant and chronometer.

Despite these studies, navigators continued to rely heavily on experience and traditional means, as most of them hailed from crews employed on the Indies run. It was customary for a ship's pilot to have worked his way up from shipboy to deckhand, able seaman and boatswain, after which he could be examined for his pilot's license if he knew how to read and write.

The House's school of cartography was also very important. Cartography in the Americas began in 1500 when Juan de la Cosa charted the Antilles and the mainland from the Amazon to Panama. Europe, Africa and part of Asia also featured in his maps. Technically speaking, however, they were more like *portolano* charts in the medieval tradition.

The nautical charts to be had in Seville at the time included written indications for determining latitude and longitude. Other annotations that were gradually added described techniques for measuring depth, currents, compass needle variations and sailing courses. However, such descriptions often differed so markedly from one chart to another, with geographical reckonings often diametrically opposed, that charts annotated in this manner actually posed a permanent hazard to navigation.

In 1512, this state of affairs prompted Ferdinand the Catholic, in the name of his daughter, Juana (Joan the Mad), to issue a royal disposition whereby Juan Díaz de Solís, a chief navigator and Juan Vespucci, a pilot, were commissioned to draw up a royal census of all discovered territories on which all subsequent sailing charts were to be based.

The royal census proved to be the most up-to-date summary of all the Spanish geographical discoveries in the New World. It was augmented with new information brought back by pilots returning from the Indies, the details being noted down by the chief navigator and the cosmographers.

No specimen of a *Padrón Real* (a royal cartographic model) has survived to the present, however, although many of the world maps made by cartographers working in the *Casa de la Contratación* may well have been based on them.

Opposite, above
The Judiciary: Judgement.

28 April 1598, Seville.
Judgement handed down by the Audiencia de la Contratación *in the lawsuit between Hernán García, first officer of the galleon, San Lorenzo, and the treasurer and deputy accountant of average, over payment of a particular sum of money.*
1 fol.
Contratación, 684.

A royal order of 26 September 1511 awarded the Casa de la Contratación *civil and criminal jurisdiction in all matters relating to the Indies trade and shipping, with the Council of the Indies acting as the court of appeal.*

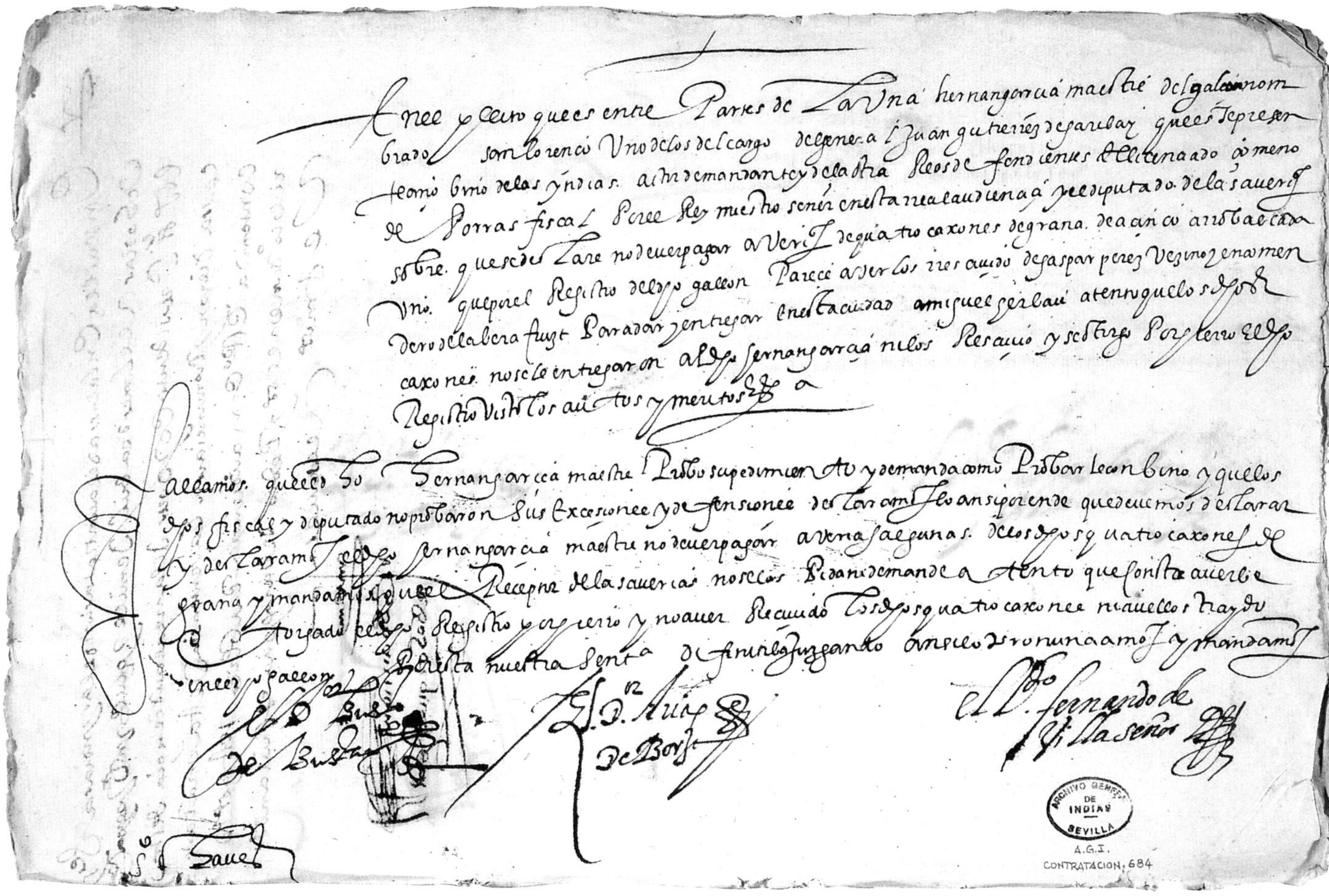

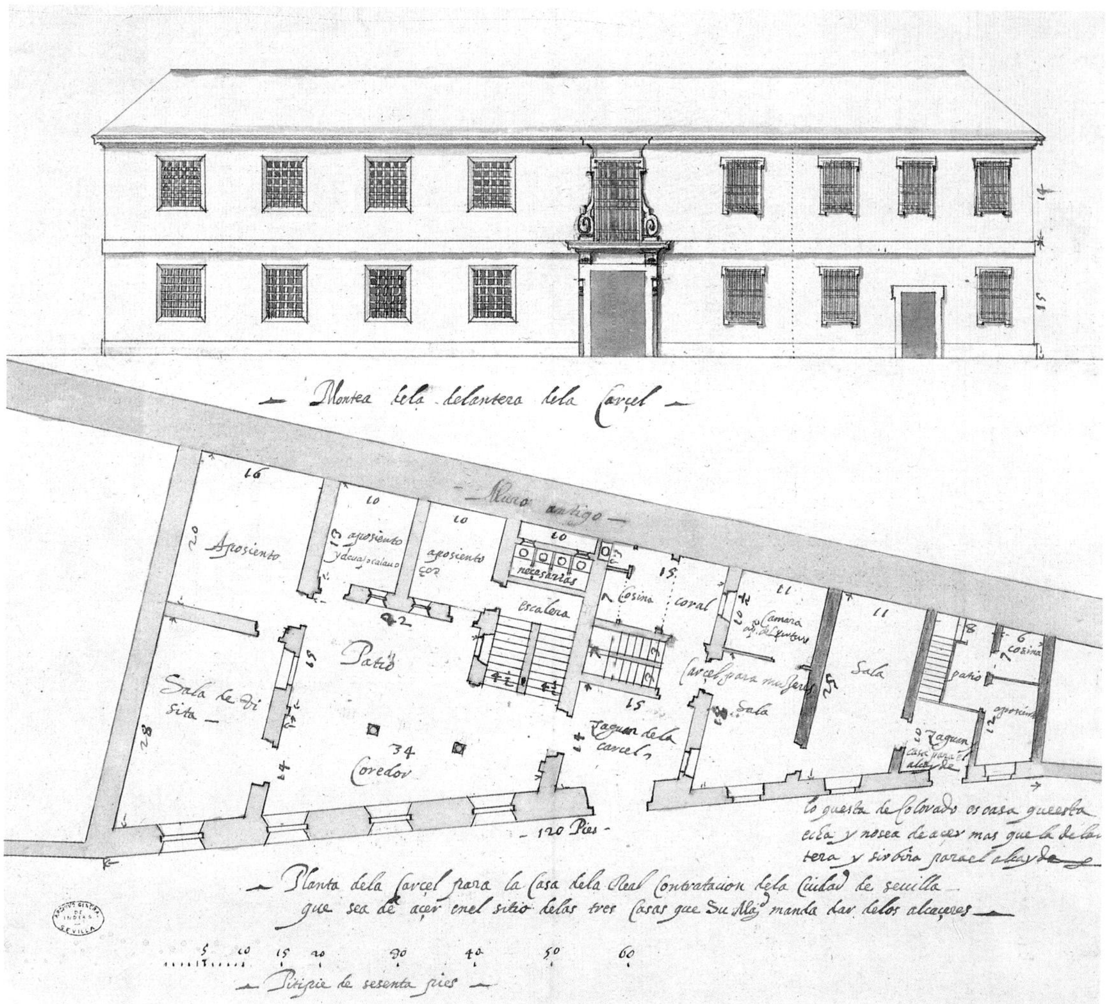

Law and order: prison

[1611]
Facade and plan of the new jail in the Casa de la Contratación, *Seville.*
489 x 417 mm.
Europa y África, 8 bis.

Although the statutes of 1503 make no mention of the House's judicial powers, from the very beginning it acted as a law court in all legal actions involving traders, freight, insurance and so on. Legal conflicts with the judicial authority of Seville were frequent, so that, following a visit by Councillor Juan Suárez de Carvajal in 1535, a special prison was built at the Casa de la Contratación *to ensure its independence and avoid further disputes.*

Some of the House's prominent cartographers were Diego de Ribero, Alonso de Santa Cruz and Andrés de Morales, from whom Juan Díaz de Solís accepted a map that became the basis of the first *Padrón Real* in 1515.

Judicial Functions

In addition to being an administrative and commercial institution, the *Casa de la Contratación* also acted as a court of law.

The statutes of 1503 do not include official mention of the House having any judicial powers and no subsequent decree was issued to that effect. Nevertheless, from the very beginning, it tried cases of infringement of its regulations and arbitrated in disputes between traders and seamen on the Indies run. Indeed, it was the only maritime and mercantile tribunal of its kind until 1543, when the Trade Consulate was formed.

The House acted as a civil court similar to that of the Consulates of Burgos and Barcelona. These had no criminal jurisdiction and for the fulfillment of their civil mandate they probably came under the aegis of municipal authorities. This would account for the long-standing disputes between the House and the city and, although the 1508 decree of Queen Joan ratified the House's judicial powers and ordered the syndic and other judges of Seville not to interfere in its affairs, it was not until 1511 that the Crown issued a decree detailing the House's exact legal competence. The decree also stipulated procedures to be followed in matters concerning contracts, trading companies, insurance, freight and so forth, in line with those operating in the Consulate of Burgos.

The House officials were thereafter known as 'judge–officials' and their lawyer and jurist assistants as 'legal advisers'.

The jurisdiction of the House was laid down definitively in laws passed in 1539, which were included in the statutes of 1552 and formed the basis of all future legislation.

All legal actions involving the Royal Treasury or pertaining to the regulations governing trade and shipping in the Indies were the exclusive jurisdiction of the House, and appeals were referred to the Council of the Indies.

In criminal proceedings, the *Casa de la Contratación* had absolute jurisdiction over any transgression of its statutes and over common law crimes committed

during voyages to and from Spanish America. Such jurisdiction came into force from the very moment passengers, crew and cargo embarked and lasted until the vessel's return and unloading.

In civil matters, it heard all cases relating to the fulfillment of the statutes and provisions regulating labor contracts, business dealings and shipping in the Indies, in addition to leases, inheritance, death duties and so forth.

In 1546, the post of prosecutor was created by royal decree. Duties associated with that position had previously been carried out by people nominated by the House. In 1553, another position of assistant judge was likewise created.

The judicial functions of the House were organized as described until 1583 when, by royal decree, a fully-fledged *sala de justicia* or 'chamber of justice' was set up. Initially, it consisted of two *oidores* or civil judges—a third *oidor* was appointed in 1596—which set it on an equal legal footing with a chancellery or *Audiencia*. From then on, it was known as the *Audiencia de la Contratación* and the House thus had two divisions: administration and justice, with the president acting as the link between both.

The tribunal was the highest judicial authority for litigation involving less than 600,000 *maravedis,* an old Spanish coin, and for all criminal proceedings, except those resulting in confiscation, death sentence and mutilation; its jurisdiction had no territorial limitations.

The Casa de la Contratación moves to Cádiz

Seville's trade monopoly was hamstrung from the outset by a serious drawback: the Guadalquivir river was only partially navigable. Clearing the Sanlúcar sandbar proved so hazardous that the spot soon became a shipping graveyard. Three solutions were put forward to overcome this: enlarging the watercourse, avoiding the river mouth by channelling it into the Guadalete river, or moving the place from which ships sailed and docked.

The last solution was deemed the most suitable and it was decreed that the point of departure for the Indies should be moved to Cádiz.

At the dawn of Modern Times, Cádiz was a relatively unimportant town lacking agriculture or industry. In the 16th century, however, it began to grow as a result of the increased shipping activity. With the discovery of the New World, its

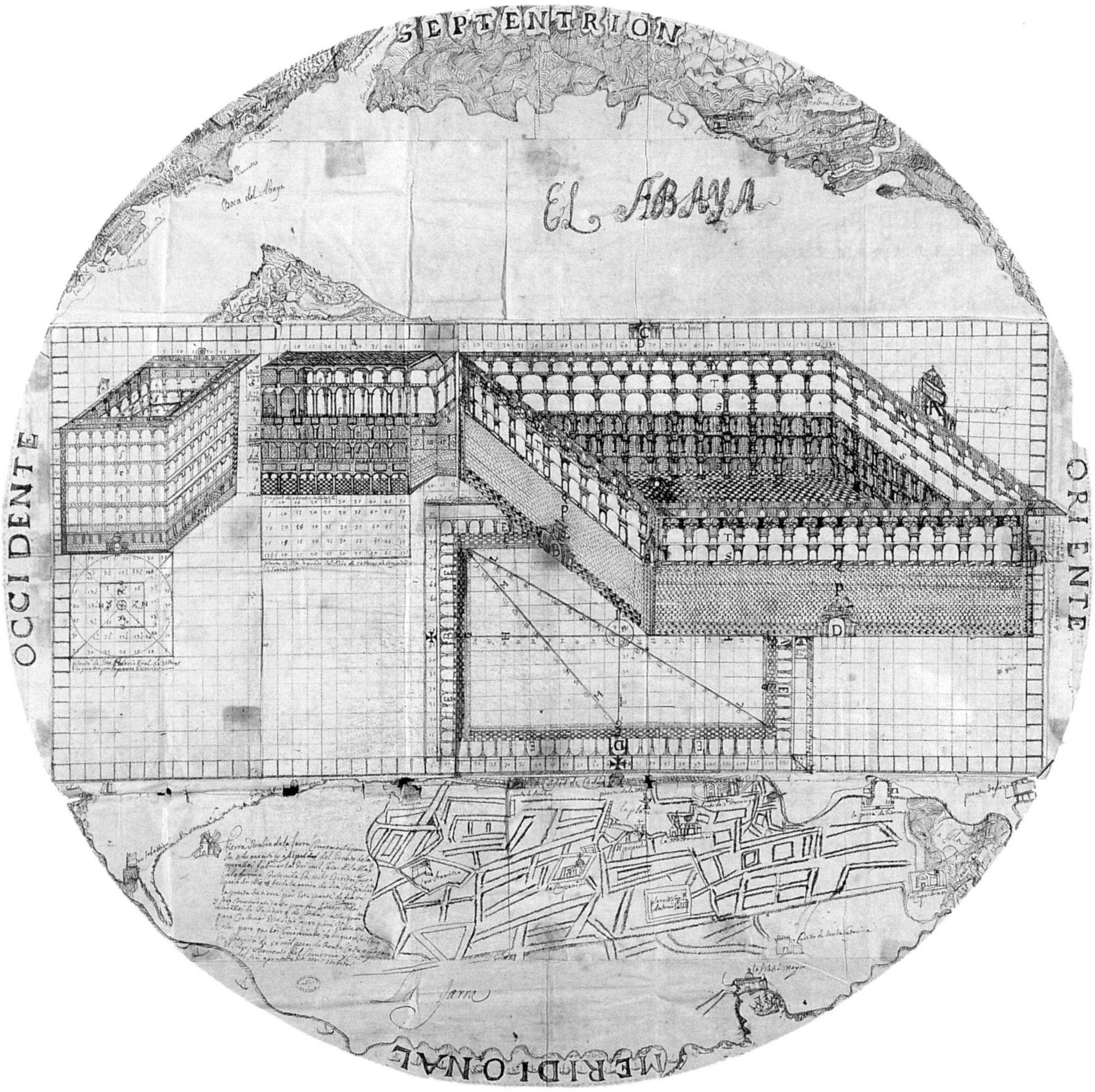

The Casa de la Contratación *moves to Cádiz.*

1675
Plan of the city of Cádiz, divided into quarters and showing blown-up details of buildings, which Juan Cano entitled Puerto Franco *or 'Free Port'.*
832 x 835 mm.
MP. Europa y África, 115.

trade potential soared and its local merchants guild, whose members were mainly Genoese, Flemish and Biscayan, were quick to seize the opportunity.

Cádiz was one of nine ports authorized by Charles V in 1529 to send ships directly to the Indies and, although the measure was overturned in 1573, Cádiz continued to enjoy the privilege. In 1558, vessels arriving from Hispaniola and Puerto Rico carrying cargoes of leather and sugar were allowed to unload in Cádiz and three years later the concession was extended to vessels that had sustained damage on the return voyage and were unable to clear the Sanlúcar sandbar. In time, it gradually became customary for one third of the fleet's tonnage to be unloaded in Cádiz.

The shift in shipping traffic was followed by that of cargoes and, eventually, by the administrative officials themselves. Although the official bodies continued to be based in Seville, they had to send staff to Sanlúcar and Cádiz, first on a temporary basis and then permanently, to oversee loading and unloading operations. By 1537, the *Juzgado de Cádiz* (Court of Justice of Cádiz), which acted as a subsidiary of the *Casa de la Contratación*, had come into being.

By the mid-17th century, Seville's monopoly had become purely symbolic, while Cádiz continued to grow. In 1664, however, Seville reacted by securing official sanction for galleons to sail to and from Sanlúcar only. Moreover, the *Juzgado de Cádiz* was abandoned and ships had to reduce their draught in order to negotiate the sandbar and receive permission to dock.

Seville's triumph was short-lived, however and, in 1679, the *Juzgado de Cádiz* was reinstated. In 1680, the town was designated as the main shipping center while Seville was kept on as the bureaucracratic center. This state of affairs lasted until 1717.

On 12 May 1717, Philip V ordered the *Casa de la Contratación* to be moved to Cádiz, thus putting an end to the long rivalry between the two cities which had begun at the very moment the House was founded.

Philip V's decision precipitated the most serious crisis the *Casa de la Contratación* had ever experienced. Apart from having to relocate to another city, a number of decrees were passed at the time that involved a major upheaval in the workings of the House. In the end, it can safely be said that the *Casa de la Contratación* of Cádiz was a completely different affair from the institution that had originally been founded in Seville.

Of the two divisions of the House that had existed in Seville—administration and judiciary—only the justice division was transferred to Cádiz and only with two of the judges, while the president of the *Casa de la Contratación* took over all powers and responsibilities originally invested in the judges.

José Patiño, who was appointed president in 1717, held the office of quartermaster general of the navy and superintendent of the kingdom of Seville. Subsequently and up until 1754, virtually all presidents of the *Casa de la Contratación* were also appointed to those offices.

In 1754, the minister, Julián de Arriaga, separated the two posts. The quartermaster general was thereafter placed in charge of all matters involved in preparing vessels sailing to the Indies, including crew and provisions, while the president of the House had to oversee loading facilities and implement measures to prevent smuggling.

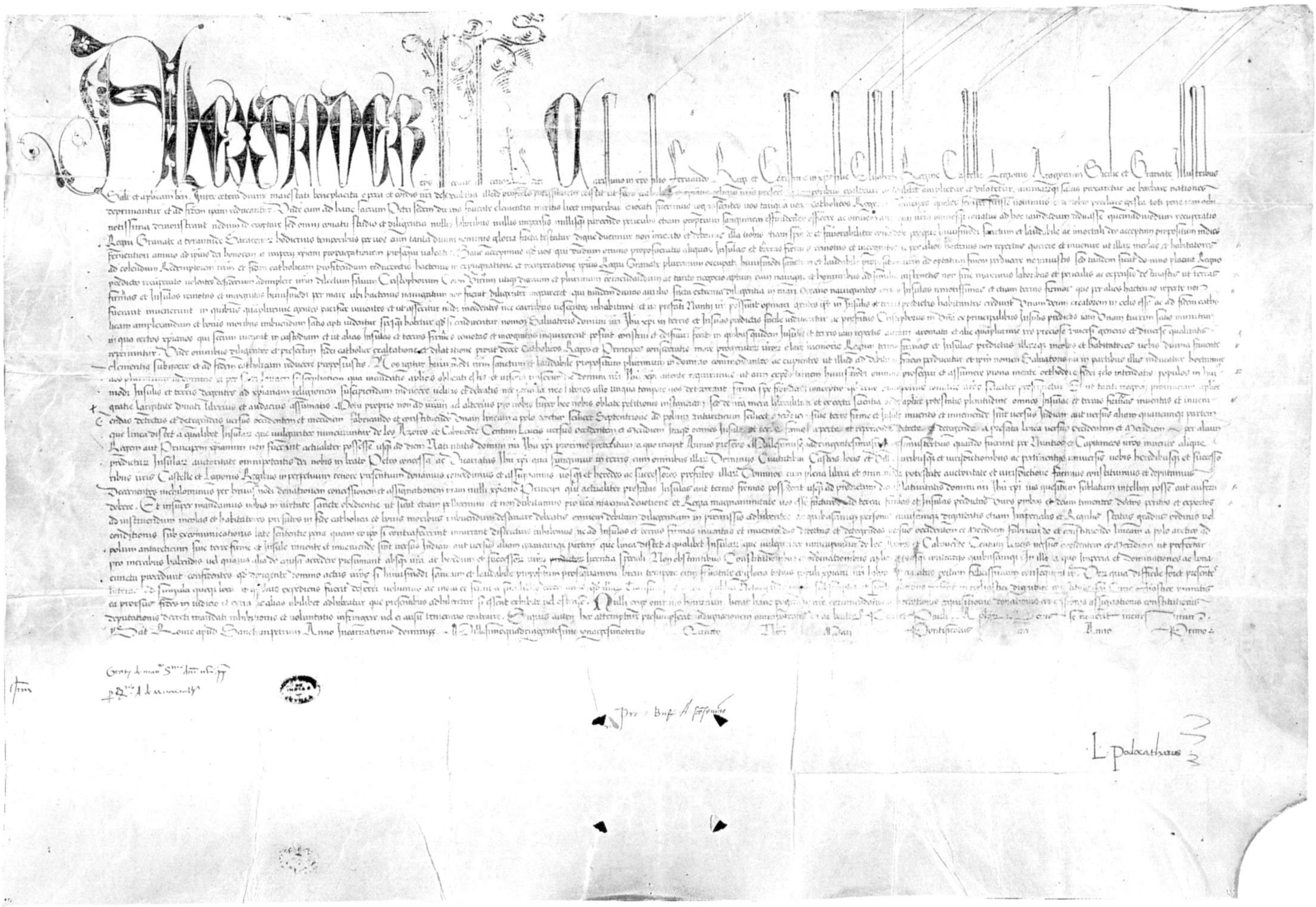

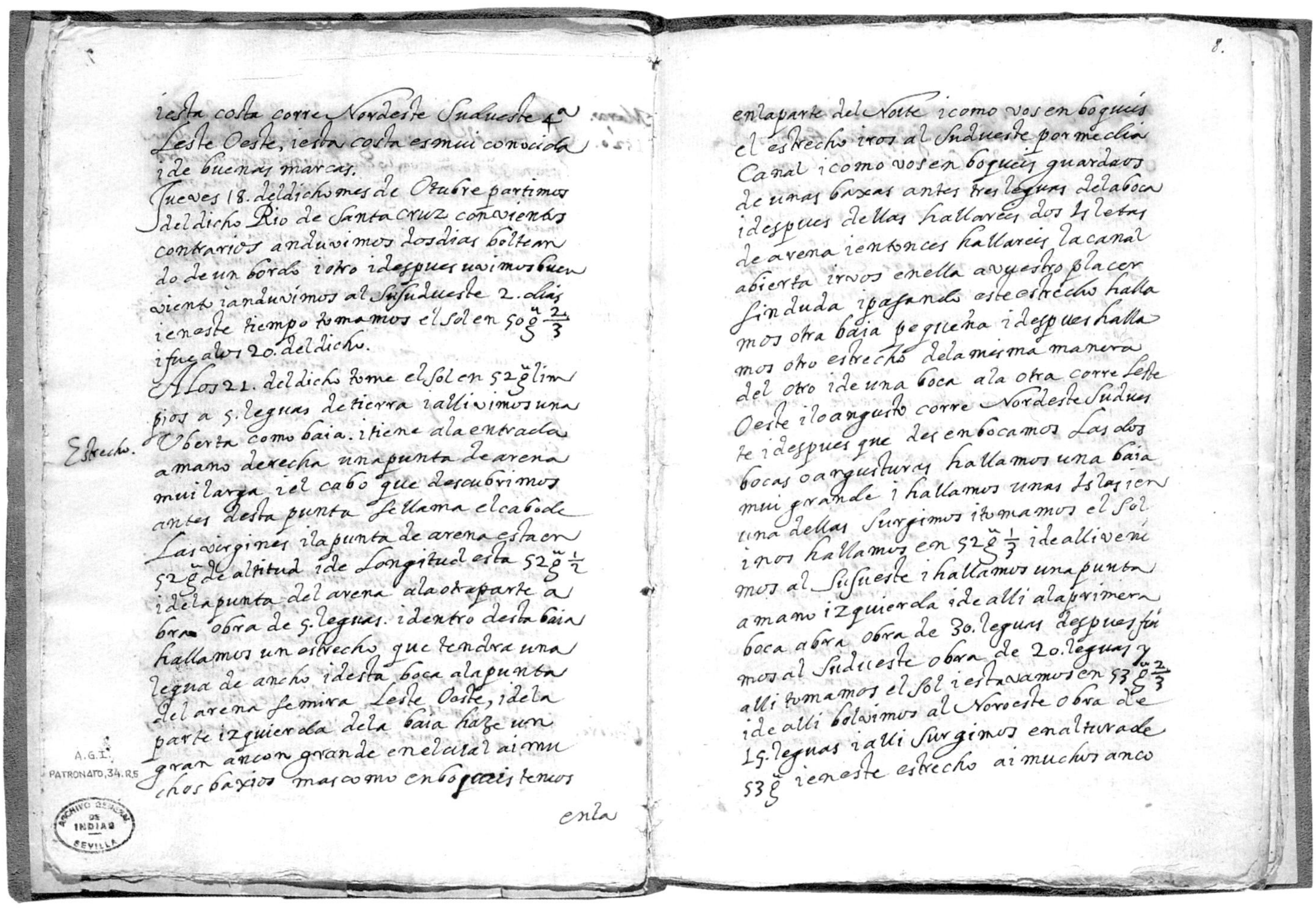
Estrecho.

iesta costa corre Nordeste Sudueste 4ª Leste Oeste, iesta costa es mui conocida i de buenas marcas.

Jueves 18. deldicho mes de Otubre partimos deldicho Rio de Santa Cruz con vientos contrarios anduvimos dos dias bolteando de un bordo i otro idespues uvimos buen viento i anduvimos al Susudueste 2. dias ienoste tiempo tomamos el sol en 50 g.^a 2/3 i fue alos 20. del dicho.

A los 21. del dicho tome el sol en 52 g.^a limpios a 5. leguas de tierra i alli vimos una Oberta como baia. i tiene ala entrada a mano derecha una punta de arena mui larga i el cabo que descubrimos antes desta punta se llama el cabo de Las virgines i la punta de arena esta en 52 g.^a de altitud i de Longitud esta 52 g.^a 1/2 i dela punta del arena ala otra parte abra obra de 5. leguas. i dentro desta baia hallamos un estrecho que tendra una legua de ancho i desta boca ala punta del arena se mira Leste Oeste, i dela parte izquierda dela baia haze un gran ancon grande en el cual ai muchos baxios mas como enboqueis tenes enla

A.G.I.
PATRONATO,34.R.5

8.

enla parte del Norte i como vos enboqueis el estrecho iros al Sudueste por medio canal i como vos enboqueis guardaos de unas baxas antes tres leguas dela boca i despues dellas hallareis dos isletas de arena i entonces hallareis la canal abierta i iros en ella a vuestro placer sin duda i pasando este estrecho hallamos otra baia pequeña i despues hallamos otro estrecho dela misma manera del otro i de una boca ala otra corre Leste Oeste i lo angosto corre Nordeste Sudueste i despues que desembocamos Las dos bocas o angosturas hallamos una baia mui grande i hallamos unas islas i en una dellas surgimos i tomamos el sol i nos hallamos en 52 g.^a 1/3 i de alli venimos al Susueste i hallamos una punta a mano izquierda i de alli ala primera boca abra obra de 30. leguas despues fuimos al Sudueste obra de 20. leguas y alli tomamos el sol i estavamos en 53 g.^a 2/3 i de alli bolvimos al Noroeste obra de 15. leguas i alli surgimos en altura de 53 g.^a i en este estrecho ai muchos anco

Opposite, above
Bull 'Inter Caetera': a papal donation.

4 May 1493, Rome.
Bull 'Inter Caetera' (II), issued by Pope Alexander VI, awarding the Catholic Kings and their successors all islands and mainlands discovered to the south and west of a line one hundred leagues from the Azores and Cape Verde islands not already possessions of any Christian king prior to Christmas Day 1492, 'so that their inhabitants might be converted to the Catholic faith'.
597 x 407 (349 x 58) mm.
MP. Bulas y Breves, 4
Patronato, 1, N. 3, r. 1.

This bull, which ratified others issued on 3 May, provided the grounds on which the Indies were legitimately incorporated into the Crown of Castile in exchange for evangelizing the lands discovered and to be discovered. Despite the controversy surrounding the import of such a fabulous donation and the Pope's right to grant it, the Spanish monarchs used it, together with other papal concessions, to assert their right to political sovereignty in the New World.

Opposite, below
The voyage of Magellan and Elcano: pilot book.

1519–1522.
Logbook or pilot book kept on Magellan's expedition from Cape Saint Augustine in Brazil until the return to Spain of the galleon Victoria, written by Francisco Albo, boatswain on the Trinidad, under the command of Ferdinand Magellan.
41 fols. in 4to + 1 blank.
Patronato, 34, N. 5.

When the fleet was being readied, the King urged Magellan and Faleiro to provide a written statement of the route they were to take. The fleet sailed from Sanlúcar de Barrameda on 20 September and reached the Canary Islands after a few days' sailing. From there, their course led through the Cape Verde islands to Brazil, where Albo's logbook begins. The specimen page recounts the crossing of the Strait of Magellan. The successful first circumnavigation of the globe paved the way for Castile to set up its vast empire.

The Council of the Indies grew gradually out of the Council of Castile. One of its councillors, Bishop Juan Rodríguez de Fonseca, was appointed in 1504 to supervise Indian affairs, initially on a personal basis and, soon afterwards, as a member of a board, together with other councillors appointed for the purpose. Thus, the so-called *Junta de Indias* was actually engendered within the Council of Castile. According to the essayist, Antonio de León Pinelo, the *Junta* was operating by 1511 and, in period documents, its members are described as 'those members of the Council concerned with the affairs of the Indies'. Having being spawned from within the supreme administrative body of Castile, the *Junta* did not have a set number of members nor specific appointments, but it may safely be assumed that its original members included men such as Francisco de los Cobos, Mercurino de Gattinara, the aforementioned Fonseca, García de Padilla and other figures close to Charles V.

The mission of that original Council of the Indies was consolidated during the early years of the monarch's reign. However, the increasingly larger tracts of land discovered, the improved socio-political organization that prevailed in the newly conquered territories—particularly in New Spain—and the complexity of the situation in the New World, must have prompted Charles V to set up an autonomous body to deal with such issues.

The official inception of the Council of the Indies or, rather, its transformation from a *Junta* into an independent body, is a subject of debate among historians. As early as 1522, in an act directed at the *Casa de la Contratación,* the Council is mentioned in passing: 'the bishop of Burgos, president of the Council of the Indies, attended the meeting and dealt with affairs awaiting his attention'. A royal provision issued in Valladolid on 8 May 1523 refers to the appointment of Doctor Diego Beltrán as the first, lifelong salaried member of the Council.

Apart from the issue of exactly when the Council was founded, what is widely accepted is the date on which its first president was appointed—1 August 1524. This coincides with the date given by the prestigious essayist and councillor of the Indies, Juan Solórzano Pereira, in his work entitled *Política Indiana* (1647). That first president was Fray García de Loaysa, a Dominican General and Emperor Charles V's confessor. The founding members of the Council were Dr. Gonzalo Maldonado, the aforementioned Diego Beltrán and Pedro Mártir de Anglería. Francisco de Prado was appointed to the post of general counsel and Francisco de los Cobos, that of secretary. From 1528 onwards, a chancellor was also appointed whose function it was to guard the royal seal, the first such official being Mercurino de Gattinara.

EL GRANDE TEMPLO DE MEXICO
1. Plan donde estaban los Idolos. 2. Escalera de 120 gradas. 3. Idolo Huitzilopösthli 4. Idolo Tlaloch. 5. Puertas, ò entradas à los quatro Vientos. 6. Habitaciones de los Sacerdotes. 7. Humilladero, ò
Sitio donde ponian las Cavezas de los Sacrificados encadenadas en unas Varas atadas a Maderos. 8. Escalera de 30 gradas para el Humilladero. 9 Figuras de Sierpes adorno de el Petril ò Muralla de la Plaza del Templo, 10 Plaza de el Templo donde danzaban ocho, ò diez mil Indios y alas Danzas llamaban Mytoies. 11. quatro Estatuas de Idolos que estaban sobre cada Puerta de la Muralla. 12 Forma de
los Sacrificios de Hombres sobre una Piedra. 13 Volcanes de Mexico. 14 Laguna de Tetzcuco. 15 Peñol de los Baños. 16. Peñol del Marques.
Navarro Sculpio en Mexico Calle de los Donzeles año 1769.

The Great Temple of Mexico.

1769.
Ritual sacrifice on the altar of 'The Great Temple', presided over by the idol, Huitziloposthli.
210 x 260 mm.
Featured in 'History of New Spain, written by the enlightened conquistador, Hernando Cortés, augmented with documents and annotations by the illustrious Don Francisco Antonio Lorenzana, Archbishop of Mexico'.
Mexico: Joseph Antonio de Hogal, 1770.
Biblioteca, L.A. S. XVIII–24.

The cultural and socio-political wealth and complexity of the Aztec civilization led the Mexican territory to be regarded as a new kingdom—that of New Spain. It was not long afterwards that an administrative body was set up to rule such vast territories—the Council of the Indies.

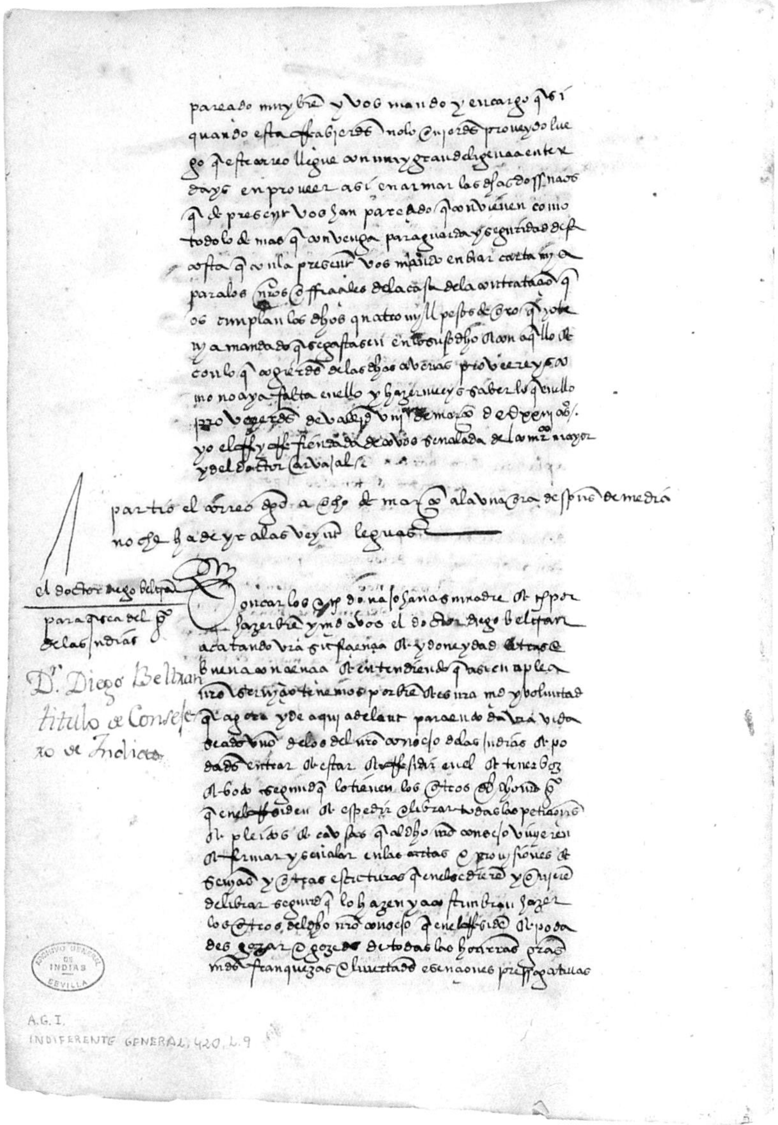

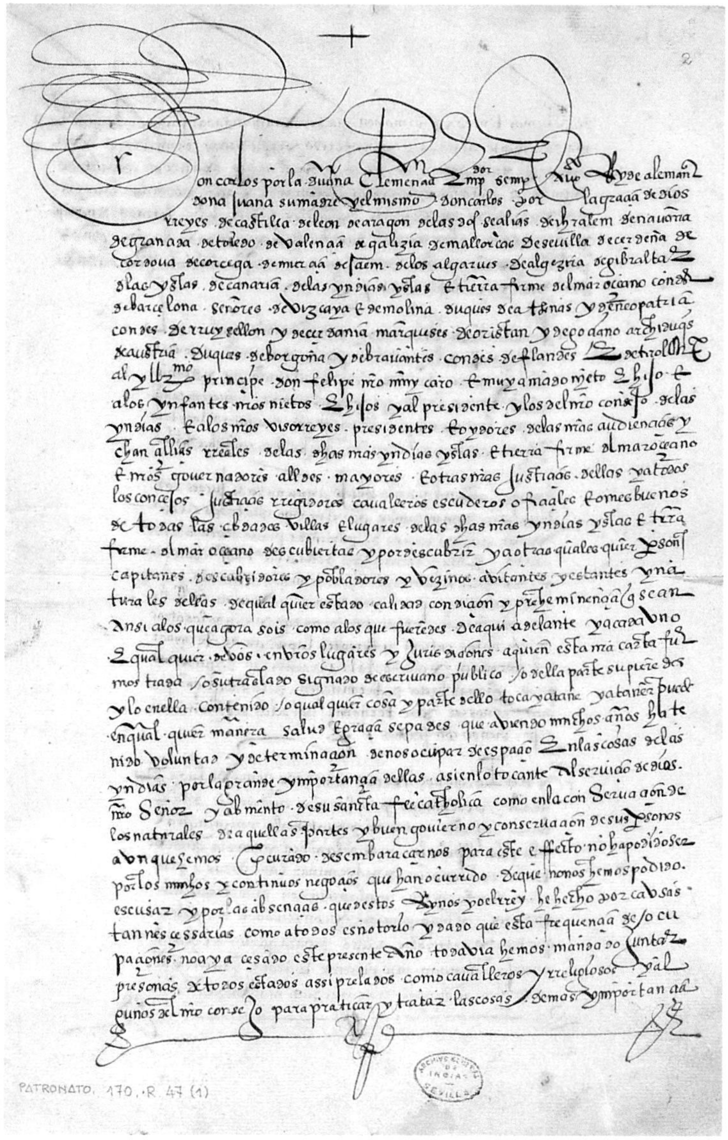

Diego Beltrán's appointment.

8 March 1523, Valladolid.
Royal provision issued by Charles V and Queen Joan appointing Doctor Diego Beltrán Councillor of the Indies.
Indiferente, 420, L. 9, fol. 91 v. to 92 r.

This was the first appointment of a salaried member of the Council of the Indies, although the earliest appointment is widely accepted to be that of its president on 1 August 1524.

The New Laws.
20 November 1542, Barcelona – 4 June 1543, Valladolid.

Royal provisions regulating procedures in the Council of the Indies and the Audiencias *for the rule and welfare of the Indians: 'New Laws' and 'Statutes of the Indies'. 15 fols., Patronato, 170, R. 47.*

Considered to be the first statutes of the Council of the Indies, most chapters actually deal with the Indians' welfare.

Hardly any provisions concerning the Council's organization and jurisdiction were issued in its early days. Instead, it was governed by statutes emanating from the Council of Castile. Similarly, it was not based anywhere in particular, but followed the Court and held its meetings in the president's house. From the outset, it had a judicial mandate as a civil and criminal appeals court and as the supreme administrative body for the New World, which entailed appointing governors and royal officials, the supervision, outfitting and preparation of fleets and legislation on the treatment of American Indians.

Concerned about the issue of protecting the natives, as well as the political unrest in the New World and the suspicion that irregularities were being committed in the Council itself, Charles V decided to pay the Council an official visit. The upshot of that visit was the drafting of what may be considered its first statutes—the so-called 'New Laws' of 1542. After an introduction in which the Emperor expresses his intention to personally take charge of affairs relating to the Indies, the laws run into a total of forty chapters covering the administrative duties of the Council (chapters 1 to 9), the *Audiencias*—the first institution exported to the Americas—and their jurisdiction (chapters 10 to 19), and the humane treatment of Indians (chapters 20 to 40), which the Council was urged to enforce.

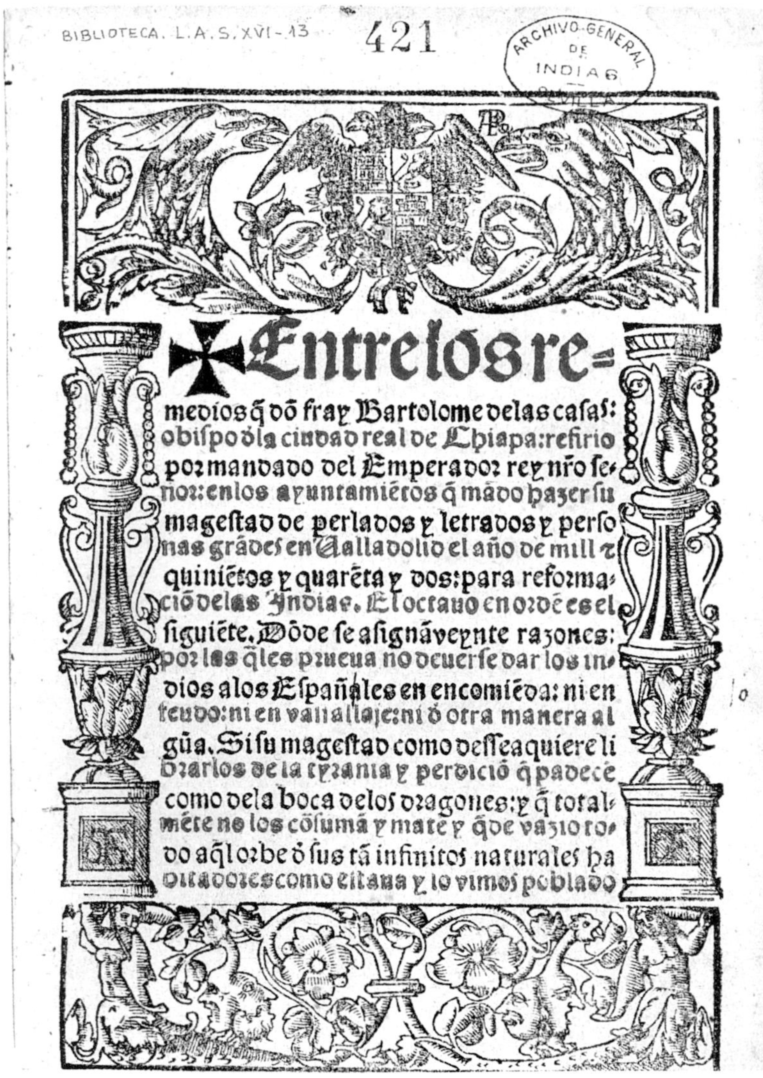

BIBLIOTECA. L.A.S. XVI-13 421

ARCHIVO GENERAL DE INDIAS

Entre los remedios q̃ dõ fray Bartolome delas casas: obispo dla ciudad real de Chiapa: refirio por mandado del Emperador rey nr̃o señor: enlos ayuntamiẽtos q̃ mãdo hazer su magestad de perlados y letrados y personas grãdes en Valladolid el año de mill y quiniẽtos y quarẽta y dos: para reformaciõ delas Indias. El octauo en ordẽ es el siguiẽte. Dõde se asignã veynte razones: por las q̃les prueua no deuerse dar los indios alos Españoles en encomiẽda: ni en feudo: ni en vassallaje: ni d otra manera alguna. Si su magestad como dessea quiere librarlos dela tyrania y perdiciõ q̃ padecẽ como dela boca delos dragones: y q̃ totalmẽte no los cõsumã y maten y q̃de vazio todo aq̃l orbe d sus tã infinitos naturales habitadores como estaua y lo vimos poblado

Fray Bartolomé de las Casas: Reforma de las Indias.

CASAS, Bartolomé de las (O.P.)
'One of the reform measures which Fray Bartolomé de las Casas, bishop of the royal city of Chiapas, instituted on behalf of the emperor... for the purpose of reform in the Indies.'
Seville: Jacome Cromberger, 1552.
54 fols., 4to.
Cover with border and imperial coat-of-arms.
Biblioteca, L.A., S. XVI–13.

Non-observance of the New Laws aroused vehement protest by Fray Bartolomé de las Casas. In this book, he sets out twenty-two reasons why Indians should not be assigned to Spanish settlers as part of the encomienda *grant of labor and tribute.*

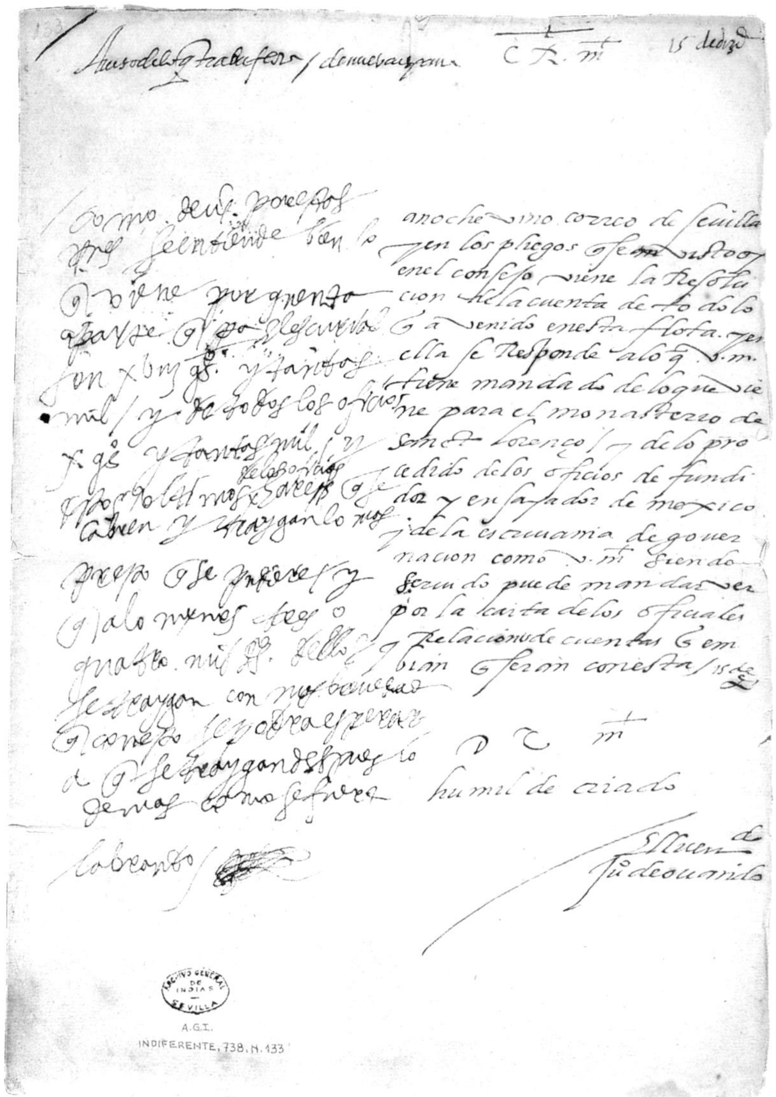

A.G.I.
INDIFERENTE, 738, N. 133

Juan de Ovando: President of the Council of the Indies.

[15 December 1574, Madrid]
Autograph letter from Juan de Ovando, President of the Council of the Indies, to H.M., rendering account of the funds transported by the fleet of New Spain, part of which have been assigned to the monastery of El Escorial.
In the margin, an autograph resolution signed by Philip II ordering consignment of the funds to be expedited.
2 fols.
Indiferente, 738, no. 133.

The lawyer, Juan de Ovando, was appointed President of the Council of the Indies on 28 August 1571, after having made his second visit to the same. He was instrumental in drawing up the Council's statutes of 1571, the first genuine laws regulating the body's composition and procedures.

Statutes regulating the 'Description of the Indies'.

3 July 1573, San Lorenzo el Real. Royal warrant, issued by Philip II, setting out laws and statutes in 135 chapters concerning the compilation, description and listing of all matters pertaining to the Indies.
Indiferente, 427, L. 29, fol. 5 v. to 66 v.

These statutes, compiled on Ovando's initiative, like those of the Council in 1571, fulfilled the need to acquire greater knowledge of New World geography and history, 'so that those who govern there, both in temporal and spiritual matters, should fully understand and rule successfully...'.

This was the main reason for the New Laws—concern for the welfare of the indigenous population and prevention of their extinction. Maltreatment had been repeatedly denounced, particularly by the Church authorities, as part of a critical trend that had emerged almost at the start of the voyages of discovery. The Crown thus faced a dual issue of a legal and theological nature—the legitimacy of the conquest and the legal and social status of the New World Indians.

In this respect, it was the repercussions of a famous sermon by the Dominican friar, Fray Antonio de Montesinos, to the authorities of Hispaniola, reprimanding them for their harsh treatment of the Indians, that led Ferdinand the Catholic to promulgate the Laws of Burgos in 1512. Those were the first laws to dictate measures regarding the freedom of the Indians, regulation of their work and their conversion. The issue that then gained currency was justification for the conquest itself, the right to which was asserted by a papal donation and the heathenism of the indigenous cultures. In 1526, Charles V himself gave instructions concerning procedures for discovery and colonization. He ordered the Indians to be well treated, so that 'it may be accomplished with no offence to God, without death nor robbery of said Indians and without enslaving them, so that the desire to spread our faith among them be achieved without grieving our consciences.'

Thus, it was the laws of 1542 that settled the issue of the status of Indian subjects in the New World. Their enslavement was abolished, as was any covert form thereof, such as employing them in the personal service of the conquistadors. The laws fixed levies and tributes the Indians were obliged to pay in lieu of such services. Similarly, wars of conquest were banned. However, they did not abolish, but merely reformed, the system of *encomiendas*. However, non-observance of the measures—repeatedly denounced by Fray Bartolomé de las Casas—ended up undermining them.

As far as the Council was concerned, the laws dealt mainly with the issues of the administration of justice and liaison with *Audiencias* in the Indies. They likewise provided specific guidelines for ensuring the councillors' impartiality and honesty. Following the Emperor's visit, some of them were found guilty of corruption, including the aforementioned Dr. Beltrán.

However, the truly constituent statutes, which defined the status, authority and procedures of the Council of the Indies, were those promulgated by Philip II on 24 September 1571 after a second visit by the Council's future president, Juan de Ovando.

Twenty-seven years had passed since Charles V's visit and, in that time, the Council's jurisdiction and the corpus of Indies legislation had grown considerably. Ovando took on the task of compiling all laws passed up until that time and, with the assistance of his secretaries, Juan de Ledesma and Juan López de Velasco, examined all the Council's registers to piece together a code of laws arranged by subject—the so-called *Código Ovandino*. Although the undertaking was never completed, he did manage to draw up a new set of Council statutes, the most authoritative and definitive code in the Council's history.

The Council was formally composed of a president, a chancellor, eight councillors, an advocate, a judicial and an administrative notary, two recorders, two accountants and an *alguacil* (constable). There were also several wardens, a receiver and a chronicler–cartographer. The 122 chapters of the *Código Ovandino* deal mainly with the councillor's duties and their performance, urging correspondence to be expedited, a rigorous study of laws and secrecy in all dealings. The statutes specify the days on which different matters are to be dealt with and the times councillors should attend, voting procedures and the manner in which dossiers should be processed, giving instructions designed to prevent favoritism. Lastly, they detail the functions of each councillor, with special emphasis on the newly created posts—those of secretary and chronicler–cartographer.

Like the New Laws, these statutes considered the main task of colonization to be the conversion and satisfactory treatment of the Indians. They also stress that, in order to administer the New World properly, the Council should have at its disposal all available information on the area's history and geography. It was precisely on Ovando's initiative that two surveys were conducted to facilitate the Council's acquisition of knowledge and organization of the Indies: a 'Survey concerning the geographical description', which all authorities in the New World were obliged to complete, and an 'Order that should prevail in all new discoveries, settlements and processes of pacification'.

The statutes of 1571 remained in force for over forty years, well into the reign of Philip IV. The most noteworthy feature of that period was the creation of a *Junta de Guerra* (War Council), *Junta de Hacienda* (Treasury Board) and *Cámara de Indias* (Chamber of the Indies).

The *Juntas* were special assemblies convened regularly during the first half of the 16th century to tackle particularly serious matters. On such occasions, in addition to members of the Council of the Indies, meetings were also attended by outside experts, theologians and members of other Councils in order to provide the monarch with the best possible advice. The assemblies held included those of Valladolid, in 1550, which again dealt with the administration and treatment of the Indians, and the *Junta Magna* of 1568, which focused on Church matters in the Indies and the *encomiendas*.

Philip II's meticulousness led to the assemblies being convened more and more frequently so that, in some instances, they became permanent institutions. Such was the case with the *Junta de Guerra de Indias*. It was actually prompted by another assembly, the *Junta de Fortificación de Puerto Rico,* called in 1583 to debate repeated protests by the governor of the island about frequent attacks by privateers. In effect, Spain's ongoing disputes with Holland, France and England throughout the 16th and 17th century encouraged the latter to harass both Spanish fleets and possessions by hiring privateers, and to attempt to set up permanent colonies in areas either unoccupied or poorly defended by Spain. In this respect, they lost the islands of Curaçao to the Dutch in 1634 and Jamaica to the English in 1655, while the French secured a foothold on Tortuga Island and the west coast of Hispaniola where they set up large pirate bases. By the last thirty years of the 17th century, the three great rivals of the Spanish empire had established a lasting presence in the Caribbean, with mainland settlements running from Belize, on the Yucatán coastline and Nicaragua, to Guayana or Surinam in South America.

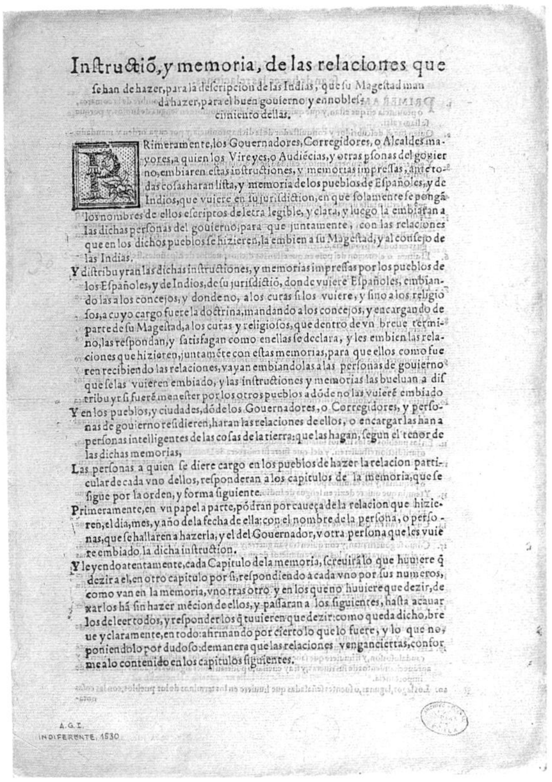

Inſtructiõ, y memoria, de las relaciones que ſe han de hazer, para la deſcripcion de las Indias, que ſu Mageſtad man da hazer, para el buen gouierno y ennobleſcimiento dellas.

PRimeramente, los Gouernadores, Corregidores, o Alcaldes mayores, a quien los Vireyes, o Audiẽcias, y otras pſonas del gouierno, embiaren eſtas inſtructiones, y memorias impreſſas, ante todas coſas haran liſta, y memoria de los pueblos de Eſpañoles, y de Indios, que vuiere en ſu juriſdiction, en que ſolamente ſe põgã los nombres de ellos eſcriptos de letra legible, y clara, y luego la embiarãn a las dichas perſonas del gouierno, para que juntamente, con las relaciones que en los dichos pueblos ſe hizieren, la embien a ſu Mageſtad, y al conſejo de las Indias.

Y diſtribuyran las dichas inſtructiones, y memorias impreſſas por los pueblos de los Eſpañoles, y de Indios, de ſu juriſdictiõ, donde vuiere Eſpañoles, embiandolas a los concejos, y donde no, a los curas ſi los vuiere, y ſino a los religioſos, a cuyo cargo fuere la doctrina, mandando a los concejos, y encargando de parte de ſu Mageſtad, a los curas y religioſos, que dentro de vn breue termino, las reſpondan, y ſatisfagan como en ellas ſe declara, y les embien las relaciones que hizieren, juntamẽte con eſtas memorias, para que ellos como fueren recibiendo las relaciones, vayan embiandolas a las perſonas de gouierno que ſe las vuieren embiado, y las inſtructiones y memorias las bueluan a diſtribuyr ſi fuerẽ meneſter por los otros pueblos a dõde no las vuierẽ embiado.

Y en los pueblos, y ciudades, dõde los Gouernadores, o Corregidores, y perſonas de gouierno reſidieren, haran las relaciones de ellos, o encargar las han a perſonas intelligentes de las coſas de la tierra: que las hagan, ſegun el tenor de las dichas memorias,

Las perſonas a quien ſe diere cargo en los pueblos de hazer la relacion particular de cada vno dellos, reſponderan a los capitulos de la memoria, que ſe ſigue por la orden, y forma ſiguiente.

Primeramente, en vn papel a parte, põdran por caueça de la relacion que hizieren, el dia, mes, y año de la fecha de ella: con el nombre de la perſona, o perſonas, que ſe hallaren a hazerla, y el del Gouernador, v otra perſona que les vuiere embiado la dicha inſtruction.

Y leyendo atentamente, cada Capitulo de la memoria, ſcreuirã lo que huuiere q̃ dezir a el, en otro capitulo por ſi, reſpondiendo a cada vno por ſus numeros, como van en la memoria, vno tras otro. y en los que no huuiere que dezir, dexarlos hã ſin hazer mẽcion de ellos, y paſſaran a los ſiguientes, haſta acauar los de leer todos, y reſponder los q̃ tuuieren que dezir: como queda dicho, breue y claramente, en todo: afirmando por cierto lo que lo fuere, y lo que no, poniendolo por dudoſo: de manera que las relaciones vengan ciertas, conforme a lo contenido en los capitulos ſiguientes.

A.G.I.
INDIFERENTE, 1530

'Instructions for the geographical description of the Indies'.

[25 May 1577]
'Survey and instructions on the procedures befitting a description of the Indies which His Majesty has ordered for the proper government and enhancement of the same.'
2 fols.
Indiferente, 1530.

The survey consisted of a questionnaire running into fifty chapters concerning the origins of a province or city, the conquistador or discoverer of the same, the pre-Hispanic settlement it belonged to, its topography, climate, crops and mines, population and administrative regime, in addition to details of local ports, coastlines and ecclesiastical status. This survey, which was sent to authorities in the Indies to be completed, was an upshot of the statutes issued by Philip II in 1573 for the purpose of drawing up a 'Description of the Indies'.

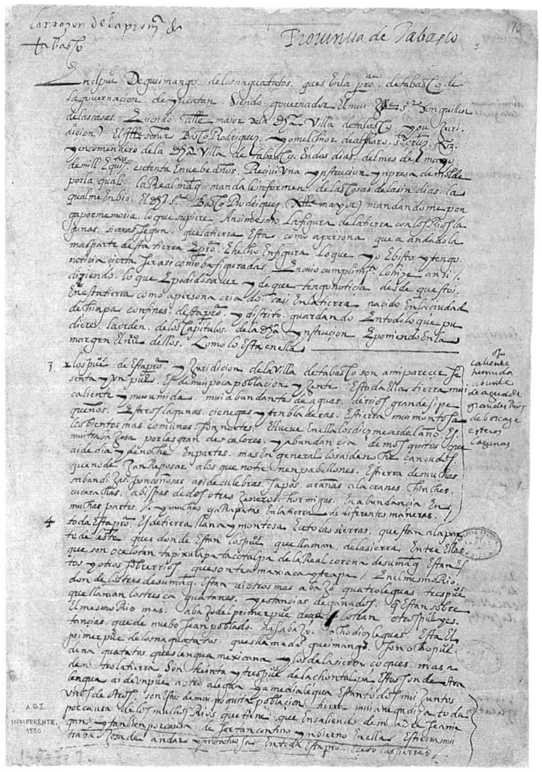

Provincia de Tabasco

A.G.I.
INDIFERENTE, 1530

Survey of the province of Tabasco.

2 May 1579, Gueimango de los Naguatatos.
Geographical survey of the province of Tabasco conducted on the orders of Guillén de las Casas, governor and captain general of the provinces of Yucatán, Cozumel and Tabasco, in fulfillment of Philip II's 'Instruction', issued in 1573 for the purpose of making a description of the Indies, by Melchor de Alfaro Santa Cruz, landowner in the town of Tabasco.
2 fols.
Indiferente, 1530.

The left-hand margin of the survey features numbers which correspond to the chapters in Philip II's 'Instruction'. The right-hand margin shows the Council's call for quality lands: '... with abundant water, large rivers, woods, marshes and lakes'.

The task of the *Junta de Hacienda de Indias,* which met from 1595 onwards, was to seek ways of increasing revenues from possessions in the Indies. Both *Juntas*—those of *Hacienda* and *Guerra*—were formally instituted in 1600, although the former was short-lived, being dissolved in 1604. The *Junta de Guerra* became a permanent institution. Its mandate covered military affairs, shipping and war, personnel and privileges, the funding of the Indies defense fleets, troop provisions and deployment, fortifications and war trials. It was composed of the president of the Council of the Indies, four councillors from the *Consejo de Guerra* and four Indies councillors. As of 1636, its activity was regulated by autonomous statutes.

A royal warrant of 25 August 1600, whereby both *Juntas* were formally instated, also provided for the foundation of a Chamber of the Indies, similar to an existing one in the Council of Castile, for 'dealing with and consulting me about clerical and lay provisions required for the sound spiritual and temporal government of the Indies'.

Its inception met the need for personal accountability when putting forward nominees for senior and honorary posts in the Indies, thus averting the dissent aroused by such proposals and by the awarding of privileges in the Council. The historian, Ernest Schäffer, also points to a maneuver by the Duke of Lerma, a royal protégé, to gain more control of appointments and awards, which was easier to achieve over the smaller number of Chamber members than over the whole Council. The former comprised the president, three councillors and the Council secretaries. They met twice a week and their organization and pay structure were modelled on those of the Chamber of Castile.

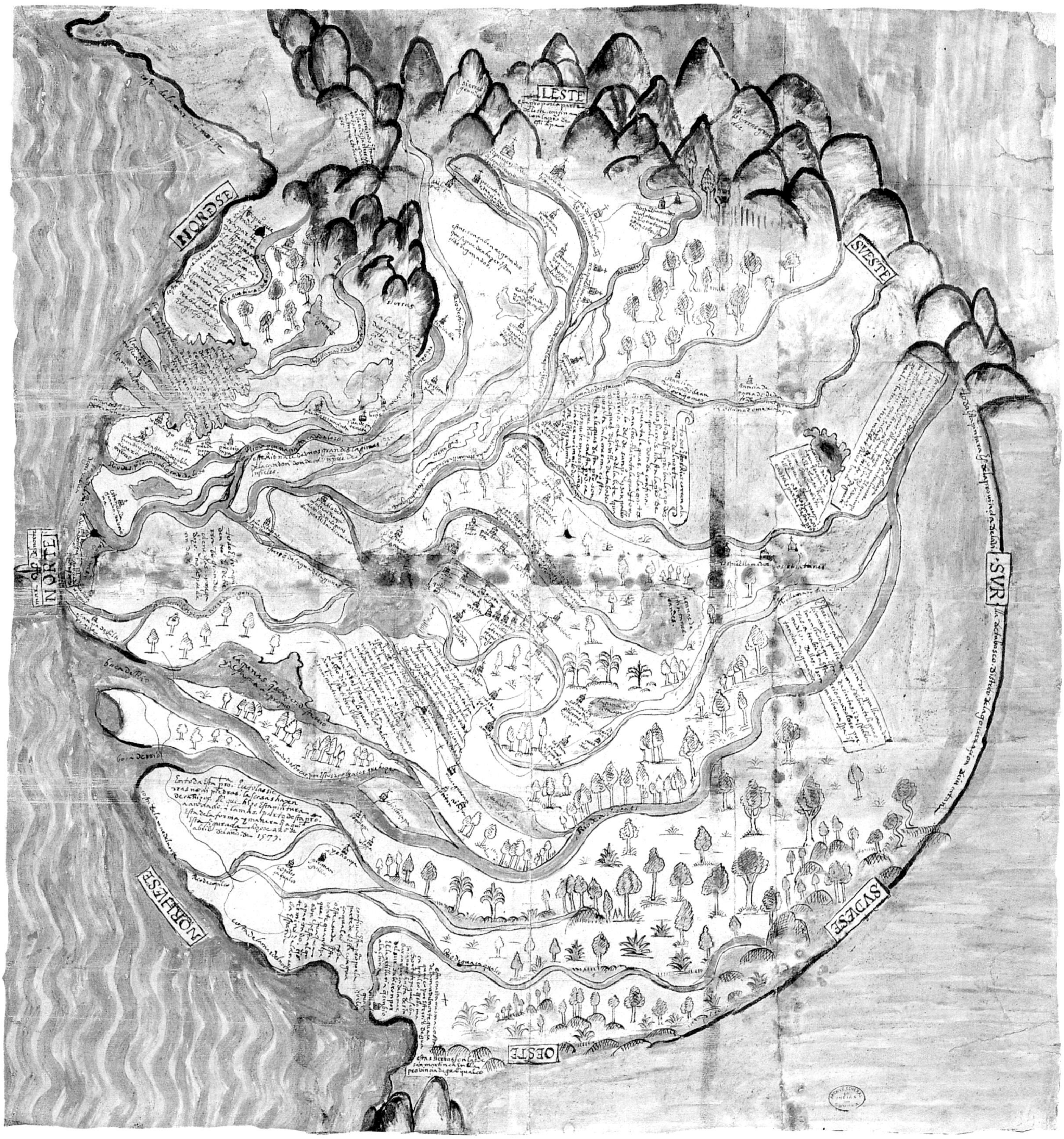

Map of the province of Tabasco.

[1579]
600 x 570 mm.
MP. México, 14.

Together with the text on the previous page, this forms part of a volume bound in parchment entitled Relaciones de la Provincia de Yucatán.

Above
Sailing manual: the Philippines.

1564–1565.
Sailing manuals kept by the pilots Esteban Rodríguez, Jaime Martínez and Diego Martín, members of the Philippine expedition under the command of Miguel López de Legazpi.
27 fols. in 4to & 6 blanks.

The Council statutes of 1571 stipulated that all sailing manuals, maps and books that might provide further knowledge of those remote lands be kept in the Archive. The above pages show drawings of the islands of Barbuda and of The Thieves (MP. Filipinas, 1 & 2).

Opposite
Description of the New World: Ortelius

ORTELIUS, Abraham.
'Theatrum orbis terrarum', by Abraham Ortelius, cartographer of His Majesty the King, with his declarations translated from Latin.
Antwerp, Christophe Plantin, 1588.
8 fols., 99 maps, with text. MS cover with engraving on back cover. Maps colored by hand, most of them engraved by Franz Hogerberg.
Biblioteca, L.A., S. XVI–1.

The Flemish cartographer, Abraham Ortelius, enjoyed great prestige in his time and was appointed royal cosmographer to Philip II in 1575. Most of his endeavors went into this great work, which was regarded as the first modern atlas and made him famous. Cristophe Plantin, a personal friend of Ortelius', printed the first edition of the atlas in 1579. The map reproduced on the following page, entitled 'Americae sive novi orbis Nova descriptio', gives us an idea of what the Council of the Indies imagined the New World to be like.

Just a few years after its inception, the Chamber of the Indies was abolished by a royal decree of 16 March 1609. It was reinstated in 1644 and continued to operate throughout most of the 17th century, when its powers were augmented after it was authorized to award Castilian titles. After a second dissolution in 1701, as part of measures designed to cut back on the number of State ministers and functionaries, it was again reinstated in 1721 on a lasting basis. Bourbon reforms did, however, curtail its powers to a large extent, as was the case with the Council.

The Council, for its part, was given new statutes in 1636. They were a revised version of the 1571 statutes and included all the royal orders that had been promulgated in the interim.

The basic text of 1571 was extended to 245 chapters, and the introduction makes mention of a project having been implemented for the purpose of compiling the Laws of the Indies. Thereafter, the chapters deal with the Council's powers and procedures, in addition to those of its members. Emphasis is laid on the secretarial posts in New Spain and Peru—and on the Audit Office, which had only been outlined in 1571 and now consisted of four members. In contrast, the number of

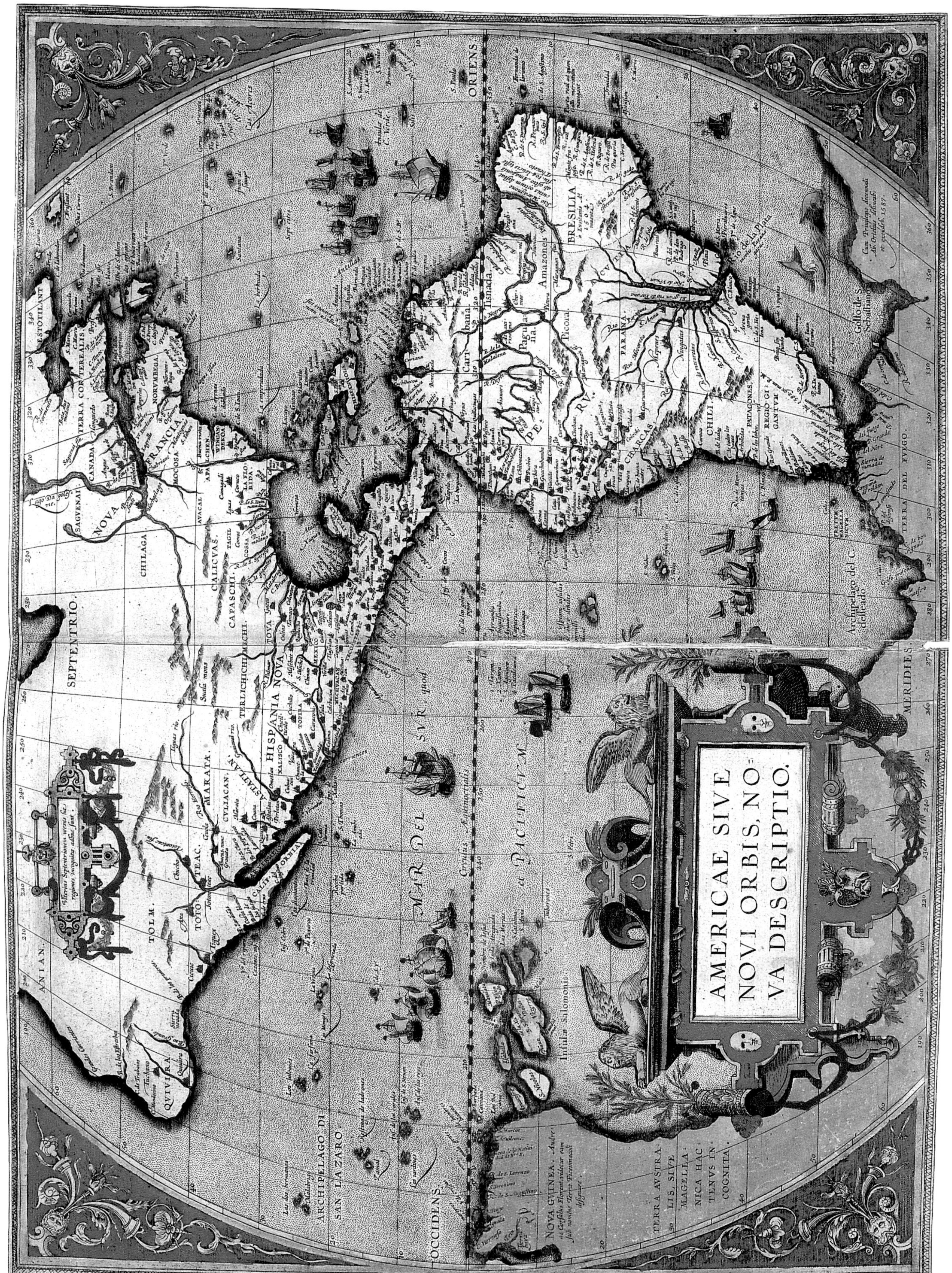
AMERICAE SIVE NOVI ORBIS, NOVA DESCRIPTIO.
SEPTENTRIO.
MERIDIES.
ORIENS.
OCCIDENS.
HISPANIA NOVA
BRESILIA
MAR DEL SVR
TERRA DEL FVEGO
ARCHIPELAGO DI SAN LAZARO
NOVA GVINEA
Insulae Salomonis
ANIAN
QVIVIRA
CHILI
PERV

古今形勝之圖

OPPOSITE
Map of China.

[1555]
Historical map of China and some neighboring islands.
1,030 x 928 mm. on 1,138 x 1,008 mm.
MP. Filipinas, 5.

Together with 'Report of the content of the chart of the Chinese to be sent to His Majesty', drawn up with the aid of Chinese interpreters and an Augustinian friar. Both the map and the report were sent to the king by the governor of the Philippines, Guido de Lavezaris, with a covering letter, on 30 July 1574. The map features historical descriptions in Chinese and later annotations in Spanish which are transcriptions of place-names and historical notes.

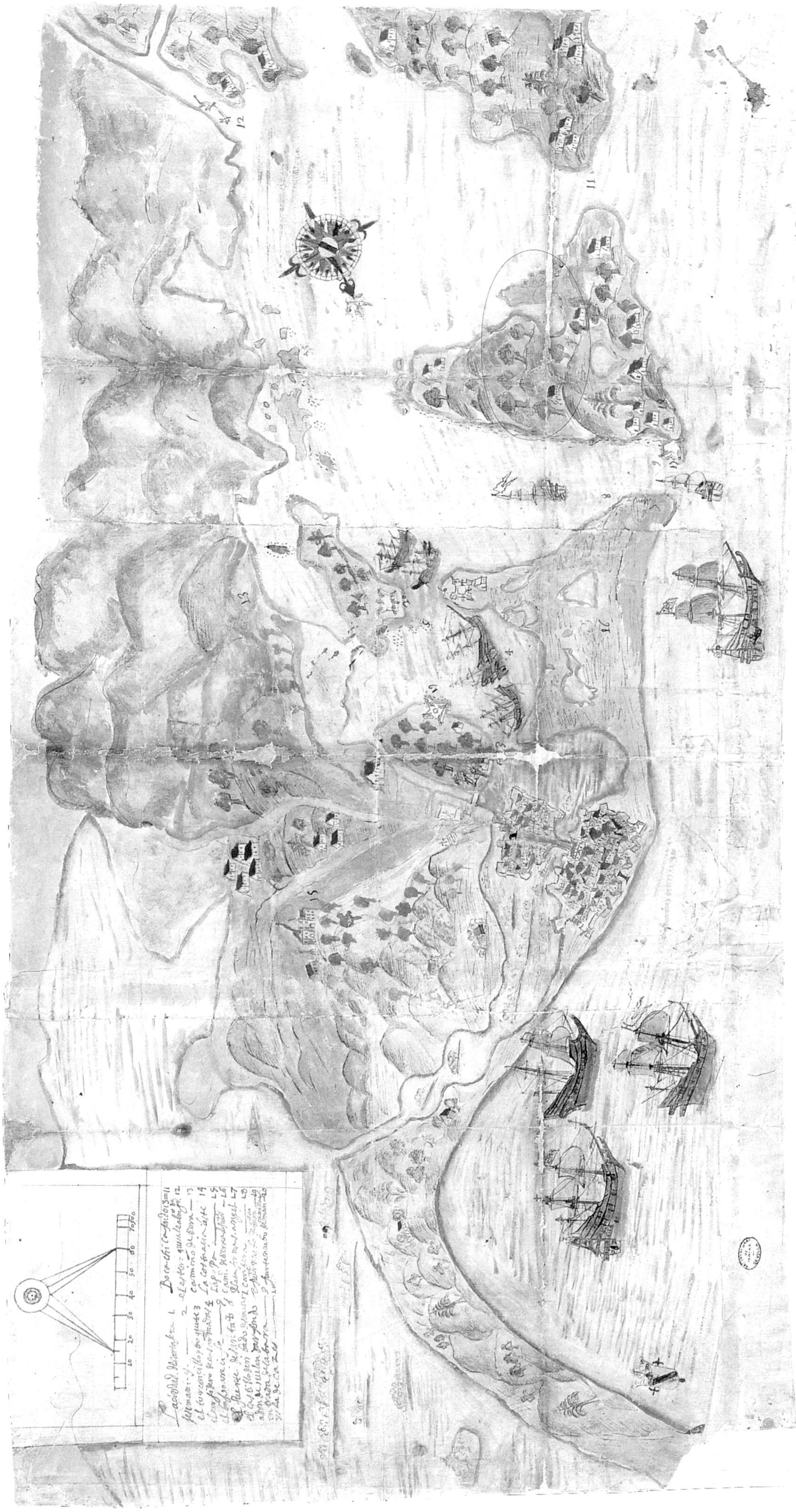

RIGHT
Plan of Cartagena de Indias.

[1628]
Plan of the city of Cartagena de Indias and its environs.
450 x 870 mm.
MP. Panamá, 45.

The plan shows the city's fortifications, some fifty years after Drake's attack, the Santangel platform at the harbor mouth and the castle of Santa Cruz on the Indio bluff. Numbers 19 & 20 indicate 'the new forts of Manzanillo and Manga'.

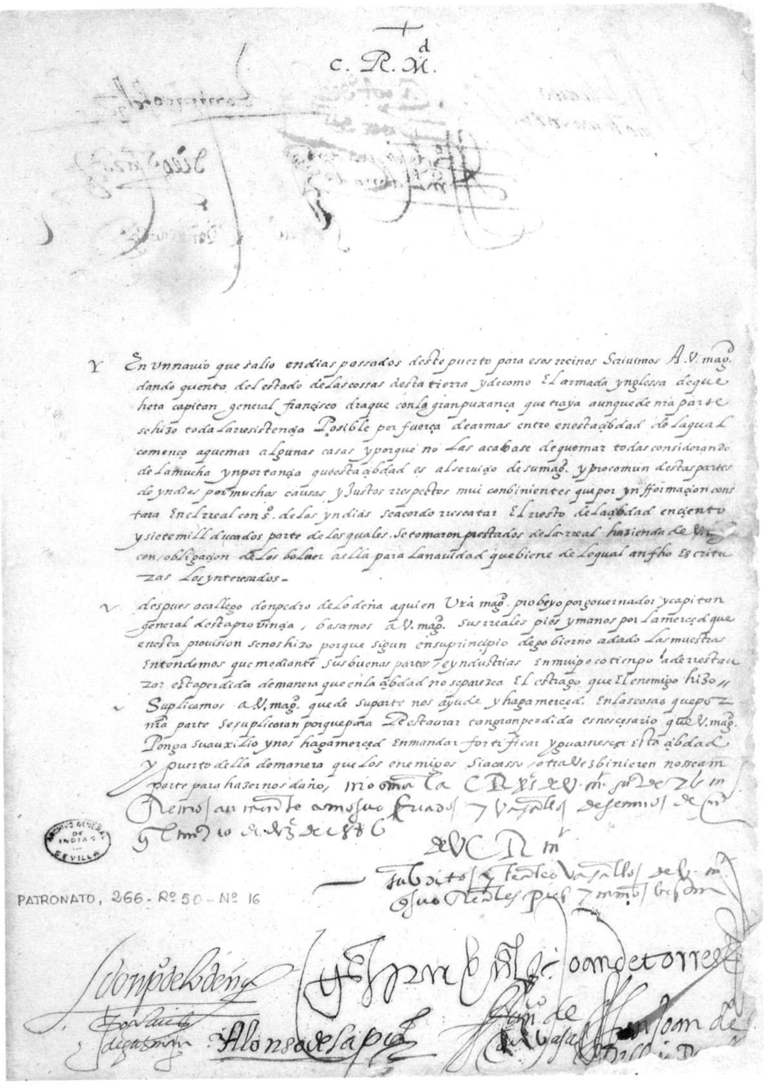
C. R. M.[d]

PATRONATO, 266 - Rº 50 - Nº 16

Drake's assault on Cartagena.

10 December 1586, Cartagena.
Letter from the Cartagena de Indias council reporting an attack by the English privateer, Francis Drake, the damage sustained and the decision taken by the council and the governor to pay a ransom of 107,000 ducats to avoid the city's total destruction.
On the back is a note from the Council: '... let it be attached to the other papers and taken to the Junta de Puerto Rico'.
2 fols.
Patronato, 266, r. 50, no. 16.

Sir Francis Drake was the most notorious English privateer of the 16th century. In 1585, he mounted an expedition to seize those key points in the Caribbean that were poorly fortified. Having conquered Santo Domingo, Drake appeared off the Cartagena coastline on Ash Wednesday, 19 February 1586, with twenty-three vessels and over a thousand men. The city fell to him with only token resistance. The frequency of pirate attacks in the Antilles and on the mainland led to an assembly in 1583 known as the Junta de Fortificación de Puerto Rico, *which later gave rise to the* Junta Permanente de Guerra.

notaries was reduced to one and he was assigned to the Justice Division. The text also draws attention to the positions of chief chronicler and cartographer of the Indies. It likewise provides for an archive to be housed in the Council itself, for which purpose an archive councillor or commissioner would be appointed. He was to keep the keys to the archive and be assisted by an official archiver or librarian. The archive was designed to hold the sailing guides, maps, books and papers concerning the Indies and everything which, in the incumbent councillor's view, ought to be purchased to broaden existing knowledge of those lands.

Those statutes, together with others pertaining to the *Junta de Guerra,* were to be inserted in the *Recopilación de Leyes de Indias* (Codification of Laws of the Indies) which was finally published in 1680.

The Council did not undergo any major changes until the end of the Habsburg dynasty. The purpose of the 1677, 1687 and 1691 reform decrees under Charles II was to reduce expenditures and the large number of officials and curb the abuse and corruption in the Council, including the sale of positions, which had serious consequences.

OPPOSITE: *The defense of the Indies: San Juan de Ulúa.*

27 January 1590, San Juan de Ulúa.
'Perspective view of the shelter, fort and settlement of San Juan de Ulúa'.
By Juan Bautista Antonelli.
410 x 550 mm.
MP., México, 36.

Fortification of the island of San Juan de Ulúa, a first line of defense for Veracruz, was undertaken repeatedly after the attack by the English privateer, Hawkins, in 1568. The Italian engineer, Giovanni Bautista Antonelli, was commissioned to design the fortifications and draw up a survey for fortifying the whole coastline, indicating the spots which he considered suitable for building forts. He made four voyages to the Americas between 1581 and 1599 and also designed forts at key points in the Caribbean: El Morro in Havana, Cartagena, El Morro in Puerto Rico, Portobelo and others.

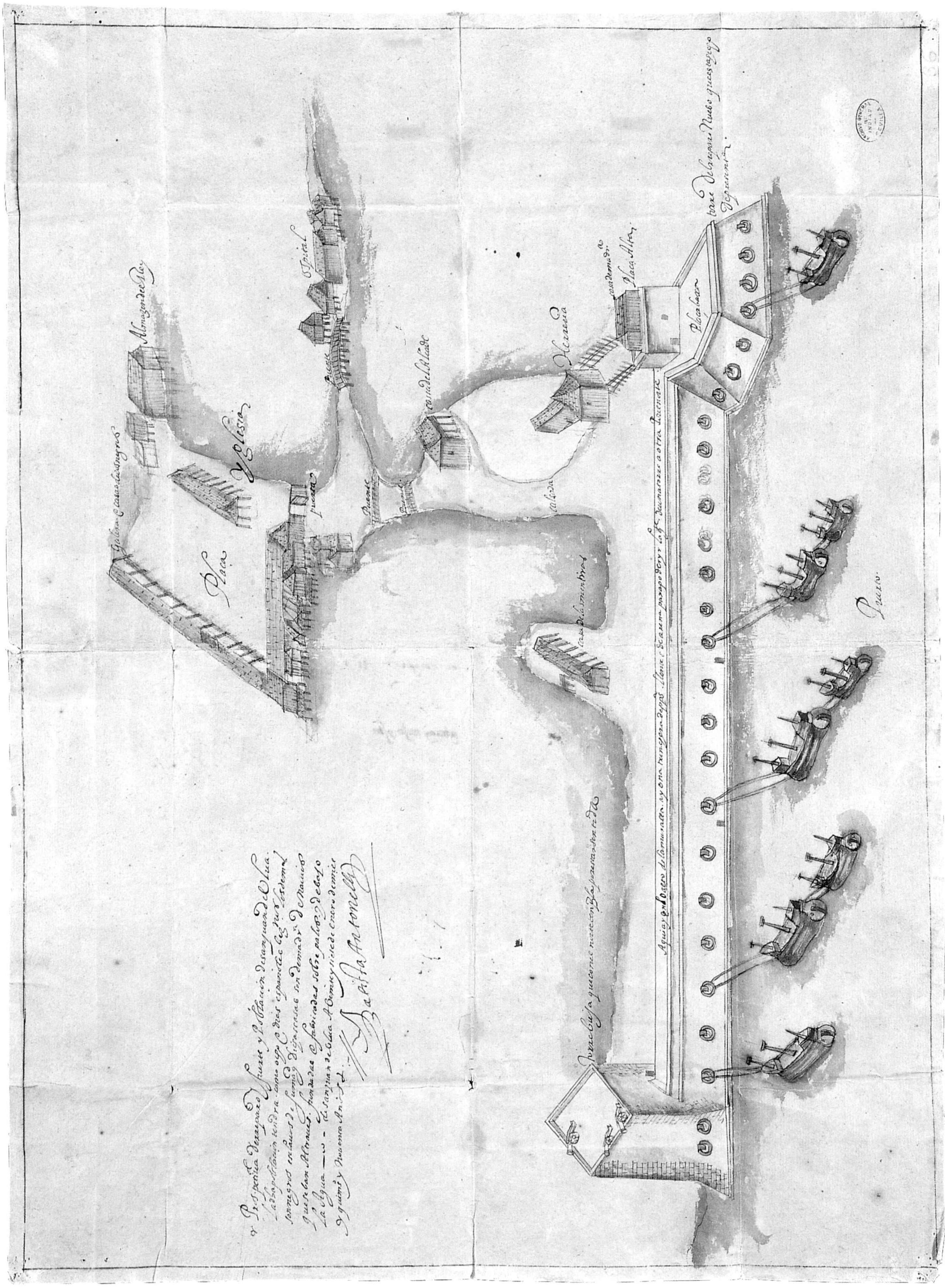

The ascent of the Bourbon dynasty led to marked changes in the Council. Decrees dating from 1714, 1717 and 1754 provided for the creation of Secretariats of State, Shipping and the Indies. The Council was relieved of its 'governmental, financial and providential' duties which were thereafter to be performed exclusively by the aforementioned secretariats or ministries. The latter were likewise empowered to appoint councillors of the Indies and the higher offices in the Americas. Other powers wrested from the Council related to the Royal Treasury, war, commerce and shipping. It was thus reduced to a an advisory body and supreme court for justice in the Indies.

Despite this, during the 18th century the number of councillors was increased on several occasions. In 1760, it had eight official and four unofficial councillors. A decree of 29 July 1773 declared the Council to be the highest rung in the civil service's chain of command, a position until then reserved for the Council of Castile, and the incumbents in such offices were entitled to the same salaries, prerogatives and exemptions as similar functionaries in the Council of Castile. Three years later, the Council was remodelled and the number of civil servants increased. It was reorganized into three permanent divisions, two executive and one judicial. As was the case with other functionaries and ministers in the Bourbon administration, its members were expected to be more highly specialized. Indeed, during that period, many councillors were highly experienced in colonial affairs. Thus, the ministers Antonio de Echavarri and Domingo Trespalacios y Escandón had served in *Audiencias* in New Spain, while José de Gálvez had held the offices of Inspector General of Mexico, Governor of the Council and Minister of the Indies.

The end of the century saw a resurgence of the Council. It became more active in administrative affairs in the Indies and eventually dealt exclusively with such matters after the demise of the *Casa de la Contratación* in 1790 and the disappearance of the *Secretaría Universal de Indias* in 1787.

During the 19th century and up until its final dissolution, the Council was abolished and reinstated several times on account of political upheaval. It was disbanded by the *Junta Central* in 1809 and the *Cortes de Cádiz* in 1812, when all consultative bodies were assimilated into the State Council. The Council of the Indies was reinstated with the return of Ferdinand VII on 2 July 1814. It again disappeared during the 'constitutional triennium' and was definitively dissolved by royal decree on 24 March 1834, when all other Councils were likewise dismantled and a Supreme Tribunal of Spain and the Indies established to deal with all matters of civil jurisdiction. The Royal Council of Spain and the Indies was instituted as the official consultative body, divided into seven sections, to advise ministers in important departmental matters.

OPPOSITE, ABOVE
Foreign occupation: Tortuga Island.

[1628]
Plan of Tortuga Island and its Dutch settlements.
310 x 430 mm.
MP. Venezuela, 24.

Despite the defense measures implemented in the Indies, involving both the founding of the Junta de Guerra *and the fortification of strategic points, the Spanish were unable to prevent privateers in the service of foreign powers from ravaging Spanish fleets and possessions and even setting up colonies in unoccupied or poorly defended areas. This plan shows the landing by Benito Arias Montano, the governor of Cumaná, and his subsequent assault on Dutch forts in an attempt to dislodge the pirates.*

OPPOSITE, BELOW
Foreign occupation: Jamaica.

[1658]
Plan of Santa Ana harbor on the island of Jamaica.
354 x 505 mm.
MP. Santo Domingo, 59.

Jamaica was occupied by the English squadron of Admiral William Penn after a failed assault on Santo Domingo in 1655. Despite resistance on the island, the invasion was brought to a successful completion by diplomacy. Jamaica then became the center of English possessions in the Indies and an excellent base for piracy and smuggling.

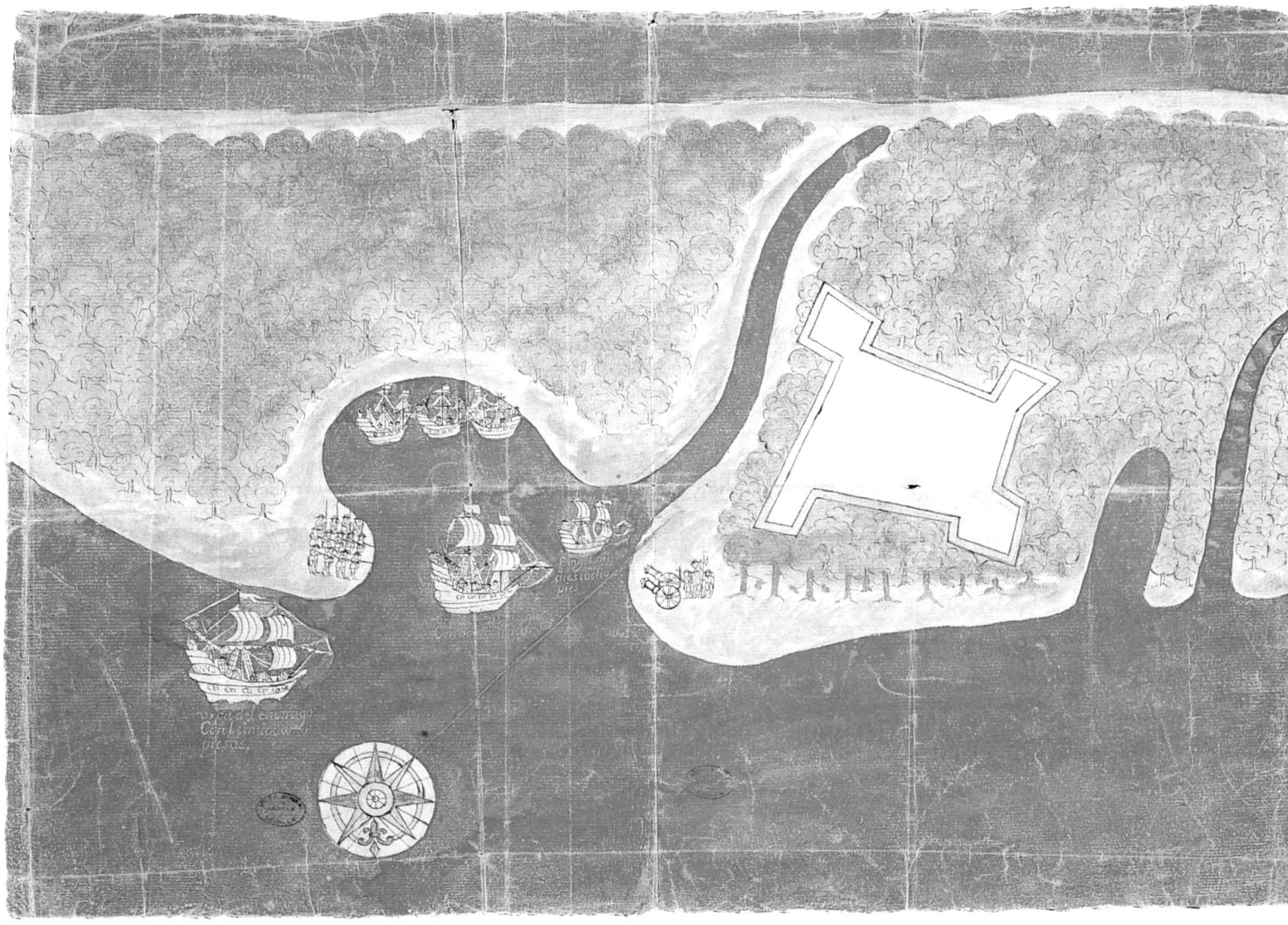

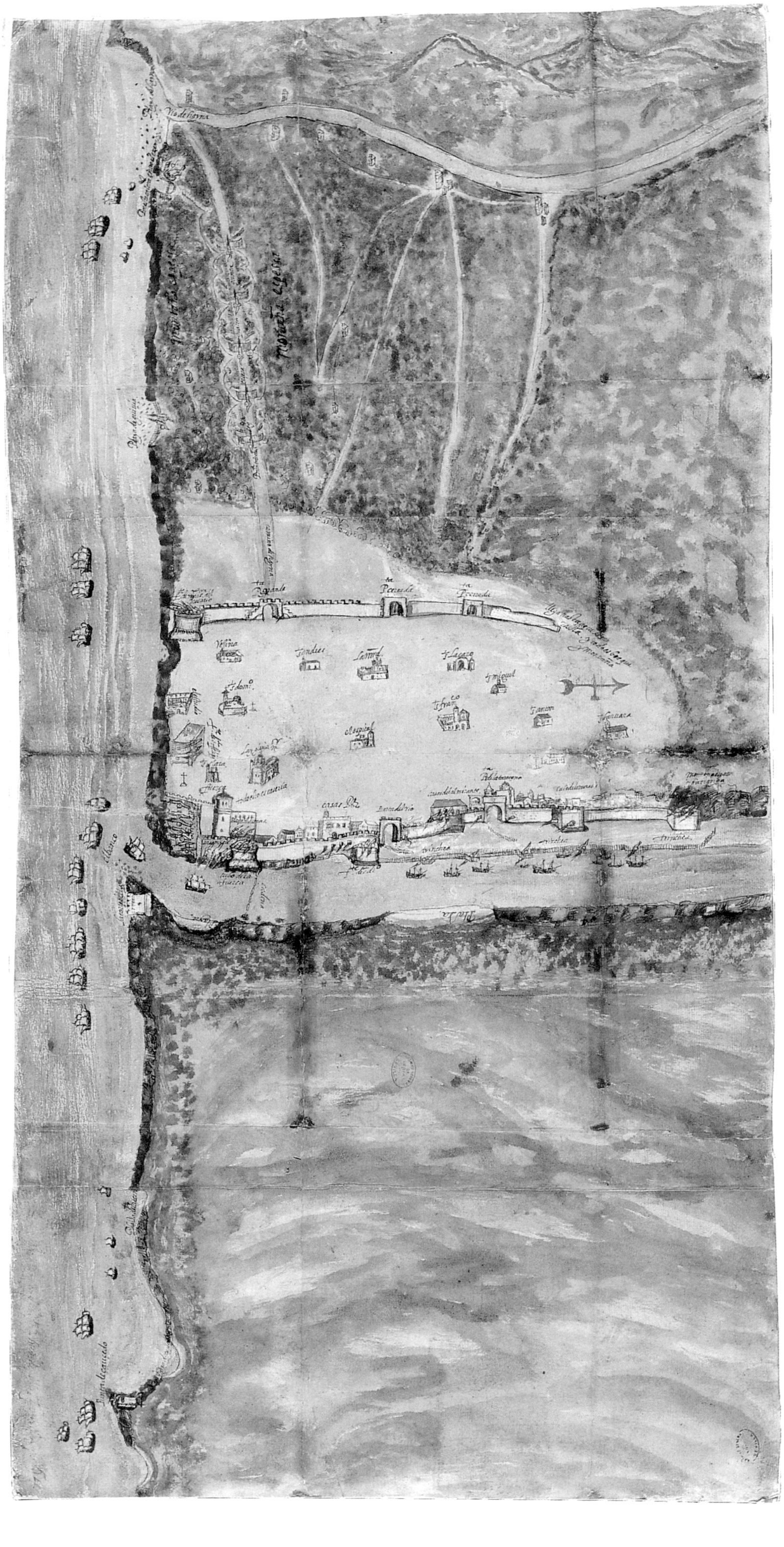

LEFT
The defense of the Indies: Santo Domingo.

1619
Plan of the defenses in the city of Santo Domingo and its environs.
415 x 827 mm.
MP. Santo Domingo, 29.

Sent by the governor, Diego Gómez de Sandoval, with an accompanying letter dated 8 February 1619 and a report on the Junta de Guerra *held there. The wall is shown in an unfinished elevation.*

OPPOSITE
Foreign occupation: Sacramento.

1681.
Plan of the San Gabriel fort, on Río de la Plata, which the Spanish wrested from the Portuguese.
Below: 'D. Bernardo Antonio Meza, 1681'.
940 x 590 mm.
MP. Buenos Aires, 27.

Like other nations, Portugal took advantage of Spain's decline in the late-17th century to claim sovereignty over the territories situated north of the Río de la Plata. Thus, in 1680, the Portuguese colony of Sacramento was founded on a spot opposite Buenos Aires, on the so-called Banda Oriental *or East Bank. Although the Spanish conquered Sacramento a year later, it was returned to Portugal by diplomatic means. It then became a major haven for smugglers and posed a threat to the Spanish possessions further south. The issue was not settled until a century later.*

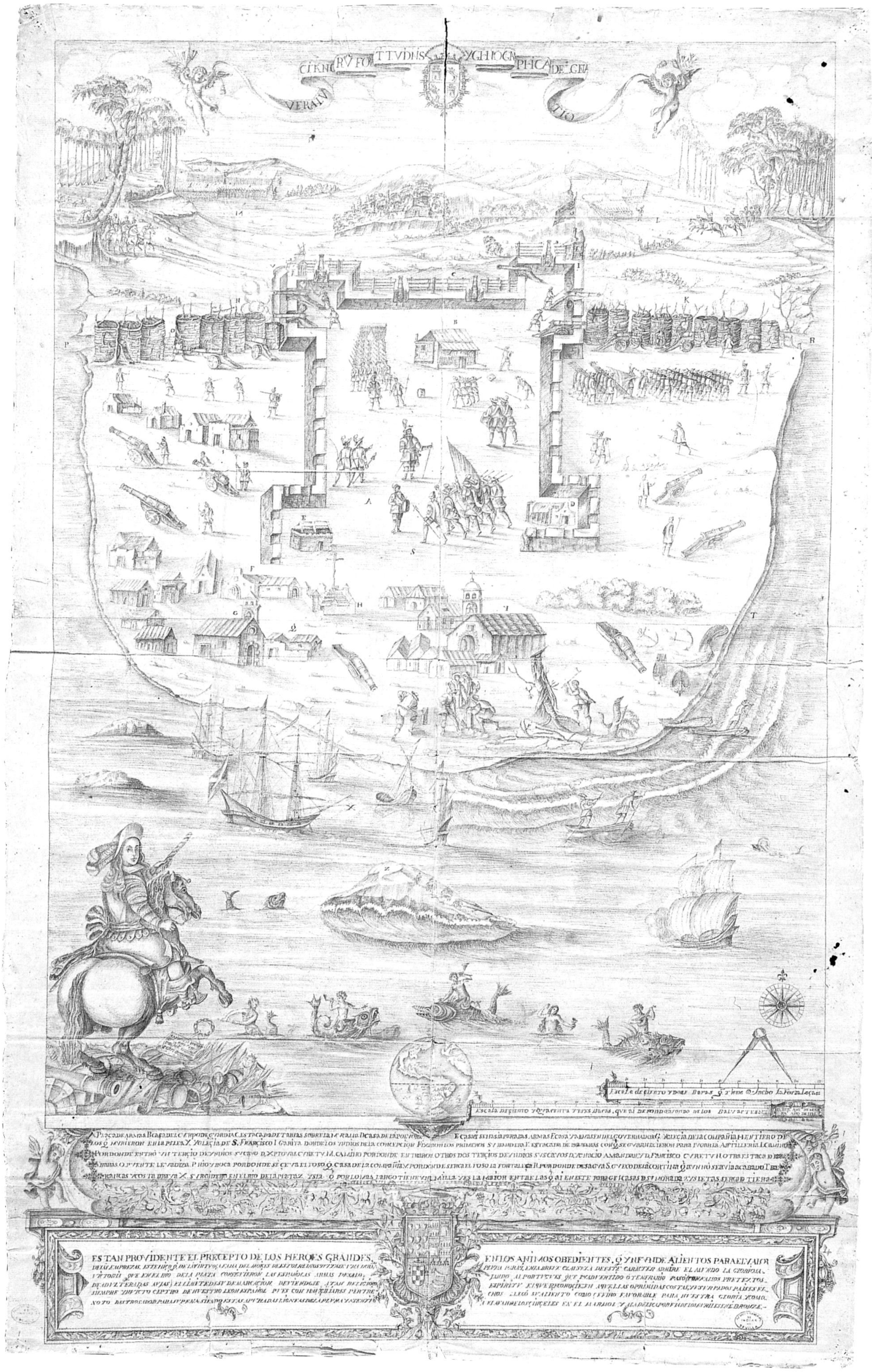
ES TAN PROVIDENTE EL PRECEPTO DE LOS HEROES GRANDES

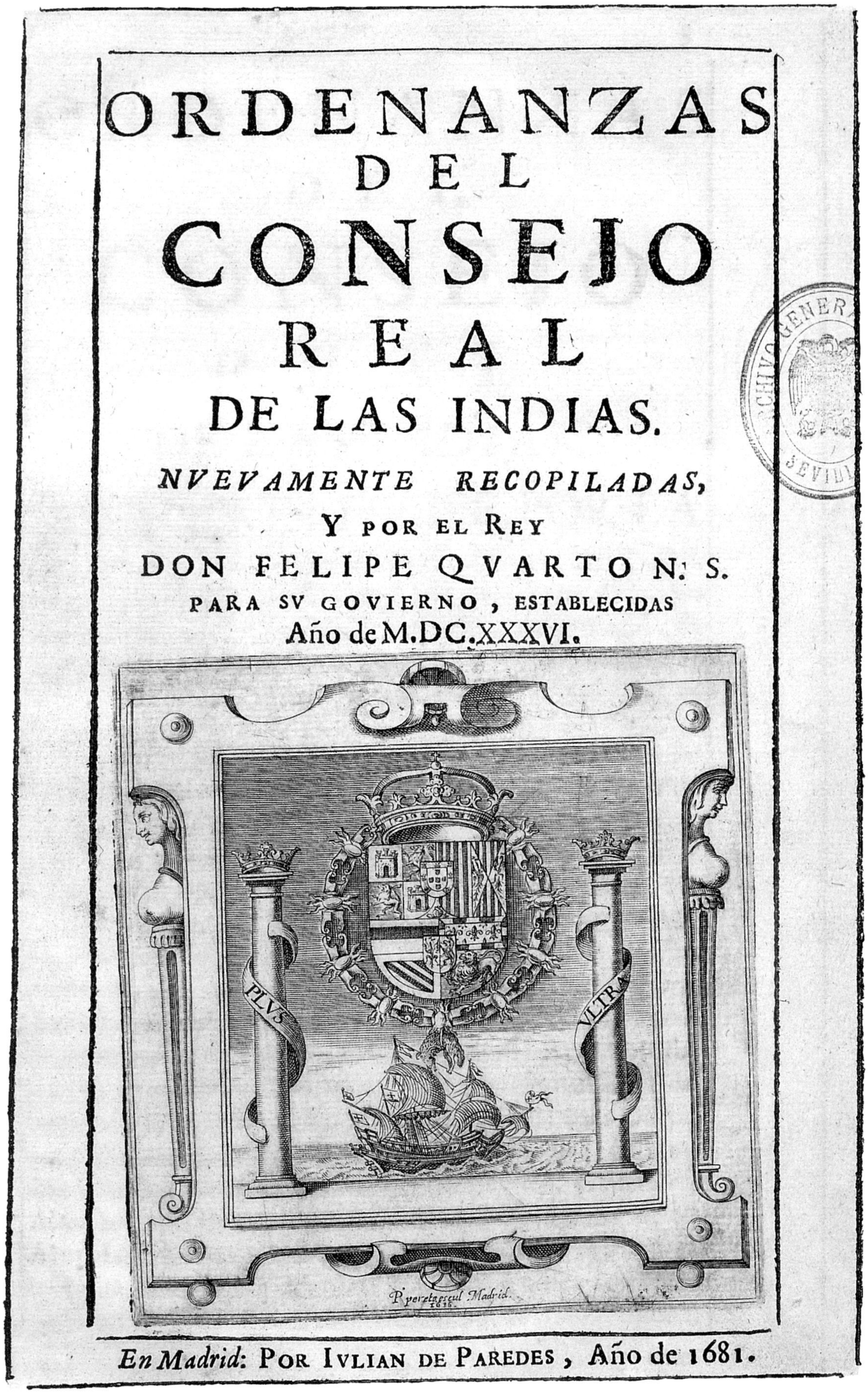

ORDENANZAS
DEL
CONSEJO
REAL
DE LAS INDIAS.
NVEVAMENTE RECOPILADAS,
Y POR EL REY
DON FELIPE QVARTO N. S.
PARA SV GOVIERNO, ESTABLECIDAS
Año de M.DC.XXXVI.

En Madrid: Por Ivlian de Paredes, Año de 1681.

The Council Statutes of 1636.

1 August 1636, Madrid.
'Statutes of the Royal Council of the Indies, newly compiled by His Majesty, Philip IV, for its government, in the year MDCXXXVI.'
Madrid: Julian de Paredes, 1681.
206 pp., 7 sheets. Cover: engraving of royal coat-of-arms for the Council by Pedro Perete in 1636.
It contains the 'Acts, agreements and decrees for governing the Royal Supreme Council of the Indies'.
Biblioteca, L.A., S. XVII–10.

These were the last statutes to be issued before the Bourbon reforms. They emphasize the role of the Secretariat, which was thereafter divided into two divisions, one for New Spain and another for Peru. Together, they were to deal with matters pertaining to all jurisdictions in the Americas. Attention is also drawn to the Contaduría *(Audit Office) and to the* Escribanía de Cámara *(Chamber of Justice).*

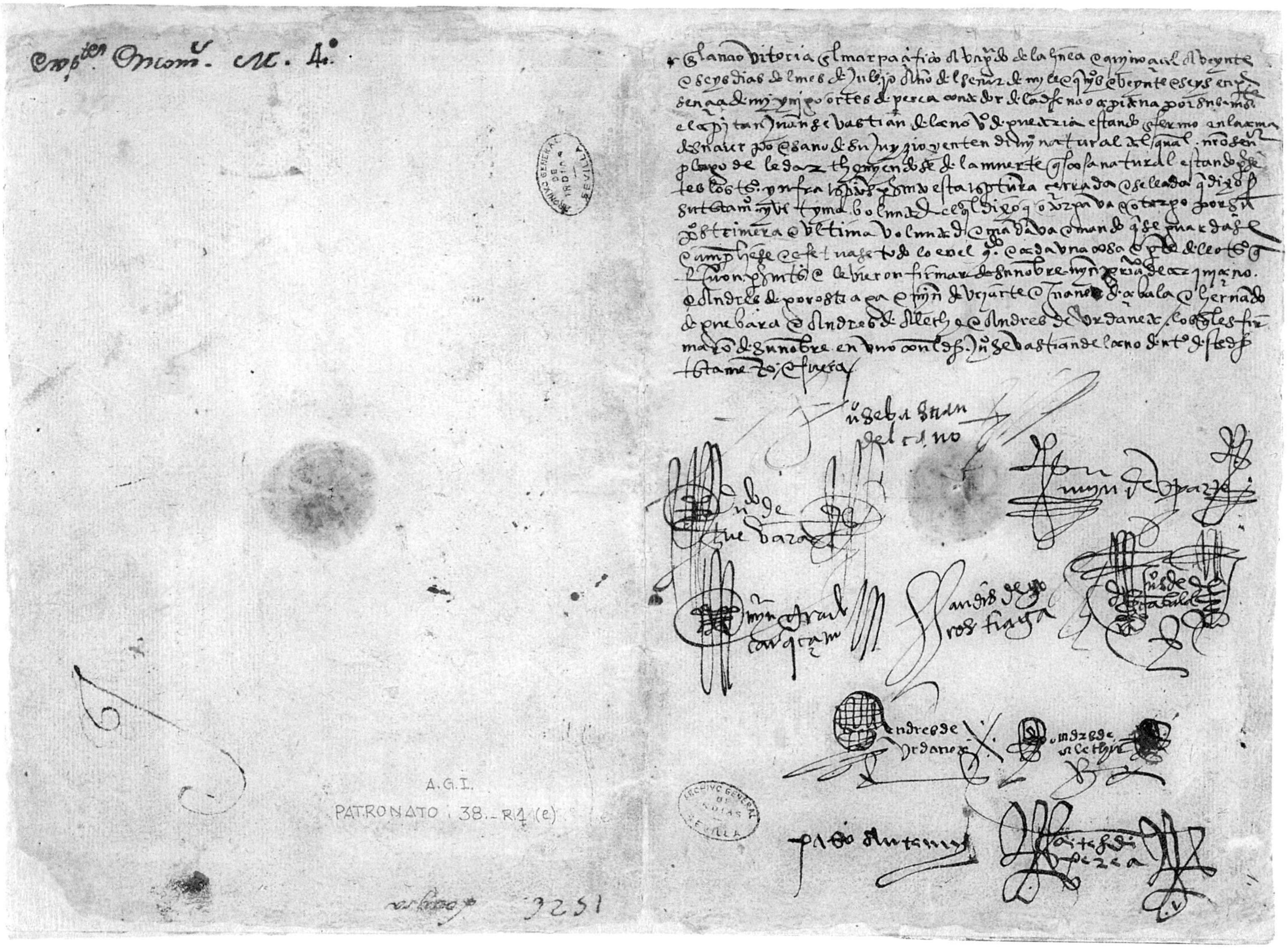

Litigation: Elcano's last will & testament.

26 July 1526, Nao Victoria.
Juan Sebastián Elcano's last will & testament.
9 fols.
Patronato, 38, r. 1 (e).

Drawn up by Elcano eleven days before his death on board the galleon, Santa María de la Victoria, flagship of the fleet which, under the command of García Jofre de Loaysa, had set sail from Corunna a year before on a second voyage to the Spice Islands. After a number of charitable bequests, some allocated to churches and shrines in his hometown of Guetaria, he appoints as heirs his son Domingo and his mother Catalina del Puerto. The will was produced, along with other documents, at a lawsuit filed by the latter with H.M.'s attorney regarding the life pension of 500 gold ducats per annum which Charles V had granted Sebastián Elcano.

Mandate of The Council of the Indies

The Council's original charge was to act as an advisory body to the monarch who, after due deliberation, would come to a decision and have the relevant orders issued.

However, in practice, the Council's powers as the supreme administrative body for the New World were extremely broad, extending to all issues associated with that administration: government, justice, war and treasury. Similarly, by virtue of the royal patronage granted to the kings of Castile by the Holy See, it had wide-ranging powers to intervene in ecclesiastical matters. Lastly, in order to perform all these functions, the Council had to undertake a great deal of research in the legislative field, as the peculiarities of the overseas territories in most cases warranted a set of laws adapted to local conditions. Let us now examine each of the legal tasks and the Indies authorities delegated by the Council to perform them.

In judicial matters, the Council of the Indies acted as the supreme civil and criminal court. It heard appeals referred from Indies *Audiencias* and trade consulates, and from the Tribunal of the *Casa de la Contratación*. It also dealt with cases

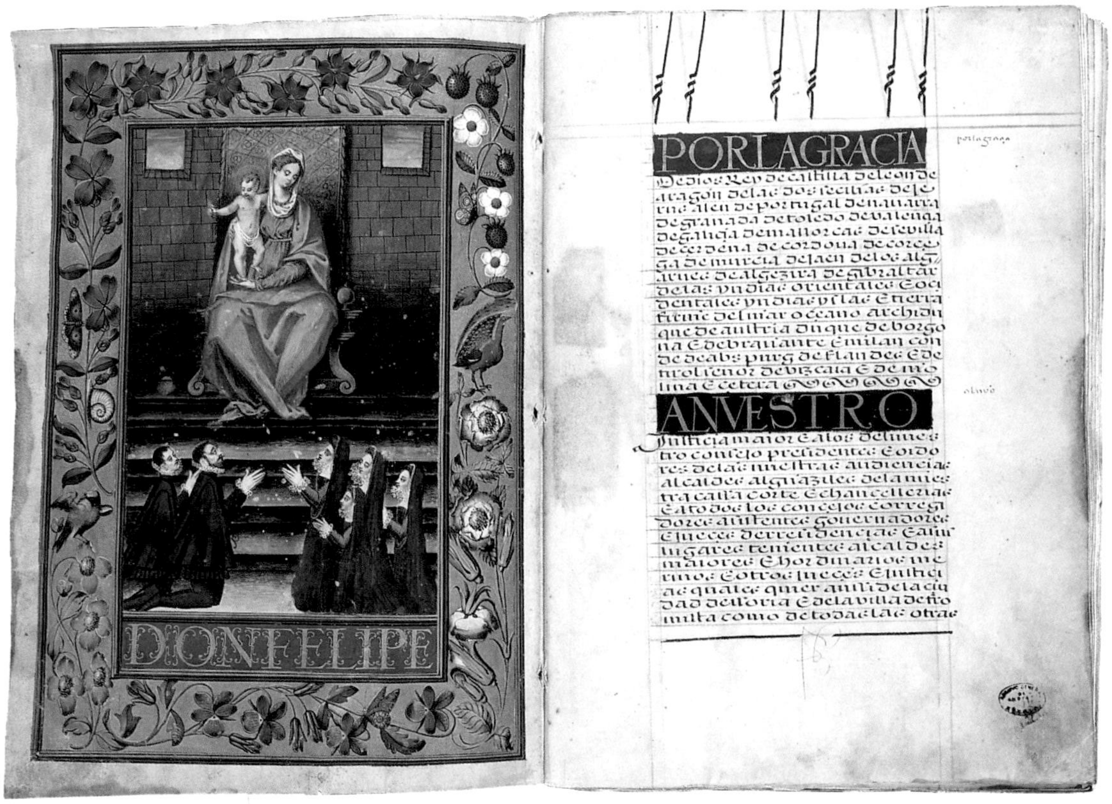

Litigation: Pedigree of the Santa Cruz dynasty.

14 March 1595, Valladolid.
Royal provision attesting the noble ancestry of Juan de Santa Cruz, an inhabitant of the town of Fromista. Headed by an image of the Virgin and Child, with Philip II and other figures in prayer.
From the book certifying the patent of nobility of the Santa Cruz family. Ornamented, leather-bound parchment. 56 fols. & 3 blank (316 x 220 mm.).
MP. Libros Manuscritos, 46.

Submitted as evidence in a suit concerning the deeds awarded to the town of Torrejoncillo and its municipality and other documents relating to the marquisate of Buena Vista (1715). The Council originally lacked jurisdiction over cases of primogeniture and hidalguía *(nobility), which were heard in the Chancellery of Valladolid.*

of impeachment and lawsuits which most of the authorities in the Indies had to submit to the Council's jurisdiction. It likewise had jurisdiction over inspection of tribunals and territories, investigations or search warrants issued for the purpose of indicting an individual. Its authority also extended to ecclesiastical issues, military trials and litigation relating to *encomiendas* in the Indies that was outside the jurisdiction of the *Audiencias.*

The Council did not, however, have legal competence in matters pertaining to primogeniture, which were heard at the Chancelleries of Valladolid and Granada, and it was prevented by statute from getting involved in legal actions between individual or business parties which could be heard in the *Audiencias*. The latter also tried criminal cases for which sentences were passed in the Indies, except in special cases of disloyalty to the Crown.

When acting in a judicial capacity, the Council met in the *Sala de Justicia.* The supreme court was composed of the president, the judges and the prosecutor. They were assisted by recorders, lawyers and duty barristers.

The highest courts of justice in the New World were those of the *Audiencias.* Modelled on courts in the Iberian Peninsular, they were set up at the very start of the process of colonization. They tried civil and criminal cases in the second and third instance referred by governors, *alcaldes mayores* and *corregidores.* The judges, known as *oidores* or *alcaldes de corte,* were also in charge of ordinary justice in the city where the *Audiencia* was sited and for five leagues around it. Lawsuits and criminal cases concerning the Indians followed special, summary procedures, as did military cases, which came under the viceroy or governor–president. The court of the *Audiencia* settled issues of mixed jurisdiction between civil and ecclesiastical judges and intervened when Church tribunals exceeded their mandate.

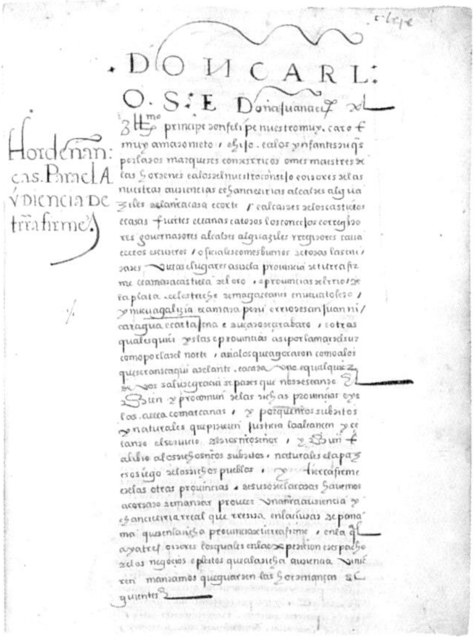

The Audiencia *of Panama.*

26 February 1538.
Royal order issued by Charles V and Queen Joan by which the Audiencia de Tierra Firme *in the city of Panama received its statutes.*
Panamá, 235, L. 6 fols. 169 r. to 182 r.

Each Audiencia *had its own constitutional statutes in which its jurisdiction, mandate and composition were laid down. The* Audiencia *of Panama had three judges and was presided over by a judge–president. Under the Laws of the Indies, it was an independent body, although this was never clearly established by the Crown. Indeed, in view of the importance of the Panama isthmus for Peru, the* Audiencia *of Panama was subordinated to the Viceroyalty of Lima. In similar fashion, the Crown granted the governor of Tierra Firme full rights in the administration of his territory.*

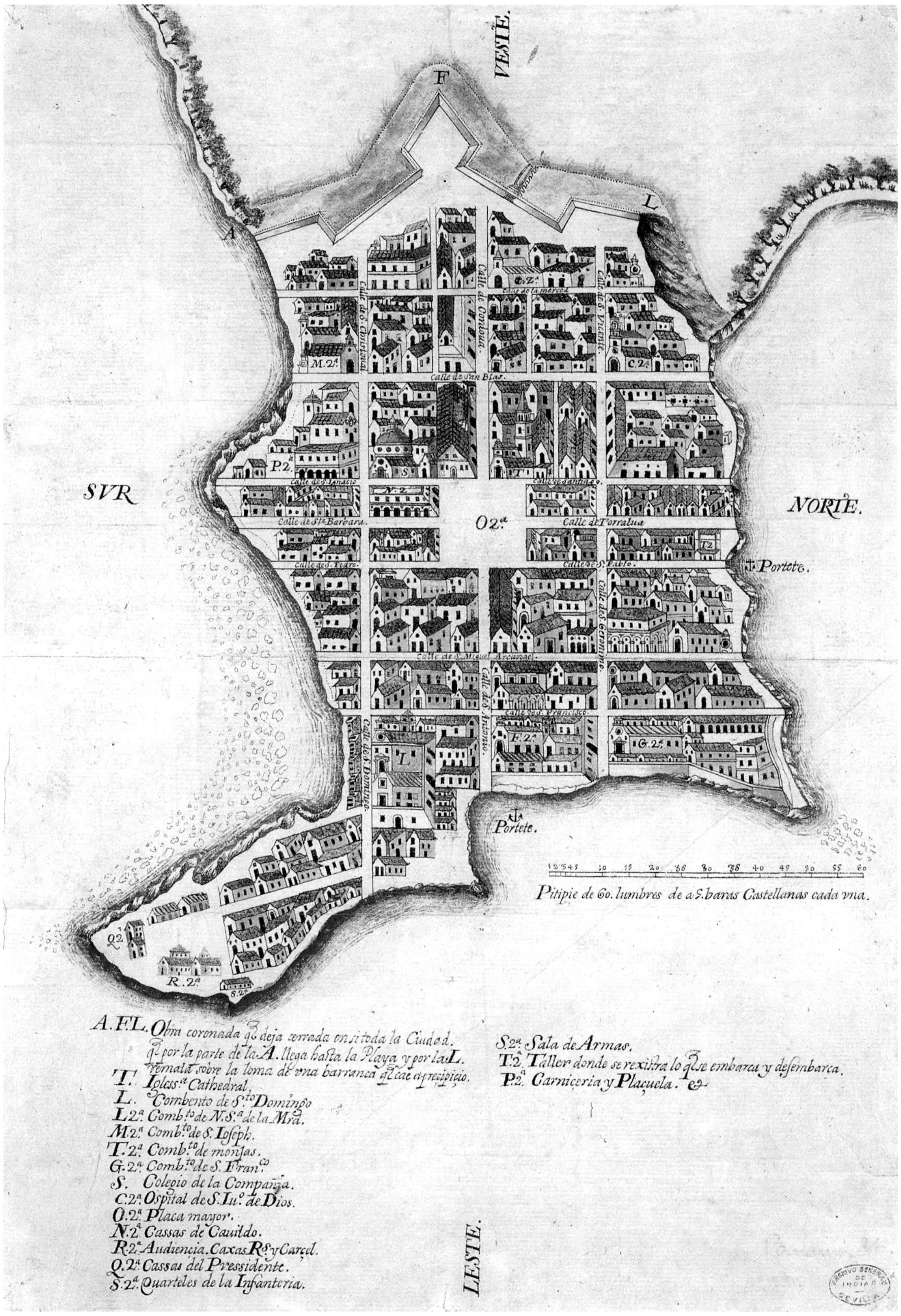

The 'ruling' Audiencia.

1673.
Plan of Panama city on its new site at Ancón.
420 x 280 mm.
MP. Panamá, 84.

Unlike the Spanish Audiencia, *those of the Americas had both judicial functions and a mandate to govern. This plan, showing the state of the city after its move, was sent by the Panama* Audiencia *on 5 June 1673, together with a letter explaining the succession after the death of the governor, Antonio Fernández de Córdoba. The* Audiencia, Cajas Reales *(offices of the Royal Treasury) and prison can be made out in the spur on the left.*

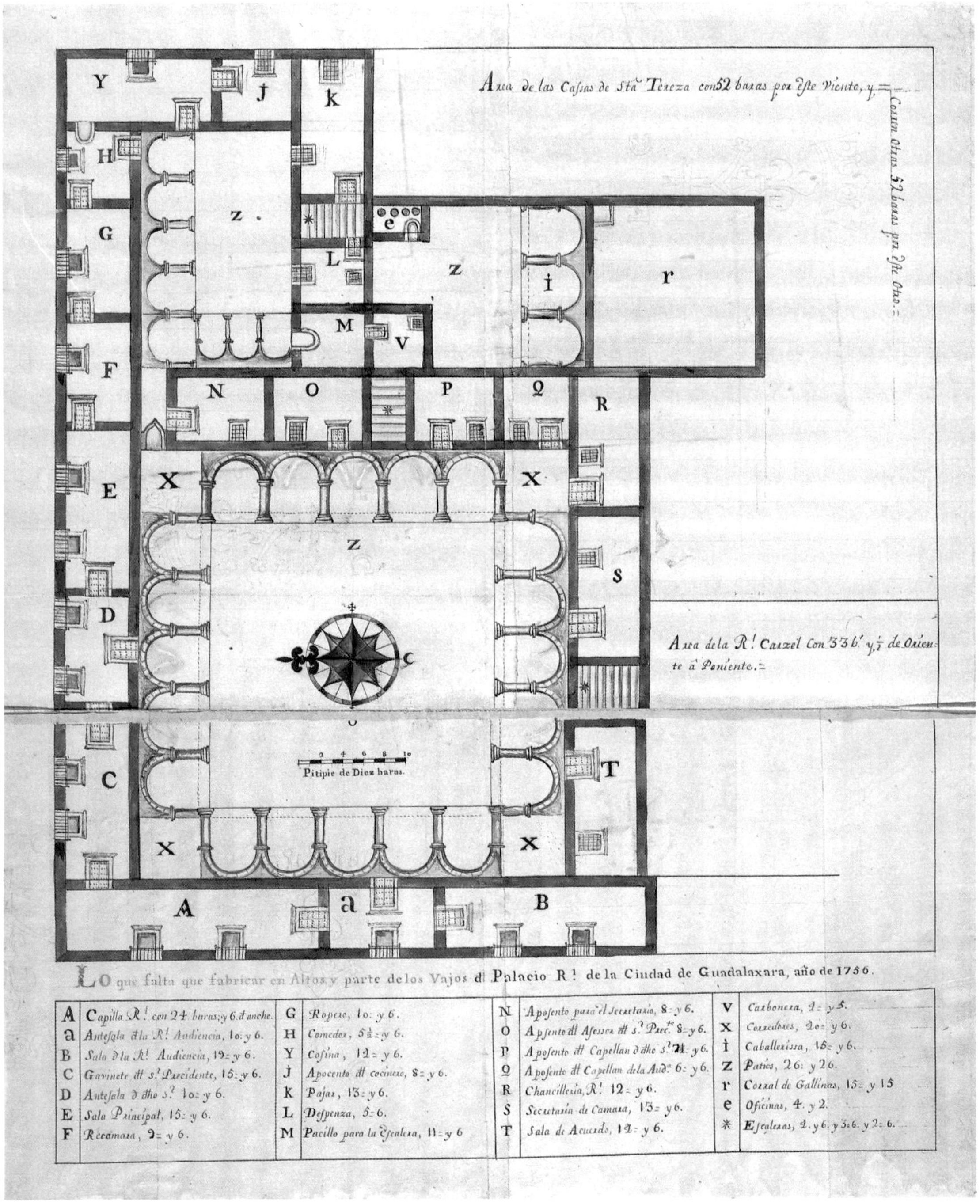

Palace of the Audiencia *of Guadalajara.*

1756.
Plan of 'what is still to be built on the upper and some of the lower parts of the Royal Palace of the city of Guadalajara, 1756.'
700 x 580 mm.
MP. México, 204.

Sent by the Audiencia, *on 13 June 1757, with an accompanying letter detailing the various chambers: Hall of Justice, Secretariat, Chancellery, Council Chamber and prison.*
The Audiencia *of Guadalajara was headed by a judge–president who was accountable in both military and political matters to the Viceroy of Mexico.*

Opposite, left
Government: instructions for the Viceroy.

14 July 1536, Madrid.
Instructions for Don Antonio de Mendoza, first viceroy of Mexico.
In a Register of Instructions, from 1509 to 1565, in the Council of the Indies.
Indiferente, 425, L. 2, fols. 65 r. to 69 r.

In addition to the wide-ranging powers, derived from his titles, the viceroy was given general instructions for governing as well as classified or secret instructions concerning especially delicate affairs, as those seen here. These deal with doctrinal matters and the treatment of the Indians, raising taxes, the administration of justice and land valuation, instructions for mayors and safeguarding of the Royal Treasury.

Opposite, right
The Viceroy's mandate: the silk statutes.

7 February 1542, Mexico.
Statutes issued by the viceroy, Don Antonio de Mendoza, concerning procedures for making silk in Mexico City, based on the statutes regulating silk production in Granada.
13 fols.
Patronato, 181, r. 3.

The viceroy was responsible for promoting and regulating agricultural, industrial and commercial activity. These statutes, drawn up by the Mexico council, were approved by the viceroy 'by the power and faculty invested in me by H.M.' They determine that silk may not be manufactured in any other town in New Spain and that it cannot be made by Indians or slaves.

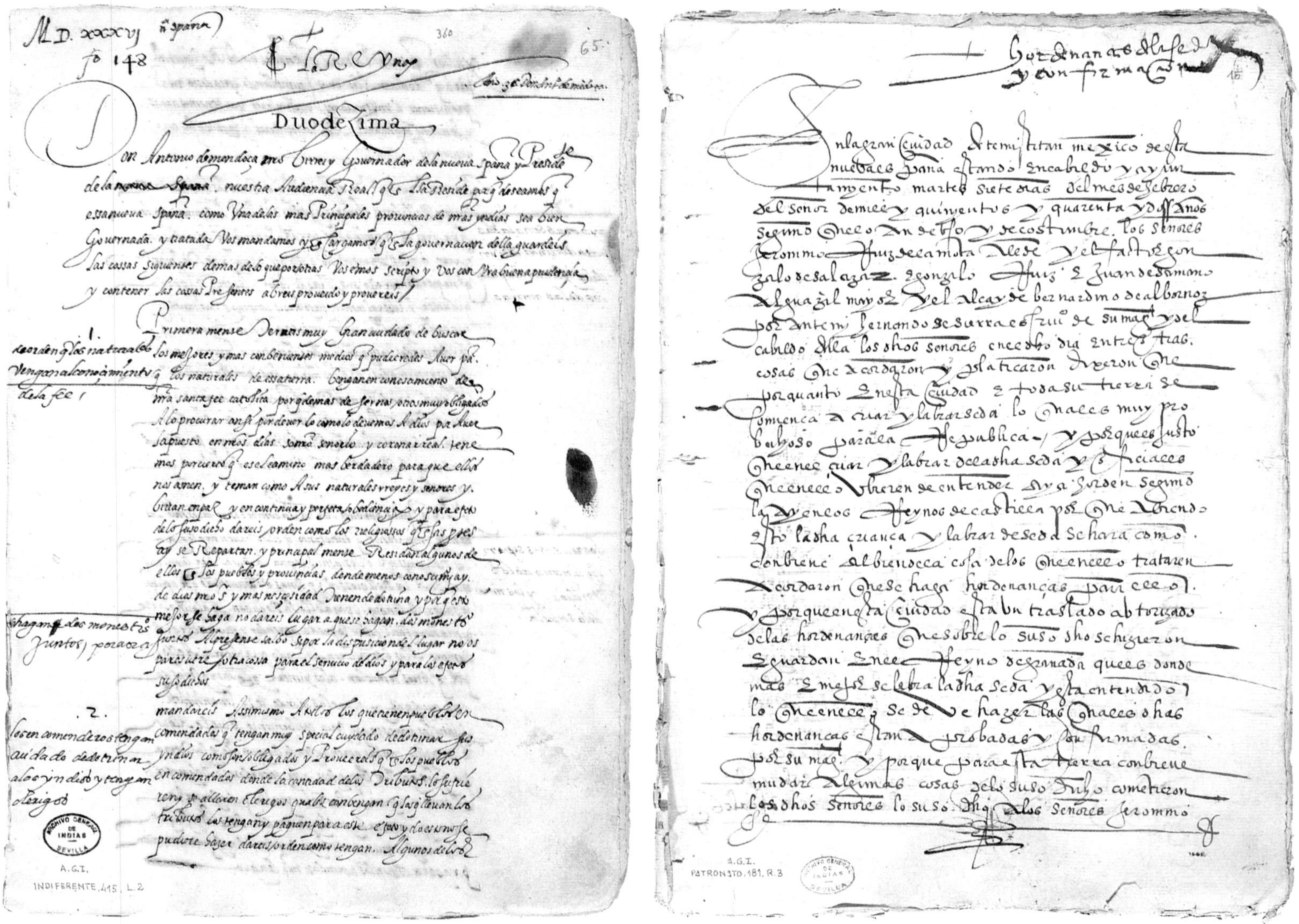

Unlike its counterpart on the Iberian Peninsular, the *Audiencia* in the Indies had a consultative and executive mandate. As a consultative body, it assisted and counselled the viceroy or governor–president on important matters. Any collaboration of this kind was known as 'royal accord'. In government affairs, the *Audiencia* had the legal duty to rule in the event of the viceroy or governor–president's absence or death. Indeed, its mandate was that of an accomplished, multi-sided administrative body which monitored the viceroy and governor–president's performance of duty and reported to the Council of the Indies on all matters of interest to the Crown. Royal officials were accountable to the *Audiencia*, which also had the power to appoint *oidores* and to oversee land surveys, and had jurisdiction over public revenue in places lacking an Audit Office.

According to the 1680 compilation of the Laws of the Indies, there were three categories of *Audiencia:* first, the viceregal, presided over by the viceroy and located in such viceregal capitals as Mexico City in New Spain and Lima in Peru in the 16th century, and Santa Fe and Buenos Aires in the 18th. Then came those

Samples of Mexican silks.

1793
Six samples of Mexican silk cloth, known as 'Popotillo velvet' (no. 1), capichola *(no. 2),* anafaya *(no. 3),* listones *(nos. 4 & 5) and* rengues *(nos. 6 & 7).*
MP. Tejidos, 15.

These were sent by the viceroy, the Count of Revillagigedo, in a letter dated 30 August 1793, reporting on the situation of trade in the viceroyalty and the number of silk workshops in the capital. Most of the raw silk manufactured there was imported from China and the most common variety was the so-called rengue, *consisting of cloth pierced with different colored silk and metal threads. Its manufacture came under the statutes passed by Viceroy Mendoza.*

subordinate to as well as answerable to the viceroy in matters of government, treasury and war, but independent in judicial matters, such as the *Audiencias* of Guadalajara, Charcas and Quito and, last, the wholly independent praetorial *Audiencias* presided over by a judge–president, as in Santo Domingo, the Philippines, Panama, Guatemala, Chile, Santa Fe, Buenos Aires, Caracas and Cuzco.

Every *Audiencia* had its own constitutional statutes establishing its powers, territorial jurisdiction and composition and was officially opened amidst much fanfare once the royal seal had been received. Account of this was given to the Council.

The first *Audiencia* in the New World was the one at Santo Domingo, set up as a result of a sentence passed in Seville in 1512 in a lawsuit between the Crown and Columbus' heirs. Its creation answered the request voiced by local inhabitants to have an appeals court in the Indies and the desire of the monarchy to curtail Columbus' prerogatives. Its statutes dated from 4 June 1528.

The *Audiencia* of New Spain was founded in Mexico City in 1527, followed by the *Audiencia* of Panama in 1538. Initially, the latter covered an enormous territory, which can only be explained by a lack of knowledge of the local geography on the part of the Spaniards. Eventually, in 1542, Panama was divided into two jurisdictions—one ranging between Guatemala and Nicaragua and another based in Lima. In the 16th century, other *Audiencias* were set up, including that of Guadalajara in 1548, Santa Fe de Bogotá in 1549, Charcas in 1551, Quito in 1563, Chile in 1567 and the Philippines in 1583. Dating from 1661 was the *Audiencia* of Buenos Aires which took over territory from Charcas, followed by Caracas in 1786 and Cuzco in 1787.

The last *Audiencias* to be set up in the New World were those of Cuba, in 1795 (first sited in Puerto Príncipe and subsequently in Havana, to replace the one in Santo Domingo, after the island had been ceded to France) and Puerto Rico in 1831.

The composition of such tribunals varied, depending on whether they were viceregal, subordinate or praetorial. It was customary, however, to have a president, a position held by the viceroy or governor, from four to eight *oidores* or criminal judges, one or two prosecutors and a number of court officials (*alguacils,* chamber secretaries, recorders, receivers, interpreters, wardens, executioners and so forth).

The *oidores* were judges with supreme authority and prestige in the Indies' administration. Appointed directly by the Council, in addition to their role as judges they acted as investigating magistrates and inspectors of the jurisdictional territory. Territorial inspections in the form of a census were carried out annually to gather information on the country's population, social regime and organization. There were many Creole judges, but they were not allowed to practise in their region of origin nor marry women from the jurisdiction of the *Audiencia,* except by royal dispensation. They were likewise forbidden to become *encomenderos* or traders, for the sake of impartiality and the continued independence of the judiciary.

All executive powers in the New World were invested in the Council of the Indies. Its duties included the appointment of all such high-ranking administrative officials as viceroys, presidents, governors, judges, mayors and magistrates, as well as less important positions in government, justice, the military and the treasury. After consultation, it also proposed nominees for posts in the *Casa de la Contratación* as well as for those of general and special territorial inspector. Likewise, it submitted proposals for the offices of archbishop, bishop and for the prebends of a diocese, the designation of which, by virtue of royal patronage, was incumbent upon the king. Proposals were made at a plenary session of the Council or by the president and, subsequently, by the Chamber of the Indies. Council assemblies were plenary when settling important issues of government, such as the establishment of *Audiencias,* the building of churches or the division of a diocese. In other matters, at least three Council members had to be in attendance. The Council was also entitled to deal with military and war matters, a task it forfeited to the *Junta de Guerra* as of 1600.

In general, all matters referred to the Council by the authorities in the Indies were decided in its administrative division. Supreme administrative power in the New World was invested in the viceroy who, as the name suggests, acted as the

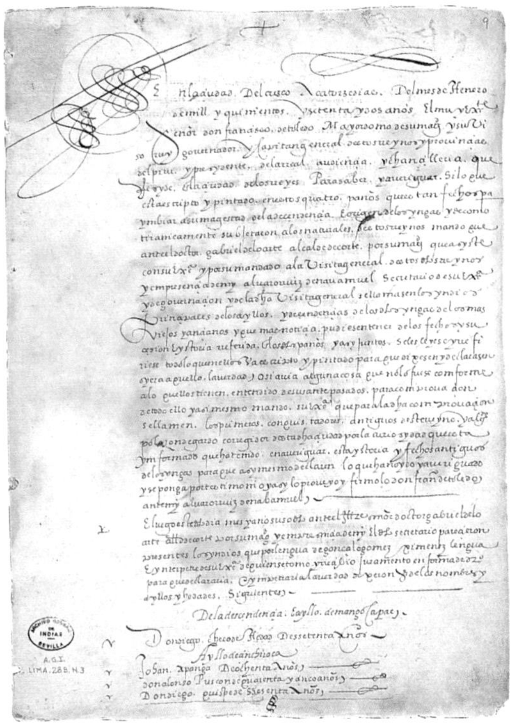

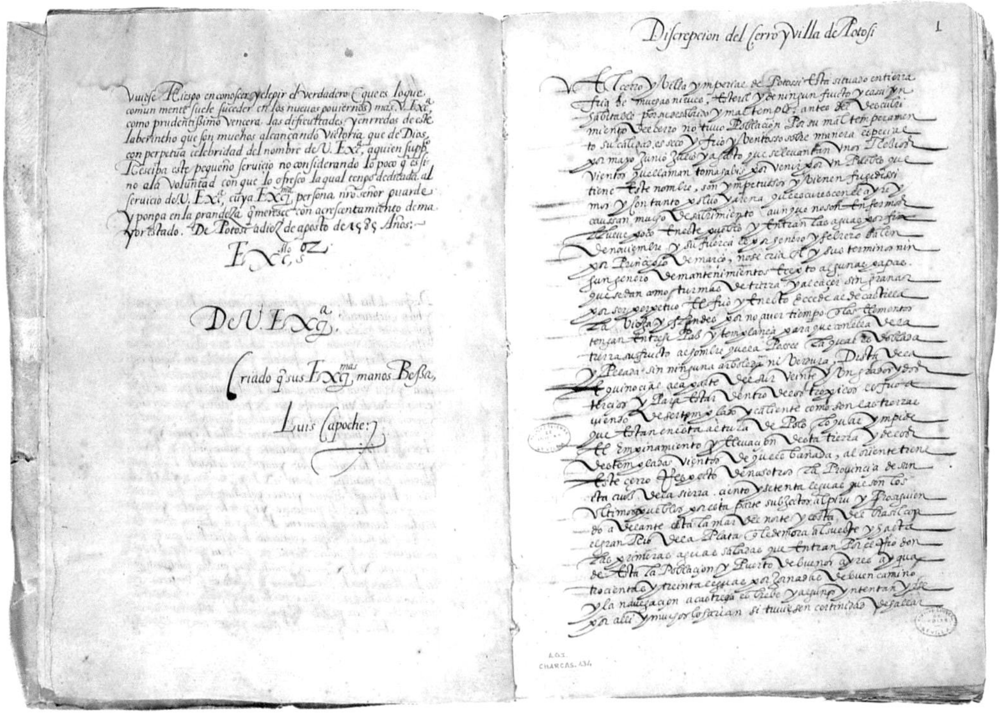

king's delegate in kingdoms where the monarch was not present. Right from the outset, Spain's major overseas possessions were not regarded as colonies but as fully-fledged kingdoms in which the monarch replaced the indigenous chieftains. Other, less important territories were considered provinces. It followed, then, that Mexico and Peru should be designated as viceroyalties. Hence, in 1535, when the Aztec empire had been conquered by Hernando Cortés, the Spanish monarchs, aware of the grandeur of the empire that had been subjected, decided to appoint a viceroy to govern in the person of Antonio de Mendoza.

The New Laws of 1542 provided for a viceroyalty to be established in Peru. There, Charles V succeeded the last of the Inca emperors, Atahualpa, while Blasco Núñez Vela was appointed the first viceroy. Mexico and Peru were the only two viceroyalties in the New World until the 18th century, when Spain's Bourbon monarchs subsequently created that of New Granada in 1717 and Buenos Aires in 1777. The former took in the provinces of Quito, Panama and Venezuela, in addition to the territory under the jurisdiction of the *Audiencia* of Santa Fe. The Buenos Aires viceroyalty comprised Río de la Plata, the jurisdiction of the *Audiencia* of Charcas and the *gobernación* of Paraguay, which included present-day Uruguay.

The viceroy, who was proposed by the Council and appointed by the king, was usually Spanish and a learned man with a military or aristocratic background, although subsequently some were of humble origin, Creole stock or churchmen. When appointed, in addition to the title of viceroy, they were granted the titles of governor, president of the *Audiencia,* captain general of the jurisdictional territory, *ordenador* of the Royal Treasury and 'deputy patron of the Church'. Viceroys were given a 'general instruction' to govern and a 'classified instruction' concerning certain secret affairs.

Information on the Incas.

14 January 1572, Cuzco.
Summary information issued by the Viceroy of Peru, Francisco de Toledo, on the origins and rule of the Incas.
Bound in parchment.
227 fols. & 9 blanks.
Lima, 28 B.

Compiled during the viceroy's tour of his dominions for the purpose of producing a factual historical account of that empire and 'to justify the magnitude of the title H.M. has conferred on this province'. In effect, by instituting viceroyalties in Mexico and Peru, the Spanish crown was doing justice to the grandeur of the Aztec and Inca empires.

Description of the town of Potosí.

10 August 1585, Potosí.
'General description of the town of Potosí and its siting and the most prominent features of its government, submitted by Luis Capoche to His Excellency, Don Hernando de Torres y Portugal, Count of Villar and Viceroy of Peru.'
Bound in parchment.
103 fols. & 3 blanks. Charcas, 134.

Promoting mining was one of the viceroy's major charges, as it was the main source of revenue for sustaining his viceroyalty. Potosí was undoubtedly the largest silver mine in South America. In the report on his term of office, the Count of Villar stressed his visit to the mines and their increased productivity during his mandate.

Potosí hill.

[1779]
'View of Potosí hill seen from the north'.
357 x 553 mm.
MP. Buenos Aires, 121.

The elevation show the hill with its seams and galleries, part of the town of Potosí and the roads to Las Lagunas and Buenos Aires.

Viceregal prerogatives were commensurate with the office. Prior to embarking in Seville, viceroys were lodged in the Alcázar and were paid the highest salaries in the Indies administration. They made the Atlantic crossing with a retinue of relatives and servants and paid no duties on the goods and slaves they took with them. Their arrival in the New World, at Portobelo or Veracruz, was met by great ceremonial fanfare and the festivities awaiting them once they had reached the capital of the viceroyalty would last for weeks. The receptions for some viceroys were so extravagant that the Council was eventually forced to issue royal warrants limiting their duration and cost. Protocol in the viceregal court was a virtual replica of royal protocol and viceroys had their own guard.

Similarly, viceroys had powers commensurate with their titles. As the supreme executive authority, they were entitled to appoint governors, *corregidores* and *alcaldes mayores* and to oversee municipal elections. They commissioned new discoveries and expeditions to neighboring territories, ordered the founding of new settlements and dictated the laws by which they were to be governed. They were empowered to distribute land and to promote agriculture, industry and commerce and had to pay special attention to mining. They determined the amount of money to be minted and placed in circulation and supervised the workings of the Royal Treasury, inspecting the transactions of royal officials and the Audit Offices.

The Huancavelica mines.

19 January 1790, Huancavelica. 'Third level of the mine, showing the first and second levels divided into three sections. Drawn up by Nicolás de Mendizábal, director of mining exploration, discovery and works at the mines separate from the main one at Santa Bárbara.' No. 3. By Pedro de Tagle. 580 x 508 mm. MP. Perú y Chile, 227.

Potosí's silver wealth was boosted by the discovery of mercury mines at Huamanga and Huancavelica in the 16th century as, until then, the mercury required for amalgamating silver was shipped to the Americas from Spain's Almadén mines. This plan was drawn up after a survey commissioned by the viceroy, the Marquis of Croix, in the 18th century. The corner shields are those of the monarchs, the town of Huancavelica, the viceroy and Pedro de Tagle.

In the social and cultural sphere, it was their duty to found universities and schools, hospitals, hospices and poorhouses, and they were entrusted with the special task of converting and protecting Indians.

As president of the viceregal *Audiencia,* the viceroy had to endorse sentences, although he did not pass them, not being a qualified lawyer. He was also empowered to pardon a private crime and to order punishment for public crimes.

In military affairs, as captain general he was the supreme commander of the armed forces and had to direct his territory's fortification and defenses, following the advise of the *Junta de Guerra*. Lastly, as deputy patron of the Church, he had to oversee the organization of clergy and lay churchmen, and to attend councils and provincial synods and promote church building.

In short, owing to their preeminence and powers, viceroys lived like kings, albeit for a limited period of time. Their term of office usually lasted six years, after which they submitted a report of their government and were subject to a *juicio de residencia,* a judicial review of their term of office, as were all Indies officials.

Mexico's Plaza Mayor.

1793.
'View of the Plaza Mayor of Mexico, remodelled and beautified on the orders of His Excellency, the Viceroy and Count of Revillagigedo in 1793.'
450 x 670 mm.
MP. México, 446.

This plan was submitted during the judicial review of the above viceroy's term of office to attest to his performance in the capital. Indeed, despite the viceroys' position and authority, which matched those of a king, once their mandate had ended their term was subject to review, as was that of all authorities in the New World. To this end, a judge was appointed, very often the incoming viceroy. A period for bringing charges was set and the viceroy had to respond to them. He was either absolved or sanctioned by the Council in the last instance.

Other territories in the New World not ranked as viceroyalties were considered major or minor provinces, depending on whether or not they had a praetorial *Audiencia*. In the former instance, the province would be governed by the judge–president of the *Audiencia*, who was also the captain general of the territory. Minor provinces, known as *gobernaciones*, usually lacked an *Audiencia*.

The major provinces were Santo Domingo, Panama, Guatemala, the Philippines, Chile, New Granada or Santa Fe, Buenos Aires (until the 18th century) and, in the 18th century, Venezuela.

A governor–president ruled over his territory with the same mandate as a viceroy, with the exception that he was not a personal representative of the monarch. His rule was totally independent and he reported directly to the king through the Council of the Indies. His term of office usually lasted eight years and he earned a salary commensurate with the importance of the province. In the 16th century, qualified jurists were usually preferred for such a post, while in the 17th century priority was usually given to noblemen experienced in command and combat. By the 18th century, most were military men. Like the viceroys, they had to present

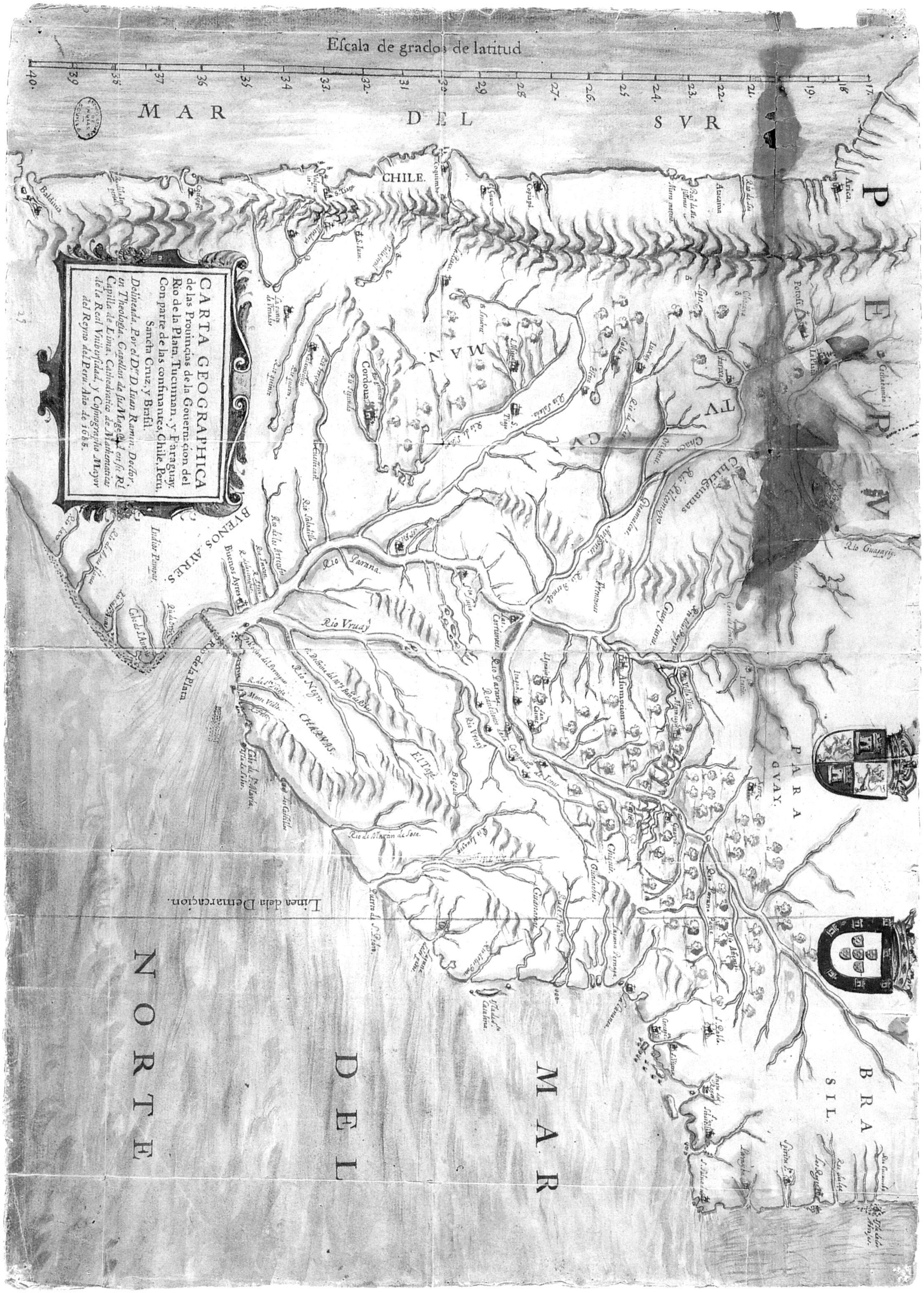

Escala de grados de latitud
MAR DEL SVR
CHILE.
CARTA GEOGRAPHICA de las Prouincias de la Gouernacion del Rio de la Plata, Tucuman, y Paraguay. Con parte de las confinantes, Chile, Peru, Sancta Cruz, y Brasil.
Delineada. Por el Dr. D. Iuan Ramon, Doctor, en Theologia. Capellan de su Magd. en su Rl. Capilla de Lima. Cathedratico de Mathematicas de la Real Vniversidad, y Cosmographo Mayor del Reyno del Peru. Año de 1685.
BVENOS AYRES.
Buenos Ayres
Rio Parana
Rio Vruay
Rio de la Plata
Asumpcion
Cordoua
CHARVAS
PARAGVAY
BRASIL
PERV
Rio Guasayis
Linea dela Demarcacion.
MAR DEL NORTE

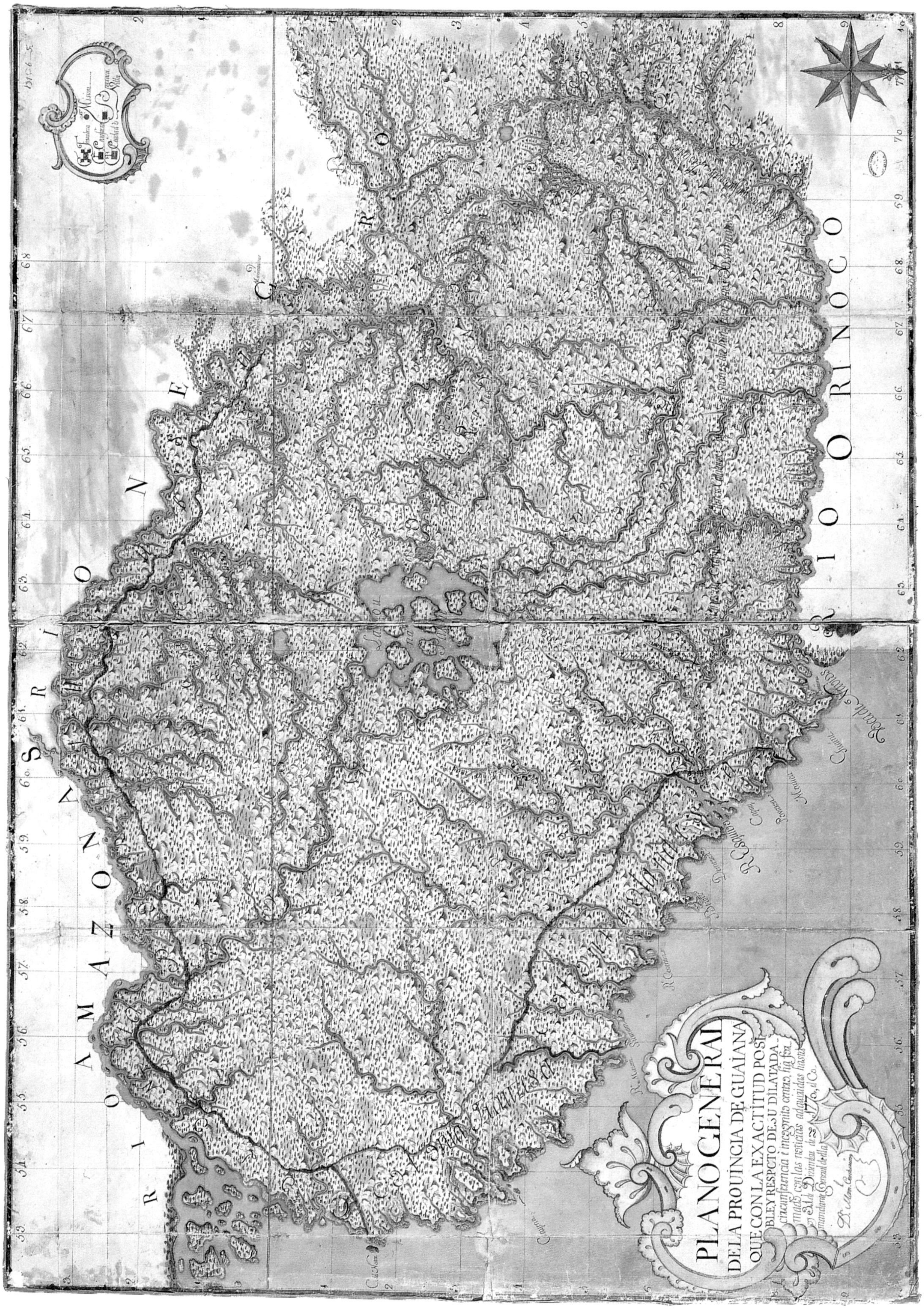
PLANO GENERAL
DE LA PROUINCIA DE GUAIANA
QUE CON LA EXACTITUD POS
IBLE Y RESPECTO DE SU DILATADA
RIO AMAZONAS
RIO NEGRO
RIO ORINOCO

Above
Founding a settlement: San Juan de la Frontera.

1562.
Plan of the town of San Juan de la Frontera, in the province of Cuyo (Tucumán), with its foundation–charter, instituted by Captain Juan de Jufre.
590 x 430 mm. MP. Buenos Aires, 9.

The establishment of a settlement followed an official procedure which was recorded in a charter drawn up by a local notary. Once the site had been chosen, the center was marked as the spot where the main square would be built and a pillory was erected. A grid plan was then drawn for the purpose of apportioning allotments according to rank. The grid pattern shown in this plan of San Juan de la Frontera was customary in the New World after first being introduced in Lima in 1535. The names of some colonists are marked on the blocks, as are the sites of the town hall, main church and convents.

Previous pages (left)
Gobernación *or minor province of Río de la Plata.*

1683.
'Map of the provinces of Río de la Plata, Tucumán and Paraguay, showing part of the neighboring provinces of Chile, Peru, Santa Cruz and Brazil. Drawn by Dr. Juan Ramón, chief cartographer of the Kingdom of Peru, 1683.'
430 x 560 mm.
MP. Buenos Aires, 29.

There were numerous minor provinces or gobernaciones *in the New World. Some, on account of their size and strategic location, were extremely important. An instance of this was Río de la Plata which in 1661 was awarded its own* Audiencia. *In the 18th century, it became a viceroyalty.*

Previous pages (right)
Guayana Province.

1770.
'General plan of the province of Guayana', by Manuel Centurión.
657 x 921 mm.
MP. Venezuela, 162.

Guayana was a huge province. Its importance lay in its role as a buffer zone against foreign expansion, particularly by the Portuguese, but also the Dutch, English and French. This map, with its minute relief and hydrographical detail, shows the boundaries of the colonies bordering on Guayana. It was drawn by Manuel Centurión, who ruled the province from 1766 to 1776 and conducted a large resettlement programme. He explored the upper reaches of the Orinoco river, reduced a host of indigenous tribes and fortified key points in the province.

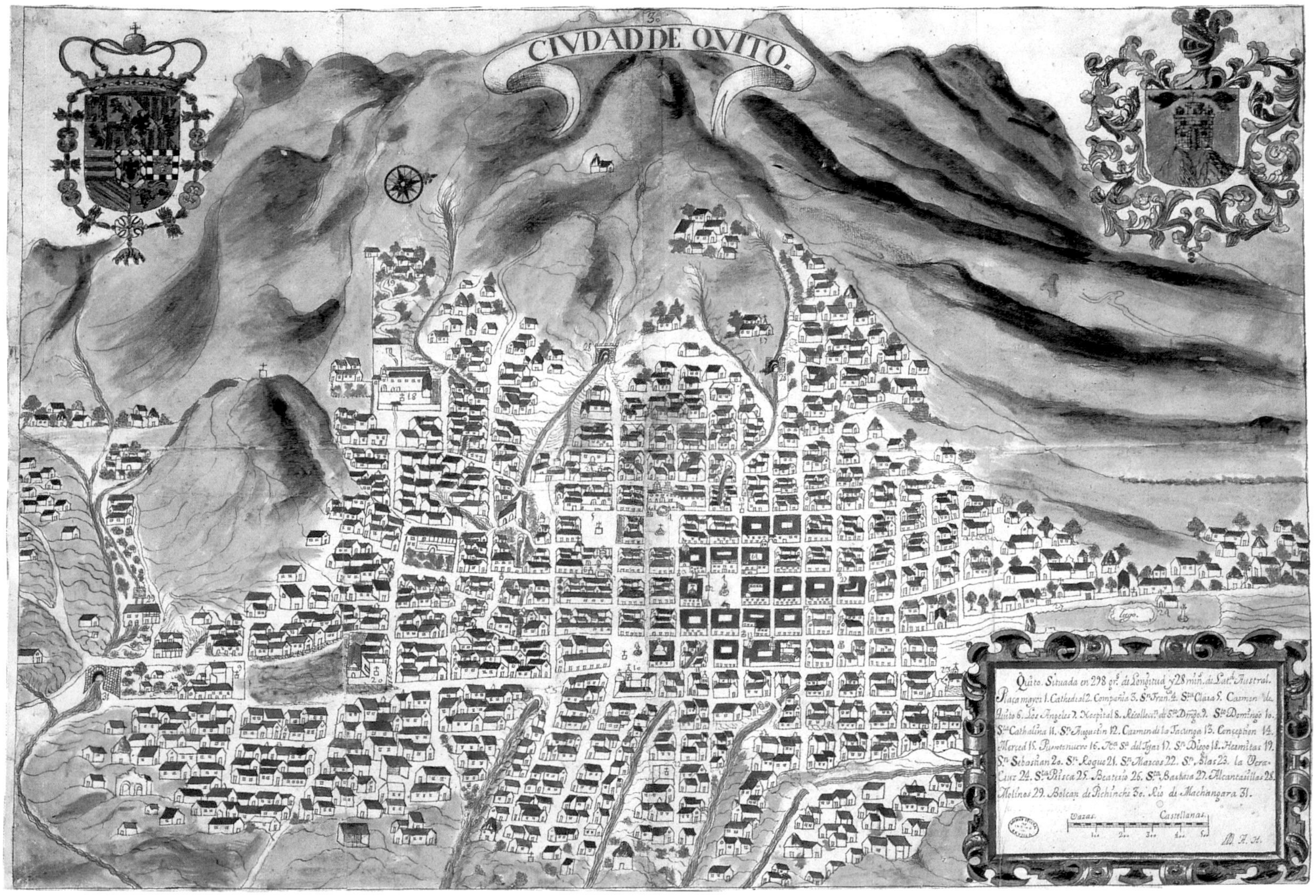

Town planning: Quito.

1734.
Plan of the city of San Francisco de Quito, by D.A.H. [Dionisio de Alcedo y Herrera?]
510 x 820 mm.
MP. Panamá, 134.

The panoramic technique used in drawing this plan provides an insight into 16th-century town planning in the New World and the adjustments made according to the lie of the land. The settlement of vast territories enabled the Spanish to apply Renaissance theories of the ideal city based on symmetry. The streets radiate out from the center to form a regular mesh, configuring an octagonal or quadrangular grid pattern. The coats-of-arms of Spain and the city are featured in the corners of the plan.

an administrative report to their successor, undergo a *juicio de residencia* or judicial review, at which the Council of the Indies passed judgement, and were liable to a general inspection at any time during their term of office.

In provinces which had an *Audiencia* subordinated to a viceroyalty, the president of the court was a judge, while the viceroy presided over affairs of higher government, war and the military.

Minor provinces which lacked an *Audiencia* were ruled by a governor. There were many such provinces and they were usually located in frontier territory bordering on uncolonized tribelands, foreign possessions or strategic enclaves used to defend colonial dominions. These governors enjoyed considerable jurisdictional freedom, unlike those appointed by viceroys or governor–presidents and subject thereto. Similarly, their rank was conditioned by their military status, and they very often held the offices of both governor and captain general.

Some of the most prominent minor provinces were Cuba, Puerto Rico, Veracruz, Yucatán, Cartagena, Popayán, Mérida de la Grita, Caracas, Cuenca, Santa Cruz de la Sierra and Tucumán.

Statutes of the city of La Plata.

5 May 1574, La Plata.
Statutes of the city of La Plata, approved by the Viceroy of Peru, Francisco de Toledo.
52 fols.
Lima, 29.

Each town was ruled according to statutes drawn up by its own council. They regulated the composition of the council, the function of each councillor, municipal elections, the use of croplands and fallow land and the festivities that could be held. The statutes had to be approved by a higher authority, in this instance the viceroy.

Governors held office for three to five years if appointed by the Council, and two years if appointed by a viceroy or governor–president. They had wide-ranging administrative and military powers, and control of the Royal Treasury. One of their tasks, for example, was to inspect the royal coffers. They were also competent in civil and criminal justice of the first instance and could hear appeals from a magistrate's court, for which purpose they could be assisted by a legal advisor.

The provincial post of *adelantado,* a royal official who headed military expeditions, lost ascendancy after the conquest was over and became an honorary position. On a local level, however, the main authorities were the *corregidor*—a magistrate with both judicial and executive powers who, as of the 18th century, was gradually replaced by the *alcalde mayor*—and the municipal councils.

Many town councils in the Indies were presided over by a *corregidor* or *alcalde mayor* who ranked higher than ordinary mayors. Their duties, as outlined in the 1680 *Recopilación de Leyes de Indias* (Codification of Laws of the Indies) were similar, but *corregidores* tended to be chosen for their executive or military background, while *alcaldes mayores* were usually qualified lawyers or judges. Those chosen to head the most important city councils were directly appointed by the king, and they were sworn in before the Council of the Indies. Most, however, were nominated by viceroys or governor–presidents. The descendants of conquistadors, discoverers or early settlers were most eligible for such positions, while *encomenderos* could not stand for office. Among their duties, they had to make at least one tour of the boundaries of their town or city and, on the basis of that visit, send a report to the *Audiencia*. Some *corregidores* and *alcaldes mayores* of territories inhabited exclusively by Indians were themselves indigenous.

OPPOSITE
The city of La Plata.

9 March 1779, La Plata.
Plan of the city of La Plata by Ildefonso Luján.
575 x 825 mm.
MP. Buenos Aires, 244 bis.

A perspective view of the city's perfect grid pattern, with a central square and parish church, as well as the characteristic layout of huge, spacious blocks enclosed on all four sides by buildings.

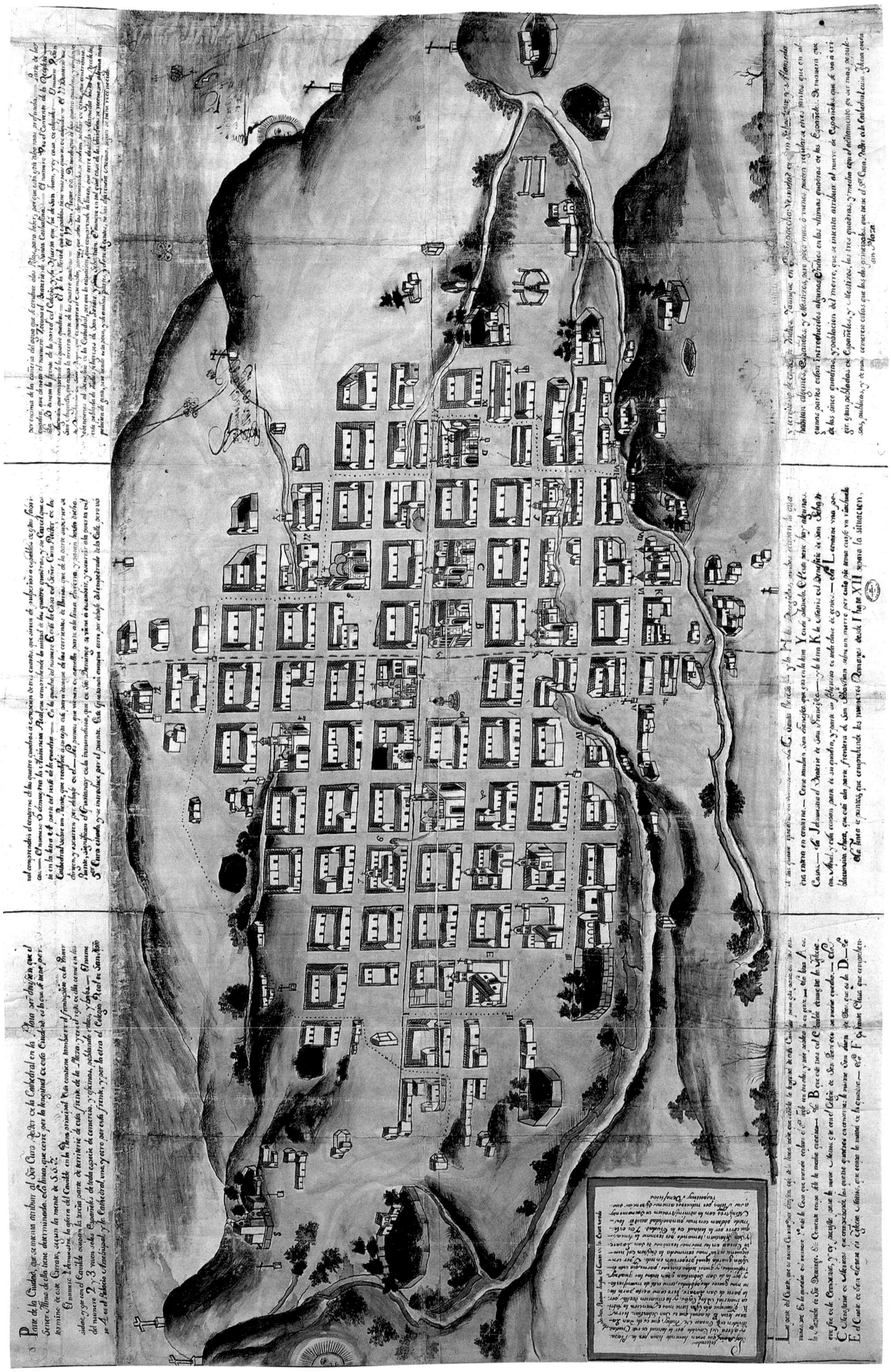

Nearly all municipalities in the New World were crown possessions, while *señoríos* (seigniories owned by the descendants of Columbus, Cortés or Pizarro) were few and far between. Nevertheless, unlike Spain, most municipalities were not *corregimientos,* that is, districts ruled by a *corregidor,* as they were governed by ordinary mayors. Together with an *alférez real* or royal yeoman, and a variable number of councillors (from four to twenty-four, modelled on the Seville city council), they made up the municipal council. Mayors were elected annually by the councillors and the result was sanctioned by the supreme authority, whether viceroy or governor–president. Mayors passed rulings on all municipal issues concerning government and the treasury and also acted as judges of the first instance. They had to be local residents, as did the councillors. The yeoman bore the royal banner at public ceremonies and commanded the local militia. Other council members included a panel of district representatives, inspectors in charge of supplies and the regulation of weights and measures, an *alguacil mayor* or bailiff who enforced the council's resolutions and patrolled the town accompanied by *alguacilillos* or wardens, the prosecutor, who acted judicially on behalf of the municipality, a secretary or clerk, a treasurer, town criers, mace-bearers, porters, a prison governor and an executioner. Most municipal offices could be voluntarily relinquished or sold at public auction, and the proceedings of such an auction went into the royal coffers.

Coat-of-arms of Zacatecas.

[1588]
Coat-of-arms of the town of Nuestra Señora de Zacatecas.
137 x 184 mm. on 310 x 217 mm. sheet.
MP. Escudos y Árboles Genealógicos, 102.

In terms of administrative status, settlements were classed as lugares *(villages),* villas *(towns) or* ciudades *(cities). Promotion to a higher status was a royal prerogative and usually went with a grant of coat-of-arms, blazon and titles. The coat-of-arms of Zacatecas features a hill surmounted by a silver cross and bearing an image of the Virgin, as the hill and mines were discovered on the feast of the birth of Our Lady. Below, portraits of the first settlers, including the town's founding father, Juan de Tolosa.*

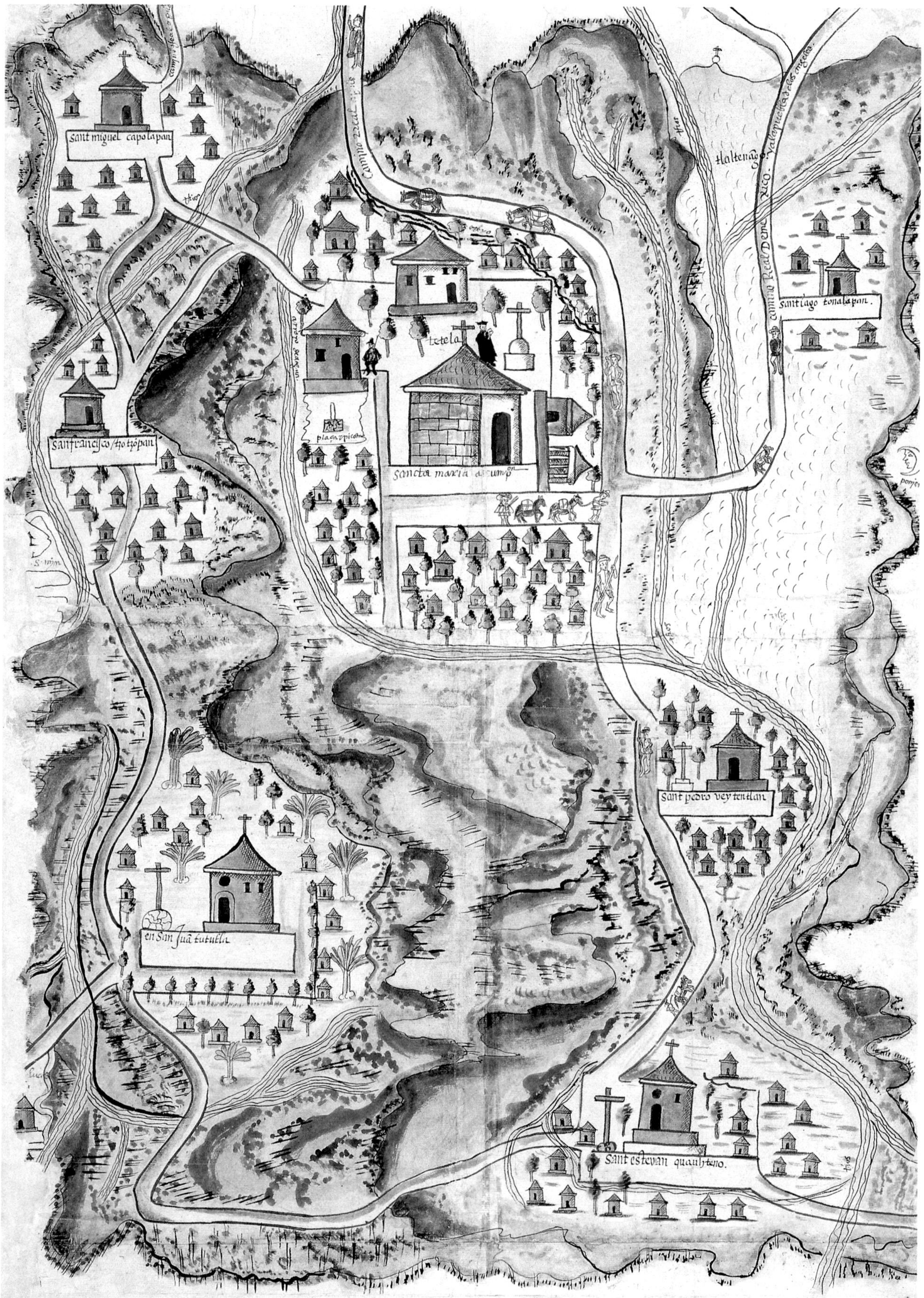
sant miguel capolapan
sanfrancisco tzotzopan
tetela
Sancta maria asump
santiago tonalapan
sant pedro vey tentlan
en San Juā tutula
sant estevan quauhteno

Each municipality drew up its own ordinances, which were then approved by the sovereign or superior government authority. In terms of administrative status, population centers were classed as *lugares* (villages), *villas* (towns) or *ciudades* (cities). Raising a town to city status was the sovereign's prerogative and an award of this kind was issued by royal warrant, usually accompanied by a grant of coats-of-arms, blazons and honorary titles for which most towns filed requests on the grounds of merit and service to the king a few years after their inception.

The process of founding a city and planning its layout in the Americas was conducted according to ceremonial and town-planning guidelines regulated by the so-called 'Statutes for discovery, new settlements and pacifications', promulgated by Philip II on 13 July 1573. As reflected in all foundation–charters, the site chosen had to comply with certain health conditions, and have an adequate water supply and good communications. Once the site had been chosen, the center of the settlement was marked as the spot for the main square to be built and the pillory to be erected. A plan, generally based on a grid, was then drawn up to divide the land into lots of varying degrees of importance and dimension. Sites were earmarked for convents and hospitals, public property, commons, meadows and communal pastureland.

Apart from Spanish towns and cities, throughout the colonized territory there were numerous exclusively Indian settlements which, as mentioned earlier, had their own municipal charter, as the Crown in many instances respected the figure of the traditional chieftain or indigenous tribal leader.

Ever since its foundation in 1524, the Council of the Indies had exclusive jurisdiction over the affairs of the Royal Treasury. From the end of the 16th century onwards, however, its task was facilitated by the assistance of a Treasury Council member who was also entitled to dispose of and administer funds received via the *Casa de la Contratación*. The Council was, however, entrusted with fiscal lawsuits, and was also assigned the important task of examining and controlling the accounts sent by royal officials from the Americas and the Philippines. It also had an auditing division known as the *Contaduría Mayor* which, as well as examining the Council's accounts, audited those of the *Casa de la Contratación* and the Consulates of Seville and Cádiz.

The functionaries in charge of treasury in the Indies were royal officials and the province over which they had jurisdiction was known as the *Caja Real*. The administrative seat of the latter was located in the capital cities of the various viceroyalties and provinces, in addition to places where the abundance of local resources—usually mineral wealth—warranted them.

Previous page
An Indian village.

1581
Map of the Indian village of Tetela.
By Cristóbal Godínez y Maldonado,
corregidor *of the village.*
700 x 420 mm.
MP. México, 31.

The process of colonization provided not only for the foundation of Spanish towns but also for that of a large number of Indian towns in order to evangelize and exercise increased control over the indigenous population. They were laid out in similar fashion to the Spanish settlements, while the sites chosen and the territorial distribution were often the same as those prevalent in pre-Hispanic times. In addition to Tetela, the map shows other villages in the jurisdiction of Sochimilco province which, as a Crown possession, was based on the original, indigenous provincial division.

The Royal Treasury: the royal fifth.

19 May 1522, Coyoacan.
Register of the gold, silver and jewels which treasurers took from the New World to H.M. in lieu of the royal fifth and other rights.
Signed by Hernando Cortés and the royal officials, Alonso de Grado and Bernardino Vázquez de Tapia, accountant and factor, respectively.
4 fols.
Patronato, 180, r. 88.

The royal fifth was one of the first tributes levied by the Crown, mainly on metals, precious stones and pearls taken from deposits, huacas *(Indian tombs) and shrines. The result was that a large part of the flood of gold and silver that arrived from the Americas in the 16th and 17th centuries ended up in the royal coffers. Between 1564 and 1624, the Kingdom of New Granada mined one and a half million pesos worth of emeralds. Pearls came mainly from Tierra Firme—in the* Cajas Reales *of Santo Domingo, San Juan and Cubagua, over eleven thousand kilos of pearls were allocated to the royal fifth in the first half of the 16th century.*

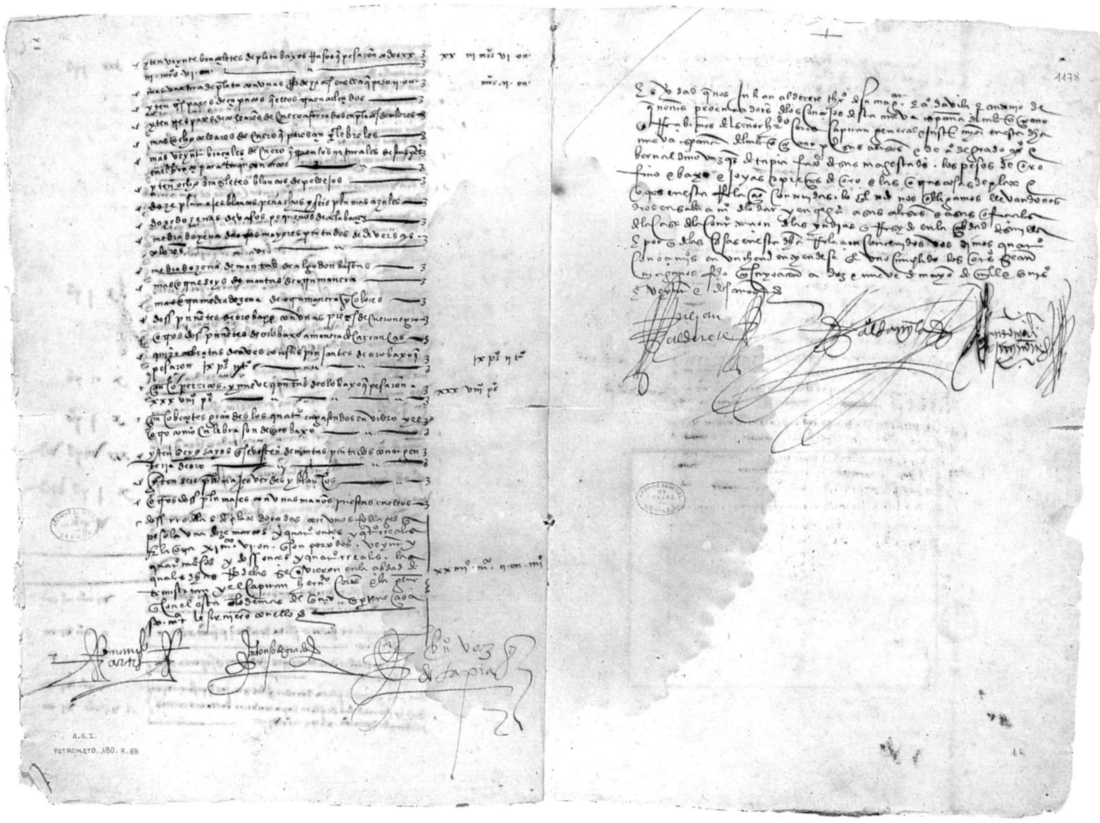

The Royal Treasury: Indian tribute.

[1550–1564]
Register of tribute paid to the Crown by some villages around the Mexico City volcano and what they might contribute if exempted from 'derramas and other tributes which governors and principals impose on them on doctrinal pretexts...'
The margin features annotations by the viceroy, Luis de Velasco, on the number of Indians in each town.
2 fols.
From a book of inspections and valuations among the Indian population in New Spain.
1550–1570.
México, 256.

16 February 1568, Mexico.
'List of the tribute which the natives of the state governed by Don Martín Cortés, the Marqués del Valle, are obliged to pay in the course of a year...'.
16 fols.
From a book of inspections and valuations among the Indian population in New Spain.
1550–1570.
México, 256.

Once their status as subjects of the Crown had been established, the Indians had to start paying a poll tax which they had previously paid to their chiefs or leaders. The list of what they paid was recorded in a valuation book.

Araya salt pan.

1623.
'Irregular ground plan of the defenses at the Ancon landing site to prevent skirmishes at the Araya saltworks, by Captain Andrés Rodríguez de Villegas, governor of this island of Margarita by the grace of H.M. the King.'
533 x 817 mm.
MP. Venezuela, 14.

The map shows the defenses proposed by the governor of Margarita Island to prevent enemy raids on the salt pan. The salt trade was one of the Crown's oldest monopolies but the revenue it generated was not large compared to the income from other monopolies such as tobacco, mercury and playing cards.

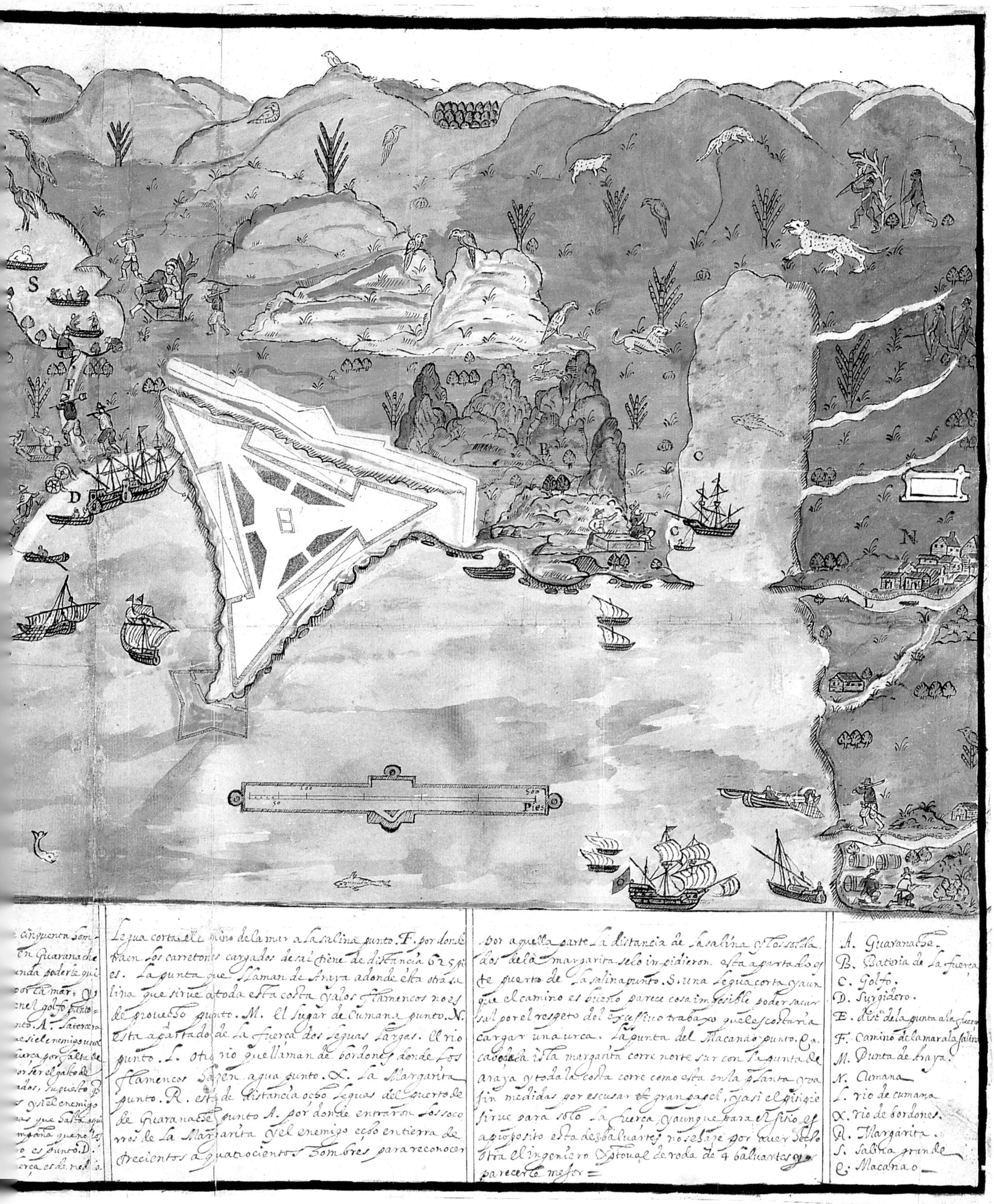
Pies
Legua corta el camino dela mar a la salina punto. F. por donde
vaen los carretones cargados de sal tiene de distancia 625 pi
es. La punta que llaman de Araya adonde esta otra sa
lina que sirue a toda esta costa y a los flamencos no es
de prouecho punto. M. el lugar de Cumana punto. N.
esta apartado de la fuerça dos leguas largas. el rio
punto. L. otro rio que llaman de bordones donde los
flamencos hazen agua punto. X. La Margarita
punto. R. esta de distancia ocho leguas del puerto de
de Guaranaese punto A. por donde entraron los soco
rros de la Margarita y el enemigo echo en tierra de
trecientos a quatrocientos hombres para reconocer
por aquella parte la distancia de la salina y los solda
dos dela margarita selo impidieron. esta apartado es
te puerto de la salina punto. S. una legua corta y aun
que el camino es bueno parece cosa imposible poder sacar
sal por el respeto del excesiuo trabajo que les costaria
cargar una urca. La punta del Macanao punto. Ç.
cabo dela isla margarita corre norte sur con la punta de
araya y toda la costa corre como esta en la planta y va
sin medidas por escusar gran papel, y asi el pitipie
sirue para solo la fuerça, y aunque para el sitio es
aproposito esta de 3 baluartes no se sabe por auer hecho
otra el ingeniero Xpstoual de roda de 4 baluartes que
parecerle mejor =
A. Guaranaese.
B. Bateria de la fuerça
C. Golfo.
D. Surgidero.
E. distª dela punta ala fuerça
F. Camino dela mar a la salina
M. Punta de Araya.
N. Cumana
L. rio de cumana
X. rio de bordones.
R. Margarita.
S. Salina grande
Ç. Macanao

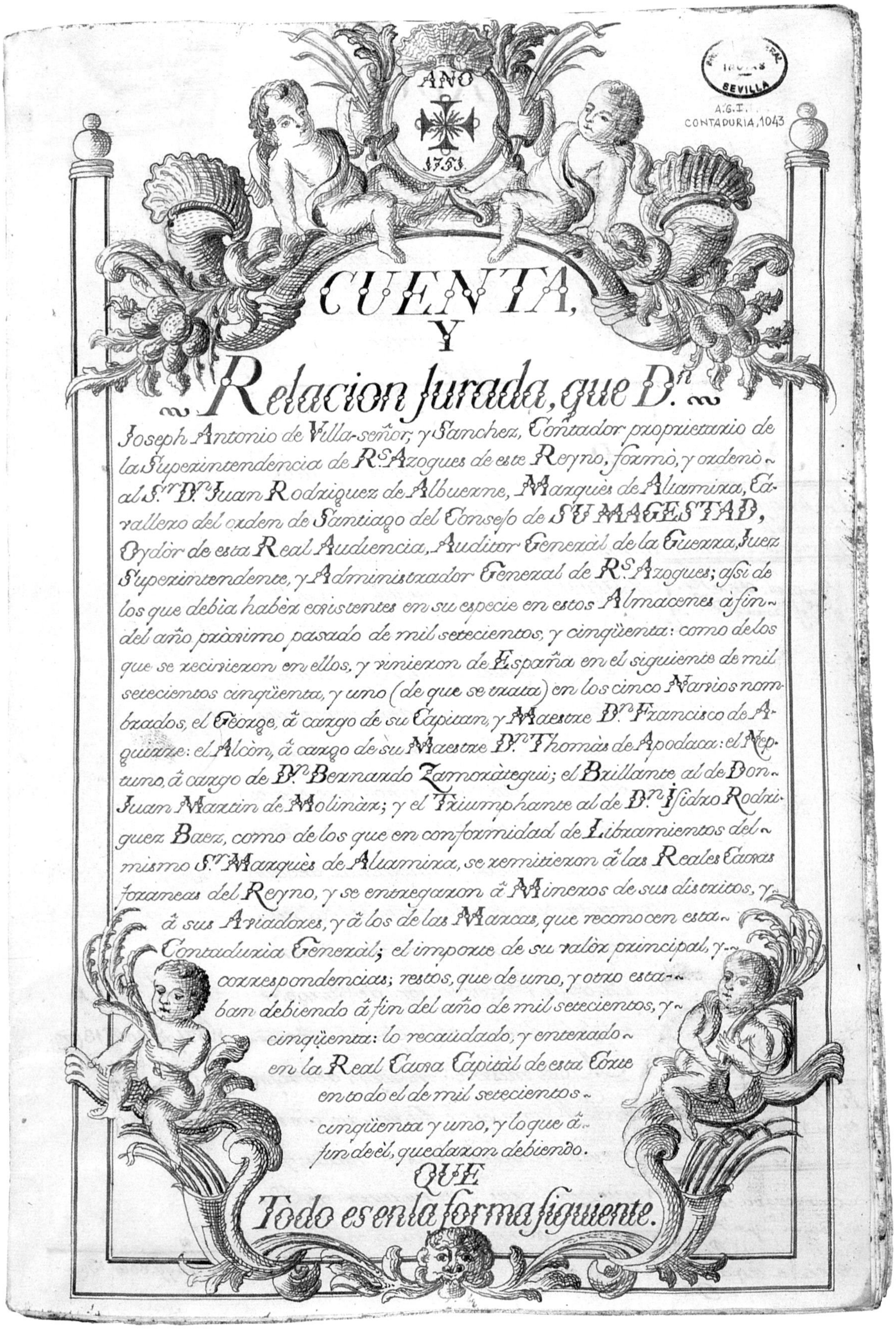

AÑO 1751

CUENTA, Y Relacion Jurada, que Dn. Joseph Antonio de Villa-señor, y Sanchez, Contador propietario de la Superintendencia de Rs. Azogues de este Reyno, formò, y ordenò al Sr. Dn. Juan Rodriguez de Albuerne, Marquès de Altamira, Cavallero del orden de Santiago del Consejo de SU MAGESTAD, Oydòr de esta Real Audiencia, Auditor General de la Guerra, Juez Superintendente, y Administrador General de Rs. Azogues; assi de los que debia habèr existentes en su especie en estos Almacenes à fin del año proximo pasado de mil setecientos, y cinqüenta: como de los que se recivieron en ellos, y vinieron de España en el siguiente de mil setecientos cinqüenta, y uno (de que se trata) en los cinco Navios nombrados, el George, à cargo de su Capitan, y Maestre Dn. Francisco de Aguirre: el Alcòn, à cargo de su Maestre Dn. Thomàs de Apodaca: el Neptuno, à cargo de Dn. Bernardo Zamorategui; el Brillante al de Don Juan Martin de Molinàr; y el Triumphante al de Dn. Isidro Rodriguez Baez, como de los que en conformidad de Libramientos del mismo Sr. Marquès de Altamira, se remitieron à las Reales Caxas foraneas del Reyno, y se entregaron à Mineros de sus distritos, y à sus Aviadores, y à los de las Marcas, que reconocen esta Contaduria General; el importe de su valòr principal, y correspondencias; restos, que de uno, y otro estaban debiendo à fin del año de mil setecientos, y cinqüenta: lo recaudado, y enterado en la Real Caxa Capital de esta Corte en todo el de mil setecientos cinqüenta y uno, y lo que à fin de èl, quedaron debiendo.

QUE

Todo es en la forma siguiente.

State monopolies: mercury.

1751
Sworn declaration by the Marquis of Altamira, Inspector General and administrator of the Reales Azogues de Nueva España *(Royal Mercury Mines of New Spain).*
105 fols.
Contaduría, 1043.

Mercury was essential for the extraction of silver in the New World, for which reason its management, transportation and sale was declared a State monopoly in 1559. It was distributed by the Cajas Reales. *On account of the considerable income it generated for the Royal Treasury, in the 18th century inspectors were appointed to oversee the trade in Mexico and Peru.*

Trade revenues: Alcabalas.

1768.
Ledger from the Real Caja de Alcabalas, *Mexico, showing accounts for the year 1768 kept by the inspector general, José Basarte, and endorsed by the viceroy, the Marquis of Criox.*
113 fols. & 27 blanks.
México, 2076.

The alcabala *was a sales tax levied on the sale of personal property, real estate and livestock. Of Moorish origin, it was eventually phased out in 1845.*

VNO QUARTILLO

CAROLUS III D. G. · AÑOS DE 1768 Y 1769 · S 4

DE EL REY NRO SEÑOR

LIBRO GENERAL, COMUN DE LA Rl. CAXA DE-
ALCAVALA para la Cuenta de su Real Hacienda, que ha de Correr: desde Primero
de Henero de 1768 de CARGO y DATA, de todas las cantidades de Pesos, que se ente-
raren en ella, pertenecientes al Real Haver, como lo que de sus productos se pagarē, en
conformidad de Ordenes de S. M. y de este Superior Govierno: Cuya Cuenta
corre à Cargo de su Superintendente D. Joseph Basarte Coronel
de los Reales Exercitos: Contador Principal D. Nicolas de
Cerquera, y Thesorero D. Domingo Ygnº de Lardizaval
Y VA ARREGLADO A REALES ORDENANZAS Y A LO
determinado en Rs. Cedulas de 28 de Junio de 1695, y 15 de Febrero de
1700, en quanto à las Cuentas de su Rl Hacienda, que sean Anuales,
con separacion de Ramos, distincion de Personas, Causas, motivos, y Ordenes de que procedieron los enteros, y pagos. Y tiene este Libro 140 fojas
firmadas y Rubricadas del
Exmo Sr D. CARLOS FRANCISCO DE CROIX MARQs
de Croix, Cavallero del Orden de Calatrava, Comendador de Molinos, y Laguna Rota en el mismo Orden, Theniente General de los
Rs Exercitos, Virrey, Governador, y Capitan General de este Reyno de
Nueva España, Presidente de su Real Audiencia, Superintendte
General de Rl. Hacienda en el, Presidente de la Junta
del Tabaco, Juez Conservador de este Ramo, y Subde-
legado General del nuevo establecimiento de Correos
Maritimos en el mismo Reyno

El Marqs. de Croix

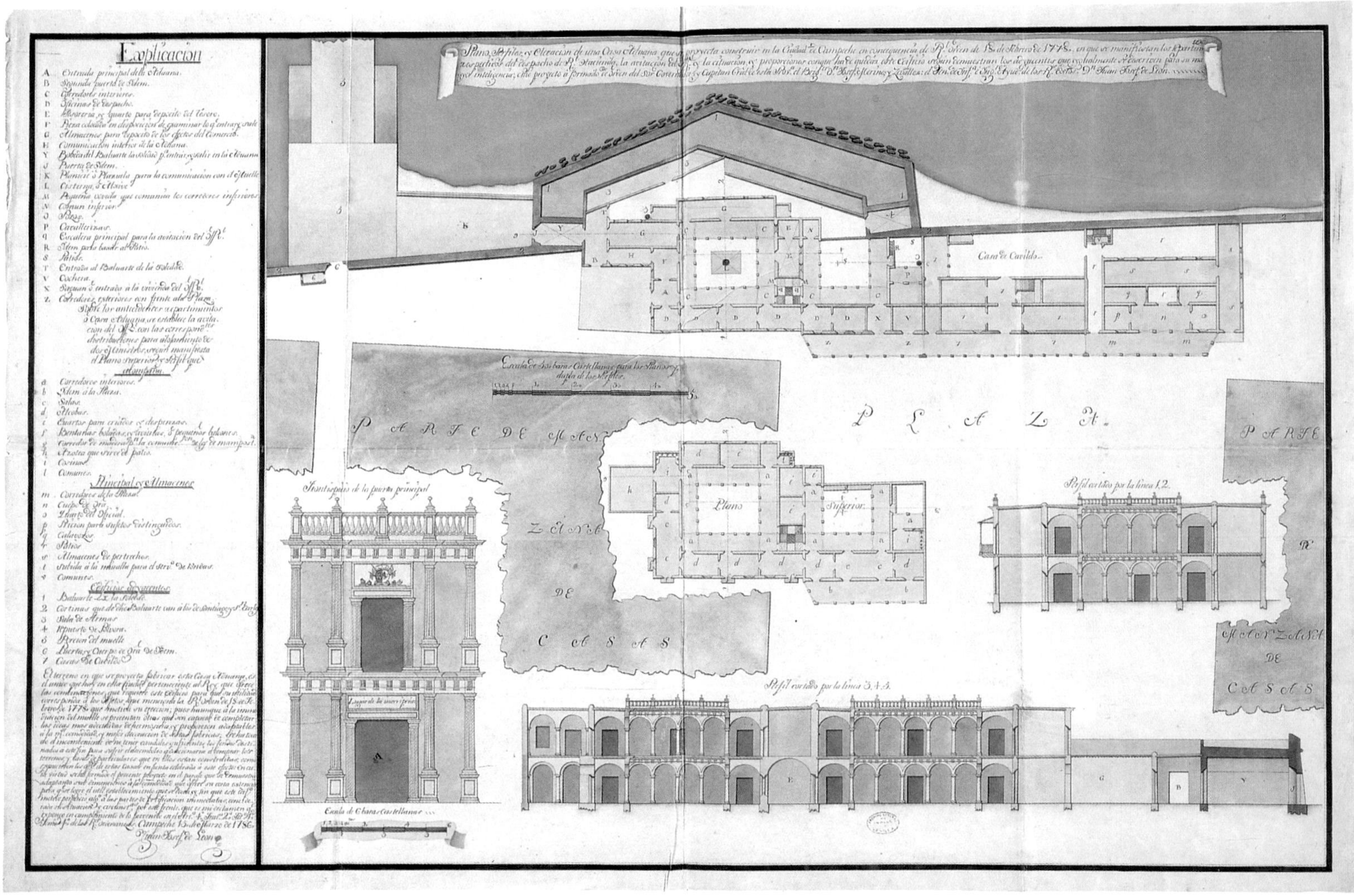

The number of *Cajas Reales* varied throughout the colonial period. When the Council was set up, they were already operating in Hispaniola, Cuba, Puerto Rico and New Spain. Each consisted of a treasurer, an accountant, a factor and an inspector. In 1563, the last two posts were abolished. These functionaries were initially appointed by the king, on the Council's advice, but their positions were later sold and traded. Their work basically involved collecting and administering Crown revenues and keeping track of both income and expenditure. The treasurer was responsible for the receipt of all income, as well as for collecting taxes and making payments. The accountant kept the books and signed orders for payment. Both were keepers of the keys to a safe with three locks where funds were deposited.

The duty of the factor was to take receipt of all goods, while the *veedor* or inspector was assigned the task of stamping gold and silver with the royal seal to certify that the 'royal fifth' had been paid. This was one of the major sources of income for the Royal Treasury. This royal tribute was levied on metals, precious stones and pearls, regardless of whether they came from mines, fisheries, burial grounds or temples.

Other items regarded as gifts to the Crown included ownerless property and, above all, State monopolies, which provided one of the major sources of State

Trade controls: the Campeche customshouse.

1786.
'Plan, outlines and elevation of a customshouse designed for the town of Campeche.'
By Juan José de León.
510 x 790 mm.
MP. México, 403.

Closely related to the treasury, customs posts were essential for collecting mercantile duties and combatting fraud and smuggling. This one at Campeche was commissioned by a royal decree of 18 February 1778 which sought to endow the town with a customshouse worthy of its mercantile standing. Owing to a lack of funds, the patios and the facade were never built.

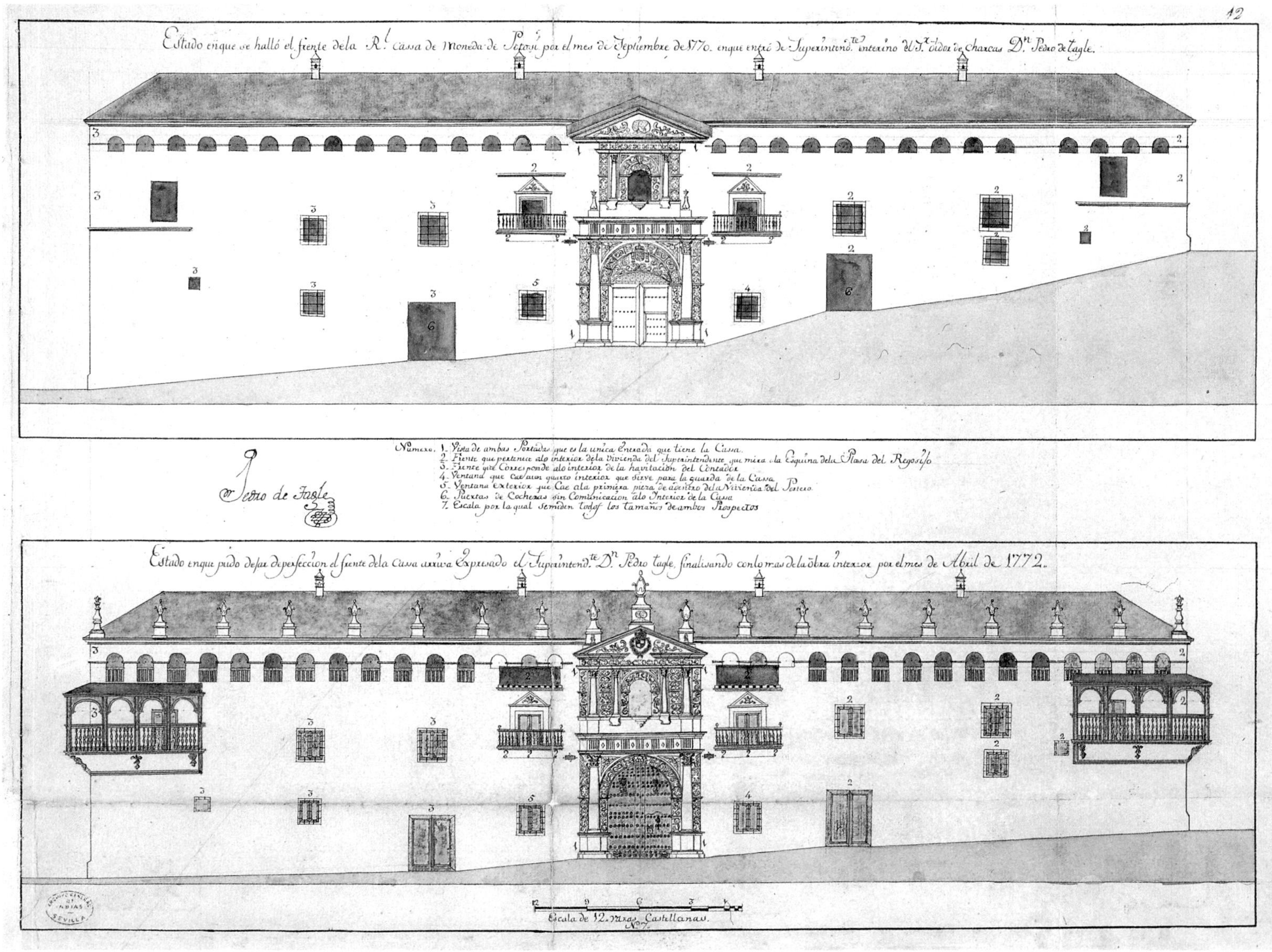

The Royal Mint, Potosí.

1772.
Plans for the facade of the Royal Mint at Potosí.
By Pedro de Tagle.
374 x 507 mm.
MP. Buenos Aires, 279.

Mints were built in the major cities and in areas of considerable mineral wealth, like the one in Potosí, which started minting coins in 1572.

income. These monopolies covered salt, gunpowder, official stamped paper, playing cards and, particularly, mercury used in the extraction of silver.

Crown subjects also contributed to State finances through the payment of levies and direct or indirect taxes. The principal taxes levied on trade were the customs duty known as *almojarifazgo,* the *alcabala, avería* or average, which contributed towards the maintenance of the navy, and *sisa,* an excise tax gauged by the weight and measure of foodstuffs.

The main direct tax was the so-called 'Indies tribute', which the Crown collected from individuals, and a poll tax which the Indians had to pay once they were recognized as royal subjects. They paid the tribute in the form of money or farm produce as they had previously done to their tribal leaders. It was calculated as a fixed amount for each male Indian above the age of fifteen. The Crown ended up assigning collection of the tribute to conquistadors and their descendants who, as *encomenderos,* exacted the tribute from the indigenous population in the form of labor or tax. The list of all contributing Indians from the *pueblos* was kept in a book of valuation which acted as a register for *corregidores* and royal officials.

Other taxes paid by individuals included *mediannatas* (semestral ecclesiastic stipends), levied on those with royal appointments, *lanzas,* paid by bearers of titles of nobility, and revenues generated by the sale of administrative posts.

Lastly, there were ecclesiastical taxes levied by virtue of the Crown's royal patronage. These included tithes, *crusades* (indulgences sold under the *Bula de Cruzada*), minor and major *vacantes* (stipends redirected to the Crown when church offices fell vacant), monthly stipends and *mediannatas, vacantia* and duties on a bishop's estate at his death.

Turning to public expenditure, the principal disbursements were for functionaries' salaries, the army and the navy, the upkeep of frontier garrisons and fortresses, fortifications and defenses and ecclesiastical expenses, including those of the clergy, missions, church building, alms and convents.

Accounts submitted by royal officials were initially inspected by the Council's auditing division, the *Contaduría,* until an intermediary auditing body was charted for the purpose—the so-called *Tribunal de Cuentas*. Auditing offices of this kind were charted by royal decree on 24 October 1605 in Mexico City, Santa Fe and Lima. Their duty was to receive and certify accounts presented by officials and other royal administrators of revenues, as well as to collect taxes, inspect the *Cajas Reales* and manage securities.

Apart from the *Cajas Reales* and *Tribunales de Cuentas,* there were other fiscal bodies such as the Customs which were essential for collecting trade duties and controlling fraud and contraband. Special courts were set up to manage royal tributes, including that of *Bienes de Difuntos* (Estate Duties Tribunal), *Lanzas y Mediannatas* and the *Tribunal de la Santa Cruzada* (Court of the Holy Crusade). The development of State monopolies in the 18th century led to the creation of a general revenues administration and such special administrative bodies as the one in charge of tobacco.

In connection with the treasury but on an autonomous, regional level were the Royal Mints which were founded by the Council of the Indies by royal decree as of 1535. The need for specie, the abundant mineral supplies and the threat of forgeries warranted the creation of mints in major cities such as Mexico City, in 1535 and Lima, in 1556 and in towns set in wealthy mining areas such as Potosí, in 1572. The main currency in circulation was the *peso fuerte* or silver *duro*.

The Council likewise had supreme authority in trade and shipping matters, although the *Casa de la Contratación* and Consulates were the direct administrators.

ORDENANZAS
PARA EL GOVIERNO
DE LA LABOR DE MONEDAS,
QUE SE FABRICAREN EN LA REAL CASA
DE MONEDA DE MEXICO,
Y DEMAS DE LAS INDIAS,
EN QUANTO FUEREN ADAPTABLES A ESTA.
MINISTROS, OFICIALES, Y OPERARIOS
que se han de ocupar; sueldos que hàn de gozar, encargos, y obligaciones de cada vno; derechos que se señalan para costèar las labores de las monedas; ensayes que hàn de hacerse de ellas, y de las barras, y piezas de oro, y plata; con lo demàs que hà de observarse.

IMPRESAS DE ORDEN DE S. M. EN LA IMPRENTA DEL REAL, y Supremo Consejo DE INDIAS. Año de M.DCC.L.

Royal Mint of Mexico.

1 August 1750, Buen Retiro.
'Statutes governing the minting of coins in the Royal Mint of Mexico and others in the Indies once they have been commissioned...'
[Madrid]: 'Imprint of the Royal and Supreme Council of the Indies, 1750'.
3 sheets, 51 pp., fol.
México, 1293.

The Royal Mint of Mexico was charted on the inception of the viceroyalty in 1535. The monetary system was based on the one prevalent in the Iberian Peninsula in the 16th century. Silver was used for minting the coins and the common unit was the peso fuerte *or* duro, *equivalent to 450 maravedis.*

The Council did not only wield executive power over civil authorities. By virtue of royal patronage, its mandate extended to the Church authorities as well. As we have seen, on the strength of the Discovery, patronage of the Church in the New World was granted to the kings of Castile in a number of papal bulls issued by Pope Alexander VI and Pope Julius II. In return for a formal pledge to convert the natives, those bulls granted the monarchs the right to set up a full-blown Church hierarchy, as well as to exact tithes; in short, to exercise their patronage. This entitled them to administer religious property, while committing them to fund and upkeep the Church in the New World. As of 1538, it also empowered them to officially approve papal bulls and briefs before their promulgation in the Indies and to withhold any documents they considered contrary to the accord of royal patronage.

The ecclesiastical presence made itself felt immediately after the Discovery. Indeed, Fray Bernardo Boyl sailed on Columbus' second voyage with express instructions to convert the natives. The Franciscan friar reached Santo Domingo in Ovando's fleet in 1502, while the Dominicans landed in 1510. Shortly after Cortés' conquest of Mexico, both orders moved there.

Nevertheless, sending priests and friars was not sufficient to establish the Church in the conquered territories. In 1504, Ferdinand the Catholic asked Rome to create ecclesiastical provinces and Pope Julius II responded by setting up three dioceses in Santo Domingo. However, the corresponding bulls made no mention of the rights associated with royal patronage, prompting the king to postpone their implementation and elicit new bulls which endorsed the original grants made by Alexander VI. Thus, in 1511, by the bull *Romanus Pontifex,* Pope Julius II dissolved the original dioceses of 1504 and created three alternative ones, in Santo Domingo, Concepción de la Vega and Puerto Rico, the first to be established in the New World. Instead of being treated as ecclesiastical provinces, they were regarded as subordinate to the metropolitan of Seville, where new bishops were to be appointed. This was specified in the contract endorsed in Seville by the Catholic King and Queen Joan, and the three bishops appointed to the new dioceses: García de Padilla, for Santo Domingo, Xuárez de Deza, for Concepción de la Vega, and Alonso Manso, for Puerto Rico.

The ecclesiastical organization in the New World made swift progress in the first half of the 16th century. The dioceses of the Antilles—Santa María de la Antigua (1513), Jamaica and Cuba (1517)—were followed by those of New Spain: Puebla (1519), Tierra Florida (1521), Mexico City (1530), Oaxaca (1535) and Michoacán (1536). Dioceses were likewise established in Tierra Firme—Nicaragua, Coro, Comayagua (1531), Santa Marta, Cartagena, Guatemala (1534) and Chiapas (1539)—and, in the kingdom of Peru, at Cuzco (1537), Lima (1541) and Quito

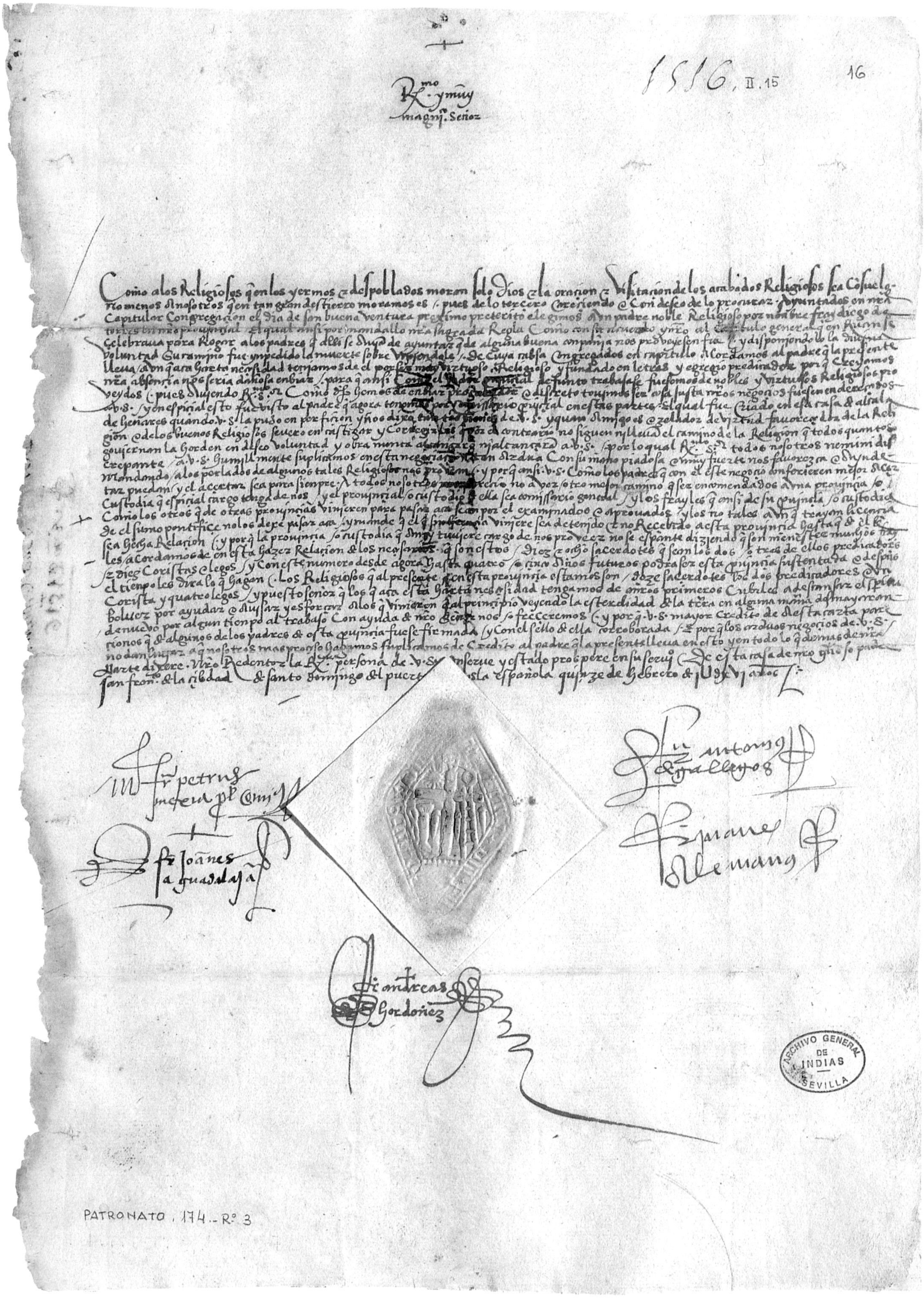
R.mo y muy magnf. Señor
1516. II.15
16
ARCHIVO GENERAL DE INDIAS SEVILLA
PATRONATO, 174.- R.º 3

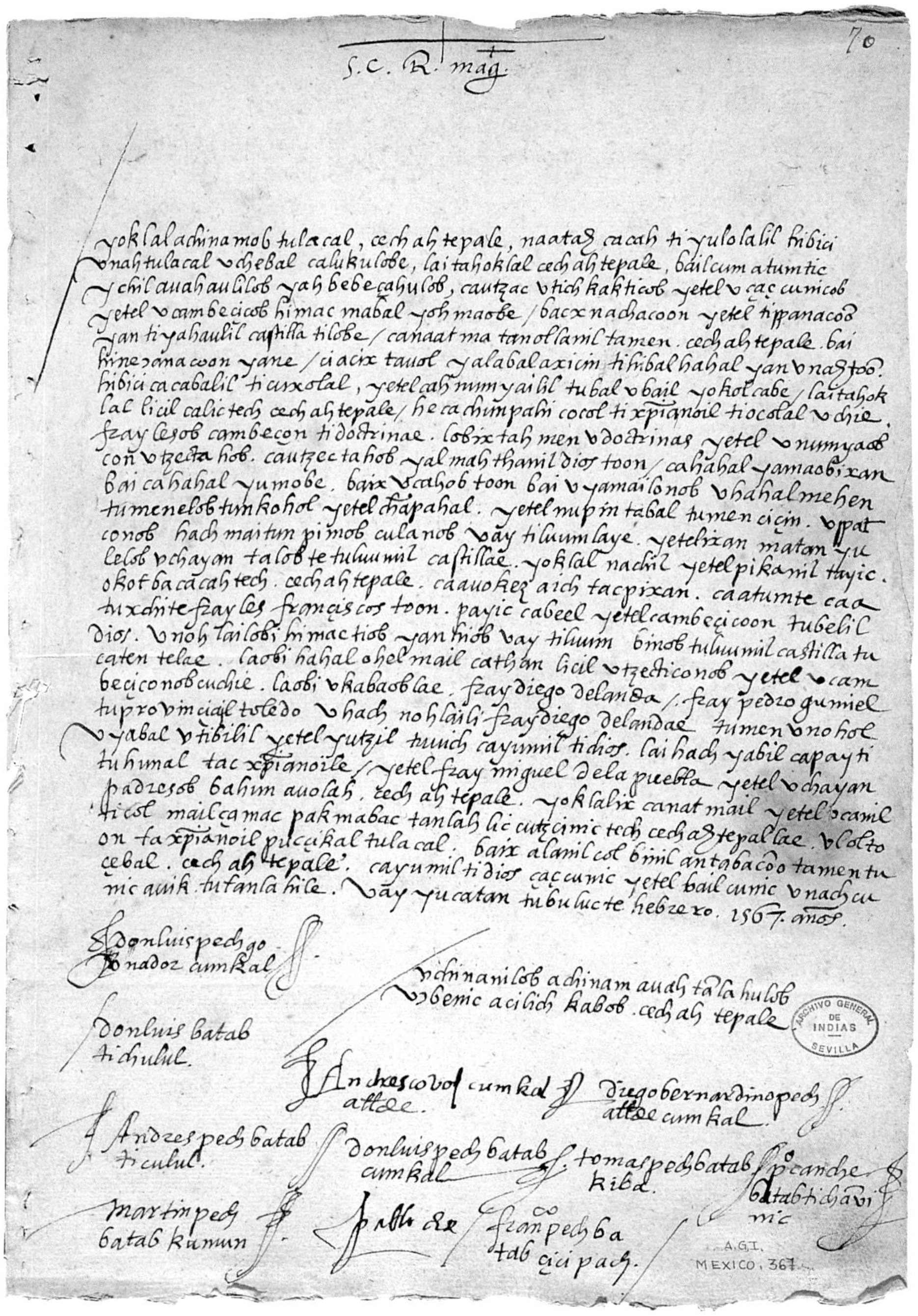

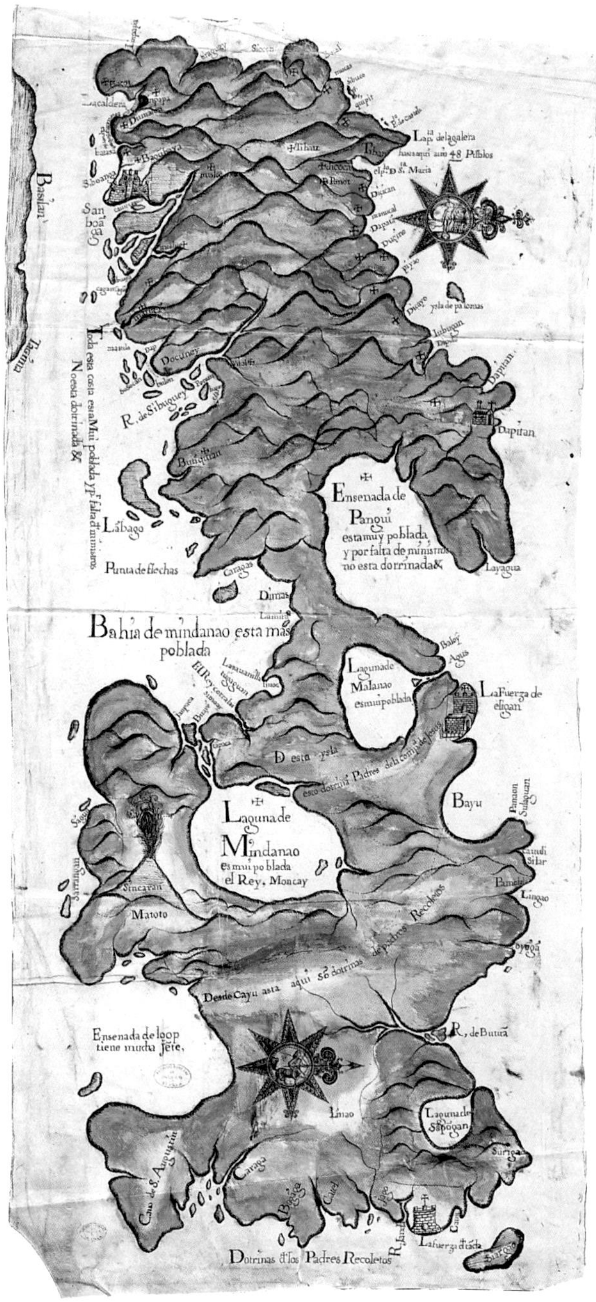

OPPOSITE: *Missionary work: the Franciscans.*

15 February 1516, Santo Domingo.
Letter from the Franciscans, Pedro de Mesía, Juan de Guadalajara, Antonio de Gallegos, Juan Alemanes and Andrés Ordóñez, to Cardinal Cisneros, Archbishop of Toledo, urging him to send missionaries and assign a province to them.
Stamp of the Order of St Francis.
1 fol. Patronato, 174, R. 3.

The Franciscans reached the New World after sailing with Fray Boyl on Columbus' second voyage in 1493. In his bull Exponi nobis *(1522), Pope Adrian VI granted them extensive privileges for conducting their missionary work, which focused on New Spain in 1524 and on Quito and Peru ten years later. By the late-16th century, there were ten Franciscan provinces in the Americas.*

Letter from the Indians of Yucatán.

11 February 1567, Yucatán.
Letter from the Indian chiefs of Yucatán to Philip II requesting him to send Franciscan missionaries, particularly those familiar with their language, such as Fray Diego de Landa and Fray Miguel de Puebla.
Written in the Mayan language.
2 fols. México, 367.

Missions on Mindanao.

[1683]
'Map of the island of Mindanao, where the Zamboanga garrison was established.'
The map shows the locations of Jesuit and Recollect missions.
940 x 422 mm.
MP. Filipinas, 11.

The Jesuits reached the Philippines in 1581 and set up their mother house in Manila. From there they ventured out to the other islands on an evangelizing mission, in similar fashion to their campaign in Mexico. In addition to the college of San Ignacio in Manila, they founded the colleges of Zamboanga, Santa Cruz, San José el Real, Cavite, Cebú and San Pedro Macutín, and the missions of Marianas, Marinduque, Pintados, Tagalos, Mindanao, Zasnal and Aetas.

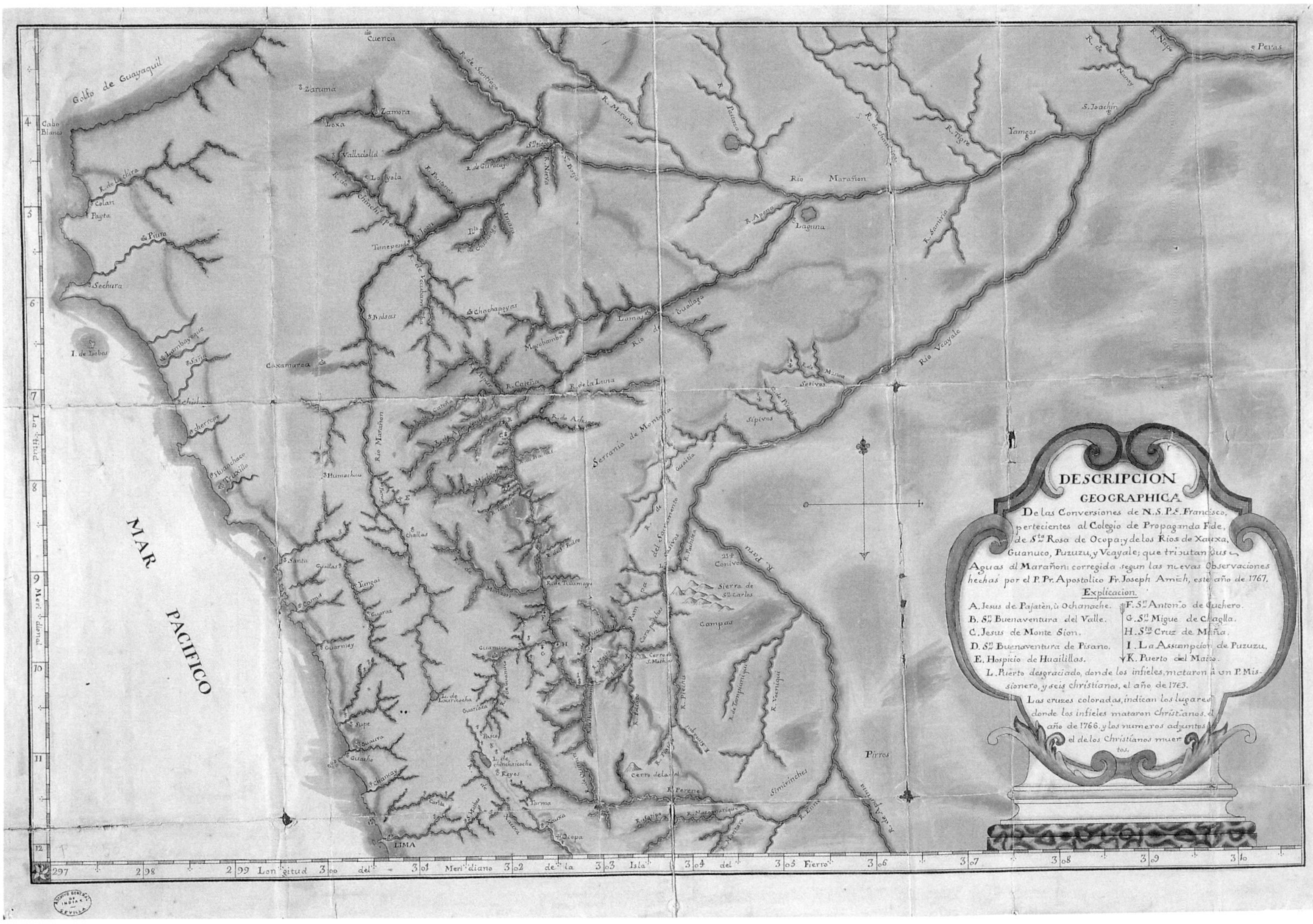

La Propaganda Fide.

1767.
'Geographical description of conversions performed by Franciscan friars from the College of La Propaganda Fide *in Santa Rosa de Ocopa...'*
630 x 420 mm.
MP. Perú y Chile, 50.

The Franciscan college of La Propaganda Fide, *in Santa Rosa de Ocopa, conducted intensive missionary work in eastern Peru between the Marañón and Ucayali rivers. The red crosses on the map mark spots where a large number of missionaries were killed by the particularly warlike tribes that inhabited the region.*

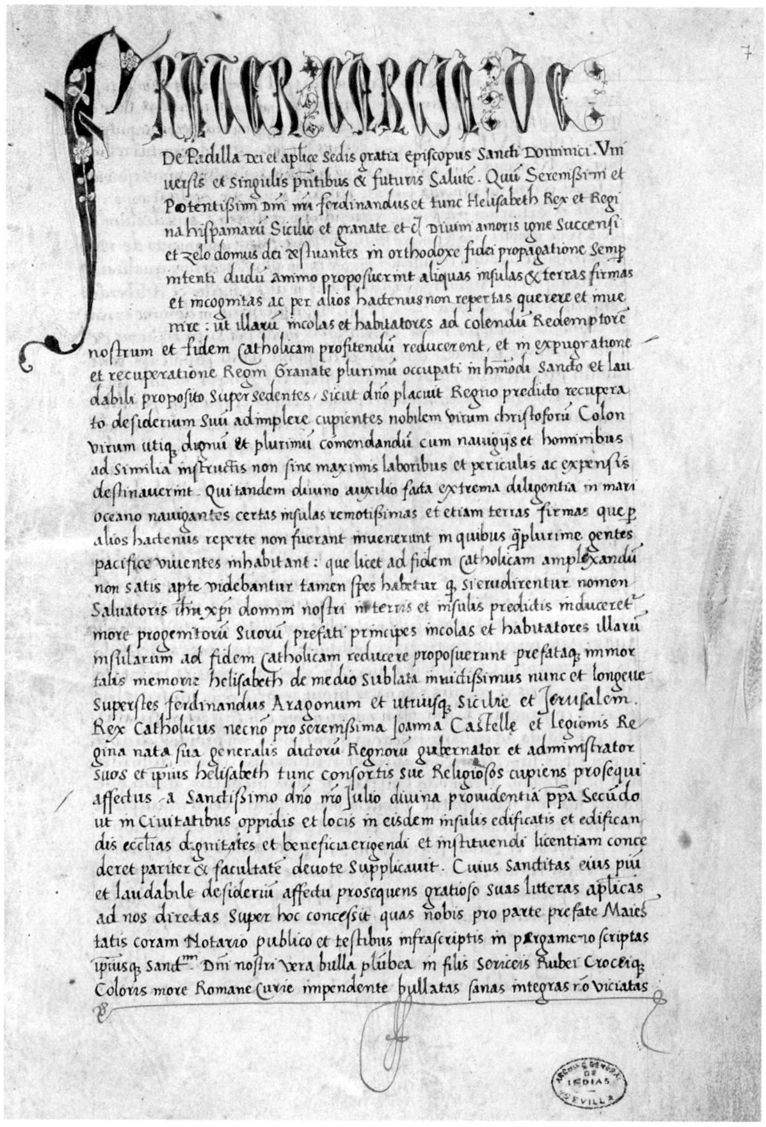

The diocesan Church: Bishopric of Santo Domingo.

12 May 1512, Burgos.
Notarial certificate endorsed by the apostolic notary, Francisco de Valenzuela, attesting to the building of the church of Santo Domingo on the island of Hispaniola, under the direction of its first bishop, García de Padilla, who officiated at the founding ceremony.
Fols. 7 r. to 13 v.
Notebook: 229 x 320 mm.
13 fols. + 1 blank, covers.
MP. Bulas y Breves, 9.

The first ecclesiastical province of the New World was founded in 1511, when Pope Julius II issued his bull Romanus Pontifex, *which provided for the creation of the first three New World dioceses at Santo Domingo, Concepción de la Vega and Puerto Rico. They were subordinate to the metropolitan of Seville where the three bishops appointed to them were consecrated. This certificate includes Julius II's bull.*

(1546). All were subordinate to the Bishop of Seville. In 1546, Pope Paul III established three legally independent ecclesiastical provinces: Mexico, which took in all dioceses from Guatemala to Florida, Santo Domingo, which included those in the Antilles and on the Caribbean coast, and Lima, to which all South American dioceses were subordinate. These were soon followed by the archdioceses of Manila, Charcas and Santa Fe.

The Council was in charge of the creation, division and organization of the dioceses. Whenever a new one was established, the first episcopal duties involved building the church and instituting both the chapter and the rules to be followed in apportioning tithes and celebrating the various services.

The chapter consisted of dignitaries—dean, archdeacon, precentor, *maestrescuela* (lecturer) and treasurer—canons, subordinates and residents. Under the diocese—the highest religious territorial unit—there were several minor divisions such as the vicariate and parish, generally located in areas inhabited mainly by Spaniards. Priests performed their duties in the Indian *pueblos* under their protection, while missions were set up among indigenous groups that were being evangelized for the first time. Separate and distinct from the missions were settlements that gathered together the natives not only for the purpose of evangelizing them but also for educating them and for promoting agricultural and industrial methods of production and, on occasion, for recruiting frontier defense forces.

Bishops in the New World had special powers granted by the pontiff, in view of the distance that separated them from Rome, both to settle issues that would otherwise have been referred to the Holy See and to convene synods and councils. These were essential instruments for the Church's consolidation—while not dogmatic, they did facilitate diocesan organization and provide the means for evangelizing, founding seminaries and other activities. The first American Council, convened by Archbishop Loaysa, was held in Lima in 1551, while the first one held in Mexico was convened by the Dominican friar, Alonso de Montufar, in 1555. In their conclusions, both stressed the need for securing the means for propagating the faith and for teaching the Cathechism in Indian languages.

As the Church hierarchy was taking shape across the New World, virtually the entire clergy was carrying out intensive missionary work. Franciscans, Dominicans, Augustinians and Mercedarians were instrumental in evangelizing the New World in the first half of the 16th century. The Jesuits arrived later in the century, first in Peru, where they had a marked influence in schools, residences and travelling missions. They reached Mexico in 1572 and were highly active as missionaries in Sinaloa, Durango and Coahuila.

The 17th century saw the rise of the *Congregatio de Propaganda Fide* (Roman Congregation of Propagation of the Faith) and the expansion of the Hospitaller orders. These were Bethlehemites, the only order indigenous to the New World, founded in Guatemala by the Canary Islander, Pedro de Bethencourt, and the Brothers of St John of God, who founded fifty–six hospitals in the Americas between 1596 and 1670.

The structure of the religious orders was based on the territorial division of ecclesiastical provinces which were established as and when the missionaries' work took them further afield. Each was headed by a 'provincial' of the order, elected by the friars for a period of three to six years. During that time, it was his task to direct the monks, guide their missionary work and convey orders from the king or the Pope.

Opposite
Archbishopric of Mexico.

17 September 1779, Mexico City. 'Geographical chart showing most of the area covered by the Archbishopric of Mexico City and part of the bishoprics of Puebla, Valladolid de Michoacán, Guadalajara and Durango, drawn up for the purpose of demarcating the territory taken in by the newly appointed bishopric, to be known as the New Kingdom of León...' By Miguel Costansó. 880 x 510 mm. MP. México, 352.

The cities of Mexico and Lima had the first metropolitan churches to be established in the New World, by order of Pope Paul III in 1546. The archbishopric of Mexico City embraced all the lands between Guatemala, the Mississippi and the Philippines. It was later divided up into various provinces that eventually became archdioceses. The Council was instrumental in setting up and determining the division of ecclesiastical provinces and this plan, commissioned in 1777, was produced by way of a Council report on the territory to be covered by the new bishopric of New León.

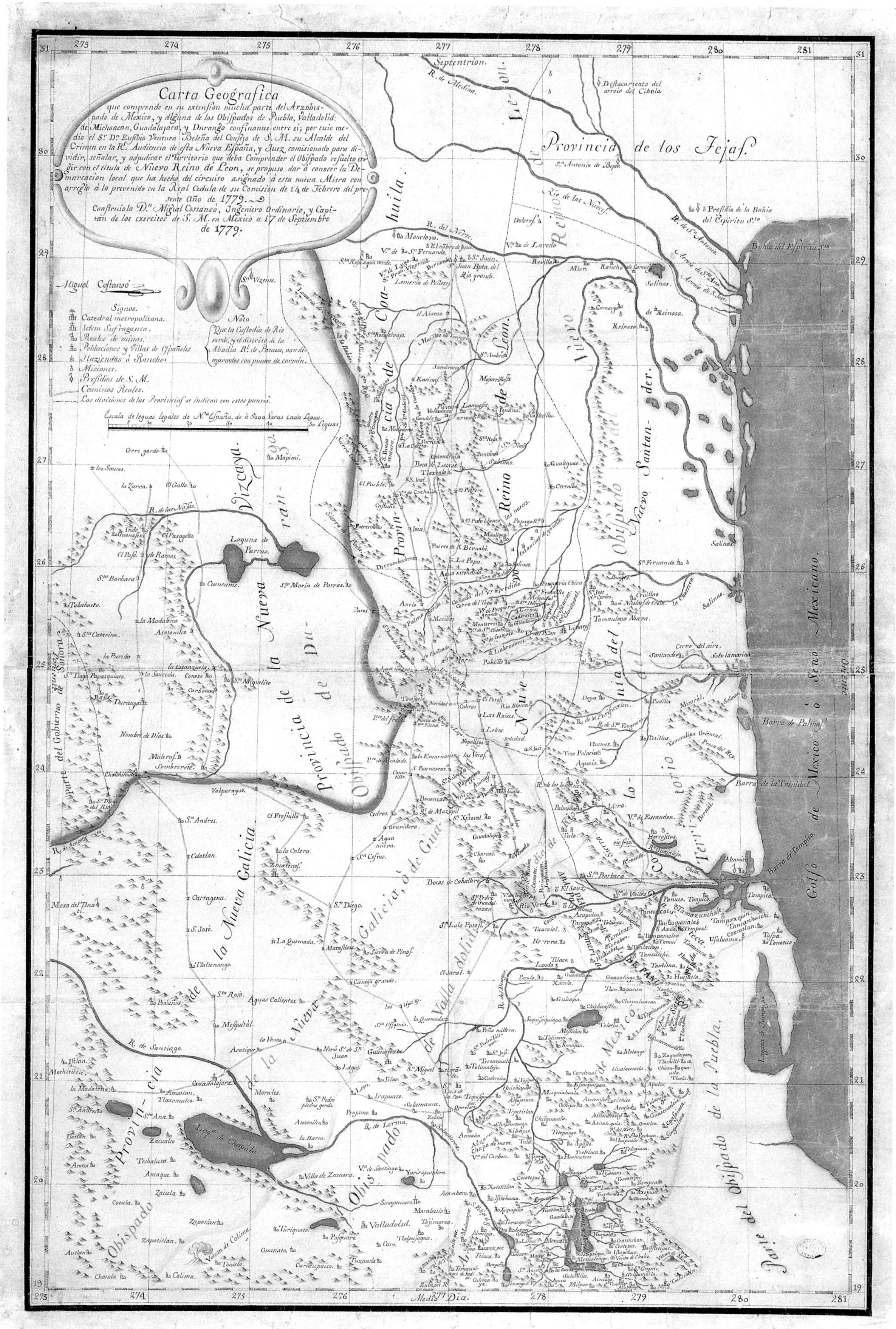
Carta Geografica
que comprende en su extension mucha parte del Arzobispado de Mexico, y alguna de los Obispados de Puebla, Valladolid de Michoacan, Guadalajara, y Durango confinantes entre si; por cuio medio el Sr. Dn. Eusebio Ventura Beleña del Consejo de S. M. su Alcalde del Crimen en la Rl. Audiencia de esta Nueva España, y Juez comisionado para dividir, señalar, y adjudicar el territorio que deba Comprender el Obispado resuelto erigir con el titulo de Nuevo Reino de Leon, se propuso dar á conocer la Demarcacion local que ha hecho del circuito asignado á esta nueva Mitra con arreglo á lo prevenido en la Real Cedula de su Comision de 14 de Febrero del presente Año de 1779.
Construiola Dn. Miguel Costansó, Ingeniero Ordinario, y Capitan de los exercitos de S. M. en Mexico a 17 de Septiembre de 1779.
Miguel Costansó
Signos.
Catedral metropolitana.
Idem Sufraganea.
Reales de minas.
Poblaciones y Villas de Españoles
Haziendas ó Ranchos
Misiones.
Presidios de S. M.
Caminos Reales.
Las divisiones de las Provincias se indican con estos puntos.
Nota
Que la Custodia de Rio verde, y el distrito de la Abadia Rl. de Panuco, van demarcados con puntos de carmín.
Escala de leguas legales de Na. España, de á 5000 Varas cada Legua.
5 10 20 30 40 50 Leguas
Septentrion.
Provincia de los Tejas.
Coahuila.
Nuevo Reino de Leon.
Nuevo Santander.
Provincia de la Nueva Vizcaya.
Obispado de Durango
Galicia, ó de Guadalajara
Golfo de Mexico ó Seno Mexicano.
Parte del Obispado de la Puebla.
Medio Dia.
273 274 275 276 277 278 279 280 281
31 30 29 28 27 26 25 24 23 22 21 20 19

The group of Church institutions in the The New World also included the Tribunal of the Inquisition, exported to Spanish America and set up in Lima in 1569 and Mexico in 1571. The few trials held there were directed mainly at foreigners, blasphemers and bigamists and at clergymen accused of vice or abuse of office. The Indians, however, did not come under the Tribunal's jurisdiction as they were regarded as novices in matters of faith.

The Church had a prominent role in Spanish America. In addition to spreading the faith, it also acted as a vehicle for acculturation—the difficulties posed by indigenous languages were soon overcome, as catechisms and collections of sermons were published in native languages, while missionaries acquired expert knowledge of indigenous cultures. In the field of education, the Church founded many schools, for both the natives and colonists. Thus, shortly after the conquest of Mexico, Fray Pedro de Gante founded a school for Indians in the convent of San Francisco. In 1536, the Colegio Imperial de Santa Cruz de Tlatelolco, which provided schooling for the sons of chieftains, was set up on the urging of the Mexican bishop, Fray Juan de Zumárraga, under the auspices of Viceroy Mendoza, who was also instrumental in commissioning the San Juan de Letrán school for those of mixed blood in 1547.

The Crown, acting through the Council of the Indies, also sanctioned and encouraged the creation of schools, colleges and universities. With statutes based on the universities of Salamanca and Alcalá de Henares, these spread across the whole of America. The Colegio de Santo Domingo on the island of Hispaniola became the Universidad de San Tomás Aquino in 1538. In 1551, with the sovereign's approval, Bishop Zumárraga founded the University of Mexico which, like all such institutions of the period, was awarded both royal and pontifical titles, as it had papal sanction. The University of Lima was founded the same year in the Convent of Nuestra Señora del Rosario, although the municipal authorities subsequently set aside another building for the institution. It was inaugurated there in 1577 on the feast day of St Mark, patron of the university.

The *universidades generales* or *mayores* enjoyed royal patronage and were supported with public funds. For this reason, the Council had a say in their statutes and curriculae and instructed viceroys to report on their progress and to settle issues and disagreements with other institutions.

Similarly, the Council also carried weight in cultural matters. It had the power to censor printed works and to decide what could be published in the Americas, where the book trade was growing steadily, as was local production thanks to the establishment of presses in Mexico City and Lima—the latter produced its first printed work in 1583.

OPPOSITE
Vicariate of San Ildefonso.

[1706]
Map of the vicariate of Villa Alta de San Ildefonso, in the province of Oaxaca, with its adjoining villages.
590 x 430 mm.
MP. México, 100.

From a religious viewpoint, the supreme territorial unit was the diocese, which was divided into parishes, vicariates, doctrinas *and missions. Their location and building often produced friction between the regular orders and secular clergy. In this case, the bishop of Oaxaca had requested the Dominicans to assign ten of the forty-five parishes they held in the bishopric to the seculars. The jurisdiction of Villa Alta was made up of five* vicarías *(vicariates) or* partidos *(districts), taking in a total of eighty-five* pueblos, *which were administered by the preaching orders.*

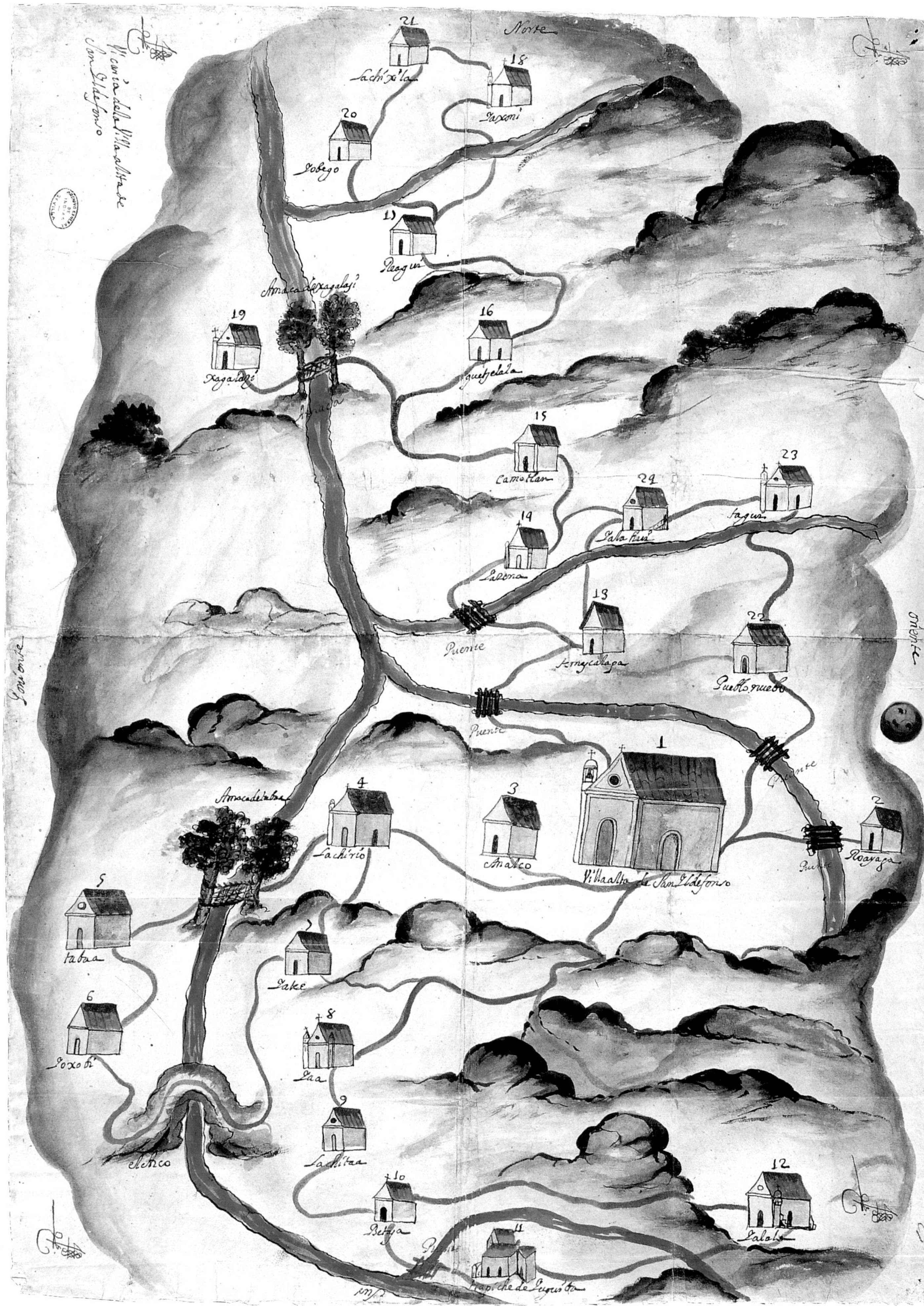

Norte
Poniente
Oriente
Puente
Camotlan
Analco
Villa alta de San Ildefonso
Roayaga
Tabaa
Yaa
Lachitaa
Betaza

As an administrative body the Council was active in the natural sciences, geography, mathematics and history. It also took part in examining technical discoveries and inventions in specific fields, such as those relating to mining, salvaging shipwrecks and fish farming. In theological law, the Council exercised a major role in affairs connected with the treatment of Indians and matters regarding royal patronage, for which it had a legislative mandate.

Indeed, in addition to all those executive functions, the Council had important legislative duties, which fell into two categories: drawing up and submitting to the king a variety of legal statutes relating to the Indies, and compiling, editing and writing a relevant legal code.

The king sanctioned laws by a procedure known as 'consultation', referring to both the act of royal consultation itself and the document derived from it. To be legally binding, all statutes had to be voted by two thirds of the councillors and a count of any votes cast against a proposal had to be submitted to the sovereign. Likewise, plenary sessions of the Council passed resolutions known as *autos acordados* concerning the enforcement of laws. After obtaining royal sanction, such *autos* became part of the mainstream legislation. All laws approved by the monarch and issued by the Council were registered in official books.

As for the task of compiling laws, in the first half of the 16th century the Council recognized the need to codify the growing volume of legislation. There are two landmarks in this respect—the *Recopilación de Leyes de Indias* (Codification of Laws of the Indies), dating from 1680, which is a compendium of legislation under the Habsburgs, and the 1797 *Nuevo Código de las Leyes de Indias* (New Legal Code of the Indies), in which the former was augmented by the addition of all the Bourbon provisions.

In the period between these two legal codes, the task of compilation undertaken by the Council produced some striking—albeit partially successful—results. Noteworthy in the 16th century were the endeavors of the *oidor* of Mexico, Vasco de Puga who, on instructions of the viceroy, Luis de Velasco, compiled all legal provisions concerning New Spain from 1525 to 1563. Equally commendable were the efforts of Juan López de Velasco who, from 1562 to 1568, under the auspices of the Council, summarized the contents of some two hundred record books, known as *cedularios*. Further to Juan de Ovando's inspection of the Council, on the orders of Philip II, came the code known as the *Código Ovandino,* a legal corpus comprising seven books dealing with spiritual government, temporal government, justice, the republic of the Spaniards, the Indians, the Royal Treasury, trade and shipping. A *cedulario* codifying all legal provisions since the time of the

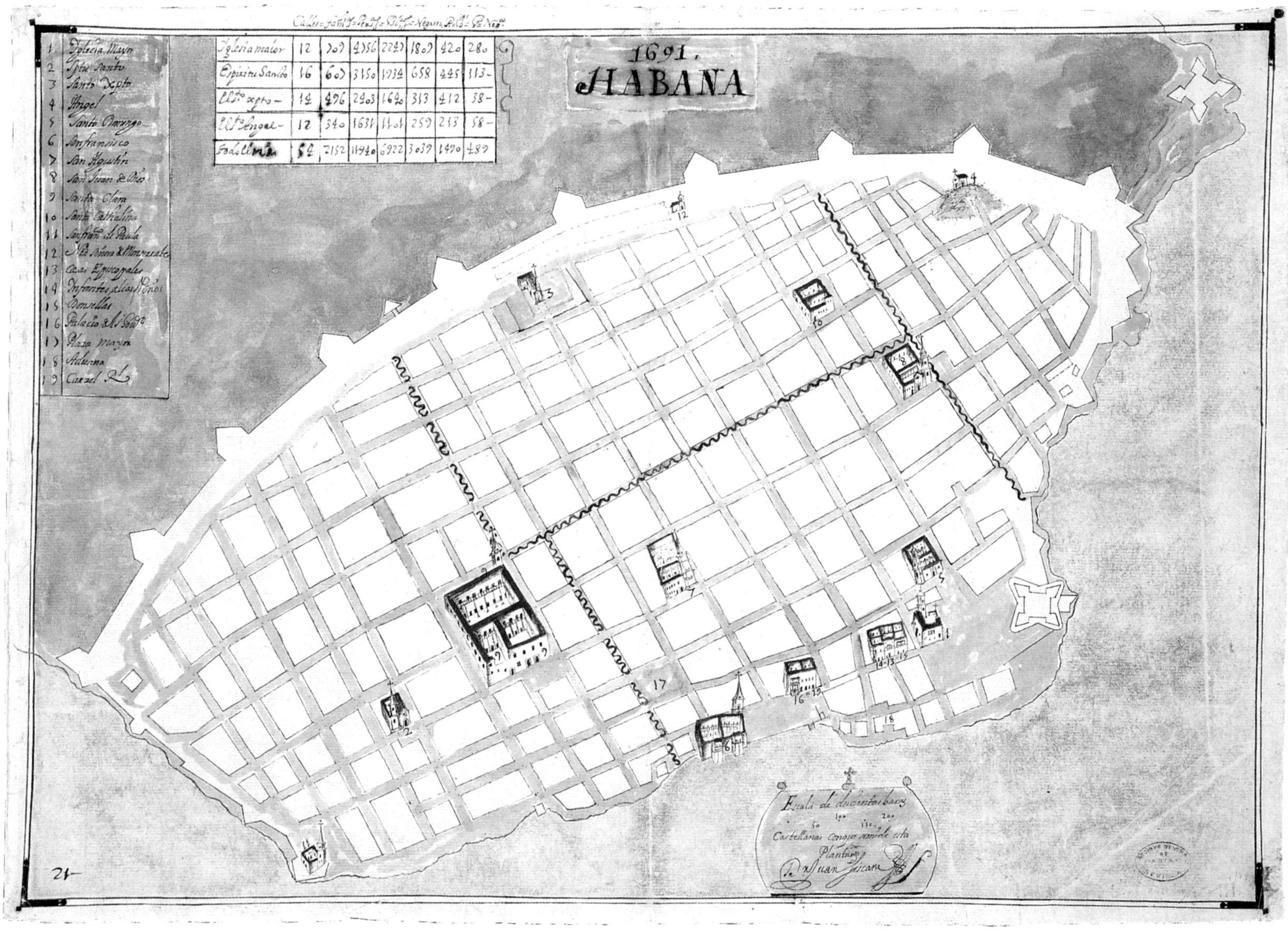

Parishes in Havana.

1691
Plan of the city of Havana showing the demarcation of its parishes.
By Juan Siscara.
312 x 430 mm.
MP. Santo Domingo, 97.

Sent by the governor, together with a record of the parishes built in the city. The table above lists the number of streets, families, black as well as white adults and children in each city.

Catholic Kings until those of Philip II was already in existence by the late-16th century, compiled by Diego de Encinas.

Notable contributions in the 17th century were those of Juan Solórzano Pereira and Antonio de León Pinelo who, in 1658, published the *Autos Acordados del Consejo de Indias,* a collection of resolutions issued by the Council of the Indies. The *Recopilación* of 1680 which, in the section citing the royal provision whereby it was instituted, contains a brief history of previous codifications, comprises a total of nine books, 218 chapters and over six thousand laws. Despite its shortcomings, it constituted a standardization of the legal diversity prevalent in the New World.

The changes that swept through all administrative fields in the 18th century, triggered by the Bourbon reforms, spawned a host of new laws that were to be added to the existing corpus of laws promulgated under the Habsburgs. In a royal decree of 9 May 1776, Charles III ordered a new code to be drawn up. The task was entrusted to Miguel José Serrador, deputy official of the Universal Secretariat

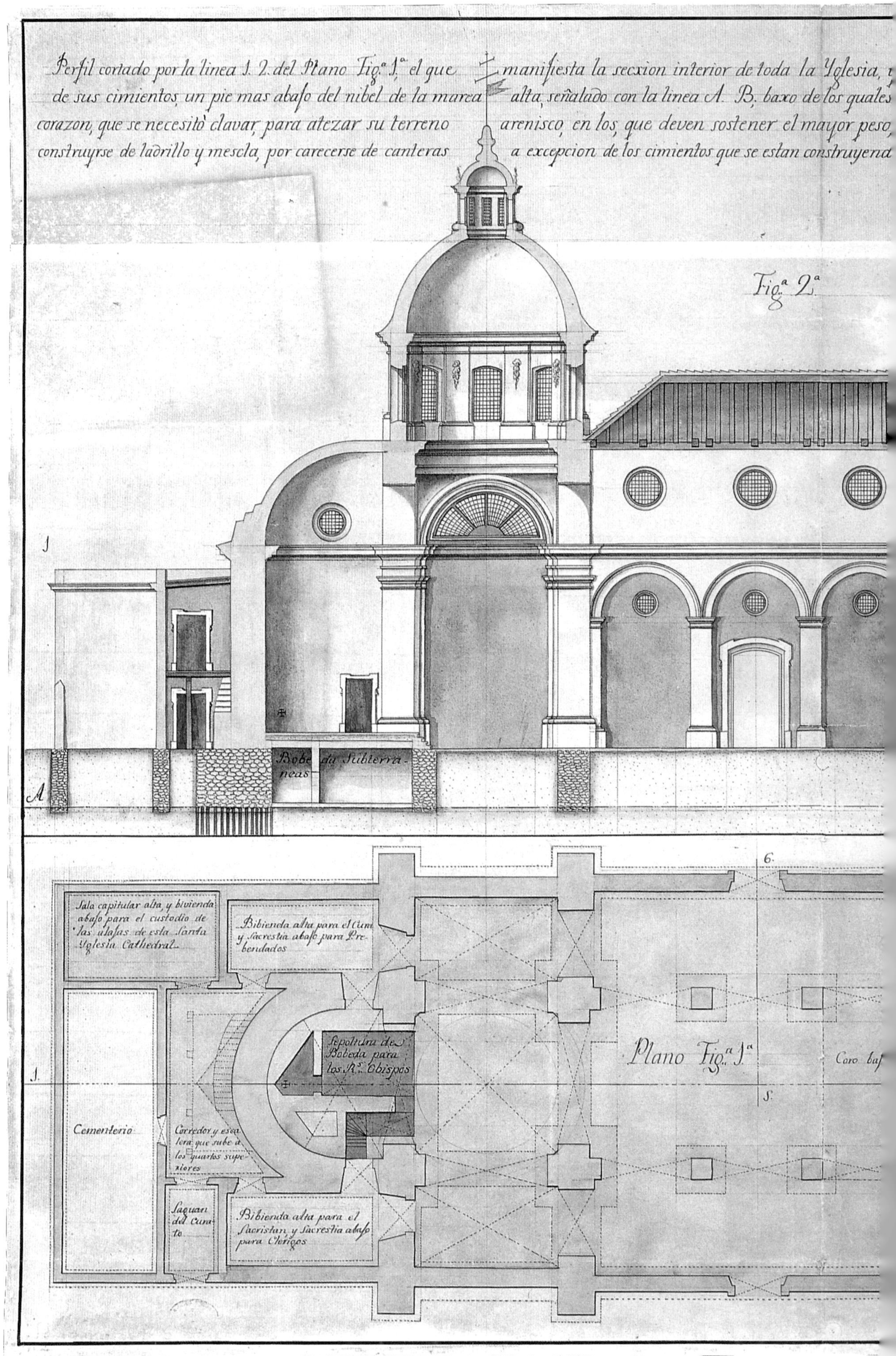
Perfil cortado por la linea 1. 2. del Plano Fig.a 1.a el que manifiesta la secxion interior de toda la Yglesia,
de sus cimientos, un pie mas abaxo del nibel de la marea alta, señalado con la linea A. B. baxo de los quales
corazon, que se necesitó clavar, para atezar su terreno arenisco, en los, que deven sostener el mayor peso,
construyrse de ladrillo y mescla, por carecerse de canteras a excepcion de los cimientos que se estan construyend
Fig.a 2.a
Bobedas Subterraneas
Sala capitular alta, y bivienda abaxo para el custodio de las alaxas de esta Santa Yglesia Cathedral.
Bibienda alta para el Cura y Sacrestia abaxo para Prebendados
Sepoltura de Bobeda para los R.s Obispos
Plano Fig.a 1.a
Coro ba
Cementerio
Corredor y escalera que sube a los quartos superiores
Saguan del Curato
Bibienda alta para el Sacristan, y Sacrestia abaxo para Clerigos

Cathedral of Santa Marta.

2 March 1767, Santa Marta.
'Plan view and elevations of the Holy Cathedral under construction in the town of Santa Martha...'
Three views: Ground plan. Cross-section cut by line 1–2, and half-view of the main facade.
By Juan Cayetano Chacón.
530 x 680 mm.
MP. Panamá, 176.

The Cathedral of Santa Marta was rebuilt after the earthquakes of 1749 and 1752 according to this plan submitted by Fray Agustín Manuel Camacho y Rojas, which included a report on the state of its plant and an estimate of the costs of same (Santa Marta, 5 March 1767). The reconstruction was completed in 1796.

Pastoral visit: parish of San Cristóbal Totonicapan.

[1770]
Map of the parish of San Cristóbal Totonicapan.
200 x 330 mm.
Featured in the 'Geographical and moral description of the Guatemala diocese, drawn up by the Archbishop, Pedro Cortés y Larraz, member of His Majesty's Council, during his visits of inspection'.
Vol. 2. 78 sheets + 2 blank + 34 maps.
Bound in parchment. Guatemala, 948.

Cortés y Larraz was appointed bishop of Guatemala on 24 August 1767. Two years later, he inspected 427 villages and 824 estates in his diocese, from Chiapas to the Gulf of Fonseca, and reported on parishes, number of inhabitants, languages spoken, the existence of idolatry and possible abuses of the indigenous peoples by Spaniards.

of the Indies, and Juan Crisóstomo Ansotegui, treasury inspector in the Council of the Indies. In addition, a *Junta de Leyes* (Council of Laws), composed of Indies councillors and with Manuel José de Ayala as secretary, was set up to produce the so-called *Diccionario de gobierno y legislación de Indias* (Dictionary of government and legislation of the Indies). By 1780, Ansotegui had completed the first tome of the new codification. The work of the *Junta* took shape in the form of the *Libro de acuerdos de la Junta nombrada para corregir y adicionar las leyes de Indias* (Book of agreements of the Council appointed to correct and amend the laws of the Indies). The new code finally came out in 1797.

The task undertaken by the Council was thus as enormous as it was innovative, bearing in mind that Castilian legislation was not always applicable to the Americas, where executive bodies, created specifically to address matters relating to local political, socio-economic and geographical conditions, issued their own laws. Similarly, existing Spanish institutions were transposed and adapted to fit New World legislation, as was the case with the labor services known as *cacicazgo* or *mita*.

Overleaf: the Provincial Council of Mexico.

1585.
'Sanctum provinciale concilium mexici celebratum Anno Domini Millessimo quingentessimo octogessimo quinto. Preasidente in eo Illustrissimo ac Reverendissimo D.D. Petro Moya de Contreras Archiepiscopo Mexicano. Romae confirmatum die vigessima septima octobris Anno.1589...'
[Mexici]: Apud Joannem Ruiz Typ., 1622
6 h., 102 fol.
Also bearing a false title page and its own folio: 'Statuta Ordinata a sancto Concilio Provinciali mexicano III. Anno Domini Millessimo Quingentessimo Octuagessimo quinto...'
38 f. 1h., Fol.
Biblioteca, L.A., S. XVII–65.

In the 16th century, following the Council of Trent, major councils were held in Lima and Mexico to analyze the spiritual status of the territory, standardize doctrine and improve means of conversion. The third Mexican Council was convened by Archbishop Pedro Moya de Contreras in 1585. The subjects dealt with were recorded in five books, viz: bk. 1, the preaching of doctrine and the competence of preachers. bk. 2, tribunals and Church litigation; bk. 5, inspections. The council agenda also featured the building of Mexico City cathedral by Fray Juan de Zumárraga in 1534.

The Synod of Chile.

20 December 1626, Santiago de Chile. The synod was convened by the bishop of Santiago de Chile, Francisco de Salcedo, on 25 February 1626, in accordance with a royal order of 8 August 1621.
23 fols. + 3 blanks.
MP. Libros Manuscritos, 4.

The Council of Trent ruled that synods or meetings of bishops with their diocesan priests should be held once a year to discuss spiritual issues. None had been held in Chile since 1612, prompting the king to order fulfillment of the directive issued at the Council of Trent. The conclusions of that 1626 synod focus on doctrinal instruction of the Indians, particularly those in the province of Cuyo, and the levies accruing to the bishoprics of La Imperial and Santiago.

The Councillors' Duties

The President, the highest-ranking officer in the Council of the Indies, was appointed directly by the king to oversee and direct the institution, and was not of necessity a lawyer. His mandate covered government, Indian affairs, the treasury, Church patronage, the distribution of supplies, the assignment of lawsuits and scheduling hearings and sentences.

The chancellor's main duty was to safeguard the seal which was stamped on royal dispatches, and to register the latter. After the first two chancellors, Mercurino de Gattinara and Francisco de los Cobos, this position was filled by Council secretaries. The office was restored under Philip IV and first awarded to the royal protégé, the Count Duke of Olivares, in 1623.

From 1524 to 1834, the number and status of councillors varied. There were usually eight ministers who had trained as magistrates in the Indies. As of 1604, with the appointment of a former Council secretary, Juan de Ibarra, ministers could also be nominated in view of their executive or military backgrounds. They often ended their career after being promoted to the Council of Castile.

The prosecutor was next-in-line after the most recently appointed councillor, a post to which he was eligible to be promoted. He was in charge of defending royal jurisdiction in any civil or ecclesiastical issue in the New World. Prosecutors acted in litigations, inspections and *residencias* instituted by the Council, and their reports on government affairs were binding.

There was originally only one secretary although, from 1596 onwards, two were appointed. One secretariat was asigned to New Spain, covering the jurisdictional districts of the *Audiencias* of Mexico City, Guadalajara, Santo Domingo, Guatemala, the Philippines and Venezuela. The other was based in Peru and took in Lima, Cuzco, Quito, Charcas, Panama, New Granada, Chile and Buenos Aires. Secretaries had the task of recording and summarizing all business transactions, both civil and ecclesiastical. They endorsed all statutes of the Indies signed by the monarch and kept the relevant books, known as *cedularios*.

Chamber scribes, first appointed in 1571, had an important executive and judicial role. They recorded executive proceedings, including privileges and pardons, prepared councillors' dispatches for the king's approval, made corresponding book entries in the *cedularios* and kept the archives until they were sent to Simancas castle for storage. Scribes ceased to have a role in executive proceedings as of 1597

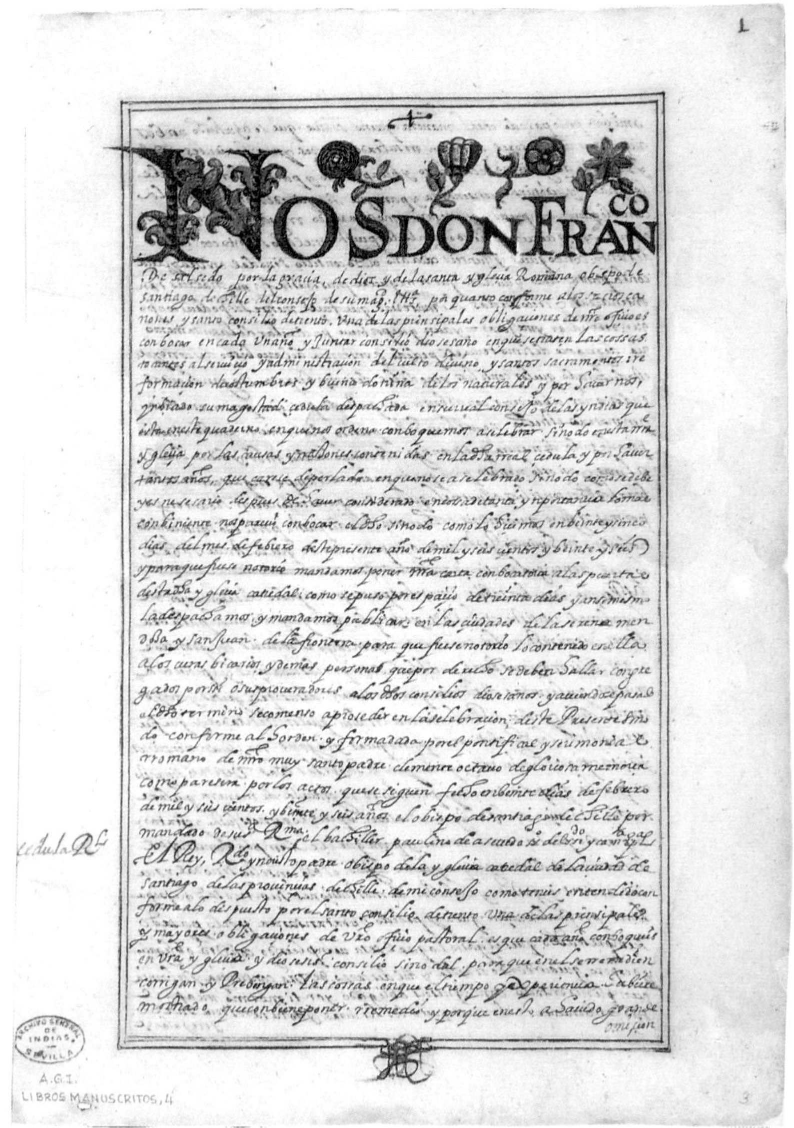

and concentrated on judicial duties related to disputes heard by the Council, as well as inspections and *residencias.*

The Council's judicial functionaries included recorders, who registered legal proceedings, a counsel of the poor, a receiver of court sentences, who also collected fines, and legal assistants to the prosecutor. Bailiffs were the executive functionaries who enforced the Council's decisions.

Separate mention must be made of the employees of the *Contaduría* (Audit Office) who enacted the judgements passed by the Council on financial matters. These were the general treasurer and keepers of accounts, whose task was to examine remittances from Indies functionaries. They were also obliged to report on and analyze all statutes of an economic nature or import.

Lastly, the Council also employed a scientific staff, including a chief chronicler of the Indies whose task it was to gather information for writing an official history of the New World. Examples of illustrious chroniclers include Gonzalo Fernández de Oviedo, author of a monumental work entitled *Historia natural y moral de las*

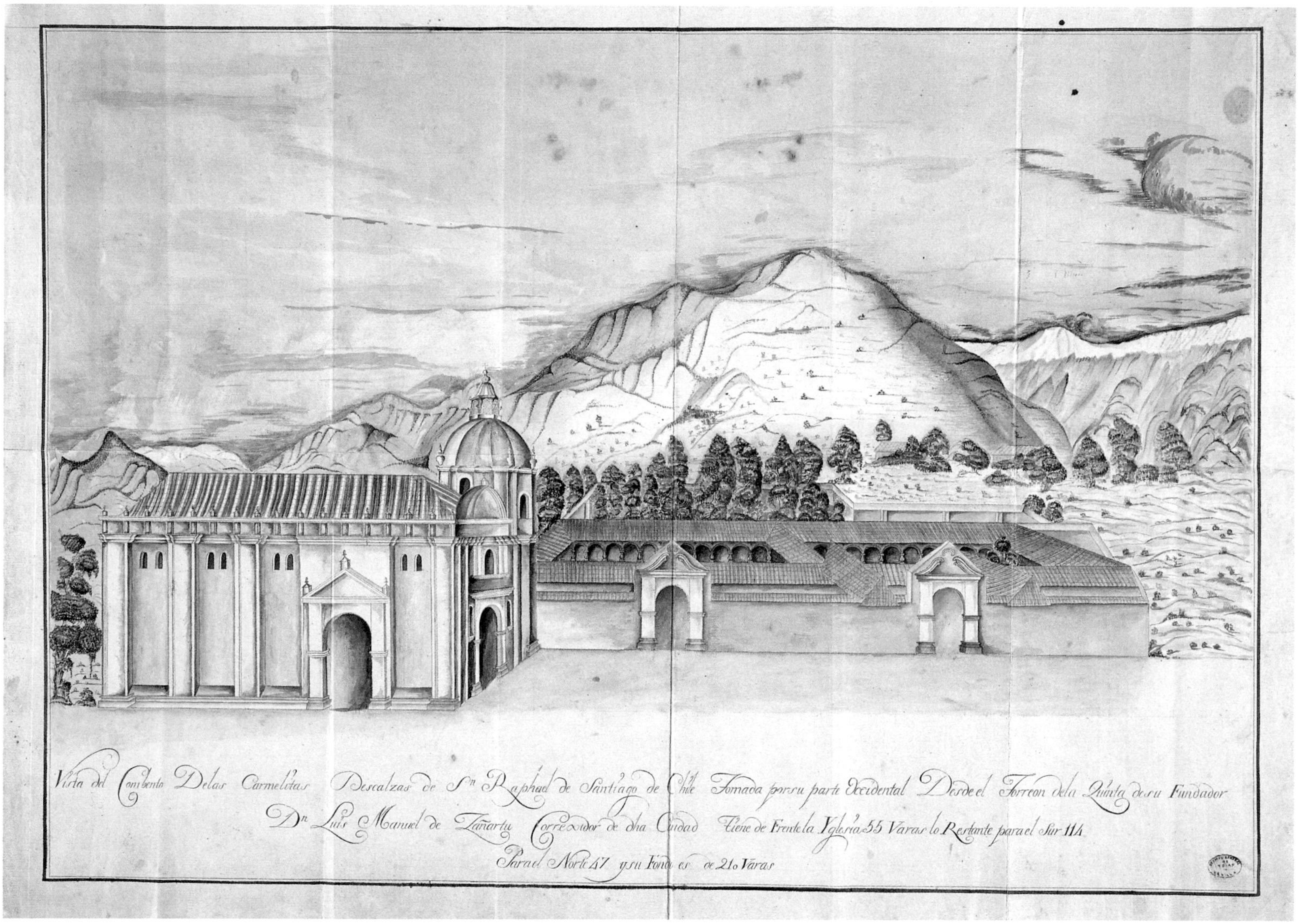

San Rafael Convent of Discalced Carmelites.

[1773]
'View of the San Rafael Convent of Discalced Carmelites, in Santiago de Chile, seen from the west-lying tower on the estate of its founder, Luis Manuel de Zañartu, corregidor *of the city...'*
542 x 752 mm.
MP. Perú y Chile, 259.

The Carmelites were late in reaching the New World and the Discalced Carmelites even more so. The first Carmelite convent in Chile dates from the late-17th century, while that of San Rafael was the second one built in Santiago. Its founder, Luis Manuel de Zañartu, who came from Oñate, was the city's corregidor *from 1762. Widowed two years later, he sought permission to found a convent where his two daughters would become nuns. A royal order of 23 June 1766 authorized him to build the convent at his own expense on his La Cañadilla estate.*

Indias, and Antonio de Herrera, who wrote the *Historia General de las Indias Occidentales o de los hechos de los castellanos en las Islas y Tierra Firme del mar Océano.* In the 18th century, the post of chief chronicler was assigned to the Academy of History. A prominent chronicler at the time was Juan Bautista Muñoz who compiled material for a history of the Americas and was appointed to head the General Archive of the Indies.

Another post in the Council was that of chief cartographer who, according to the *Recopilación* (Codification) of 1680, had to be a professor of mathematics. It was his task to investigate and record eclipses and other phenomena to facilitate measurement of the earth's longitude and to notify authorities in the Indies of such events. He was also commissioned to compile sailing charts, make maps of the American continent and produce a book featuring descriptions of all its provinces, lands, coastlines, islands and harbors.

The Council also had its own chaplain who said Mass every day for the staff. While it lacked a chapel, it did have the necessary liturgical vessels, as attested to in inventories of the *Contaduría.*

Finally, the Council's auxiliary staff included four wardens, the prison governor, and a crier, among others.

According to the statutes, Council ministers worked three hours in the morning and three in the afternoon every day except Sundays and holidays. They first dealt with executive matters, starting with a compulsory reading of all correspondence in the possession of the president and the councillors. A fixed weekly schedule determined just when other matters were to be seen to. These included disputes, *visitas* or inspections, *residencias,* treasury affairs, and attending to poor prisoners.

The system was sluggish. Minutes of meetings were left unwritten. When it came to executive matters, which councillors were instructed to deal with in strict secrecy, the secretary made brief notes of proceedings or abstracts of documents, noting the author and date of the dossier in question. Treasury officials decided which dossiers were to be sent from the secretariats to the council chamber for reading, together with any available antecedents. The prosecutor examined them and passed a ruling which the Council had to approve. The dossier was then either deemed completed or re-opened for further deliberation or referred to the king by consultation, a process endorsed by all councillors. Subsequently, the names of the councillors consulted were entered in the left-hand margin of the document. The royal reply was noted down in another margin or on the back of the document and taken as a basis for drawing up a royal warrant, decree or statute which would then be entered in a register.

In addition to letters and dossiers remitted by the authorities, the Council reviewed all applications and memoranda submitted by private individuals, accompanied by reports on personal merits and service, for the purpose of requesting favors or pardons, or reparation for some injustice. The Council also had to be consulted on confirmation of titles or positions that were up for sale, or of *encomiendas* granted by viceroys or governors, and had jurisdiction in all cases of appeal in the last resort.

Council ministers originally earned the same salary as those employed by the Council of Castile: 200,000 maravedis per annum for the president and 100,000 for the councillors, prosecutor and secretaries. In 1546, the salary of the president or 'grand chancellor' was increased to 500,000 maravedis, and that of the other ministers to 200,000. Strangely enough, their earnings remained at that level until the 18th century. However, all Council members were entitled to occasional or set perquisites. Apart from special, temporary grants of incomes or allowances for duty in the Indies, they were paid a fixed sum of money known as the *salario de casa*

Opposite
Bethlehemite hospital of San Miguel in Guadalajara.

[1757]
'Geometrical plan of the factory site where the Royal Hospital of San Miguel is to be located in the city of Guadalajara.'
680 x 1240 mm.
MP. México, 597.

The Royal Hospital of San Miguel of Guadalajara was built at the expense of Bishop Antonio Alcalde and run by the Bethlehemite order, founded by Pedro de Bethencourt in Guatemala in 1653. The vast construction was based on a cruciform ground plan introduced in hospitals in Spain by the Catholic Kings. The highly elongated wards met at a transept crossing and, at the other end, were joined by two other, similarly elongated wards. The areas for men and women are shown in different colors.

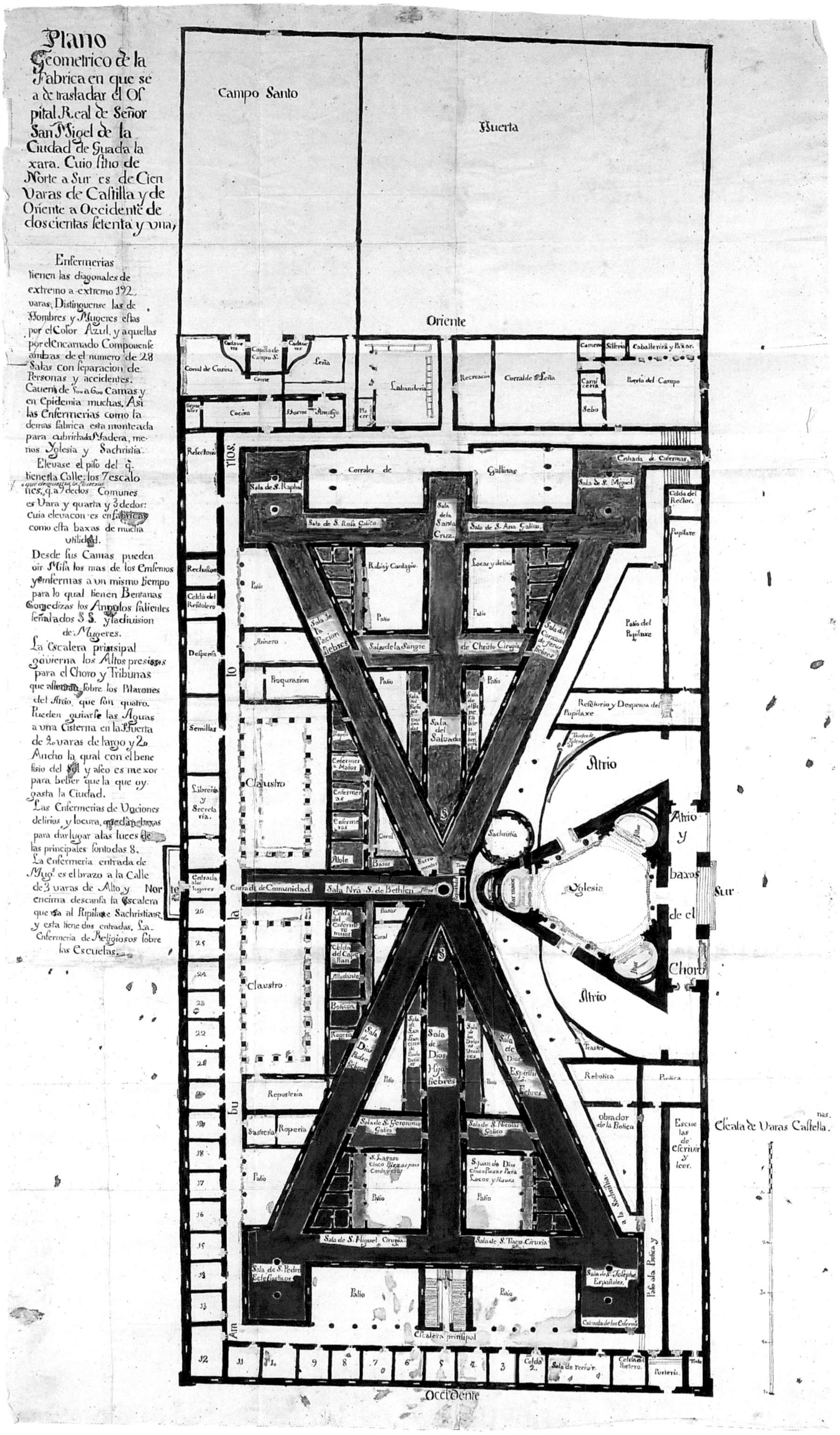
Plano
Geometrico de la Fabrica en que se a de trasladar el Ospital Real de Señor San Migel de la Ciudad de Guadalaxara. Cuio sitio de Norte a Sur es de Cien Varas de Castilla y de Oriente a Occidente de doscientas setenta y una,
Enfermerias tienen las diagonales de extremo a extremo 192 varas; Distinguense las de Hombres y Mugeres estas por el Color Azul, y aquellas por el Encarnado Componense ambas de el numero de 28 Salas con separacion de Personas y accidentes. Cauen de 500 a 600 Camas y en Epidemia muchas. Asi las Enfermerias como la demas fabrica esta monteada para cubrirla de Madera, menos Yglesia y Sachristia.
Elevase el piso del q. tiene la Calle: los 7 escalones, q. a 9 dedos Comunes es Vara y quarta y 3 dedos: Cuia elevacion es en fabricas como esta baxas de mucha utilidad.
Desde sus Camas pueden oir Misa los mas de los Enfermos y enfermas a un mismo tiempo para lo qual tienen Bentanas Corredizas los Angulos salientes señalados S.S. y la diuision de Mugeres.
La Escalera prinsipal govierna los Altos presisos para el Choro y Tribunas que asientan sobre los Pilarones del Atrio que son quatro.
Pueden guiarse las Aguas a una Cisterna en la Huerta de 20 varas de largo y 20 Ancho la qual con el benefisio del Sol y aseo es mexor para beber que la que oy gasta la Ciudad.
Las Enfermerias de Unciones delirios y locura, quedan baxas para dar lugar a las luces de las principales son todas 8.
La Enfermeria entrada de Mugs. es el brazo a la Calle de 3 varas de Alto y encima descansa la Escalera que va al Pupilaxe Sachristia, y esta tiene dos entradas. La Enfermeria de Religiosos sobre las Escuelas.
Campo Santo
Huerta
Oriente
Corral de Cocina
Capilla de Campo S.
Leña
Cocina
Labanderia
Recreacion
Corral de Leña
Caballeriza y Paxar
Puerta del Campo
Refectorio
Corrales de Gallinas
Entrada de Enfermas
Sala de S. Raphael
Sala de S. Miguel
Celda del Rector
Sala de S. Rosa Galico
Sala de la Santa Cruz
Sala de S. Ana Galico
Pupilaxe
Patio del Pupilaxe
Reclusion
Despensa
Semillas
Procuracion
Salade la Sangre
de Christo Cirugia
Sala del Salvador
Refitorio y Despensa del Pupilaxe
Atrio
Claustro
Libreria y Secretaria
Sachristia
Yglesia
Atrio y baxos de el Choro
Sur
Norte
Sala Nra. S. de Bethlen
Claustro
Reposteria
Roperia
Sastreria
Rebotica
obrador de la Botica
Escuelas de Escrivir y leer.
Sala de S. Geronimo Galico
Sala de S. Nicolas Galico
Sala de Dios Hyjo fiebres
Sala de S. Miguel Cirugia
Sala de S. Tiago Cirugia
Sala de S. Pedro Eclesiasticos
Sala de S. Joseph Españoles
Patio
Escalera principal
Sala de recibir
Porteria
Occidente
Escala de Varas Castellanas

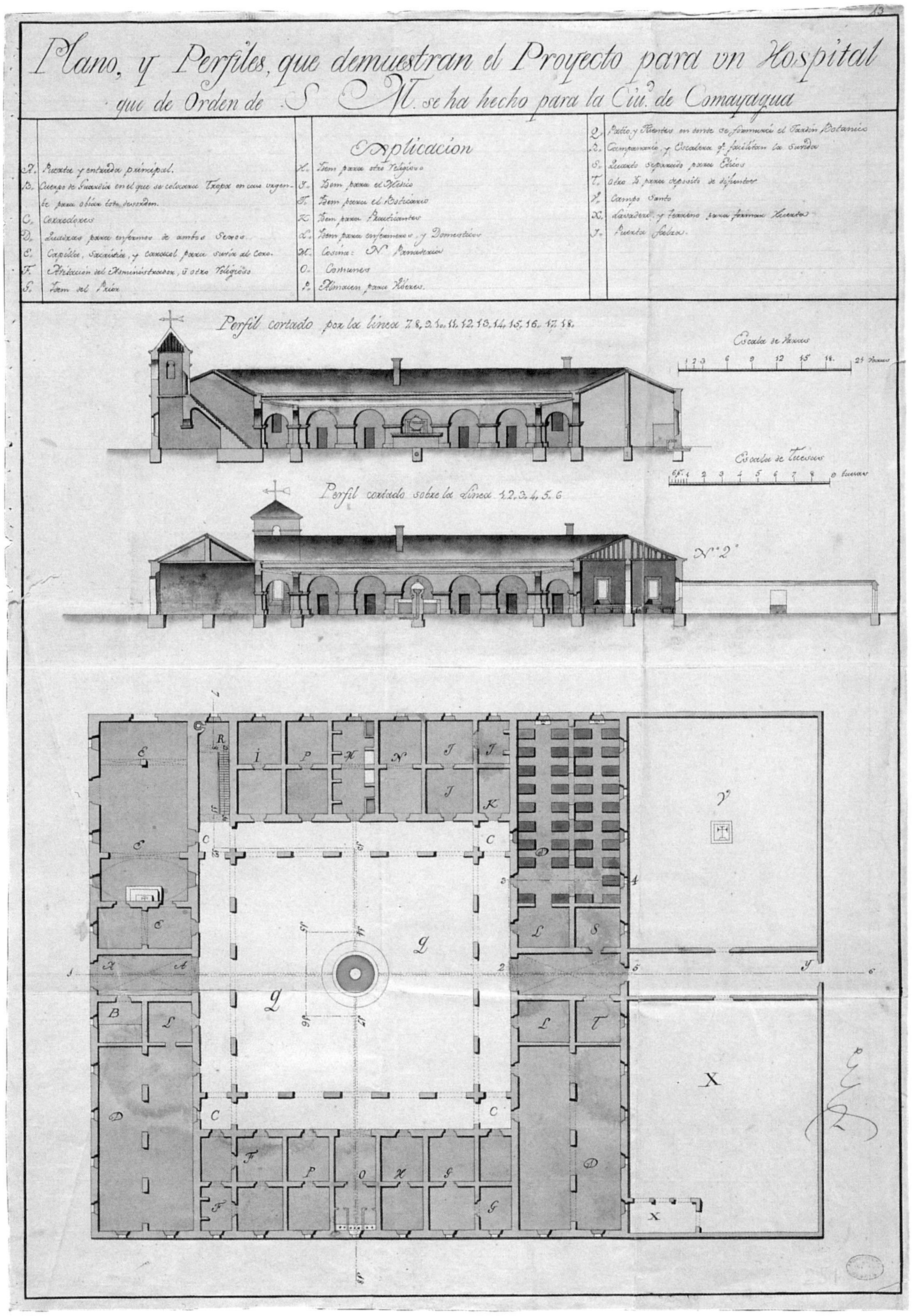

Hospital of San Juan de Dios, Comayagua.

6 August 1783, Comayagua.
Plan and elevations of the hospital which the monarchs ordered to be built in the town of Comayagua.
By Juan de Ampudia y Valdéz.
660 x 450 mm. MP. Guatemala, 251.

The Hospital Order of St John of God, founded in the mid-16th century, opened hospitals in Mexico City, Nombre de Dios and Lima in the last three decades of that century. A century later, the Hospitallers had fifty-seven hospitals in the Americas.

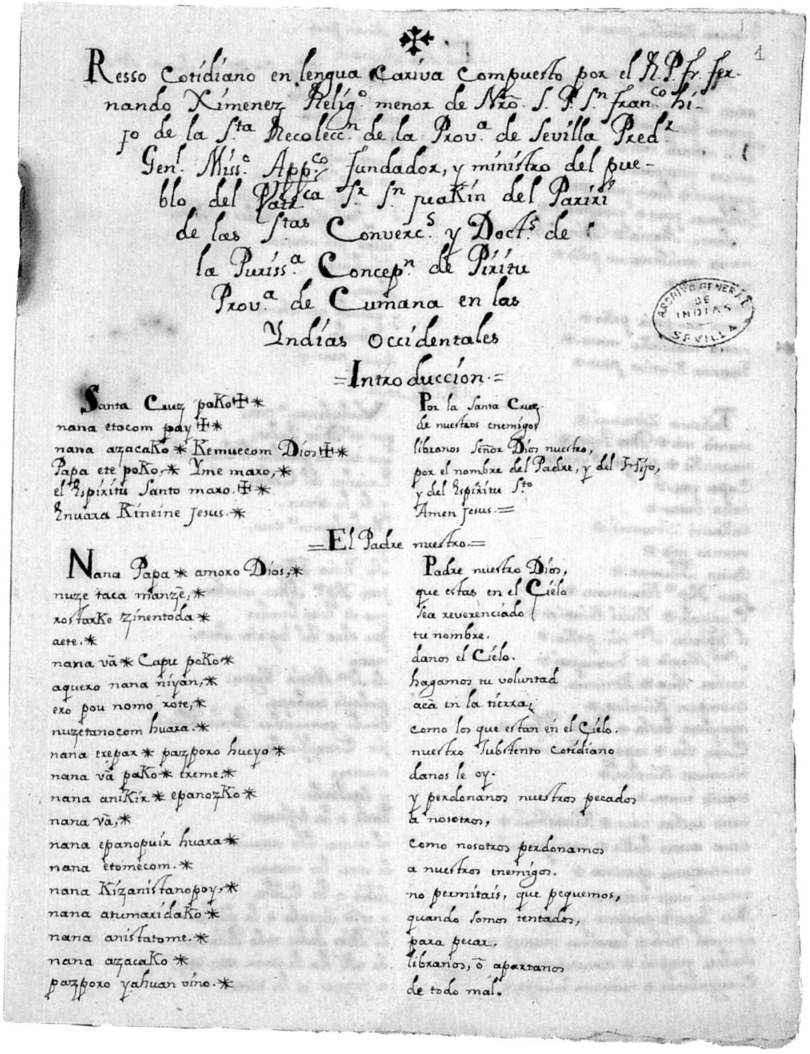
1

Resso Cotidiano en lengua Cariva compuesto por el R. P. fr. Fernando Ximenez Relig.o menor de Nro. S. P. Sn Franco. hijo de la Sta Recolecc.n de la Prov.a de Sevilla Pred.r Gen.l Miss.o Appco. fundador, y ministro del pueblo del Patca Sr Sn Juakin del Pariri de las Stas Converc.s y Doct.s de la Puriss.a Concep.n de Piritu Prov.a de Cumana en las Indias Occidentales

=Introduccion=

Santa Cruz poKo ✠ *
nana etocom pay ✠ *
nana azacaKo * Kemuecom Dios ✠ *
Papa ete poKo, * Yme maro, *
el Espiritu Santo maro. ✠ *
Enuara Kineine Jesus. *

Por la Santa Cruz
de nuestros enemigos
libranos Señor Dios nuestro,
por el nombre del Padre, y del Hijo,
y del Espiritu Sto
Amen Jesus. =

=El Padre nuestro=

Nana Papa * amoro Dios, *
nuze taca manze, *
rostarKe zinentoda *
aere. *
nana vã * Capu poKo *
aquero nana niyan, *
ero pou nomo zote, *
nuzetanocom huara. *
nana trepar * parzporo hueyo *
nana vã poKo * treme. *
nana aniKir * epanozKo *
nana vã, *
nana epanopuir huara *
nana etomecom. *
nana Kizanistanopoy, *
nana atumaridaKo *
nana anistatome. *
nana azacaKo *
parzporo yahuan vino. *

Padre nuestro Dios,
que estas en el Cielo
sea reverenciado
tu nombre.
danos el Cielo.
hagamos tu voluntad
acà en la tierra,
como los que estan en el Cielo.
nuestro sustento cotidiano
danos le oy.
y perdonanos nuestros pecados
à nosotros,
como nosotros perdonamos
a nuestros enemigos.
no permitais, que pequemos,
quando somos tentados,
para pecar.
libranos, ò apartanos
de todo mal.

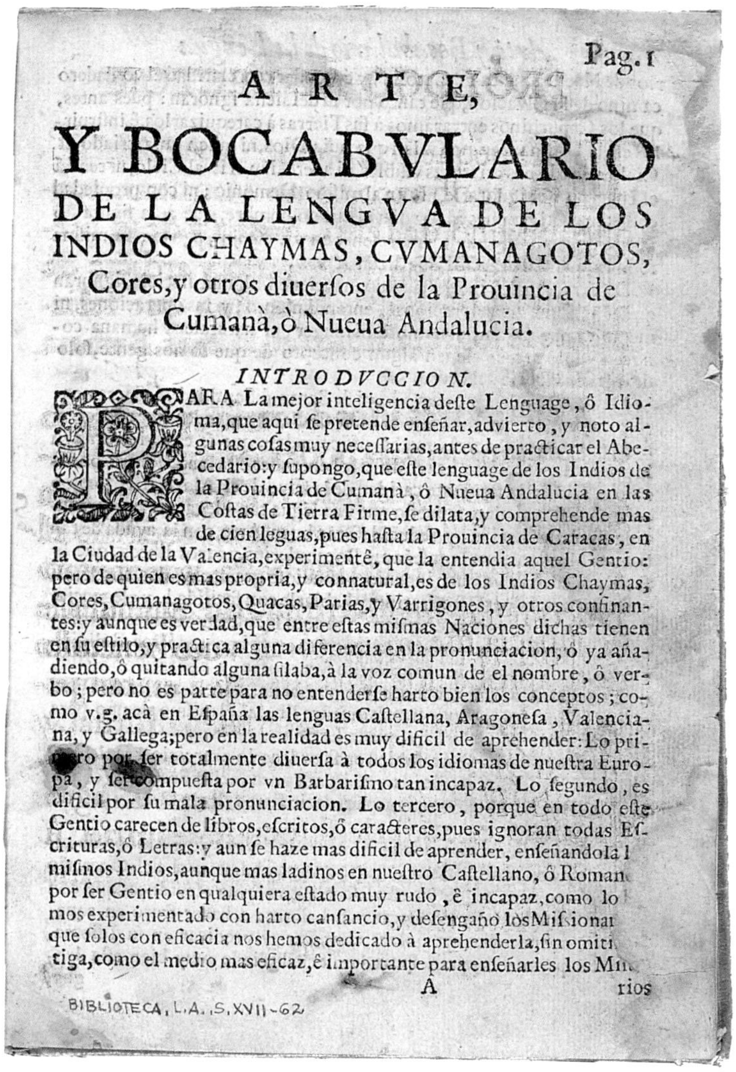
Pag. 1

ARTE,
Y BOCABVLARIO
DE LA LENGVA DE LOS
INDIOS CHAYMAS, CVMANAGOTOS,
Cores, y otros diuerſos de la Prouincia de
Cumanà, ò Nueua Andalucia.

INTRODVCCION.

PARA La mejor inteligencia deſte Lenguage, ô Idioma, que aqui ſe pretende enſeñar, advierto, y noto algunas coſas muy neceſſarias, antes de practicar el Abecedario: y ſupongo, que eſte lenguage de los Indios de la Prouincia de Cumanà, ô Nueua Andalucia en las Coſtas de Tierra Firme, ſe dilata, y comprehende mas de cien leguas, pues haſta la Prouincia de Caracas, en la Ciudad de la Valencia, experimentê, que la entendia aquel Gentio: pero de quien es mas propria, y connatural, es de los Indios Chaymas, Cores, Cumanagotos, Quacas, Parias, y Varrigones, y otros confinantes: y aunque es verdad, que entre eſtas miſmas Naciones dichas tienen en ſu eſtilo, y practica alguna diferencia en la pronunciacion, ò ya añadiendo, ô quitando alguna ſilaba, à la voz comun de el nombre, ô verbo; pero no es parte para no entenderſe harto bien los conceptos; como v.g. acà en Eſpaña las lenguas Caſtellana, Aragoneſa, Valenciana, y Gallega; pero en la realidad es muy dificil de aprehender: Lo primero por ſer totalmente diuerſa à todos los idiomas de nueſtra Europa, y ſer compueſta por vn Barbariſmo tan incapaz. Lo ſegundo, es dificil por ſu mala pronunciacion. Lo tercero, porque en todo eſte Gentio carecen de libros, eſcritos, ô caracteres, pues ignoran todas Eſcrituras, ô Letras: y aun ſe haze mas dificil de aprender, enſeñandola l[illegible] miſmos Indios, aunque mas ladinos en nueſtro Caſtellano, ô Roman[illegible] por ſer Gentio en qualquiera eſtado muy rudo, ê incapaz, como lo[illegible] mos experimentado con harto canſancio, y deſengaño los Miſsionar[illegible] que ſolos con eficacia nos hemos dedicado à aprehenderla, ſin omiti[illegible] tiga, como el medio mas eficaz, ê importante para enſeñarles los Mi[illegible]

A rios

ABOVE, LEFT
Daily prayer in the Carib language.

[S.F.]
'Daily prayer in Carib, composed by Fray Fernando Ximénez, a Franciscan friar, founder and minister of the new Mission of the Patriarca Señor San Juakin del Pariri, de las Santas Conversiones y Doctrinas de Puríssima Concepción de Piritu *in Cumaná province, West Indies...'*
Sent by the Bishop of Puerto Rico, Pedro Martínez de Oneca, in a letter dated 14 April 1760, in which he recounts his pastoral visit to the diocese.
Manuscript. 5 sheets in 4to + 1 blank.
MP. Escritura y Cifra, 49 bis.

The province of Piritu, on the Venezuelan coast, was evangelized by a group of Franciscans from the Recolección de la Concepción de España *in the second half of the 17th century after the Capuchins had abandoned the area. The mission of the* Puríssima Concepción *was the first to be founded in that province.*

ABOVE, RIGHT
Vocabulary of the Chayma, Cumanagota and Core Indians.

TAUSTE, Francisco de (O.F.M.).
*[*Arte y vocabulario de la lengua de los indios chaymas, cumanagotos, cores, parias y otros diversos de la provincia de Cumaná o Nueva Andalucía. *Madrid: Bernardo de Villa-Diego. 1680]*
4 sheets, 182 pp., 4to. Cover, prelims & end pages missing.
Biblioteca, L.A. S. XVII-62.

The Capuchins were the last order to arrive in the New World, in the mid-17th century, and they focused mainly on Venezuela. In 1649, they settled in Cumaná and from there spread to Los Llanos, Trinidad, Guayana and Maracaibo. Like the other orders, they made a considerable effort to learn local languages, as attested to in this grammar of the Chayma language.

OVERLEAF
College of San Juan de Letrán.

14 September 1549, Rome.
Rescript from the Chapter and Canons of St John Lateran to the viceroy, Antonio de Mendoza, and the Audiencia *of Mexico, authorizing the founding and building of a church and hospital, alongside the college, under the name San Juan de Letrán, with the same privileges and exemptions as other Church foundations of the kind.*
666 x 519 mm. (459 x 60).
MP. Bulas y Breves, 37.

The College of San Juan de Letrán was founded in Mexico City in 1547 on the urging of Fray Juan de Zumárraga and the viceroy, Antonio de Mendoza, for orphans of mixed blood and poor children. Throughout the colonial period, it was held in esteem by the Crown, while Popes granted it privileges commensurate with Lateran foundations.

CAPITVLVM ET CANONICI

Constituciones De la universidad De Los Reyes, Hechas Por el Illustre Señor Retor, y Doctores, y maestros de la dicha Universidad:—

1. Como se a de elegir el rretor cada año, y q̄ sea lego:—

Primeramente el Retor a de ser lego, elegido por votos del claustro, y por cedulas secretas, y ha de ser añal, que se elija cada año. De manera que des de la una elecion a la otra de rretor ha de ser tiempo de un año, y no mas. y antes que se elija aquella mañana, diran una missa al spiritu Sancto; y elegirsehan dos consiliarios por votos del claustro, y mientras no ay copia de Graduados, seran los deanes mas antiguos:—

2. A lo que esta obligado el rretor:—

Sera obligado el Retor a mandar que todos los graduados y estudiantes se vengan a matricular ante el Notario, so pena que los cursos no valdran ni se Graduaran:—

3. A lo que es obligado el rretor para las cathedras:—

Sera obligado el Retor a mirar las catedras y lectiones como se leen, y se ha de hallar en todos los actos publicos, secretos, y llamar (Por lo menos) de quinze A quinze dias a claustro para ver lo que es menester en la Universidad:—

4. Officio del Bedel:—

El Bedel o Bedeles que fueren de la dha universidad, sean obligados à asistir en actos publicos de la universidad con sus maças, Guardando el decoro y autoridad que se deue ala Universidad, y quando convenga echar a las fiestas por los generales en latin por la orden que sele dara:—

5. Officio del Notario:—

El Notario sea obligado a hallarse en los actos publicos, y secretos, y en los claustros, y en todos los grados de tal manera ha de estar en los claustros q̄ no este dentro, sino que le den la peticion decretada escripta por el menos antiguo:—

University of Lima.

[1571]
'Charter of the University founded by H.M. in the Monastery of El Señor Santo Domingo in this city of Kings.'
9 fols. + 1 blank.
Patronato, 191, R. 1 (4).

The Crown, acting through the Council of the Indies, encouraged and promoted the establishment of universities and colleges throughout the New World. The University of Lima was founded by a royal decree of 12 May 1551 and was housed in the convent of Santo Domingo in that city. It enjoyed the same privileges and exemptions as the University of Salamanca. Twenty years later, the city council provided other premises built for this purpose: they came into commission on the feast day of St Mark, the patron of the university.

Overleaf, above
The legislative task—León Pinelo.

LEÓN PINELO, Antonio de.
Autos, Acuerdos i decretos de gobierno del Real i Supremo Consejo de las Indias *(Proceedings, Agreements and Government Decrees of the Royal and Supreme Council of the Indies). Transmitted by Luis Méndez de Haro, the Count Duke of Olivares and compiled by Antonio de León Pinelo,* oidor *of the* Casa de la Contratación, *Seville. Madrid, Diego Diáz de la Carrera, 1658.*
2 sheets, 47 fols., bordered cover. Title page bearing the coat-of-arms of the Council and bordered with two fillets. Biblioteca, L.A. S. XVII–24.

In 1624, Antonio de León Pinelo set about compiling the laws of the Council of the Indies. For over ten years he worked on the Registers of Orders under the direction of the lawyer Aguiar and Juan Solórzano. His death in 1660 prevented him from seeing publication of his full work. The Autos, Acuerdos y decretos de gobierno... *was published after León Pinelo's appointment as* oidor *of the* Casa de la Contratación *and covers the period 1594 to 1658.*

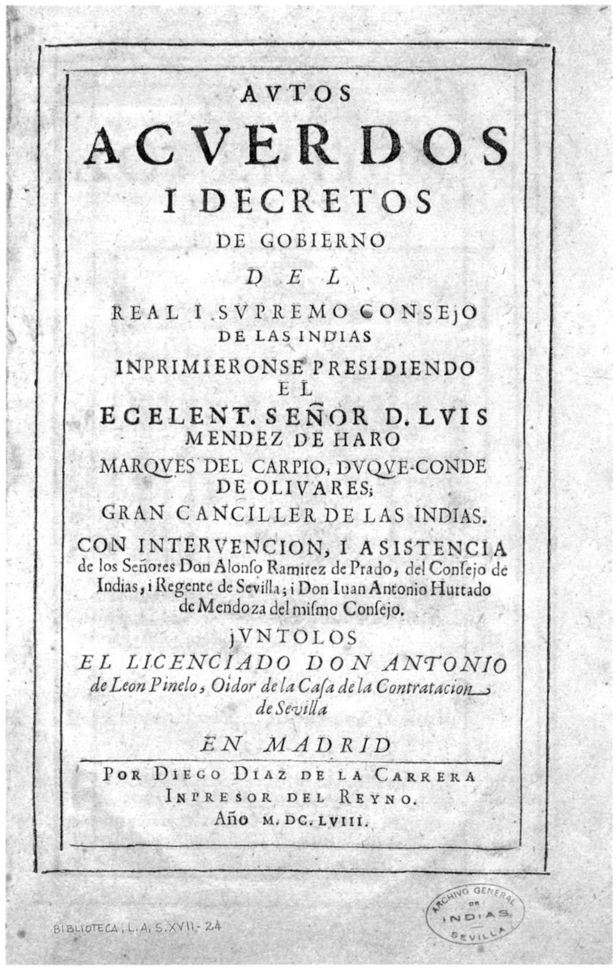

AVTOS
ACVERDOS
I DECRETOS
DE GOBIERNO
D E L
REAL I SVPREMO CONSEJO
DE LAS INDIAS
INPRIMIERONSE PRESIDIENDO
E L
ECELENT. SEÑOR D. LVIS
MENDEZ DE HARO
MARQVES DEL CARPIO, DVQVE-CONDE
DE OLIVARES;
GRAN CANCILLER DE LAS INDIAS.
CON INTERVENCION, I ASISTENCIA
de los Señores Don Alonso Ramirez de Prado, del Consejo de Indias, i Regente de Sevilla; i Don Iuan Antonio Hurtado de Mendoza del mismo Consejo.
JVNTOLOS
EL LICENCIADO DON ANTONIO
de Leon Pinelo, Oidor de la Casa de la Contratacion de Sevilla
EN MADRID
POR DIEGO DIAZ DE LA CARRERA
INPRESOR DEL REYNO.
Año M. DC. LVIII.

Codification of the Laws of the Indies.

1680.
'Codification of the Laws of the Kingdoms of the Indies, commissioned by Charles II and divided into four parts, with a general Table of Contents and, at the beginning of each Volume, a special Table of Contents of the titles contained therein'. Madrid: Julián de Paredes, 1681.
4 Vols. I: 6 sheets, 299 fols.; II: 3 sheets, 298 fols.; III: 3 sheets, 302 fol. & IV: 2 sheets, 364 fol. The covers of all four volumes bear an embossed, royal coat-of-arms produced by Gregorio Fosman for the Council publications in 1681. A motto printed on the inside cover of the first three volumes reads: Soy de la Librería del Sr. Marqués de Perales *('I belong to the bookshop of the Marquis of Perales').*
Bilbioteca, L.A. S. XVII–20/1-4.

This definitive codification of the Laws of the Indies, known as the Recopilación, *includes all legislation applicable to the New World promulgated under the Habsburgs. The royal order of 18 March 1680, whereby the new code came into effect, also features a description of the work involved in its making. The code is divided into 9 chapters as follows: ch. I: Church Matters; ch. II: The Council of the Indies & the* Audiencias; *ch. III: Political Administration, Viceroys and Governors; ch. IV: Discoveries, Colonization, Municipalities & Public Works; ch. V: Government & Civil Justice; ch. VI: Issues relating to the Indies; ch. VII: Judges & Investigators, Vagrants & Miscreants & the Penal Code; ch. VIII: Treasury Administration; ch. IX:* Casa de la Contratación, *Trade & Shipping. In all, the code comprises a total of 218 sections and over six thousand laws.*

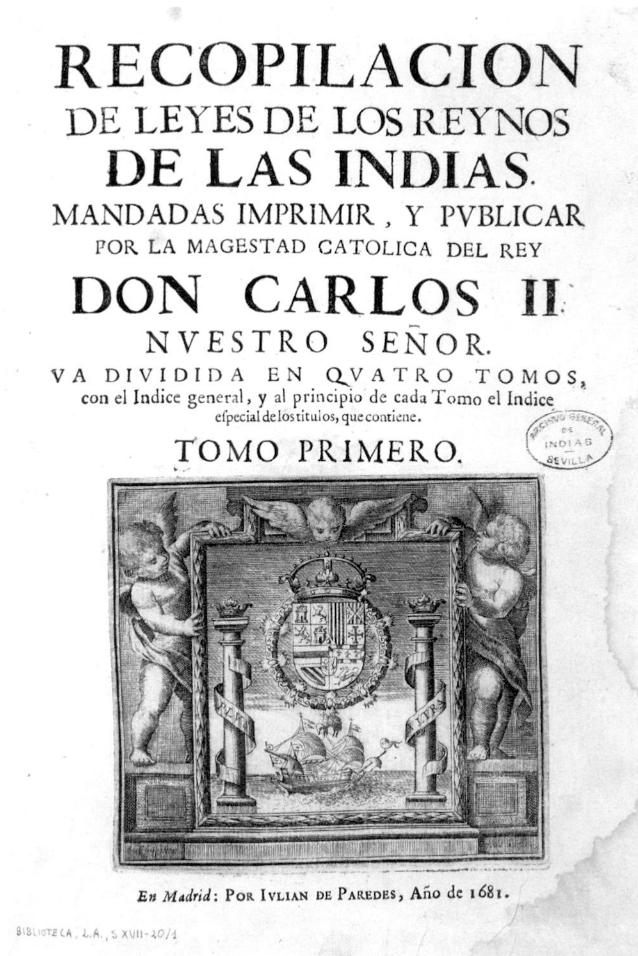

RECOPILACION
DE LEYES DE LOS REYNOS
DE LAS INDIAS.
MANDADAS IMPRIMIR, Y PVBLICAR
POR LA MAGESTAD CATOLICA DEL REY
DON CARLOS II.
NVESTRO SEÑOR.
VA DIVIDIDA EN QVATRO TOMOS,
con el Indice general, y al principio de cada Tomo el Indice especial de los titulos, que contiene.
TOMO PRIMERO.
En Madrid: POR IVLIAN DE PAREDES, Año de 1681.

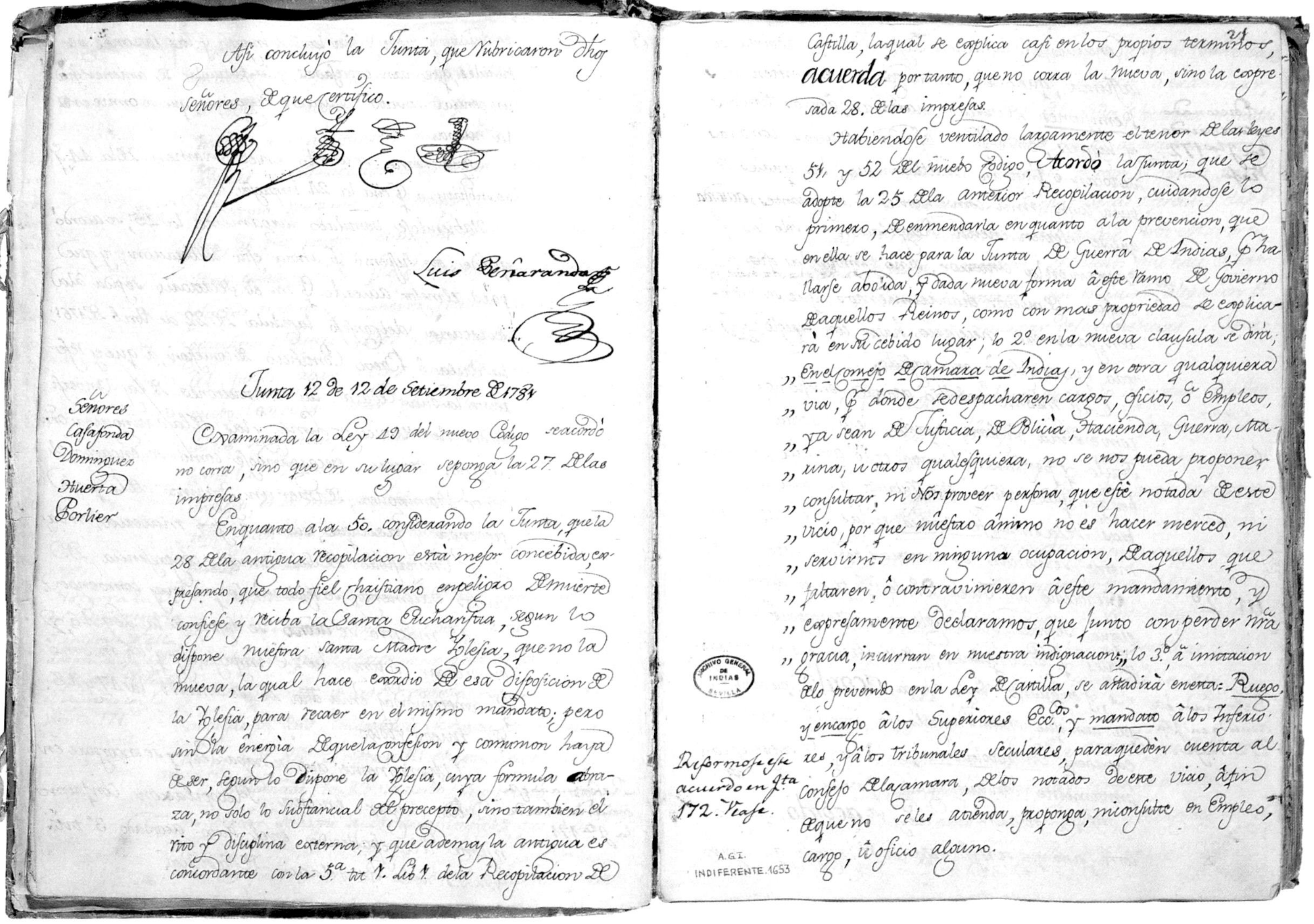
Así concluyó la Junta, que rubricaron dhos
señores, de que certifico.

Luis Peñaranda

Junta 12 de 12 de Setiembre de 1784

Señores
Casafonda
Dominguez
Huerta
Porlier

Examinada la Ley 19 del nuevo Código se acordó
no corra, sino que en su lugar se ponga la 27 de las
impresas.

En quanto a la 50. considerando la Junta, que la
28 de la antigua Recopilacion está mejor concebida, ex-
presando, que todo fiel christiano en peligro de muerte
confiese y reciba la Santa Eucharistia, segun lo
dispone nuestra santa Madre Iglesia, que no la
nueva, la qual hace exordio de esa disposicion de
la Iglesia, para recaer en el mismo mandato; pero
sin la energia de que la confesion y comunion haya
de ser, segun lo dispone la Iglesia, cuya formula abra-
za, no solo lo substancial del precepto, sino tambien el
rito y disciplina externa, y que ademas la antigua es
concordante con la 5.ª tit. 1. Lib. 1. de la Recopilacion de

Castilla, la qual se explica casi en los propios terminos, 21
acuerda por tanto, que no corra la nueva, sino la expre-
sada 28. de las impresas.

Habiendose ventilado largamente el tenor de las leyes
51, y 52 del nuebo Codigo, Acordó la Junta, que se
adopte la 25 de la anterior Recopilacion, cuidandose lo
primero, de enmendarla en quanto a la prevencion, que
en ella se hace para la Junta de Guerra de Indias, por hallarse abolida, y dada nueva forma a este ramo de Govierno
de aquellos Reinos, como con mas propriedad se explica-
rá en su cebido lugar; lo 2.º en la nueva clausula se dirá;
„ En el Consejo de Camara de Indias, y en otra qualquiera
„ via, por donde se despacharen cargos, oficios, ó Empleos,
„ ya sean de Justicia, de Policia, Hacienda, Guerra, Ma-
„ rina, u otros qualesquiera, no se nos pueda proponer,
„ consultar, ni Nos proveer persona, que esté notada de este
„ vicio, por que nuestro animo no es hacer merced, ni
„ servirnos en ninguna ocupacion, de aquellos que
„ faltaren, ó contravinieren a este mandamiento, y
„ expresamente declaramos, que junto con perder nra.
„ gracia, incurran en nuestra indignacion;„ lo 3.º á imitacion
de lo prevenido en la Ley de Castilla, se añadirá en esta: Ruego,
y encargo a los Superiores Eccos., y mandato a los Inferio-
res, y a los tribunales seculares, para que den cuenta al
Consejo de la Camara, de los notados de este vicio, a fin
de que no se les atienda, proponga, ni consulte en Empleo,
cargo, ú oficio alguno.

Reformose este
acuerdo en Jta
172. Vease.

ARCHIVO GENERAL DE INDIAS SEVILLA

A.G.I.
INDIFERENTE.1653

Book of amendments to the legal code.

16 June 1776–18 May 1785.
'Book of resolutions issued by the Committee appointed to amend & augment the Laws of the Indies.'
416 fols. + 10 blanks.
Indiferente, 1653.

In 1771, the Council of the Indies instructed a new legal code to be drawn up that would include all legislation passed after the Recopilación *(Codification) of 1680. Miguel José Serrador, an official of the Indies Secretariat, and Crisóstomo de Ansotegui, the Council's treasury agent, were commissioned to perform the task. A legal committee was set up to supervise the work of the two commissioners and to submit the new codification at a plenary session of the Council for the latter's approval. The* Nuevo Código de Leyes *(New Code of Laws) appeared in 1797.*

y aposentos (household and lodgings allowance), in addition to the emoluments awarded for each bullfight staged in the Court and subsequently at celebrations, such as those on the feasts of SS Isidore, John and Ann. One part of councillors' salaries was known as *luminarias* (illuminations). Originally measured as a number of large candles given to ministers to be lit on major feasts, in time an equivalent amount of money was given instead.

Once the Council had fixed premises, its members lived in rented accommodation paid for monthly by royal stewards with public funds. At the end of the 16th century, the Council moved to the ground floor of the old Madrid Alcázar and, in the 17th century, to the east wing of the Royal Palace. There it remained for over a century, until 1717, when Philip V ordered it to be moved to the palace occupied by Queen Mariana at the end of the Calle Mayor in Madrid.

Council business was conducted in a number of chambers or offices. Wardens were in charge of their upkeep and, judging from surviving inventories, the rooms

Chroniclers of the Indies: Fernández de Oviedo.

FERNÁNDEZ DE OVIEDO Y VALDÉS, Gonzalo.
Book XX of the second part of Historia General y Natural de las Indias. *Written by Captain Gonzalo Fernández de Oviedo y Valdés, governor of the fort and harbor of Santo Domingo on the island of Hispaniola, His Majesty's chronicler, on the subject of the Strait of Magellan.*
Valladolid: Francisco Fernández de Cordova, 1557.
64 fols., 3 engravings. Cover bearing bordered, royal coat-of-arms.
Biblioteca, L.A. S. XVI–7.

Gonzalo Fernández de Oviedo (1478–1557) first sailed to the Americas on an expedition commanded by Pedrarias Dávila in 1514. There he held various offices, including that of governor of Santo Domingo. In 1526 he was commissioned to write a history of the Indies in ten years, although in 1535 the period was extended. By that time he had already published the first part of his Historia General y Natural de las Indias. *This Book XX of Part Two had just gone to press in 1557 when its author took ill and died in Santo Domingo. Fernández de Oviedo bore the title of 'Chronicler of the Indies', although the post was not institutionalized within the Council until the statutes of 1571.*

Chroniclers of the Indies: Antonio de Herrera.

HERRERA TORDESILLA, Antonio.
Historia General de los hechos de los castellanos en las Islas i Tierra Firme del Mar Océano, *written by the chief chronicler of His Majesty of the Indies and chronicler of Castile. Covering four decades, from 1492 until 1531.*
First Decade. *To His Majesty the King.*
Madrid: Royal Printing Works, 1601.
4 Vols. I: First Decade–4 sheets, 371 pp., 11 sheets. Cover with engravings of scenes and portraits. Second Decade–1 sheet, 368 pp., 8 sheets (end).
Madrid. By Juan Flamenco, 1601.
Biblioteca, L.A. S. XVII–21/1.

Antonio de Herrera was appointed Chronicler of the Indies in 1596 and did justice to his office by publishing this work in 1601 after spending nineteen years on it. The work is divided into eight decades, spanning the period from 1492 to 1544. This first decade runs from the Discovery up until Pedrarias Dávila's expedition to Castilla del Oro. The cover, flanked by portraits of the Catholic Kings, Christopher Columbus and Bartolomé Columbus, shows different scenes from Columbus' epic voyage.

were lavishly decorated. The council and justice chambers were adorned with crimson and green damask and velvet wall hangings, paintings and tapestries, one of which depicts the story of King Xerxes in eight panels. Other trappings included the Council's coat-of-arms embroidered in gold and silver on velvet, taffeta or linen curtains, Turkish carpets, desktop drapes and a cast-iron royal coat-of-arms on the fireplace in one of the two chambers. The furniture included walnut tables, desks and consoles, quilted velvet councillors' benches, chairs upholstered in green silk, and cabinets for classified papers. Other items listed in the inventories include writing cases, inkstands, silver bells and candelabra, bronze braziers, clocks, maps and globes of the world.

The inventories also mention the library housing the books and manuscripts which the councillors used as reference material for their reports. The Council was likewise documented as having a large selection of books on civil and canon law, codifications of the Laws of the Indies, the *Partidas de Alfonso X* (the Laws of Castile compiled by King Alfonso X), the proceedings of the Council of Trent, and a wealth of geographical and historical works, such as those by Pedro Mártir de Anglería, Gonzalo Fernández de Oviedo, López de Gomara and Bernal Díaz del Castillo. Sailing charts, indigenous dictionaries, books on navigation and a host of material on economics and fiscal administration completed the library's reference sources.

The inventories kept by Council wardens also describe the ornaments and hangings used on feast days. In addition to the aforementioned feasts of SS Isidore, John and Ann and regular court celebrations such as Corpus Christi, the Council had its commemorative day on 21 November, the feast of the Presentation of the Virgin.

Surviving accounts of the protocol observed during those festivities and in the course of the Council's normal business give us an idea of just how important such pomp and circumstance was to the Spanish authorities at the time.

One's proper place at public events, seating arrangements, suitable decoration and dress, including headgear, caps or swords, as well as forms of address commensurate with each occasion, were meticulously laid down. The slightest breach of protocol elicited an immediate reprimand or sanction and sometimes led to a full-scale dispute. Such excessive formality and etiquette often detracted from the efficient rendering of services, a fact which earned the Council a reputation for being a stilted and unwieldy administrative body and had a great deal to do with subsequent reforms in the 18th century.

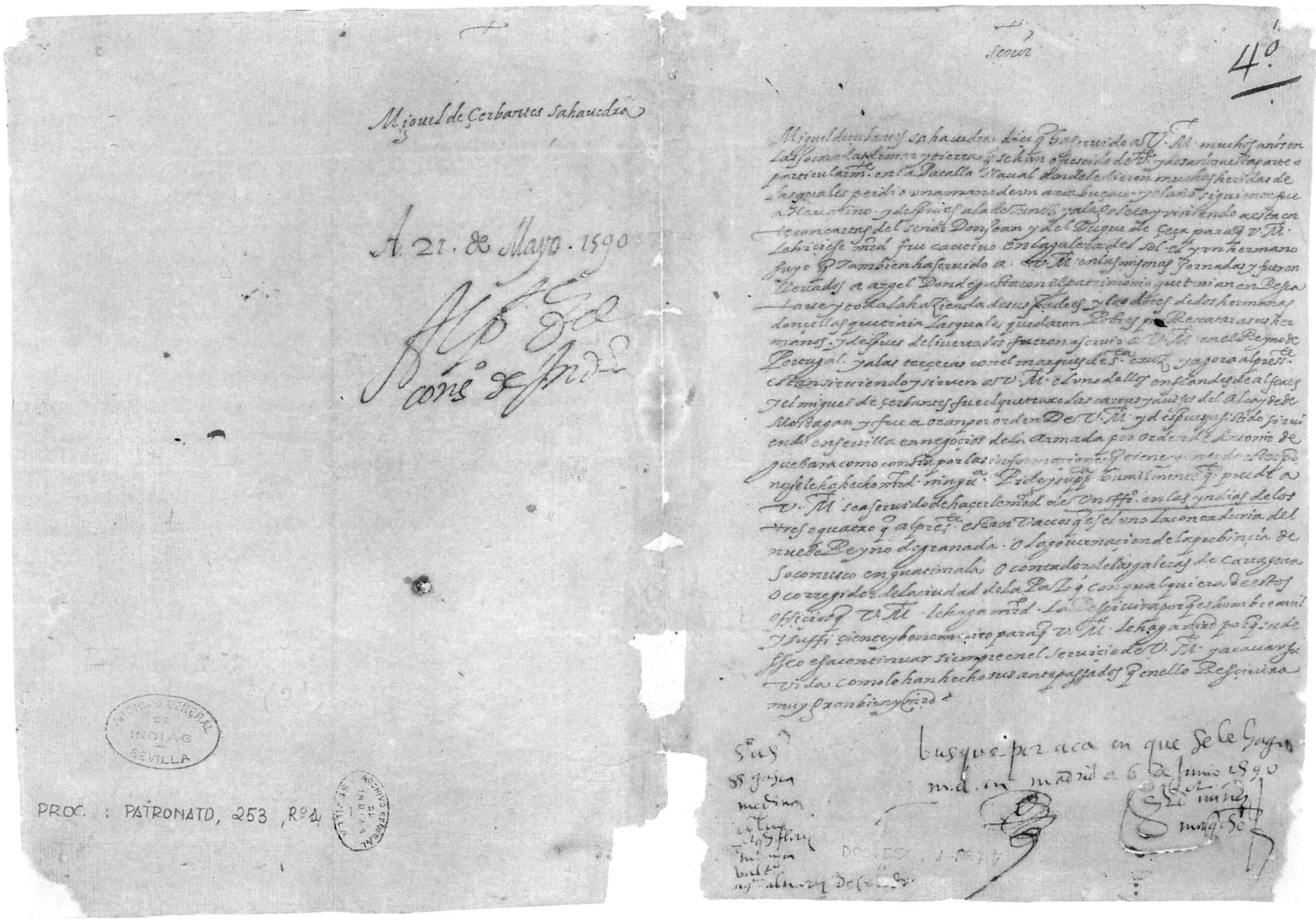
Miguel de Cerbantes Sahavedra

A 21 de Mayo 1590

PROC. : PATRONATO, 253, R°1

Memorandum book of Miguel de Cervantes.

[21 May 1590, Madrid]
In this book, Cervantes describes his merits and services and requests employment in the Indies, either in the Counting House of New Granada, the administration of Soconusco, the audit office for Cartagena-based galleys or the corregimiento *or municipality of La Paz. 2 sheets in 4to. Patronato, 253, R.1.*

Individuals were entitled to petition the Council for a privilege or grant by submitting a memorandum. The date of this submission appears on the back. Featured in the lower margin are the names of the councillors and their decision not to award the employment sought by Cervantes.

Nevertheless, despite its shortcomings, the Council of the Indies gradually assumed a more far-reaching mandate than other Councils of the time and over much vaster territories. Council members stated as much in a report submitted to Philip V in 1714. After dispensing with normal business, they conclude: 'The aforementioned issues, and those which have been omitted, give rise to so many courses of action and exemptions to be transacted in the Council Chamber that it is well nigh impossible to determine their number and kind and one would be hard put to find another Council or Tribunal in Spain, or even all of them together, comparable to the Council in the amount of business they transact'.

The magnitude of the Council's work is evident when poring over the 25,000 surviving bundles. Currently housed in this General Archive of the Indies, they provide an essential reference for anyone wishing to learn about the history of the New World.

POLITICA INDIANA.
COMPUESTA POR EL DOTOR
DON JUAN
DE SOLORZANO
PEREIRA,
Cavallero del Orden de Santiago, del Consejo del Rey Nuestro Señor en los Supremos de Castilla, y de las Indias.
Dividida en Seis Libros.
EN AMBERES.
Por HENRICO Y CORNELIO VERDUSSEN;
Mercaderes de Libros. Año M.D.CC.III.
Con Gracia y Privilegio.
DON JUAN DE SOLORSANO PEREIRA

'Policy in the Indies.'

SOLÓRZANO PEREIRA, Juan de:
Política indiana compuesta por el Dotor [sic] Don Juan de Solórzano Pereira... dividida en Seis Libros...
Amberes: Henrico y Cornelio Verdussen, 1703.
(Policy in the Indies, compiled by Dr Juan de Solórzano Pereira... divided into Six Books...
Antwerp: Henrico & Cornelio Verdussen, 1703.)
1 sheet, 1 engraving, 8 sheets, 536 pp., 42 sheets.

This was one of the most frequently consulted works in the Council library. It was written by Juan de Solórzano (1575–1655) who was appointed Councillor of the Indies in 1629. His reputation as a legal expert led him to be placed in charge of compilations up until 1680. The fruit of his undertakings was this work, written in Latin and subsequently translated into Castilian Spanish. It was first published under the title, Política Indiana, *in 1647. Divided into six books, it constitutes the best justification of Spain's intervention in the Americas. It also features a detailed history of the Council and its functions.*

PRIMERA PARTE
DELOS VEINTE IUN LIBROS RITUALES I MONARCHIA
Indiana, con el origen y guerras, delos Indios Ocidentales, de
sus Poblaçones, Descubrimiento, Conquista, Conuersion y
otras cosas marauillosas dela mesma tierra distribuydos
en tres tomos.
COMPUESTO POR F. JUAN DE TORQUEMADA
Ministro Prouincial dela Orden de Nuestro Serafico Padre.
San Francisco en la Prouincia del Santo Evangelio de
Mexico en la Nueba España.
DICO EGO OPERA MEA REGI
Sæculorum immortali et inuisibili
CON PRIVILEGIO
En Madrid en la Oficina y acosta de Nicolas Rodriguez Franco
Año de 1723
Irala inv.t del.t & Sculp.t

The Council library: 'Indies Monarchy'.

TORQUEMADA, Juan de (O.F.M.).
'Part I of the twenty-one Ritual Books & the Indies Monarchy, *on the origins and wars in the West Indies, their peoples, discovery, conquest, conversion and other marvels of those lands, distributed in three volumes... Madrid: Micolás Rodríguez Franco, 1723.'*
3 vols.
I: 20 sheets, 1 map, fold-out. 768 pp., 36 sheets.
Biblioteca, L.A. S. XVIII–109/1.

The Council library provided a wealth of source material for Councillors' reports, as attested by surviving inventories, which list this work, among others.

THE SECRETARIATS OF STATE AND THE INDIES

The ascent to the Spanish throne of the Bourbons after the War of the Spanish Succession and the Treaty of Utrecht (1713) involved not only a change of dynasty but a renewal of ideological precepts and the way the monarchy saw itself. Indeed, the traditional idea of the monarchy was replaced with an absolutist one.

After Philip V's rise to power, a number of reforms were ushered in and were to last throughout the 18th century. State structure was completely overhauled and the foundations were laid for the administrative organization of contemporary Spain. The reformist trends of Philip V and Ferdinand VI were but the first step towards the more far-reaching changes wrought by Charles III.

The administrative reforms grew out of the inherently new approach to monarchy and out of political necessity. Indeed, the idea of the monarchy as the supreme embodiment of sovereignty and the State, in which all power was invested, was bound to clash with the administrative system of the Habsburgs which was based on the Councils, corporate and consultative bodies which also acted as supreme executive bodies.

Moreover, the political climate, both on the domestic front (the inception of the Bourbon dynasty after the civil war) and abroad, where relations between the major powers were becoming increasingly more complex, called for a more modern, rationalized and agile form of administration able to respond quickly and effectively to any problem. This required unity of thought and swift action which would have been unthinkable under the old corporate system of the Councils. Additionally, the king could not attend to all matters personally, and delegating decisions to a secretary with broad-based powers was both an inadequate and dangerous solution, as the system of protégés had proved under the Habsburgs. The solution, then, was to appoint not one but a number of secretaries with proven experience in particular fields of administration. They would be directly answerable to the king and meet with him in the Cabinet Assembly.

Reform entailed building up a larger body of centralized administration and introducing standardization in all territories. This was achieved through the so-called Decrees of *Nueva Planta,* whereby the *fueros* (local privileges) were abolished in virtually all the Spanish kingdoms. The newfound consolidation of centralized power was rounded off by reforms in municipal government and the introduction of *intendencias,* a system of government in which provinces were ruled by a royal official known as an intendant.

The Indies played a decisive role in this process of reform. On the one hand, Spain's possessions in the New World were becoming increasingly more important in international relations. They were often the scene of military confrontation with other nations, who had designs on a variety of places in Spain's empire. Moreover, the Americas were viewed as a huge marketplace with resources that had to be guarded and nurtured.

The Bourbon reforms in the New World thus involved a two-pronged thrust—the defense and safeguarding of possessions, and the development and exploitation of their economic wealth. In both instances, reforms were directed at both central and provincial government, in addition to the application of specific measures in the spheres of fortifications, naval and military affairs and the introduction of new economic policies that wrought profound changes in trade and navigation.

The State Secretariat and the Universal Secretariat of the Indies

The first move in reforming the central administration came when Philip V issued a royal decree on 11 July 1705 whereby the only existing Secretariat was divided into two. That initial period was marked by French influences in the guise of Philip V's lawyer–administrator, Jean-Henri-Louis Orry. In effect, the French administration was the source of inspiration for the royal decree of 30 November 1714, by which the *Nueva Planta de las Secretarías del Despacho* (New Regime of Secretariats) became the core of Spain's new administrative regime. Four such Secretariats were created: a State Secretariat, which acted as a foreign ministry, another which dealt with Church matters, justice and the jurisdiction of councils and courts, a War Secretariat and the Department of the Navy and the Indies. The treasury, headed at the time by a *veedor general* or inspector general, was placed in the hands of a 'general intendant of the treasury... who alone is to render account before my Cabinet of all matters pertaining to the Treasury, and to express his view on each of them, thereby facilitating the resolutions that the Ministers in attendance submit to me, so that I may judge them more intelligently'.

In charge of each Secretariat was a person 'bearing the title and office of State Secretary, who is to comply with the regulations I have ordered to be drawn up, so that each is aware of the duties assigned to him, the salary he is to earn and the number of officials assigned to each office'. The first secretaries to be appoin-

'Allegory of Spanish America.'

[1786]
'Allegory of Spanish America,' engraved by J. Camarón and J. Joaquín Fabregat.
235 x 340 mm.
Featured on the back cover of the 'Royal Statute providing for the appointment and training of provincial and military Intendants in the Kingdom of New Spain... on His Majesty's orders.'
Madrid, 1786.
Biblioteca, L.A. S. XVIII–16.

This allegorical illustration is highly representative of the role played by the Americas in the Bourbon dynasty's yearnings for imperial renewal. Young America, attired in Indian apparel, is shown reclining on a horn of plenty, an alligator and a tobacco plant, an allusion to the wealth of her produce. Guarding her from behind is the coat-of-arms of Charles III and the imperial lion.

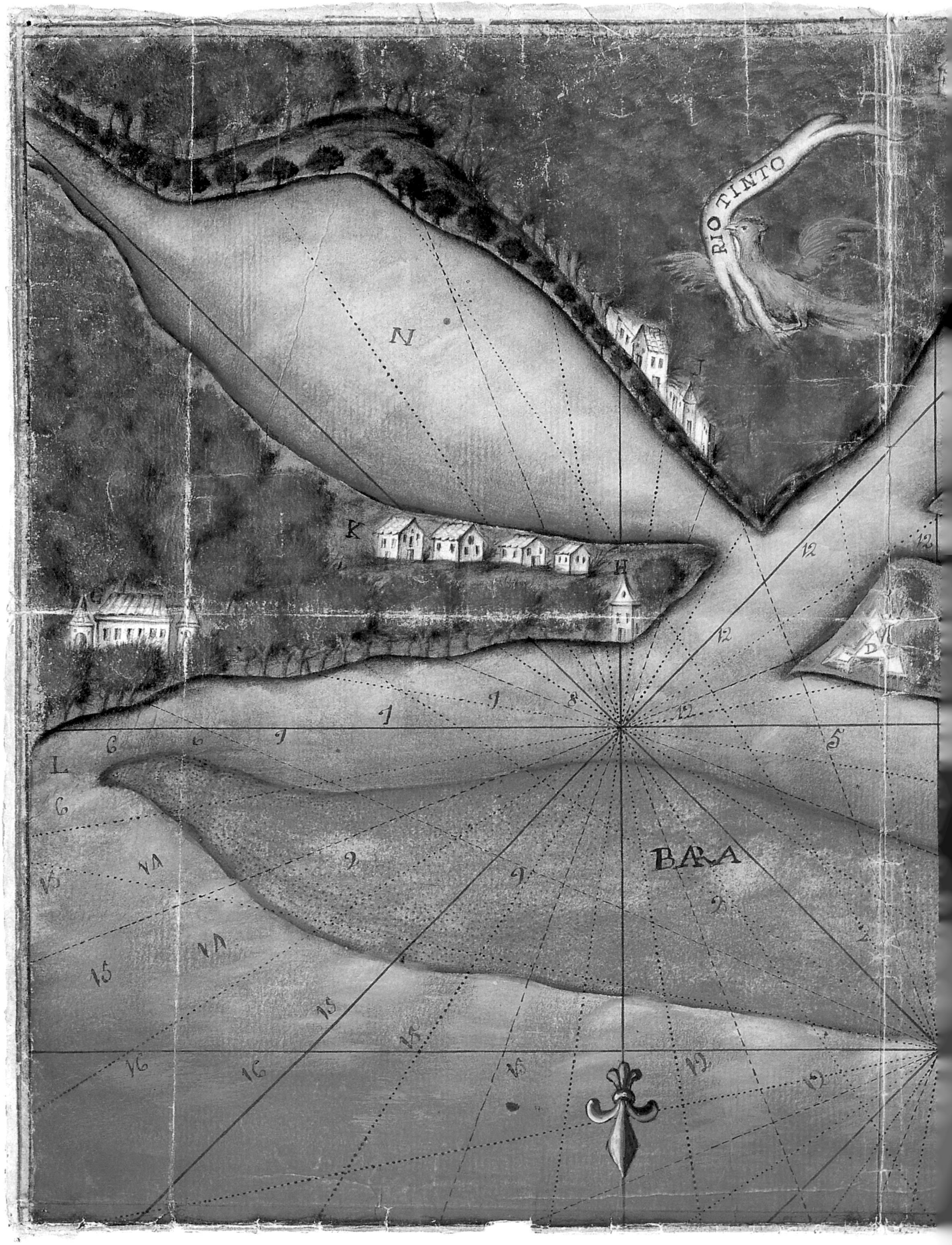
RIO TINTO
N
K
H
D
L
BARRA

English settlements: Mosquitos.

1758
'Río Tinto: Plan of Río Tinto, showing the settlement and the sandbar at the river mouth. Depths of the seabed are marked in feet, while the letters of the alphabet indicate fortifications. Occupied by the English.'
316 x 449 (630 x 458) mm.
MP. Guatemala, 51.

One cause for the strained Anglo–Spanish relations throughout the 18th century was the presence of English settlements in the Gulf of Honduras which, since the end of the 17th century, had been a haven for banished cutters of dyewoods and buccaneers. With the support of the Mosquito Indians, who had long rebelled against Spanish authority, they built fortifications in the Tinto river mouth, as shown in the plan.

DON CARLOS, POR LA GRACIA DE DIOS,
REY DE CASTILLA, DE LEON, DE ARAGON, DE LAS DOS SICILIAS, DE JERUSALEN, DE NAVARRA, DE GRANADA, DE TOLEDO, DE VALENCIA, de Galicia, de Mallorca, de Sevilla, de Cerdeña, de Cordova, de Corcega, de Murcia, de Jaén, de los Algarves, de Algecira, de Gibraltar, de las Islas de Canarias, de las Indias Orientales, y Occidentales, Islas, y Tierra-firme del Mar Oceano, Archiduque de Austria, Duque de Borgoña, de Brabante, y Milán, Conde de Abspurg, Flandes, Tirol, y Barcelona, Señor de Vizcaya, y de Molina, &c.

Yo El Rey

Joseph de Galvez

José de Gálvez's signature.

2 January 1787, Madrid.
Autograph of the Secretary of State and the Indies Department, José de Gálvez, on a shipping patent with an ornate border, engraved by Francisco Muntaner in Madrid in 1781, bearing the seal of Charles III.
1 sheet (372 x 500 mm).
Indiferente, 2271.

José de Gálvez was appointed minister of the Indies in 1776, a position he held together with the office of governor of the Council of the Indies. He had direct experience of Indies affairs, having been a visitador general *or inspector general in New Spain from 1765 to 1771. It was during his mandate that the major reforms were introduced, characterized by the Intendancy, the Bill of Free Trade, the new viceroyalty of Buenos Aires and the 'General Command of the Internal Provinces', the Captaincies General of Caracas, Cuba, Guatemala and the Philippines, fortifications and agricultural development. 'Everything came to life and was set in motion by a single minister' (José Pablo Valiente to the king. Seville, 16/9/1809).*

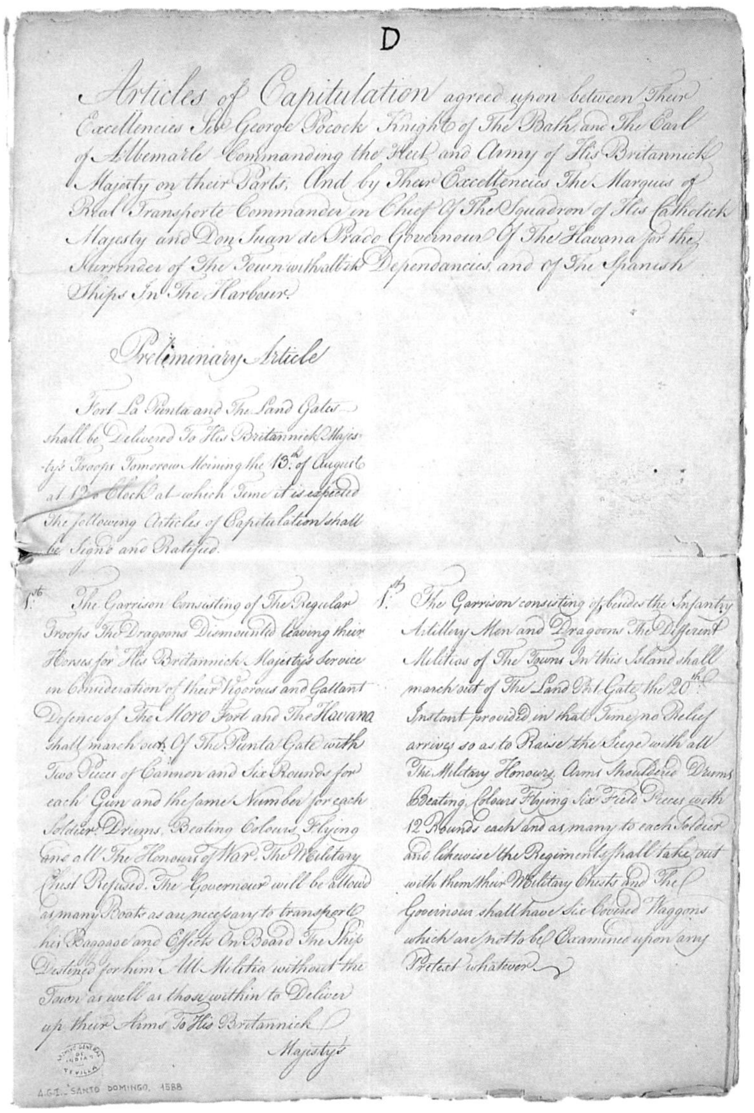

D

Articles of Capitulation agreed upon between Their Excellencies Sir George Pocock Knight of The Bath, and The Earl of Albemarle Commanding the Fleet and Army of His Britannick Majesty on their Parts, And by Their Excellencies The Marquis of Real Transporte Commander in Chief Of The Squadron of His Catholick Majesty and Don Juan de Prado Governour Of The Havana for the Surrender of The Town with all its Dependancies and of The Spanish Ships In The Harbour.

Preliminary Article

Fort La Punta and The Land Gates shall be Delivered To His Britannick Majesty's Troops Tomorrow Morning the 13th of August at 12 o'Clock at which Time it is expected The following Articles of Capitulation shall be Signed and Ratified.

1st The Garrison Consisting of The Regular Troops The Dragoons Dismounted (leaving their Horses for His Britannick Majesty's Service in Consideration of their Vigorous and Gallant Defence of The Moro Fort and The Havana) shall march out Of The Punta Gate with Two Pieces of Cannon and Six Rounds for each Gun and the same Number for each Soldier Drums Beating Colours Flying and all The Honours of War. The Military Chest Refused. The Governour will be allowd as many Boats as are necessary to transport his Baggage and Effects On Board The Ship Destined for him. All Militia without the Town as well as those within to Deliver up their Arms To His Britannick Majesty.

1st The Garrison consisting of besides the Infantry Artillery Men and Dragoons The Different Militias of The Towns In this Island shall march out of The Land Port Gate the 20th Instant provided in that Time no Relief arrives so as to Raise the Siege with all The Military Honours, Arms Shouldered Drums Beating Colours Flying Six Field Pieces with 12 Rounds each and as many to each Soldier and likewise the Regiments shall take out with them their Military Chests and The Governour shall have Six Covered Waggons which are not to be Examined upon any Pretext whatever.

The Seven Years' War: the capture of Havana.

12 August 1762, Havana.
Articles of capitulation for the surrender of Havana, signed by Sir George Pocock and the Earl of Albemarle, commanding the fleet and army of His Britannick Majesty, and the Marquis of Real Transporte, commander-in-chief of the squadron of His Catholic Majesty, and Juan de Prado, the governor of Havana.
In English.
5 sheets + 1 blank (425 x 280 mm).
Santo Domingo, 1588.

After signing a treaty with France in 1761, Spain first clashed with England on the island of Cuba where the reinforced garrison was unable to withstand the overwhelming might of the English fleet (26 warships, 15 frigates and 200 transport vessels) which reached Havana on 7 June 1762. After intense bombardment, the governor surrendered the stronghold on 12 August. Both he and the Marquis of Real Transporte were subsequently court-martialled and severely punished.

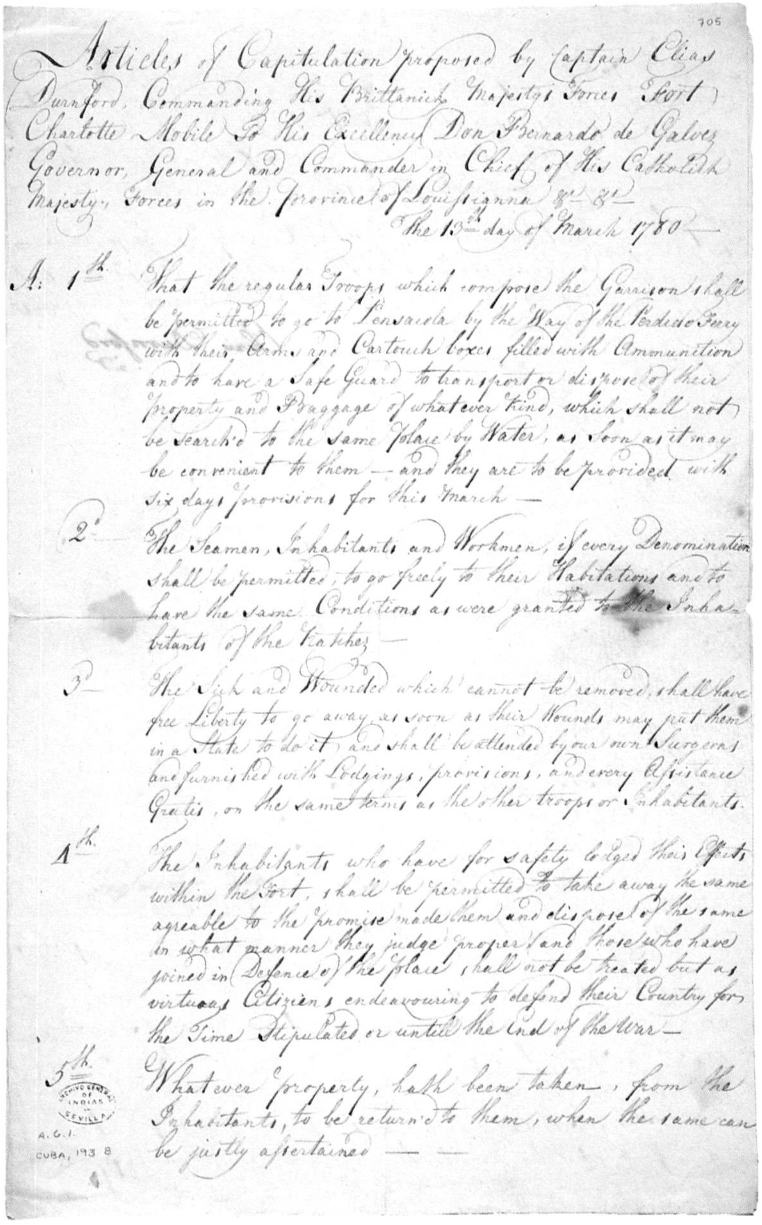
705

Articles of Capitulation proposed by Captain Elias Durnford, Commanding His Brittanick Majestys Forces Fort Charlotte Mobile To His Excellency Don Bernardo de Galvez Governor, General and Commander in Chief of His Catholick Majesty's Forces in the Province of Louisianna &c &c

The 13th day of March 1780

Art: 1st That the regular Troops which compose the Garrison shall be permitted to go to Pensacola by the Way of the Perdido Ferry with their Arms and Cartouch boxes filled with Ammunition and to have a Safe Guard to transport or dispose of their property and Baggage of whatever kind, which shall not be search'd to the same place by Water, as soon as it may be convenient to them — and they are to be provided with six days provisions for this March —

2d The Seamen, Inhabitants and Workmen, of every Denomination shall be permitted to go freely to their Habitations and to have the same Conditions as were granted to the Inhabitants of the Natchez —

3d The Sick and Wounded which cannot be removed, shall have free Liberty to go away as soon as their Wounds may put them in a State to do it, and shall be attended by our own Surgeons and furnished with Lodgings, provisions, and every Assistance Gratis, on the same terms as the other troops or Inhabitants.

4th The Inhabitants who have for safety lodged their Effects within the Fort, shall be permitted to take away the same agreable to the promise made them and dispose of the same in what manner they judge proper and those who have joined in Defence of the place, shall not be treated but as virtuous Citizens endeavouring to defend their Country for the Time Stipulated or untill the End of the War —

5th Whatever property, hath been taken, from the Inhabitants, to be return'd to them, when the same can be justly ascertained — —

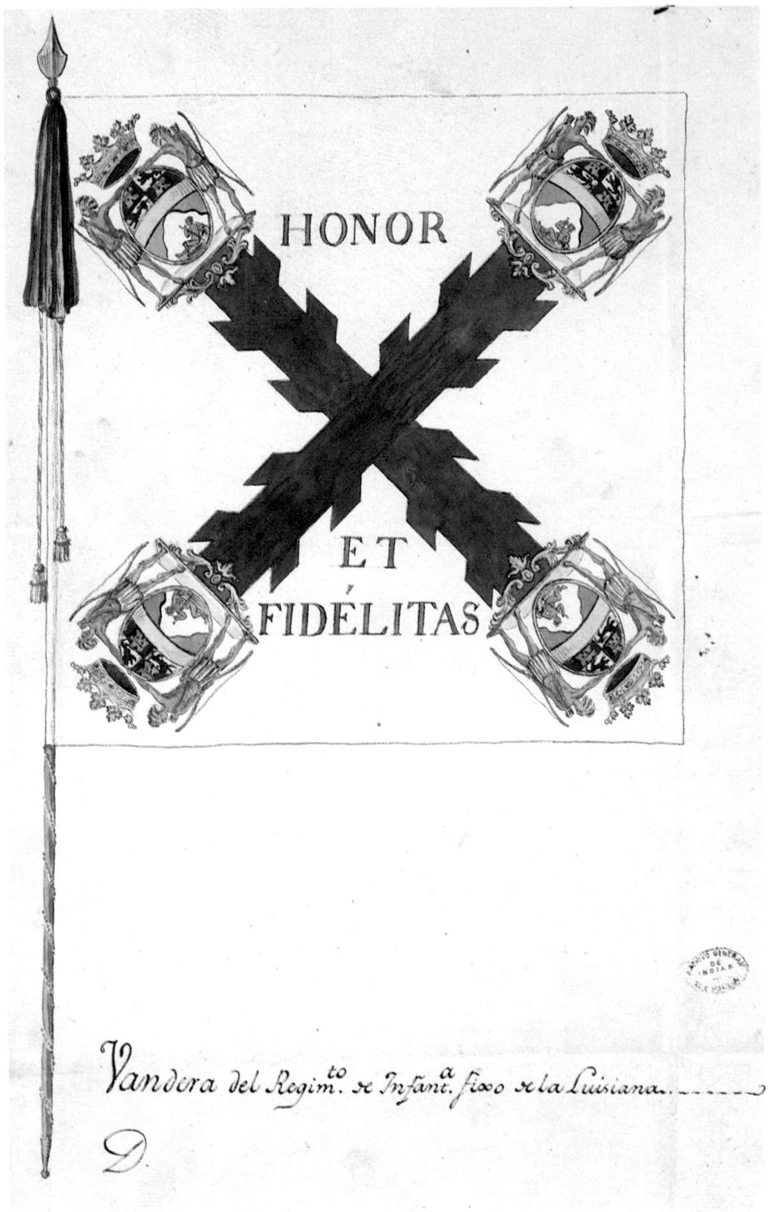

The Spanish assault on Mobile.

13 March 1780, Mobile.
Articles of capitulation proposed by Captain Elias Durnford, commanding His Britannick Majesty's forces at Fort Charlotte, Mobile, to Bernardo de Gálvez, governor general and commander of His Catholic Majesty's forces in the province of Louisiana.
In English.
1 sheet + 1 blank (375 x 231 mm.).
Cuba, 193 B.

The revolution staged by English settlers in North America gave Spain a pretext to regain the territorial losses suffered as a result of the Treaty of Paris. It assisted the settlers by supplying them with weapons and funds, first sporadically, through the Gardoqui trading company and the governors of Louisiana, and subsequently by openly assaulting the English troops. In 1779, Bernardo de Gálvez seized the forts of Baton Rouge and Natchez, followed by those of Mobile, Alabama, in 1780 and Pensacola, Florida, in 1781. For his heroism in battle he was awarded the motto: 'I alone'.

Flag of the Louisiana Regiment.

[1786]
Design for the permanently stationed Infantry Regiment of Louisiana.
229 x 335 mm.
MP. Banderas, 4.

Like all regimental flags from the time of Philip V onwards, the design features a St. Andrew's cross on a white ground. According to statutes dating from 1768, the corners had to bear the royal coat-of-arms or, as in this case, that of the province or city where the regiment was stationed. The shield of Louisiana which appears here is the same as the one used before the Spanish occupation, although the original fleurs-de-lis have been replaced by castles and lions.

ted were José Grimaldo for State, Manuel Vadillo for Justice, Miguel Fernández Durán for War, and Bernardo Tinajero de la Escalera for Navy and the Indies.

All East and West Indies affairs were transferred to this Secretariat, to the detriment of the Council of the Indies which, until then, had been the all-powerful administrative body in that field. The latter did, however, retain its judicial authority and its consultative role. This period also saw the introduction of a *vía reservada,* a confidential channel of direct communication between the king and his secretaries and from these to the Spanish American authorities. After the monarch, the Secretary of the Navy and the Indies was now the supreme authority in matters of government, war, revenues, trade and shipping in the Indies and likewise had the important task of counselling the sovereign on appointments to the highest-ranking offices abroad. Although still operating, the Chamber of the Indies was left with the sole task of proposing nominees to the judiciary.

The number of Secretariats and their mandates varied throughout the 18th century. A special Secretariat was set up to deal with Spain's American affairs during certain periods, while at other times such matters came under the jurisdiction of several other Secretariats.

The first such change occurred in 1717, when the number of Secretariats was reduced to three: a state and foreign affairs department, a Secretariat in charge of war, the navy and justice in Spain and the Indies, and a third covering political administration and the treasury in both Spain and the Indies.

The definitive shape and mandate of the Secretariats was eventually determined during the reign of Ferdinand VI, who settled for a total of five: State, Justice, the Navy and the Indies, the Treasury and War.

By royal decree of 15 May 1754, Don Ricardo Wall was nominated State Secretary with a foreign affairs portfolio. The other secretaries were appointed in a decree dating from 26 August of that year. Courts of law, chancelleries, the *Audiencias* and ministerial appointments came under the Justice Department, as did the Supreme Tribunal of the Inquisition and the appointment of the Grand Inquisitor. The War Department was in charge of all military affairs including personnel, garrisons, campaigns, artillery and fortifications. Appointments of military officers, courts-martial and intendants were made in consultation with the Treasury Department. The latter administered the Royal Treasury and controlled public expenditure, trade and manufacture, in addition to appointing ministers to the Treasury Council. It also received funds sent from the New World after being cleared by the General Depository in Cádiz.

The Department of the Navy and the Indies handled all New World affairs, which is why it soon came to be known as the 'Universal Secretariat of the Indies'. Its mandate covered everything relating to government, war, revenues, trade and shipping, and it submitted proposals for the appointment of councillors, prosecutors, secretaries and accountants in the Council of the Indies, the president and ministers of the *Casa de la Contratación*, and the major posts in the Indies. Military nominations were made in consultation with the War Secretary. It also had exclusive powers to inspect the Armada's arsenals and shipyards, consignments, supplies, equipment and munitions and had jurisdiction over economic, political and military naval matters.

Similarly, the Department had legal competence over royal officials and all posts in the Royal Treasury in the Americas, as the Secretary of the Indies was also the Inspector General of the Royal Treasury. Ecclesiastical presentations under Crown jurisdiction, by virtue of royal patronage, were also among his duties. Lastly, the office included the administration of the Almadén mines and the conveyance of mercury to Seville and Cádiz for subsequent shipment to the Americas.

Also in 1754, Fray Julián de Arriaga y Rivera was appointed minister of the department. He held office until 1776, when he was replaced by José de Gálvez, who was also President of the Council of the Indies. Together, their terms of office spanned the entire period of existence of the Indies Department and coincided with the height of institutional reform in the New World. Arriaga's term heralded the first stage in the application of reforms championed by the all-powerful Marquis of Esquilache, the Secretary of the Treasury and War, who was the leading figure in Charles III's cabinet. Gálvez, who had direct experience of Indies affairs from his stint as inspector of New Spain from 1765 to 1771, saw a term of office in which the reforms were consolidated. As mentioned above, both ministers had as their priority military and economic reinforcement through the rationalization of the administration and increased trade between Spain and the Americas. The ultimate goal was to win Spain a place among the powerful nations on the basis of absolute control over its overseas colonies. In short, foreign policy, directed by the State minister, the Count of Floridablanca, had as its main asset Spain's American territories administered by José de Gálvez.

In the international arena, Spain's hegemony under the Habsburgs had given way to a new balance of power that would gradually be broken during the 18th century by the emergence of the new European powers—Russia and Prussia—and by Great Britain's imperialist policy, based on its rule of the seas and trade expansion. The century was marked by four major armed conflicts: the War of the Spanish Succession (1700–1713), the War of the Austrian Succession (1740–1748), the Seven

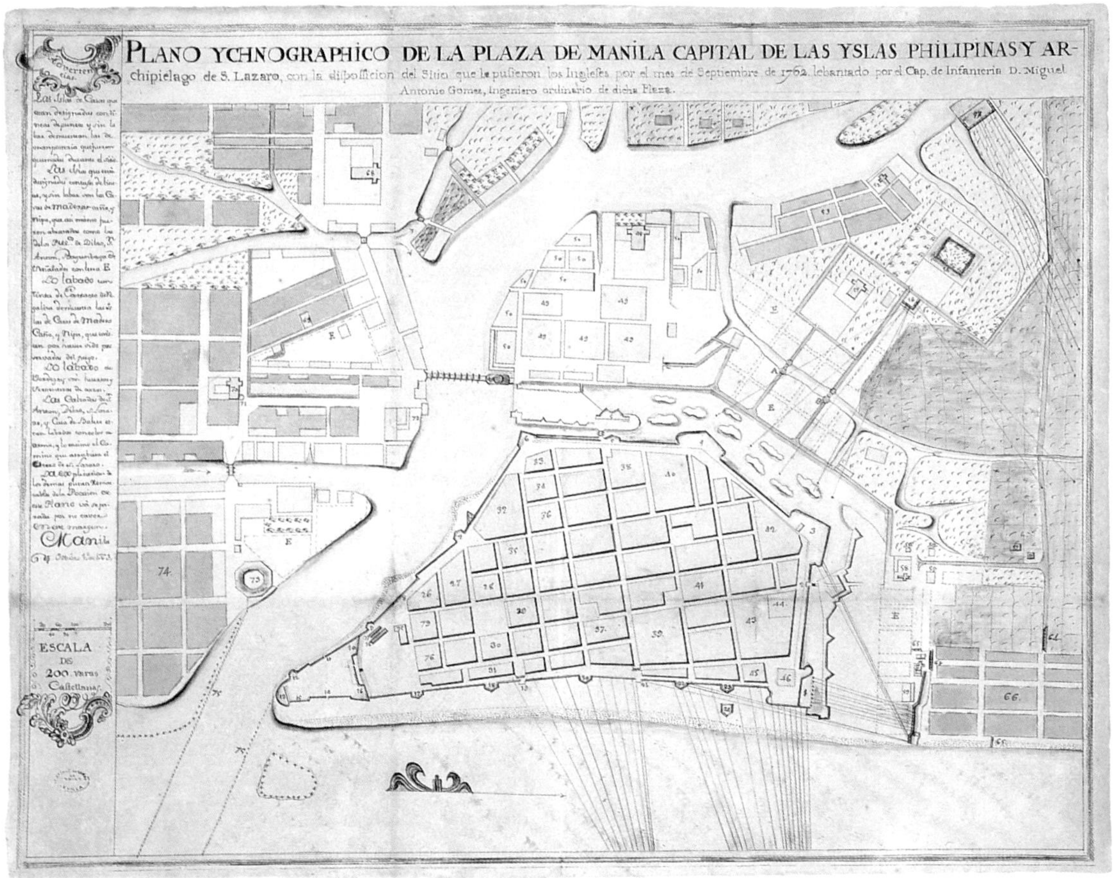

The siege of Manila.

1763
'Ground plan of the stonghold in Manila, capital of the Philippines and the San Lazaro archipelago, showing the points where the English laid siege to the city in September 1762'.
By Miguel Antonio Gómez.
482 x 597 mm.
MP. Filipinas, 42–Ter.

Submitted by the governor of the Philippines, Francisco de la Torre, to the Minister of the Indies. The ground plan shows the layout of the siege mounted by Admiral Cornix's English squadron. The city capitulated on 22 September and was sacked by the English for three days. The guerrilla forces that were mustered in the interior of Luzón island by the oidor, *Simón de Anda, held out until the signing of the Treaty of Paris in 1763, by which Spain recovered Manila.*

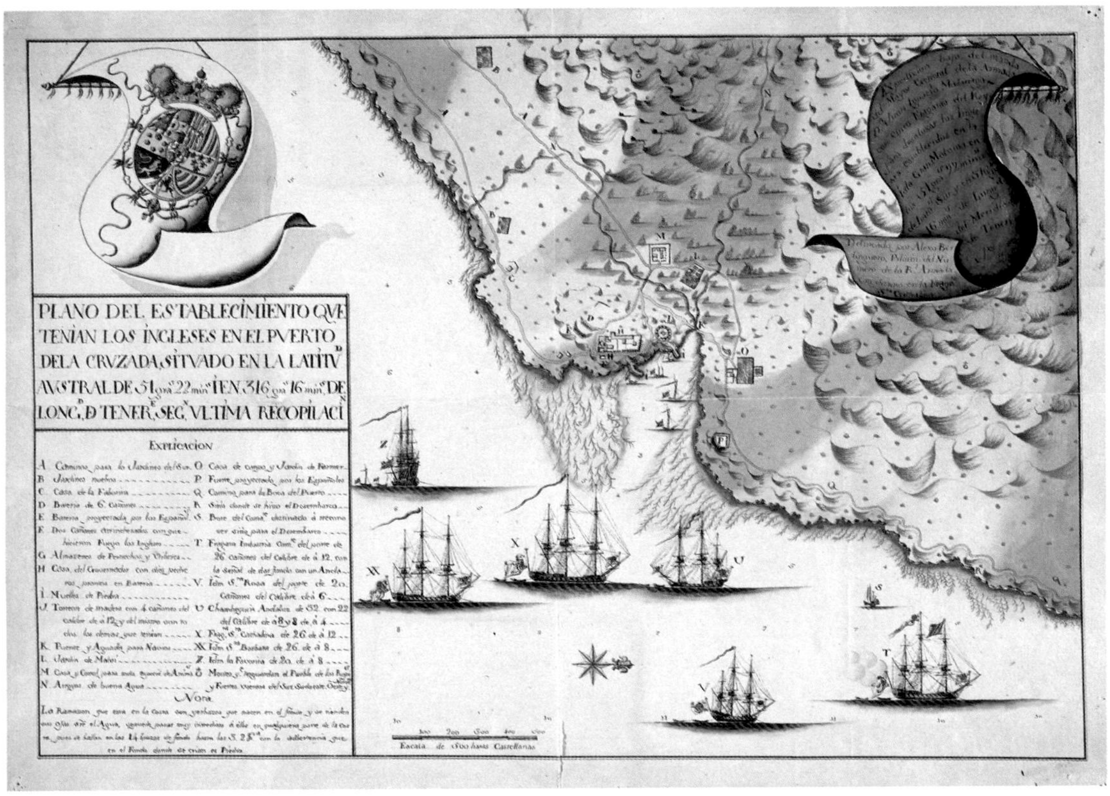

English settlements: the Falklands.

[1770]
'Plan of the English settlement at Puerto de la Cruzada, situated 51 degrees 22 minutes south and 316 degrees 16 minutes from the Tenerife meridian.'
By Alexo Berlinguero, pilot's assistant in the Armada.
366 x 513 mm.
MP. Buenos Aires, 89.

The Treaty of Paris was not at all favorable to Spain's interests after having been through an unfortunate war, and it did not serve to settle disputes with England and Portugal. Moreover, the issue of Honduras was compounded by English occupation of the Falklands (or Malvinas) in 1768. The Spanish government mounted an expedition to flush out the English in 1770, as shown in the plan. The Falklands had considerable strategic value for shipping around Cape Horn and the defense of the southern reaches of the South American continent.

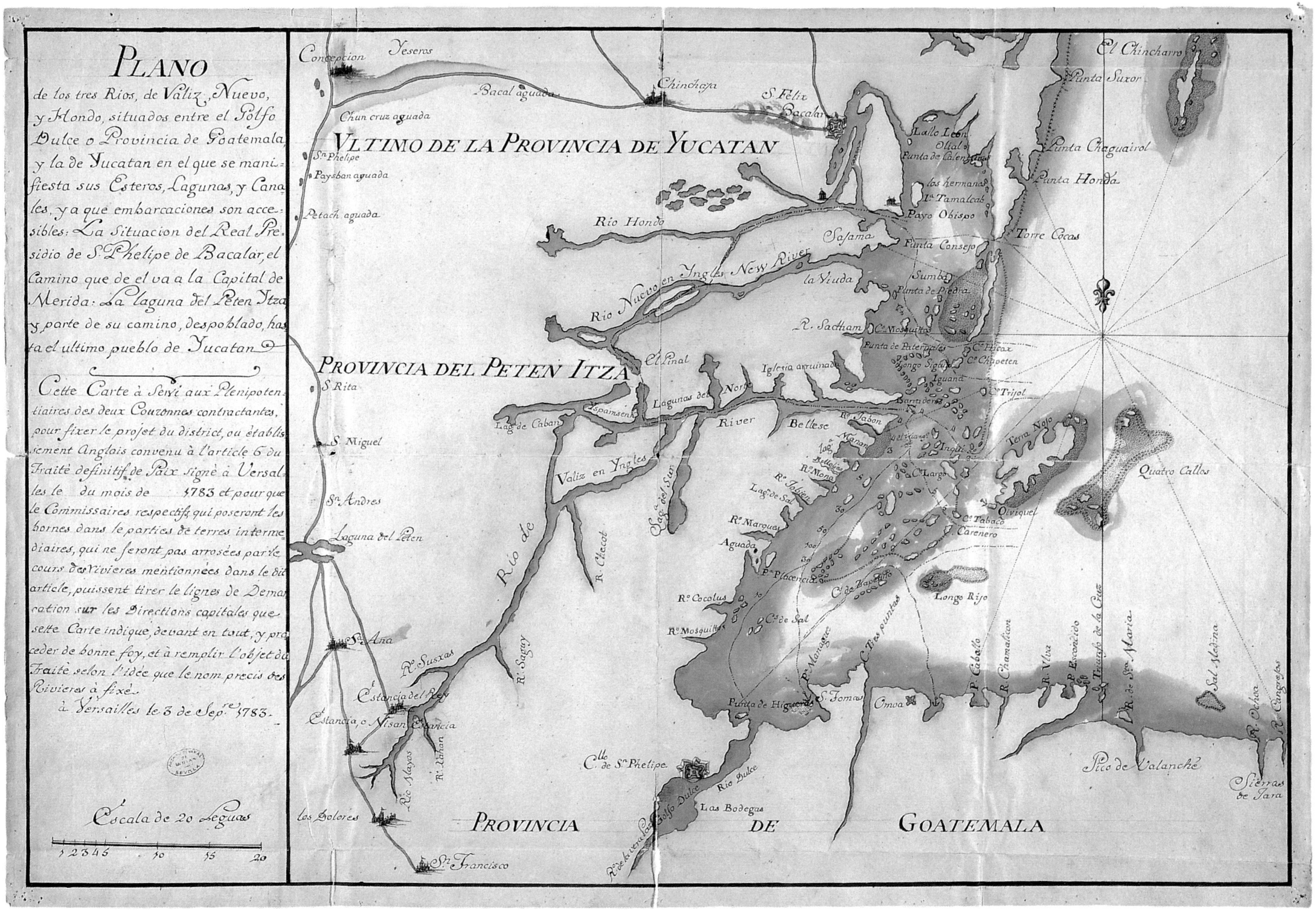
PLANO
de los tres Rios, de Valiz, Nuevo, y Hondo, situados entre el Golfo Dulce o Provincia de Goatemala, y la de Yucatan en el que se manifiesta sus Esteros, Lagunas, y Canales, y a que embarcaciones son accesibles: La Situacion del Real Presidio de S. Phelipe de Bacalar, el Camino que de el va a la Capital de Merida: La laguna del Peten Itza, y parte de su camino, despoblado, hasta el ultimo pueblo de Yucatan
Cette Carte à servi aux Plenipotentiaires des deux Couronnes contractantes, pour fixer le projet du district, ou établissement Anglois convenu à l'article 6 du Traité definitif de Paix signé à Versailles le du mois de 1783 et pour que le Commissaires respectifs qui poseront les bornes dans le parties de terres intermediaires, qui ne feront pas arrosées par le cours des Rivieres mentionnées dans le dit article, puissent tirer le lignes de Demarcation sur les Directions capitales que sette Carte indique, devant en tout, y proceder de bonne foy, et à remplir l'objet du Traité selon l'idée que le nom precis des Rivieres à fixé.
à Versailles le 3 de Sepre 1783.
Escala de 20 Leguas
1 2 3 4 5 10 15 20
VLTIMO DE LA PROVINCIA DE YUCATAN
PROVINCIA DEL PETEN ITZA
PROVINCIA DE GOATEMALA
Concepcion
Yeseros
Bacal aguada
Chinchaja
S. Felix
Bacalar
Chun cruz aguada
Sn Phelipe
Paysban aguada
Petach aguada
Rio Hondo
Rio Nuevo en Ynglés New River
Sasama
la Viuda
R. Sactham
El Pinal
Iglesia arruinada
Lagunas del Norte
River
Bellese
Lag. de Caban
Valiz en Yngles
Rio de
R. Chacot
R. Sagny
R. Susxas
S. Rita
S. Miguel
Sn Andres
Laguna del Peten
Sn Ana
Estancia del Rey
Estancia, o Nisan Estancia
R. Mayas
R. Lutan
los Dolores
Sn Francisco
Cll. de Sn Phelipe
Rio Dulce
Golfo Dulce
Las Bodegas
Punta de Higuera
S. Tomas
Omoa
Tres puntas
P. Manague
Cs. de Sal
R. Mosquitos
R. Cocolus
P. Placencia
Aguada
Lag. de Sal
Longo Rijo
Carenero
Cs. Tabaco
Oviquel
Terra Nojo
Quatro Callos
El Chincharro
Punta Suzor
Punta Chaguairol
Punta Honda
Torre Cocas
Payo Obispo
Punta Consejo
Sumba
Punta de Piedra
Punta de Calentura
los hermanas
Lallo Leon
P. Caballo
R. Chamalicon
R. Vlva
P. Escondido
Triunfo de la Cruz
R. de Sn Maria
Sal Medina
R. Ocha
R. Cangrejos
Pico de Valanche
Sierras de Jara

Previous page: *the Valiz, Nuevo and Hondo rivers.*

3 September 1783, Versailles.
'Map showing the rivers Valiz, Nuevo and Hondo, situated between the Golfo Dulce *or Guatemala Province and Yucatán. Also shown are marshes, lagoons and channels and which vessels can navigate therein, the S. Phelipe de Bacalar garrison, the road to the capital, Mérida, Lake Petén Itzá and part of the deserted road to the last village in Yucatán.'*
430 x 630 mm.
MP. México, 390.

This map was used by the plenipotentiaries of Spain and England to delimit the areas where the English were allowed to fell dyewood trees, as regulated in the sixth clause of the Versailles Treaty. The issue had been pending since the 1763 Treaty of Paris, which had provided for the demolition of English fortifications but permitted them to fell logwood, leading to continued incursions and the founding of new settlements along those three rivers.

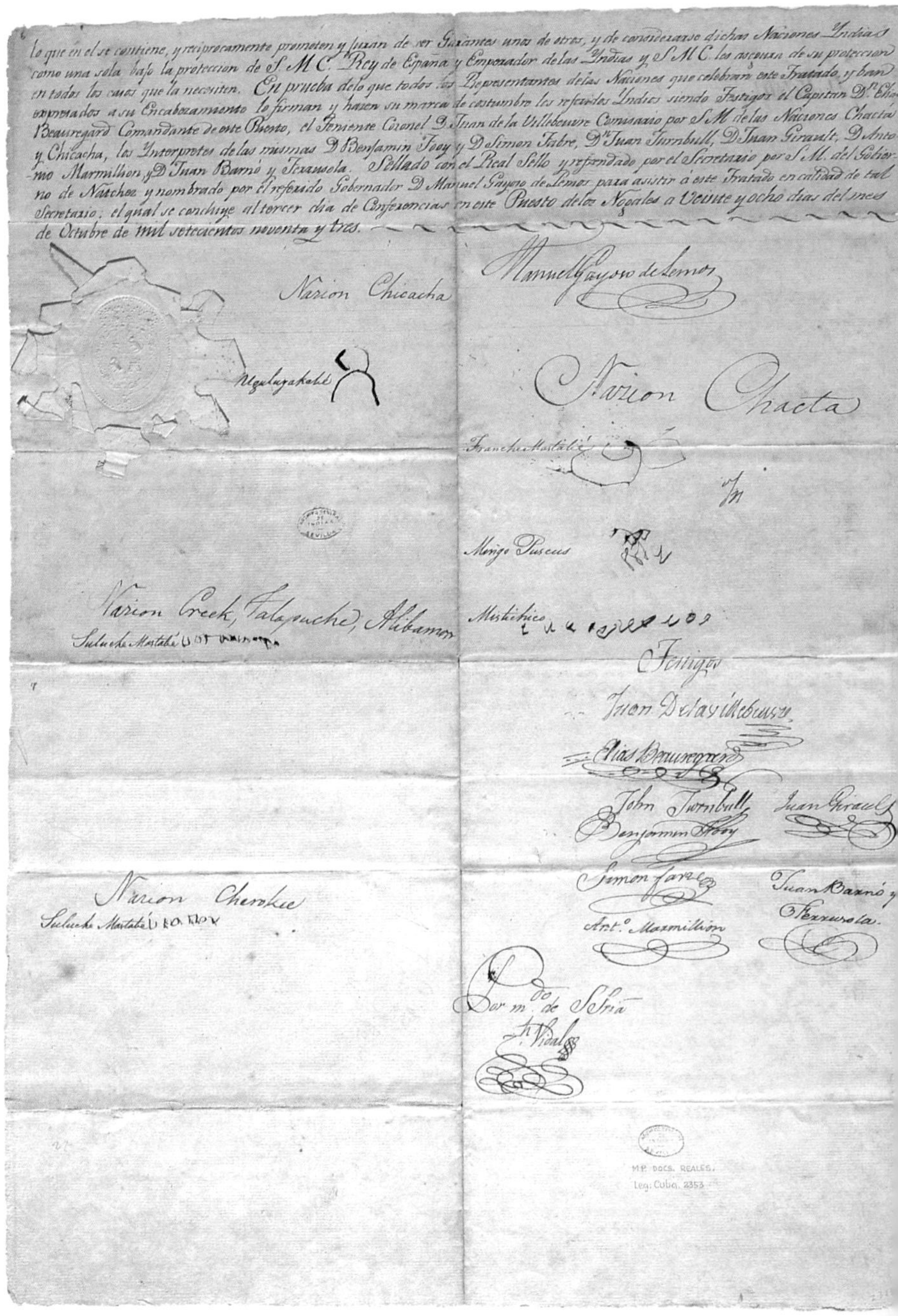
lo que en el se contiene, y reciprocamente prometen y juran de ser Garantes unos de otros, y de considerarse dichas Naciones Indias como una sola bajo la proteccion de S. M. C. Rey de España y Emperador de las Indias y S. M. C. los asegura de su proteccion en todos los casos que la necesiten. En prueba de lo que todos los Representantes de las Naciones que celebran este Tratado, y van expresados a su Encabezamiento lo firman y hazen su marca de costumbre los referidos Indios siendo Testigos el Capitan Dn. Elias Beauregard Comandante de este Puesto, el Teniente Coronel D. Juan de la Villebeuvre Comisario por S. M. de las Naciones Chacta y Chicacha, los Interpretes de las mismas D. Benjamin Fooy y D. Simon Fabre, Dn. Juan Turnbull, D. Juan Girault, D. Antonio Marmillion, y D. Juan Barnó y Ferrusola. Sellado con el Real Sello y refrendado por el Secretario por S. M. del Gobierno de Natchez y nombrado por el referido Gobernador D. Manuel Gayoso de Lemos para asistir a este Tratado en calidad de tal Secretario: el qual se concluye al tercer dia de Conferencias en este Puesto de los Nogales a Veinte y ocho dias del mes de Octubre de mil setecientos noventa y tres.

Manuel Gayoso de Lemos

Nacion Chicacha

Nacion Chacta

Nacion Creek, Talapuche, Alibamon

Testigos

Juan D. la Villebeuvre

Elias Beauregard

John Turnbull

Juan Girault

Benjamin Fooy

Simon Fabre

Juan Barnó y Ferrusola

Ant.o Marmillion

Nacion Cherokee

Por m.do de S. Sria

MP. DOCS. REALES.
Leg. Cuba, 2353

The Indian nations: The Treaty of Nogales.

28 October 1793, Nogales.
'Treaty of friendship and security between His Catholic Majesty, the King of Spain... of the one part, and, of the other, the Chicacha, Creek, Talapuche, Alibamones, Cherokee and Choctaw nations...' from the provinces of Louisiana and Western Florida.
1 sheet (543 x 375 mm.).
Cuba, 2353.

Maintaining good relations with Indian tribes was crucial for settling the provinces of Lousiana and Florida and for controlling border areas, particularly after the independence of the United States. The treaty in question was an offensive–defensive alliance with the Indian nations, who appointed the king of Spain to mediate with the United States over their common borders. The document features autograph signatures of the governor of Natchez, Manuel Gayoso de Lemos, and various tribal chiefs.

Opposite: *Power of attorney granted by Napoleon.*

6 June 1803, Saint Cloud.
Power of attorney awarded by Napoleon Bonaparte, as First Consul of France, to Pierre Clement Laussat, the French government commissioner who took possession of Louisiana when it was ceded by Spain in fulfillment of the terms of the Treaty of San Ildefonso.
Bearing Bonaparte's signature and seal.
Parchment, 375 x 475 mm.
Documentos Escogidos, 1, N. 119.

Private agreements and the alliance with Napoleon put paid to the territorial recovery achieved under Charles III. The 1801 Treaty of San Ildefonso forced Spain to hand Louisiana over to the French. However, the latter never took possession of the territory as the United States, alarmed at the thought of losing the Mississippi outlet, encouraged Napoleon to instead purchase New Orleans or the land east of the river. To their surprise, he sold them the whole of Lousiana for sixty million francs.

Years' War (1756–1763) and the American War of Independence (1776–1783). These were not triggered so much by religious or national sentiments as by dynastic issues and a redistribution of power, and all had repercussions in the New World.

The Spanish Crown realized how the strategic status of its American dominions had been undermined since the decline of the Habsburgs, the War of Succession and the Treaty of Utrecht in 1713. The last had enabled England to gain a territorial and, above all, economic foothold in the New World thanks to its slave trade and the concession of a *navío de permiso* (courtesy vessel), which, for every Spanish fleet bound for Veracruz and Portobelo, allowed a 500-ton English vessel to sail laden with duty-free goods, a measure which encouraged smuggling. The reigns of Philip V and Ferdinand VI saw endeavors to regain lost sovereignty and

Bonaparte Premier Consul, au nom du Peuple Français, ayant pour but d'opérer la prise de possession de la Louisiane, cédée à la République Française par Sa Majesté Catholique, en vertu du Traité conclu à Saint-Ildephonse, le neuf Vendémiaire, an neuf, entre les deux Gouvernemens, le quel Traité a été confirmé par celui d'Aranjuez du trente Ventôse suivant; ayant, de plus, pris connaissance de l'ordre par le quel Sa Majesté Catholique charge le Gouverneur actuel de la Louisiane de remettre cette Colonie aux agens Français envoyés pour la recevoir, nomme le citoyen Pierre Clément Laussat Commissaire du Gouvernement Français, lui donne plein et absolu pouvoir, commission et mandement spécial pour recevoir, au nom de la République Française, des mains des officiers et autres agens préposés à cet effet par Sa Majesté Catholique, la Colonie ou province de la Louisiane; pour prendre toutes les mesures relatives à l'évacuation de ce pays par les troupes Espagnoles, et pour passer tous les actes aux quels pourront donner lieu les dites remise et évacuation. En foi de quoi sont données les présentes, signées, contresignées et munies du Sceau de la République.

A Saint-Cloud, le dix-sept Prairial, an onze de la République Française (six Juin, mil huit cent trois).

Bonaparte

Le Ministre de la
Marine & des Colonies
Decrès

Par le Premier Consul,
Le Secrétaire d'État
Hugues B. Maret

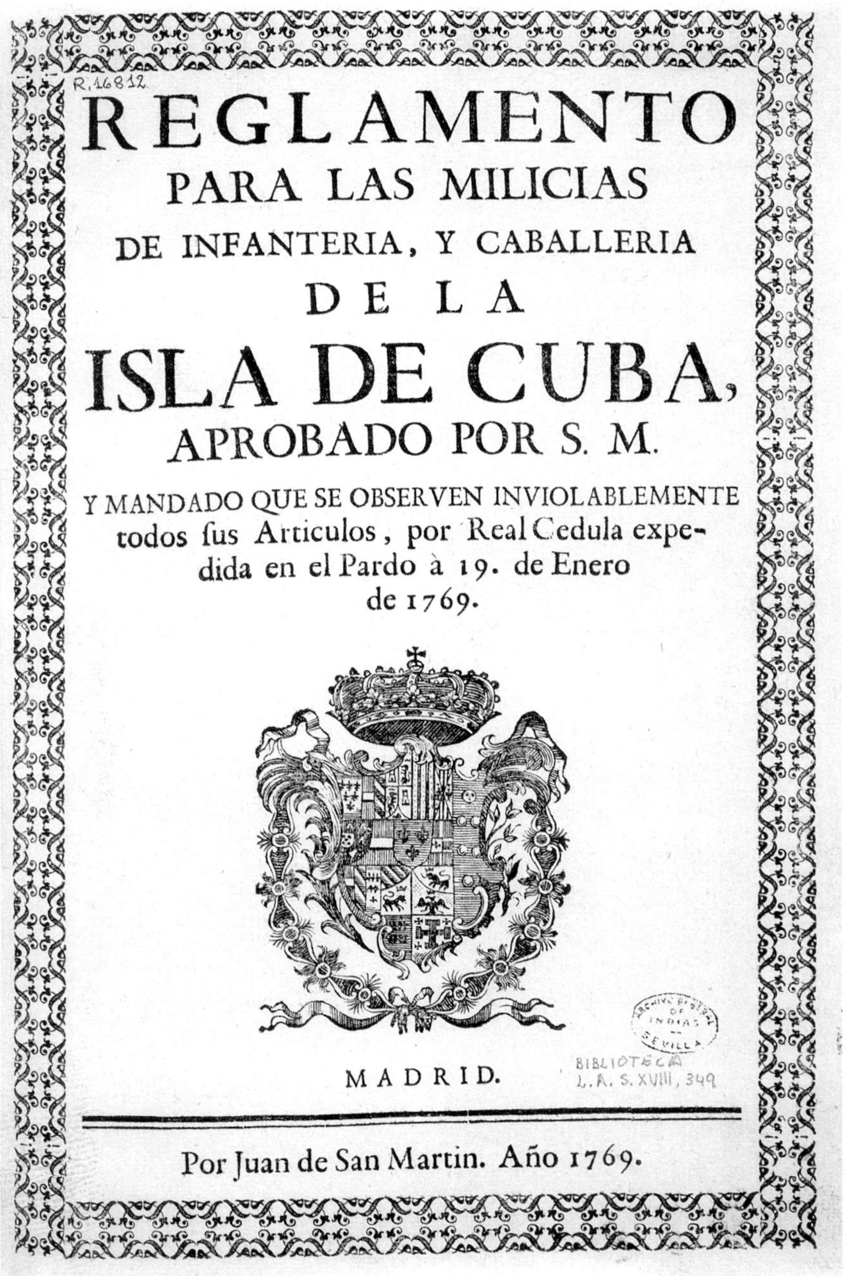

R. 16812

REGLAMENTO
PARA LAS MILICIAS
DE INFANTERIA, Y CABALLERIA
DE LA
ISLA DE CUBA,
APROBADO POR S. M.
Y MANDADO QUE SE OBSERVEN INVIOLABLEMENTE
todos ſus Articulos, por Real Cedula expedida en el Pardo à 19. de Enero de 1769.

MADRID.

Por Juan de San Martin. Año 1769.

O'Reilly's visit.

19 January 1769, El Pardo.
'Regulations for the Infantry and Cavalry militia of the island of Cuba, approved by H.M., who, in view of its return to Spain as stipulated in the Treay of Paris, instructed all its articles to be strictly observed. Royal warrant issued at El Pardo on 19 January 1769.'
By Juan de San Martín, 1769, Madrid.
37 pp., 14 sheets (1 fold-out). Bordered cover. Royal coat-of-arms of Ferdinand VI. Biblioteca, L.A., S. XVIII–349.

One of the first reforms to be implemented by Alejandro O'Reilly on his visit to Cuba, after the island's return to Spain under the terms of the Treaty of Paris, was to commission and regiment the urban militia sent to reinforce the comparatively small garrison of regular troops. The commission provided for the dispatch of 6,700 blanco, pardo y moreno *(white, mulatto and black) militiamen, distributed in eight battalions, and 800 cavalry troops and dragoons, distributed in two regiments.*

Dress uniform of the Morenos *of Havana.*

[1763]
Dress uniform of the Morenos *of Havana [designed by José Nicolás Escaler].*
450 x 240 mm.
MP. Uniformes, 25.

Sent by Alejandro O'Reilly to the Indies minister, Julián de Arriaga, on 21 December 1763 and incorporated into the 'Militia Regulations' of 1769. This infantry battalion of 'free blacks' from Havana played a prominent role in the war with England, coinciding with the independence of the United States, particularly during the Pensacola campaign.

the Indies trade monopoly. The English model had highlighted the benefits to be had from properly governed colonies within the capitalistic framework of a colonial agreement, in which the colonies acted as producers of raw materials and importers of manufactured goods from the homeland. The message finally came home to the Spanish government after they sustained severe losses during the Seven Years' War, when, in 1762, the powerful English navy seized the vital enclaves of Manila and Havana without encountering much opposition. Both strongholds were returned to Spain with the signing of the Treaty of Paris on 10 February 1763. However, Spain then forfeited Florida, which became a buffer zone between the English and Spanish empires after the latter had been compensated by France's cession of Louisiana. The Spanish authorities heeded the warning of 1762 and, during the period leading up to the decisive confrontation with England, when the United States won its independence, they set about instituting the necessary reforms to bolster Spanish America's defensive capability.

The reforms were implemented on a tentative basis in a few territories and, on the basis of the results achieved, applied to the remaining territories thereafter. Thus, shortly after the war, Ricla was sent to Cuba as newly appointed captain general, while General O'Reilly was sent to conduct an inspection of the island in 1763 and 1764, and Puerto Rico in 1765. The upshot of his visit was the commissioning of the militias, the reinforcement of defenses and the submission of proposals for economic recovery. In 1769, O'Reilly also carried out an important mission in Louisiana where he was sent to restore order and Spanish government after an uprising by French inhabitants of the province. The corpus of regulations, statutes and instructions concerning all aspects of public life, which he drew up after his inspection, attest to the major role he played in settling the colony. A similar process ensued in the Antilles, where Ricla was appointed to direct the newly established captaincy general in Havana. Its jurisdiction now also took in Louisiana and its presence ensured Spanish sovereignty over all Mexican territory and the Caribbean. The strategic importance of the region and the results of the reforms instituted there were put to the test in the war with England, triggered when the North American settlers won their independence; Spanish forces seized the English strongholds of Mobile and Pensacola and the island of Providence. After the Treaty of Versailles, which marked the end of the war in 1783, Spain recovered Florida in exchange for some minor concessions to English timber merchants in Campeche and Honduras. That marked the height of the Spanish Bourbons' imperial recovery. However, the Spanish presence in the region was to be short-lived—under the terms of the Treaty of San Ildefonso, endorsed in 1801, Spain returned the province of Louisiana to the French, who then sold it to the United States for fifteen million dollars.

No less important than O'Reilly's visit was that of José de Gálvez to New Spain in 1765. He was granted sweeping powers to conduct thorough inspections of all offices of the Royal Treasury and to study the prospects for introducing the system of intendancies in the viceroyalty. He made some outstanding policy decisions about securing the northern border against raids by Indian tribes, the threatening presence of French and English troops in the Mississippi area and Louisiana and the build-up of the Russian and English presence along the Pacific coastline, lured by the fur trade. Gálvez successfully restored peace to Sonora, Sinaloa, Nueva Vizcaya, New Mexico, Coahuila and Texas through a series of personal visits. He provided for all those territories to be fortified with a frontier line of small but strategically placed garrisons known as *presidios* designed to keep the local, indigenous population in check. After the expulsion of the Jesuits, he was likewise active in promoting the missionary work of the Franciscans, led by Fray Junípero Serra, who replaced the Jesuits in the task of exploring and evangelizing California. The port of San Blas, one of the Spanish navy's largest arsenals as of 1767, was the point of departure for a number of expeditions that sailed along the Pacific coastline as far as San Diego, Monterrey and, eventually, the bay of San Francisco. The year he was appointed minister of the Indies, Gálvez decided to reinforce that frontier by setting up the so-called 'General Command of the Internal Provinces of New Spain'. Based at Arispe, it took in the major provincial jurisdictions of Sonora, California and Nueva Vizcaya and the subordinate, minor provinces of Coahuila, Texas and New Mexico. He appointed the Caballero de Croix to rule over them and granted him such wide-reaching powers that the provinces became virtually independent from the viceroyalty of Mexico.

Many new commands and captaincies general were established at the time for the purpose of strategic territorial defense and expansion. In 1777, the Captaincy General of Caracas was formed, the territory having previously been part of the viceroyalty of New Granada. This, the third viceroyalty, had been tentatively set up in 1717 and permanently so in 1739. It embraced the jurisdictions of the *Audiencias* of Panama, Santa Fe and Quito and the *gobernación* (minor province) of Venezuela. The foundation–charter gives as reasons for establishing the viceroyalty the benefit to be had by such large regions and the need to improve the organization of territorial defense. To this end, military commands were set up in Cartagena, Panama and Caracas. When the latter became a captaincy general, it was awarded jurisdiction over the *gobernaciones* of Guayana, Margarita Island, Cumaná, Coro and Mérida. In 1786, it acquired an *Audiencia* and was granted independence from the viceroyalty of New Granada.

For strategic reasons, the captaincies general of Guatemala, Yucatán, Chile and the Philippines were also established.

Opposite
Inspections: 'Internal Provinces of New Spain'.

[1777]
'Map of that part of the kingdom of New Spain falling between the latitudes of 19 and 42 degrees north and the longitudes of 249 and 289 degrees west of the Tenerife meridian. Prepared on the orders of His Excellency, Fray Antonio Maria Bucarely y Ursua, to show the boundaries of the Viceroyalty of Mexico and of the Internal Provinces established by virtue of the royal decree of 1777.'
By Miguel Costansó.
1,000 x 1,250 mm.
MP. México, 346.

A prominent feature of the inspection of Mexico conducted by José de Gálvez in 1765 was the implementation of his policy designed to protect the northern border from raids by Indian tribes and counteract the presence of the English and French in Louisiana and that of the English and Russians on the Pacific seaboard. For this purpose he provided for a frontier line of garrisons or presidios *to be built in the provinces of Sonora, Sinaloa, Nueva Vizcaya, New Mexico, Coahuila and Texas and actively promoted Franciscan exploration and missionary work in California. After his appointment as minister of the Indies, Gálvez secured the whole of that frontier by creating the so-called General Command of the Internal Provinces.*

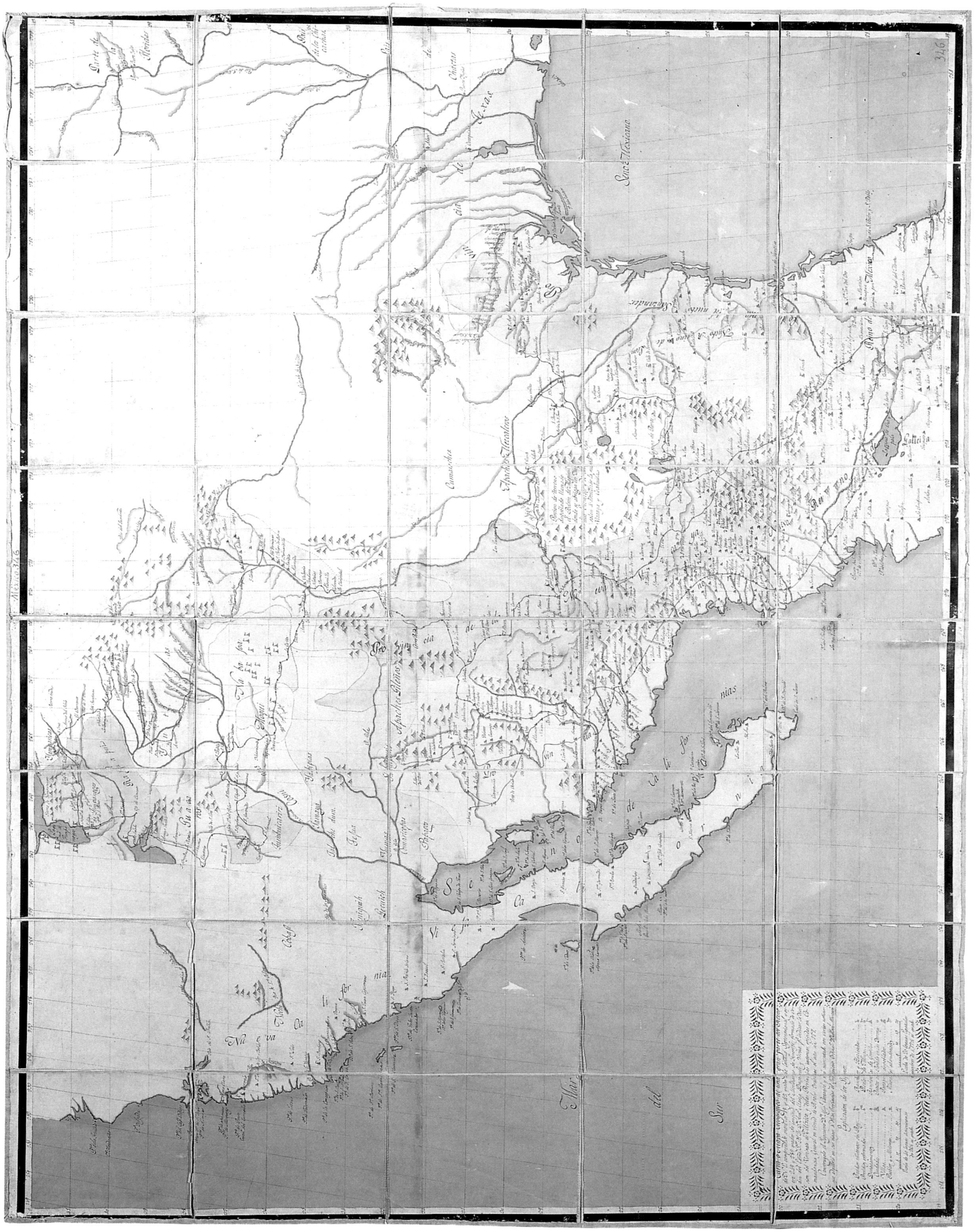
Seno Mexicano
Mar del Sur

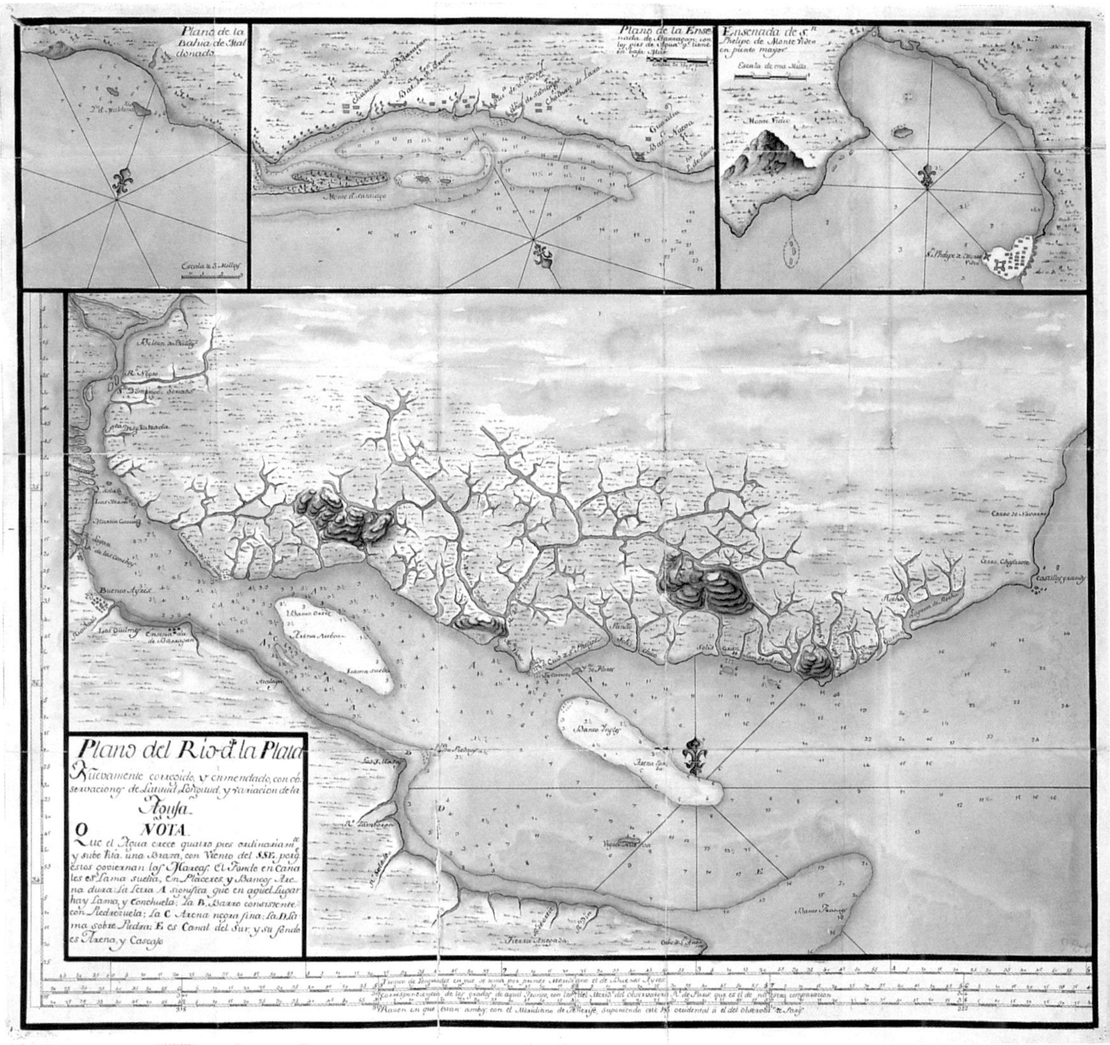

Opposite, above
Uniforms: the Philippines.

[1797]
'Panels showing the uniforms worn by His Majesty's troops stationed at the Manila garrison and outlying batteries, with a description of the arms and rank of each. The number of soldiers, excluding officers, amounts to 13,887.'
515 x 754 mm.
MP. Uniformes, 62.

Bourbon military reform was directed at dignifying the image of the institution and special emphasis was laid on the uniform, regarded as a mark of standardization and identification of each unit. The most striking examples shown here are the cavalry units, particularly the Cazadores *or 'Chasseurs', founded by Philip V in 1701 to pursue an enemy in retreat and 'hunt them down in the field'. Their horses, known as a* regular marca fatiga *(regular fatigue breed), were indigenous to the country. A curiosity is the* Compañía de Faginantes *(Company of Brushwood Gatherers) whose task it was to extinguish fires and act as bearers in the event of the stronghold being placed under siege. The uniform was adapted from local dress, as all soldiers in this company were natives.*

Río de la Plata.

[1771]
'Revised and amended plan of Río de la Plata, with indications of latitude, longitude and compass needle variations.'
The three plans featured above are Maldonado Bay, the Barragán inlet and the Bay of San Felipe de Montevideo.
820 x 840 mm.
MP. Buenos Aires, 92 B.

The map shows the Río de la Plata estuary and the Portuguese settlement of Sacramento. The creation of the viceroyalty of Buenos Aires and its consolidation after the Treaty of Limits, signed with Portugal in 1777, secured the whole region for Spain and settled once and for all the issue of the Portuguese colony on the so-called Banda Oriental *(the east bank of the Uruguay river).*

Opposite, below
The fortification of Talcaguano.

[1785]
'Map of Talcaguano bay and harbor, showing the forts of San Agustín and Gálvez.'
'Plan of the San Agustín fort, built of brushwood, on Talcaguano beach.'
'Plan of Gálvez fort on the slopes of Zerro de Talcaguano.'
310 x 410 mm.
MP. Perú y Chile, 80.

Spain's defense of its possessions in the New World was a three-pronged initiative: the establishment of commands and captaincies general, military reform and the fortification of strategic points. These forts at Talcaguano, a town near Concepción in Chile, were erected in anticipation of an enemy landing during the war with England. The San Agustín fort protected the beach, while that of Gálvez, excavated in a half-moon shape on a hillslope, commanded a general view of possible enemy movements. Crossfire from both forts covered the whole bay and all possible anchorages.

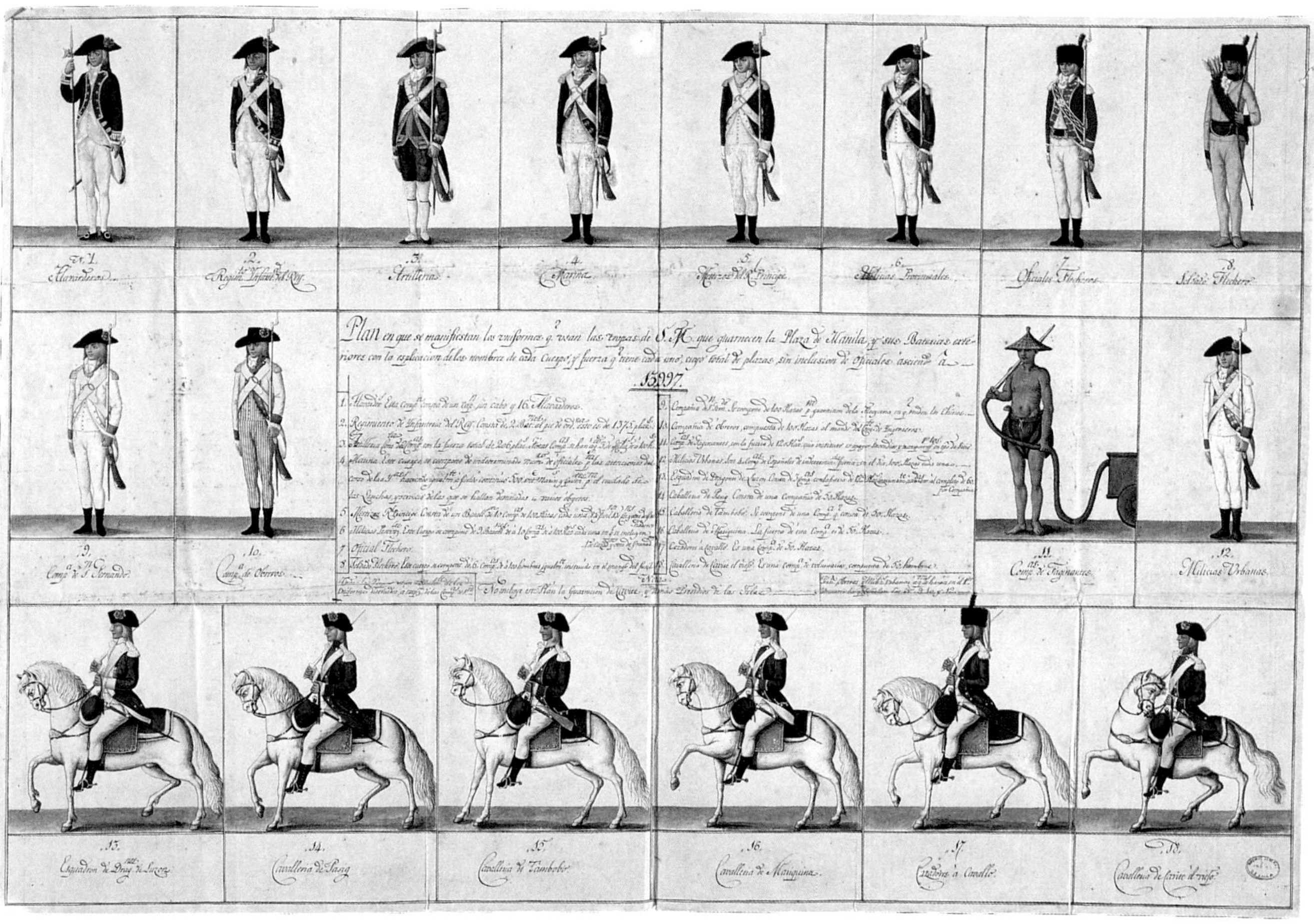
Plan en que se manifiestan los uniformes q. usan las tropas de S. M. que guarnecen la Plaza de Manila, y sus Baterias exteriores con la esplicacion de los nombres de cada Cuerpo, y fuerza q. tiene cada uno, cuyo total de plazas, sin inclusion de Oficiales asciende á
15997.
3. Artilleria.
4. Marina.
5. Mozos del R.l Principe
6. Milicias Provinciales.
11. Comp.a de Fajinantes.
12. Milicias Urbanas.

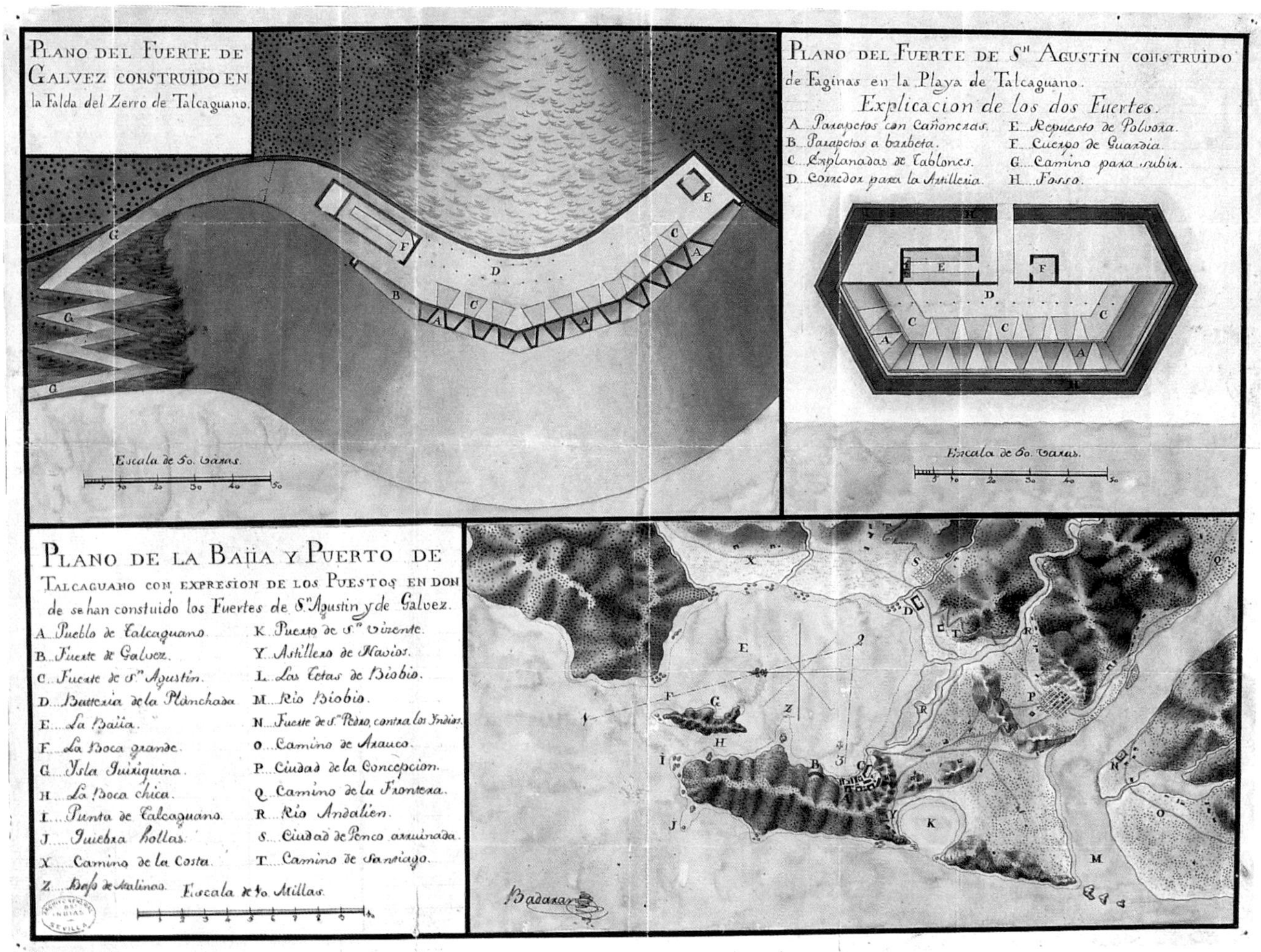
Plano del Fuerte de Galvez construido en la Falda del Zerro de Talcaguano.
Plano del Fuerte de S.n Agustin construido de Faginas en la Playa de Talcaguano.
Explicacion de los dos Fuertes.
A. Parapetos con Cañoneras.
B. Parapetos a barbeta.
C. Explanadas de Tablones.
D. Corredor para la Artilleria.
E. Repuesto de Polvora.
F. Cuerpo de Guardia.
G. Camino para subir.
H. Fosso.
Escala de 50. Varas.
Escala de 50. Varas.
Plano de la Bahia y Puerto de Talcaguano con expresion de los Puestos en donde se han construido los Fuertes de S.n Agustin y de Galvez.
A. Pueblo de Talcaguano.
B. Fuerte de Galvez.
C. Fuerte de S.n Agustin.
D. Bateria de la Planchada.
E. La Bahia.
F. La Boca grande.
G. Isla Quiriquina.
H. La Boca chica.
I. Punta de Talcaguano.
J. Quiebra Hollas.
X. Camino de la Costa.
Z. Bajo de Molinos.
K. Puerto de S.n Vizente.
Y. Astillero de Navios.
L. Las Tetas de Biobio.
M. Rio Biobio.
N. Fuerte de S.n Pedro, contra los Indios.
O. Camino de Arauco.
P. Ciudad de la Concepcion.
Q. Camino de la Frontera.
R. Rio Andalien.
S. Ciudad de Penco arruinada.
T. Camino de Santiago.
Escala de 10 Millas.

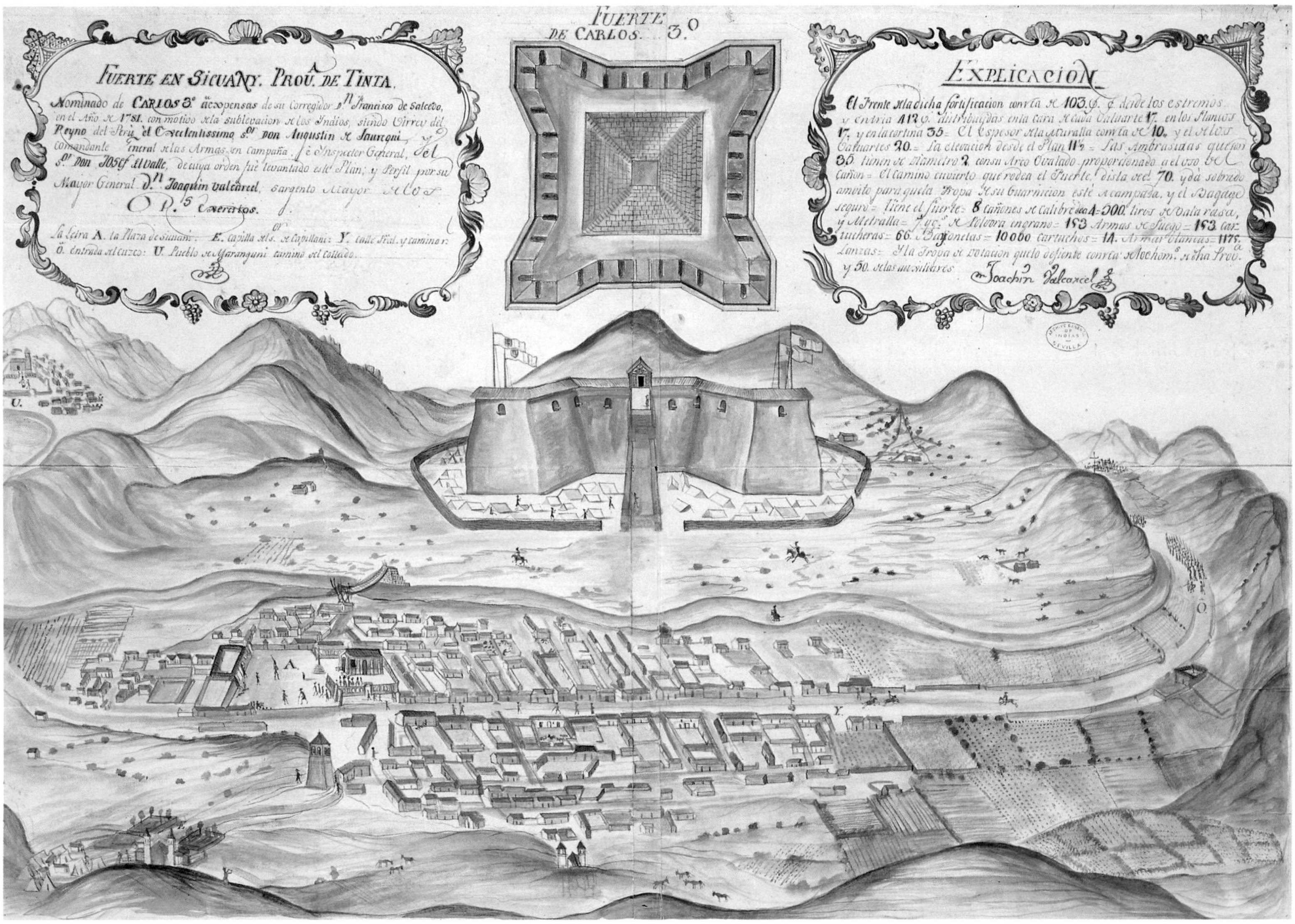

Fort Sicuany.

[1781]

'Fort Sicuany, Tinta province, built on the orders of Charles III and at the expense of its corregidor, *Francisco de Salcedo, in 1781, during the Indian uprising.'*

500 x 420 mm.

MP. Perú y Chile, 187.

Areche, the visitador *or 'inspector' of Peru, implemented taxation that sparked a number of uprisings, starting in Arequipa in 1780 and spreading to La Paz, Cochabamba and Cuzco. The fiercest uprising, which began in the province of Tinta, was staged by Tupac Amaru, a local chieftain. He resolved to rid the indigenous peoples of the onerous system of taxes and forced labor* (mita y obrajes) *and, after hanging the corregidor, mounted the largest armed rebellion against Spanish administration prior to 1810.*

However, the most far-reaching territorial reform was the establishment of the viceroyalty of Río de la Plata in 1776. It took in the *gobernaciones* of Tucumán, Buenos Aires, Paraguay the Falklands, the Cuyo *corregimiento* (annexed to Chile), the Banda Oriental (the area between the Río de la Plata estuary and the Brazilian border) and Charcas, one of the most important mining centers and most densely populated Indian towns on the continent. The viceroyalty was first set up on a temporary basis when Pedro Cevallos mounted an expedition against the Portuguese of the Banda Oriental, who were constantly raiding Spanish territory. With the outbreak of the independence movement in the English colonies of North America, the Spanish took advantage of the predicament in which Portugal's British ally found itself by sending an expedition to Río de la Plata, granting its commander viceregal authority. The viceroyalty was finally consolidated with the signing of the Treaty of Limits in 1777 which put an end to the disputes over the territory bordering on Brazil and settled once and for all the problem of the Sacramento colony, on which Portugal withdrew its claim.

The creation of the viceroyalty was a highly successful measure in that it guaranteed Spain a foothold in the Río de la Plata estuary and therefore its defense of the South Atlantic, with the Falklands as the key to Pacific access. It also boosted

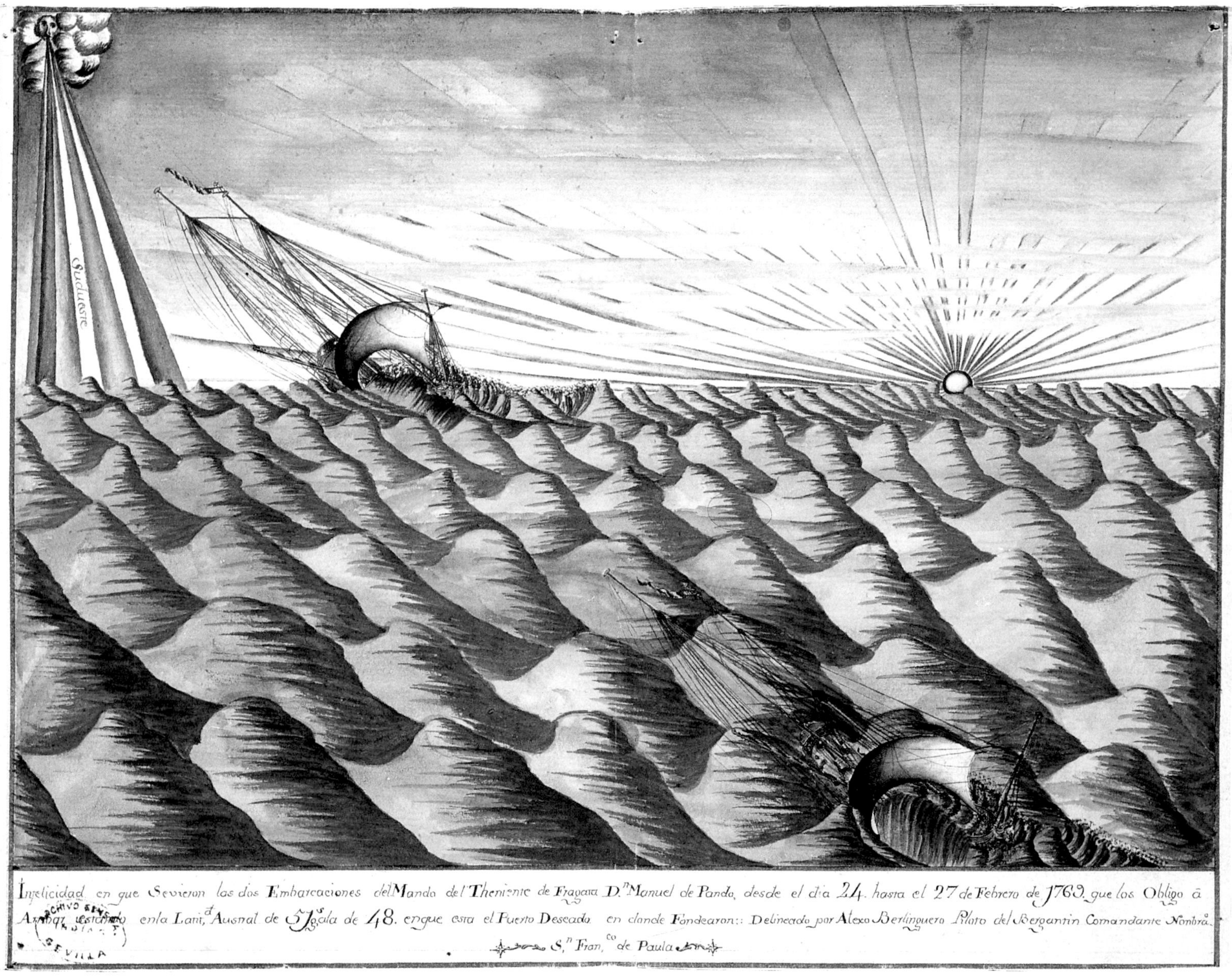

Sudueste
Infelicidad en que Se vieron las dos Embarcaciones del Mando del Theniente de Fragata D.n Manuel de Pando, desde el dia 24. hasta el 27 de Febrero de 1769. que los Obligo á
Arribar estando en la Lati.d Austral de 51.s á la de 48. en que esta el Puerto Deseado en donde Fondearon:: Delineado por Alexo Berlinguero Piloto del Bergantin Comandante Nombrã.
S.n Fran.co de Paula

Expedition to Tierra del Fuego.

[1769]

'Misfortune befell the two vessels under the command of Lieutenant Manuel de Pando, from 24 to 27 February 1769 when, having reached 51 degrees latitude south, they were driven back to 48 degrees, where Puerto Deseado is located and where they were able to cast anchor.'
By Alexo Berlinguero, pilot on the brig San Francisco de Paula.
195 x 251 mm.
MP. Buenos Aires, 80.

In 1766, the strategic importance of the Patagonian coast and Tierra del Fuego as the gateway to the Pacific prompted the Crown to commission the establishment of a 'colony and port of call' there. It was also to act as a base for exploring the coastline, reducing the Indian population and preventing other European powers from settling the region. This expedition sailed from Buenos Aires in December 1768 under the command of Lieutenant Manuel Pando. This drawing was found in the ship's logbook which carries a description of how the objective of the expedition could not be fulfilled on account of the adverse sea conditions, which forced the vessels to make a landfall at Puerto Deseado.

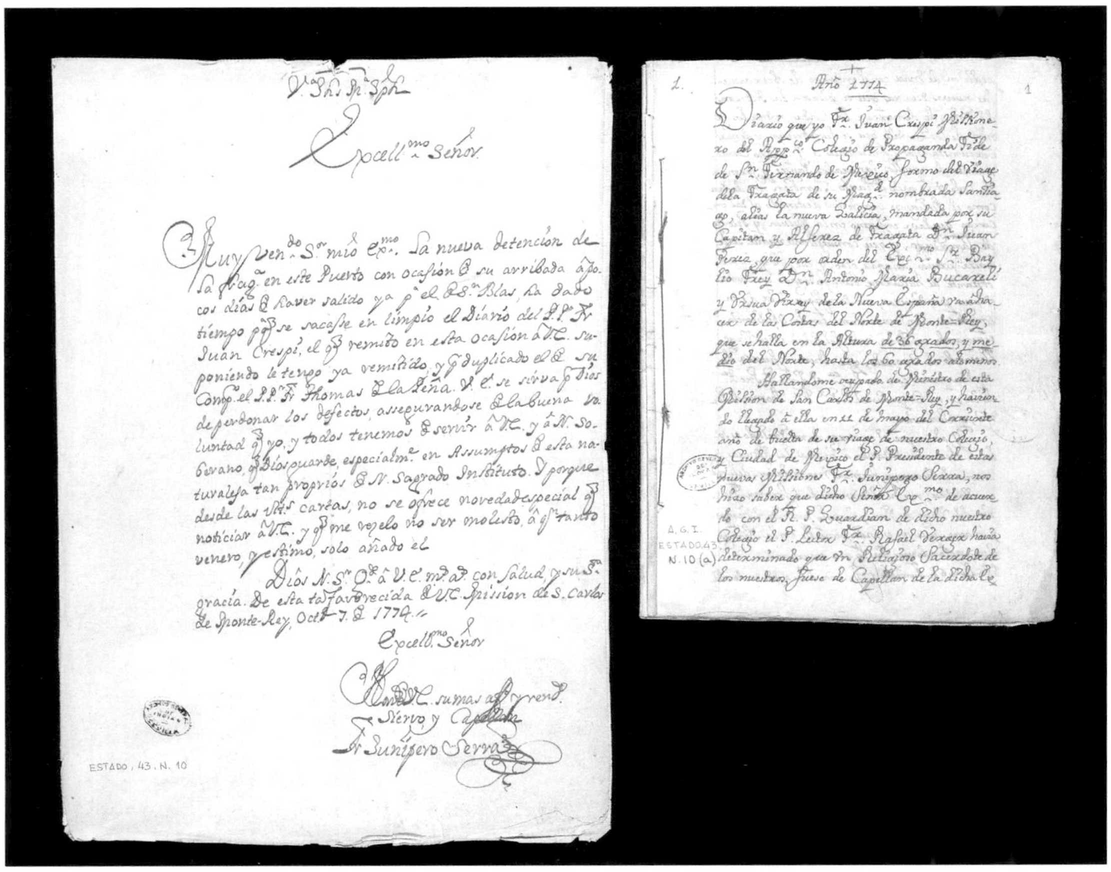

The California expedition.

7 October 1774, mission of San Carlos de Monterrrey.
Autograph letter by Fray Junípero Serra accompanying Fray Juan Crespi's logbook, kept on board the frigate Santiago, which sailed from the port of Monterrey to 60º latitude north on a voyage that took from 6 June to 27 August 1774.
1 fol. + 1 blank; 42, 4to sheets + 4 blanks.
Estado, 43, N. 10 & 10 a.

The purpose behind the colonization of Upper California was twofold: politically, to counteract the English and Russian influence on the Pacific seaboard and, on the religious front, to resume the missionary work that had come to a standstill after the expulsion of the Jesuits in 1767. An outstanding figure in this respect was the Majorcan friar, Junípero Serra. From 1774 onwards, a number of expeditions were readied in the port of San Blas. They led to the establishment of missions and garrisons spanning the entire coastline of California. The land route from Sonora, opened up by Juan Bautista Ansa, linked all the missions in Upper California with Mexico, with Monterrey acting as the communications junction. By the time of Fray Junípero's death in 1784, the Franciscan mission was well under way.

The Gran Chaco expedition.

1774
'Map marking the landing by the governor of Tucumán province, Don Gerónimo Matorras, on the coast of the fertile and extensive lands of the Gran Chaco Gualamba, in observance of the Royal Contract of 1774.'
By Julio Ramón de César.
540 x 375 mm. MP. Buenos Aires, 107.

Territorial expansion was directed at both frontier lands 'to be discovered' and the underpopulated or sparsely colonized interior. The Gran Chaco Gualamaba was a vast region between the Andes, Panama and the Argentine Pampa inhabited by a large number of tribes, among which the Jesuits had some reducciones *or villages of converted Indians. The governor of Tucumán was commissioned to pacify the region and to found a settlement with people from Santiago del Estero. The drawing shows the meeting between Matorras and Paikin, leader of the numerous Indian nations in the Chaco.*

the economy of the Andean regions. At the same time, however, it precipitated the decline of the viceroyalty of Peru by removing large areas under its jurisdiction. New Granada was dismembered in similar fashion. Gálvez decided to commission an inspection of these two viceroyalties before implementing territorial and economic changes. For this purpose he sent Juan Francisco Gutiérrez de Piñeres to New Granada and Juan Antonio de Areche to Lima. Both met with severe difficulties and their endeavors triggered the uprisings of Socorro in the viceroyalty of Santa Fe, and that of Tupac Amaru in Peru, more in protest over the tax burden and abuses committed by local authorities than over the issue of royal authority.

While the administrative reforms were under way, a number of specific measures were adopted to reinforce existing defenses at strategic points. In the Caribbean, these were carried out in Havana, Veracruz, Omoa and Cartagena and, on the coast of South America, in the areas stretching from Maracaibo to the Orinoco and from Montevideo to Patagonia. On the Pacific seaboared, an entire line of fortresses was set up between Chiloé and Callao in the south and Acapulco and San Blas in the north. Equally important reforms were introduced in the armed forces, particularly the decision to station a permanent militia, divided into battalions, between various towns and provinces, alongside the comparatively small number of regular troops, numbering 6,000 in New Spain, 3,000 in New Granada and 1,500 in Peru.

Implementation of the territorial defense plan likewise involved considerable territorial expansion with the aim of reinforcing border areas and pushing back the boundaries of colonized provinces by jointly sending out missionaries with military escorts and settling new colonies. The expeditions ventured into uncharted territories such as southern Chile and Patagonia, with the Jesuits and Franciscans paving the way for colonization of vast tracts of land in the eastern Andes and California. Simultaneously, peaceful but deserted areas were also settled, often by whole families from mainland Spain and the Canary Islands. Such resettlement projects, the steep cost of which was met by the Royal Treasury, were put into practice by both the authorities and private concerns. Private colonial initiatives were undertaken in exchange for land grants, tax exemptions and, quite often, titles, such as that of the Marquis of Sierra Gorda, in New Santander, the Count of San Juan de Jaruci, in Cuba and the Count of Osorno in Chile.

Complementary to and no less important than the measures implemented for the defense and fortification of Spain's strategic position in the Americas were those related to the promotion of economic and financial resources. In this respect, the major administrative reform was the establishment of the system of intendancies which, like other Bourbon institutions, was French in origin. It was formally

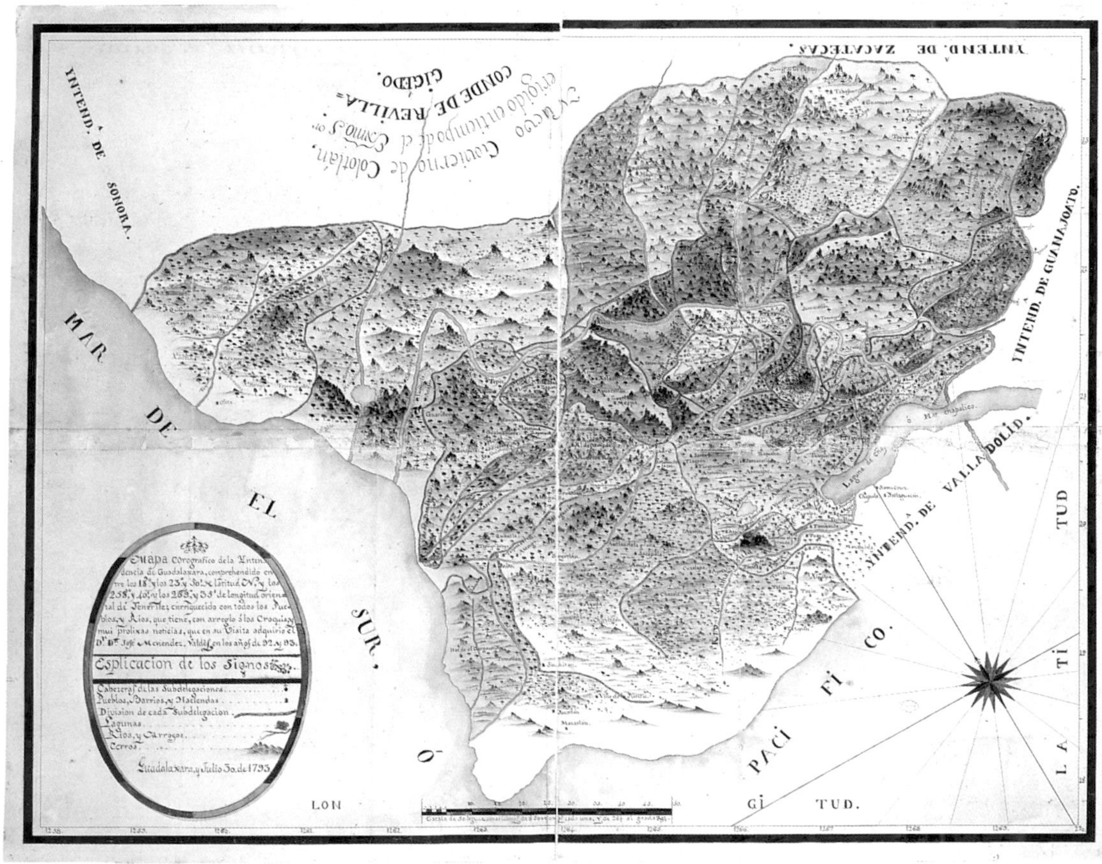

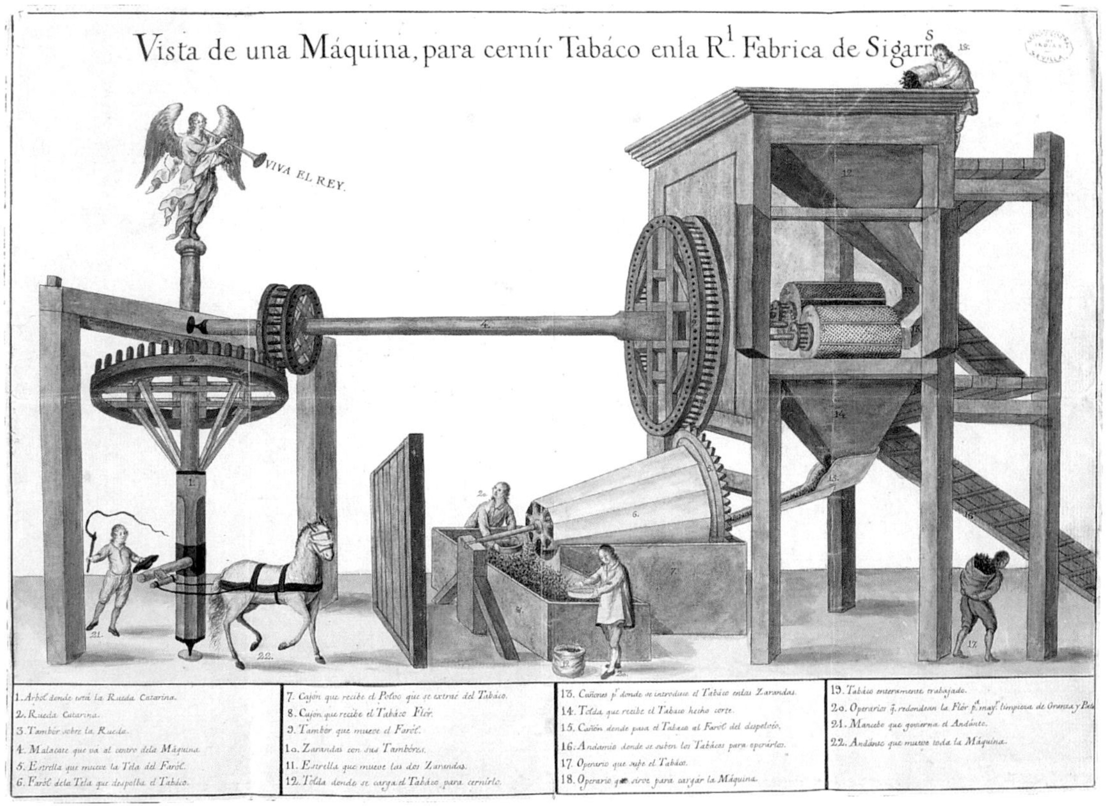

ABOVE: *The Guadalajara intendancy.*

30 June 1793, Guadalajara.
'Chorographic map of the Guadalajara intendancy... replete with rivers and towns, an accurate rendering of the sketches and accounts presented to Don José Menéndez Valdés in the years 92 and 93.'
933 x 1176 mm.
MP. México, 547.

Among the objectives of José de Gálvez's visit to New Spain was that of testing the system of intendancies. Viceroy Bucarely's opposition led Gálvez to postpone his plans and it was not until 1786 that he won approval for his 'Statute for the Intendants of New Spain', where the newly created intendancies were: México, Guadalajara, Puebla, Veracruz, Mérida, Oaxaca, Guanajuato, Valladolid de Michoacán, San Luis Potosí, Zacatecas, Durango and Sonora.

BELOW: *Tobacco-shredding machine.*

[1787]
'View of a tobacco-shredding machine in the Royal Cigar Factory (Mexico).'
By Alonso Francisco González?
307 x 425 mm.
MP. Ingenios y Muestras, 162.

18th-century fiscal policy tended towards an increase in State control and royal revenues. Given the importance of the tobacco business, a separate administrative body, the Directorate General of Tobacco, was set up to protect the royal tobacco monopoly and to oversee cigarette manufacture. This sketch was submitted together with a letter to the Subdelegate of the Royal Treasury of New Spain describing the experiments conducted with this machine, designed by Alonso Francisco González, a merchant from Mexico (México, 21 July 1787).

OPPOSITE: *Mines in New Spain.*

1787
'Plan showing a mining complex, known as a real, *located in Villaalta province and owned by Juan Francisco Echarri, Colonel of Oaxaca City's Provincial Militia, near the towns of San Miguel Talea and San Bartolomé Yatani.' By Manuel Antonio Jixon y Sivaxa.*
594 x 443 mm. MP. México, 721.

A view of the San Anselmo, Concepción, San Ignacio, San Francisco de Asís, Quagüote and La Cata mines, including shafts, machinery, water channels and roads. The plan was remitted together with a letter from the aforementioned Echarri, the owner of the mining company, requesting privileges for having restored the mining complex.

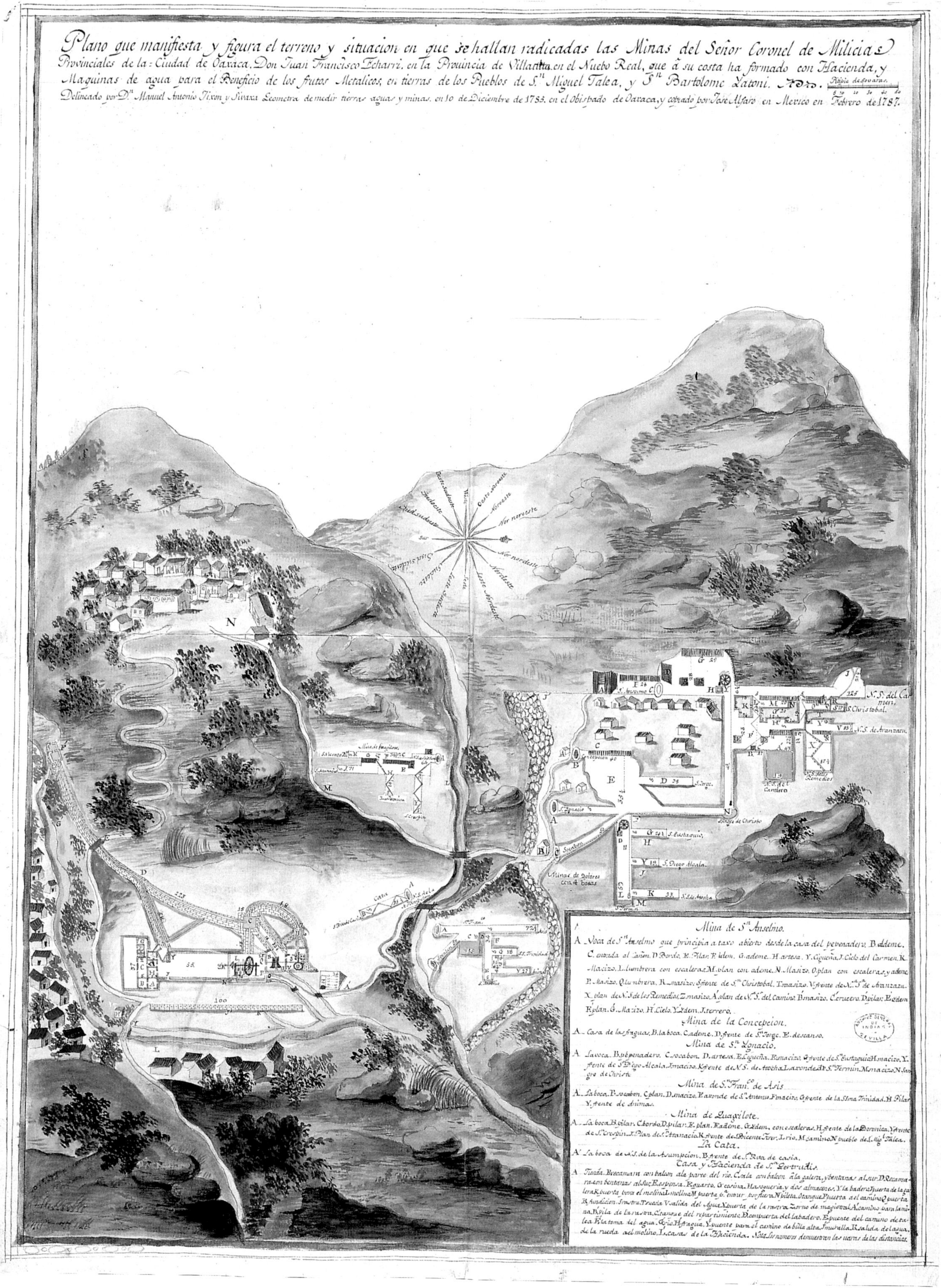
Plano que manifiesta y figura el terreno y situacion en que se hallan radicadas las Minas del Señor Coronel de Milicias Provinciales de la Ciudad de Oaxaca, Don Juan Francisco Echarri, en la Provincia de Villaalta en el Nuebo Real, que à su costa ha formado con Hacienda, y Maquinas de agua para el Beneficio de los frutos Metalicos, en tierras de los Pueblos de Sn. Miguel Talea, y Sn. Bartolome Zatoni.
Pitipie de varas.
Delineado por Dn. Manuel Antonio Tixon y Sivaxa Geometra de medir tierras aguas y minas, en 10 de Diciembre de 1783, en el Obispado de Oaxaca, y copiado por Jose Alfaro en Mexico en Febrero de 1787.
N
Minas de Dolores con 4 bocas
N. S. de Atocha
Mina de Sn. Anselmo.
A. Boca de Sn. Anselmo que principia a taxo abierto desde la casa del pepenadero. B. ademe. C. entrada al cañon. D. Bordo. E. Pilar. F. idem. G. ademe. H. artesa. Y. Cigueña. J. Cielo del Carmen. K. Macizo. L. lumbrera con escaleras. M. plan con ademe. N. Masizo. O. plan con escaleras, y ademe. P. Masizo. Q. lumbrera. R. masizo. S. frente de Sn. Christobal. T. masizo. V. frente de Nra. Sra. de Aranzazu. X. plan de N. S. de los Remedios. Z. masizo. A'. plan de N. S. del Camino. B'. masizo. C'. crucero. D'. pilar. E'. idem. F'. plan. G'. Masizo. H'. Cielo. Y'. Ydem. J. terrero.
Mina de la Concepcion.
A. Casa de las fraguas. B. la boca. C. ademe. D. frente de Sn. Jorge. E. descanso.
Mina de Sn. Ygnacio.
A. La boca. B. pepenadero. C. socabon. D. artesa. E. Cigueña. F. macizo. G. frente de Sn. Eustaquio. H. macizo. Y. frente de Sn. Diego Alcala. J. macizo. K. frente de N. S. de Atocha. L. aronde de Sn. Fermin. M. macizo. N. Sangre de Christo.
Mina de Sn. Franco. de Asis
A. La boca. B. socabon. C. plan. D. macizo. E. aronde de Sn. Antonio. F. macizo. G. frente de la Sma. Trinidad. H. Pilar. Y. frente de Animas.
Mina de Quagilote.
A. La boca. B. pilar. C. bordo. D. pilar. E. plan. F. ademe. G. Ydem, con escaleras. H. frente de la Beronica. Y. frente de Sn. Crespin. J. Plan de Sn. Atanacio. K. frente de Sn. Bicente Frer. L. rio. M. camino. N. pueblo de Sn. Migl. Talea.
La Cata.
A'. La boca de N. S. de la Asumpcion. B. frente de Sta. Rita de casia.
Casa y Hacienda de Sta. Gertrudis.
Archivo General de Indias. Sevilla

New mining techniques.

[1790]
'Plan showing the new mining technique invented by the sergeant major of the Canta Dragoons, Gaspar Sabugo.'
616 x 386 mm.
MP. Perú y Chile, 121.

The illustration shows the situation of and entrance to mines, with cross-sections of the interior. The caption contains a description of the procedures followed by the Royal Mining Tribunal of Lima to test the new mining technique, which Gaspar Sabugo claimed to have verified in Pomacancha and San Silvestre Huarochiri. Sabugo's claims to the mines were finally rejected by the tribunal.

COPIA
DE LA REAL CEDULA
DE SU MAGESTAD,
EXPEDIDA PARA QUE EN LA
Ciudad de San Chriſtoval de la Habana ſe forme una Compañia, à cuyo cargo eſtè la conduccion de tabacos, azucar, corambres, y otros frutos de la Isla de Cuba; con la direccion, reglas, exempciones, y obligaciones, que ſe expreſſan.

AÑO 1740.

EN MADRID: En la Imprenta de Antonio Sanz, Impreſſor del Conſejo.

Real Compañía de la Habana.

18 December 1740, Buen Retiro.
'Copy of His Majesty's royal warrant, instructing a company to be established in the city of San Christoval de la Habana [Havana] for conveying tobacco, sugar, hides and other produce from the island of Cuba under the terms, rules, obligations and exemptions stipulated herein.'
Madrid: Antonio Sanz, 1740.
1 sheet, 17 fols. Cover bearing the royal coat-of-arms.
Biblioteca, L.A. S. XVIII–349.

Trading companies were a novelty in 18th-century Spain. Their emergence was a tentative first step towards trade liberalization achieved by partially breaking up the monopoly held by the port of Cádiz. The Havana company, as shown in its foundation–charter, was entitled to export Cuban produce. In exchange, the island could receive supplies from mainland Spain and was awarded a number of privileges relating to shipbuilding and shipping. The company, which was founded with a share capital of one million pesos, was governed by a board of directors made up of a chairman, five directors, an accountant, a treasurer and a factor based in Cádiz.

Cigarette boxes made in Cuba.

1864
Album of labels from different brands of cigarette boxes made in Havana.
30 sheets, 4to.
MP. Estampas, 254.

Cigar production in Cuba was controlled by the Royal Tobacco Factory of Havana, ever since its establishment in 1760. However, factories of this kind only lasted as long as the royal monopoly, that is until 1821. Thereafter, cigar and cigarette production diversified into a wide variety of brands, as shown in this album of labels.

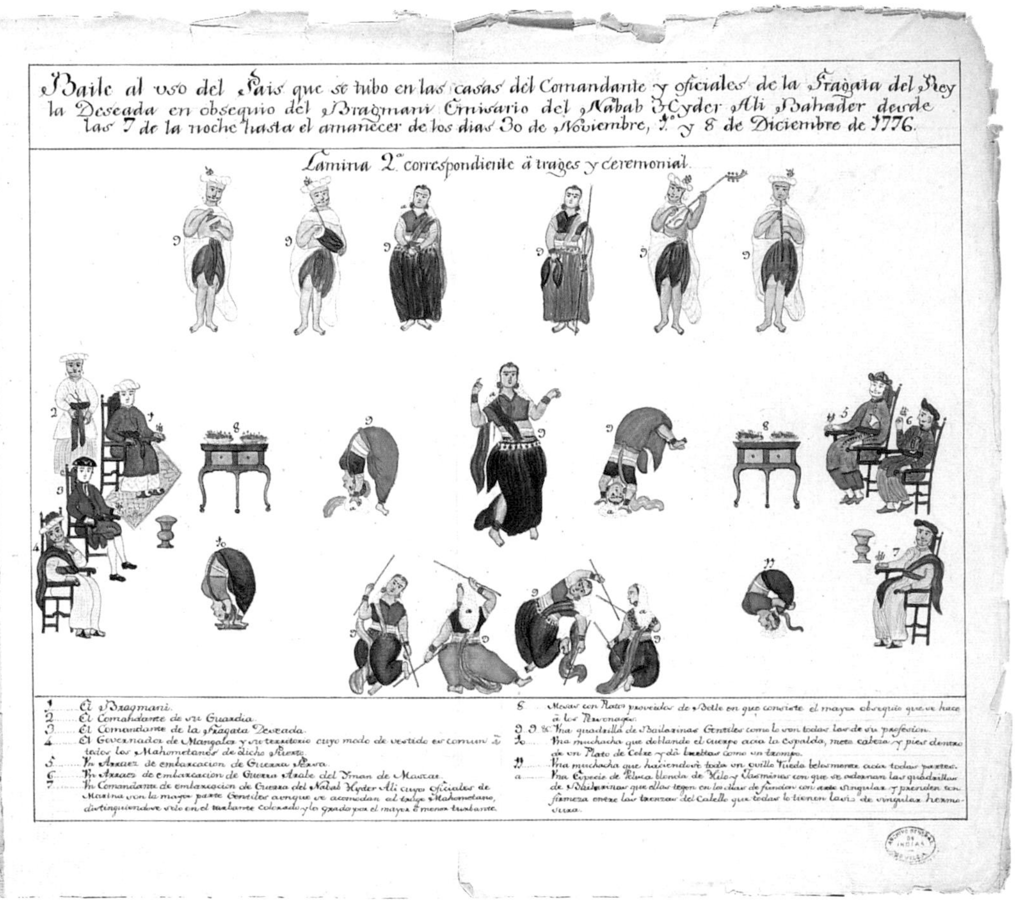

instituted in Spain on 4 July 1718 in Philip V's 'Statutes for Military and Provincial Intendants' which were subsequently amended by Ferdinand VI in 1749. After their successful implementation in Spain, they were applied in the Americas during the time of the Universal Secretariat of the Indies.

The first New World intendancy was established in 1764 on the island of Cuba after O'Reilly's visit. On 8 October 1776, the 'Statutes for Military and Provincial Intendants of Venezuela' were instituted, as were those for Louisiana and Florida. Intendancies were set up at Río de la Plata in 1782 and in Peru the following year. New Spain and the Philippines followed suit in December 1786. By the time of Gálvez's death, the intendancy system had taken root across most of the New World.

The system of intendancies was an important step forward in the articulation of territorial administration in Spanish America. The secretary of the *Despacho Universal de Indias* (Universal Secretariat of the Indies) was in charge of overall organization. Each of the viceroyalties or presidencies was divided into a number of provinces placed under the jurisdiction of a provincial intendant, under which came the district sub-delegates, while intendants residing in the capital of a viceroyalty or presidency had seniority over other intendants.

Their authority ranged over economic development, public works, finance, war and justice. They were expected to oversee financial matters and boost revenues by combating tax evasion and creating an efficient organization of tax collection.

Trade expeditions.

[1778]
'Govari, an idol worshipped by a caste of gentiles named the Gauris, who claim to descend from the ancient Persians...'
[By Miguel Antonio Gómez]
332 x 207 mm.
MP. Filipinas, 92.

[1778]
'Traditional dance performed in the quarters of the skipper and officers of the royal frigate, La Deseada, in honor of the Brahman ambassador of Nabab Hyder Ali Bahader, from 7 o'clock in the evening to dawn the following day on 30 November and 8 December 1776.'
[By Miguel Antonio Gómez]
333 x 417 mm.
MP. Filipinas, 90.

These drawings, together with the logbook from the frigate Nuestra Señora del Carmen, also known as La Deseada, were sent to the port of Mangalore with a view to establishing trade relations with Hyder Aly Khan.

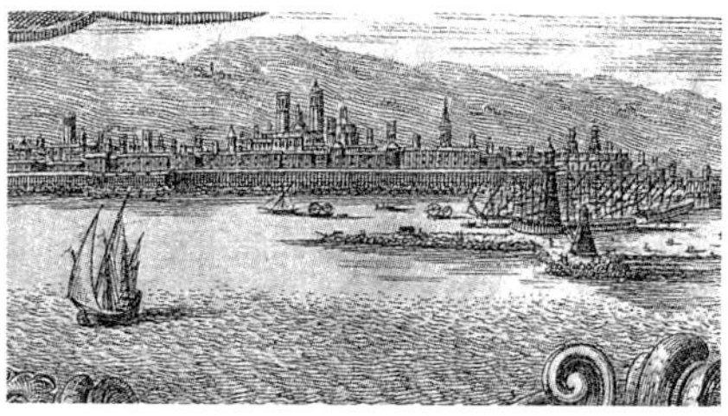

Backed by a provincial board of the Royal Treasury, they audited accounts and made decisions regarding the use of public funds for incidental expenses. They also supervised and provided considerable impetus to the treasury offices in charge of collecting sales taxes, customs duties and revenues from the State monopolies.

The advent of the intendancies did away with the figures of the *corregidor* and the *alcalde mayor* whose duties, including the administration of justice, were assumed by intendants or sub-delegates under the guidance of legal advisors. Lastly, the military jurisdiction of the intendants covered all matters relating to finance and war, and intendants also acted as deputy patrons of the Church in their provinces.

Intendants were royally appointed officials, proposed by the Secretary of the Indies, and no fixed term of office was attached to their duties. On taking office, they were required to pay a deposit and to draw up an inventory of their belongings. On the whole, the institution of the intendancy was a successful venture in that it achieved greater efficiency in the administration of revenues and led to the economic reactivation of all branches of production and the exploitation of natural resources.

In this respect, the Universal Secretariat of the Indies instituted other reforms, including the implementation of highly successful measures in trade and shipping. The first such measures had been adopted under Philip V, although the latter's ministers had actually tended to patch up rather than mend existing structures. Thus, when the *Casa de la Contratación* was moved from Seville to Cádiz in 1717, they missed their chance to do away with the traditional shipping system and open other harbors on the Iberian peninsula to the sea trade. The tax reform of 1720 replaced the complicated customs regime with a simpler system of fixed-rate tariffs on the volume of goods shipped, measured in spans or palms and known as *palmeo,* a move which facilitated registration. Similarly, the establishment of trading companies partially eased the monopoly held by the port of Cádiz, as the companies were authorized to trade with certain territories from their ports of origin. A novelty as far as the 18th-century was concerned, the companies had shareholders. The main ones were the *Compañía Guipuzcoana de Caracas* (1728), which had exclusive trading rights on Venezuelan cacao, tobacco, leather and indigo, the company known as *La Habana* (1740), which had a monopoly of Cuban tobacco and was authorized to export sugar and hides, and the *Compañía de Barcelona* or *Cumaná,* which traded in Cuban cotton. Slightly later came the *Cinco Gremios* and the *Compañía de Filipinas* (1785) which merged the remains of *La Guipuzcoana* and the *San Fernando* of Seville to boost trade in commodities from the East.

Nevertheless, a trading system that would exploit to greatest advantage the potential of the colonies as producers of raw materials and consumers of manufactured goods could only be achieved by abolishing Cádiz's monopoly and the existing system of fleet sailings. Moreover, while free trade was first introduced in 1765, with seven Spanish ports (Santander, Gijón, Corunna, Málaga, Alicante, Cartagena and Barcelona) being readied to trade directly with the islands of Cuba, Puerto Rico, Santo Domingo, Trinidad and Margarita, the 'separate registration' system of sailing to South America and that of fleet-sailings to New Spain remained in force. Subsequently, however, the success of the Caribbean system led to it being gradually extended to other provinces. It was applied in Lousiana in 1768, with more of a political than an economic purpose, given the dearth of commercial products in that colony, and from there it was taken to Yucatán and Campeche with the aim of boosting exports of dyewood to Spain. Finally, on 12 October 1778, Gálvez's endeavors were rewarded with the publication of the Free Trade Regulations whereby direct trade was authorized and facilitated between twelve Spanish and twenty–four American ports, and a variety of levies were replaced by a single, less costly trade tariff. The system was only comparatively 'free' in that such trade applied solely to Spanish nationals, totally excluded all foreigners, and had clear-cut geographical limitations both in Spain and the Americas. Nonetheless, the new regulations were successful in expediting commercial transactions and fostering economic growth on both sides of the Atlantic.

As a result, in agriculture, traditional crops such as cacao, sugar, tobacco, cotton and dyewoods were grown more intensively, while experimentation began on new crops such as flax and hemp. Mining was also given renewed impetus, particularly in Mexico, which by the end of the century had registered production levels of over 22 million pesos (two thirds of the overall production of the Americas). In 1777, during Gálvez's time, the Royal Mining Tribunal of New Spain was set up to deal with mining affairs and to settle disputes.

Lastly, provisions for development of the Indies were reinforced by State support for two non-governmental institutions, the Consulates and the Economic Associations. The former, which appeared as an upshot of the new Free Trade Regulations under the auspices of the Finance Minister, Diego Gardoqui, had spread along the entire American coastline by the end of the 18th century: to Caracas and Guatemala in 1793, Buenos Aires and Havana in 1794, and Cartagena, Veracruz, Guadalajara and Santiago de Chile in 1796. The Economic Associations of the Indies, for their part, submitted proposals for improving trade, tapping new sources of wealth and introducing innovative industrial techniques. Their scope spilled over into cultural promotion, as evinced in the appearance of newspapers such as the various 'Gacetas' and 'Mercurios', and into the field of science, prompting the

The quinine expedition.

[1769]
Map of Loja province and the mountains where Cinchona bark is found.
300 x 410 mm.
MP. Panamá, 179.

Quinine, obtained from the Cinchona bark found in the province of Loja, has long been used to combat fever, first by the indigenous peoples and subsequently by Europeans. The Crown commissioned several expeditions to locate and study the trees and shrubs, the most celebrated of these being the expedition led by the physician, José Celestino Mutis. In 1783 he set out with a large team to survey the botany, geography and meteorology of various regions in the viceroyalty of Santa Fe. The venture continued after his death and went on to compile a collection of over six thousand engravings, known as the 'Flora of Bogotá'.

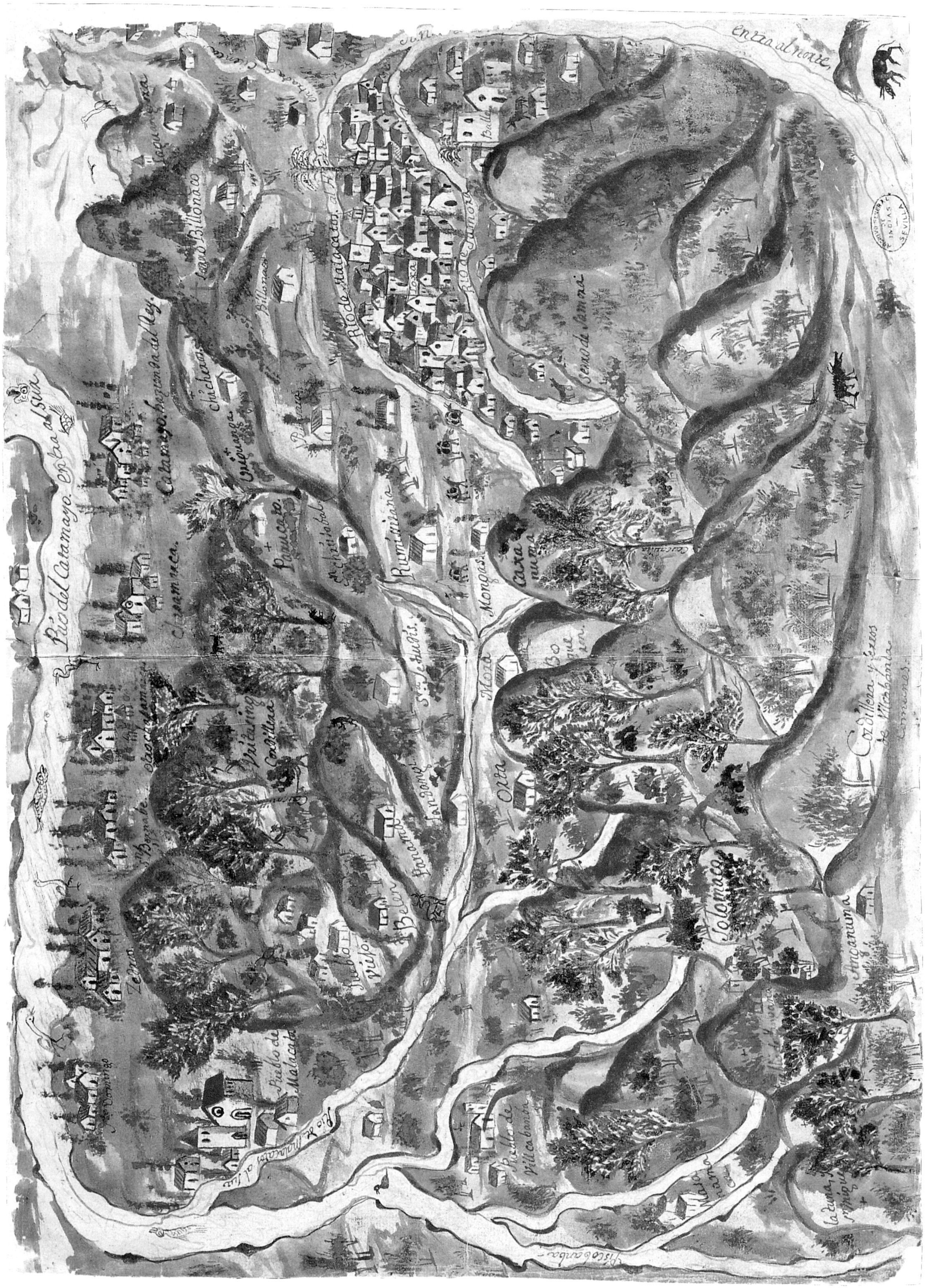
Rio del Catamayo entra al Sur
entra al norte
Solomaco
Belen
Mongas

R. 9744

OBSERVACIONES
ASTRONOMICAS, Y PHISICAS
HECHAS
DE ORDEN DE S. MAG.
EN
LOS REYNOS DEL PERÙ

Por D. JORGE JUAN, Comendador de Aliaga en el Orden de S. Juan, Socio Correspondiente de la R. Academia de las Ciencias de Paris, y D. ANTONIO DE ULLOA, de la R. Sociedad de Londres, ambos Capitanes de Fragata de la R. Armada.

DE LAS QUALES SE DEDUCE
LA FIGURA, Y MAGNITUD
DE LA TIERRA,
Y SE APLICA
A LA NAVEGACION.

IMPRESSO DE ORDEN DEL REY NUESTRO SEÑOR
EN MADRID
Por JUAN DE ZUÑIGA, Año M.D.CC.XL.VIII.

Scientific expeditions: Jorge Juan and Antonio de Ulloa.

JUAN Y SANTACILIA, Jorge: Astronomical and physical observations, commissioned by H.M. to be conducted in the kingdoms of Peru by Don Jorge Juan and Don Antonio de Ulloa... from which the shape and magnitude of the earth might be determined and applied to navigation. Printed on the orders of H.M. the King. *Madrid, Juan de Zúñiga, 1748. 1 sheet, 1 engraving, 7 sheets, XXVIII, 396 pp., 9 engravings, 1 fold-out, 7 sheets. Cover featuring two-color allegorical vignette and royal coat-of-arms. Inside cover bearing allegorical engraving on earth measurements. Biblioteca, L.A. S. XVIII–18.*

One of the first scientific expeditions of the 18th century was the Franco–Spanish venture, authorized by Philip V in 1734, set up for the purpose of determining the exact measurement of a meridian degree on the equator. Under the command of the Frenchman, La Condamine, the expedition included the Spaniards Jorge Juan and Antonio de Ulloa. They worked intensively in territories in the jurisdiction of the Quito Audiencia. *On their return, ten years later, they published the results of their research in three volumes: 'Historical account of the journey to South America' (1748), 'Astronomical observations' (1748) and 'A historical and geographical essay on the meridian' (1749).*

establishment of institutions such as botanical gardens or the San Carlos Academy of New Spain, the astronomical observatory of Bogotá or the Academy of Natural Sciences of Guatemala.

The end-of-century scientific expeditions had a considerable impact in intellectual circles. Under the direction of Spanish and European experts and with State patronage, their aim was to carry out cultural, scientific and geographical surveys of the continent. Thus, from 1735 to 1744, a Franco–Spanish expedition set out to measure a degree of the earth's meridian. The results of their endeavors were published by the Spaniards, Jorge Juan and Antonio de Ulloa, in their *Relación Histórica del viaje a la América Meridional.* Several botanical expeditions were mounted under Charles III, including one led by Hipólito Ruiz and José Pavón to Chile and that of José Celestino Mutis to New Granada. In 1787, the naturalist Martín Sessé set off on a similar expedition through New Spain, while the last few years of the century saw an expedition conducted to vaccinate the population against smallpox.

The expedition that sailed around the Río de la Plata and Pacific coastlines between 1789 and 1795 in the corvettes *Descubierta* and *Atrevida,* under the command of Alessandro Malaspina, conducted geographical and historical surveys. No less important to Hispano–American geography and politics were the results of the expedition of the German explorer Alexander Humboldt.

The political reforms of the Bourbons, which were highly successful in many spheres, foundered when it came to relations with the Church, particularly during the period of the Universal Secretariat of the Indies. Those relations were conditioned by the absolutist monarchy's attempt to become wholly independent of the pontificate and to establish the political principle that the king had jurisdiction over all non-spiritual Church matters. The mounting climate of regalism prompted the

Scientific expedition to New Spain.

[1793]
'Crater in the Txtla (sic, Tuxtla) volcano, seen from the east, 1793.'
294 x 420 mm.
MP. México, 445.

The third great botanical expedition to America was organized early in the reign of Charles IV. Commanded by the physician, Martín Sessé, its dual objective was the scientific exploration of New Spain, Central America and the Antilles, and the establishment of botanical gardens and a chair of botany in Mexico City. Sessé was assisted in his task by José Mariano Mociño, also a physician, the naturalist, José Longinos and the draughtsman, José Vicente de la Cerda, among others. The above illustration was sent by José Mociño with a report on the origins of the Tuxtla mountain range, near the coast of Veracruz, volcanic eruptions and his observations in the field (San Andrés de Tuxtla, 27 November 1793). In 1804, Sessé and Mociño returned to Spain with herbaria and drawings currently housed in the Botanical Gardens of Madrid.

Crown to curtail the Church's judicial mandate by calling ecclesiastical immunity into question. Despite having always collected tithes and so-called *vacantes mayores* (a bishop's stipend, redirected to the Crown when the office fell vacant), the monarch now sought to seize those of the dignitaries or canons *(vacantes menores),* a move that met with papal approval, sanctioned in a Concordat of 1753. Royal intervention even began to be felt in spiritual matters when royal warrants were issued to convene provincial councils throughout America. Such was the case of the Councils of Mexico in 1771, Lima in 1772 and Charcas in 1773.

However, the most striking expression of Bourbon regalism was undoubtedly the expulsion of the Jesuits, decreed by Charles III on 27 February 1767 after precedents in France and Portugal. The order, the reasons for which the king kept to himself, was enforced throughout Spain's empire—over two thousand Jesuits resident in the Americas were led back to Spain and had their possessions confiscated and sold, with the proceeds being distributed by the Church.

The expulsion had serious consequences in the Americas as it involved losing ministers of outstanding spiritual value, who had until then performed some vital functions. Creole society gazed on in disbelief as the colleges and universities where Spanish America's young had been educated were closed down. Indeed, there was the widespread feeling that such measures were the work of a tyrant. Moreover, the missions directed by the Society of Jesus in northern Mexico and

Paraguay were abandoned to their fate, while the *reducciones,* where thousands of Indians had been educated in the faith, had become familiar with urban mores and had engaged in productive work, slipped into decline.

Gálvez's death, on 17 June 1787, coincided with the demise of the Universal Secretariat of the Indies, which Charles III split into two organizations—one, headed by Antonio Porlier, was placed in charge of Church matters and justice, while the other, led by Antonio Valdés, was appointed to deal with government, finance, trade and shipping in the Indies.

The reason given for that division was that it would expedite the large backlog of business that had built up in Spain's vast dominions. The mandates of both Secretariats, which were dubbed 'Ministries', were laid down in royal decrees of 8 July and 29 September and in a royal order of 11 November 1787, which also stipulated affairs that were to be processed jointly, such as new discoveries, resettlement and the demarcation of frontiers.

The Supreme Council of State was likewise founded by a royal decree of 8 July 1787. Made up of all the secretaries from the State and Universal Secretariats, it was established for the purpose of dealing with new laws, or amendments to existing laws, jurisdictions between Secretariats, appointments to high-ranking office and other issues. It was subsequently abolished by Charles IV and replaced by the Council of State.

Another major reform of the central administration was undertaken during the monarch's reign when the Secretariat of the Indies was abolished on the pretext of the motto: 'One king, one law'. In effect, on 25 April 1790 it was decreed that 'all the divisions of every Department in the Universal Secretariat of Spain and the Indies are to be merged into a single Secretariat so that, by reducing the various departments to those of State, Justice, War, the Navy and Finance, there should be perfect equality, unity and reciprocity in the administration and transaction of business in all dominions and among their respective inhabitants'. In other words, Spanish Americans were classed as citizens of equal status to the mainland Spanish and their affairs were to be processed exclusively in terms of the Secretariat they related to.

No other ministry dealing exclusively with American affairs was to emerge until the promulgation of the *Cortes de Cádiz* in 1812, at which the *Gobernación de Ultramar* or 'Overseas Department' was established as one of seven Secretariats.

After the return to power of Ferdinand VII, the Overseas Department was abolished and replaced by the Universal Ministry of the Indies, restored to its former

Church revenues.

15 December 1781, Mexico.
'Register of tithes at the Holy Metropolitan Church of Mexico for the year 1780, including that of anniversaries for the same year.' Submitted by the royal registrars of Church tithes to the Audit Office of New Spain.
30 fols. + 1 blank.
México, 2728.

In addition to tithes, the Crown was paid other Church dues which were increased under Bourbon rule. Thus, in 1750, Benedict XIV authorized the king to collect vacantes mayores *(the vacantia or stipend that went with a bishop's office when the latter fell vacant) and, subsequently,* vacantes menores *(the stipend attached to chapter offices). The sovereign was also entitled to receive the stipends earned by all Church dignitaries and, from 177 onwards, all* mediannata *over 300 pesos. Lastly, the Crown was empowered to inherit all the possessions in a bishop's estate.*

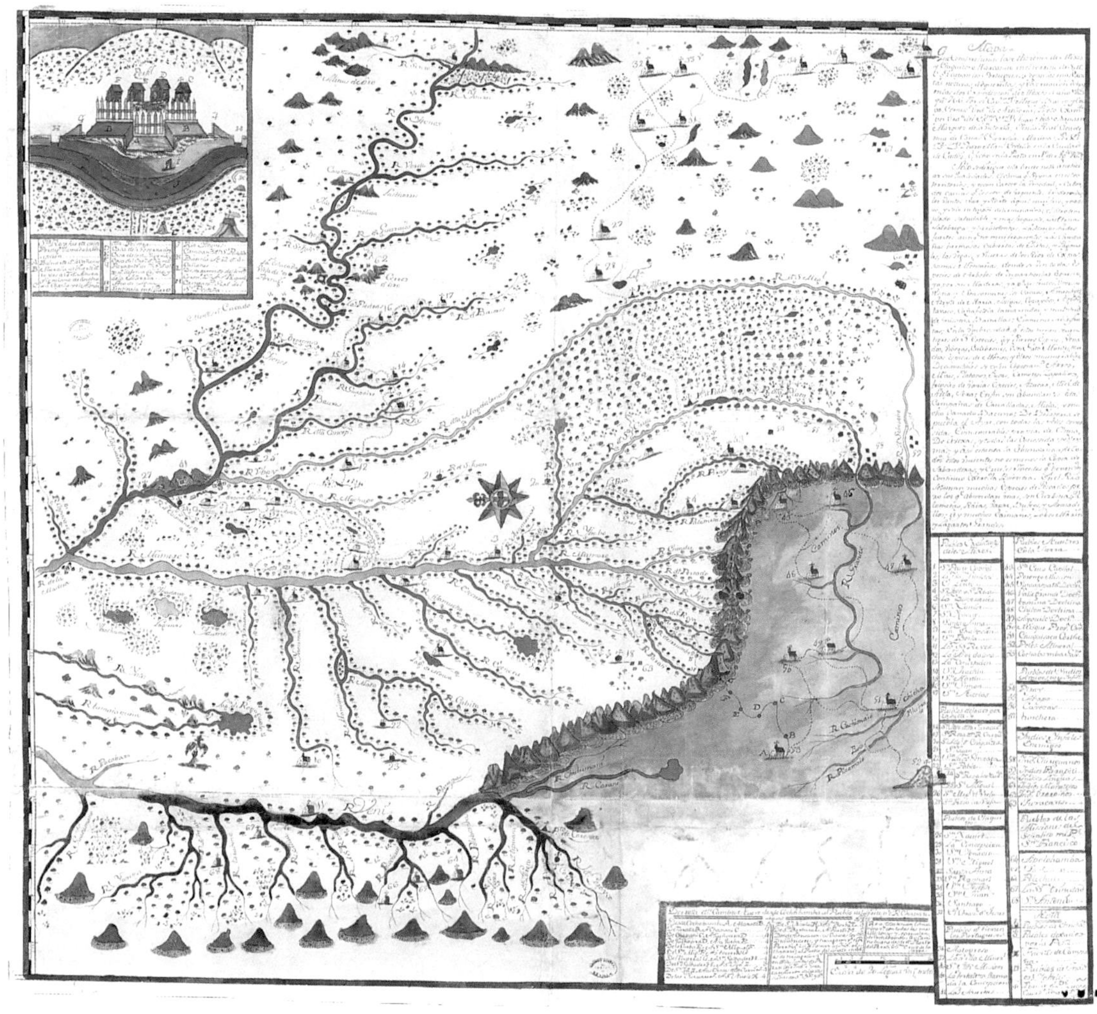

Jesuit missions.

1 August 1769, La Plata.
'Map showing the missions of Moxos and Chiquitos and the areas of His Catholic Majesty's territory occupied by the Portuguese, according to the latest observations and accounts reported from the two expeditions to Moxos, in 1763 and 1766.'
By Miguel Blanco y Crespo.
660 x 620 mm.
MP. Buenos Aires, 78.

Most missions on this map belonged to the Jesuits, as borne out by a comparison with another, very similar map submitted in 1764 in a report on the suspicious conduct of the Jesuits in those provinces during the indigenous unrest that followed the treaty with Portugal (1750). The Society of Jesus had first entered Moxos in 1595 in an expedition under Suárez de Figueroa, although their first reducciones, *or Christian settlements, were only set up in the late-17th century. The province of Chiquitos was spiritually conquered by the Jesuits of Paraguay. At the time of their expulsion, they had thirty-five mission villages in this area.*

state prior to the reform of 1787. This was to be short-lived, however, as the idea of setting the business dealings of Spain and the Indies on an equal footing, as parts of a single nation, gained ascendancy once more with the issuing of a royal decree of 23 February 1816.

The Overseas Department reemerged during the 'Liberal triennium'. By that time the independence movements had spread like wildfire across Latin America. The decline of the Spanish monarchy, aggravated in 1795 by Napoleon's interference in Spain's internal affairs and, eventually, a full-scale invasion of the Iberian peninsula by French troops; the effect on trade with the Indies of the ongoing wars in Europe, which worked in the United States' favor (Trade & Shipping Treaty of 1795), the territorial losses of Santo Domingo in 1795, Trinidad in 1802 and Louisiana in 1801, and the Spanish Peninsula War all conspired to debilitate Spain's ties to its overseas possessions. Those factors also fostered a thirst for independence in the colonies which, after Hidalgo's uprising in Mexico in 1810 and Simón Bolívar's successful campaign in Venezuela in 1813, turned into a full-scale war of independence against Spain. The former viceroyalties of New Spain and Peru declared their independence in 1821, while Bolívar and San Martín's campaigns were stepped up, until the independence of the whole of South America was decided at the battles of Junín and Ayacucho in 1824.

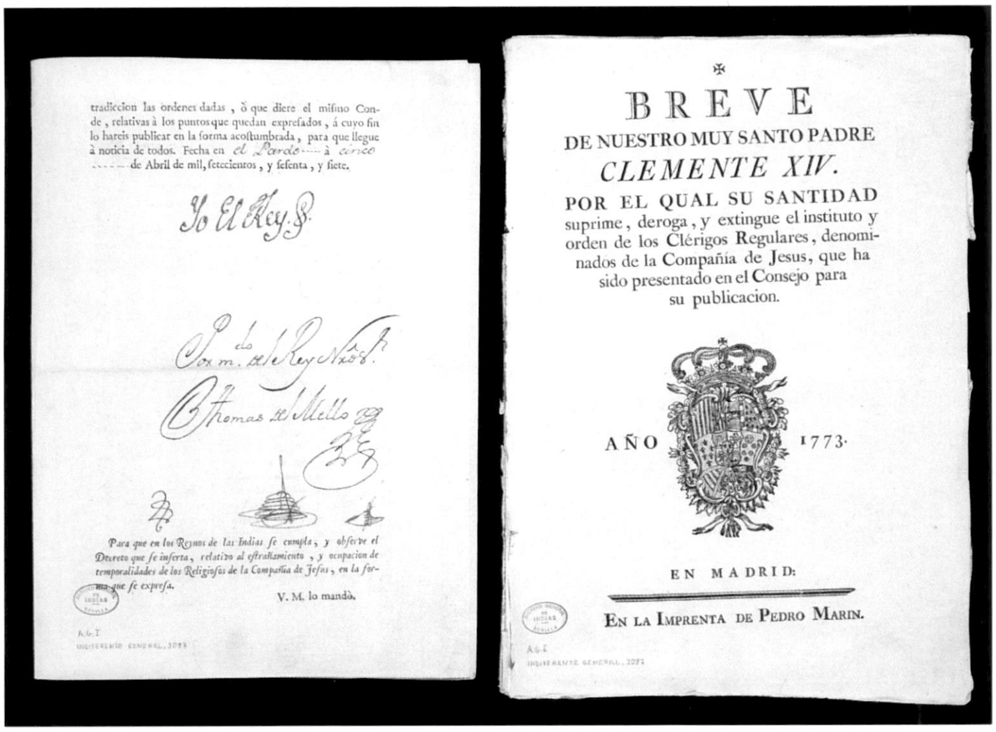

tradiccion las ordenes dadas, ò que diere el mismo Conde, relativas à los puntos que quedan expresados, á cuyo fin lo hareis publicar en la forma acostumbrada, para que llegue à noticia de todos. Fecha en el Pardo à cinco de Abril de mil, setecientos, y sesenta, y siete.

Yo El Rey.

Para que en los Reynos de las Indias se cumpla, y observe el Decreto que se inserta, relativo al estrañamiento, y ocupacion de temporalidades de los Religiosos de la Compañia de Jesus, en la forma que se expresa.

V. M. lo mandò.

BREVE
DE NUESTRO MUY SANTO PADRE
CLEMENTE XIV.
POR EL QUAL SU SANTIDAD
suprime, deroga, y extingue el instituto y orden de los Clérigos Regulares, denominados de la Compañia de Jesus, que ha sido presentado en el Consejo para su publicacion.

AÑO 1773.

EN MADRID:
EN LA IMPRENTA DE PEDRO MARIN.

The expulsion of the Jesuits.

5 April 1767, El Pardo.
Royal warrant urging the observance and fulfillment of an attached decree ordering the abolition of the Society of Jesus and expropriation of its members' goods and chattels.
Printed matter. 4 sheets. Indiferente, 3087.

21 July 1773, Rome.
'Brief from the Holy Father, Pope Clement XIV, by which His Holiness suppresses, revokes and extinguishes the institute and order of the regular clergy of the Society of Jesus, as submitted to the Council for publication.'
Madrid, Pedro Marin, 1773.
1 sheet, 52 pp., 5 sheets.
Indiferente, 3087.

The expulsion of the Jesuits, for which no reasons were given, was decreed by Charles III on 27 February 1767. The president of the Council of Castile, the Count of Aranda, was granted special powers to execute the order. The eviction from America of some 2,500 Jesuits was expeditious. Expulsion orders came into force in Mexico on 25 June 1767, in Buenos Aires and Paraguay in July, Santa Fe in August and Lima in November. The Spanish monarchy and others that expelled the Jesuits had made concerted representations to the Holy See in support of abolition of the order, particularly after the death in 1769 of Pope Clement XIII who had been opposed to such a measure. Charles III presented the papal successor, Clement XIV, with a report in favor of expulsion endorsed by forty-six Spanish prelates. He also appointed as his ambassador to Rome the forceful José Moñino who, after the publication of the above brief dissolving the Society, was awarded the title of Count of Floridablanca for his successful negotiations.

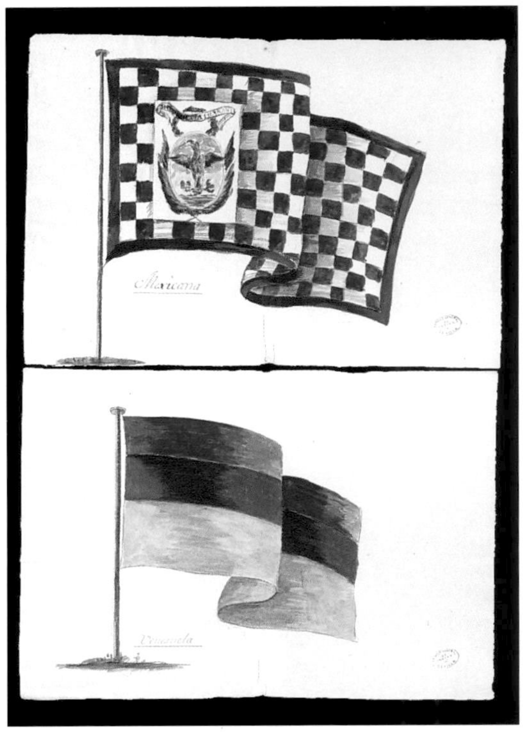

The flags of Mexico and Venezuela.

[1817]
Flag designs for the rebels of Mexico and Venezuela.
212 x 311 & 214 x 310 mm.
MP. Banderas, 25 & 26.

The decline of Spain as a major power during the reign of Charles IV and the power vacuum produced by the Napoleonic invasion of the Iberian peninsula led to the disintegration of the colonies where, for a variety of reasons, the first independence movements were emerging. In 1810, Miguel Hidalgo staged an uprising in Mexico. A year later, he convened a Congress at which, in the presence of Francisco de Miranda and Simón Bolívar, the independence of Venezuela was declared. Fifteen years of war ensued before the whole of America became independent.

After most of Spain's American possessions had won their independence, the affairs of the remaining colonies—Cuba, Puerto Rico and the Philippines—were placed under the jurisdiction of the various Secretariats (Presidency, State, Justice, War, the Navy and Finance), which endured throughout the 19th century in one form or another. There was then no specific body for Indies' affairs until the Foreign Directorate General, a division of the Presidency of the Council of Ministers, was established on 30 September 1851.

Finally, a decree was passed on 20 May 1863 whereby the Overseas Ministry was created for the purpose of governing and administering the islands of Puerto Rico, Cuba and the Philippines. It lasted until its dissolution on 25 April 1899, as decreed by the Presidency of the Council of Ministers, owing to the loss of those last remaining overseas provinces.

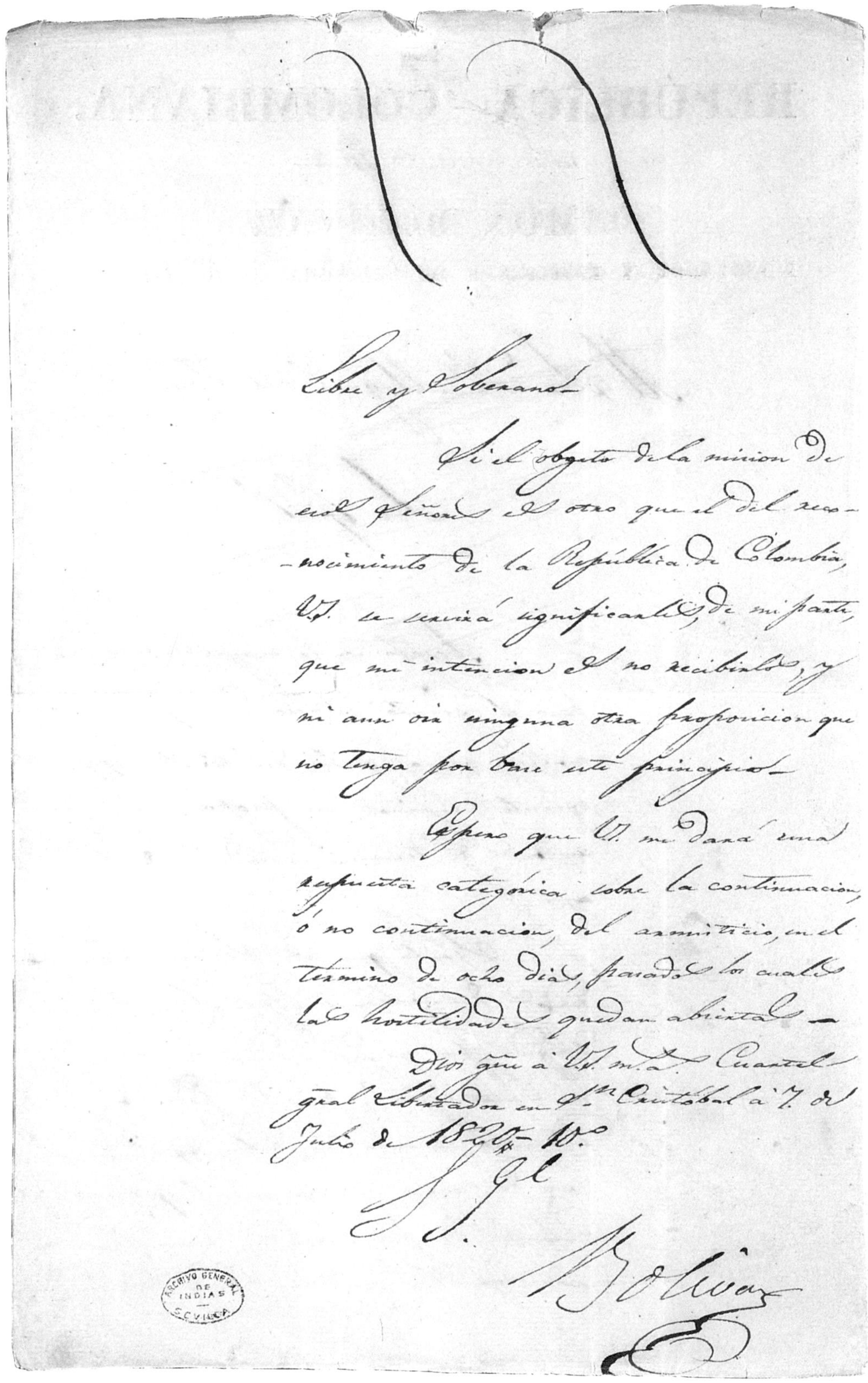

Libre y Soberano —

Si el objeto de la mision de ese Señor es otro que el del reco-nocimiento de la República de Colombia, V.S. se servirá significarle, de mi parte, que mi intencion es no recibirlo, y ni aun oir ninguna otra proposicion que no tenga por base este principio —

Espero que V.S. me dará una respuesta categórica sobre la continuacion, ó no continuacion, del armisticio, en el término de ocho dias, pasados los cuales las hostilidades quedan abiertas —

Dios gũe á V.S. m.s a.s Cuartel gral Libertador en S.n Cristobal á 7 de Julio de 1820 — 10.º

S. Gl.

Bolívar

Simón Bolívar's signature.

17 July 1820, San Cristóbal.
Autograph memorandum from Simón Bolívar to Miguel de la Torre accepting the armistice proposed by the latter on behalf of the commander of the Spanish army and demanding, for its continuity, recognition of the Republic of Colombia as an independent state.
2 fols. Documentos Escogidos, 1, N. 169.

Bolívar accepted the armistice while preparing for the final military campaign in Venezuela's independence. A year after the term had expired, the campaign was resumed on the Carabobo plain, where Bolívar's troops crushed the enemy. In late 1821, he convened a Congress at Cúcuta for the drafting of the Constitution of the newly independent country.

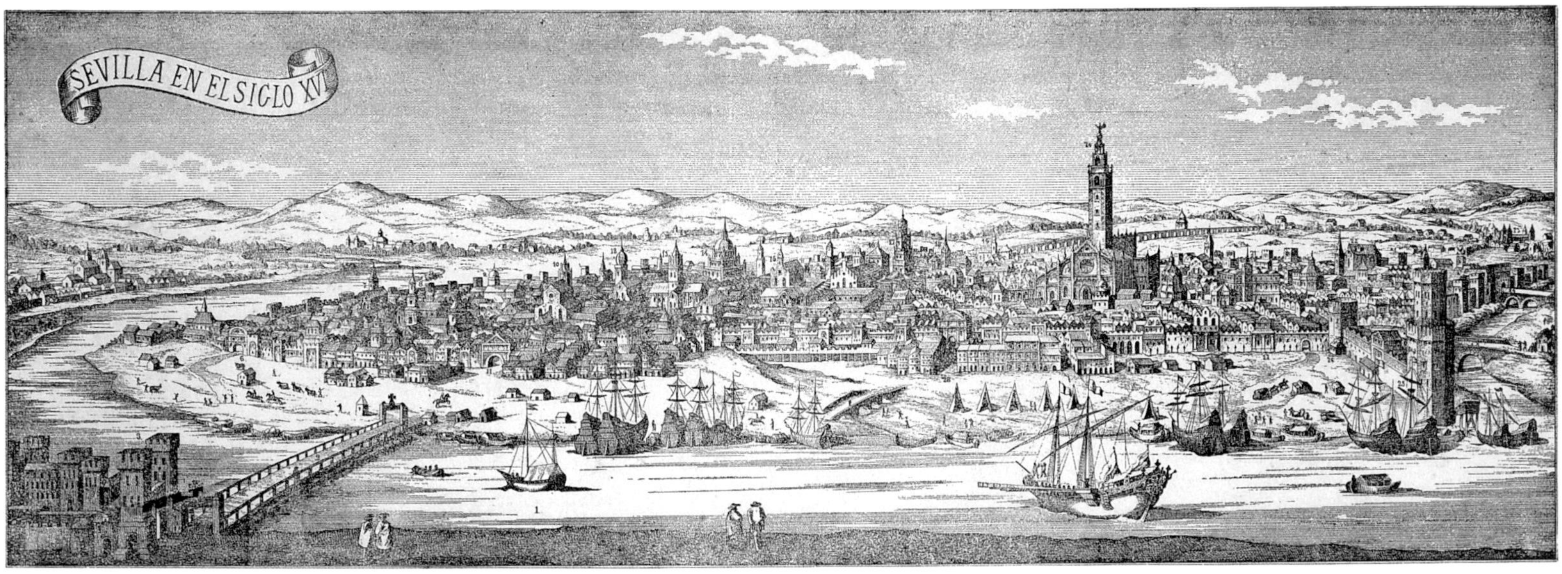

Trade activity in the port of Seville in the 16th century.

[1878]
'Seville during the 16th century.'
220 x 520 mm.
Featured in a work by Francisco de Borja: Historia crítica de las riadas o grandes avenidas del Guadalquivir
(A critical review of spates and massive flooding on the Guadalquivir.)
Seville, Francisco Álvarez, 1878, plate V.

In the 16th century, Seville became the major trading port and gateway to the Indies and it was there that the leading institutions for controlling the sea trade were established. Merchants, traders, brokers, factors, skippers, pilots and others thronged the streets of Seville as they negotiated deals and secured contracts. The harbor was studded with a motley variety of sailing vessels ready to make the Atlantic crossing once the requisite bureaucratic paperwork had been completed. In the words of Domínguez Ortiz, Seville 'had the picturesque appearance of a forest of sails and El Arenal that of a permanent fairground.'

THE CONSULATES OF SEVILLE AND CÁDIZ

Two completely different but similarly named institutions were established in Seville and Cádiz. One was a merchant guild known as the *Consulado de la Universidad de Cargadores a Indias* (Consulate of the University of Indies Merchants). Originally located in Seville, the Consulate was a division of the *Casa de la Contratación*. However, when the latter moved to Cádiz in 1717, the Consulate became a separate institution. The other was the *Consulado Nuevo de Sevilla* (New Consulate of Seville), founded in 1784 after the Free Trade Regulations had come into force in 1778, precipitating the demise of a minor offshoot of the Seville Consulate—the *Diputación de Comercio* or Trade Delegation. Both Consulates coexisted until the promulgation of the Code of Commerce in 1829, which relegated them to the status of Tribunals. These important merchant associations were eventually dissolved in the decree of regional charters issued on 6 December 1868.

From Merchant Guild to Consulate

Ever since the late Middle Ages, merchants of different nationalities accompanied Castilian monarchs during their sojourns in Seville, as attested to in the city's street-names, bearing their nationalities or places of origin: Alemanes, Génova, Francos, etc. Foreign merchants, factors and agents flocked to the city in even greater numbers after Seville's designation as the port of the Indies. In the words of Professor Domínguez Ortiz, Seville 'had the picturesque appearance of a forest of sails and El Arenal that of a permanent fairground.'

With the growth in trade activity around the port of Seville, merchants soon encountered obstacles when it came to pressing litigation before competent authorities: the municipal courts, the *Audiencia de Grados* (Tribunal of Degrees) and the court of the *Casa de la Contratación.* Paradoxically, when settling issues relating to trade and shipping in the Indies, merchants would appear indiscriminately before any of those authorities, leading to considerable friction and confusion. This state of affairs worsened to such an extent that, in 1539, the Crown had to intervene by creating statutes in the *Casa de la Contratación* regulating that House's legal competence and the duties incumbent on its officials. Thus, the *Casa de la Contratación* became the only body with jurisdiction over civil litigation. The *Audiencia de Grados* was designated as the appeal court for claims of less than

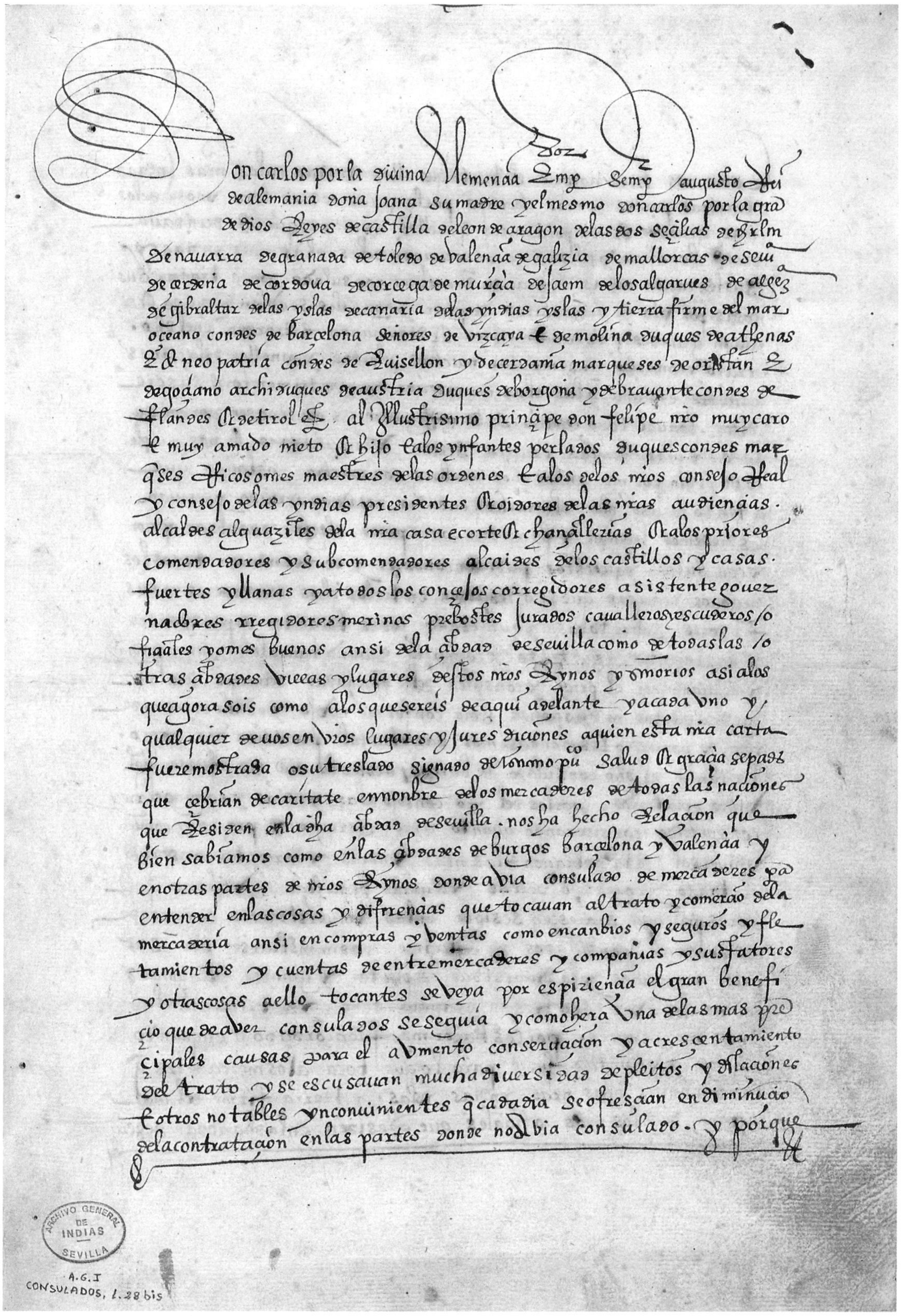

Don carlos por la diuina clemencia emp[erad]or semp[er] augusto Rey
de alemania doña joana su madre y el mesmo don carlos por la gra[cia]
de dios Reyes de castilla de leon de aragon de las dos secilias de jerusalem
de nauarra de granada de toledo de valencia de galizia de mallorcas de seuilla
de cerdeña de cordoua de corcega de murcia de jaen de los algarues de algezira
de gibraltar de las yslas de canaria de las yndias yslas y tierra firme del mar
oceano condes de barcelona señores de vizcaya e de molina duques de atenas
e de neopatria condes de Ruisellon y de cerdania marqueses de oristan e
de goçiano archiduques de austria duques de borgoña y de brauante condes de
flandes e de tirol etc. al Illustrisimo principe don felipe n[uest]ro muy caro
e muy amado nieto e hijo e a los ynfantes perlados duques condes mar
queses Ricos omes maestres de las ordenes e a los de los n[uest]ros consejo Real
y consejo de las yndias presidentes e oidores de las n[uest]ras audiencias
alcaldes alguaziles de la n[uest]ra casa e corte e chancillerias e a los priores
comendadores y subcomendadores alcaides de los castillos y casas
fuertes y llanas y a todos los concejos corregidores asistente gouer
nadores e regidores merinos prebostes jurados caualleros escuderos o
ficiales y omes buenos ansi de la cibdad de seuilla como de todas las o
tras cibdades villas y lugares destos n[uest]ros Reynos y señorios asi a los
que agora sois como a los que sereis de aqui adelante y a cada vno y
qualquier de vos en v[uest]ros lugares y jure diciones a quien esta n[uest]ra carta
fuere mostrada o su treslado signado de escriuano publico salud e gracia sepades
que cebrian de caritate en nonbre de los mercaderes de todas las naciones
que residen en la dicha cibdad de seuilla nos ha hecho Relacion que
bien sabiamos como en las cibdades de burgos barcelona y valencia y
en otras partes de n[uest]ros Reynos donde auia consulado de mercaderes para
entender en las cosas y diferencias que tocauan al trato y comercio de la
mercaderia ansi en compras y ventas como en cambios y seguros y fle
tamientos y cuentas de entre mercaderes y compañias y sus fatores
y otras cosas a ello tocantes se veya por espiriencia el gran benefi
cio que de auer consulados se seguia y como hera vna de las mas prin
cipales causas para el aumento conseruacion y acrescentamiento
del trato y se escusauan muchas diuersidad de pleitos y dilaciones
e otros notables ynconuinientes que cada dia se ofrescian en diminucion
de la contratacion en las partes donde no auia consulado. y porque

Foundation–charter of the Consulate of Indies Merchants.

23 August, 1543, Valladolid.
Royal order, issued by Charles V, sanctioning the foundation of the Consulate of Indies Merchants of Seville.
6 fols. + 10 interleaved blanks.
301 x 207 mm.
Leather-bound, with floral decoration.
Consulados, L. 28 bis.

Cebrián de Caritate, on behalf of all merchants of all nations residing in Seville, urged the monarch to order the creation of a Consulate, similar to the ones in Burgos, Barcelona and Valencia, which might 'arbitrate in the issues and disputes pertaining to trade dealings and sales, money changing and insurance, freight, brokerage accounts, companies and their factors and other related issues'. Once royal sanction had been secured, the Consulate was born as an institution.

40,000 maravedis, while appeals in excess of that figure were referred to the Council of the Indies. Moreover, when the defendant lived in Seville, merchants could choose to argue their claim either before the *Casa de la Contratación* or the city's lawcourts.

However, despite having clearly established the jurisdictional limits of each body, commercial transactions were in no way expedited and merchant's claims were often left unsettled. The *Casa de la Contratación* took so long over its deliberations that the merchants of Seville gradually warmed to the idea of setting up their own tribunal, similar to ones operating in Valencia, Majorca, Barcelona and Burgos which rapidly expedited all claims brought before them.

The merchant community persevered with its objective until Cebrián de Caritate, 'on behalf of all merchants of all nations residing in Seville', submitted his report on the subject to the Council of the Indies, requesting permission to found a Consulate that would be able to arbitrate in commercial disputes, change money, deal in insurance and freight, broker transactions and handle other matters essential to trade.

The Council came out in favor of this initiative, although, understandably, it voiced reservations over the creation of yet another lawcourt in the city. However, the importance of Indies merchants to Spain's economic policy led to the granting of the concession without restrictions. The institution was modelled along the lines of the Consulate of Burgos and, in exchange for the Council's concession, 'the merchants were expected to render certain services in return for the demands they present', as Charles V's secretary, Francisco de los Cobos, put it.

The *Consulado de la Universidad de Cargadores a Indias* (Consulate of the University of Indies Merchants) was founded by a royal decree of 23 August 1543. The text of the decree was published by J.J. Real. Subsequently, the institution came to be known as the 'Old Consulate of Seville' and all cases associated with the dealings of Indies merchants were heard before that tribunal.

The Statutes of the Consulate

The election of a prior and consuls posed several problems on account of the large number of people involved. A set of statutes was drawn up by the prior and the consuls to address that and other issues. Included in the task was Dr. Hernán Pérez de la Fuente, of the Council of the Indies. The statutes were modelled on

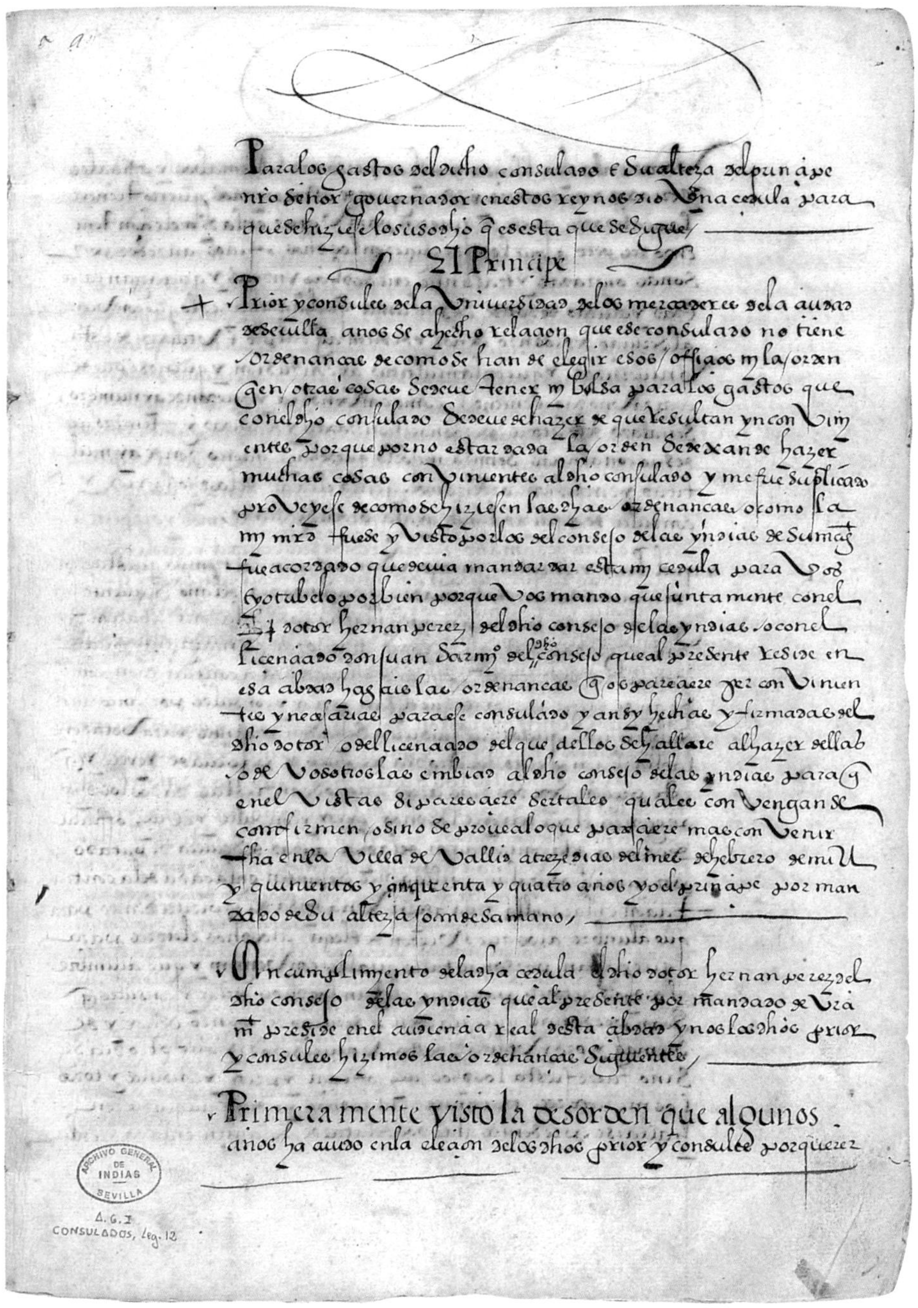

Left
Regulating consular activity: the statutes.

14 July 1556, Valladolid.
Royal provision, issued by Philip II, endorsing statutes for the Consulate of Indies Merchants in Seville.
Traces of the seal.
26 fols. + 4 blanks (304 x 210 mm.)
Consulados, 12.

The Consulate's foundation–charter provided for drawing up 'perpetual or fixed-term' statutes, as long as they were submitted to the Council of the Indies for approval. The first such statutes were printed by José de Blas y Quesada in 1739, some years after the Consulate had moved to Cádiz. The second set of statutes was printed in Cádiz by Juan Ximénez Carreño in 1787.

Opposite, above
The venue for commercial dealings, past and present.

[18th century?]
'Perspective view of Seville Cathedral, seen from the back, and the Commodity Exchange.'
140 x 195 mm.

The triangle formed by the Cathedral, the Casa de la Contratación *(then in the hall of the Alcázar), and the Guadalquivir river was the heart of Seville's business center in the 16th and 17th centuries. That was the area where, after a long controversy with the Cathedral chapter, the Commodity Exchange was eventually built on the site of the Royal Ironworks, part of the Mint, the Hospital de las Tablas and some quarters belonging to the Cathedral chapter.*

those of the Consulate of Burgos, drawn up in 1538. After completion, they were approved by a royal sanction issued in Valladolid on 14 July 1556.

The statutes comprise a total of 60 chapters, as do those of Burgos. Antonia Heredia divided them into two major sections, the first dealing with the institution's internal regime—elections, agreements, archives, *avería,* and brokerage—and a considerably larger second section devoted to marine insurance.

As a result of the activities generated by the Consulate and its staff, the merchants soon realized that they needed their own premises. Until then they had been given the use of a room in the *Casa de la Contratación,* but they generally dealt on the Cathedral steps, drawing serious complaints from the Church, as the merchants took shelter inside the building during bad weather. Thus, a suitable site for a commodity exchange had to be found near the river, the *Casa de la Contra-*

Opposite, below
Electing the Consulate officials.

[18th century?]
'The Consulate (Seville).'
Lithograph by F. Crosa, under the direction of F.J. Parcerisa.
201 x 295 mm.
MP. Europa y África.

Perspective de l'Eglise Cathedrale de SEVILLE, vue par derriere, et de la Bourse des Marchands.

tación and the Cathedral steps. Eventually, the Crown gave over a plot of land known as *Las Herrerías* (The Ironworks) and building of a new Commodity Exchange got under way in 1584; by 1598, it was in use. Adjoining the Exchange, on the Cathedral facade, is the so-called 'Cross of Oaths', intended to preside over trade deals.

Consulate Elections

As of 1596, records of meetings and transactions were kept in separate books. The minute book provided concise details of attendance and the issues discussed. Written in 'old lettering and barely intelligible' and in a sorry state of disrepair, the members of the Consulate who attended a session held on 18 July 1787 decided to copy these and, having done so, promptly proceeded in rather non-archivistic fashion to destroy the originals.

The 'rectors' of the Consulate of Seville—the prior and two consuls—were elected on 2 January each year in the *Casa de la Contratación.* Owing to the large number of people that presented their candidature, the election rules contained in the foundation–charter had to be modified. Until then, the procedure had been hampered by the fact that those who stood for election even included foreign merchants and their servants, as attested to in eight chapters devoted to the issue in the Statutes of 1556.

The main novelty in those statutes was that they provided for the creation of an electoral body to serve for a two-year term which was responsible for choosing the prior and two consuls. Antonia Heredia, who studied that electoral system, recalls how the annual electoral procedure first involved announcing the forthcoming elections on the Cathedral steps and in other public places. After that, a thanksgiving mass was held on the monarch's feast day and, the following day, in the presence of the outgoing prior and consuls, a presiding judge and the recorder of the *Casa de la Contratación* would oversee voting in a thirty-man electoral body. The following day, these people would elect the highest-ranking officials of the Consulate.

Consular elections were first held in the *Casa de la Contratación,* and were at times clouded by bribery and irregularities, particularly in 1685. When the House was moved to Cádiz in 1717, twenty members still voted in Seville while the balance cast their ballot in Cádiz. In 1744, ten voted in Cádiz, ten in Seville and the balance in Puerto de Santa María, Sanlúcar de Barrameda and Jerez. After that, the

'The long-standing practice of recording the agreements reached at trade assemblies, with passing reference to the attendants, eventually led to the minute books falling into disrepair, so in 1787 the books were copied and the old originals destroyed forthwith. Two scribes, on a stipend of 20 pesos each, were engaged for the purpose. In a letter from Cádiz dated 30 August 1794, the Consulate's advisor notified the prior and consuls of the scribes having completed the process of copying all the books in their possession, yielding twelve or thirteen folio-size books in good handwriting containing the agreements made between 1596 and 1704, except for the year 1701, for which no record has ever come to light. This is explained in clean, uniform handwriting in the books documenting the agreements negotiated in the Consulate. The time at which they were copied does not correspond to the dates of the books now housed in the 'Consulates' Section.
'We do not know why that process of copying did not go beyond the year 1705. All we know is that neither the copies nor the originals for the remaining years have ever come to light among the Consulate documents. An unbridgeable gap remains between 1705 and 1788, so that we can only accurately account for the merchants' presence and activity over a period of four years.' HEREDIA HERRERA, Antonia: *Sevilla y los hombres del Comercio (1700–1800).* Seville, Editorial Andaluzas Unidas, S.A., 1989, pp. 41; and 'Regulations and Statutes of the Consulate of Cádiz in the 18th century', in the *Jornadas de Andalucía y América.* Seville, Escuela de Estudios Hiapanoamericanos, 1985, pp. 67.

elections took place entirely in Sanlúcar, marking the end of Seville's importance as a trade center.

The Consulate statutes were taken into consideration when the first trade institutions were set up in the Americas, beginning with the Consulates of Lima and Mexico City. The monarch sanctioned the creation of the Mexican Consulate in 1592 in view of the thriving trade between New Spain and the Iberian peninsula. In 1594, the Lima *Audiencia* requested a Consulate along the lines of the one in Seville, an initiative the King endorsed in 1595. However, differences between the merchants and the Lima traders postponed its inauguration until 1613.

Fleet Dispatch

Regular commercial fleet sailings between Spain and the New World were a logical development from the outset. As the conquest of American territory expanded, supplies had to be sent to an increasing number of European settlers across Spanish America. And, owing to the hazards posed by pirates, corsairs and accidents at sea, the merchant vessels sent to convey those supplies had to be escorted.

At the request of the Consulate of Seville, in 1554 Charles V issued a royal warrant instituting two important annual sailings; to New Spain in January and Tierra Firme in September, each of which would be protected by four naval vessels. The cost of the operation was met by receipts from *avería* or average tax. As of 1572, the fleets sailed to New Spain in early April and to Tierra Firme in early August to take advantage of fair weather.

Sailings could not be undertaken on a more active basis due to the lack of funds from merchants, inadequate knowledge of the New World market and the general economic climate at the time. Royal receipts, the upkeep of Seville and part of the business structure in Spain and the rest of Europe depended on the safe arrival of merchant vessels from the Indies. A glance at the Consulate minute book reveals how anxiously those arrivals were awaited by traders, who held masses and festivities to celebrate such events.

One of the services provided by the Consulate was to assign merchant vessels to a fleet sailing. However, the tonnage involved was decided by the merchants. Another service was to appoint a consul to supervise sailings, for which he was paid three ducats a day.

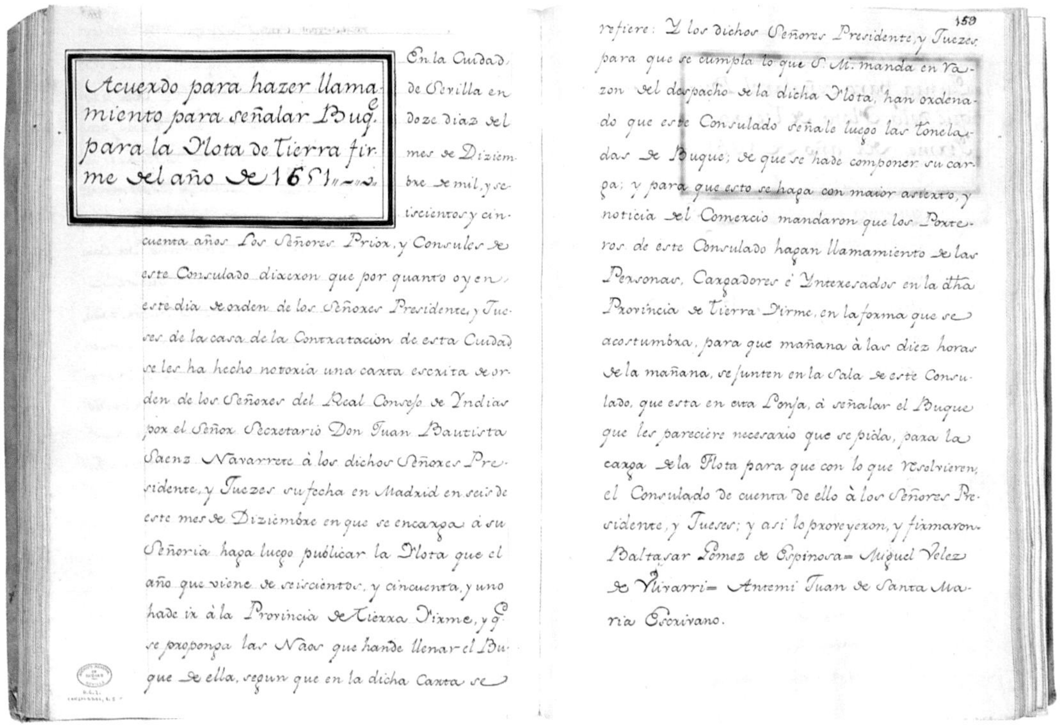

The role of the Consulate in dispatching fleets.

12 December 1650, Seville.
Minutes of the Consulate Assembly at which vessels on the Tierra Firme run were designated.
Signed in 1651.
18th-century facsimile.
497 x 285 mm.
Consulados, L. 5, fol. 158 v.–159.

One of the functions of the Consulate was to appoint the vessels to be included in the fleet dispatch. The above document was drawn up after a session at which 3,000 tons were requested of the king, 2,000 tons of which corresponded to Seville trade and the remaining 1,000 tons to merchants from Cádiz.

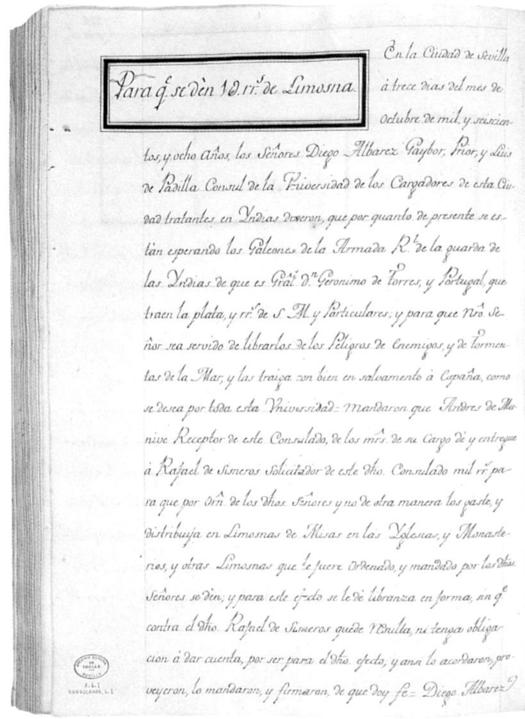

Prayer for a safe arrival.

13 October 1608, Seville.
Document attesting the allocation of 1,000 reales, to be used by Rafael Cisneros for defraying the cost of masses and alms at a thanksgiving service for the safe arrival of galleons in the fleet of General Jerónimo de Torres y Portugal.
18th-century facsimile.
497 x 285 mm.
Consulados, L. 1, fol. 196 v.

Fleet departures and arrivals used to arouse a flurry of trade activity in the city. Consignments of money, gold and silver and various commercial products were eagerly awaited, as was news of a fleet's safe arrival, for which it was customary for the Consulate to hold thanksgiving ceremonies.

The Consulate handled a large volume of business during its Seville period and the merchants made handsome profits on their cargoes, enabling them to extend loans to the Crown and thus alleviate the monarchs' financial hardship. In this respect, it was common for merchants to expedite sailings even in adverse weather conditions when the cargoes were to bring in large sums of money.

Operating along with the fleet sailings were dispatch boats whose duties included conveying news of a fleet's imminent arrival, the dispatch of official and private correspondence and warning of the presence of foreign vessels or enemy warships. These were sent out by the *Casa de la Contratación* and paid for by average tax or the Royal Treasury.

In the 16th century, the Consulate was commissioned to send out dispatch vessels on specific occasions, but it was not until 1628 that it was expected to outfit them. The Consulate was always reluctant to undertake such services on account of the costs involved, despite the fact that it was authorized to take the odd paying passenger on board or carry cargo to offset the expense incurred.

El Rey
1690 Carlos 2º
quedo con gran seguridad de conseguir mi deseo mediante el amor de tan buenos vasallos
Yo el Rey
DOC. ESC. 2. nº 26

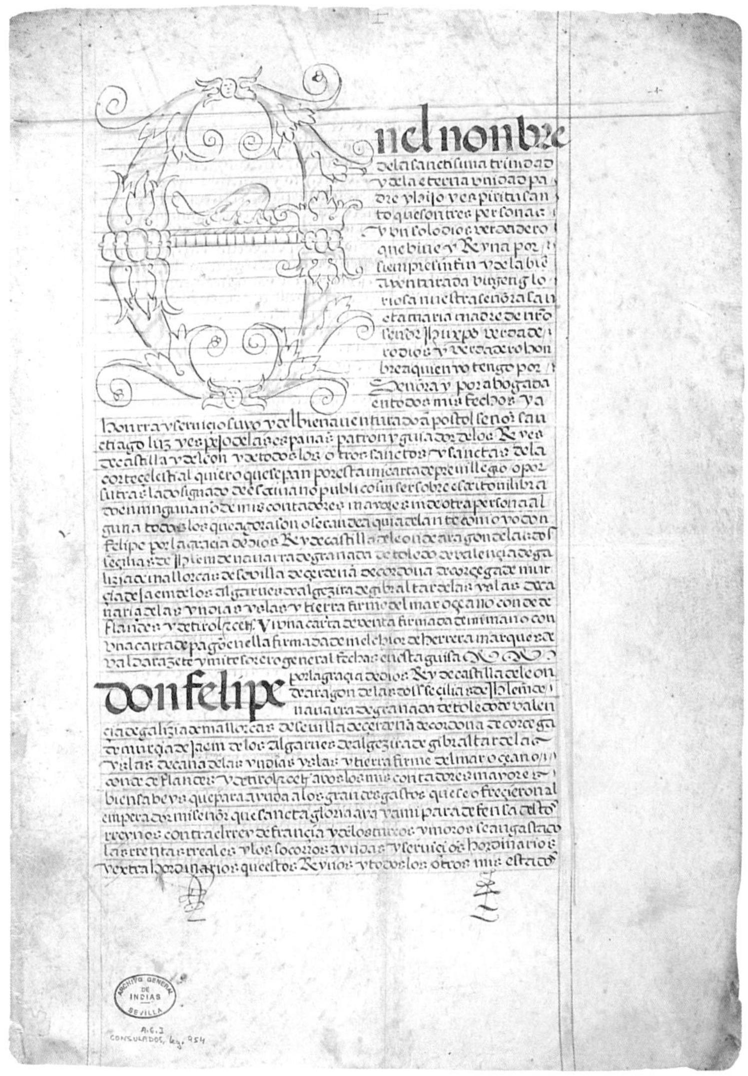

The Crown's financial difficulties and Consulate loans.

26 December 1690, Madrid.
Royal warrant issued by Charles II applying for a loan of 500,000 pesos from the Consulate.
Royal seal.
295 x 205 mm.
Consulados, 689.

Ever since the Crown had awarded the consular concession, it expected Seville's merchants and traders to provide financial assistance in return. Massive aid of this kind was provided by merchants from both Seville and Cádiz until the 19th century. In this instance, the king writes in his own hand to give due weight to his request: 'I am certain my request will be met by the love of such devoted subjects'.

Consulate investments: annuities.

10 August 1571, Madrid.
Annuity issued to Alonso de Ojeda by the Almojarifazgo *of Seville, a customs institution.*
4 fols. (337 x 240 mm)
Consulados, 954.

Surplus Consulate funds were invested in debentures or annuities guaranteed by national and local contributions. The Consulate's investment in the Almojarifazgo *of Seville and the* Almojarifazgo *of the Indies has been documented since the institution's inception. On other occasions, the funds were invested in Seville real estate.*

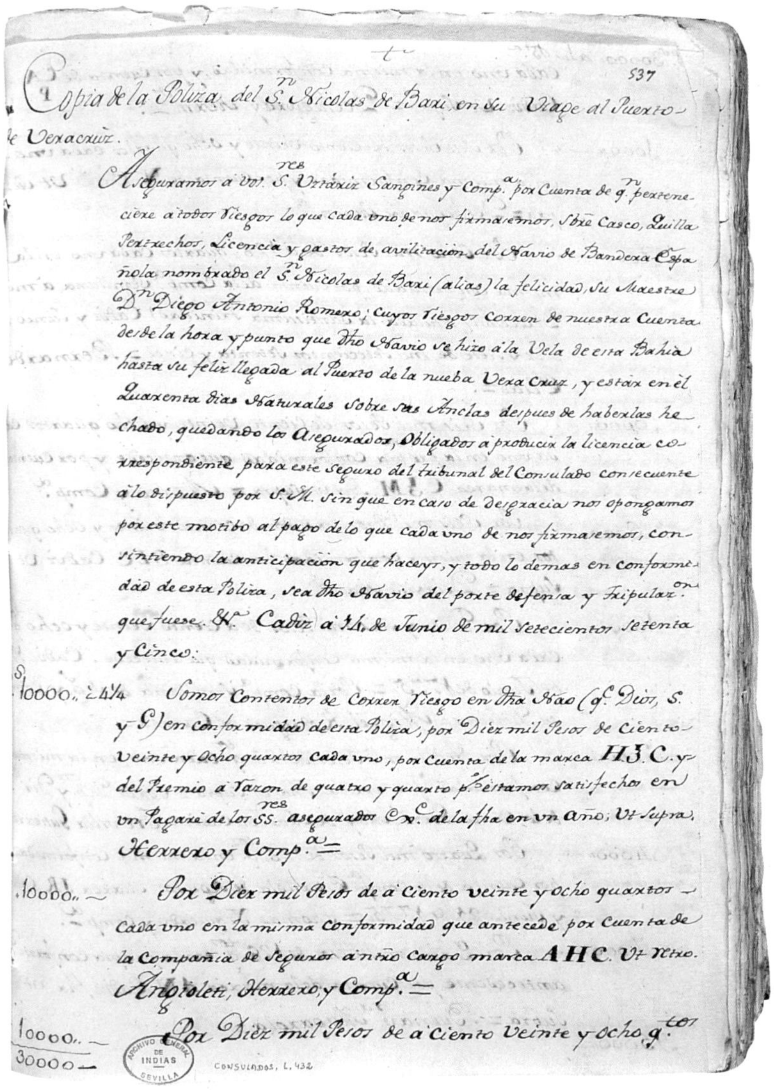

Marine insurance contract.

19 June 1775, Cádiz.
Insurance policy for the vessel, San Nicolás de Bari, during its voyage to the port of Veracruz.
18th-century facsimile.
310 x 203 mm.
Consulados, L. 432, fols. 537–538 v.

Shipping insurance regulations were a major part of the Consulate's statutes and methods for assessing different types of contracts were meticulously laid down. Such regulations were strict, as it had been common practice to file exorbitant insurance claims.
It was illegal to insure freight, military supplies and rigging. Only the ship's hull could be insured at partial value.

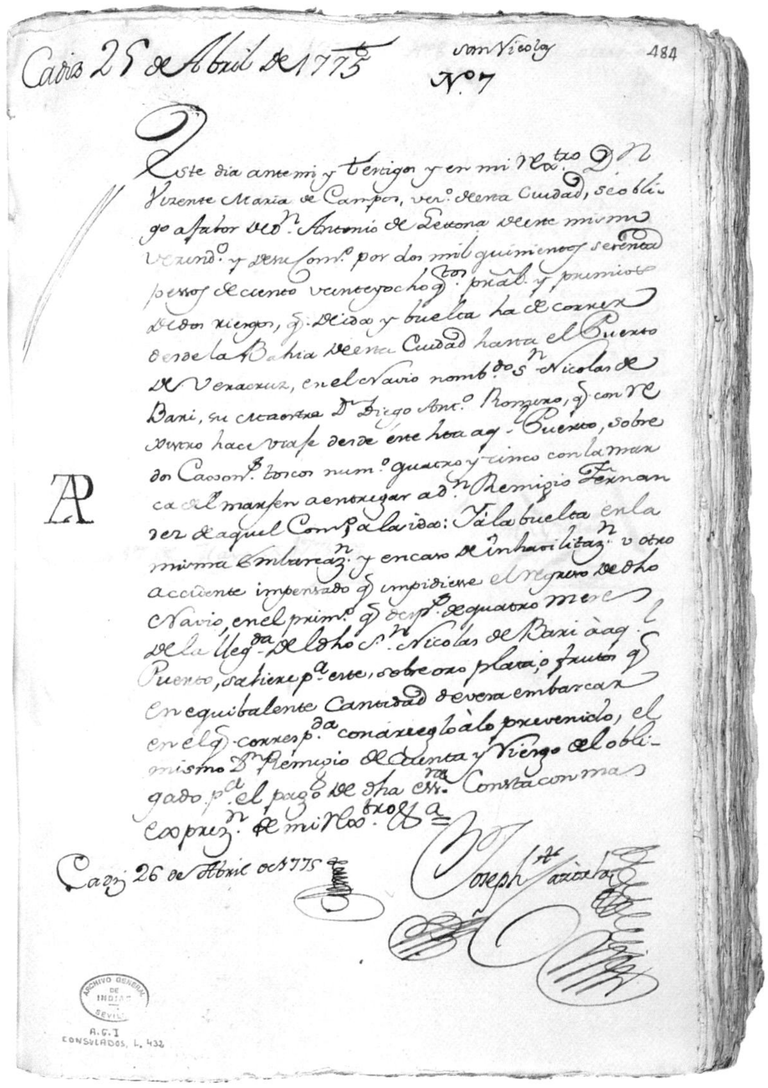

Insuring risk: freight insurance.

25 April 1775, Cádiz.
Risk cargo certificate covering the vessel, San Nicolás de Bari, on its voyage to the port of Vera Cruz.
310 x 203 mm.
Consulados, L. 432, fol. 484.

Insurable freight value was reduced by shipping loans when the vessel acted as security. The limit was between one and two thirds of the actual value. These loans required approval of the prior and consuls, and were registered with the Consulate.

The service reached its height in 1720 when the Crown assigned to the Consulate the task of sending four dispatch boats on a periodical basis to Tierra Firme and four to New Spain: their principal mission was to carry correspondence. From studies undertaken by Antonia Heredia, it appears that, although merchants were initially reluctant to accept the terms imposed by the Crown, it was two trade consuls of Cádiz, Antonio Pardo and Adrián Ignacio Delgado, that persuaded them of the consequences of refusing to perform such duties. In exchange, the Consulate was authorized to traffic in cargoes on both the outgoing and return voyages and to make stopovers. It also received tax exemptions.

Making Loans to the Crown

The Consulate and the *Casa de la Contratación* were jointly responsible for the trade monopoly of the Indies. The former acted in its members' interests while the officials of the *Casa de la Contratación* carried out royal orders. The overlapping mandates of the two bodies led at times to a certain amount of friction, otherwise they cooperated in matters of common interest. The Crown felt it was entitled to request loans from merchants in exchange for granting privileges and while merchants accepted the idea of assisting the Crown, they were by no means prepared to pay for the financial disasters of the Royal Treasury.

The Consulate's receipts grew throughout the 16th century and in the last two decades reached the sum of 400,000 maravedis. However, these were hard hit by an economic crisis in the 17th century, when they dropped to little more than 100,000 maravedis per year.

As it had done throughout the 16th century, the Crown continued to request loans from merchants. However, in the 17th century, the monarch's demands were stepped up in view of Spain's economic difficulties. The reiterated requests for financial aid to meet political and military needs and to bail out the Royal Treasury elicited complaints, opposition and resignation on the part of the merchants.

The only course of action open to them was to accede to the monarch's demands and try to find other means of income including the implementation of new tariffs, the reintroduction of old ones and legalized fraud. This became the customary response at the Consulate.

As A.M. Bernal pointed out, loans to the Crown were offset by awarding privileges, particularly when it came to cargo inspections and to regulations concerning bankruptcies, insurance and exchange rates. This new state of affairs led to the decline of the once all-powerful *Casa de la Contratación,* while the Consulate gained control of sea trade on the Indies run.

Taxes and Tariffs Administered by the Consulate

To finance construction of the Commodity Exchange, in 1582 an *impuesto de lonja* (commodity tax) of one third of a percent was levied on all goods entering or leaving Seville. However, despite the Exchange having already started trading at the end of the 16th century, the tax in question continued to be collected until early in the 19th century.

A 1% *impuesto de infantes* (infantry tax), similar to the above, was first levied in 1632 and originally intended to remain in force until 1638. It was related to the Crown concession of a 360,000-ducat consular subsidy used to defray the cost of supporting 500 infantrymen. A royal decree of 1637 perpetuated collection of the tax, as an additional amount of 800,000 ducats had to be raised. Like the commodity tax, it remained in force until the first two decades of the 19th century.

In 1625, a special loan of 400,000 ducats for equipping a fleet of three galleons and ten tenders gave rise to an average of 1% known as the 'tonnage tax'. It remained in force until 1627. In 1642, another similar tax was instituted as a result of the 200,000-ducat outlay required for military expenses in Catalonia.

Tax evasion was legion: for instance, it was common practice in Seville to import goods without registering them. Aware of the situation, the king would negotiate a settlement with the merchants in exchange for a general pardon. The price of a pardon was established by the same merchants that had benefitted from the tax evasion. On one occasion, a settlement of this kind was financed by the Consulate's issuing debt certificates and mortgages collateralized by a form of customs duty, the *impuesto de balbas,* which consisted of levying 1.5% on all imports from the Americas. In 1695, Charles II borrowed 500,000 pesos from the Consulate to defray military costs in Catalonia. In return, he gave merchants permission to export so-called 'illicit goods'.

Based on assessed value, an average tax was instituted to pay for fleet organization and defense and was levied on all goods conveyed to or from the New World. It was administered by the merchants until 1573, and by the *Casa de la Contratación* until 1591, when it was placed under the control of the Consulate, returning to the *Casa de la Contratación* in 1640. Apart from the administration of other tariffs, partial control over average tax turned the Consulate into an impor-

'In view of the uncontrolled smuggling of slaves by foreign agents, which had a great impact on the official trade, and of pressure brought by private, well-to-do entrepreneurs and the administrative bodies that governed the Indies, the Consulate had no alternative but to intervene and take over control of the trade. The first stage of intervention, lasting until 1678, was marked by the Consulate reacting arrogantly at its lack of power to control the traffic. That later led to a realistic compromise, when it accepted the offer of a trader from Cádiz, Juan Barroso del Pozo, to operate 6,000 of the 10,000 tons the Consulate had committed itself to. The final stage was one of resignation, when the Consulate took stock of its failure and realized that foreign control of the trade was irreversible.'
(VILA VILAR, E. *El Consulado de Sevilla, asentista de esclavos: una nueva tentativa para el mantenimiento del monopolio comercial.* Huelva, Instituto de Estudios Onubenses, 1981, pp. 183–195.)

tant Crown agent. The Consulate's so-called ordinary expenditure—personnel, lawyers' fees, almsgiving, masses and so on—was met by a tax of 0.05% on all exports.

The Consulate also made a handsome profit on the sale of cargo licenses and notarial privileges. It had widespread powers to appoint public notaries, particularly in three trade categories with notarial status—the chief recorder of navies and fleets, the paymaster and the purveyor.

Part of the profit made by the Consulate was invested in debentures and in Seville real estate. However, the Consulate's financial administration was widely criticized by its creditors who, on examining its books, were astonished by 'the chaos and confusion', either caused wilfully or by the continued collection of taxes beyond their stipulated lifespan.

Marine Insurance and Risk Cargo Certificates

Maritime risk goes back to ancient times. According to M. Ravina, in Spain there has always been some confusion as to the difference between maritime risk and maritime insurance. Maritime risk consisted of one party (the insurer) lending money to another (the shipper). The insurer would assume all risks and contingencies on or from the sea, from which the shipper was exempted in case of an accident at sea. Consequently, upon safe arrival, the principal was returned to the first party, along with a stipulated premium. A contract of this kind was formalized before a public notary. An abridged copy was registered in the Consulate's accounting department and many such contracts are now housed in the General Archive of the Indies.

In marine insurance, there was no loan. One of the parties to the agreement—the insurer—was obliged to pay compensation up to the limit of the value insured, for the damages to a vessel or its cargo incurred by the other party in the course of a shipping accident. In return, the insured party paid the insurer a premium. Their agreement was formalized before a broker at the Commodity Exchange and simply recorded by filling in a form.

Problems arose in connection with a practice, regarded as fraudulent, whereby merchants and shippers each insured their vessels and cargo for the same amount. If the vessel went down, they were exempted from paying their creditors but, as beneficiaries, they were entitled to collect the insurance paid out by the insurers.

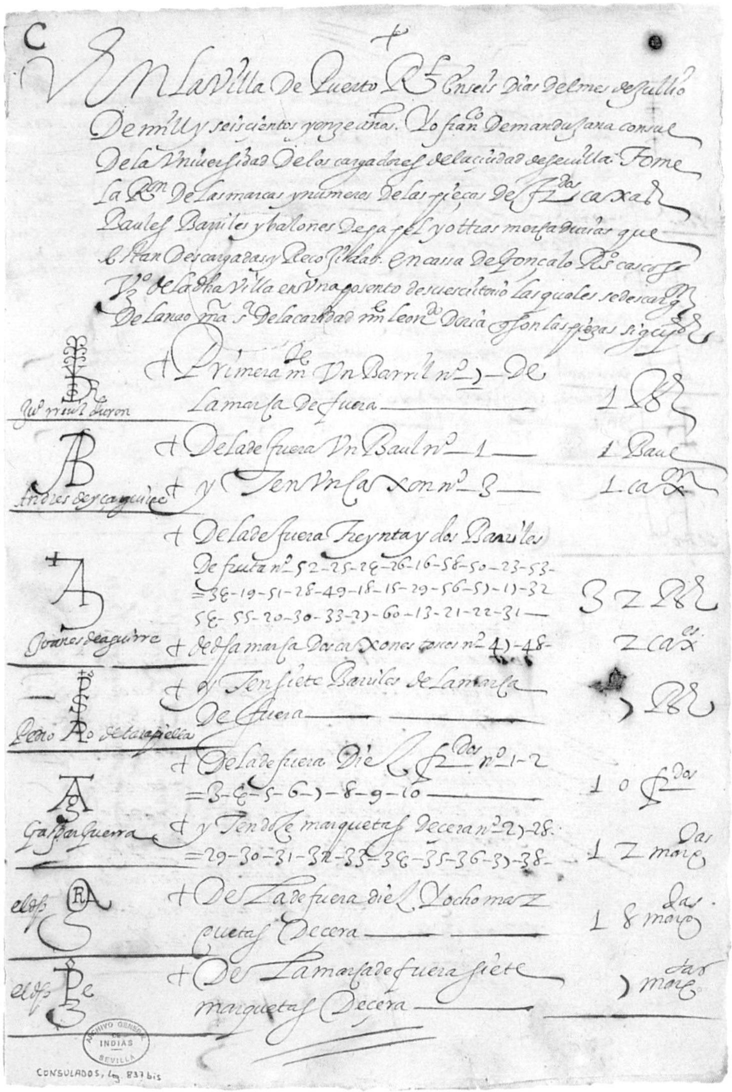

Shipwrecks on the Indies run.

6 July 1611, Puerto Real.
Report drawn up by Francisco de Mandajana, consul of the Consulate of Indies Merchants of Seville, listing salvage from the vessel, Nuestra Señora de la Caridad, *which sunk in the Bay of Cádiz. The cargoes salvaged were stored in the home of Gonzalo Rodríguez Cascojo in Puerto Real.*
2 fols.
310 x 215 mm.
Consulados, 837 bis.

The number of shipwrecks was directly related to the risks taken by shipowners, skippers and pilots on the Indies run. Sailing charts of the period were studded with markings showing dangerous areas. One such place was the Bay of Cádiz with its numerous shoals. From the very beginning, the Consulate was legally entitled to undertake salvage operations, as provided for in its statutes.

The first set of Consulate statutes mentioned insurance and risk as follows: '*They are legally competent in dealings and trade in merchandise and in purchases and sales, insurance and freightage and accounts between merchants and companies and their factors and other things associated with them*'. The *Casa de la Contratación*, for its part, was left to act as an appeals court whenever an issue exceeded the jurisdiction of the prior and consuls.

The 1556 Consulate statutes strictly prohibited their insurance of cargo, artillery or rigging on either outbound or return Indies voyages. All that could be insured by them on the outbound voyage was two thirds of the hull value and insurance of this kind had to be formalized in a different policy from the one used for insuring cargoes. On the return voyage, the value exposed had to be established by the prior and consuls.

Brokers at the Commodity Exchange

The *Diccionario de Autoridades* defines a broker as 'one who assists merchants in dispatching their goods, in engaging people to purchase them and in arranging things'. A dispute arose in 1574 between brokers and the Chapter over ownership of the titles to brokerage. The brokers paid the city council 24,000

Identifying salvage.

30 May 1756, Barcelona.
'Angel marking cargo crates'. Detail from a Compañía de Barcelona *share certificate.*
MP. Monedas, 39.

The list of all rescued cargo from shipwrecks was essential for assessing losses. The first step in the process was to identify the marks on every 'crate' or 'package' and the resulting information was later compared to entries in the Consulate register.

ducats for the right to such titles, while the city reserved the right to issue them to new brokers in the event of a vacancy.

In 1634, the Crown attempted to institute a new profession concerned exclusively with insurance policies, but the brokers of Seville responded by asserting that since the time of Philip II it had always been their business to draw up insurance deals, as there was no reason for them to be transacted before a notary. No 'foreigner, Portuguese or Genoese' was allowed to become a broker, 'on account of the disservice that might do to the Crown'.

The commodity traders were entitled to all rights of brokerage on insurance policies, the sale of slaves, annuities, exchange deals, barter in copper, silver and gold, letters of exchange and other effects. The Crown attempted to raise the existing number of sixty brokers by ten, to which end a title was sold to the Portuguese trader, Juan Bispo. However, this raised heated objection, and the Crown was forced to withdraw it. That brush with the Crown prompted it to implement a number of measures regulating the brokerage trade, including barring access to brokers with fixed residence in the vicinity of the Exchange. Sanctions were likewise established for intruders in the profession—known as *zánganos* or 'drones'—and a judge of the Royal *Audiencia* was appointed to try such cases of intrusion.

Salvaging Shipwrecks

Chapter 22 of the Consulate Statutes referred to 'what might be lost or salvaged on the voyage to the Indies'. The Consulate was directly responsible for following up on such losses on the Indies run. Its mission was to salvage as much of the cargo as it could and to distribute the value received among the merchants. It was likewise required to keep a register of all incidents and losses affecting trade with the New World. Salvage operations sometimes required official royal sanction and usually involved sending out dispatch boats. The Consulate also explored the idea of setting up shipyards to improve the quality of galleons. The Indies run was fraught with perils and accidents: apart from the mouth of the Guadalquivir, the most dangerous areas included the Caribbean and the shallows around Argentina.

Merchants and Traders

As pointed out by Antonia Heredia, a description of the merchants behind the Indies trade is no easy matter, as they did not form part of a fully-fledged business partnership and there are no surviving records of their names and dealings.

It appears that the merchants that originally became involved in the Indies trade in the 16th century were wholesalers who gradually adapted to the new commercial horizons opened up by the discovery of the New World. The Statutes of 1556 did not evidently exclude the participation of foreign traders, as the person who, on behalf of all the merchants of Seville, first voiced the need for a Consulate, Cebrián de Caritate, was not Spanish. Thus, as stated by Heredia, 'what qualified a trader was taking up residence in Seville and being regularly involved in overseas trade'. After the Consulate was founded in 1543, however, the informal qualification as a trader was formalized by the new institution.

Consulate membership implied eligibility to take part in the election of a prior and consuls, a right open only to merchants. From 1686 onwards, an eligible merchant was defined as one who traded an annual cargo of over 200,000 maravedis. Merchants engaged in other activities: some were landowners, and special importance was attached to those who produced grapes or olives. Produce yielded by their crops usually became the content of regular consignments in fleet sailings known as 'the fruit third'. Other traders engaged in the sale of textiles, manufactured goods or farm produce.

The power wielded by the Consulate is borne out in many instances of struggle for control of the institution, which was commonplace among various groups of merchants. Hardly any names of merchants belonging to the Consulate prior to the 18th century are known, as few relevant documents have survived. This is not the case as far as directors of the institution is concerned. Heredia was able to reconstruct a roster of all such high-ranking officials after studying minute books and election dossiers. The top members of the Consulate formed a social elite. They were awarded titles, military honors and appointments in the Cathedral chapter, and they married into the aristocracy of Seville. The mercantile dynasties of the Ortiz de Sandoval, Delgado y Ayala, Torre Cossío and Céspedes families acted as powerful lobbies in 18th-century Seville, and their high status had its roots in their activity during the previous century.

St Leander, patron of commodity traders.

1745
St Leander, Archbishop of Seville and patron saint of commodity traders.
Seville, 1745.
290 x 200 mm.
Included in the reprint of the Royal Provision of 27 October 1637 in which the Consulate of Indies Merchants of Seville had its privileges and statutes ratified. Fol. IV.
MP. Estampas, 222.

The commodity traders formed a guild around the figure of their patron, St Leander. Any merchant who failed to attend a guild meeting was fined two ducats, and all proceeds from such fines were used to pay for the celebrations held on the saint's feast day, at which the main attraction was a procession that ended at the nuns' convent of the same devotion.

The Consulate Moves to Cádiz

The headquarters of the mercantile fleet was transferred from Seville to Cádiz in 1680, heralding the start of a shift in the entire colonial trade structure and administration. The transfer of the *Casa de la Contratación* to Cádiz in 1717 was therefore part and parcel of the geographical shift that had begun several decades earlier. The royal warrant of 8 May 1717, drawn up on the initiative of José Patiño, President of the *Casa de la Contratación,* stated categorically that the Consulate

'Of all the factors affecting the company's financial results, which brought about its untimely downfall, the most important one was inordinately high overheads. Next in importance was the lack of sufficient share capital, which never reached the total of one million pesos (4,000 shares), the original target set by the founding members. Indeed, by 1745, no more than 3,334 shares had been sold. Other factors included unprofitable factory production which was unable to compete on the colonial market, and unpaid debts incurred on mercantile expeditions to the American continent, compounding the vicissitudes that marred the business record of the *Compañía de San Fernando*.
Like all other Spanish initiatives prompted by the Bourbon reforms, the untimely Sevillian scheme was doomed to failure. According to Matilla Quizá, those companies did not set up businesses commensurate with their share structure. Neither did they implement new production techniques or a sufficiently dynamic marketing network. They did, however, achieve one of the declared objectives of the Bourbons—that of limiting the port of Cádiz's exclusive monopoly of Indies trade.'
GONZÁLEZ SÁNCHEZ, C.A.: *La Real Compañía de Comercio y Fábricas de San Fernando de Sevilla (1747–1787)*, Seville: City Council, 1994, pp. 125–126.

and the *Casa de la Contratación* should be located 'from this day on, in the city of Cádiz, so that the rank and file of commerce may have at their disposal the resources they require'. Thus began the Cádiz phase of the Consulate which had been founded in Seville. This marked the beginning of a long-standing dispute between the inhabitants of the two cities over the control of trade. The dispute lasted well into the 18th century.

In business terms, the relocation affected certain trading practises, but not their essentials. As A.M. Bernal stated quite correctly, the merchants considered the move as a temporary measure. This perception is confirmed by the absence in Cádiz of any of the large mercantile squares so common in Europe at the time, or of such grand buildings as the Commodity Exchange or the Royal Mint in neighboring Seville. Indeed, the city did not even have an equivalent of the legendary Cathedral steps of Seville.

Seville retained its commercial hegemony in the first few years after the Consulate and the *Casa de la Contratación* had moved to Cádiz. Nevertheless, it slowly went into decline. Its trade activity was hampered by the limitations of its river port on the Guadalquivir, and by the hazards of the Sanlúcar de Barrameda sandbar. Cádiz, on the other hand, was a seaport and could offer safe berth to any kind of vessel, a situation that gradually turned it into the most cosmopolitan city on the Iberian peninsula.

The Diputación de Comercio

After the Consulate had moved to Cádiz, a *Diputación de Comercio* or 'Trade Delegation' was established on the premises of the Commodity Exchange in Seville and acted as a court of law with jurisdiction over New World trade. Two delegates or deputies were placed in charge of the newly founded institution. At first, they were nominated by the first consul but, as of 1758, annual elections were held at the same time as those for the prior and consuls. According to Antonia Heredia, from 1719 to 1783, office-holders were distinguished members of the Consulate.

The other members of the *Diputación*, all commodity traders, were nominated by their directors and, in principle, their appointment had to meet with the approval of the Consulate in Cádiz. However, that approval was not always sought, particularly since the positions in question were unremunerated. However, the incentive for merchants to seek office was that they could then take up residence in the Commodity Exchange at a time when it was difficult to find housing in Seville.

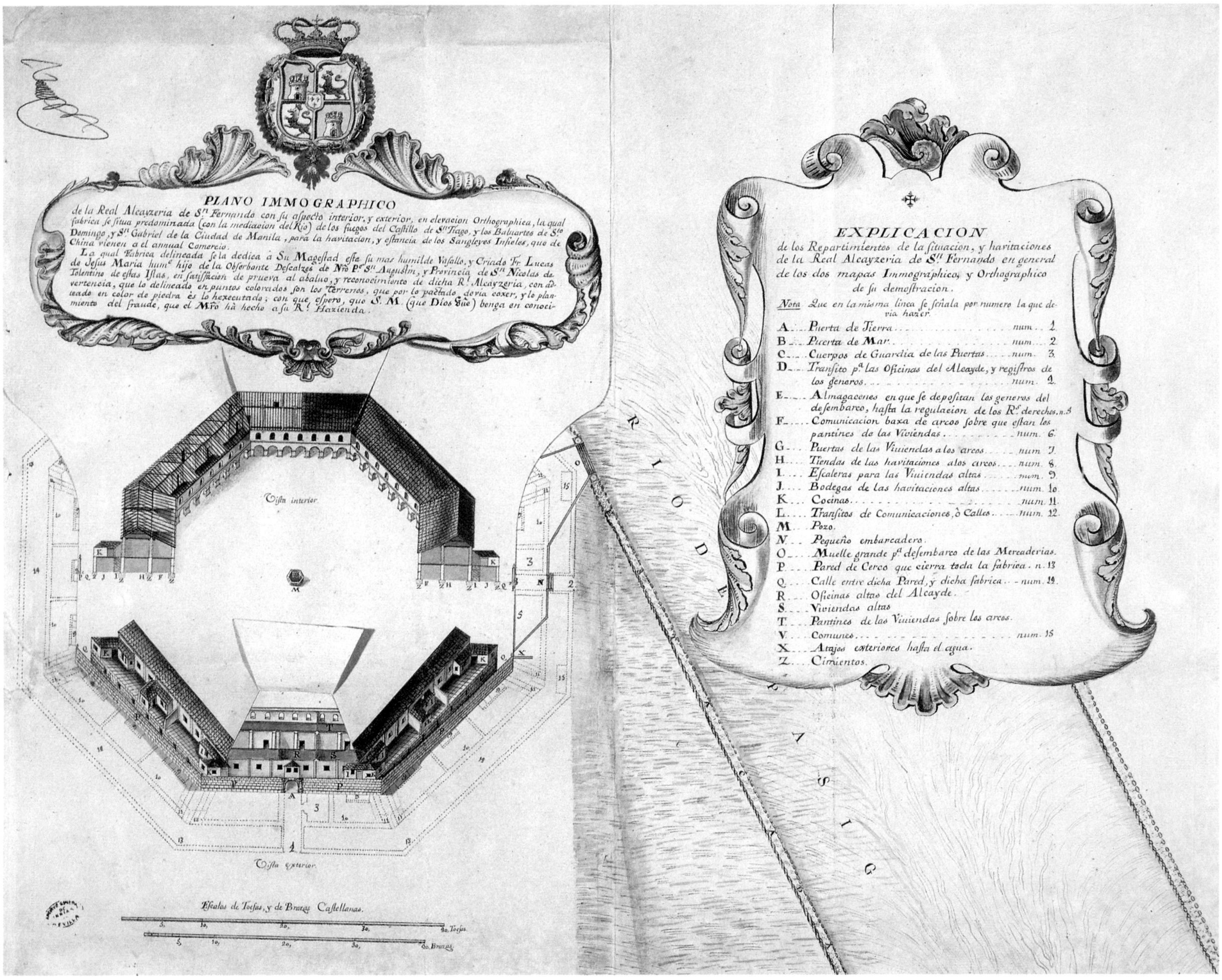

By the mid-18th century, activity at the *Diputación* had slowed down to a bare minimum, the Commodity Exchange had fallen into disrepair and the merchants that had been operating under its auspices started looking for alternative lines of trade. On a visit to the Exchange in 1784, the syndic Pedro López de Lerena notified the merchants that, from then on, the chambers in the *Diputación* were to house the so-called 'New Consulate of Seville'. Gálvez issued an order to that effect and the news was confirmed on 4 December 1784. After the building had been vacated, the *Consulado Marítimo y Terrestre* (Sea and Land Consulate) moved into the ground floor, while the General Archive of the Indies was set up on the first floor, marking a new period in the life of the building.

Trade control: the alcaicería (raw silk exchange) *of San Fernando de Manila.*

[1760 or 1771]
'Ground plan of the Real Alcaicería of San Fernando de Manila.'
By Fray Lucas de Jesús María, a Discalced Augustinian.
476 x 593 mm. (ground plan);
383 x 295 mm. (overlay).
MP. Filipinas, 176.

Published in the report filed by the Bishop of Cebu in which he rendered account of the excesses committed by Fernando de Mier y Noriega, governor of the fortress, when building the alcaicería, *the silk traders' quarters. They were built to house Sangleys (people of mixed Chinese and Indian blood) who travelled to Manila each year to conduct trade dealings. The elevation contains two small overlays revealing the interior of the quarters.*

Trading Companies

The ascent to the Spanish throne of the Bourbon dynasty ushered in sweeping reforms in all spheres of State administration. Among the most important of the new directives concerning the country's economic policy were those intended to

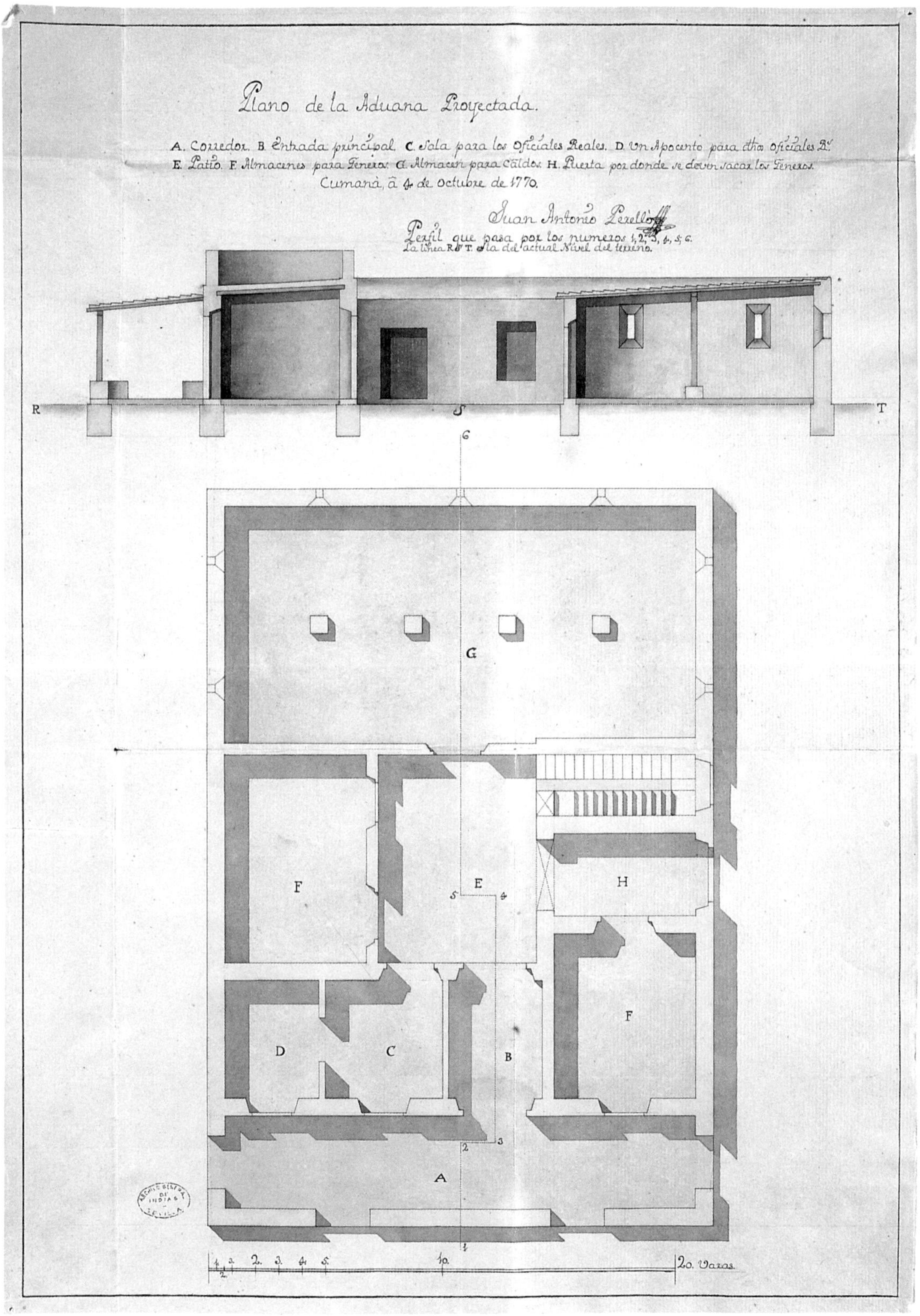

Trade control: The Cumaná customshouse.

4 October 1774.
'Plan of the Cumaná customshouse.'
Signed by Juan Antonio Perelló.
475 x 331 mm.
MP. Venezuela, 160.

The royal officials of Cumaná did not attend the loading and discharge of merchant vessels on the grounds that they had no customshouse. A royal warrant of 24 March 1774 ordered one to be built at a cost not to exceed 3,000 pesos. A tariff of 1% was levied on all trade in Cumaná to defray the expense. Building was completed in 1776 at a cost of 4,650 pesos, while 21,012 pesos had been collected through taxation. By royal order of 21 November 1791, the balance remaining, once the construction work had been paid for, was returned to the merchants who had been unduly taxed.

reactivate agriculture, trade and industry. Spain's trade and industry at the time had fallen behind other European powers. The major reason for this was that the nation's industry was still largely based on a guild structure, had enjoyed little technical progress and, finally, that the private sector was lethargic.

The Crown redoubled its efforts to regain control of its overseas empire by supporting the new mercantilist trend of developing the Spanish economy. One such initiative was to provide such incentives as tax exemptions and franchises to stimulate private investment in trade and industry, a move that led to a spate of new companies with trade privileges and factories with royal patronage.

Spain's colonial trade policy now showed a definite shift in emphasis, based on a decision to break Cádiz's trade monopoly and to adopt a *laissez faire* attitude in commerce. To achieve this, a number of new practices were instated, including dispatching sailing vessels that were independent of any particular fleet or port, and granting licenses and naturalization papers more readily to foreign traders.

Newly formed and especially privileged shareholding companies attempted to spread the shipping monopoly throughout Spain and to attract the interest of the middle classes throughout the Iberian peninsula. Several such moves took place during the 17th century, but none of them achieved their objective, and Spain had to wait until the 18th century before the idea became a reality.

The first enterprises to emerge were large companies that acquired trade monopolies with the New World. Encouraged by tax exemptions and other privileges, these quickly gained control of trade with the Indies. One of the leading companies of this kind was *La Guipuzcoana de Caracas,* founded in 1728, which secured exclusive rights to Venezuelan cacao, in addition to tobacco and leather. In 1785, the company was absorbed by the *Real Compañía de Filipinas* (The Royal Philippines Company) with the aim of contributing to the economic development of Asia. Another commercial giant was the *San Cristóbal de La Habana,* founded in 1740, which exercised a monopoly over Cuban tobacco and was licensed to export sugar and leather from the island. Finally, there was the *Compañía de Barcelona,* set up in 1755 to trade with Santo Domingo, Puerto Rico and Margarita Island, which ended up dealing mainly in cotton from Cumaná and Guayana.

A second group was made up of trading companies directed by merchants from a particular region of Spain, although these likewise enjoyed royal patronage and employed people from other regions. Their main aim was to stimulate industrial activity with a view to marketing Spanish goods in the Americas and vice versa, and they went a long way in reactivating the textile industry and reestablish-

'The rhythm of life in Cádiz was dictated by the very sun rising and setting over the sea. Cádiz had little more than sea. It had no hinterland, because that was no longer Cádiz, but Puerto de Santa María, Sanlúcar de Barrameda or Jerez de la Frontera. Cádiz was unique in a markedly agricultural region in that it lacked any farmland. Its wealth and economic activity and its rhythm of life were based more on the daily cycle of nature than a seasonal agricultural one. Its pulse was dictated by its port, as it was open to the sea and to all maritime activity. More than Seville, Cádiz would have been a natural choice for focusing New World trade and using the profits derived from it to develop its industry. Lacking any agriculture, it would have been the ideal alternative. But industry required knowledge and know-how, as well as capital investment and the right frame of mind. And that was either unavailable or in short supply.
The La Carraca naval shipyards, founded by José Patiño on the island of León (San Fernando) in 1729, only had one smelting furnace in 1786. A factory producing copper sheeting for lining naval vessels was established shortly afterwards in Puerto Real. In response to the increase in shipping, the *Fábrica de la Jarcia y Lona* was set up there, too. According to A. Ponz, by the end of the century the factory was churning out some 2,500 sheets of canvas and 1,400 to 1,600 pounds of rigging. This, in addition to the 408 caulkers and 291 shipwrights and other craftsmen in the area, amounts to a total of 40% of the population of Puerto Real being engaged in industrial or craft activities, a unique instance in the region. Cádiz, for its part, only had consumer craft workshops.'
RUIZ RIVERA, J.B. & GARCÍA BERNAL, M.C.: *Cargadores a Indias*. Madrid, Mapfre, 1992, pp. 335–336.

'**A**s was the case with emigration, the right to trade with the New World was, from the outset, considered to be a privilege for which only citizens of Spain's kingdoms were eligible. As Antúñez y Acevedo points out, "citizens" were considered to be "those whose parents and grandparents had also been born in the kingdoms of Castile, León and Navarre, the inhabitants of which had the exclusive right to trade with the Indies". That state of affairs lasted until 1620, when a royal order issued on 14 August of that year introduced the novelty whereby foreigners born of Catholic parents and resident in Spain for over ten years were also classed as "citizens".

'Another restrictive factor was the consolidation of all colonial sea trade in a single port. Not content with legally barring foreigners from emigrating to and trading with the New World, in its endeavors to possess and secure exclusive rights over the wealth of the New World, the Crown imposed stringent control over trading in the Indies and that was more likely to be achieved by channelling trade through a single harbor.'

GARCÍA–BAQUERO GONZÁLEZ, A.: *Cádiz y el Atlántico (1717–1778). El comercio colonial español bajo el monopolio gaditano*. Cádiz, Diputación Provincial, 1988, pp. 98–99.

ing trade links. Some of the major initiatives of this kind were implemented in Extremadura and Zaragoza in 1746, Granada and Seville in 1747, Toledo and La Unión in 1748, Requena in 1753, and Burgos in 1767.

The *Real Compañía de San Fernando* of Seville, the object of a study by C.A. González, was a case apart. In addition to attempting to reactivate the textile industry, its aim was to engage in colonial trade. In some respects this was the most ambitious project to emerge from Seville's middle classes following the transfer of the fleet's headquarters to Cádiz. The initiative probably stemmed from the links between the promoters and the Consulate and might have been based in part on a desire to restore the city's former splendor.

Records of the balance of trade in Veracruz, which the Consulate had started in 1809, provide a clear picture of the imports and exports registered at that Mexican port. The leading imports were cooking oil, steel, spirits, almonds, saffron, Spanish lace, knitted garments, silk ribbons, damask, iron, fretwork from Granada, cotton and silk stockings, paper, taffeta, velvet and wine. The major exports were indigo, sugar, cacao, coffee, cochineal, Jalapa purgative, quinine, leather soles and sarsaparilla.

Bankruptcy

Most of the business operations transacted in Seville and the Indies were based on credit. The high rate of accidents registered by shipping on the Indies run, along with other factors, conspired to undermine the mercantile venture. Those contributing factors were delays in fleet arrivals, poor sales in the Americas, accidents at sea and shipwrecks, Crown seizures of remittances, poor business forecasts and other misjudgements.

The relocation of the *Casa de la Contratación* and the Consulate to Cádiz attracted merchants in droves from various parts of the Iberian peninsula and Europe. The city was soon bustling with activity, despite its lack of space, a drawback it had inherited from the late Middle Ages. In the words of J. Ruiz, the city thereafter became 'the epitome of a free port; indeed, a port and nothing but a port, where goods were exchanged, shipped and discharged'.

Seville rode out its decline as best it could. Ever since 1608, the year in which the highest volume of goods was exported to Spanish America, trade had gradually taken a downturn. This is attested to by a significant figure: in the 17th century, untilled and fallow land together accounted for over half the total farmland, while export cargoes included only one genuinely Sevillian product—olive oil.

The Consulate moves to Cádiz: the consular building.

19th century.
Elevation of the consular building in Cádiz.
308 x 485 mm. MP. Europa y África, 70.

Seville's trade monopoly was phased out in the second half of the 17th century. The transfer of fleet headquarters to Cádiz in 1680 foreshadowed the order, in 1717, for the Casa de la Contratación *and the Consulate to follow suit. This marked a new era in the life of the 'Old' Consulate, far removed from the ambience of Seville's Cathedral steps and the Guadalquivir river.*

Cádiz—city of merchants.

1735
Crest and blazons of the city of Cádiz.
Inscribed: 'Fr. Francisco Rodríguez Parra, ordinis minoris delineavit et esculpsit, anno 1735'.
270 x 186 mm. (293 x 210 mm).
Part of the royal warrant, issued in San Lorenzo on 19 November 1734, decreeing that all members of the Cádiz city council should be of noble birth.
MP. Escudos y Árboles genealógicos, 291.

The city, with its millennial history, welcomed the relocation of the Consulate and the Casa de la Contratación, *taking it to be an assertion of Cádiz's supremacy over Seville. Thus began the political and economic ascendancy of a city that was to play a vital role in the 19th century.*

In the final analysis, it appears that by allowing itself to be taken in by the promise of quick profits and monopolistic control of the Indies trade, Seville had neglected modernization and the development of its agricultural and industrial sectors. Only the textile industry had maintained reasonable levels of production, despite a sharp drop in the number of looms in operation. The only other enterprises of any note were State-owned concerns in tobacco, minting coins, saltpeter, timber and artillery.

Founding New Consulates

The 'Free Trade Regulations' of 12 October 1778, which were a codification of measures suggested in 'The Decree and Instruction' of 16 October 1765, marked the peak of deregulation of trade with the Indies, a process which had been quite gradual. In late 1778, Charles III asked the Church authorities of Seville to study the feasibility of establishing another consulate and propose appropriate members. As a result, the *Consulado Marítimo y Terrestre de Sevilla,* (Sea and Land Consulate of Seville), known as the New Consulate of Seville, was founded on 24 November 1784.

The statutes of the New Consulate were adopted both in Spain and in New World port cities where the Indies trade was centered: Caracas and Guatemala in 1793, Buenos Aires and Havana in 1794, and Cartagena, Veracruz, Guadalajara and Santiago de Chile in 1796. The new Spanish American consulates embodied the Bourbon aim of stimulating colonial trade in areas previously ostracized or overshadowed by the two great trade centers—Lima and Mexico City.

The New Consulate's territorial jurisdiction included the Archbishopric of Seville and all towns and villages that did not come under the jurisdiction of the

The Consulate moves to Cádiz: the Diputación del Comercio, *Seville.*

[undated]
Lithograph of the Consulate by Santigosa.
460 x 617 mm.

Once the Consulate and Casa de la Contratación *had been transferred to Cádiz, a trade delegation known as the* Diputación del Comercio *was held over in Seville. Its function was to exercise judicial authority in disputes related to New World trade. Despite an ongoing relationship between the two institutions, relations gradually deteriorated and, by the mid-18th century, activity at the* Diputación *had virtually come to a standstill.*

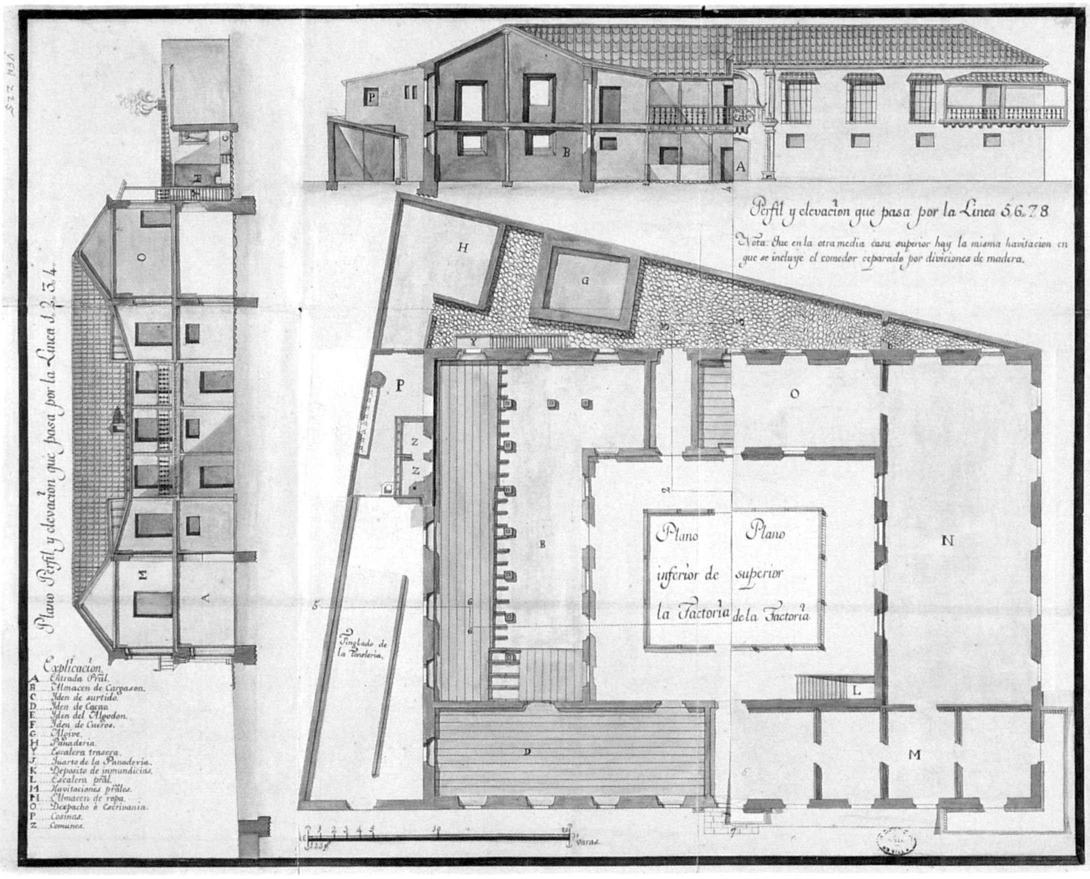

'The Philippines Company': The Maracaibo factory.

7 September 1790, [Maracaibo].
Plan of the Real Compañía de Filipinas *factory in Maracaibo, showing elevations and plans of the ground and first floors.*
By the engineer, Francisco Jacot.
429 x 539 mm.
MP. Venezuela, 225.

The building was purchased by the Royal Treasury to house armaments and artillery supplies and as office premises for the customs and the tobacco monopoly. It included the administrator's house and tobacco warehouses.

Consulate of Cádiz. A royal order was issued on 21 December 1784 by which Sanlúcar de Barrameda was likewise placed under its jurisdiction until the town acquired its own consulate in 1805.

Unlike the old consulates, which had been established in response to a need voiced by merchants, the New Consulate was a Crown initiative. It was placed under royal patronage and was funded by the *Sociedad Económica del País* (Economic Association of the Nation). Although the Consulate was ostensibly expected to perform the traditional consular function of intervening in disputes between merchants and expediting settlements, its ultimate purpose was to stimulate the local economy in such sectors as agriculture, factories and industry and to reinstate active trade between Seville and the New World.

Reactivation of the agricultural sector led to a closer working relationship between landowners and merchants. In keeping with the provisions of the Consulate statutes, the marketing of farm produce created a need for public works to facili-

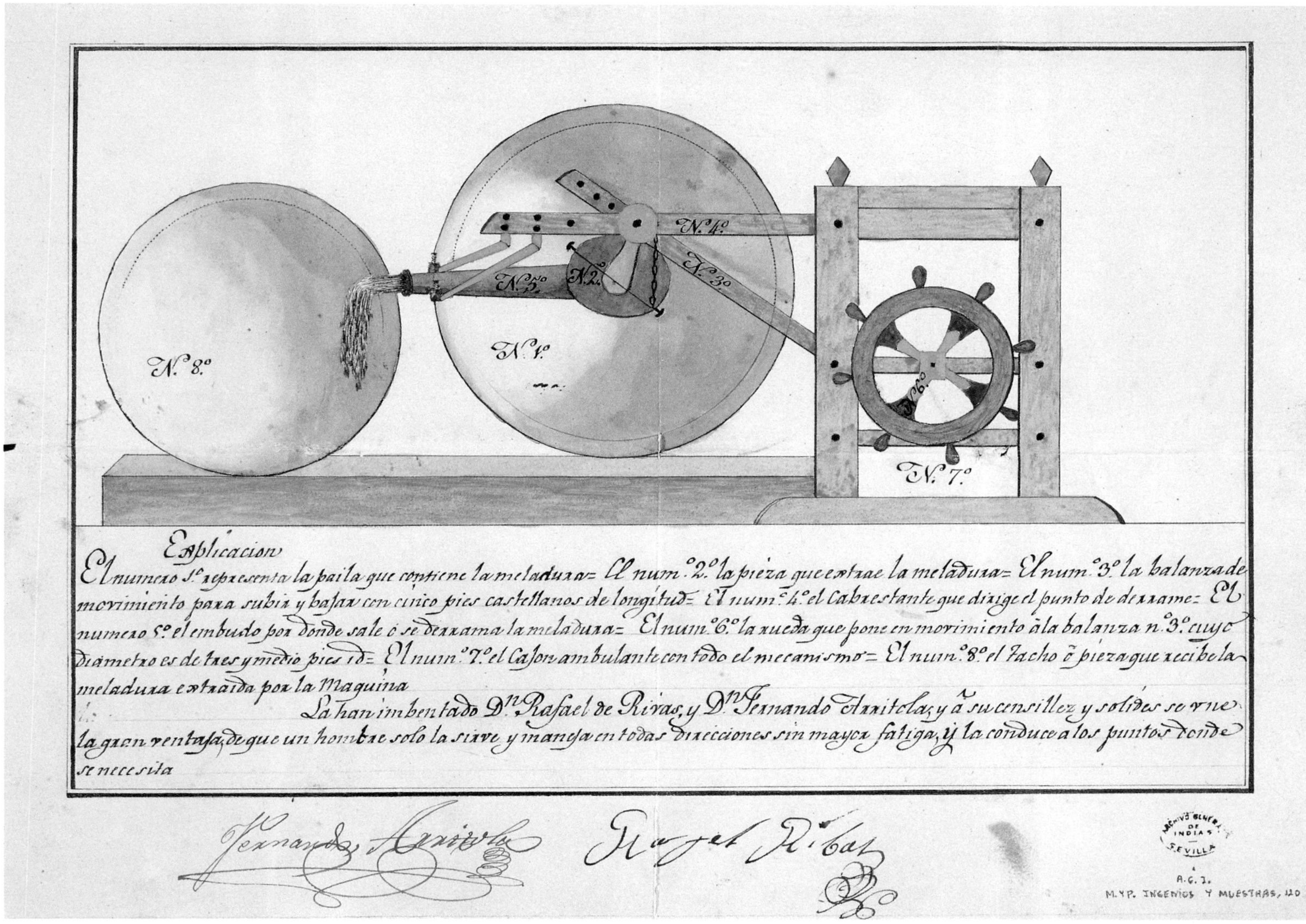

Trade commodities: sugar.

28 August 1826.
Device for decanting molasses.
Built by Fernando Arritola and Rafael Ribas.
290 x 375 mm.
MP. Ingenios y Muestras, 120.

Sugar was one of the main commodities imported from the New World. The Captaincy General of Cuba granted the inventors of the device shown above an eight-year license to build and sell it. The legend featured under the diagram states that 'it is simple and robust and has the advantage that any man may operate it on his own without untoward fatigue and direct it to wherever it is required'.

N.º 256.

ACCION DE LA COMPAÑIA REAL DE ZARAGOZA

Ynteresa D.n Juan Lorenzo de Galarraga Contad. Princip.l de esta R.l Comp.a y Vezino de Zarag.a En esta Accion de doscientos cinquenta Pesos de á ciento veinte y ocho quartos, que ha entregado en la Caxa de la Compañia. Y Nosotros los Directores de ella le otorgamos obligacion de contribuir las Cantidades, que de las ganancias se repartieren, à quien se presentare con ella à los tiempos que se señalaren: Y para cumplirlo assi, mandamos dár esta Declaracion à su favor firmada por Nosotros, sellada con el Sello de la Compañia, y refrendada por el Secretario de ella. En Zaragoza à treinta dias del mes de Agosto de mil setecientos quarenta y ocho años.

Trading companies: the Real Compañía de Zaragoza.

30 August 1748, Zaragoza.
Share certificate no. 256 issued by the company.
165 x 250 mm. (200 x 294 mm).
MP. Monedas, 36.

In the upper, central portion of the border, the Virgin of the Pillar is shown standing above the coat-of-arms of Zaragoza. The figures of SS James and George appear in the upper corners. One noteworthy feature is the well-preserved white wax Company seal which features the bridge in Santiago over the river Ebro. Beneath it is a boatman, with the towers of the Cathedral of El Pilar in the background. This share certificate belonged to the chief accountant of the company, a native of Zaragoza, who bequeathed it to the king in his will.

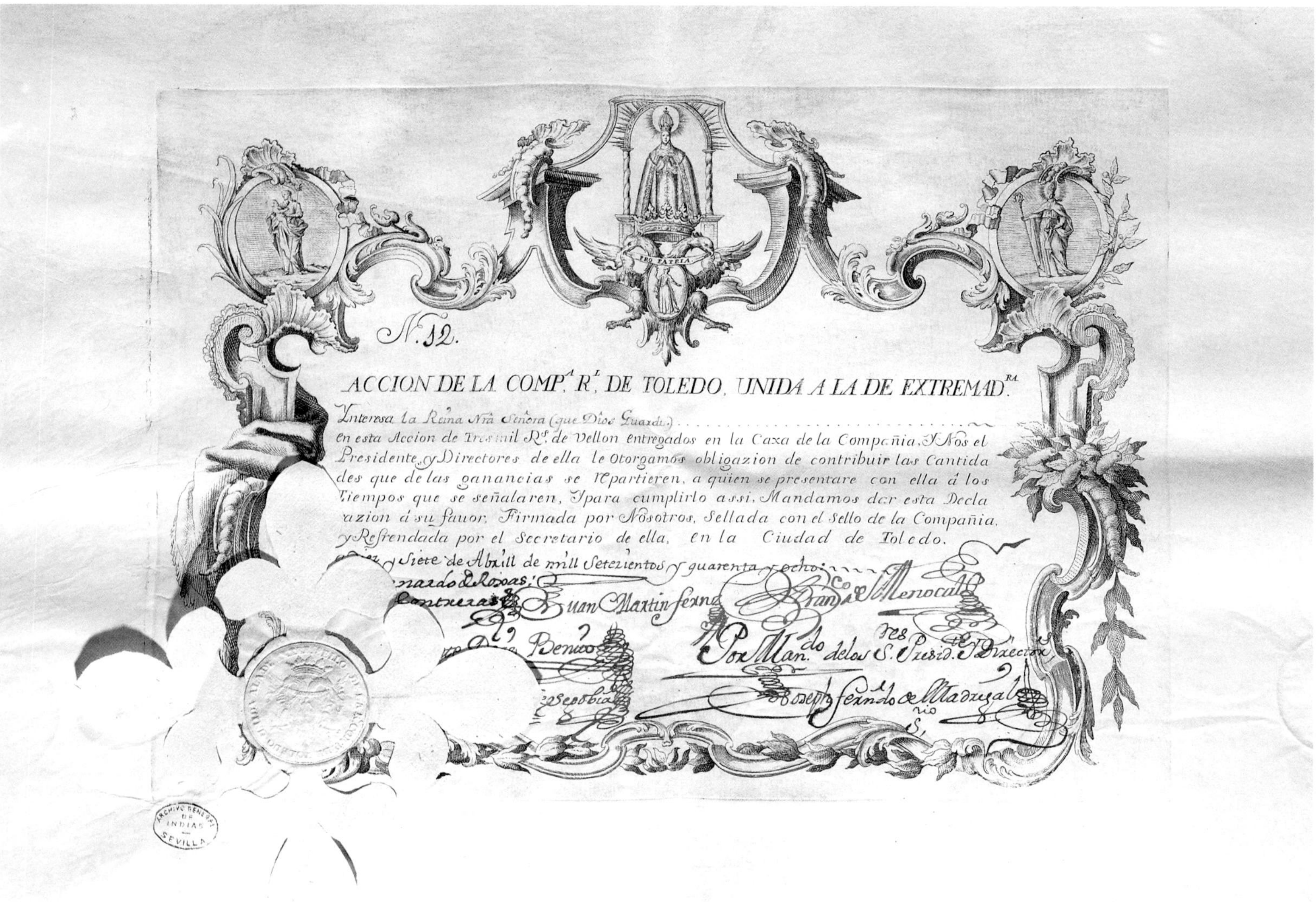

N.º 12.

ACCION DE LA COMP.A R.L DE TOLEDO, UNIDA A LA DE EXTREMAD.RA

Interesa la Reina Nra Señora (que Dios Guarde) .... en esta Accion de Tres mil R.s de Vellon entregados en la Caxa de la Compañia, Y Nos el Presidente, y Directores de ella le Otorgamos obligazion de contribuir las Cantidades que de las ganancias se repartieren, a quien se presentare con ella a los Tiempos que se señalaren, Y para cumplirlo assi, Mandamos dar esta Declarazion a su favor, Firmada por Nosotros, Sellada con el Sello de la Compañia, y Refrendada por el Secretario de ella, en la Ciudad de Toledo. ... y Siete de Abrill de mill Setezientos y quarenta y ocho.

Trading companies: the Real Compañía de Toledo.

17 April 1748, Toledo.
Share certificate no. 12 issued by the Real Compañía de Toledo, *in conjunction with that of* Extremadura.
203 x 290 mm. (296 x 423 mm).
MP. Monedas, 42.

This share certificate belonged to the queen and was worth 3,000 copper reales. In the upper central portion of the border stands Our Lady of the Tabernacle, the patroness of Toledo. Beneath her is St Leocadia and, on either side, SS Joseph and Ildefonsus. The seal features the coat-of-arms of Toledo with similar motifs to those found on the border.

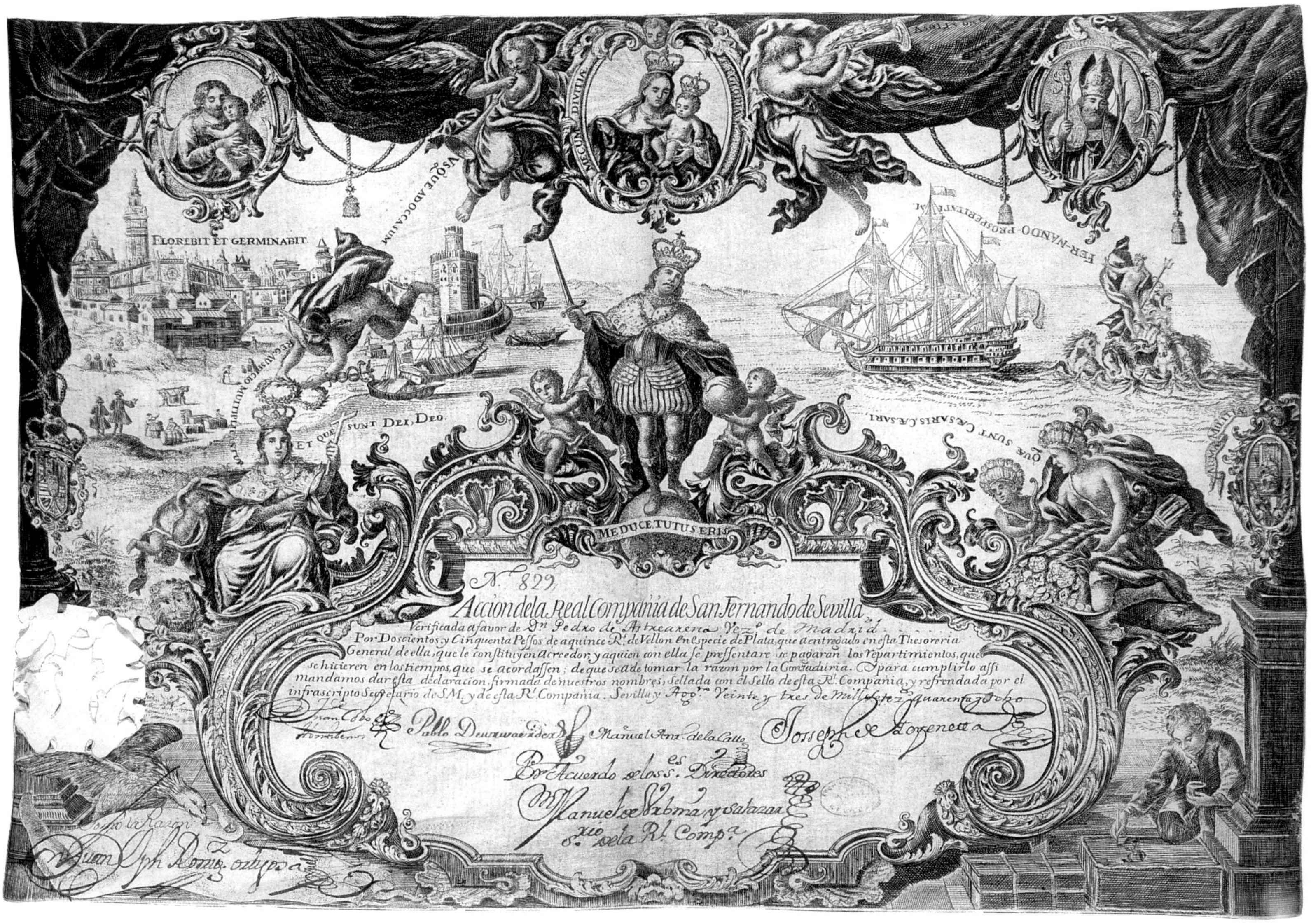

Trading companies: the Real Compañía de San Fernando.

23 August 1748, Seville.
Share certificate no. 829 issued by the company.
By Pedro Tortolero.
283 x 405 mm.
MP. Monedas, 33.

'The aim of this company is to establish factories producing pure silk, and mixtures of silk with gold and silver, in addition to wool and hemp. It is also the company's intention to extract all the surplus fruit of the kingdom, both for foreign kingdoms and for the kingdoms and provinces of America, on the terms expressed below.' (GONZÁLEZ SÁNCHEZ, C.A.: La Real Compañía de Comercio de San Fernando de Sevilla. *Seville, City Council, pp. 133.)*

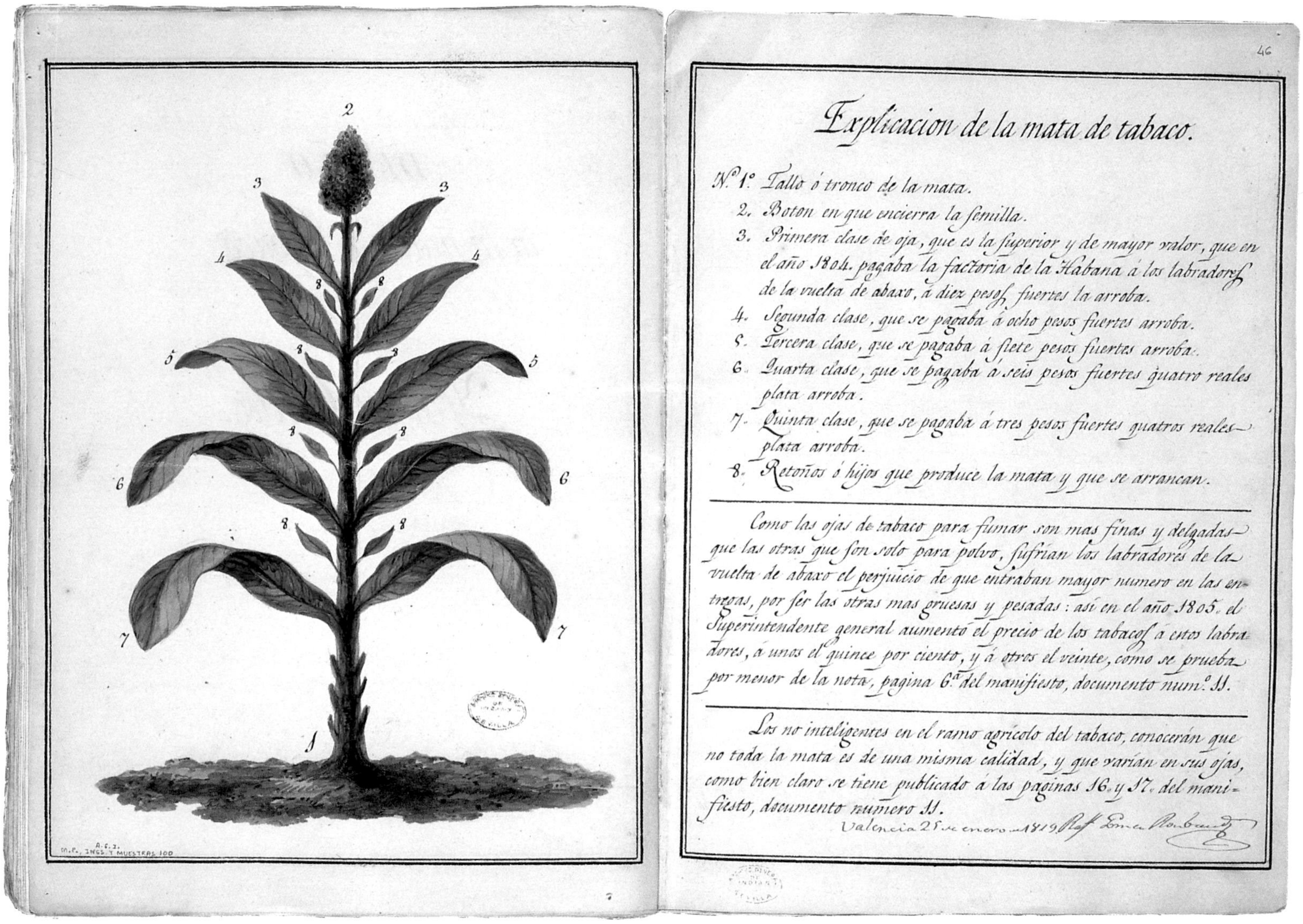

46

Explicacion de la mata de tabaco.

N.º 1.º Tallo ó tronco de la mata.
2. Boton en que encierra la semilla.
3. Primera clase de oja, que es la superior y de mayor valor, que en el año 1804. pagaba la factoria de la Habana á los labradores de la vuelta de abaxo, á diez pesos fuertes la arroba.
4. Segunda clase, que se pagaba á ocho pesos fuertes arroba.
5. Tercera clase, que se pagaba á siete pesos fuertes arroba.
6. Quarta clase, que se pagaba á seis pesos fuertes quatro reales plata arroba.
7. Quinta clase, que se pagaba á tres pesos fuertes quatros reales plata arroba.
8. Retoños ó hijos que produce la mata y que se arrancan.

Como las ojas de tabaco para fumar son mas finas y delgadas que las otras que son solo para polvo, sufrian los labradores de la vuelta de abaxo el perjuicio de que entraban mayor numero en las entregas, por ser las otras mas gruesas y pesadas: así en el año 1805. el Superintendente general aumentó el precio de los tabacos á estos labradores, á unos el quince por ciento, y á otros el veinte, como se prueba por menor de la nota, pagina 6.ª del manifiesto, documento num.º 11.

Los no inteligentes en el ramo agrícolo del tabaco, conocerán que no toda la mata es de una misma calidad, y que varían en sus ojas, como bien claro se tiene publicado á las paginas 16. y 17. del manifiesto, documento numero 11.

Valencia 25 de enero de 1819

Trade commodities: tobacco.

25 January 1819, Valencia.
Tobacco factory on the island of Cuba, with a report on its cultivation and processing.
305 x 425 mm.
Featured in a report by Rafael Gómez Rombaud, honorary minister of the Council of the Indies, on tobacco and the factory in Havana. Fols. 45 v.–46 r.
MP. Ingenios y Muestras, 100.

Tobacco became popular in Spain after being introduced as a medicinal plant. The Fábrica de Tabacos de Sevilla, *founded in 1620, was the first such production facility in Europe. The* Compañía de San Cristóbal *of Havana was placed in charge of the tobacco trade monopoly in Cuba. Apart from that privilege, the company was entitled to export sugar and leather from the island.*

Trade commodities: cochineal.

29 April 1620.
'This is a diagram of a nopal, cultivated in many areas, to which the cochineal has swarmed. The Indians are harvesting to their delight.'
288 x 218 mm.
Quoted from a description of how the nopal or prickly pear is used to breed cochineal.
MP. Estampas, 70.

The aforementioned document mentions large areas along the Hacha river, Santa Marta and the provinces of Caracas and Venezuela given over to this type of cultivation. Cochineal breeding is directly related to nopal farming in Spanish America. The cochineal is an insect which reveals marked sexual dimorphism: the male is whitish, while the female varies in color from red to blood-red. (GOMIS BLANCO, A.: 'Tinctures and American Dye-plants', in La agricultura viajera. *Barcelona, Lunwerg, 1990, pp. 200.)*

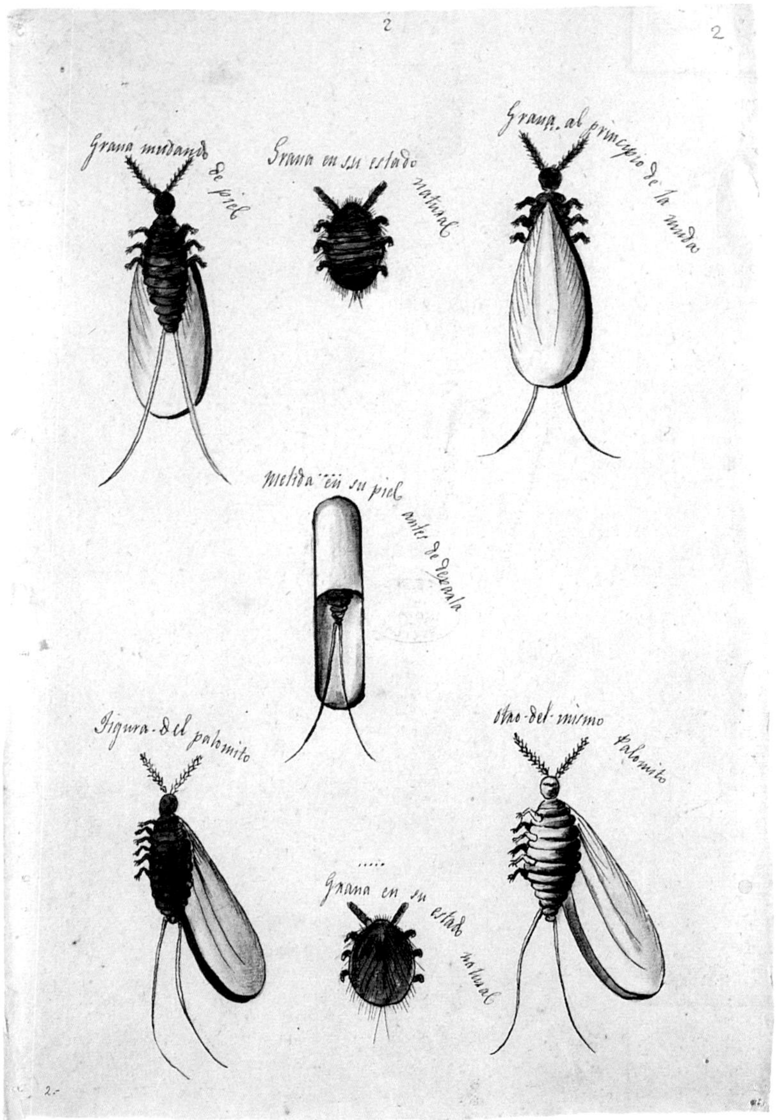

Cochineal: breeding, harvesting and processing.

29 October 1821.
The production of cochineal, from harvest to processing.
3 sheets (305 x 210 mm).
MP. México, 515.

There were those who thought cochineal to be the fruit of the prickly pear. The best way of killing the insects was to heat them in an oven. The Creole, José Antonio de Alzate y Ramírez (1737–1799), provided a full description of the insect's nature and breeding habits in his work, Memoria. *(Gomis Blanco, A.: op. cit. pp. 201.)*

tate navigation along the Guadalquivir river. In 1794, the authorities decided to build hydraulic works, including a canal. All river traffic and related affairs were controlled by the Consulate of Seville, at least until 1817, after which they were placed under the direction of the newly formed *Compañía de Navegación del Guadalquivir* (Guadalquivir Shipping Company).

The fact that the Consulate had an express mandate to develop trade with the New World was enshrined in its statutes, which stated that managerial posts could only be filled by those who traded with the Americas. The need to restore those links is borne out by trade figures, which show to what extent Seville had become cut off from the overseas possessions with which it had once had close commercial ties.

Like its predecessor, the New Consulate acted as a financial resource for the Crown to fall back on in times of need, although to a considerably lesser degree

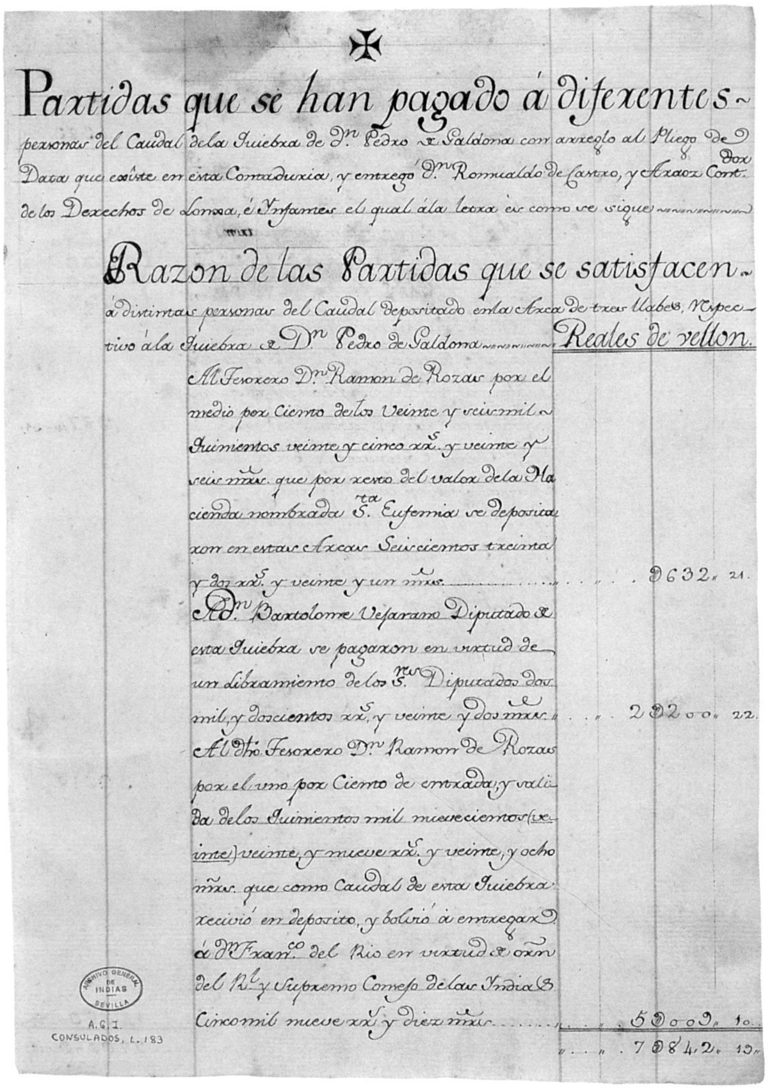

Partidas que se han pagado á diferentes personas del Caudal de la Quiebra de Dn. Pedro de Galdona con arreglo al Pliego de Data que existe en esta Contaduria, y entregó Dn. Romualdo de Castro, y Arroz Contor. de los Derechos de Lonxa, é Infames el qual á la letra es como se sigue

Razon de las Partidas que se satisfacen á diversas personas del Caudal depositado en la Arca de tres llaves, respectivo á la Quiebra de Dn. Pedro de Galdona ... Reales de vellon.

Al Tesorero Dn. Ramon de Rozas por el medio por Ciento de los Veinte y seis mil quinientos veinte y cinco rs. y veinte y seis mrs. que por resto del valor de la Hacienda nombrada Sta. Eufemia se depositaron en estas Arcas Seiscientos treinta y dos rs. y veinte y un mrs. ... 9632. 21.

A Dn. Bartolome Vesarano Diputado de esta Quiebra se pagaron en virtud de un Libramiento de los Sres. Diputados dos mil, y doscientos rs. y veinte y dos mrs. ... 2200. 22.

Al dho Tesorero Dn. Ramon de Rozas por el uno por Ciento de entrada, y salida de los Quinientos mil novecientos sesenta y nueve rs. y veinte, y ocho mrs. que como Caudal de esta Quiebra recivió en deposito, y bolvió á entregar á Dn. Franco. del Rio en virtud de orn. del Rl. y Supremo Consejo de las Indias Cinco mil nueve rs. y diez mrs. ... 5009. 10.

... 7842. 19.

The trade crisis: bankruptcies.

2 May 1785, Seville.
Amounts paid to various people after liquidating Pedro de Galdona's assets.
The payments were made by the accountant of the Commodity Exchange, Romualdo de Castro y Arroz.
340 x 238 mm.
Bound in parchment.
Consulados, L. 183, fol. 1.

In the 18th century, the original system of a 'waiting period', whereby merchants were granted a loan extension by the Consulate, gave way to rapid liquidation when a contract had been broken.
The Consulate attempted to reach out-of-court settlements, but the increase in bad debts and liquidation proceedings made it difficult to reach such agreements, and led to bankruptcies.

A Seville industry: silk manufacture.

1785
Seville silk ribbon manufacturers' trademarks.
305 x 210 mm.
MP. Ingenios y Muestras, 60.

Seville had a flourishing, traditional textile industry which was boosted by demand from the American market. Domínguez Ortiz estimates that, at the height of its production, the industry had over 16,000 looms in operation and engaged 130,000 silk workers.

The Consulate's participation in public festivities: the coronation of Charles III.

11 November 1759, Cádiz.
Facade of the Consulate of Indies Merchants on the day Charles III was crowned.
580 x 390 mm.
MP. Estampas, 56.

The frontispiece of the building bore the following quatrain written in the form of an acrostic in praise of the monarch:

C on propensión bien constante
O bsequíolo el gyrasol
N o pierde de vista a el sol
S iguiéndole más amante
V iva expressión, y elegante
L eal demuestra el Consulado
A Carlos que proclamado
D emuestra su luz brillante.

The Consulate's participation in public festivities: the princes' weddings.

1816
Monument raised by the Consulate in San Antonio square to commemorate the royal weddings of Prince Ferdinand VII and his brother Charles to María Isabel and María Asís de Braganza.
220 x 262 mm (435 x 278 mm).
MP. Europa y África, 100.

Work on the monument was directed by Juan de Lizasoaín, Director of the Academy of Sculpture of Cádiz, and Miguel Zumalave, a master builder from the same city and member of the Sociedad de Amigos del País. *The figure of Felicity and the lions were sculpted by José Giscardi and those of Justice and Prudence by José Fernández Guerrero, Deputy Director of the Cádiz Academy.*

than before. The Consulate's financial contributions to the Crown included two million reales to fund the war with France, a similar amount for war with England, fourteen million reales raised as a 'compulsory national subsidy loan' and funds to finance the Peninsular War.

As Antonia Heredia concluded in her study of the period, the institution was directed by an administrative board which met twice a year and was made up of a prior, consuls, councillors, a secretary, an accountant and a treasurer. The shareholders also met twice a year. The New Consulate remained in existence from 1784 to 1860. During that period, a key date was 1829, when the Code of Commerce was published.

The Haulers of Cádiz

Loading and unloading cargo in the ports of Seville and Cádiz created a small army of haulers or porters, all of whom needed a license that cost 15 ducats. The license entitled its holder to *'load, unload, fetch and bring, on a cart or on horseback, any goods to be loaded on any vessel in the municipality and port of Cádiz'.* The occupation was handed down from father to son.

The regulations dating from 1719 stipulated the number of haulers and carts that could pass through customs at any one time, in addition to the fee haulers could charge and the number of licenses to be offered by the Consulate, which was in charge of the whole operation.

The Consulate started exercising these duties in 1743. After reviewing the work carried out by the four existing teams of haulers, it proposed implementing a number of measures that would first have to be approved by the Crown. Among those was the drafting of a new set of tariffs, which was approved on 24 October 1746.

Since taking on its supervisory role, the Consulate attempted to settle disputes between the haulers. In 1749, it managed to persuade the three teams of haulers and porters to reach an agreement on fees and the distribution of work, although a subsequent attempt to bring draymen into the agreement failed on account of their different resources and working conditions.

Concerned about safety in the transportation of goods, the Consulate presented the city council and syndics with a scheme for replacing the system of conveyance on horseback by another, safer method. After several meetings with the associations of haulers and customs workers, on 26 April 1804 the Tribunal issued a law barring the use of panniers or hand conveyances, which were to be replaced by horse-drawn carts or drays. The new regulation was ratified by a royal order of 23 November 1815.

Efforts to Rescue Trade

When economic relations between Spain and its colonies started breaking apart due to competition from other European countries, proposals were put forward to reactivate trade. One such proposal was to found schools of commerce in Seville and Cádiz. In the words of R. Fernández and S. Tinoco, it was a case of 'resorting to education to develop productive forces'. The thinking behind the proposal was to focus on developing and perfecting 'human capital'. In short, the idea was to educate merchants so that they would acquire a greater degree of confidence, effectiveness, skill and ultimately profit in their activity. The move was directed both at those wishing to take up trade as a career and those who were already working in the field. Also included were people active in production and manufacturing, for whom the faculties of Agriculture and Physical-Chemical Sciences were established.

The Crown urged the Consulates to bring these educational projects to completion by the late-18th or early-19th century. However, the Consulates of both Cádiz and Seville dragged their feet, and it was only at the end of the 18th century that the project got under way. A modest school of commerce and mathematics was opened in Cádiz; nothing of the sort happened in Seville.

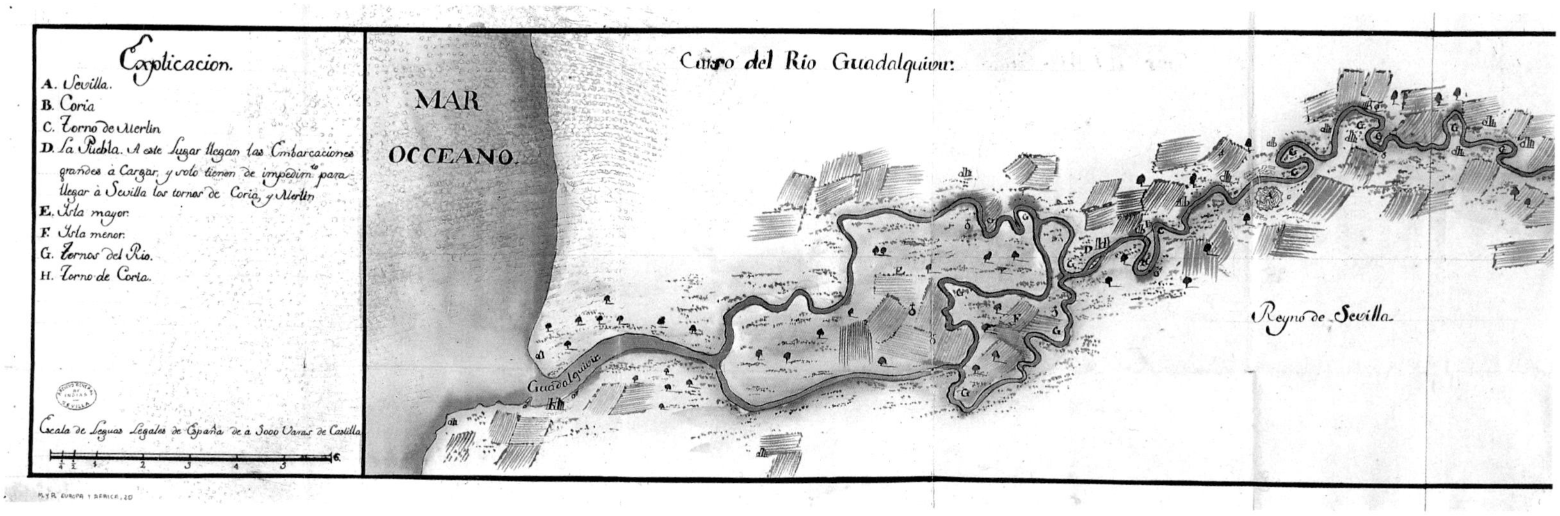

A natural trade route:
the Guadalquivir river.

14 November 1757.
Lower course of the Guadalquivir river, from the provincial border between Córdoba and Seville (Peñaflor).
238 x 990 mm.
MP. Europa y África, 20.

The Guadalquivir had acted as a natural trade route for Seville since Roman times. Sailing upstream, it was navigable from there as far as Córdoba. The loss of the port's Indies monopoly, the increase in the tonnage of ships, smuggling, navigational hazards along the winding river and the perilous Sanlúcar sandbar led to the decline of Seville's harbor. Seville eventually relinquished its calling as 'a port and gateway to the Atlantic ocean', a status wrested from it by Cádiz.

A variety of reasons was put forward to account for the failure of the venture: war, epidemics and lack of funds. However, such cities as Barcelona and Alicante, which were affected by the same constraints, managed to successfully carry off similar projects.

The Decline of the Consulates

Under the Code of Commerce of 1829, so-called 'Trade Tribunals' were appointed to replace the old consulates. They were empowered to settle mercantile issues, while the *Audiencias* acted as appeals courts. The Tribunals were made up of a prior, appointed annually, two consuls and a legal consultant. The prior and consuls had to be professional merchants. The Tribunals were dissolved by a decree, issued on 6 December 1868, and their jurisdiction transferred to judges of the first instance. A royal decree of 9 April 1886 provided for the establishment of Chambers of Commerce, Industry and Shipping that acted as arbitrators in matters brought to them by traders, industrialists and shipowners, actively seeking amicable agreements and settlements between interested parties. From the founding of the original Consulate of Indies Merchants until the dissolution of the last of the consulates, four centuries of the history of Seville and Cádiz had gone by. The mark left by those institutions in both cities can still be seen today in the Commodity Exchange and the Archive of the Indies.

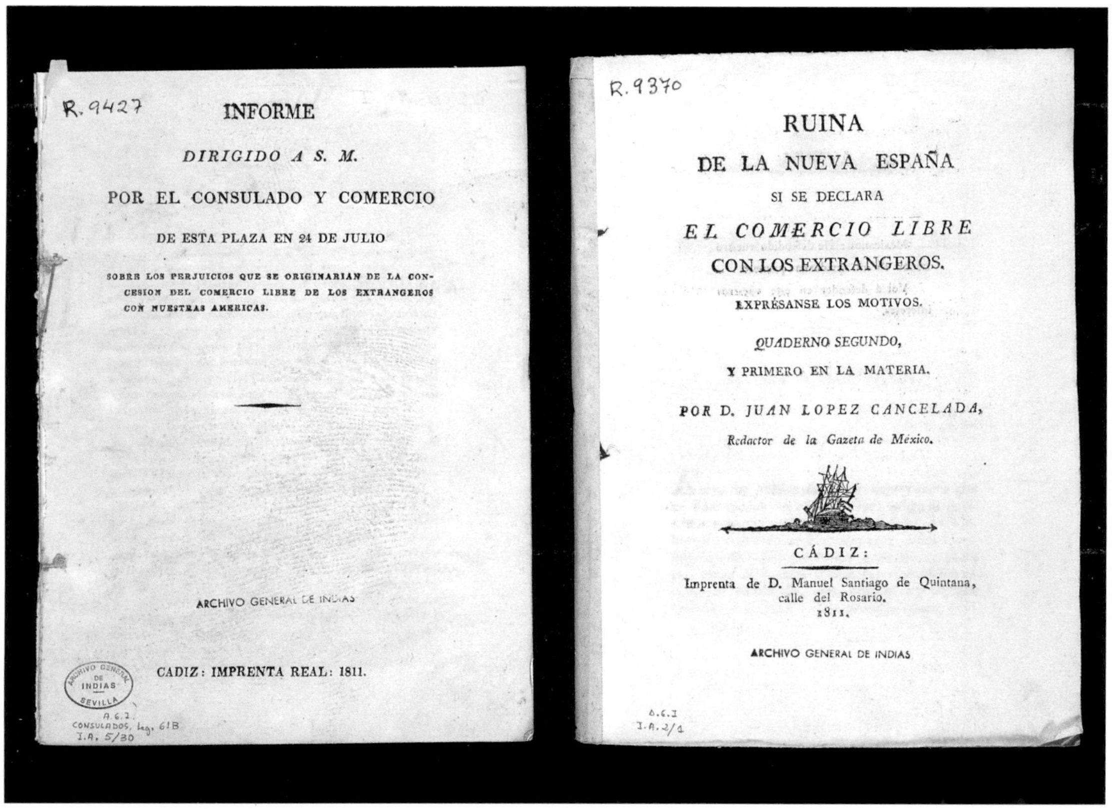
R. 9427

INFORME

DIRIGIDO A S. M.

POR EL CONSULADO Y COMERCIO

DE ESTA PLAZA EN 24 DE JULIO

SOBRE LOS PERJUICIOS QUE SE ORIGINARIAN DE LA CONCESION DEL COMERCIO LIBRE DE LOS EXTRANGEROS CON NUESTRAS AMERICAS.

ARCHIVO GENERAL DE INDIAS

CADIZ: IMPRENTA REAL: 1811.

R. 9370

RUINA

DE LA NUEVA ESPAÑA

SI SE DECLARA

EL COMERCIO LIBRE

CON LOS EXTRANGEROS.

EXPRÉSANSE LOS MOTIVOS.

QUADERNO SEGUNDO,

Y PRIMERO EN LA MATERIA.

POR D. JUAN LOPEZ CANCELADA,

Redactor de la Gazeta de Mexico.

CÁDIZ:

Imprenta de D. Manuel Santiago de Quintana, calle del Rosario. 1811.

ARCHIVO GENERAL DE INDIAS

Extending free trade to foreigners.

1811
'Free trade with foreigners would bring about the downfall of New Spain.'
By Juan López Cancelada.
Cádiz: printed by Manuel Santiago de Quintana in 1811.
84 pp. (20.3 x 14.5 cm).
Biblioteca, L.A. 2/1.

In the foreword to the above title, the author states: 'Of all the issues dealt with in Congress, none has such grave consequences as the proposal to allow foreigners to trade with New Spain. Those who have requested the privilege and those prepared to grant it may be acting in good faith, without realizing that their acts will bring about the downfall of that country'.

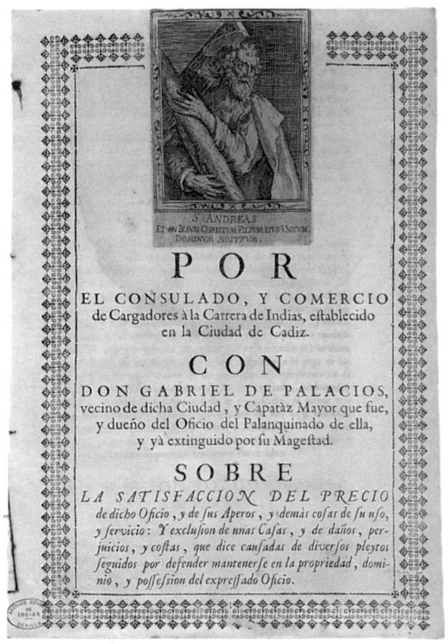
POR

EL CONSULADO, Y COMERCIO de Cargadores à la Carrera de Indias, establecido en la Ciudad de Cadiz.

CON

DON GABRIEL DE PALACIOS, vecino de dicha Ciudad, y Capatàz Mayor que fue, y dueño del Oficio del Palanquinado de ella, y yà extinguido por su Mageftad.

SOBRE

LA SATISFACCION DEL PRECIO de dicho Oficio, y de sus Aperos, y demàs cosas de su uso, y servicio: Y exclusion de unas Casas, y de daños, perjuicios, y costas, que dice causadas de diversos pleytos seguidos por defender mantenerse en la propriedad, dominio, y possession del expressado Oficio.

Haulage: haulers and porters.

Circa 1735.
Lawsuit between the prior and consuls of the Consulate of Indies Merchants and Gabriel de Palacios Agudo, foreman of a haulage business, concerning the annulment of that occupation.
1 sheet, 20 fols.
Consulados, 1775.

In 1690, Charles II authorized Cristóbal de Palacios Agudo to work as foreman of a haulage business. Seven years later, the latter provided for passing on the privilege to his descendants. In the early-18th century, the business was inherited by his son, Gabriel de Palacios, under whose administration it underwent marked changes, as attested to in a protracted litigation with the Consulate.

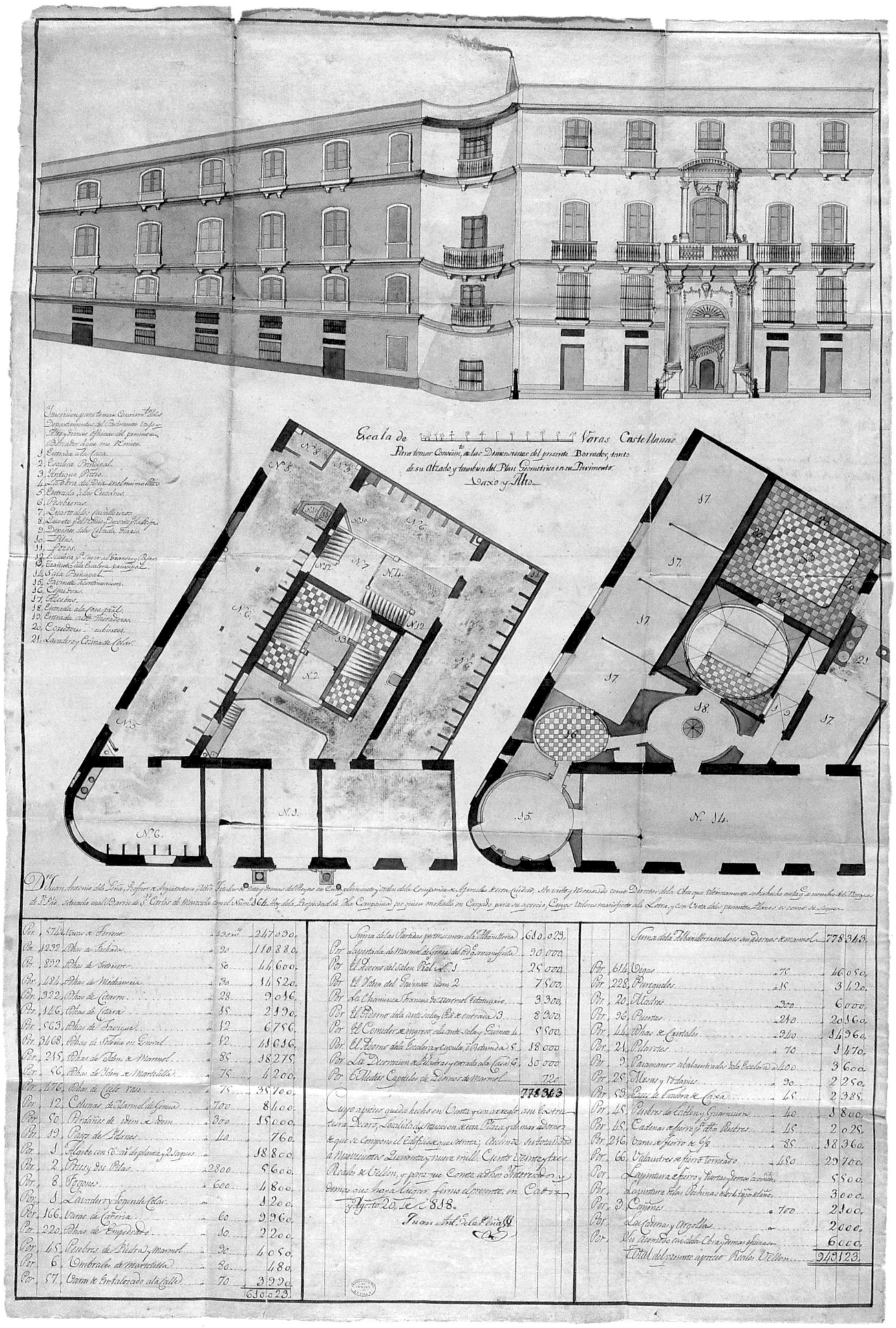

Haulage: the Draymen's Guild.

20 August 1818, Cádiz.
Plan of the building acquired by the Draymen's Guild of Cádiz, in the San Carlos quarter no. 164.
By Juan Antonio de la Peña, architect.
1,018 x 675 mm.
MP. Europa y África, 71.

Since being in charge of haulage, the Consulate attempted to settle differences between rival teams of porters, draymen and stevedores. Its endeavors failed, however, on account of the different working conditions and resources of the various trades.

Haulage: new regulations.

26 April 1804, Cádiz.
View of the new cart designed for urban transport.
275 x 440 mm.
Included in a Consulate by-law regulating haulage in the city of Cádiz.
MP. Ingenios y Muestras, 299.

The existing system of haulage in Cádiz was fraught with practices that led to damaged goods and trade losses, in addition to a large number of accidents involving haulers and passers-by. Consulate representatives and city councillors met to seek solutions. They also conferred with the Draymen's and Customs Workers Guilds. It was not long before an agreement was drawn up whereby the system of using panniers on horseback was replaced by horse-drawn carts like the one shown in the illustration.

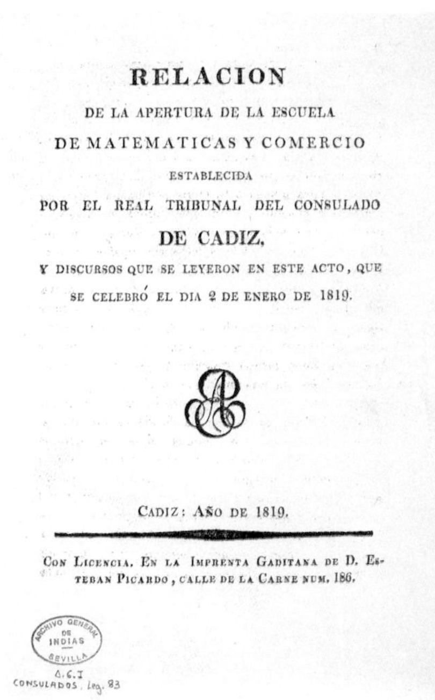
RELACION
DE LA APERTURA DE LA ESCUELA
DE MATEMATICAS Y COMERCIO
ESTABLECIDA
POR EL REAL TRIBUNAL DEL CONSULADO
DE CADIZ,
Y DISCURSOS QUE SE LEYERON EN ESTE ACTO, QUE SE CELEBRÓ EL DIA 2 DE ENERO DE 1819.

CADIZ: AÑO DE 1819.

CON LICENCIA. EN LA IMPRENTA GADITANA DE D. ESTEBAN PICARDO, CALLE DE LA CARNE NUM. 186.

The opening ceremony at the School of Commerce, Cádiz.

1819
'Report on the opening of the School of Mathematics and Commerce, established by the Tribunal of the Consulate of Cádiz, and the speeches that were delivered during the ceremony, held on 2 January 1819.'
200 x 145 mm.
Consulados, 83.

'Nodoby doubts that, in order to exercise a profession in commerce, apart from being endowed with a flair for that occupation, one requires a broad knowledge of the different fields it encompasses. However, most believe that practice is sufficient to become accomplished in the profession, while only those familiar with the benefits of a methodical training, wherein the various disciplines of art or science are reduced to set principles and general rules, know that practice alone is insufficient when not grounded in the theoretical principles that precede it' (pp. 10).

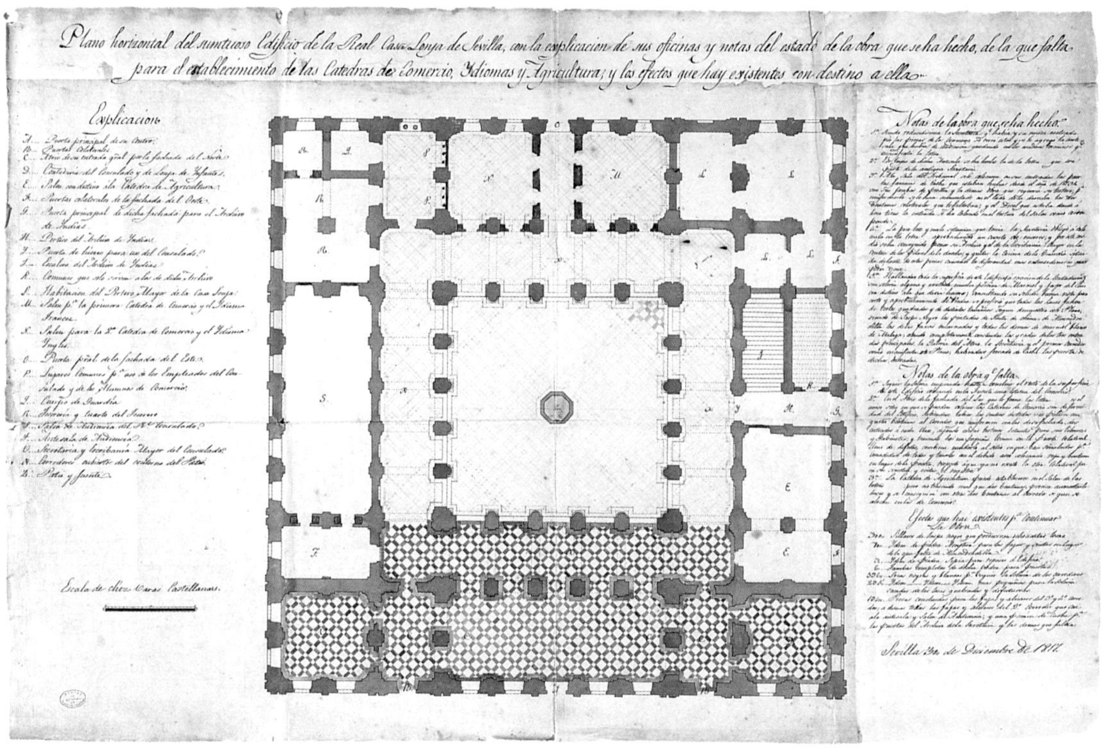

Attempts to rescue the economy: the Seville School of Commerce.

30 December 1817, Seville.
'Ground plan of the luxury "Royal Commodity Exchange of Seville", with a description of its offices and a progress report on building work and the tasks remaining to complete the faculties of Commerce, Languages and Agriculture, with a list of the fittings to be included.'
By Francisco González de Haro.
552 x 820 mm.
MP. Europa y África, 110.

The Seville School of Commerce was founded as a result of the royal decree governing the founding of the New Consulate: 'The Consulate shall determine the resources required for establishing the Schools of Commerce and Agriculture and for revealing and conveying the chemical secrets required for perfecting the Arts and, having drawn up the corresponding plans, shall submit them to me for approval (Article 4)'.

Attempts to rescue the economy: the Cádiz School of Commerce.

1815
The Cádiz School of Commerce.
125 x 175 mm. (200 x 280 mm).
Figure no. 9 of the 'Collection of views of important buildings in Cádiz, with a brief account of their foundation, purpose and artistic value'.
Cádiz: Hércules printworks, 1815.
MP. Europa y África, 95.

In 1804, the Consulate decided to found a School of Commerce to raise the standards of trade and commerce, as lack of training had been identified as one of the reasons for a decline in the sector. The school was built in San Francisco Street, next to the old customshouse, under the direction of Pedro Albisu.

Opposite
Merchant opposition to the Code of Commerce.

24 November 1829, Madrid.
Communiqué issued by Luis López Ballesteros, State and Treasury Secretary, notifying the Consulate of Cádiz of the implementation of the royal order of 16 November 1829 concerning the Trade Tribunals.
300 x 207 mm.
Bound in pasteboard, with parchment spine and corners.
Consulados, L. 1083, fol. 18.

Despite the Consulate's protests, the Trade Tribunals were effectively instated to replace the old consulates. However, their activity was short-lived—by a decree of 1868, issued for the purpose of standardizing local charters, their powers were transferred to judges of the first instance. The Code of Commerce, promulgated in 1885, failed to reinstate the mercantile jurisdiction.

18

MINISTERIO
DE
HACIENDA DE ESPAÑA.

Cadiz 7. de Diciembre de 1829.

Al Ministro respectivo expediente dirigiendose á S.M. la conveniente exposicion acerca de las dificultades que ofrece el cumplimiento de esta R.l orden.

R.

He dado cuenta al Rey N. S. de la exposicion hecha por V.S. en 27 de Octubre ultimo por la cual solicitaba que sin perjuicio de establecerse en esa Ciudad el Tribunal de Comercio que debe haber con arreglo al Código de este ramo se conservase la Junta de gobierno de ese Consulado con las Oficinas necesarias para el desempeño de los encargos que le están confiados; y enterado S. M. ha tenido á bien mandar se diga á V. S. que por real orden de 16 de este mes está yá mandado que en los puntos donde hay Consulados subsistan las Juntas directivas ó de Comercio que están unidas á ellos, despues que cesen en sus funciones dichos Consulados en virtud del nuevo Código; y que por consiguiente quedando remediada con esta disposicion la falta que haria el de esa Ciudad para el desempeño de los encargos que V.S. menciona en dicho escrito, solo tiene S. M. que prevenir que el actual Prior y Consules, pasando á ser individuos de la Junta de Comercio que ha de quedar desde 1º de Enero de 1830 sean individuos de la Junta directiva del puerto-franco y de los demas encargos de aquella. De real orden lo comunico á V. S. para su inteligencia y efectos consiguientes. Dios guarde á V. S. muchos años. Madrid 24. de Noviembre de 1829.

Ballesteros.

Sr. Prior y Cónsules del Consulado de Cadiz.

BIBLIOGRAPHY

BAUDOT, Georges et al (1985): *El Archivo General de Indias en mi recuerdo.* Seville, Consejería de Cultura, 1985.

BERNARD, Gildas (1972): *Le Secretariat d'Etat et le Conseil espagnol des Indes: 1700-1808,* Genève, Librairie Drie.

BERNAL, Antonio Miguel & GARCÍA BAQUERO, Antonio (1976): *Tres siglos de comercio sevillano (1598-1868). Cuestiones y problemas.* Seville, Chamber of Commerce.

BERNAL, Antonio Miguel (1993): *La financiación de la Carrera de Indias 1492-1824: dinero y crédito en el comercio colonial español con América.* Seville, Tabapress.

BURKHOLDER, M.A. (1976): "The Council of the Indies in the late eighteenth century: A new perspective", in *Hispanic American Historical Review,* 56, no. 3 (August 1976), pp. 404–423.

CASTAÑEDA DELGADO, Paulino & MARCHENA FERNÁNDEZ, Juan (1992): *La jerarquía de la Iglesia en Indias: el episcopado americano, 1500–1850.* Madrid, Mapfre.

CASTRO, Javier de (1990): *La recuperación de pecios en la Carrera de las Indias.* Lleida, Espai–Temps.

CESPEDES DEL CASTILLO, Guillermo (1945): *La avería en el comercio de Indias.* Seville, (C.S.I.C.–Tall. I.G.A.S.A.).

Colección de documentos inéditos relativos al descubrimiento, conquista y colonización de las posesiones españolas en América y Oceanía: Sacados en su mayor parte del Real Archivo de Indias, under the direction of Joaquín F. Pacheco, Francisco de Cárdenas & Luis Torres de Mendoza. Madrid, printed by Manuel B. de Quirós, 1865–1884. 42 vols.

Colección de documentos inéditos relativos al descubrimiento, conquista y organización de las antiguas posesiones españolas de Ultramar: [Recogidos del Archivo de Indias de Sevilla], published by the Real Academia de la Historia. Madrid, Est. Tipográfico, sucesores de Rivadeneyra, 1885–1932. 25 vols.

COLUMBUS, Christopher (1982): *Textos y documentos completos: Relaciones de viajes, cartas y memoriales;* editing, foreword & annotations by Consuelo Varela. Madrid, Alianza Editorial (Alianza Universitaria, 320).

COS GAYON, Fernando (1976): *Historia de la Administración Pública de España en sus diferentes ramos de Derecho Político, Diplomacia, Organización administrativa y Hacienda desde la dominación romana hasta nuestros días.* Madrid, Instituto de Estudios Administrativos.

CHAUNU, Huguette et Pierre (1957): *Seville et l'Atlantique (1504-1650).* Paris, SEVPEN. 7 vols.

ELLIOT, John H. (1970): *The Old World and the New, 1492-1650.* Cambridge, Cambridge University Press.

ESCUDERO, José Antonio (1979): *Los orígenes del Consejo de Ministros en España: la Junta Suprema de Estado.* Madrid, Editora Nacional.

ESCUDERO, José Antonio (1976): *Los Secretarios de Estado y del Despacho.* Madrid, Instituto de Estudios Administrativos.

FERNANDEZ-ARMESTO, Felipe (1991): *Columbus*. Oxford, 1991.

FERNANDEZ DE NAVARRETE, Martín (1825-1837): *Colección de los viages y descubrimientos que hicieron por mar los españoles desde fines del siglo XV, con varios documentos inéditos concernientes a la historia de la marina castellana y de los establecimientos españoles en Indias, De orden de S.M.* Madrid, Royal Printworks, 1825–1837. 5 vols.

GARCÍA BAQUERO GONZÁLEZ, Antonio (1988): *Cádiz y el Atlántico (1717–1778). El comercio colonial español bajo el monopolio gaditano.* Cádiz, Diputación Provincial.

GARCIA GALLO, Concepción (1973): 'La información administrativa en el Consejo de Indias', in *III Congreso del Instituto Internacional de Historia del Derecho Indiano.* Madrid, Instituto Nacional de Estudios Jurídicos.

GONGORA, Mario (1975): *Studies in Colonial History of Spanish America.* New York, Cambridge University Press, (Cambridge Latin American Studies, vol. 20).

HARING, Clarence Henry (1918): *Trade and navigation between Spain and the Indies in the time of the Hapsburgs.* Cambridge, Harvard University Press.

HEREDIA HERRERA, Antonia (1992): 'El Consulado de Mercaderes de Sevilla: una institución "retrasada" del Descubrimiento', in *Congreso de Historia del Descubrimiento, 1492–1556.* Madrid, Real Academia de la Historia, pp. 35–51.

HEREDIA HERRERA, Antonia (1986): 'El Consulado Nuevo de Sevilla y América', in *V Jornadas de Andalucía y América;* vol. I. Seville, Escuela de Estudios Hispanoamericanos, pp. 287–301.

HEREDIA HERRERA, Antonia (1973): 'Las ordenanzas del Consulado de Sevilla', in *Archivo Hispalense,* vol. LVI, no. 171–173. Seville, Diputación Provincial, pp. 152–183.

LOCKHART, James (1968): *Spanish Peru, 1532-1560: A Colonial Society.* Madison, Univesity of Wisconsin Press.

MADARIAGA, Salvador de (1949): *Christopher Columbus.* London.

MANZANO MANZANO, Juan (1989): *Colón y su secreto: el predescubrimiento,* 3rd edn. Madrid, Ediciones de Cultura Hispánica (Colección colombina).

MANZANO MANZANO, Juan (1989): *Cristóbal Colón: siete años decisivos de su vida, 1485–1492,* 2nd edn. Madrid, Ediciones de Cultura Hispánica (Colección colombina).

MANZANO MANZANO, Juan (1981): *Historia de las Recopilaciones de Indias.* Málaga, Gráficas Urania.

MORALES PADRÓN, Francisco (1988): *Atlas Histórico–cultural de América.* Las Palmas de Gran Canaria, Gobierno de Canarias, Consejería de Cultura y Deportes, Comisión de Canarias para la conmemoración del V Centenario del descubrimiento de América. 2 vols.

MORALES PADRÓN, Francisco (1971): *Historia del descubrimiento y conquista de América,* 2nd edn. Madrid, Editora Nacional (Mundo Científico, Serie Historia).

MORALES PADRÓN, Francisco (1974): *Los conquistadores de América.* Madrid, Espasa Calpe (Colección Austral, 1565).

MORALES PADRÓN, Francisco (1979): *Teoría y Leyes de la conquista.* Madrid, Cultura Hispánica del Centro Iberoamericano de Cooperación.

MORRISON, Samuel Eliot (1972): *The European discovery of America*. New York, Oxford University Press. 2 vols.

MORRISON, Samuel Eliot (1942): *Admiral of the Ocean Sea: A life of Christopher Columbus*. Boston, Little, Brown and Company.

MURO OREJÓN, Antonio (1980): *Los libros impresos y manuscritos del Consejo de Indias*. Seville, Escuela de Estudios Hispanoamericanos.

MURO OREJÓN, Antonio (1945): *Las Leyes Nuevas, 1542–1543: Reproducción de los ejemplares existentes en la Sección de Patronato del Archivo General de Indias*. Transcription & annotations by the author. Seville, Consejo Superior de Investigaciones Científicas.

MURO OREJÓN, Antonio (1957): 'Las Ordenanzas del Consejo de 1571, ediciones de 1585 y 1603', in *Anuario de Estudios Americanos*, XIV Seville. Facsimile edn.

MURO OREJÓN, Antonio (1957): 'Ordenanzas Reales sobre los indios (Las Leyes de 1512-1513)'; a study by the author in *Anuario de Estudios Americanos*, XIV. Seville, Escuela de Estudios Hispanoamericanos.

MURO OREJÓN, Antonio (1983): 'La Recopilación de Indias de 1680', in *Justicia, Sociedad y Economía en la América española (siglos XVI, XVII y XVIII), VI Congreso del Instituto Internacional de Historia del Derecho Indiano*. Valladolid, Seminario Americanista de la Universidad de Valladolid.

NAVARRO GARCIA, Luis (1975): *La Casa de la Contratación en Cádiz*. Cádiz, Instituto de Estudios Gaditanos.

Ordenanzas del Archivo General de Indias, facsimile edn. Preliminary studies by Francisco de Solano et al. Seville, Consejería de Cultura, 1986.

PADDEN, R.C. (1970): *The Hummingbird and the Hawk: Conquest and Sovereignity in the Valley of Mexico, 1503–1541*. New York, Harper & Row.

PEÑA Y CAMARA, José de la (1958): *Archivo General de Indias. Guía del Visitante*. Madrid, Dirección General de Archivos y Bibliotecas.

PRADO Y ROZAS, Antonio de (1982): *Dos estudios sobre Historia de la Administración: las Secretarías del Despacho*. Madrid, Instituto de Administración Pública.

PRESCOTT, William H. (1857): *History of the conquest of Mexico with a preliminary view of the ancient Mexican civilization and the life of the conqueror Hernando Cortez*. Boston, Phillips, Sampson and Company.

PRESCOTT, William H. (1847): *History of the conquest of Peru with a preliminary view of the civilization of the Incas*. Paris, Baudry's European Library.

PUENTE Y OLEA, Manuel de la (1900): *Los trabajos geográficos de la Casa de la Contratación de las Indias Occidentales*. Seville, Tipografía Salesiana.

PULIDO RUBIO, José (1950): *El Piloto Mayor de la Casa de la Contratación de Sevilla. Pilotos mayores, Catedráticos de Cosmografía y Cosmógrafos*. Seville, Escuela de Estudios Hispanoamericanos.

RAMOS, Demetrio (1981): *Audacia, negocio y política en los viajes españoles de 'descubrimiento y rescate'*. Valladolid, Casa–Museo de Colón (Colección Tierra Nueva o Cielo Nuevo).

RAMOS, Demetrio, PEREZ DE TUDELA, Juan et al (1970): *El Consejo de las Indias en el siglo XVI*. Valladolid, University of Valladolid, Secretariado de Publicaciones.

REAL DÍAZ, José Joaquín (1962): *El Consejo de Cámara de Indias: génesis de su fundación*. Seville, G.E.H.A.

RUIZ RIVERA, Julián Bautista (1988): *El Consulado de Cádiz. Matrícula de comerciantes, 1730–1823*. Cádiz, Diputación Provincial.

RUIZ RIVERA, Julián Bautista & GARCÍA BERNAL, Manuela Cristina (1992): *Cargadores a Indias*. Madrid, Mapfre.

RUIZ DEL SOLAR Y AZURIAGA, Manuel (1900): *La Casa de la Contratación*. Seville, Escuela, Tipografía y Librería Salesianas.

SAUER, Carl Ortwin (1966): *The Early Spanish Main*. Berkeley, University of California Press.

SCHÄFER, Ernesto (1935): *El Consejo Real y Supremo de las Indias. Su historia, organización y labor administrativa hasta la terminación de la Casa de Austria*. Seville, Imprenta Carmona.

THOMAS, Hugh (1994): *La conquista de México*. Barcelona, Ed. Planeta.

VEITIA LINAGE, José de (1981): *Norte de la Contratación de las Indias Occidentales. Sevilla, Juan Francisco de Bras, 1672*. Madrid, Ministerio de Hacienda, Instituto de Estudios Fiscales. Facsimile edn. with a preliminary study by Francisco Solano & Pérez Lila entitled 'Nota sobre la vida y obra del autor del Norte de la Contratación de las Indias Occidentales'.

VEGA FRANCO, María Luisa (1984): *El tráfico de esclavos en América (Asiento de Grillo y Lomelín, 1663–1674)*. Seville, Escuela de Estudios Hispanoamericanos, C.S.I.C.

VERLINDEN, Charles (1970): *The Beginnings of Modern Colonization*. Ithaca, Cornell Univesity Press.

VILA VILAR, Enriqueta (1973): 'Algunos datos sobre la navegación y los navíos negreros en el siglo XVII', in *Historiografía y Bibliografía Americanistas*. Seville, vol. XVII, no 3, pp. 219–232.

VILA VILAR, Enriqueta (1981): *El Consulado de Sevilla asentista de esclavos: una nueva tentativa para el mantenimiento del monopolio comercial*. Huelva, Instituto de Estudios Onubenses.

VORSEY, L. & PARKER, J. (1985): *In the Wake of Columbus*. Detroit.

INDEX

Spanish Edition:

LUNWERG EDITORES, S.A.

Editor-in-Chief
JUAN CARLOS LUNA

Art Director
ANDRÉS GAMBOA

Production Manager
MERCEDES CARREGAL

Layout
FRANCISCO COLACIOS

Coordination
MARÍA JOSÉ MOYANO

Photography
JOAQUÍN CORTÉS

Some photographs supplied
by courtesy of
LUIS ARENAS